Professional Graphics Programming
in the
X Window System

Eric F. Johnson

Kevin Reichard

MIS: PRESS

A Subsidiary of
Henry Holt and Co., Inc.

First Edition—1993

ISBN 1-55828-255-6

Printed in the United States of America.

10 9 8 7 6 5 4 3 2 1

MIS:Press books are available at special discounts for bulk purchases for sales promotions, premiums, fund-raising, or educational use. Special editions or book excerpts can also be created to specification.

For details contact: Special Sales Director
MIS:Press
a subsidiary of Henry Holt and Company, Inc.
115 West 18th Street
New York, New York 10011

Development Editor, Laura Lewin
Production Editor, Patricia Wallenburg
Copy Editor, Andrea Salvatore

Dedication

From Kevin:
For Penny, Sean, and Geisha—as always.

Table of Contents

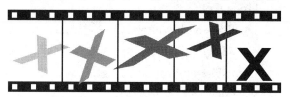

Chapter 2: Drawing with X 27

Chapter 3: The Graphics Context 5I

Chapter 25: Double Buffering for Smooth Animation 1005

Introduction

Welcome to *Professional Graphics Programming in the X Window System*! This book is meant for the serious programmer: The programmer who has a job to do and is looking for the most efficient way to do it. We've combined a lot of hands-on tips and shortcuts with appropriate overviews to create a book meant for the serious programmer.

Because this book is geared toward the professional programmer, we've made some assumptions as to your skill level. Although we're covering the creating of professional-quality graphics programming from the ground up, we're not covering every aspect of the X Window System, Motif and Open Look in depth. (If you need to get up to speed on these programming topics, check out the list of recommended books in Appendix E.) And while it's not necessary for you to have a ton of experience with X Window before tackling this book, you should at least be an experienced C programmer. Most of the advanced topics in this book are not for the faint of heart, so experience is necessary.

What sort of advanced topics are we talking about? Essentially, the areas of X that contribute to a polished, professional-quality application. We're talking the smooth and accomplished treatment of bitmaps and bitmaps. We're talking about support for various aspects of multimedia: animation, for instance. And we're talking about the small touches that make your software appear smoother and slicker to the average user: A more polished approach to colors and fonts, for instance.

Because this book is already big enough, we won't go into an expanded explanation of X Window and how it works. Instead, we'll cover such topics as they are first needed throughout this book. For instance, we'll explain the various X toolkits when that information is needed by you; we'll skip the big picture for now.

Typographical Conventions

In this book, the following typographical conventions have been used:

- ✦ C program references (such as function names and filenames) within a text paragraph will appear in a monospaced typeface, as in the following example:

  ```
  To   allocate   a   standard   colormap   structure,   use
  XAllocStandardColormap.
  ```

- ✦ Actual program examples and listings will appear in monospaced type.

Feedback

If you want to send us comments about this book, feel free to drop us via electronic mail on the Internet (kreichard@mcimail.com) or CompuServe (73670,3422).

X Basics: From Drawing to Menus

The first six chapters of this book encompass the basics for X Window graphics. The rest of the book's advanced topics build on the foundation built in this section.

We begin our exploration of the X graphics-programming field by starting with an fast-paced overview of X programming concepts, including the entire notion of event-driven programming, as well as how X treats displays, screens, and windows.

From there we proceed directly into some practical programming techniques in Chapter 2, examining how X treats basic drawing functions— and how you can most efficiently use these functions.

In Chapter 3, the graphics context, or GC, is introduced. Much of X graphics programming lies in the effective use of the graphics context.

Chapter 4 covers events—and most specifically, those events that relate to graphics. At its heart X is an event-driven environment, and so your graphics applications must be optimized to handle events.

We introduce Motif programming in Chapter 5, explaining its basic concepts and then putting together a sample Motif program.

Finally, the section ends in Chapter 6 with an overview of the Open Look Intrinsics Toolkit, or OLIT. Again, we explore basic concepts in OLIT and then put together a sample OLIT program.

Graphics Programming with X

This chapter introduces basic X Window concepts, such as:

- ✦ Displays
- ✦ Screens
- ✦ Windows
- ✦ The root window
- ✦ Mapping windows to the screen
- ✦ Save unders and backing store
- ✦ The X Window coordinate system
- ✦ X display information
- ✦ The graphics context, or GC
- ✦ Using color with X
- ✦ Event-driven programming
- ✦ Working with X toolkits

Introducing the X Window System

The X Window System uses a client-server architecture for distributed graphics applications. X divides the workload into two parts: the *X server* controls a display screen (or screens), while *clients* (or application programs) request services from the server, such as opening windows and drawing lines or text into the windows. All X applications, such as text editors, spreadsheets, and clock displays, are clients of the X server. As a programmer, however, you won't need to do anything special to take advantage of the distributed graphics; X takes care of it for you.

Throughout this book we'll refer to *applications* and *clients* interchangeably.

N O T E

The X server is also called a *display*. Each display manages a keyboard, a pointing device (usually a mouse), and one or more physical monitors, called *screens*. The server allows multiple applications to share the same graphics hardware while managing the task of sending keyboard input to the proper applications.

The X server is normally a separate UNIX process. Clients communicate to the server through a connection, usually a network link.

Since the X server is a separate process, the first step in any X program is opening a network connection to the server, which is done with the XOpenDisplay function. This connection could be a TCP/IP socket, a DECnet connection, or perhaps a shared memory link on a local machine, depending on the machine running the X server. (Don't worry about the mechanism—XOpenDisplay will set up the proper connection. This is part of the X Window System's much-vaunted portability.)

XOpenDisplay is part of the *X library*, or *Xlib*, which is the low-level C graphics library for the X Window System:

```
#include <X11/Xlib.h>


Display* XOpenDisplay(char* display_name)
```

`XOpenDisplay` takes one parameter: the name of the display (server) you want to talk to. This name is a specially formatted character string, which is normally *hostname:0* (the first X server on machine *hostname*), such as `nicollet:0` for a workstation with a network name of `nicollet`. The actual format of display names doesn't really matter in this discussion, as your X toolkit normally takes care of this for you.

N O T E Every C source file that calls the X library routines should include the header file `<X11/Xlib.h>`. By convention, this file will be located in the directory `/usr/include/X11` on machines running the UNIX operating system or close variants. Sun Microsystems workstations usually place X include files in `/usr/openwin/include/X11`. On Hewlett-Packard systems, look in `/usr/include/X11R4/X11` for HP-UX 8.0 with X11 Release 4, and in `/usr/include/X11R5/X11` for HP-UX 9.0 with X11 Release 5. Consult your system documentation for more information on your local configuration. Some of the other header files in the X11 directory will be introduced later, as needed, as well as Motif and Open Look Intrinsics Toolkit (OLIT) headers.

If you use an X toolkit, like Motif or OLIT, you normally won't have to worry about opening a display connection. The function `XtAppInitialize` takes care of this for you. If you need to access more than the default visual or create your own colormap, however, you may need to call `XtOpenDisplay`, which we cover in Chapter 5 on the Motif toolkit.

Screens

Each X server can control multiple *screens*, or physical monitors on a multiheaded system. This is *not* the same as multiple users at separate X terminals—reusing common terminology like screens is often very confusing.

An X server controls the graphics hardware for a single user. With a powerful multiuser UNIX system, you need to run a separate X server process for each user running X. Therefore, if you want to write a multiuser X application, your application must connect to multiple X servers, not screens.

A single-user X application can place windows on more than one screen controlled by the same X server. To make things a little less confusing, keep in mind that every user runs an X server—even lowly X terminals have their own X server software. Each of these X servers may control one or more physical monitors, but only one keyboard and mouse. Popular for CAD systems, a multiheaded workstation has multiple X screens (if it runs X, of course).

Sometimes an X server supports two wildly different screens, such as one monochrome and one color screen. Older Sun-3 workstations, for example, often provided color and monochrome frame buffers. Or, perhaps, one of the screens supports 24 bit-planes of color, while the second screen only has 8 bit-planes of color. In all cases, you can tell how many screens are available using the `ScreenCount` macro:

```
int  ScreenCount(Display* display)
```

`ScreenCount` returns the number of screens supported by your X server.

Each screen is numbered, starting with zero for the first screen. X, true to its C bias, normally starts counting at zero (0). The `DefaultScreen` macro returns the screen number for the default screen. Since 99 percent of all X servers support just one screen, chances are the number returned is zero.

```
int DefaultScreen(Display* display)
```

In addition to screen numbers, some X functions and macros take a pointer to a `Screen` structure, which contains further information about an individual screen. To get the `Screen` pointer for a given screen number, use the `ScreenOfDisplay` macro:

```
Screen* ScreenOfDisplay(Display* display, int screen)
```

Each screen supports a hierarchy of windows.

For most X Library macros, anything ending in *OfScreen* usually takes a `Screen` pointer. `HeightOfScreen`, for instance, takes a `Screen` pointer. `DisplayHeight` takes a `Display` pointer with a screen number.

N O T E

Windows

The X Window System supports a hierarchy of overlapping windows and sub-windows on each screen. A *window* in X terminology is a rectangular area treated as a logical unit by the X server. Each window has its own local coordinate system, and all graphics output is clipped to the window boundaries. Windows may have *child windows*—also called *subwindow*s, which are clipped to their bounds, or the bounds of their parents, whichever is smaller.

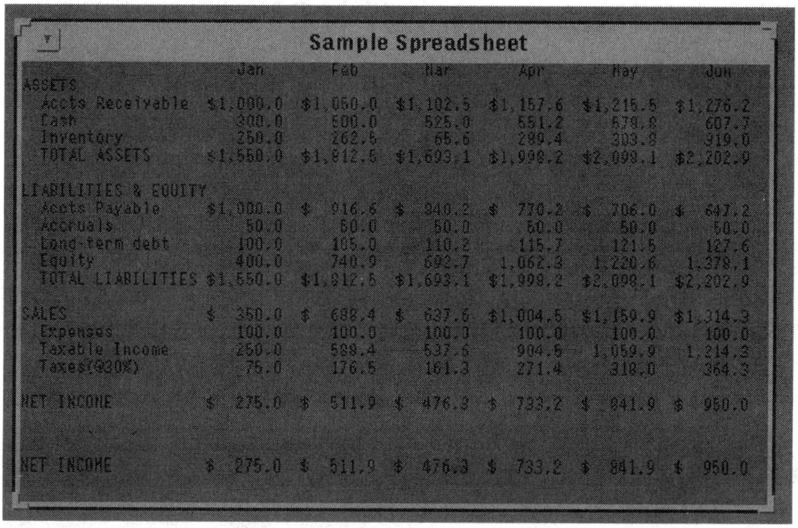

Figure 1.1 *A window under the Open Look window manager.*

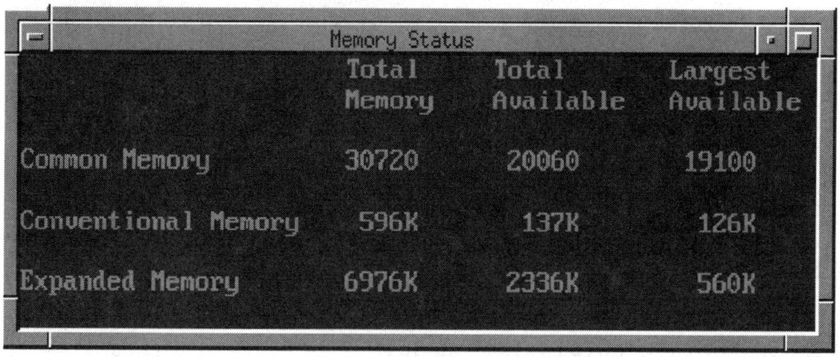

Figure 1.2 *A window under the Motif window manager.*

The SHAPE extension first introduced in X11 Release 4 allows for the creation of windows with rounded corners.

NOTE

Each window is identified by a *window ID*. This ID, a typedef for a long integer, is unique for a screen, but is not persistent. If you create a window and later destroy it, the X server is free to reuse the destroyed window's ID.

Windows are arranged in a hierarchy. Each screen has its own independent window hierarchy. (Unlike the Macintosh, no window in X may span multiple screens.) At the top of the hierarchy sits the root window.

The Root Window

Each X screen contains a root window covering the entire screen. The bounds of this window are the physical pixel resolution of the screen. You can think of the root window as a screen background, in reality. When you want to change your screen background, using a program such as xset-root, you're really changing the background of the root window.

Some window managers, such as olvwm or Hewlett-Packard's vuewm, support the concept of very large virtual windows that are larger than the root window. In these cases, the window manager covers the root window with a virtual desktop window. If you use xsetroot to change the root window, you won't see the changes because the virtual desktop layer hides the root window.

NOTE

You can determine the root window's ID with the RootWindow macro. RootWindow returns the root window ID for a given screen on a given display:

```
Window RootWindow(Display* display,
         int screen_number)
```

Every window created by X applications is a child window of the root window. Most X applications create a large number of windows: windows are considered relatively cheap in terms of memory resources and they're convenient. One example of this convenience is that the X server sends applications events based on window IDs. If you create a separate window for the arrowheads at the top and bottom of a scroll bar, your code is much simpler, because the X server will handle the hit detection: you will get events for the top arrowhead when the user clicks the mouse in that area. This eliminates the need for your code to handle the task of determining where in the scroll bar the user clicked the mouse.

Of course, saying that windows in X are cheap is a bit of an euphemism. Most UNIX/X systems don't run well unless you have at least 16 megabytes of memory. While RAM prices have generally gone down, we don't consider the term *cheap* appropriate for multiple-megabyte programs. X programs tend to be huge, and part of the reason is that X programs create a large number of windows. Window managers, in particular, are likely to place a number of windows surrounding your application's top-level windows.

Just to see how many X windows you'll see on your display, we took a typical low-end X workstation, running just four X applications: the `mwm` window manager, `oclock`, and two copies of `xterm`, a client that opens a terminal window. We then listed all the windows on the display with the `xwininfo` program, using the `-tree` command-line parameter. We counted 54 windows for just four X applications. The vast majority of these windows were placed by `mwm`. Try running the command `xwininfo -tree` on your system and you'll see what we mean.

The X Window Coordinate System

Important in any introduction to X graphics programming is the sometimes-confusing X coordinate system. In the X Window System, the origin (0,0) is located in the *upper left* corner of the screen. x values increase going to the right. y values increase going *down*. You may be more used to an origin in the lower left corner with y values increasing going up.

Every window in X also has its own local coordinate system, with a local origin, again located in the upper left corner. All drawing output in X is measured in pixels.

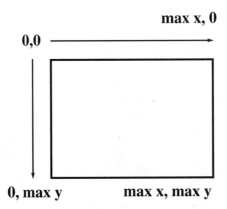

Figure 1.3 *The X coordinate system.*

Mapping Windows to the Screen

Each window on an X display may be in one of the following states, defined in `<X11/Xutil.h>`, and listed in Table 1.1.

Table 1.1 *Window states.*

State	Value	Meaning
WithdrawnState	0	Window is not visible (unmapped)
NormalState	1	Window is visible (mapped)
IconicState	3	Window is replaced by an icon (if supported)

When first created, windows are in the `WithdrawnState`. You can later *map* a window to the screen, changing it to `NormalState`. You can *unmap* a window to change it back to `WithdrawnState`. In `IconicState`, the window is replaced with an icon.

Most window managers, including the Motif window manager (mwm), the Open Look window manager (olwm), and the Tab window manager (twm), support icons. Users can *iconify* or *minimize* a window, and the window manager replaces the window with its associated icon. This icon can be in itself another window or it can be a monochrome bitmap. (We cover icons and icon windows in Chapter 20.)

Windows in the withdrawn state exist in a sort of limbo. These windows are not visible on the screen, but they still count as a window and you can perform operations on such a window—although any graphics drawn to a withdrawn window will be ignored.

To change the state of a window from withdrawn to normal (visible on the screen), use the Xlib function XMapWindow:

```
XMapWindow(Display* display, Window window)
```

The XMapWindow function maps the window to the screen. At this point, the window manager may intervene and change the placement of your window. Until this time, the window existed in a sort of never-never land (in withdrawn state), never appearing on the screen.

XMapWindow has no defined return type in <X11/Xlib.h> and therefore uses the default X return type of int. In real life, we treat this function and those like it as if they have a void return value. Other functions without a listed return type are treated the same way.

N O T E   If you use the Xt Intrinsics with a toolkit such as Motif or OLIT, you do not have to map your widgets. By default, all managed, realized widgets are mapped to the screen. You can change this default by setting the mappedWhenManaged *resource* (XmNmappedWhenManaged in Motif and XtNmappedWhenManaged in OLIT) to False. We'll use this technique later in toolkit-based programs.

If you do prevent a widget (normally a top-level shell widget) from being mapped, you need to later map this widget to the screen, using the Xt macro XtMapWidget:

```
XtMapWidget(Widget widget)
```

We'll cover this in more detail in Chapters 5 and 6.

Xlib functions normally begin with *X*. X Toolkit Intrinsics functions begin with *Xt*. Motif functions begin with *Xm* and most OLIT functions begin with *Ol*.

NOTE

Mapping and Raising Windows

XMapRaised acts the same as XMapWindow, but it also raises the new window to the top, making it appear over other windows that may be in the way. In most cases, XMapWindow will seem to act the same way, but XMapRaised is explicit about the placement. XMapRaised takes the same parameters as XMapWindow:

```
XMapRaised(Display* display, Window window)
```

You can later unmap a window, undoing the effects of XMapWindow, with the XUnmapWindow function, using the same parameters:

```
XUnmapWindow(Display* display, Window window)
```

Unmapping a window returns it to the withdrawn state.

Clearing Windows

You can clear a window to its background color (or pixmap) using XClearWindow:

```
XClearWindow(Display* display, Window window)
```

Save Unders and Backing Store

The X server demands that your X applications always be able to redraw the contents of any of your application windows—at any time. X does not save the contents of any obscured windows. Even so, there are two techniques you can use to optimize performance and cut down on the number of redraw requests (called Expose events).

First, you can ask for *backing store* on any window. Backing store is where the X server provides offscreen storage for any obscured parts of the window. Any graphics drawn to the window, obscured or not, is saved in the backing-store memory. When you ask for backing store on a window, you are not guaranteed *anything*. The X server may provide backing store for a while and then later give it up (due to low memory conditions, for example). In all cases, remember that backing store is a request and that the X server may or may not provide it.

Backing store is a window attribute. You place the desired backing-store flag into the XSetWindowAttributes structure that is passed to XCreateWindow for a new window or NOTE XChangeWindowAttributes for existing windows.

Second, the *save-under* attribute is like backing store on other windows. If you ask for the save-under attribute for your window, the X server will try to save the area *underneath* your window. Save under is extremely useful for menu windows or other windows that you intend to be on the screen for a very short time. If you have a menu or another window that will be visible for only a short time, you want the menu to appear and disappear as fast as possible. Once the menu is drawn on the screen, however, the menu will obscure the pixels underneath. When the menu goes away, the applications that own the windows underneath your menu need to redraw the formerly obscured pixels. This can take time. One way to speed this up is to ask the X server to save the area under the menu (hence, the term *save under*) and then restore that area when the menu goes away.

Without save under enabled, browsing through a menu bar of pulldown menus is a painfully slow operation. You can check if an X server provides backing store or save unders with the DoesSaveUnders and DoesBackingStore macros:

```
Bool DoesSaveUnders(Screen* screenptr)

int DoesBackingStore(Screen* screenptr)
```

DoesSaveUnders returns True if the X server supports save unders and False otherwise. The DoesBackingStore macro returns WhenMapped, NotUseful, or Always, constants defined in <X11/X.h>, which is automatically included in <X11/Xlib.h>. These constants indicate what kind of backing store may be available. You get the `Screen` pointer with the `ScreenOfDisplay` macro introduced above.

Note that both backing store and save under are just requests—the X server isn't obligated to honor your requests.

X Display Information

Once you've established a connection to the X server, you should ask if it supplies color planes (or supports only monochrome) and how big the display screen is. If you have a VGA (video graphics array) screen with only 640 x 480 pixel resolution (considered very confining for running X), you don't want to create a window at pixel location (800, 800), as it wouldn't be on the screen.

The size of the screen in pixels is returned from two macros: `DisplayWidth` and `DisplayHeight`:

```
int  DisplayWidth(Display* display,
        int screen_number)
```

```
int DisplayHeight(Display* display,
        int screen_number)
```

These macros return the size of the display in pixels as well as the number of dots on the screen in the vertical (`DisplayHeight`) and horizontal (`DisplayWidth`) directions.

You can check for the actual size of the monitor, in millimeters, by using the `DisplayHeightMM` and `DisplayWidthMM` macros:

```
int  DisplayWidthMM(Display* display,
        int screen_number)
```

```
int  DisplayHeightMM(Display* display,
        int screen_number)
```

WARNING Creating true WYSIWYG (or what-you-see-is-what-you-get) applications depends on knowing the size of the output monitor. Unfortunately, the values returned by these macros are fraught with error. On some Sun systems, for instance, these numbers are hard-coded, and both the 16-inch and 19-inch monitor returns the same size in millimeters. You can never depend on the values returned by `DisplayHeightMM` and `DisplayWidthMM`.

The number of bit-planes (for color or gray-scale monitors) is returned by the `DefaultDepth` macro:

```
int  DefaultDepth(Display* display,
       int screen_number)
```

The number of bit-planes returned may be deceiving. If the depth is 1, you have a monochrome system (or at least a monochrome default visual, which we'll cover later). In order to determine if you have a color system, though, you must also determine which visuals are supported. (A visual is an X abstraction that hides some of the differences in color graphics hardware.) If the depth is greater than 1, you may have a color system or a gray-scale system with a number of shades of gray.

Closing the Display Connection

When you are done with the connection to the X server (usually at the end of your program), it is a nice practice to close the connection gracefully. `XCloseDisplay` closes a connection to an X server. Once you call `XCloseDisplay`, the `Display` pointer is no longer valid.

```
XCloseDisplay(Display* display)
```

When your program terminates under most versions of UNIX, the operating system usually breaks all connections by closing all open file descriptors. This makes the call to `XCloseDisplay` technically unnecessary. Since X runs on more than one operating system, though, and you don't know if this capability is built into the operating system (in theory, your applications shouldn't depend on a particular operating system), it's a good idea to close your X session gracefully. Note that if you use an X toolkit, your toolkit may have its own function to end an X session and close the display connection.

Drawing with X

Of course, all this work setting up a display connection is done so we can get to the meat of our programs and draw graphics into X windows.

In X, you can draw into windows and into offscreen drawing areas called *pixmaps*. Both pixmaps and windows are considered *drawables*. Each drawable is a structure in the X server and is represented in your programs with a long-integer ID number. Most X drawing functions, which we introduce in the next chapter, take a `Drawable` ID as a parameter to tell the X library where you want to draw.

All drawing with X also uses a *graphics context* to hold the pen parameters, like drawing color and line width. Each GC has a structure in the X server and a shadow structure within your program. To improve performance, both the X server and the X library in your program cache a number of GCs and GC parameters. Because of this, it is important to never try to modify a GC structure directly. Instead, always use the utility functions for changing the pen, or GC parameters. We cover the graphics context and these utility functions in depth in Chapter 3.

The Display/Window/GC Triumvirate

To do any drawing in X, you need:

  ✦ A display pointer, which represents the X-server connection;
  ✦ A window or pixmap ID, which represents where to draw; and
  ✦ A graphics context, which describes how to apply the drawing.

Most drawing is done to windows, obviously, since windows are on-screen while pixmaps are off. This display, window, GC triumvirate is used in just about every function to draw graphics. The key is to get, create, or otherwise commandeer the proper three values.

When you work with most X toolkits, the toolkit will take care of the display pointer. You generally create a special toolkit object for the window to draw in, which takes care of that. But in most cases, you have to create your own graphics context, which we cover in Chapter 3. In the next few chapters, watch carefully how we extract the display pointer and window IDs, because this is a key for graphics in X when you use any toolkit.

Using Color

There's a wide variety of hardware implementations of color graphics. In fact, all the really cool workstations always sport a large color display adapter card, full of big macho-looking heat sinks and other big chips, which should impress the heck out of you.

Unfortunately, there is a great variance in how these macho graphics cards work. Because of this, programming color in X is one of the most frustratingly complex endeavors.

X encapsulates color under a concept called a *visual*. A visual is supposed to hide the messy details of the underlying color implementation. With six main visual types, though, you end up writing a lot of code to handle the differences in color implementations—which was exactly what visuals were supposed to avoid.

A second and easier technique is to ignore the wide variety of visuals and instead concentrate on the simplest color visual type, called PseudoColor. Since most workstations provide a default PseudoColor visual, you can usually get away with this.

Each visual supports a number of *colormaps*. Your programs then allocate colors from these colormaps. You can create new colormaps or reuse existing ones. Because most workstation color hardware still supports only one colormap at a time, you tend to get annoying flashing or "technicolor" effects as the window manager swaps in and out colormaps. Since most users don't like this, it's a good idea to try to reuse the default colormap instead of creating your own colormaps—if at all possible.

We delve into the messy details of visuals, colormaps, and colors in Chapter 7.

Black and White

Every X server preallocates at least two colors: black and white. These colors may not even look like the black and white we're all used to. In fact, they may be red and green, but at the very least these colors are supposed to contrast, so you can write text in one color on a background of the other color and have the text be viewable to a human observer.

If you use just the preallocated black and white colors, you can create a monochrome X application with a minimum of work. Using color, though, is a much more complex procedure, which we cover in Chapter 7.

Different X servers allocate different spots in their color tables for black and white, so you cannot depend on black having a color number of 0 and white 1. Some systems reverse this. Some, like the Data General Aviion, use 0 for black and 255 for white. Other odd systems may use any value they desire for black and white. There's nothing wrong with this, but you can't assume black and white will be assigned to any particular color index numbers. Thus, your application always needs to inquire the values for black and white on a given screen of a given display (X server).

The macros `BlackPixel` and `WhitePixel` return the default color indexes in the default colormap for black and white, respectively. These color indexes are unsigned long integers (*ints*).

```
unsigned long BlackPixel(Display* display,
       int screen_number)
```

```
unsigned long WhitePixel(Display* display,
       int screen_number)
```

Many times these numbers will be 0 and 1 (or 1 and 0, respectively), since black and white are usually the first two colors allocated.

OLIT provides two utilities to get the black and white pixels for the colormap associated with a widget:

```
unsigned long OlBlackPixel(Widget widget)
unsigned long OlWhitePixel(Widget widget)
```

Assigning Colors to GCs

You assign a color to a graphics context with the XSetForeground function:

```
XSetForeground(Display* display,

    GC gc,

    unsigned long foreground)
```

The *foreground* parameter is the color index you want to draw with, such as the color index from the BlackPixel macro:

```
Display*    display;
GC          gc;
int         screen_number;


XSetForeground(display, gc,
    BlackPixel(display, screen_number) );
```

We cover the graphics context in depth in Chapter 3.

Event-Driven Programming

Event-driven programs are literally driven or controlled by incoming events from the X server. Event-driven programs are not like traditional noninteractive UNIX batch programs like ls, tr, and who. A batch program, such as a program to strip out all the control characters from a text file, takes in user input only at the beginning, usually to get the names of the input and output files. The batch program then chugs away on the input and produces the output. The program is in total control of itself.

In an event-driven application, however, the program cedes control to the user. The user drives the actions of the program through a series of many events. The program is really still in control, but it gives the user the feeling that the user is running the show. This is very important if your applications support users who are new to computing. The big difference with event-driven programming is that events can come in at any time and in any order. This places the meat of most event-driven programs in a central loop that takes each event as it comes in and responds to that event in some way.

The X Toolkit Intrinsics, used by Motif and OLIT, provides the `XtAppMainLoop` and `XtMainLoop` functions to handle this central event loop. These functions accept input events from the X server and then dispatch the events to the proper Xt widgets (we'll cover widgets more in Chapters 5 and 6).

Working with X Toolkits

Throughout this book, we bandy about terms like X toolkits, Motif, and OLIT. That's because we assume most X programmers use some form of toolkit to speed the development of X applications. The most popular X toolkits, or function libraries, are written in the C language and are based on the X Toolkit Intrinsics (or Xt for short), a pseudo-object-oriented layer provided with the X Window System.

Xt programs use the concept of a *widget* to encapsulate an interface element, such as a scroll bar, menu, or push button. The most popular Xt-based toolkits include:

✦ *Motif* from the Open Software Foundation, or OSF.

✦ The *Open Look Intrinsics Toolkit*, or *OLIT*, from Sun Microsystems.

✦ The *Athena* widget set, free with the X Window System, but not supported by many vendors.

Another popular Open Look toolkit is XView, which builds on the old SunView programming model. XView, though, according to Sun Microsystems, has a limited life and should not be used. (New Open Look applications should be written using OLIT—and OLIT itself has a limited life, according to Sun.)

For C++ toolkits, the main contenders are InterViews, a free toolkit from Stanford University, and Object Interface (or OI) from ParcPlace. You can also use C++ with most C-based X toolkits.

All told, there are literally hundreds of X toolkits. Because of this, we aimed this book as generically as possible. The techniques we describe, for the most part, go beyond what any X toolkit offers. Hence, we must drop down beneath the toolkit layer to the low-level X library to implement most graphics techniques. This has the advantage of working just about any X toolkit. In fact, most of the source code example functions we provide should work just fine with Motif, OLIT, and most other X toolkits. We take no position in the often nasty toolkit wars.

We wrote the full example programs, though, using Motif and OLIT. We did this for two main reasons. First, most UNIX workstations come with one or the other. Sun and Univel systems, for example, provide OLIT. Most of the rest, such as Hewlett-Packard, IBM, Digital Equipment, SCO, and Silicon Graphics, ship with Motif libraries. Second, if you develop commercial-grade X applications, you're probably already using OLIT or Motif. A key concept here is how to connect graphics with your toolkit to build a complete application.

What is an X Toolkit?

An *X toolkit* is a software library aimed at speeding application development under the X Window System. Essentially, X toolkits are preprogrammed graphics routines usually written in C. The whole idea is to build up your user interface from prebuilt high-level components instead of drawing every menu, push button, and slider using the low-level X drawing routines. Both Motif and OLIT are based on a underlying layer called the *X Toolkit Intrinsics*, a look-and-feel independent software layer (or *C library*) that sits above the low-level X library.

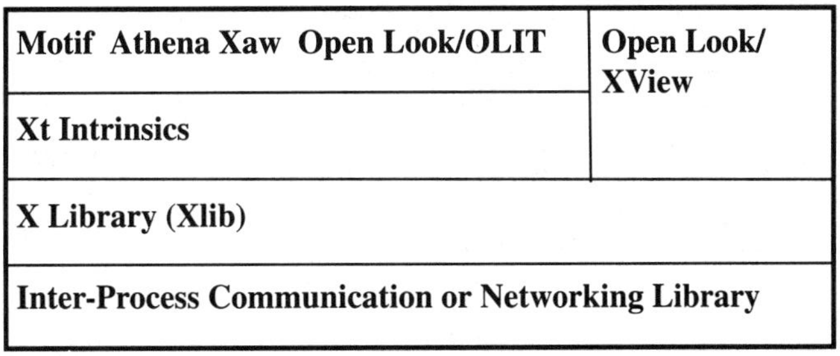

Motif Athena Xaw Open Look/OLIT	Open Look/ XView
Xt Intrinsics	
X Library (Xlib)	
Inter-Process Communication or Networking Library	

Figure 1.4 *X software layers.*

The Xt Intrinsics provide a look-and-feel neutral base for creating high-level X toolkits. Both Motif and OLIT, then, share Xt as a common base, while both also provide different look-and-feel interfaces on top of that base. Xt is like an erector set; you can put together different parts to form your user interface. With Xt, these parts are basic data types called widgets. If you're familiar with object-oriented programming, a widget is akin to an object.

The widget is the main concept introduced by Xt. Xt provides the basic concept of widgets, but leaves it to the higher-level toolkits, also called *widget sets*, to flesh out the widgets and provide a real user interface. Both Motif and OLIT provide a widget set, which is the way both can be layered on top of Xt.

A widget, then, is a user-interface object, dynamically allocated with `malloc`. A widget encapsulates a user-interface element, like a menu, slider, scroll bar, or text-entry field.

At the base level, each widget is built on top of an underlying window. (Motif gadgets and OLIT flat widgets are exceptions to this rule.) Because of this one-to-one connection between widgets and windows, most Motif and OLIT applications tend to create *huge* numbers of windows on the X display.

In the end, all this means the key to Motif and OLIT applications is understanding how to work with widgets.

Like a window, each widget requires a parent, except for the very first widget your application creates. This widget is normally returned by `XtAppInitialize`, a function that initializes the Xt Intrinsics, starts up your widget set (e.g., Motif) and establishes the connection to the X server (by calling `XOpenDisplay` under the hood). OLIT programs provide their own initialization functions, such as `OlInitialize` and `OlToolkitInitialize`. Motif uses plain old `XtAppInitialize`.

In a fashion similar to how child windows are clipped by their parent windows, parent widgets control the layout (called *geometry* in widgetese) of child widgets. Following this simple rule, there are a number of geometry-manager widgets that exist for the sole purpose of laying out child widgets. The OLIT `ControlArea` and Motif `XmForm` widgets fall into this category.

Part of the key to working with widgets is understanding this widget hierarchy. User-interface widgets must be created in a top-down fashion, with the parents created first, and then the children.

Why Toolkits?

There are a number of reasons for using an X toolkit, including:

✦ X designers worked hard to ensure software portability, so it shouldn't be surprising that they included guidelines for prewritten graphical user interfaces—why should software designers reinvent the wheel?

✦ The toolkit is the easiest way to provide consistent user interfaces from system to system and from implementation to implementation.

✦ Writing a complete application interface using Xlib forms a significant task. Xlib isn't known for brevity. You can save a lot of coding time by using a toolkit.

Few X toolkits, though, offer anything at all in terms of sophisticated graphics. Most X toolkits merely provide utilities to create your user interface. The rest is left to you. Therefore we divide our code along these natural lines: we use the X library for drawing, but the toolkit, for instance, Motif, for the interface.

To make this work, we need to get hooks into the low-level X library and especially to an X window for this technique to work. Motif, for example, provides a `XmDrawingArea` widget, which allows us access to the underlying window ID. OLIT similarly provides the `DrawArea` and older `Stub` widgets.

In the next chapter, we cover the basics of drawing into windows on the X display from any X toolkit. We continue on with a discussion of graphics techniques in Chapters 3 and 4. In Chapter 5, we introduce programming with the Motif toolkit. Chapter 6 covers programming with OLIT. (You may want to skip these two chapters if you're already familiar with an X toolkit.)

Summary

This chapter covers the basics of programming in the X Window System. Important points of terminology to remember include:

✦ X splits the computing into two parts: The client (application) and the server. The clients requests services from the server. As a programmer, you won't need to worry about this split.

✦ The server (also called a display) manages a number of screens, which may or may not be located on one physical monitor.

✦ Every X application must begin by opening a connection to the server, with the XOpenDisplay function.

✦ Sometimes an X server supports two wildly different screens, such as one monochrome and one color screen. You can tell how many screens are available using the ScreenCount macro.

✦ The X Window System supports a hierarchy of overlapping windows and subwindows on each screen. A window in X terminology is a rectangular area treated as a logical unit by the X server. Each window has its own local coordinate system, and all graphics output is clipped to the window boundaries. Windows may have child windows—also called subwindows, which are clipped to their bounds, or the bounds of their parents, whichever is smaller.

✦ Each X screen contains a root window covering the entire screen. The bounds of this window are the physical pixel resolution of the screen. You can think of the root window as a screen background.

✦ In the X Window System, the origin (0,0) is located in the upper left corner of the screen. *x* values increase going to the right. *y* values increase going down.

✦ The X server demands that your X applications always be able to redraw the contents of any of your application windows—at any time. X does not save the contents of any obscured windows. Even so, there are two techniques you can use to optimize performance and cut down on the number of redraw requests: save under and backing store.

✦ Before you can draw anything in X, you must determine what sort of display is being used. A number of functions and macros return the size of the display, as well as if it's color or black and white.

✦ In X, you can draw into windows and into offscreen drawing areas called pixmaps. Both pixmaps and windows are considered drawables. Each drawable is a structure in the X server and is represented in your programs with a long-integer ID number. Most X drawing functions, which we introduce in the next chapter, take a drawable ID as a parameter to tell the X library where you want to draw. All drawing with X also uses a graphics context to hold the pen parameters, like drawing color and line width.

✦ X encapsulates color under a concept called a *visual*. A visual is supposed to hide the messy details of the underlying color implementation. It's easiest to ignore the wide variety of visuals and instead concentrate on the simplest color visual type, called PseudoColor. Since most workstations provide a default PseudoColor visual, you can usually get away with this.

✦ Every X server preallocates at least two colors: black and white. These colors may not even look like the black and white we're all used to. In fact, they may be red and green, but at the very least these colors are supposed to contrast, so you can write text in one color on a background of the other color and have the text be viewable to a human observer.

✦ Event-driven programs are literally driven or controlled by incoming events from the X server. Event-driven programs are not like traditional noninteractive UNIX batch programs like ls, tr, and who. A batch program, such as a program to strip out all the control characters from a text file, takes in user input only at the beginning, usually to get the names of the input and output files. The batch program then chugs away on the input and produces the output. The program is in total control of itself. In an event-driven application, however, the program cedes control to the user. The user drives the actions of the program through a series of many events. The X Toolkit Intrinsics, used by Motif and OLIT, provides the XtAppMainLoop and XtMainLoop functions to handle this central event loop.

• The most popular X toolkits, or function libraries, are written in the C language and are based on the X Toolkit Intrinsics (or Xt for short), a pseudo-object-oriented layer provided with the X Window System. Xt programs use the concept of a widget to encapsulate an interface element, such as a scroll bar, menu, or pushbutton.

X Library Functions and Macros Introduced in This Chapter

```
BlackPixel
DefaultDepth
DefaultScreen
DisplayHeight
DisplayHeightMM
DisplayWidth
DisplayWidthMM
DoesBackingStore
DoesSaveUnders
RootWindow
ScreenCount
ScreenOfDisplay
WhitePixel
XClearWindow
XCloseDisplay
XMapRaised
XMapWindow
XOpenDisplay
XSetForeground
XUnmapWindow
```

X Toolkit Intrinsics Functions and Macros Introduced in This Chapter

```
XtMapWidget
```

OLIT Functions and Macros Introduced in This Chapter

```
OlBlackPixel
OlWhitePixel
```

Chapter 2

Drawing with X

This chapter covers:

- ✦ X drawing basics
- ✦ Drawing lines and points
- ✦ Drawing and filling rectangles
- ✦ Drawing arcs
- ✦ Drawing ovals
- ✦ Filling polygons
- ✦ Drawing line segments
- ✦ Drawing multiple lines, arcs, rectangles, and points
- ✦ When to draw
- ✦ Drawing efficiently

X Drawing Basics

The X Window System provides a number of drawing functions. But if you use an X toolkit exclusively, you may never see these drawing functions—that's because they're part of the low-level X library.

If you lean on public opinion when making your programming decisions, you may find a lot of partisan advice floating around. Many toolkit proponents will tell you that you can use Motif exclusively, or only Open Look Intrinsics Toolkit (OLIT) or XView or whatever toolkit is being pushed. In real life, though, we've found that most sophisticated applications require dropping down to the X library, or Xlib, level. Relying exclusively on a toolkit for complex animation or graphics just won't cut it.

A good rule in this situation is to use Motif (or your favorite toolkit) to provide the majority of the user interface, and then use the low-level Xlib functions for any raw graphics you need. For example, Motif won't help you display computer-aided design (CAD) drawings, computerized axial tomography (CAT) scans, or weather maps.

The usual technique, which we cover in Chapters 5 and 6, is to create a "raw" drawing widget (e.g., `XmDrawingArea` in Motif), and then draw all your graphics into that raw widget.

Basic Drawing Guidelines

When you draw with X, you must draw into a data type called a *drawable*. Drawables are an X catchall term for windows and pixmaps (offscreen drawing areas). In place of the drawable data type, really an unsigned long integer (*int*), you can pass either a window or pixmap ID.

The file `<X11/X.h>`, automatically included in `<X11/Xlib.h>`, defines types for `Drawable`, `Window`, and `Pixmap`:

```
typedef unsigned long XID;

typedef XID Drawable;

typedef XID Window;

typedef XID Pixmap;
```

In most cases, you'll draw into windows. (We cover pixmaps in Chapter 17.)

There are a few basics for drawing with Xlib that should help you better understand and use the functions introduced in this chapter. For example, just about every X drawing function uses the same parameter order:

✦ A `Display` pointer for the connection to the X server.

✦ A drawable ID (`Window` or `Pixmap`).

✦ A graphics context, or GC, which controls pen parameters.

✦ Required coordinates or values describing for what to draw.

For the coordinates, there are also a few simple rules:

✦ The location, x, y, comes first.

✦ x always comes before y.

✦ The size, width, height, come after the location.

✦ The width always comes before the height.

All rectangular shapes in X are defined in terms of the location of the shape (the upper left corner) and a size (the width and height of the shape).

The function names follow guidelines as well:

✦ XDraw*Something* functions, like XDrawRectangle, draws the outline of the shape.

✦ XFill*Something* functions, like XFillRectangle, fills in the shape.

The Graphics Context

We mentioned a graphics context, or GC, above. GCs are catchall data structures that contain almost everything needed to specify pen parameters for drawing. The GC contains the foreground and background colors, the width of the pen for drawing lines, whether lines should be dashed or solid, and so on. We'll cover GCs in depth in the next chapter. For now, just assume that you must create a GC and set up the colors and other drawing attributes you want.

X Toolkit Basics

If you use a toolkit based on the Xt Intrinsics, you'll deal primarily with *widgets* instead of *windows*. To use the functions in this chapter, you must extract the display pointer and window ID for a given widget.

`XtDisplay` returns the display pointer for a given widget:

```
Display* XtDisplay(Widget widget)
```

If you have a gadget or flat widget instead of a full-blown widget, use `XtDisplayOfObject`:

```
Display* XtDisplayOfObject(Widget widget)
```

`XtDisplayOfObject` is intended for those widgets that don't have an underlying X window, called *gadgets* in Motif and *flat widgets* in OLIT.

`XtWindow` returns the window ID for a given widget:

```
Window XtWindow(Widget widget)
```

Even though you can get the window ID, though, it is considered bad form to do so unless you're using a widget designed for drawing, such as the Motif `XmDrawingArea` or the OLIT `DrawArea` widgets.

Sometimes, you don't even have a widget, but instead a *gadget*, or light-weight widget, as mentioned above. For performance reasons, the Motif toolkit sometimes shares a window ID between a number of user-interface objects—gadgets. The purpose of gadgets is to avoid the window overhead in the X server when creating small, simple objects. Unfortunately, some gadget implementations are less efficient than using plain widgets. In addition, the X server has been optimized over the course of time so that each window takes up a lot less memory resources than in previous releases.

OLIT uses the term *flat widget* instead of gadget, but the basic concept is the same.

If you have one of these gadgets or flat widgets, you need to use the `XtWindowOfObject` function to get the window ID:

```
Window XtWindowOfObject(Widget widget)
```

`XtWindowOfObject` returns the window ID of the parent widget, or the parent's parent widget, and so on if you have gadgets within gadgets.

N O T E

The Xt Intrinsics do not create windows for widgets until you call `XtRealizeWidget` on a high-level parent widget. Until you call `XtRealizeWidget`, `XtWindow`, and `XtWindowOfObject` will return NULL. See Chapters 5 and 6 for more information on `XtRealizeWidget`.

After all those basics, you're probably anxious to get into actual functions for drawing.

X Drawing Functions

The X library provides drawing functions for common basic shapes, as listed in Table 2.1.

Table 2.1 *Xlib drawing functions.*

Drawing and Filling Functions

XDrawArc

XDrawLine

XDrawRectangle

XFillArc

XFillPolygon

XFillRectangle

Multiple-Item Functions

XDrawArcs

XDrawLines

XDrawPoints

XDrawRectangles

```
XDrawSegments
XFillArcs
XFillRectangles
```

We'll start by drawing lines.

Drawing Lines and Points

X defines a line as going from one pixel location (x1,y1) to another (x2,y2). XDrawLine draws such a line:

```
XDrawLine(Display* display,
     Drawable drawable,
     GC gc,
     int x1, int y1, /* starting point */
     int x2, int y2) /* ending point */
```

XDrawLine, and most other X drawing functions defined in <X11/Xlib.h>, have no defined return type and therefore use the default C return type of int. In real use, we treat these functions as if they have a void return type.

XDrawLine draws a line from (x1,y1) to (x2,y2) into the given *drawable* using the graphics context gc. The GC controls the pen, or drawing, parameters. Remember that the X Window coordinate system places the origin in the upper left corner. Y values increase going down. Depending on what graphics systems you're used to, the origin location may fool you for a while.

NOTE X coordinate values are usually converted to 16-bit signed integers, so you should keep your starting and ending coordinates within 0 to 32,767. The Xlib functions still take normal int (usually 32-bit) values, but convert internally to 16 bits. Since most monitors provide under-2,000-pixel resolution in x and y, you really shouldn't have a problem here for at least a few years. There is another problem with the width and height of windows and rectangles. These values should be kept under 16,000. Again, these size limitations shouldn't be a problem.

You can draw a single point with XDrawPoint:

```
XDrawPoint(Display* display,

    Drawable drawable,

    GC gc,

    int x, int y) /* 16-bit ints */
```

Drawing Multiple Points and Lines

If you intend to draw more than one point or line, you should consider using one of the functions that batches up multiple drawing requests into one function call. Sometimes, using these functions requires too many changes to your source code to be worthwhile. But if you're just starting out and you intend to draw 10 or more lines or points in a row, you should look into using XDrawLines or XDrawPoints. (We chose 10 as a arbitrary number. Up to 10 points or lines, it probably isn't worth converting your code. At some point after 10 lines or points, though, you should see a performance boost using XDrawLines or XDrawPoints.)

Both functions take a similar set of parameters:

```
XDrawLines(Display* display,

    Drawable drawable,

    GC gc,

    XPoint* points,

    int number_points,

    int mode)


XDrawPoints(Display* display,

    Drawable drawable,

    GC gc,

    XPoint* points,
```

```
        int number_points,
        int mode)
```

XDrawLines connects all the points in the XPoint array. You might consider the use of XDrawLines to create a form of polyline. XDrawPoints draws unconnected points; use XDrawSegments, below, for drawing multiple unconnected lines.

To use these functions, you need to fill in the array of XPoint structures and then call the drawing function. The XPoint structure is defined as:

```
typedef struct {
        short           x, y;
} XPoint;
```

You must allocate your own array of XPoint structures and then pass a pointer to the first array item to XDrawPoints or XDrawLines.

Coordinate Modes

The coordinate *mode* used with XDrawPoints and XDrawLines specifies how the coordinate values in the XPoint array should be interpreted. You need to pass CoordModeOrigin or CoordModePrevious.

CoordModeOrigin means that all coordinates are defined in terms of the window's origin.

CoordModePrevious means that each point is merely an offset from the previous point in the XPoint array (the first point is then an offset from the origin). This mode can be good for drawing lines in *turtle graphics*, where the ending point of one line is the starting location for the next, and all movements are described as the motion from the last point (i.e., relative to the last point). This mode is often useful for displaying CAD drawings. We normally use CoordModeOrigin, but CoordModePrevious may better fit into your coding style or needs.

Drawing and Filling Rectangles

As you'd expect, X provides functions for drawing rectangles. XDrawRectangle draws the outline of a rectangle:

```
XDrawRectangle(Display* display,

    Drawable drawable,

    GC gc,

    int x, int y,          /* 16-bit int */

    unsigned int width,    /* 16-bit unsigned int */

    unsigned int height)   /* 16-bit unsigned int */
```

XFillRectangle fills in a rectangle:

```
XFillRectangle(Display* display,

    Drawable drawable,

    GC gc,

    int x, int y,          /* 16-bit int */

    unsigned int width,    /* 16-bit unsigned int */

    unsigned int height)   /* 16-bit unsigned int */
```

Drawing Multiple Rectangles

Much like you can draw multiple lines or points, you can also draw multiple rectangles. XDrawRectangles draws the outline of the rectangles in an array of XRectangle structures:

```
XDrawRectangles(Display* display,

    Drawable drawable,

    GC gc,

    XRectangle* rectangles,

    int number_rectangles)
```

Like XDrawLines, you must allocate your own array of XRectangle structures. The XRectangle structure looks like:

```
typedef struct {

    short          x, y;
```

```
    unsigned short  width, height;
} XRectangle;
```

`XFillRectangles` fills in each rectangle in an array of rectangles:

```
XFillRectangles(Display* display,
    Drawable drawable,
    GC gc,
    XRectangle* rectangles,
    int number_rectangles)
```

Unlike `XDrawLines`, `XDrawRectangles` and `XFillRectangles` do *not* connect the rectangles. Each rectangle in the `XRectangle` array is drawn separately.

Drawing Arcs

Every graphics system seems to define arcs differently. In X, an *arc* is bounded by a rectangle, and the sweep of the arc is limited to the box formed by the rectangle. The arc begins at a *start angle* and draws an arc for a distance specified by a *path* or *sweep angle*. If that isn't confusing enough, the angle values are given in 64ths of a degree—meaning a full circular path is 360 degrees times 64—or 23,040.

`XDrawArc`, as the function name seems to imply, draws an arc:

```
XDrawArc(Display* display,
    Drawable drawable,
    GC gc,
    int x, y,                /* 16-bit int */
    unsigned int width,      /* 16-bit unsigned int */
    unsigned int height,     /* 16-bit unsigned int */
    int start_angle,         /* 16-bit int, degrees * 64 */
    int sweep_angle)         /* 16-bit int, degrees * 64 */
```

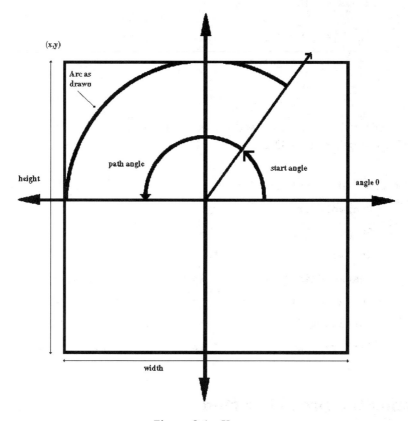

Figure 2.1 *X arcs.*

XDrawArc draws an arc that fits in a rectangle, from *start_angle* to *sweep_angle*. Angles are in 1/64 degrees. That is, multiply the degrees by 64 to get the value to place into *start_angle* and *sweep_angle*.

The *width* and *height* parameters must be positive numbers, or you can get in trouble, especially with shared-library X servers. You may want to test the *width* and *height* parameters each time you try to draw or fill an arc:

N O T E

```
if ( width < 1 ) {
    width = 1;
}
```

```
if ( height < 1 ) {
    height = 1;
}
```

XFillArc fills in an arc based on the graphic context's arc-filling mode (ArcChord or ArcPieSlice):

```
XFillArc(Display* display,
    Drawable drawable,
    GC gc,
    int x, y,                /* 16-bit int */
    unsigned int width,      /* 16-bit unsigned int */
    unsigned int height,     /* 16-bit unsigned int */
    int start_angle,         /* 16-bit int, degrees * 64 */
    int sweep_angle)         /* 16-bit int, degrees * 64 */
```

Setting the Arc-Filling Mode

You can change a GC's arc-filling mode with XSetArcMode:

```
XSetArcMode(Display* display,
    GC gc,
    int arc_mode)
```

XSetArcMode sets the mode for filling arcs in the graphics context to ArcChord (draw chords or circle segments) or ArcPieSlice (fill in slices of circles).

The figure on the next page describes ArcPieSlice fairly well. ArcChord, though, isn't so clear. ArcChord works by drawing a line segment between the ends of the arc and then filling in the resulting shape.

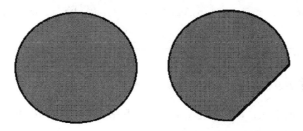

Figure 2.2   *Arc-filling modes: ArcChord on left, ArcPieSlice on right .*

Drawing Multiple Arcs

You can draw multiple arcs with XDrawArcs:

```
XDrawArcs(Display* display,
    Drawable drawable,
    GC gc,
    XArc* arcs,
    int number_arcs)
```

You can fill multiple arcs with XFillArcs:

```
XFillArcs(Display* display,
    Drawable drawable,
    GC gc,
    XArc* arcs,
    int number_arcs)
```

XFillArcs uses the graphic context's arc mode (ArcChord or ArcPieSlice), described above. Both functions use an array of XArc *structures*:

```
typedef struct {
    short          x, y;
    unsigned short  width, height;
```

```
short              angle1, angle2; /* Degrees * 64 */
} XArc;
```

Drawing Multiple Arcs Example

Here's an example for drawing multiple shapes with X. It shows that when drawing multiple shapes with X, you must first allocate an array of the proper size to hold the parameters for the shapes you want to draw. In this case, we allocate an array of XArc structures (structs), with at least as many elements as we plan on drawing. The example code draws two arcs:

```
Display*   display;
Drawable   drawable;
GC         gc;
int        number_arcs;
XArc       arcs[ 2 ];
arcs[ 0 ].x      = 10;
arcs[ 0 ].y      = 142;
arcs[ 0 ].width  = 50;
arcs[ 0 ].height = 50;
arcs[ 0 ].angle1 = 0;       /* start angle */
arcs[ 0 ].angle2 = 360*64; /* sweep angle: full circle */
arcs[ 1 ].x      = 200;
arcs[ 1 ].y      = 221;
arcs[ 1 ].width  = 50;
arcs[ 1 ].height = 50;
arcs[ 1 ].angle1 = 0;       /* start angle */
arcs[ 1 ].angle2 = 180*64; /* sweep angle: half circle */

number_arcs = 2;

XDrawArcs(display, drawable, gc,
          arcs, number_arcs);
```

Drawing Ovals

The X library provides no means for drawing or filling circles, ovals, and ellipses. Instead, you must write your own functions. The basic idea is simple—we can draw an oval using an arc with a sweep angle that goes 360 degrees around a circle. By convention, we use 0 for the start angle and 360 * 64 for the sweep angle.

To make the code clearer, we use two constants, START_CIRCLE (0) and FULL_CIRCLE (360*64):

```
#define START_CIRCLE    0
#define FULL_CIRCLE     (360*64)
```

For performance reasons, we could define FULL_CIRCLE to be 23040 (the value of 360*64), but we wanted to highlight the fact that X defines arc angles in terms of 1/64 degrees. We've created two convenience functions for drawing ovals, DrawOval and FillOval. The file drawoval.c contains these functions:

```
/*
 *  drawoval.c
 *  Routines to draw and fill ovals.
 *
 */
#include "draw.h"

/*
 *  Angles for drawing an arc around a circle.
 *  X angles are defined in 64ths of degrees.
 */
#define START_CIRCLE    0
#define FULL_CIRCLE     (360*64)


void DrawOval(Display* display,
```

```
        Drawable drawable,
        GC gc,
        int x, int y,
        int width, int height)

{   /* DrawOval */

    if (width < 1) {
        width = 1;
    }

    if (height < 1) {
        height = 1;
    }

    XDrawArc(display, drawable, gc,
        x, y, width, height,
        START_CIRCLE,
        FULL_CIRCLE);

}   /* DrawOval */

void FillOval(Display* display,
        Drawable drawable,
        GC gc,
        int x, int y,
        int width, int height)

{   /* FillOval */

    if (width < 1) {
```

```
        width = 1;
    }


    if (height < 1) {
        height = 1;
    }


    XFillArc(display, drawable, gc,
        x, y, width, height,
        START_CIRCLE,
        FULL_CIRCLE);


}        /* FillOval */


/* end of file drawoval.c */
```

The header file `draw.h` provides standard C function prototypes and includes the necessary Xlib header file, `<X11/Xlib.h>`. We cover `draw.h` in Appendix B.

Filling Polygons

Up to now, we've discussed drawing fairly common shapes like rectangles, lines, and arcs. Not all your drawing needs may be met by these functions, though, as you may need to fill arbitrary polygon shapes. For this need, use `XFillPolygon`:

```
XFillPolygon(Display* display,
    Drawable drawable,
    GC gc,
    XPoint* points,
    int number_points,
```

```
    int shape,

    int mode)
```

Set the *shape* parameter to `Complex`, `Convex`, or `Nonconvex`. These values are used by `XFillPolygon` to optimize performance for simple cases. `Complex` means that edges in the polygon may intersect. If you know this is not true, then pass `Nonconvex`, which means that the edges do not intersect, but the polygon is not known to be convex. `Convex` means that for any two points inside the polygon, a line connecting the two points will not intersect any edge.

Using `Convex` as the shape should speed up the performance of `XFillPolygon`, but be careful. If you try to fool `XFillPolygon` by passing an incorrect *shape* parameter, the results are undefined and probably not what you wanted.

The *mode* parameter should be `CoordModeOrigin` or `CoordModePrevious`, as defined above.

 There is no XDrawPolygon. Use XDrawLines instead.

NOTE

Drawing Line Segments

To draw multiple unconnected lines, use `XDrawSegments`:

```
    XDrawSegments(Display* display,

        Drawable drawable,

        GC gc,

        XSegment* segments,

        int number_segments)
```

Unlike `XDrawLines`, discussed earlier, `XDrawSegments` does not connect the lines it draws. The lines are drawn in the order they appear in the `XSegment` array. Each line segment is stored in an `XSegment` structure, which is defined below:

```
typedef struct {
        short      x1, y1, x2, y2;
} XSegment;
```

All numbers in the XSegment structure are signed 16-bit integers.

Drawing Multiple Lines, Arcs, Rectangles, and Points

The X library converts all X drawing requests into network packets to send out "over the wire" to the X server. Remember that the X server normally is a distinct process separate from your application and that all X requests are sent out to the X server over an interprocess communication channel, usually a network link. Due to operating-system (usually some incarnation of UNIX, although you're not supposed to take this into account) limitations, there are only so many requests that you can bundle together into one network packet. Newer versions of the X library will automatically break up very large requests, but older X libraries didn't break up big requests into packets. The danger is that you may exceed the operating-system buffer size with your large packet.

If you're using a lot of combined drawing requests, such as XDrawLines, or one of the other multiple-item drawing functions and have a large array of items to draw, you should check on the largest size you can safely send out at once. XMaxRequestSize returns the largest supported packet size, in units of 4 bytes:

```
long XMaxRequestSize(Display* display)
```

You can then add up the size of each element in one of your arrays, using the standard C *sizeof operator*, for example:

```
#include <stddef.h>

size_t array_element_size;

array_element_size = sizeof(XRectangle);
```

Once you have the size of one element, you can figure out how many elements you can send. Each X network packet will have its own header and may require extra padding bytes, so a good rule of thumb is to never get too close to the maximum request size. Leave yourself some room to spare.

When to Draw

As we stated in Chapter 1, X Window applications are event-driven. One of the event types defined by X is the `Expose` event. This event arrives when your application needs to redraw part of a window. Each `Expose` event contains a single rectangle that your application needs to redraw. X, unlike other windowing systems, does not automatically protect obscured parts of windows. When part of your window becomes unobscured, your application is responsible for redrawing that formerly obscured area.

The save-under and backing-store requests, covered in Chapter 1, may cut down the number of `Expose` events, but you cannot depend on these requests. Consequently, your applications are still responsible for redrawing `Expose`d areas.

Additionally, because X is an asynchronous windowing system, there can be a delay between the time you create and map your windows and when they actually appear on the screen. (Most window managers also intercept your requests and place a window-manager title bar or other so-called "decorations" around your window.)

There are a few simple rules for drawing any graphics with X:

✦ Don't draw *anything* until your application gets the first `Expose` event.

✦ Anything you try to draw into a window before it is fully mapped may be lost.

✦ Be prepared to redraw any area of any window at any time.

We'll cover `Expose` events in more depth in Chapter 4. At that point, we'll also discuss a number of techniques for efficient handling of `Expose` events. For now, though, the rules above should suffice.

Drawing Efficiently

X is an asynchronous windowing system, and the X library batches up drawing requests. The XFlush function flushes out the batched drawing requests and sends them to the X server:

```
XFlush(Display* display)
```

Because each batch you send to the X server may result in a network communication packet, judicious use of XFlush can make your programs work a lot better. If you call XFlush after every drawing function, you'll get your graphics out to the screen as soon as possible—remember the asynchronous delay imposed by X's distributed nature. Each time you call XFlush, though, your application incurs a network packet overhead. You probably don't want to call XFlush after every drawing function.

Instead, the best time to call XFlush is after you've drawn a logical grouping of items. For example, if you are drawing out a whole windowful of spreadsheet cells, call the Xlib drawing functions for the whole window and only then call XFlush to send out all the output. This way, it looks like the whole window was updated at once. This generally looks better than drawing and flushing each cell one at a time—even if the total time for the drawing is the same. This difference is in the user's perception of the speed. If it looks like all the items are drawn at the same time, the perceived speed is enhanced.

Because XFlush incurs the network transmission overhead, though, you'll probably increase more than the user's perception of speed if you batch your Xlib drawing requests.

Synchronizing the Display

To make sure that all your drawing requests are actually drawn to the screen before going on, you can use the XSync function:

```
XSync(Display* display, Bool discard_events)
```

XSync flushes the output buffer and waits for the server to process events. Also, XSync calls the error-handling function for each Xlib error (see below).

If the *discard_events* parameter is True, XSync discards all events in the queue. We almost always pass False, so that the events are merely queued up and not discarded.

XSync is also very useful for debugging purposes.

N O T E

Don't confuse the XSync function mentioned above with the similarly named XSynchronize. XSynchronize places your program into synchronous mode, which is also useful for debugging, but slows your programs down dramatically.

Summary

The X Window System provides many drawing tools that should be indispensable for any graphics programmer. The key to using them, though, is to use the low-level X library, as opposed to higher-level X toolkits (e.g., Motif or OLIT).

This chapter covered Xlib tools for drawing:

✦ Lines and points;
✦ Rectangles;
✦ Arcs;
✦ Ovals;
✦ Polygons;
✦ Line segments;
✦ Multiple lines; and
✦ Points.

In addition, we covered Xlib tools that allow for more efficient communications: XSync, which flushes the output buffer and waits for the server to process events; and XFlush, which flushes out the batched drawing requests and sends them to the X server.

X Library Functions and Macros Introduced in This Chapter

XDrawArc

XDrawArcs

XDrawLine

XDrawLines

XDrawPoint

XDrawPoints

XDrawRectangle

XDrawRectangles

XDrawSegments

XFillArc

XFillArcs

XFillPolygon

XFillRectangle

XFillRectangles

XFlush

XMaxRequestSize

XSetArcMode

XSync

X Toolkit Intrinsics Functions and Macros Introduced in This Chapter

XtDisplay

XtDisplayOfObject

XtWindow

XtWindowOfObject

C h a p t e r   3

The Graphics Context

This chapter covers:

+ Controlling pen parameters with the graphics context, or GC
+ Creating GCs
+ GC values in depth
+ Setting the foreground and background colors for drawing
+ Dashed lines and other drawing parameters
+ Drawing modes or functions
+ Using the XOR mode for rubber-banding lines
+ Plane masks for drawing to a single color plane
+ Clipping and clip masks
+ Freeing GCs
+ Modifying GCs
+ Using GCs with X toolkits
+ Using GCs efficiently

51

Controlling Pen Parameters with the Graphics Context

The *graphics context*, or *GC*, is a catchall data structure that contains almost everything needed to specify "pen" parameters for drawing. The GC contains the foreground and background colors, the width of the pen for drawing lines, and the arc-filling mode (ArcChord or ArcPieSlice, as covered in the last chapter). The GC controls the *graphics pipeline*, the set of tasks that convert your drawing functions into pixels on the screen. This graphics pipeline includes clipping, line widths, colors, tiling, and stippling.

Each Xlib drawing function introduced in the last chapter requires a GC. In this chapter, we cover how to create, modify, and efficiently use GCs for your graphics. While most X toolkits will take care of the display pointer and window ID, you will generally create a graphics context by hand.

Xlib Functions for GCs

The functions in Table 3.1 operate on graphics contexts.

Table 3.1 *Functions that operate on graphics contexts.*

GC Functions

XChangeGC	XSetFillStyle
XCopyGC	XSetFont
XCreateGC	XSetForeground
XFreeGC	XSetFunction
XGetGCValues	XSetGraphicsExposures
XSetArcMode	XSetLineAttributes
XSetBackground	XSetPlaneMask
XSetClipMask	XSetState
XSetClipOrigin	XSetStipple
XSetClipRectangles	XSetSubwindowMode
XSetDashes	XSetTile
XSetFillRule	XSetTSOrigin

Creating GCs

Before you can use a GC, you must create it. Create a graphics context with
XCreateGC:

```
GC XCreateGC(Display* display,
    Drawable drawable,
    unsigned long valuemask,
    XGCValues* gcvalues)
```

XCreateGC creates a new graphics context for the given *drawable* (a
window or a pixmap). The drawable parameter is important because GCs
are tied to drawables. When creating a graphics context, you must specify
which window (or pixmap) it is created for. Once created, you can use the
GC to draw into the given drawable, or if it is a window, into subwindows
of the window passed to XCreateGC as well.

You can create multiple graphics contexts for a given window or
pixmap. In fact, this technique often leads to performance boosts. Watch
out, though: too many GCs eat up too many resources in the X server and
within your program (see the section called Using GCs Efficiently, near the
end of this chapter).

For efficiency, you can set up the initial pen parameters for the newly
created GC and create the GC all in one operation—using the aforemen-
tioned XCreateGC function. To do so, you fill in the desired parameters
into the XGCValues structure and then set the *valuemask* to hold the
proper flags. The reason for the *valuemask* is that you don't have to fill in
all the values into the XGCValues structure—just the values you want.
The *valuemask* then contains a set of bit-flags, indicating which fields of
the XGCValues structure you filled in. The bit-flags contain the inclusive
OR of a set of predefined flags.

Use these values with care, or you can mess up your application—be sure to set the bits in the valuemask for only those
fields in the XGCValues structure that you actually filled in.

WARNING

In the code below, we show how to create a GC and set the foreground and
background drawing colors, all in the same call to XCreateGC:

```
GC CreateGC(Display* display,
    Drawable drawable,
    unsigned long forecolor,
    unsigned long backcolor)


{   /* CreateGC */
  XGCValues       xgcvalues;
  GC              gc;
  unsigned long   valuemask;


  xgcvalues.foreground = forecolor;
  xgcvalues.background = backcolor;


  /* OR together the proper bit-flags */
  valuemask = GCForeground | GCBackground;


  gc = XCreateGC(display,
        drawable,
        valuemask,
        &xgcvalues);


  return gc;


}   /* CreateGC */
```

In most cases, the GC can be created with the default values. If you need more than the defaults, you must fill fields in the XGCValues structure.

The XGCValues Structure

If you want to use different values than the defaults when you create a GC, you need to fill in the proper values in the XGCValues structure:

```
    typedef struct {
        int             function;       /* e.g. GXxor */
        unsigned long   plane_mask;
        unsigned long   foreground;
        unsigned long   background;
        int             line_width;     /* (in pixels) */
        int             line_style;
        int             cap_style;
        int             join_style;
        int             fill_style;
        int             fill_rule;
        int             arc_mode;
        Pixmap          tile;
        Pixmap          stipple;        /* 1 plane pixmap */
        int             ts_x_origin;
        int             ts_y_origin;
        Font            font;
        int             subwindow_mode;
        Bool            graphics_exposures;
        int             clip_x_origin;
        int             clip_y_origin;
        Pixmap          clip_mask;
        int             dash_offset;
        char            dashes;
    } XGCValues;
```

If you create a GC and change some of the defaults in the XGCValues structure, you also need to set the proper bits in the *valuemask*. The *valuemask* is the inclusive OR of the bit-flags for the fields you fill in. In the chart below, we present the XGCValues field, the default value, and the bitmask name.

Use the proper bit-flags for the fields you fill in the XGCValues structure. You can also use one of many GC convenience functions to change the GC's attributes, which we describe below. In many cases, though, you can just stick with the default GC values.

Default GC Values

The default values are listed in Table 3.2.

Table 3.2   *GC default values and bitmasks.*

XGCValues Field	Default Value	Bitmask Name
arc_mode	ArcPieSlice	GCArcMode
background	1 (sometimes white)	GCBackground
cap_style	CapButt	GCCapStyle
clip_mask	None	GCClipMask
clip_x_origin	0	GCClipXOrigin
clip_y_origin	0	GCClipYOrigin
dashes	[4,4]	GCDashList
dash_offset	0	GCDashOffset
fill_rule	EvenOddRule	GCFillRule
fill_style	FillSolid	GCFillStyle
font	fixed	GCFont
foreground	0 (sometimes black)	GCForeground
function	GXcopy	GCFunction
graphics_ exposures	True	GCGraphics Exposures
join_style	JoinMiter	GCJoinStyle
line_style	LineSolid	GCLineStyle
line_width	0	GCLineWidth
plane_mask	all planes (all 1s)	GCPlaneMask
stipple	pixmap with all 1s	GCStipple
subwindow_mode	ClipByChildren	GCSubwindowMode
tile	pixmap with foreground	GCTile
ts_x_origin	0	GCTileStipXOrigin
ts_y_origin	0	GCTileStipYOrigin

The default foreground and background colors (0 and 1, respectively) sometimes equate to white and black. But you cannot depend on this across computer systems. Always set the foreground and background color to values valid for your system. See Chapter 7 on color for more on this.

Newly created GCs have a default font, usually the font named *fixed*. On some systems, though, trying to use this default font generates an X error. So never try to use a font with a GC unless your application loads the font first. See Chapter 14 for more on fonts.

The default line width of zero does not imply invisible lines. A zero line width means that any hardware line-drawing acceleration may be used. For more information, see the line width section, later in this chapter, under Setting the Line Attributes.

Don't use tiling or stippling without setting up the proper tile or stipple masks.

GC Values in Depth

In order to change GC values, you need to know exactly what all the fields in the XGCValues structure mean and how to change them. The next sections in this chapter cover that. Along with the fields in the XGCValues structure, we also cover the GC convenience functions used to change the settings for already-created GCs. For most common settings, such as the foreground drawing color, the X library provides handy utility functions to set the value, in this case, XSetForeground.

Arc Mode

We covered the arc-filling mode in the last chapter when we discussed filling ovals. You can set the *arc_mode* field in the XGCValues structure or call XSetArcMode:

```
XSetArcMode(Display* display,
      GC gc,
      int arc_mode)
```

The allowable values for the *arc_mode* are ArcChord (draw chords or circle segments) or ArcPieSlice (fill in slices of circles). The *valuemask* bit-flag is GCArcMode.

Background Color

The background color is used for drawing the background of text, when you draw text with the XDrawImageString or XDrawImageString 16 functions. You can set the *background* field to any valid *color index* (also called a *pixel value* in a confusing rehash of common terminology) in the current colormap. (Each window may have its own associated colormap.) The values returned by the BlackPixel and WhitePixel macros are valid color indexes for the default colormap. Unless you mess with colormaps, you're using the default colormap.

```
XSetBackground(Display* display,

    GC gc,

    unsigned long background)
```

The bit-flag for the *valuemask* is GCBackground.

Dashing

X allows you to define how dashed lines are drawn, but take note that dashed lines are much more expensive to draw than normal solid lines. The *dash list* is a character array where each character is treated as a number— the number of pixels for that element of dashing. That is, the first character holds the number of pixels drawn for the first dash, the second character in the dash list holds the number of pixels drawn for the second dash, and so forth.

If this isn't complex enough, the *dash offset* determines how many pixels into the dash list that the dashing should start. The dash offset is also called the *phase* of the dashing. You can fill in the *dash_offset* and *dashes* fields of the XGCValues structure, or call XSetDashes to change the definition of dashing:

```
XSetDashes(Display* display,
```

```
GC gc,

int dash_offset,

char* dash_list,

int number_in_list)
```

The *number_in_list* parameter is how many characters are in the *dash_list*. Most of the time, though, you won't need to change the definition of dashing.

Note that lines won't be drawn dashed unless you also set the line style to LineOnOffDash or LineDoubleDash. The *valuemask* bit-flags are GCDashList and GCDashOffset.

Fill Rule

The *fill rule* determines how filled objects will be drawn, especially complex polygons. You can set a GC's fill rule to EvenOddRule or WindingRule. Both rules are used to determine if a point is inside or outside a polygon.

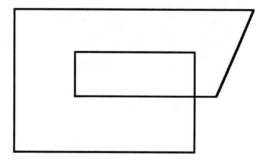

Figure 3.1   *A polygon.*

The EvenOddRule determines that a point is inside the polygon if a ray with the point as its origin crosses the path of the polygon an odd number of times.

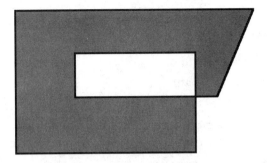

Figure 3.2   The EvenOddRule.

The `WindingRule` determines that a point is inside the polygon if a ray with the point as its origin crosses an unequal number of clockwise and counterclockwise path segments.

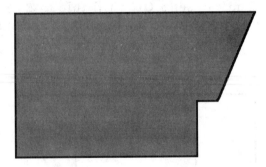

Figure 3.3   The WindingRule.

To set the fill rule, fill in the *fill_rule* field of the XGCValues structure, or use the XSetFillRule function:

```
XSetFillRule(Display* display,
    GC gc,
    int fill_rule)
```

The *valuemask* bit-flag is GCFillRule.

Fill Style

The *fill style* controls whether tiling or stippling will be used. The default, a fill style of `FillSolid`, acts like you would expect: filled objects are filled as solid objects with the foreground color. You can also set the fill style to `FillTiled`, which uses the GC's tile pixmap as a form of brush. With `FillStippled`, the foreground color is masked by the GC's stipple. The `FillOpaqueStippled` style acts like a tile, where the foreground color is drawn for every one bit in the stipple mask and the background color is drawn for every zero bit in the stipple mask.

You can set the `fill_style` field of the `XGCValues` structure or call the `XSetFillStyle` function:

```
XSetFillStyle(Display* display,

    GC gc,

    int fill_style)
```

The *valuemask* bit-flag is `GCFillStyle`.

N O T E   When drawing double dashes, a fill style of `FillSolid` draws the background color for the odd dashes. A fill style of `FillStippled` masks the background color with the GC's stipple and draws this for the odd dashes. For `FillTiled` and `FillOpaqueStippled`, the odd and even dashes are drawn the same.

Font

The *font* field of the `XGCValues` structure controls which font the GC draws with. That is, when you draw text, the GC determines which font is used. The `XSetFont` function sets the font used by a GC:

```
XSetFont(Display* display,

    GC gc,

    Font font)
```

The *font* parameter is a font ID, which we'll cover in depth in Section 3 when we discuss fonts and text. Even though the GCs often have a default font set up, many X implementations don't provide a proper default font. To avoid nasty X errors, always be sure to set the GC's font before drawing any text.

The *valuemask* bit-flag is GCFont.

Foreground Color

The foreground color is used to draw. When you call XDrawLine, for example, the new line is drawn in the GC's foreground color. You can set the *foreground* field in the XGCValues structure or call XSetForeground with any valid color index—or pixel—value:

```
XSetForeground(Display* display,
     GC gc,
     unsigned long foreground)
```

The bit-flag for the *valuemask* is GCForeground.

GC Drawing Functions

X provides 16 GC raster graphics modes or *drawing functions*, although the name *function* is misleading, since most C programmers already have a working definition of the word *function*. The GC function is more like a drawing mode, such as drawing in XOR mode—used commonly for rubber-band lines.

To change the GC's drawing function or mode, you can set the *function* field of the XGCValues structure or call the XSetFunction function:

```
XSetFunction(Display* display,
     GC gc,
     int function)
```

The *valuemask* bit-flag is GCFunction.

The most commonly used GC drawing mode or function is GXcopy, which merely draws your graphics to a window or pixmap—just like you'd expect. GXcopy is, in fact, the default. The other modes tend to the obscure.

The GC function names are defined in the include file <X11/X.h>, usually included automatically from the file <X11/Xlib.h>.

Table 3.3 *GC functions or modes.*

GC Function Name	What it Does
GXand	ANDS source and destination bits
GXandInverted	Inverts source (NOT source), then ANDS with destination bits
GXandReverse	ANDS source with inverted destination bits (([NOT dest] AND source)
GXclear	Clears out area (not portable!)
GXcopy	Places down source, wipes out destination bits (default)
GXcopyInverted	Inverts the source (NOT source), wipes out destination bits
GXequiv	Inverts the source (NOT source), then XORs with destination bits ([NOT source] XOR dest)
GXinvert	Inverts the destination bits (NOT dest)
GXnand	Inverts the source (NOT source), inverts the destination (NOT dest), then ORs the two ((NOT source) OR (NOT dest))
GXnoop	Leaves the destination bits alone
GXnor	Inverts the source (NOT source), inverts the destination (NOT dest), and ANDs the two together ([NOT source] AND [NOT dest])
GXor	ORs the source and the destination bits (source OR dest)

`GXorInverted`	Inverts the source (NOT source), then ORs with the destination bits ([NOT source] OR dest)
`GXorReverse`	ORs the source with the inverted destination bits (source OR [NOT dest])
`GXset`	Sets all the bits in the drawing area (not portable!)
`GXxor`	Exclusive-ORs the source and the destination bits (used for rubber-band lines)

NOTE

Be careful when using the GC functions `GXclear` and `GXset`, as these functions do not necessarily work the same way on every machine. They depend on the use of 1 and 0 for the values of `BlackPixel` and `WhitePixel`—and these values do not hold true on all X servers. In fact, the only modes most people will ever use are `GXcopy` and `GXxor`. And you'll use `GXcopy` 99 percent of the time. Also, be careful to distinguish between `GXor` and `GXxor`—it's easy to type one when you mean the other!

Notes on GC Raster Functions

Many of the GC drawing modes or functions execute logical operations on the pixels you're drawing and on the pixels already in the drawable (pixmap or window) you're drawing to. The problem is that (unless you carefully check) you normally have no idea what the pixel values for colors really are. The pixel for red, for example, could be 5, 15, or 55 (or anything else), depending on how—and when—the color red was originally allocated. Green could have a pixel value of 2, 3, or 33 (or anything else). If you draw with a red pixel onto an existing green pixel and apply an XOR operation, then the result may be some odd color in the colormap—nearly any color.

The GC functions `GXcopyInverted`, `GXequiv`, `GXinvert`, `GXnand`, `GXnor`, `GXorInverted`, and `GXorReverse` all output some variety of odd colors on a color system (depending on what color cells are already allocated and what placement these colors have in the colormap you're using).

In fact, unless you have a monochrome system, you're never sure of exactly *what* will happen when you use the more obscure GC raster drawing modes. When inverting colored pixels, you get other colors, depending on the positions of colors in the colormap you're using. When inverting pixels on a monochrome system, you can only get black or white. Using any raster operation other than GXcopy can result in a confusing display.

Even with this caveat, though, the GC raster operations are all you have, so generally, you can either query all the colors defined in the colormap (see Chapter 10) or just live with the results.

Using the XOR Mode for Rubber-Banding Lines

If drawn twice, a line drawn in exclusive-OR mode will disappear, leaving the original drawing intact. This is the basic means to create *rubber-band lines*, which are used in most graphics drawing packages.

The term *rubber-band* is used because the lines look like a rubber band is stretched between the starting and ending points. As the user moves the mouse, the ending point constantly changes to reflect the current mouse position. The rubber-band line provides feedback to the user, telling, in effect, what the line would look like if the user locked in the line to the current position. Of course, you can also draw rubber-band rectangles, ovals, and anything else you care to. Starting with lines is just easier.

To draw rubber-band lines (or any other sort of rubber-band shape), you need to first set up a graphics context for drawing rubber-band lines, which we show below. From there, the basic method is simple:

- ✦ Select an anchor point and store the x, y coordinates.

- ✦ Draw the line from the anchor point to the current mouse pointer location, which forms the endpoint of the line. Also store this endpoint.

- ✦ When the mouse pointer moves, redraw the old line to erase it (drawing anything twice in GXxor mode erases it). Then, draw a new line from the anchor point to the new mouse pointer location.

- ✦ When the user finally selects the endpoint (usually by releasing a mouse button), you need to erase the last rubber-band line you drew, in order to get rid of any XOR pixels, and redraw the line using the permanent drawing mode (usually GXcopy).

Setting Up an XOR GC

There are a few rules you need to follow to properly set up an XOR graphics context for drawing rubber-band lines:

1. Set the *foreground* color to the exclusive OR of the desired foreground and background colors:

```
xgcvalues.foreground = forecolor ^ backcolor;
```

2. Set the *background* color to 0:

```
xgcvalues.background = 0;
```

3. Set the *function* field to GXxor:

```
xgcvalues.function  = GXxor;
```

4. Pass the proper flags to XCreateGC: GCBackground, GCForeground, and GCFunction:

```
Display*        display;
Drawable        drawable;
unsigned long forecolor;
unsigned long backcolor;
XGCValues       xgcvalues;
GC              gc;


xgcvalues.foreground = forecolor ^ backcolor;
xgcvalues.background = 0;
xgcvalues.function  = GXxor;


gc = XCreateGC( display,
        drawable,
```

```
( GCForeground | GCBackground | GCFunction ),
&xgcvalues );
```

Once the rubber-band GC is set up, use the normal drawing functions, such as XDrawLine, XDrawRectangle, and XDrawArc.

NOTE

If other drawing takes place between the time the line is first drawn in XOR mode and the time the line is redrawn (to clear it out), the original picture may not be restored. This method of drawing rubber-band lines using GXxor depends on the original picture not changing between calls. Normally, no other program will be drawing to your windows, so this shouldn't be a problem. If you intend to draw using GXxor over other windows, you should be aware of this. Window managers typically allow you to move windows about the screen. These window managers often use GXxor to draw a ghost outline of the window, showing its size and shape, so you can better place it. These window managers need to stop all other graphics output while this takes place, or the screen will tend to look messy. All graphics output from other programs can be held up by grabbing the X server exclusively for your program during this time.

Graphics Exposures

When you copy areas of drawables (windows or pixmaps), there is always the chance that some of the source area is not visible. For windows, this source area could be covered by another window, or the source area could be outside of the window's bounds. For pixmaps, you can also have a source that transcends the pixmap's bounds. In this case, you application may receive GraphicsExpose events that describe the empty areas of the *destination* drawable.

GraphicsExpose events arrive in batches, like Expose events.

If there is no problem with the source area for copying, your application receives a single NoExpose event.

Whether or not your application receives GraphicsExpose and NoExpose events is determined by the graphics context used for the copy operation. To receive such events, you can set the *graphics_exposures* field in the XGCValues structure to True, or call the XSetGraphicsExposures function:

```
XSetGraphicsExposures(Display* display,

    GC gc,

    Bool graphics_exposures)
```

The *valuemask* bit-flag is GCGraphicsExposures. See the next chapter for more on GraphicsExpose events.

Setting the Line Attributes

There are a number of GC attributes that control how X draws lines. These attributes include:

✦ The *cap style*, which controls how the endpoints of lines are drawn.

✦ The *join style*, which controls how lines are joined together.

✦ The *line style*, which sets up dashed or solid lines.

✦ The *line width*, which controls the pen width as lines are drawn.

These line attributes can be changed by filling in the proper fields in the XGCValues structure, or by calling the XSetLineAttributes function. XSetLineAttributes changes the GC values for drawing lines:

```
XSetLineAttributes(Display* display,

    GC gc,

    unsigned int linewidth,

    int linestyle,

    int capstyle,

    int joinstyle)
```

Cap Style

The *cap style* defines how the endpoints of lines are drawn. The default, CapButt, squares lines at their endpoints (perpendicular to the slope of the line). No pixels are projected beyond the end of the line.

CapNotLast is like CapButt, but when the line width is 0 (an odd-looking parameter for improving performance; see Line Width below), the very last pixel is not drawn.

CapProjecting sets the line squared at the ends, but the line is drawn beyond the ending point a distance of one-half the line width.

CapRound draws a circular arc at the endpoint. The diameter of this arc is the line width.

To set the cap style, you can fill in the *cap_style* field, or call XSetLineAttributes.

The *valuemask* bit-flag is GCCapStyle.

Join Style

The *join style* determines how corners are drawn for wide lines. You can set the *join_style* field of the XGCValues structure to JoinBevel (draws a line, using CapButt cap style, between the endpoints and then fills in the triangular notch between the endpoints), JoinMiter (which extends the outer edge of both lines to meet at an angle), or JoinRound (where the corners are rounded off with a circle centered on the point where the two lines join). The function XSetLineAttributes also sets the join style.

The *valuemask* bit-flag is GCJoinStyle.

Line Style

You can set the GC's *line style* to LineSolid, LineOnOffDash, or LineDoubleDash. LineSolid, as the name implies, draws solid lines. LineOnOffDash draws even dashes (see Dashing, above). LineDoubleDash fills even dashes differently than odd dashes, using the current fill style (see Fill Style, above).

To set the line style, fill in the *line_style* field of the XGCValues structure, or call XSetLineAttributes. The *valuemask* bit-flag is GCLineStyle.

Line Width

The *line width*, obviously, controls how wide a pen is used for drawing. The line width is specified in pixels.

You can draw wide lines, or normal 1-pixel-wide lines. The default line width of 0 seems odd, but is a special case. Many workstations provide optimized graphics hardware, but it's unlikely that the graphics hardware was designed with X's complex drawing rules in mind. Because of this, the special line width of 0 draws 1-pixel-wide lines, using any hardware acceleration that is available. This can result, though, in lines that are drawn slightly differently on different platforms.

If you really need exact lines, use a line width of 1 instead of 0. You can set the `line_width` field in the XGCValues structure or call XSetLineAttributes to change the line width. The `valuemask` bit-flag is GCLineWidth.

Clipping and Clip Masks

X provides a number of features to aid in clipping graphics output. All drawing is automatically clipped to the boundaries of the window (or pixmap) you draw to. In addition, if you draw into windows, all your drawing is clipped to the boundaries of any parent windows, all the way up the window hierarchy to the root window. Depending on the GC's subwindow mode (see below), if you draw into a parent window, the child windows may clip your output, too. You can also set up extra clipping in the GC, should you want to clip within a window or pixmap. The GC controls this clipping.

With a GC, you either clip to a *clip mask*, which is a bitmap to clip to, a *clip region*, or a set of *clip rectangles*. We'll cover bitmaps in depth in Chapter 17 and clip regions in the next chapter as part of handling Expose events.

Clipping Mask

You can clip to a bitmap, a pixmap with a depth of one, using the XSetClipMask function, or by setting the `clip_mask` field of the XGCValues structure before calling XCreateGC or XChangeGC (see below, under Modifying GCs).

```
XSetClipMask(Display* display,
    GC gc,
    Pixmap clip_mask)
```

`XSetClipMask` constrains your graphic output to all the 1 bits in the pixmap. All the 0 bits in the pixmap are the area you *don't* want to draw to. The *valuemask* bit-flag is `GCClipMask`.

Turning Off Clipping

You turn off a GC's clipping by setting a clip mask of None (a constant for zero):

```
Display*    display;
GC          gc;

XSetClipMask(display, gc, (Pixmap) None);
```

This also undoes a call to `XSetClipRectangles` or `XSetRegion`.

Using a clipping bitmap forces a rather expensive performance hit. It is usually more efficient to use a set of clip rectangles instead of a clip mask or bitmap. (Of course, there's a wide variance in X, so the best thing to do is to test performance on your systems.)

The `XSetClipRectangles` function sets a GC to clip to a set of rectangles:

```
XSetClipRectangles(Display* display,
    GC gc,
    int clip_x_origin,
    int clip_y_origin,
    XRectangle* rectangles,
    int number_rectangles,
    int ordering)
```

The rectangle ordering is a flag that you can use to help the X library improve performance. If you sort the rectangles passed in the `XRectangle` array, you can speed up the GC's clipping. The rectangle ordering can be one of Unsorted (you don't have a clue if the XRectangle array is sorted in any fashion), YSorted (nondecreasing in the y origin from the beginning of the XRectangle array to the end), YXSorted (YSorted with the constraint that all rectangles with the same y origin are sorted with x origins nondecreasing) or YXBanded (YXSorted with the constraint that for every possible y scanline, all rectangles that include this scanline have an identical y origin and y extent).

In the constants above, the y comes before x. This is one of the few places where the order is yx and not xy. We mention it because this led us to a number of dumb typos over the years.

N O T E

Clipping Origin

When you use a GC to clip your graphics, the clipping mask, rectangle list, or region is set to the origin of the window or pixmap you're drawing to—by default. That is, position 0,0 in the clipping bitmap equates to position 0,0 in the output window. You can also change this clipping origin by setting the *clip_x_origin* and *clip_y_origin* fields of the XGCValues structure or with the XSetClipOrigin function:

```
XSetClipOrigin(Display* display,
    GC gc,
    int clip_x_origin,
    int clip_y_origin)
```

The *clip origin* then becomes the starting point to apply the clip region, mask (pixmap), region, or set of rectangles. The *valuemask* bit-flags are GCClipXOrigin and GCClipYOrigin.

Subwindow Mode

The *subwindow mode* controls whether the graphics you draw into a window are clipped by child windows. Normally, you want this to be so—otherwise there isn't much point in creating child windows. Set the subwindow mode to ClipByChildren.

In some cases, though, you want to draw into sub or inferior windows. In this case, set the subwindow mode to IncludeInferiors. For example, when you move a window from the window manager, the window manager draws a ghosted outline of your window over all other windows—in other words, child windows of the root window.

You can set the *subwindow_mode* field of the XGCValues structure or call XSetSubwindowMode:

```
XSetSubwindowMode(Display* display,
    GC gc,
    int subwindow_mode)
```

The *valuemask* bit-flag is GCSubwindowMode.

Tiling and Stippling

Tiling is the process of painting a brush pattern or tile when drawing. Instead of drawing in a given color, you draw with a given picture—an X pixmap. *Stippling* is the process of drawing only in the shape of a one-plane pixmap (also called a bitmap). In effect, stippling provides and additional GC clip mask. In the stipple bitmap, all the 1 bits allow drawing to go through, all the 0 bits stop drawing.

Both tiling and stippling act as though the tile or stipple is an infinitely large pixmap. Since you don't use an infinitely large pixmap—but a pixmap with a width and a height—X in effect replicates your tile or stipple across any target drawing area in a window or pixmap. By default, the tile or stipple is replicated from the target window or pixmap's origin, but you can change this *tile and stipple origin*.

Stippling

When you use a stipple bitmap, all your graphics output is clipped to the 1 bits in the bitmap. Every place you draw where there is a 1 bit, the GC foreground is drawn. The 0 bits appear transparent if you use a fill style of FillStippled. The 0 bits are painted with the current GC background color if you use a fill style of FillOpaqueStippled. If the fill style is

FillSolid, then no stippling takes place. (You can change the fill style with the XSetFillStyle function.)

To set the stipple bitmap, set the *stipple* field of the XGCValues structure or use the XSetStipple function:

```
XSetStipple(Display* display,
     GC gc,
     Pixmap stipple)
```

The stipple pixmap must be a 1-bit-deep pixmap, or you will generate an X error.

The *valuemask* bit-flag is GCStipple.

Tiling

Tiling is a lot like stippling, except that instead of painting the foreground color, you paint the pixels in the tile pixmap. Tiling effectively makes the GC into a form of brush, and you can paint a complex shape to the screen. Tiling is very popular in painting programs.

To tile, you must set the GC's fill style to FillTiled and set up the tiling pixmap. Unlike the stippling pixmap, your tiling pixmap may be more than one bit deep. In fact, the tiling pixmap must match the depth of any window or pixmap you draw to using the tile.

To set up the tiling pixmap, either set the XGCValues tile field or call XSetTile:

```
XSetTile(Display* display,
     GC gc,
     Pixmap tile)
```

We cover how to create pixmaps at various depths in Chapter 17.

The *valuemask* bit-flag is GCTile.

The Tile and Stipple Origin

As we stated above, both tiling and stippling act as though the tile or stipple is an infinitely large pixmap. Since you don't use an infinitely large pixmap, but a pixmap with a width and a height, X replicates your tile or stipple across any target drawing area in a window or pixmap.

By default, the tile and stipple origin is the target window or pixmap's origin, so the tile or stipple is replicated as if the pixmap started at this position.

You can change this tile and stipple origin, though, by setting the *ts_x_origin* and *ts_y_origin* XGCValues fields or by calling XSetTSOrigin:

```
XSetTSOrigin(Display* display,
    GC gc,
    int tile_stipple_x,
    int tile_stipple_y)
```

The *valuemask* bit-flags are GCTileStipXOrigin and GCTile-StipYOrigin.

Tiling and Stippling Efficiently

Graphics hardware accelerators make dramatic improvement in tiling and stippling operations. If you use these operations frequently, you should query the X server to find out the best supported sizes for the tiling and stippling pixmaps. Since many of the sizes are limited in the graphics hardware, using the best size can result in improved performance, while using nonoptimal sizes can seriously degrade your application.

To determine the best sizes for the tile and stipple pixmaps, X provides the XQueryBestSize, XQueryBestStipple, and XQueryBestTile functions.

XQueryBestSize is the most generic:

```
XQueryBestSize(Display* display,
    int query,
    Drawable drawable,
    unsigned int width,
    unsigned int height,
```

```
    unsigned int* best_width,
    unsigned int* best_height)
```

By specifying the proper query, XQueryBestSize can be used to determine the best cursor (CursorShape), stipple (StippleShape), or tile (TileShape) size. The *drawable* can be any window or pixmap for querying the best cursor size—the *drawable* is used to determine which screen you're on, and nothing more. For the stipple and tile sizes, though, the depth and class of your window may make a difference. The *width* and *height* are the desired values you want. The *best_width* and *best_height* are the returned best values.

XQueryBestStipple determines the best size for a stipple pixmap:

```
XQueryBestStipple(Display* display,
    Drawable drawable,
    unsigned int width,
    unsigned int height,
    unsigned int* best_width,
    unsigned int* best_height)
```

XQueryBestTile determines the best size for a tile pixmap:

```
XQueryBestTile(Display* display,
    Drawable drawable,
    unsigned int width,
    unsigned int height,
    unsigned int* best_width,
    unsigned int* best_height)
```

Drawing to Individual Bit-Planes

By default, all graphics output gets drawn into all of the color bit-planes, assuming you have a color workstation. Like most other features of X, though, you can change the *plane mask* a GC draws to. The plane mask controls which of the bit-planes are drawn into, for those systems that have pixels with multiple bit-planes. Every 1 bit in the plane mask corresponds to a color plane that is drawn to. Every 0 bit in the plane mask corresponds to a color plane that is left untouched. Note that not all graphics hardware supports this type of system, although most do.

The most common use for the plane mask is to copy a 1-bit-deep bitmap, such as an icon, into an 8-bit-deep color window, using XCopyPlane, which we cover in Chapter 17. Other common uses for the plane mask include drawing into color overlay planes or performing smooth rotation. See Chapter 11 for using overlay planes.

Plane Mask

You can set the plane mask using the *plane_mask* field of the XGCValues structure, or by calling XSetPlaneMask:

```
XSetPlaneMask(Display* display,

    GC gc,

    unsigned long  plane_mask)
```

The default GC plane mask contains all ones to draw into all available bit-planes. The *valuemask* bit-flag is GCPlaneMask.

In addition to XSetPlaneMask, you can also use XSetState, which sets the foreground and background colors, the drawing function or mode, such as GXcopy and GXxor, and the plane mask, all in one fell swoop:

```
XSetState(Display* display,

    GC gc,

    unsigned long foreground,

    unsigned long background,

    int function,

    unsigned long planemask)
```

XSetState is a very handy convenience function if you use color overlay planes, which we cover in Chapter 11.

Freeing GCs

When you finish with a GC, you should free the resources in the X server with XFreeGC:

```
XFreeGC (Display* display, GC gc)
```

Once freed, you should never attempt to use this GC again.

Modifying GCs

In addition to all the functions for changing individual GC values, you can change GC values *en masse* using XChangeGC:

```
XChangeGC(Display* display,
     GC gc,
     unsigned long valuemask,
     XGCValues* xgcvalues)
```

XChangeGC changes the items flagged in *valuemask* and stored in *xgvalues*. The *valuemask* and XGCValues structure act just like in XCreateGC.

N O T E   While it might be tempting to try and avoid the function-call overhead described above and just set the values into a GC structure directly, you should *not* do this. The X library caches graphics contexts, so you should never try to modify the contents of the GC directly. Instead, always use the supported functions for modifying a GC. Even so, it's sometimes tempting to examine the current values for a GC. The actual structure looks like:

```
typedef struct _XGC {
    XExtData*     ext_data;
    GContext      gid;
    Bool          rects;
```

```
    Bool          dashes;
    unsigned long dirty;
    XGCValues     values;
} *GC;
```

Remember that the structure may not be current, due to caching.

Copying GCs

You can copy the attributes of one created GC to another using XCopyGC:

```
XCopyGC(Display* display,
    GC src_gc,
    unsigned long valuemask,
    GC dest_gc)
```

Again, the bit-flags in the *valuemask* determine which values are copied from the *src_gc* to the *dest_gc*. This is very useful for copying the line attributes of one GC to another, or the plane mask, and so on.

Finding Out GC Settings

The FillRoundRect function we cover in Appendix B calls XGetGCValues to query the contents of the GC passed to the function. The purpose was to set up the proper arc-filling mode (ArcPieSlice) needed by the FillRoundRect function. You can call XGetGCValues to query any GC and discover what values it holds:

```
Status XGetGCValues(Display* display,
    GC gc,
    unsigned long valuemask,
    XGCValues* gcvalues)      /* RETURN */
```

Like XChangeGC and XCreateGC, you fill in a *valuemask* of the values you want. In this case, though, you don't fill in the XGCValues structure, as XGetGCValues will do that for you. XGetGCValues will only fill in the fields for which you asked with the *valuemask*.

XGetGCValues returns a nonzero value if the routine succeeded and filled in the values you asked for. XGetGCValues returns zero otherwise. This routine is new in X11 Release 4.

GCs and X Toolkits

You can call XCreateGC from within X toolkit programs, such as Motif and Open Look programs, just like you can from within any X program. Be sure that you've realized your widgets (see Chapters 5 and 6) before making any X calls, because realizing the widgets creates the X window IDs associated with Motif and OLIT widgets.

Because using a lot of graphics contexts can slow down the X server, the X Toolkit Intrinsics provides a cache of GCs. To use this cache, you can call XtGetGC to acquire a read-only shared GC:

```
GC XtGetGC(Widget widget,

    XtGCMask valuemask,

    XGCValues* xgcvalues)
```

The *valuemask* and *xgcvalues* parameters act the same as in XCreateGC and XCopyGC, except that all values must match in the *xgvalues*, regardless of the valuemask, in order to share a GC. We've found it a good idea to make sure the given *widget*, or a parent widget, is realized first, before calling XtGetGC. Remember that XtGetGC returns a read-only shared GC.

Because of this fact, XtGetGC is not very useful. In X11 Release 5, the XtAllocateGC function allocates a modifiable GC:

```
GC XtAllocateGC(Widget widget,

    Cardinal depth,

    XtGCMask valuemask,

    XGCValues* xgcvalues,
```

```
XtGCMask modifiable_mask,

XtGCMask never_used_mask)
```

XtAllocateGC returns a GC that you can change. The GC is initialized with the values specified by *valuemask* and stored in the XGCValues structure. This is still a shared GC, though, so you must follow certain rules. You can only modify the values listed in the *modifiable_mask*. The *never_used_mask* specifies the GC attributes your application won't ever use. This enables XtAllocateGC to more efficiently share GCs.

Because the returned GC is still shared, and since other functions and widgets may modify this GC, you'll need to reset the GC values you need before drawing—every time.

If you use XtAllocateGC or XtGetGC, you should release the GC with XtReleaseGC when you're through—don't free a shared GC on your own, let the X toolkit do it:

```
void XtReleaseGC(Widget widget, GC gc)
```

Using GCs Efficiently

The proper use of graphics contexts can make a big difference in the performance of your applications. Take care when planning your software that uses GCs. Remember that GCs are resources in both your application and in the X server, so using a lot of GCs is discouraged. What exactly is a lot of GCs, though, is up to debate. One thousand GCs are a lot. Ten GCs are not.

One way to use multiple GCs is to have one GC to draw red shapes and one to draw blue, for example. If you use the GXxor mode described above to draw rubber-band lines, you should have a separate GC for this and another GC to draw permanent shapes.

GC values are cached both by the X library and by the X server. To take advantage of the way both caches work, you should draw as much as possible using the same GC settings, such as the same color and line width. Then, change the GC and draw other items.

If you can arrange your drawing in this fashion, such as drawing all the red items first, you should see a nice performance gain. Unfortunately, to do this might require a complete redesign of your software.

Summary

Any successful graphics program needs a solid foundation, and this solid foundation can be your use of the graphics context, or GC. The GC is a catchall data structure that contains almost everything needed to specify "pen" parameters for drawing. The GC contains the foreground and background colors, the width of the pen for drawing lines, and the arc-filling mode. The GC controls the graphics pipeline, the set of tasks that convert your drawing functions into pixels on the screen. This graphics pipeline includes clipping, line widths, colors, tiling, and stippling.

We ran down the steps needed to create a GC, starting with XCreateGC, and covers such specific tasks as:

✦   Dashing;
✦   Filling;
✦   Setting fonts;
✦   Drawing, including rubber-band lines;
✦   Setting specific line attributes;
✦   Tiling;
✦   Stippling;
✦   Copying; and
✦   Modifying.

Finally, the chapter ended with a discussion of the wise use of GCs—wise in the sense of using as few system resources as possible without cutting short your applications.

X Library Functions and Macros Introduced in This Chapter

```
XChangeGC
XCopyGC
XCreateGC
```

```
XFreeGC
XGetGCValues
XSetBackground
XSetClipMask
XSetClipOrigin
XSetClipRectangles
XSetDashes
XSetFillRule
XSetFillStyle
XSetFont
XSetForeground
XSetFunction
XSetGraphicsExposures
XSetLineAttributes
XSetPlaneMask
XSetState
XSetStipple
XSetSubwindowMode
XSetTile
XSetTSOrigin
```

X Toolkit Intrinsics Functions and Macros Introduced in This Chapter

```
XtAllocateGC
XtGetGC
XtReleaseGC
```

Chapter 4

X Events For Graphics

This chapter covers:

- ✦ Event-driven applications
- ✦ Events in the X Window System
- ✦ The `Expose` event
- ✦ Working with X regions
- ✦ The `GraphicsExpose` and `NoExpose` events
- ✦ Window-resizing events
- ✦ Mouse events
- ✦ Colormap and visibility events
- ✦ Events and X toolkits
- ✦ Asking for events

Event-Driven Applications

Event-driven programs, as we mentioned in Chapter 1, are literally driven by incoming events from the X server. Event-driven programs are not like traditional noninteractive UNIX batch programs such as `ls`, `tr`, and `who`.

A batch program, such as a program to strip out all the control characters from a text file, takes in user input only at the beginning, usually to get the names of the input and output files. The batch program then chugs away on the input and produces the output. The program is in total control of itself.

In an event-driven application, however, the program cedes control to the user. The user drives the actions of the program through a series of many events. The program is really still in control, but it gives the user the feeling that the user is running the show. This is very important if your applications support users who are new to computing. The big difference with event-driven programming is that events can come in at any time and in any order. This places the meat of most event-driven programs in a central loop that takes each event as it comes in and responds to that event in some way.

It is extremely important when designing the event-driven user interface to provide some feedback for each user-initiated event. The user needs to know that your program received the event and is doing something. Highlighting a choice or beeping the speaker are common ways to provide the feedback. This feedback must appear as soon as possible, even if the action to be taken on the event will take a long time. You need to let the user know that the event is received and understood—otherwise the user will probably try the event again and again, pounding on the same key until a response is seen.

Typical event-driven programs have an initialization section in the beginning, then an event loop, and finally a section to perform any necessary cleanups at the end. Programmers experienced with Microsoft Windows, IBM Presentation Manager, or the Apple Macintosh will feel right at home with event-driven programming.

When working with X toolkits, much of this event processing is done for you. The X Toolkit Intrinsics, used by Motif and Open Look Intrinsics Toolkit (OLIT), provides the `XtAppMainLoop` and `XtMainLoop` functions to handle the central event loop. These functions accept input events from the X server and then dispatch the events to the proper Xt widgets.

The method used by `XtAppMainLoop` is simple (ignoring timers and other sources of input for now): wait for an event to arrive, then dispatch the event to the proper widget. Each class, or type, of widget has functions to handle incoming events. These automatic event-handling functions work up to a point. We've found that most toolkit-based programs also need to draw their own data into windows, and therefore must handle events for those windows. Hence, this chapter's coverage of X events. We concentrate on those events that pertain most to the type of program described above.

A word processor, for example, may use an X toolkit like OLIT for most of the user interface, but in the end, the central part of a word processor is the display of the documents the user is editing. Since most word processors go far beyond what is offered by X toolkits, you have to program your own routines to display documents and handle user-generated events in the document windows.

Events in the X Window System

X events are messages generated by the X server (or other applications) and sent to your program. The user creates events (which are technically generated by the X server acting for the user) by pressing on keyboard keys, clicking mouse buttons, and moving the mouse pointer about the screen. X even goes a step further: a `KeyPress` is one event; the corresponding `KeyRelease` is another. Your applications can track mouse `ButtonPress` and `ButtonRelease` events as well.

An event occurs when a window-manager program works with the user to change the size of a window on the screen. And an event happens when one program sends an event to another program.

Events tell your application programs exactly what is happening on the display screen. More technically, an event is a fixed-size packet of information sent to your program by the X server. X provides many different types of events, and each one interprets the contents of the data packet differently. X uses these events to such an extent that your programs will become driven by these events.

The X Event Model

Events in X are generated from windows, which means an X program without any windows normally has a difficult time receiving events from the X server. The X server provides each connection (i.e., each application program) an event queue. This is a first-in, first-out list of all events generated for the program's windows. Application programs read events from this queue and respond to them in some way. A word-processor application, for instance, receives keypress events and then displays each character pressed in the word processor's window (or windows).

Keys pressed on the keyboard go to whatever window currently has the *keyboard focus*. This focus window is normally whatever window the mouse pointer is in. Most X toolkits, though, support complex means for changing which window has the keyboard focus. (In Motif terminology, this is called *keyboard traversal*.)

In all cases, though, it is the window manager that determines which top-level application window has the keyboard focus. Some window managers support an active window. The user must click a mouse button in a window, which normally raises that window and gives the window the keyboard focus. This type of interaction is called *click to type*. Another type of interaction is called *focus follows mouse*. In this style of interaction, the keyboard focus follows the mouse pointer. Whatever top-level window the mouse is in gets the keyboard focus. If the window manager allows both types of interaction, the user can configure the choice. Your applications, however, must deal with the user's choice.

While the window manager controls which top-level application window has the keyboard focus, your applications can control which subwindow has the focus. Both OLIT and Motif make extensive use of this feature.

But before you worry about the keyboard focus, you need to determine what type of event was sent from the X server.

Types of X Events

The XEvent type is a C language union, a union of C structures. Each type of event has its own structure—its own interpretation of the XEvent data, layered on top of the XEvent union. The actual XEvent union is rather long:

```
typedef union _XEvent {
    int                 type;
    XAnyEvent           xany;
    XKeyEvent           xkey;
```

```
        XButtonEvent              xbutton;

        XMotionEvent              xmotion;

        XCrossingEvent            xcrossing;

        XFocusChangeEvent         xfocus;

        XExposeEvent              xexpose;

        XGraphicsExposeEvent      xgraphicsexpose;

        XNoExposeEvent            xnoexpose;

        XVisibilityEvent          xvisibility;

        XCreateWindowEvent        xcreatewindow;

        XDestroyWindowEvent       xdestroywindow;

        XUnmapEvent               xunmap;

        XMapEvent                 xmap;

        XMapRequestEvent          xmaprequest;

        XReparentEvent            xreparent;

        XConfigureEvent           xconfigure;

        XGravityEvent             xgravity;

        XResizeRequestEvent       xresizerequest;

        XConfigureRequestEvent    xconfigurerequest;

        XCirculateEvent           xcirculate;

        XCirculateRequestEvent    xcirculaterequest;

        XPropertyEvent            xproperty;

        XSelectionClearEvent      xselectionclear;

        XSelectionRequestEvent    xselectionrequest;

        XSelectionEvent           xselection;

        XColormapEvent            xcolormap;

        XClientMessageEvent       xclient;

        XMappingEvent             xmapping;

        XErrorEvent               xerror;

        XKeymapEvent              xkeymap;

        long                      pad[24];

    } XEvent;
```

The first element of the XEvent union is the *type*. The *type* field tells, surprisingly enough, what type of event has been received.

Each type of event has its own structure, part of the XEvent union. All structures share a common part, which is held in the XAnyEvent structure:

```
typedef struct {
    int          type;
    unsigned long serial;
    Bool         send_event;
    Display*     display;
    Window       window;
} XAnyEvent;
```

The *serial* field is a request number generated by the X server. The *send_event* flag is True if the event was generated by another X application and sent via the XSendEvent function. The *display* field indicates which display connection the event came from (any X program may connect to multiple X servers, although the vast majority of X programs connect to just one X server). Finally, the *window* field indicates on which window the event was generated.

Toolkits and Event-Handling

Most X toolkits manage the events for all the windows created with the toolkit. This frees you, the application writer, from having to write code to handle all these event types, which is, of course, one of the reasons to use an X toolkit. Even so, if you want to create sophisticated graphics with your toolkit programs (the main reason you picked up this book), you'll need to create a "raw" toolkit window in which to draw your graphics, be they fractal landscapes, video games, or geographic information systems (GISs). In these raw toolkit windows (such as the OLIT DrawArea widget), your application will need to handle a number of events, especially Expose events.

The Expose Event

Expose events are requests from the X server indicating that your application needs to redraw parts of one of its windows (see When to Draw in Chapter 2). Every time a new window appears on the screen, it generates Expose events to tell your application that it is time to draw the window for the first time. Expose events are also generated later when windows disappear or are moved about the screen, obscuring and unobscuring other windows.

Because windows in X can overlap and most users run more than one X application at a time, it is very likely that another program's window will at some time obscure your application's window (or windows). If this overlapping window is moved away and no longer covers your window, the covered part of your window is considered *exposed*.

This exposed or damaged area must be redrawn. In the X world, your applications are entirely responsible for redrawing this exposed area. (Your applications can ask the X server to do it for you, via the *backing-store hint* we covered in Chapter 1, but you cannot depend on this. Low memory conditions usually make X servers give up backing store to use the precious memory for something considered more important. Consequently, your applications must be ready to redraw any part of any window at any time.)

Even if you ask for backing store, your application can still expect to receive Expose events, if only to draw the window's contents for the first time. All X applications should expect—and handle—exposure events.

When an area becomes exposed, the X server will send your application an Expose event. When your program receives an Expose event, it should redraw the area that was previously covered up. Each of these events arrives with a rectangle (all rectangles in X are identified by their x,y location and size—width and height) that bounds the exposed area.

All X applications that create windows are required to check for expose events and redraw the proper areas of their windows. As we stated above, your X toolkit, such as Motif, will handle most X events, including Expose events. It's only when you create raw toolkit windows, like the XmDrawingArea, that you need to worry about handling Expose events.

NOTE Each X toolkit uses its own means for your application to receive events like the Expose event. Many toolkits use the concept of callback functions: Your application registers a function to be called on some event. When this event happens, your function is executed. This is how Motif and OLIT work, but your toolkit may act differently. Because of the wide variance in X toolkits, we cannot cover all the means for setting up event-handling functions. Instead, we present a generic introduction to the events your applications will need to handle, so that you can work with any toolkit. We also provide examples of how Motif and OLIT handle this task. If you use a different toolkit, such as OI, you'll need to consult your toolkit documentation.

The XExposeEvent Structure

The Expose event arrives in an XExposeEvent *structure:*

```
typedef struct {
    int             type;
    unsigned long   serial;
    Bool            send_event;
    Display*        display;
    Window          window;
    int             x, y;
    int             width, height;
    int             count;
} XExposeEvent;
```

For Expose events, the important fields are:

- ✦ *type*;
- ✦ *window*;
- ✦ *x,y*;
- ✦ *width*;

✦ `height;` and

✦ `count;`

The `type` field is set to `Expose`. The `window` field contains the ID of the window in which the event occurred. The `x,y`, `width`, and `height` fields contain the rectangular area that needs to be redrawn. Finally, the `count` field indicates how many more `Expose` events are expected to arrive. When the `count` field is zero, the last `Expose` event in a given sequence has arrived. All `Expose` events arrive in batches.

Expose events are guaranteed to be generated in a sequence. That is, if a window moves about on the screen and this movement uncovers part of your application's window, all the `Expose` events for that movement will arrive as part of one group. The `count` field counts down the events in the batch, until zero, the last event in the group.

This helps your application efficiently update the display. If you wait until all `Expose` events arrive in a batch, you could, for example, then update the smallest rectangle that encloses *all* the damaged area. (Or you could use an advanced X tool, regions, which we describe below.) Lazy applications could just redraw the entire window when the `count` field becomes zero.

Which of these redraw policies makes the most sense for your application is up for debate. As always, though, you are the best judge for your code. Try the different refresh policies and choose the one that works best for your applications.

 As we described in Chapter 2, do not draw to any window until the first `Expose` event arrives. This is because X is an asynchronous windowing system, with a delay between the time you create and map your windows and when they actually appear on the screen. (Most window managers also intercept your requests and place a window manager title bar or other so-called "decorations" around your window.)

N O T E

There are a few simple rules for drawing any graphics with X:

✦ Don't draw *anything* until your application gets the first `Expose` event.

✦ Anything you try to draw into a window before it is fully mapped may be lost.

✦ Be prepared to redraw any area of any window at any time.

Working with X Regions

One technique to handle Expose events is to collect all the rectangles for one batch of events into an X structure called a *region*. Regions are opaque data types that hold odd shapes, such as collections of rectangles.

On the first Expose event, create a new region, adding in the Expose event's rectangle to the region. On every Expose event following, add in the new rectangle to the original region. Then, when the Expose event count field is zero, use this region as the clipping area for the window. Redraw the contents of the window, clipping to the region.

This gets a little more complex when we write the code, however. From <X11/Xutil.h>, we see the obscure definition of a region:

```
typedef struct _XRegion *Region;
```

The _XRegion structure is not defined in <X11/Xutil.h>. You're supposed to treat a region as an opaque data structure.

You create a new, empty region with XCreateRegion:

```
Region XCreateRegion()
```

You can then fill in a region with a number of functions. XUnionRectWithRegion adds a rectangle to a region and creates a new output region that is the union of the input region and the input rectangle:

```
XUnionRectWithRegion(XRectangle* input_rectangle,
      Region input_region,
      Region output_region)
```

Intersect two regions with XIntersectRegion:

```
XIntersectRegion(Region input_region1,
```

```
        Region input_region2,

        Region output_region)    /* RETURN */
```

To clear out a region, intersect the region with a null region.

When you're all done, destroy the region with `XDestroyRegion`:

```
XDestroyRegion(Region region)
```

This frees up the memory held in the region data structure.

N O T E   `XCreateRegion` calls `malloc` to allocate memory. Thus, the importance of `XDestroyRegion` for reclaiming that memory. This may also impact your decision to use regions, because `malloc` often becomes a performance bottleneck.

To use regions with `Expose` events:

1. For each new batch of `Expose` events, create a new region.
2. For each `Expose` event in a batch, add the exposed rectangle to the region.
3. When all the `Expose` events are in (when the count field is zero), then either set a graphics context (GC) clip mask to the region, or set the clip mask to the smallest rectangle that bounds the region.
4. Then, redraw all your graphics, using the GC clipping functions to display only what is necessary.

To make a GC clip to a region, use `XSetRegion`:

```
XSetRegion(Display* display, GC gc,

        Region region)
```

This sets the GC's clipping mask to the region, which may be quite complex. Sometimes, though, you want a simpler clipping structure. Instead, you can figure the smallest rectangle that bounds a region entirely with `XClipBox`:

```
XClipBox(Region region,

        XRectangle* output_rectangle) /* RETURN */
```

`XClipBox` determines the smallest rectangle enclosing the region and fills in the *output_rectangle* with the result.

When you're done drawing, it's a good idea to reset the GC's clipping mask, by using a mask of None:

```
Display*  display;
GC        gc;
XSetClipMask(display, gc, (Pixmap) None);
```

To keep track of our exposed area, we can build a simple utility function to add the rectangular area in an `Expose` event to an existing X region. When all the `Expose` events are then in, we should have the total exposed area collected into the region.

The function `UnionExposeWithRegion`, below, calls `XUnionRectWithRegion` on the rectangular area in an `Expose` event structure and a region passed to the function. The region is both an input and an output parameter, in that it first contains the initial region and after `UnionExposeWithRegion`, it contains the new total region:

```
void UnionExposeWithRegion(XExposeEvent* event,
    Region region)


{   /* UnionExposeWithRegion */
    XRectangle rectangle;

    rectangle.x = event->x;
    rectangle.y = event->y;
    rectangle.width = event->width;
    rectangle.height = event->height;

    XUnionRectWithRegion(&rectangle,
        region, region);


}   /* UnionExposeWithRegion */
```

Once we have all the `Expose` events, we then can set the clipping region of a GC with `XSetRegion`. The function `ClipToRegion`, below, does this.

`ClipToRegion` supports two means to clip. First, you can clip to the actual region built up from the batch of `Expose` events. Second, you can get the smallest rectangle that encloses this region and clip to that rectangle. In the code below, define *CLIP_REGIONS* to clip to the region. Comment out the *#define CLIP_REGIONS* to use the smallest rectangle approach.

The file `region.c` contains both the `UnionExposeWithRegion` and `ClipToRegion` functions:

```
/*
 * region.c
 * Routine to collect Expose events into regions.
 */
#include <X11/Xlib.h>
#include <X11/Xutil.h>

void UnionExposeWithRegion(XExposeEvent* event,
    Region region)

{   /* UnionExposeWithRegion */
    XRectangle    rectangle;

    rectangle.x = event->x;
    rectangle.y = event->y;
    rectangle.width = event->width;
    rectangle.height = event->height;

    XUnionRectWithRegion(&rectangle,
        region, region);

}   /* UnionExposeWithRegion */


/* Set a GC to clip to a region. */
```

```
void ClipToRegion(Display* display, GC gc, Region region)


{    /* ClipToRegion */
     XRectangle   rectangle;


#define CLIP_REGIONS


#ifdef CLIP_REGIONS
     XSetRegion(display, gc, region);


#else /* Clip by smallest enclosing rectangle. */


     /*
      * Get the smallest rectangle that
      * bounds the region.
      */
     XClipBox(region, &rectangle);


     XSetClipRectangles(display, gc,
         0, 0,    /* clip origin */
         &rectangle,
         1,       /* one rectangle */
         YXBanded);


#endif   /* !CLIP_REGIONS */


}    /* ClipToRegion */


/* end of file region.c */
```

N O T E

Under X11 Release 4, we found bugs on some X servers when using clip regions for graphics contexts. We found problems with clipping arcs and points, for example, when drawn with XDrawArcs and XDrawPoints on Interactive/SunSoft SVR3.2 version 3.0. Everything worked fine, however, on other systems, such as Hewlett-Packard 705 workstations. If the above code doesn't work for you, try using XClipBox and XSetClipRectangles, as we presented in region.c, above.

With the above two functions, we can then put together a C function to handle Expose events on a window. The HandleExpose function collects the total area in a batch of Expose events by building up a region using UnionExposeWithRegion. When all the Expose events in a batch are in, (i.e., when the count field is zero), HandleExpose sets the GC to clip to the region with ClipToRegion and redraws the window. Finally, HandleExpose calls XSetClipMask with a mask of None to reset the GC's clipping mask to include the whole window.

```
/*
 * Globals
 */
Display*    global_display;
Window      global_window;
GC          global_gc;
Region      global_region = (Region) NULL;

/* Redraw the drawing area. */
void HandleExpose(XExposeEvent* event)

{       /* HandleExpose */
    XRectangle    rectangle;

    /*
     * Add each rectangle to the region.
```

```
    */
   if (global_region == (Region) NULL) {
       global_region = XCreateRegion();
   }


   UnionExposeWithRegion(event,
       global_region);


   /*
    * Redraw the entire contents
    * of the window, relying on the
    * clipping to improve performance.
    */
   if (event->count == 0) {
       ClipToRegion(global_display, global_gc,
           global_region);

       XDestroyRegion(global_region);

       global_region = (Region) NULL;

       /* redraw window... */

       /*
        * Restore clip mask.
        */
       XSetClipMask(global_display,
           global_gc, (Pixmap) None);
   }


} /* HandleExpose */
```

Regions and the Xt Intrinsics

The Xt Intrinsics provides the XtAddExposureToRegion function to help automate the process of collecting regions:

```
void XtAddExposureToRegion(XEvent* event,
    Region region)  /* input/output */
```

The *region* parameter holds the input region as well as the output region. The *event* parameter must be an Expose or GraphicsExpose (see below) event.

The NoExpose and GraphicsExpose Events

In addition to Expose events, there's another odd event pair called GraphicsExpose and NoExpose. Normally, you'd figure that you wouldn't worry about nonexposures, but these events do make sense, in the same sort of twisted way that X makes sense.

X allows you to copy the pixels from one drawable (window or pixmap) to another, using the XCopyPlane or XCopyArea functions (which we describe in depth in Chapter 17). You normally select a rectangular source area and then copy the pixels to a rectangular destination area.

When you copy areas of drawables, there is always the chance that some of the source area is not visible. For windows, this source area could be covered by another window, or the source area could be outside of the window's bounds. For pixmaps, you can also have a source that transcends the pixmap's bounds. In this case, your application may receive GraphicsExpose events that describe the empty areas of the *destination* drawable. These empty areas are the holes in the destination drawable left from the holes in the source drawable.

GraphicsExpose events arrive in batches, like Expose events. Each GraphicsExpose event describes one rectangular hole.

If there is no problem with the source area for copying, your application receives instead a single NoExpose event.

Whether or not your application receives GraphicsExpose and NoExpose events is determined by the graphics context used for the copy operation. To receive such events, you call the XSetGraphicsExposures function:

```
XSetGraphicsExposures(Display* display,
    GC gc,
    Bool graphics_exposures)
```

Pass True for *graphics_exposures* to receive GraphicsExpose and NoExpose events. Pass False if you don't want to receive these events.

The GraphicsExpose Event Structure

GraphicsExpose events arrive in the XGraphicsExposeEvent structure:

```
typedef struct {
    int           type;
    unsigned long serial;
    Bool          send_event;
    Display*      display;
    Drawable      drawable;
    int           x, y;
    int           width, height;
    int           count;
    int           major_code;
    int           minor_code;
} XGraphicsExposeEvent;
```

GraphicsExpose events are very similar to Expose events, except for the *major_code* field. The *major_code* is either X_CopyArea or X_CopyPlane, indicating the X function, XCopyArea or XCopyPlane, that created the hole. The *minor_code* field is not yet defined. The *type* field is set to GraphicsExpose.

The NoExpose Event Structure

The NoExpose event provides a similar structure, the XNoExposeEvent structure:

```
typedef struct {
    int           type;
    unsigned long serial;
    Bool          send_event;
    Display*      display;
    Drawable      drawable;
    int           major_code;
    int           minor_code;
} XNoExposeEvent;
```

The *type* field is set to NoExpose. The rest of the fields mimic the XGraphicsExposeEvent structure presented above.

Window-Resizing Events

When working with X toolkit windows, you need to know when the window changes size. Normally, though, you don't worry about the position of the window, as your toolkit no doubt controls the window's placement.

In X, the ConfigureNotify event describes any change in your window's configuration, such as a size or position change. You can select this event with StructureNotifyMask, although Motif, for instance, already provides resize events for the XmDrawingArea widget (you do need to set up a XmNresizeCallback callback, though). ConfigureNotify events use the XConfigureEvent structure:

```
typedef struct {
    int           type;
    unsigned long serial;
    Bool          send_event;
```

```
        Display*        display;
        Window          event;
        Window          window;
        int             x, y;
        int             width, height;
        int             border_width;
        Window          above;
        Bool            override_redirect;
    } XConfigureEvent;
```

If the window's size or position changed, the *x,y*, *width*, and *height* fields have new values. Most window managers allow users to resize and move windows about the screen. By watching for ConfigureNotify events, your application can keep track of changes to its windows. Note that you should normally ignore the x,y fields. (Most window managers will reparent your application windows, so the x and y values will be local to its new parent window and thus, often 0,0. Check out the Inter-Client Communications Conventions Manual, or ICCCM, which describes how well-behaved X applications must act, for more information.)

The *window* field holds the ID of the window that changed. The *event* field holds either the window that changed (if the event was requested with StructureNotify, see below) or the parent window (if the event was requested with SubstructureNotify). The *above* field is either None if the window is on the bottom of all sibling windows or the ID of a sibling window. If a window ID is present, the *above* field holds the window ID of the sibling window that the window which changed state is above. In other words, the *above* field indicates a sibling window that is below the window listed in the *window* field. Confusing?

The *type* field is set to ConfigureNotify.

Mouse Events

X, like most recent computer graphics packages, requires a mouse for efficient use. (Anywhere the word *mouse* is used, you could replace it with trackball, joystick, graphics pad, or whatever pointing device your system has.) Most X software, though, seems to assume a three-button mouse. X itself defines up to five mouse buttons, but most software only assumes a left, middle, and right mouse button.

X provides a number of mouse-tracking events. X mouse-button events are generated when the user:

✦ Presses down a particular mouse button;

✦ Releases the button;

✦ Moves the mouse pointer; or

✦ Moves the mouse pointer while holding down a mouse button within an active window or within the child of an active window.

You can ask for mouse-button events, such as `ButtonPress` and `ButtonRelease`, that indicate when mouse-buttons are pressed, as well as mouse motion events. For mouse motions, you can get an event for every pixel the mouse pointer moves (although this tends to generate a lot of events), or just get events when the mouse is moved and one or more of the mouse buttons are held down, typically in a drag operation. There's also a motion hint that compresses the motion events. If you can use this hint, your applications may perform faster.

Depending on the events you ask for, the events your program will receive are listed in Table 4.1.

Table 4.1 *Mouse events.*

Event	Meaning
ButtonPress	For button pressings
ButtonRelease	For releasing buttons that were pressed
MotionNotify	For any of the motion masks

The key to these mouse events includes finding out which window the event took place in, determining the `x,y` location of the event, and determining which mouse buttons were pressed at the time of the event.

Mouse Button Events

A ButtonPress event is generated every time the user presses a mouse button while in one of your application's windows. A ButtonRelease event is generated when the user releases a mouse button—again, in one of your application windows. (Yes, it's up to your application to deal with the fact that users can press a mouse button in one of your application windows and then move the mouse outside of your windows, releasing the button there.)

Most X toolkits provide extensive mouse-handling functions, so that you should only work with mouse events that happen inside of raw X windows your application creates, such as XmDrawingArea or DrawArea widgets.

NOTE

ButtonPress and ButtonRelease Events

ButtonPress and ButtonRelease events share the same XButtonEvent *structure*:

```
typedef struct {
        int           type;
        unsigned long serial;
        Bool          send_event;
        Display*      display;
        Window        window;
        Window        root;
        Window        subwindow;
        Time          time;
        int           x, y;
        int           x_root, y_root;
        unsigned int  state;
        unsigned int  button;
        Bool          same_screen;
```

```
} XButtonEvent;

typedef XButtonEvent        XButtonPressedEvent;
typedef XButtonEvent        XButtonReleasedEvent;
```

The *type* field is set to ButtonPress or ButtonRelease. The *window* field is the window for which you asked for mouse events. The event is reported relative to this window. The *subwindow* field is the child of *window*, if any, that the mouse event really occurred in. The *x* and *y* fields are the coordinates of the mouse pointer when the event occurred—in the *window*. The *root* field indicates the root window for the event, and the *x_root* and *y_root* are the global coordinates for the mouse event.

The *same_screen* field is set to True if the *root* and *window* fields indicate windows that are on the same screen, and False otherwise. Most X servers support only one screen, so this is normally not an issue.

The *time* field is a timestamp in milliseconds so that you can place X events in their proper order.

Because of its asynchronous network-based nature, X events may arrive at any time. If you are trying to detect a double-click event, for example, you'll want to look for a ButtonPress, ButtonRelease, and ButtonPress event sequence that all occur within a given short period of time and for which the *x,y* coordinates are within a certain tolerance. (X provides no standard means to detect double-click events otherwise.)

The button field will contain which button caused the event: Button1, Button2, Button3, Button4, or Button5. Button1 is usually the leftmost mouse button. Button2 on a three-button mouse is the middle button (or, in the case of a two-button mouse, both buttons pushed simultaneously), and Button3 the rightmost mouse button.

Modifier Keys

The XButtonEvent state field indicates which mouse buttons and modifier keys, such as the **Shift**, **Caps Lock**, **Control**, or **Meta** (**Alt**, **Extend Char**, or strange pretzel-like character, depending on your keyboard) keys, were held down at the time the event was generated (for a ButtonRelease event, the event is assumed to be the moment *before* the user released a mouse button—otherwise you'd never know for sure which button was released). The state field is set to the inclusive OR of the following bitmasks listed in Table 4.2.

Table 4.2   *The state field.*

Mask	Meaning
Button1Mask	The first mouse button was down
Button2Mask	The second mouse button was down
Button3Mask	The third mouse button was down
Button4Mask	The fourth mouse button was down (usually not available)
Button5Mask	The fifth mouse button was down (usually not available)
ControlMask	**Control** key was down
LockMask	**Caps Lock** was down
Mod1Mask	Typical **Meta** key was down
Mod2Mask	Second **Meta** key
Mod3Mask	Another **Meta** key often not found on the keyboard
Mod4Mask	Another **Meta** key often not found on the keyboard
Mod5Mask	Another **Meta** key often not found on the keyboard
ShiftMask	A **Shift** key was down

Most of these modifier keys are self-explanatory, save for the *Meta key*. The Meta key is typically a key that performs an alternative function and is often labeled as the **Alt** key. Most Meta keys are located next to the space bar on the keyboard.

On the Sun Type 4 keyboard, for instance, the **Meta** key is the left diamond-shaped key next to the space bar and not the key next to it labeled **Alt**. On a Sun 3 keyboard, the meta keys are the **Left** or **Right** keys. On the HP 9000 Series 700, the **Extend Char** key performs this function, and on the

Apple Mac IIx, it is the **Command** key (labeled with an apple outline and a pretzel shape). The Data General Aviion and SCO OpenDesktop both use the **Alt** key as the Meta key. You can use the standard X client program xev to find out the special mappings on your keyboard.

Mouse Movement Events

You can ask for mouse motion events to be generated only while the user holds down a mouse button, or generated all the time the mouse moves. Obviously, if you ask for all mouse motion, regardless of button presses, you'll see a *lot* of mouse motion events.

All these events arrive in the XMotionEvent structure:

```
typedef struct {
     int           type;
     unsigned long serial;
     Bool          send_event;
     Display*      display;
     Window        window;
     Window        root;
     Window        subwindow;
     Time          time;
     int           x, y;
     int           x_root, y_root;
     unsigned int  state;
     char          is_hint;
     Bool          same_screen;
} XMotionEvent;
typedef XMotionEvent    XPointerMovedEvent;
```

The *type* field is set to MotionNotify. Other than the *is_hint* field, the rest of the structure mimics the XButtonEvent structure presented above. The *is_hint* field is set to NotifyNormal or NotifyHint. This indicates whether mouse motion hinting is taking place.

If the *is_hint* field is NotifyHint, then you know that the mouse has moved, but the x and y fields may be out of date. Use XQueryPointer (see below, under Determining the Mouse Pointer Position) to get the current mouse location. If the *is_hint* field is NotifyNormal, then you have a normal mouse event.

Mouse-Motion Hinting

Because a mouse-motion event is generated for every pixel of mouse movement, the X event queue can get completely bogged down processing mouse motion events. To compress this stream of events, you can use the PointerMotionHintMask when asking for mouse events. In this case, the X server is allowed to send you a single mouse-motion event. The hint asks the X server to compress the event stream.

Some applications require every mouse event. In that case, don't hint. But, you'll find you can often speed things up by using mouse motion hinting.

Different X servers may implement motion hinting differently. Because of this, you should only depend that you'll get a mouse-motion event on mouse movement. Query the current mouse-pointer location if necessary.

N O T E

Determining the Mouse Pointer Position

You can track the mouse position with MotionNotify events, or you can query the current location of the mouse with XQueryPointer:

```
Bool XQueryPointer(Display* display,
    Window window,
    Window *root,           /* RETURN */
    Window *child,          /* RETURN */
    int* root_x,            /* RETURN */
    int* root_y,            /* RETURN */
    int* window_x,          /* RETURN */
    int* window_y,          /* RETURN */
    unsigned int* buttons)  /* RETURN */
```

XQueryPointer returns True if the pointer is on the same screen as *window*, False otherwise. If the pointer is on the same screen as *window*, the *window_x* and *window_y* parameters represent the current mouse location in terms of coordinates local to *window*. The location in terms of the *root* window is returned in root_x and root_y. If the mouse is in a *child* window, child holds this window ID, or 0 otherwise.

The *buttons* parameter is filled in with the current modifier key and button state, using an inclusive OR of the bitmasks from Table 4.2.

You should call XQueryPointer (or the often-not-implemented XGetMotionEvents) for every MotionNotify event that arrives with the *is_hint* field set to NotifyHint.

N O T E

Mouse Event Masks

To ask for the various kinds of mouse-motion events, there are a number of event masks. Use these event bitmasks to ask for events in functions like XtAddEventHandler (see Table 4.3).

Table 4.3 *Pointer event masks.*

Mask	Meaning
ButtonMotionMask	The mouse is moved while a button is pressed
Button1MotionMask	The mouse is moved while button I is pressed
Button2MotionMask	The mouse is moved while button 2 is pressed
Button3MotionMask	The mouse is moved while button 3 is pressed
Button4MotionMask	The mouse is moved while button 4 is pressed
Button5MotionMask	The mouse is moved while button 5 is pressed

ButtonPressMask	A mouse pointer button is pressed down
ButtonReleaseMask	A mouse pointer button that was pressed down was released
PointerMotionHintMask	Special mask that asks X to compress a number of mouse movements into one event
PointerMotionMask	The mouse pointer was moved (which happens very often)

Programming Button Events

For user-interface design, a quick ButtonPress, then ButtonRelease is usually referred to as a button *click*. When checking for these events, it is a good idea to provide some user feedback when the first event comes in—the ButtonPress. This is so the user doesn't repeatedly press the mouse button (or hold it down for a long time) under the mistaken impression that the application didn't notice the ButtonPress. The fact that many X connections are over a network introduces a potential time lag between the arrival of the ButtonPress and ButtonRelease.

In addition to mouse events, other graphics-related events include ColormapNotify and VisibilityNotify events.

Colormap Events

The ColormapNotify *event* charts changes in the colormap attribute or to the attribute itself in a particular window. Since most UNIX workstations provide only one hardware colormap, if your application creates a colormap, only one X colormap can be "active" at a time. If your application creates a colormap, part of the time your colormap will be active, and part of the time your colormap will not be active. Each time this changes, your application receives a ColormapNotify event (if the application asked for that event, see below). You can select for this event with the ColormapChangeMask. ColormapNotify events use the XColormapEvent structure:

```
typedef struct {
    int          type;
    unsigned long serial;
    Bool         send_event;
    Display*     display;
    Window       window;
    Colormap     colormap;
    Bool         new;
    int          state;
} XColormapEvent;
```

The *colormap* field is set to a valid colormap ID if a colormap was changed, installed, or uninstalled, or None if a colormap was freed. The *new* field is set to True if the colormap changed and False if the colormap was installed or uninstalled. The *state* field indicates ColormapInstalled or ColormapUninstalled. The *type* field is set to ColormapNotify.

Visibility Events

A VisibilityNotify *event* occurs when a window's visibility changes. This does not include changes in any subwindows. If you ask for the VisibilityNotify event (with the VisibilityChangeMask), you'll get the event data in an XVisibilityEvent *structure*:

```
typedef struct {
    int          type;
    unsigned long serial;
    Bool         send_event;
    Display*     display;
    Window       window;
    int          state;
} XVisibilityEvent;
```

The *window* field indicates the window for which the visibility changed. The *state* field is set to either `VisibilityFullyObscured`, `VisibilityPartiallyObscured`, or `VisibilityUnObscured`. The *type* field is set to `VisibilityNotify`.

Events and X Toolkits

X toolkits process most events, and this is good. Your application doesn't have to mess with events for each interface widget. Instead, you only need to deal with events sent to raw graphics windows.

The basic Xt event-handling loop is the simple function `XtAppMainLoop`:

```
void XtAppMainLoop(XtAppContext appcontext)

{
    XEvent      event;

    for (;;) {
        XtAppNextEvent(appcontext, &event);
        XtDispatchEvent(&event);
    }
}
```

`XtAppNextEvent` blocks until the next event arrives from the X server (or another input source, such as a timer, generates an event). `XtDispatchEvent` then sends this event to the proper Xt widget.

For your applications, you have three routes to get at X events. First, you can use callbacks, such as the `XmNexposeCallback`, which is called when `Expose` events arrive for an `XmDrawingArea` widget. Second, you can write your own version of `XtAppMainLoop`. This way, you can intercept every X event that arrives and decide whether or not to dispatch this event via `XtDispatchEvent`. Third, you can call `XtAddEventHandler` to set up a callback for additional events on a widget:

```
void XtAddEventHandler(Widget widget,
    EventMask eventmask,
    Boolean nonmaskable,
    XtEventHandler callback,
    XtPointer client_data)
```

The EventMask is an unsigned long integer (int) and holds the inclusive OR of the bit-flags for the events you want. XtPointer is a typedef for *char** or *void**, depending on your system. The *client_data* parameter is a pointer to any extra data you want to pass to the callback function. The *callback* function should then take the following parameters:

```
void callback(Widget widget,
    XtPointer client_data,
    XEvent* event,
    Boolean* continue_to_dispatch)
```

Generally, don't mess with the *continue_to_dispatch* parameter. If you set the Boolean pointed at by *continue_to_dispatch* to False, none of the remaining callback functions will get executed. The *client_data* parameter points at the data passed to XtAddEventHandler.

Asking for Events

X follows a simple model for events: your application only gets the events it asks for. Because there are so many kinds of events supported by X, this makes sense in that it produces more efficient applications. If you use an X toolkit, most of the event processing will be taken care of. But if you want to get additional events on various toolkit widgets, use a function such as XtAddEventMask.

Event Types and Structures

The following two tables list the X event types, the masks you use to ask for events of that type, and the event structures you get for the events. Table 4.4 starts with the point of view of the event type.

Table 4.4 *Event types, masks, and structures.*

Event Type	Mask to Ask for Event	Event Structure
ButtonPress	ButtonPressMask	XButtonPressedEvent
ButtonRelease	ButtonReleaseMask	XButtonReleasedEvent
CirculateNotify	StructureNotifyMask,	XCirculateEvent
	SubstructureNotifyMask	XCirculateEvent
CirculateRequest	SubstructureRedirectMask	XCirculateRequestEvent
ClientMessage	None	XClientMessageEvent
ColormapNotify	ColormapChangeMask	XColormapEvent
ConfigureNotify	StructureNotifyMask,	XConfigureEvent
	SubstructureNotifyMask,	XConfigureEvent
ConfigureRequest	SubstructureRedirectMask	XConfigureRequestEvent
CreateNotify	SubstructureNotifyMask	XCreateWindowEvent
DestroyNotify	StructureNotifyMask,	XDestroyWindowEvent
	SubstructureNotifyMask	XDestroyWindowEvent
EnterNotify	EnterWindowMask	XEnterWindowEvent
Expose	ExposureMask	XExposeEvent
FocusIn	FocusChangeMask	XFocusInEvent
FocusOut	FocusChangeMask	XFocusOutEvent
GraphicsExpose	(Graphics exposure in GC)	XGraphicsExposeEvent
GravityNotify	StructureNotifyMask,	XGravityEvent
	SubstructureNotifyMask	XGravityEvent
KeymapNotify	KeymapStateMask	XKeymapEvent
KeyPress	KeyPressMask	XKeyPressedEvent
KeyRelease	KeyReleaseMask	XKeyReleasedEvent
LeaveNotify	LeaveWindowMask	XLeaveWindowEvent
MapNotify	StructureNotifyMask,	XMapEvent
	SubstructureNotifyMask	XMapEvent
MappingNotify	None	XMappingEvent
MapRequest	SubstructureRedirectMask	XMapRequestEvent
MotionNotify	ButtonMotionMask,	XPointerMovedEvent
	Button1MotionMask,	XPointerMovedEvent
	Button2MotionMask,	XPointerMovedEvent
	Button3MotionMask,	XPointerMovedEvent
	Button4MotionMask,	XPointerMovedEvent
	Button5MotionMask,	XPointerMovedEvent

	PointerMotionMask,	XPointerMovedEvent
NoExpose	(Graphics exposure in GC)	XNoExposeEvent
PropertyNotify	PropertyChangeMask	XPropertyEvent
ReparentNotify	StructureNotifyMask,	XReparentEvent
	SubstructureNotifyMask	XReparentEvent
ResizeRequest	ResizeRedirectMask	XResizeRequestEvent
SelectionClear	None	XSelectionClearEvent
SelectionNotify	None	XSelectionEvent
SelectionRequest	None	XSelectionRequestEvent
UnmapNotify	StructureNotifyMask,	XUnmapEvent
	SubstructureNotifyMask	XUnmapEvent
VisibilityNotify	VisibilityChangeMask	XVisibilityEvent

The event masks of None indicate that your application always gets those events, even if you don't ask for them.

Event Masks

Table 4.5 starts from the event mask.

Table 4.5   *Event masks and types.*

Mask	Asks for Event Type
ButtonMotionMask	MotionNotify (any button)
Button1MotionMask	MotionNotify
Button2MotionMask	MotionNotify
Button3MotionMask	MotionNotify
Button4MotionMask	MotionNotify
Button5MotionMask	MotionNotify
ButtonPressMask	ButtonPress
ButtonReleaseMask	ButtonRelease
ColormapChangeMask	ColormapNotify
EnterWindowMask	EnterNotify
ExposureMask	Expose
FocusChangeMask	FocusIn, FocusOut
KeymapStateMask	KeymapNotify
KeyPressMask	KeyPress

KeyReleaseMask	KeyRelease
LeaveWindowMask	LeaveNotify
NoEventMask	None
OwnerGrabButtonMask	None
PointerMotionHintMask	None
PointerMotionMask	MotionNotify
PropertyChangeMask	PropertyNotify
ResizeRedirectMask	ResizeRequest
StructureNotifyMask	CirculateNotify, ConfigureNotify, DestroyNotify, GravityNotify, MapNotify, ReparentNotify, UnmapNotify
SubstructureNotifyMask	CirculateNotify, ConfigureNotify, CreateNotify, DestroyNotify, GravityNotify, MapNotify, ReparentNotify, UnmapNotify
SubstructureRedirectMask	CirculateRequest, ConfigureRequest, MapRequest
VisibilityChangeMask	VisibilityNotify

Summary

In an event-driven application, such as those found in the X Window System, the program cedes control to the user. The user drives the actions of the program through a series of many events. The program is really still in control, but it gives the user the feeling that the user is running the show. This is very important if your applications support users who are new to computing. The big difference with event-driven programming is that events can come in at any time and in any order.

That's why it's up to you to prepare for these events. This chapters covers graphics-related events, such as:

✦ Expose events, requests from the X server that your application needs to redraw parts of one of its windows;

✦ Regions, which are opaque data types that hold odd shapes, such as collections of rectangles;

✦ Window-resizing events;

✦ Mouse and button-press events;

✦ The `ColormapNotify` event, which charts changes in the colormap attribute or to the attribute itself in a particular window; and

✦ A `VisibilityNotify` event, which occurs when a window's visibility changes.

Finally, X follows a simple model for events: your application only gets the events it asks for. Because there are so many kinds of events supported by X, this makes sense in that it produces more efficient applications. If you use an X toolkit, most of the event processing will be taken care of. But if you want to get additional events on various toolkit widgets, use a function such as `XtAddEventMask`.

In the next two chapters, we introduce two of the most popular X toolkits, Motif (Chapter 5) and OLIT, the Open Look Intrinsics Toolkit (Chapter 6), and finally get down to writing real X programs. If you use an X toolkit other than Motif or OLIT, or if you're already very familiar with your toolkit of choice, you probably want to skip ahead to Chapter 7, which discusses color.

X Library Functions and Macros Introduced in This Chapter

```
XClipBox

XCreateRegion

XDestroyRegion

XIntersectRegion

XQueryPointer

XSetRegion

XUnionRectWithRegion
```

X Toolkit Intrinsics Functions and Macros Introduced in This Chapter

```
XtAddEventHandler
XtAddExposureToRegion
```

C h a p t e r 5

Graphics Programming with the Motif Toolkit

This chapter covers:

- ✦ X Window toolkits
- ✦ The Motif toolkit
- ✦ The X Toolkit Intrinsics
- ✦ Widgets and windows
- ✦ Programming with X toolkits
- ✦ The basic format of Motif programs
- ✦ Creating basic Motif widgets
- ✦ X graphics from the point of view of Motif
- ✦ The Motif drawing area widget
- ✦ A sample Motif program
- ✦ Compiling Motif programs

What is an X toolkit?

An *X toolkit* is a software library aimed at speeding application development under the X Window System. The whole idea is to avoid making low-level calls to the X library and instead work at a higher level of abstraction. In this regard, the Motif toolkit works very well, except when you need to go beyond the toolkit when programming applications for such needs as computer-aided design (CAD), geographic information systems, or even traditional word processors or spreadsheets.

X toolkits normally provide a lot of help when creating the user interface of your application, but they don't work well for creating the inner workings, or base code, of your application. When your application's basic functions involve graphics, such as image processing or data display, X toolkits don't tend to provide much help. In those cases, you have to drop down to the low-level X library.

In fact, every sophisticated, commercial-grade X application we've ever come across used the X library as well as a toolkit. Because of this, we've aimed this book squarely at X application developers who *do* need to go beyond what their toolkit provides. And one of the most commonly used X toolkits is the Motif toolkit. This chapter presents a whirlwind introduction to Motif. We also provide a set of Motif utility functions to speed development of the sample programs in the rest of the book.

If you're already well-versed in Motif, you can skip ahead to Chapter 6 on Open Look Intrinsics Toolkit (OLIT) or to Chapter 7 on X color. If you're not well versed in Motif, read on. You may also want to read a tutorial specifically on Motif, as we're not going to make you Motif experts with one chapter.

What we will do, though, is briefly cover a common set of Motif widgets used for things like pulldown menus. We then will briefly explain utility functions that create menus and prompted text entries, which should save you from writing extra code.

If you are new to Motif or OLIT, though, you'll be at a slight disadvantage. There's simply too much material to cover in this book to also provide a full-blown tutorial an Motif and OLIT.

N O T E

Because Motif and OLIT are so similar, we develop the same set of utility functions for both. This makes the sample programs much more generic and less dependent on toolkits—at least as much as possible. In the real world, you need to take advantage of what your toolkit offers. We struck a middle ground: for simple things like pulldown menus and pushbuttons, we develop generic utility functions that act the same for Motif and OLIT. (The implementation under the hood is different for both, of course.) For complex graphics, we tie the solution to the toolkit where necessary.

What is Motif?

Motif was developed by the Open Software Foundation (OSF), an industry consortium that includes Digital Equipment Corp. (DEC), Hewlett-Packard, and IBM. Actually, there's no such *thing* as Motif (much the same as there's no such *thing* as Open Look); instead, when someone refers to Motif, he or she can be referring to any one of the following:

- ✦ A look-and-feel Style Guide for applications, based on IBM's Common User Access (CUA).
- ✦ A Motif window manager, mwm, to help enforce the Style Guide.
- ✦ A User Interface Language (UIL) interpreter, which places much of the user interface code into interpreted files.
- ✦ A toolkit (C library) for building Style Guide-compliant applications, also called a widget set. This toolkit is based on the Xt Intrinsics, as are the Athena widgets and OLIT toolkits.

Why Use Motif?

There are a number of reasons why you might want to use the Motif toolkit:

- ✦ Motif is one of the major interface standards in the UNIX world.
- ✦ Motif provides nice-looking 3D effects.
- ✦ Motif compliance is needed for selling to many big firms and organizations.

✦ Using a toolkit—any toolkit—speeds programming.

✦ Motif fits in reasonably well with X standards (e.g., window managers and resource files).

A lot of people try to push the idea of a war between Motif and OLIT for market share. We hold the position that you'll choose the toolkit that works best for you. Other than availability, there are no real technical reasons for using Motif over OLIT. Both toolkits provide the same basic framework for your applications.

Why Should You Avoid Motif?

There are also a number of reasons why you might want to run for the hills upon seeing Motif. First and foremost is the fact that the Xt Intrinsics enforce an odd pseudo-object-oriented code style. Designed at a time when C++ or other object-oriented languages were not as widely available as today, the Xt Intrinsics includes an odd object-oriented layer. Contrast this with other object-oriented toolkits like InterViews and Object Interface (OI), which were based on C++.

While Xt's object-oriented layer may seem like an advantage, programming with the Xt Intrinsics is a bear, especially if you want to create your own subclasses of existing widgets. So far, there's no decent C++ interface to Motif or the Xt Intrinsics.

It's an understatement to note that Motif programs tend to be large. Very few Motif programs clock in at under 1 megabyte in size, unless you use shared libraries. The X Window System and Motif constitute one reason why you're probably buying double the RAM in your workstations than you were just a few short years ago.

Motif and all Xt-based programs also tend to call `malloc` and other memory-allocation functions far too often. This tends to become a performance bottleneck. Xt-based programs, for example, allocate more than 50 kilobytes of random access memory (RAM) at start-up time. For this and other reasons (mainly the high overhead), Motif programs tend to be slow.

And finally, Motif and all Xt-based programs make extensive use of X resource files. X resources form a handy means to customize applications—without access to source code—but also tend to be impossible to debug. The X world has only recently moved in the direction of graphical resource editors.

X Toolkit (Xt Intrinsics)

The Xt Intrinsics, as we described in Chapter 1, is an independent software layer that sits above the low-level X library. It provides a base for creating high-level X toolkits, like Motif or OLIT, without imposing a specific look and feel. Xt presents an odd but reasonably consistent programming style. This style, especially in the use of XtSetArg, is unique to X.

The main concept introduced by Xt is the idea of a widget. Xt provides the basic concept of widgets and a set of functions for manipulating widgets, but leaves it to the higher-level toolkit, also called a *widget set*, to layer on the actual look and feel. This is the way that both OLIT and Motif can provide different user interfaces and yet both be based on the Xt Intrinsics.

Other common widget sets include the free Athena widgets (Xaw) and the Motifized version of OLIT called MoOLIT (available as part of UNIX System V Release 4.2).

Widgets

A *widget* is a named user-interface object, dynamically allocated via malloc. The names are important when working with X resources files. A widget encapsulates a user-interface element, like a menu, scroll bar, slider, or text-entry field. At the base level, each widget has an underlying X window (Motif *gadgets* are exceptions). Because of this, Motif applications tend to create a *lot* of windows on the X display. Even so, the key to Motif is understanding how to work with widgets.

Each widget has a parent, except for the top-level widget returned by XtAppInitialize or OlIntialize (covered in the next chapter), much like each X window has a parent except for the root window.

This parent widget controls the layout (called the *geometry* in widget terminology) of its child widgets. Following this simple rule, there are a number of geometry-manager widgets that exist for the sole purpose of laying out child widgets. The Motif paned-window widget, for instance, lays out child widgets vertically, in panes. The form widget, on the other hand, allows a fine grain of control over the placement of child widgets.

Part of the key to X application development is understanding the top-down approach to creating interface elements. Not only are widgets arranged in a hierarchy, they must be created in the hierarchical order as well.

Motif widgets are organized into widget classes or types (note the object-oriented terminology).

Motif Widget Classes

Motif widgets fall into certain classes. The major widgets are listed in Table 5.1 (some of the abstract classes and gadgets are skipped for clarity). The basic types of Motif widgets include managers, primitives, shells, and Xt-provided widgets.

Table 5.1 *Major Motif widgets.*

Widget	Function
Managers	Widgets that hold other widgets
Primitives	Widgets that don't hold other widgets, e.g., a text label (`XmLabel`)
Shell widgets	Manager widgets that interact with the window manager. This has nothing to do with UNIX shells like csh and ksh
Xt widgets	Provided in the base Xt Intrinsics

Primitive Widgets

The primitive widgets are listed in Table 5.2.

Table 5.2 *The Motif primitive widgets.*

Widget	Function
`XmArrowButton`	Holds an arrow tip; used for the ends of scroll bars
`XmCascadeButton`	Used to pull down menus
`XmGadget`	Superclass for Motif gadgets (windowless widgets)

`XmLabel`	Displays a text message
`XmList`	Presents a list of choices
`XmPushButton`	Activates a callback when "pushed" with the mouse
`XmScrollBar`	Used for scroll bars
`XmSeparator`	Provides a horizontal line; used to separate menu items
`XmText`	Text-entry field; can be a multiline or a single-line entry field
`XmTextField`	Single-line text-entry field
`XmToggleButton`	Pushbutton that holds a state ("on" or "off"); used for radio buttons

Manager Widgets

The manager widgets are listed in Table 5.3.

Table 5.3 The Motif manager widgets.

Widget	Function
`XmBulletinBoard`	Primitive manager widget; used for dialogs
`XmCommand`	Used to hold commands
`XmDrawingArea`	"Raw" window onto which you can draw
`XmDrawnButton`	Combination of `XmPushButton` and `XmDrawingArea`
`XmFileSelectionBox`	Used to ask the user to select a file name from a list of files
`XmForm`	Subclass of `XmBulletinBoard`; has complex layout rules
`XmFrame`	Surrounds a widget with a 3D beveled frame
`XmMainWindow`	Used to hold elements of the application's main window, e.g., the menu bar

`XmPanedWindow`	Lays out child widgets vertically in "panes"; may have sashes to separate
`XmRowColumn`	Lays out widgets in rows or columns; used to hold menus
`XmScale`	A valuator widget
`XmScrolledWindow`	Presents a viewport onto a very large child widget

Shell Widgets

The name *shell* is a bit of a misnomer. A *shell widget* is a top-level widget that is originally created as a child of a screen's root window. The shell provides functions to interact with window managers, special X programs that control the layout of top-level windows on the screen.

The shell widgets are listed in Table 5.4.

Table 5.4 *The Motif shell widgets.*

Widget	Function
`XmDialogShell`	Used to hold dialogs; subclass of `TransientShell`
`XmMenuShell`	Used to hold menus; subclass of `OverrideShell`

Xt Classes

Motif also uses a number of Xt widgets directly, although you should note that Motif customizes these widgets. They are listed in Table 5.5.

Table 5.5 *The Xt classes.*

Class	Function
`ApplicationShell`	Shell returned by `XtAppInitialize`

OverrideShell	Holds menus
TopLevelShell	Subclass of VendorShell; used for top-level windows
TransientShell	Used to hold "transient" windows, e.g., dialogs
VendorShell	Subclass of WMShell that has toolkit-specific (e.g., Motif) features
WMShell	Superclass for shells that need to interact with the window manager

The ApplicationShell and the XmDrawingArea are the two most important widget classes for working with graphics and Motif.

Xt Event Handling

As mentioned in the last chapter, Xt and Motif intercept and handle most X events, freeing your code from this responsibility. If you wish to be notified of an event, though, you can set up an event-handling *callback function* to handle an event. Motif makes heavy use of these callback functions to notify your application code when a higher-level event occurs. For example, a pushbutton widget generates an *activate callback* when activated (the user presses the leftmost mouse button over it). When this happens, your function is "called back" (executed).

Basic Format of Motif Programs

Motif programs usually follow six basic steps:

- ✦ Initialize the Xt Intrinsics (which also sets up connection to the X server).
- ✦ Creates widgets.
- ✦ Sets up any needed callback functions.
- ✦ Realizes the widget hierarchy with XtRealizeWidget.
- ✦ Enters the event-handling loop.
- ✦ Loops forever—yes, forever.

The *loop-forever* part is serious. Because of this, you'll need to set up at least one callback function to exit your program.

N O T E

When programming with the Xt Intrinsics and Motif, it's easy to get confused as to which function comes from which library. Just like most X functions begin with *X*, Xt functions begin with *Xt* and Motif functions begin with *Xm*. (OLIT functions begin with *Ol*.)

Motif Header Files

All Motif programs require the header file `<Xm/Xm.h>`. Plus, every Motif widget has its own header file. (You can find the names of the necessary header files in the OSF/Motif Programmer's Reference.) In all the code examples below, we assume `<Xm/Xm.h>` is included.

XtAppInitialize

The first step in any Motif program is to initialize the Xt Intrinsics. The function `XtAppInitialize` does this:

```
Widget XtAppInitialize(
    XtAppContext* appcontext,  /* RETURN */
    String app_class_name,
    XrmOptionDescList xrm_options,
    Cardinal number_xrm_options,
    int* argc,          /* input/output */
    String* argv,    /* input/output */
    String* fallback_resources,
    ArgList args,    /* hard-coded resources */
    Cardinal number_args)
```

The application context is set up by `XtAppInitialize`. You use the `appcontext` in the call to `XtAppMainLoop`.

For most of the parameters, you can pass NULLs to XtApp-Initialize. That's because few programs will need all the options and these are advanced features.

N O T E

In X11 Release 4, the argc pointer was a Cardinal (unsigned integer [int]) pointer. In X11 Release 5, this is a normal int pointer. If you compile with both R4 and R5 and use ANSI/ISO C, you'll have to put in some code to cast to the proper type.

We use the #defined symbol XtSpecificationRelease to tell if we are at X11 Release 4 or higher. The following code sets up the macro ARGC_PTR to an int or unsigned int pointer as necessary:

```
#if XtSpecificationRelease > 4

#define ARGC_PTR     (int*)

#else   /* X11R4 */

#define ARGC_PTR     (unsigned int*)

#endif  /* X11R4 */
```

We can then cast the pointer to argc, above, to the ARGC_PTR type, without worrying which version of the Xt library we're compiling under.

XtAppInitialize in Real Use

In your code, you can call XtAppInitialize, passing mostly null values:

```
int main(int argc, char** argv) {
Widget          parent;
XtAppContext    app_context;
```

```
Arg             args[20];
int             n;


n = 0;


parent = XtAppInitialize(&app_context,
            "ProX",                          /* app class */
            (XrmOptionDescList) NULL,        /* options */
            0,                               /* num options */
            ARGC_PTR &argc, argv,            /* cmd line */
            (String*) NULL,                  /* fallback res. */
            args, n);


    /* ... */

}
```

Managing Widgets

Managing a widget makes that widget visible. Technically, managing a widget places that widget under control of its parent's geometry management. If a widget is unmanaged, it will not be visible at all. If you manage a widget, then that widget will be made visible if the parent allows it.

Dialog widgets, for example, are usually left unmanaged. You do manage all the children of the dialog widgets, though. To show a dialog, you simply manage the dialog shell widget. To hide a dialog, you unmanage the dialog shell widget.

XtManageChild manages a widget. By default, all Motif-created widgets are created unmanaged, unless you use the XtCreateManagedWidget function. An unmanaged widget will not be made visible when your application calls XtRealizeWidget, so you must manage most widgets after you create them—that is, if you want those widgets to become visible in your application's interface.

`XtManageChild` takes one parameter, the widget to manage:

```
void XtManageChild(Widget widget)
```

XtRealizeWidget

`XtRealizeWidget` realizes a widget and all of its child widgets. Normally, you must realize all top-level shell widgets, except for popup windows like dialogs and menus. For simple programs, you call `XtRealizeWidget` on the top-level shell widget returned by `XtAppInitialize`. `XtRealizeWidget` creates the actual window IDs used under the hood by Motif widgets. If you ever want to do advanced operations on the windows associated with Motif widgets, you must realize the widgets first. This forms a common stumbling block when programming Motif applications.

```
void XtRealizeWidget(Widget parent)
```

Mapping Windows

A very common Motif programming technique involves creating the top-level window but not managing it. The reasoning is simple: you need to get a valid X window ID to work with colormaps, create graphics contexts (GCs), and work with window options, but you normally want to do this *before* the application appears on the screen. Because of this, you need to go through an odd sequence.

First, set the `mappedWhenManaged` resource to `False` on the top-level shell widget created by `XtAppInitialize`. (This forces the widget to remain unmapped when you manage it, as the top-level shell is by default created managed.) Then call `XtRealizeWidget` to actually create the top-level widget's associated window. After working with the window ID, you finally map the top-level widget to make it appear on the screen.

The function `XtMapWidget` will map a widget:

```
XtMapWidget(Widget widget)
```

The whole code sequence to initialize the toolkit looks like the following:

```
Widget        parent;
XtAppContext  app_context;
Arg           args[20];
int           n;


n = 0;


XtSetArg(args[n], XmNmappedWhenManaged, False); n++;


/* ... */


parent = XtAppInitialize(&app_context,
          "ProX",                     /* app class */
          (XrmOptionDescList) NULL,   /* options */
          0,                          /* num options */
          ARGC_PTR &argc, argv,       /* cmd line */
          (String*) NULL,             /* fallback res. */
          args, n);


/* Create the windows */
XtRealizeWidget(parent);

/*
 * You can now use the window IDs
 * to set up graphics contexts, etc...
 */


/* map the window. */
```

```
XtMapWidget(parent);


/* Enter the main loop. */
XtAppMainLoop(app_context);
```

XtAppMainLoop

`XtAppMainLoop` executes the main event-handling loop of a Motif application. This loop executes forever, so you must set up at least one callback function that will exit your program. (You could create your own event loop, but that is an advanced topic.)

```
void XtAppMainLoop(XtAppContext appcontext)
```

If you develop with Motif 1.0, you won't have an application context and you should use `XtMainLoop` instead of `XtAppMainLoop`.

N O T E

Creating Widgets

There are two main ways to create Motif widgets. First, you can use the Xt-provided functions `XtCreateWidget` (and a host of variants). Second, you can use the Motif-provided functions, one for each widget type, to create widgets. In most cases, this is all a matter of your preferred coding style.

There are a few exceptions, though, where it pays to use the Motif toolkit functions. Menus, dialogs, scrolled text widgets, and other combinations have Motif front-ends to a complex set of code hidden under the hood. If you use the Xt functions, you must mimic this code on your own. In those cases, we strongly urge you to use the Motif convenience functions.

Among the built-in Motif functions is `XmCreatePushButton`.

XmCreatePushButton

XmCreatePushButton creates a pushbutton widget. You'll find all Motif XmCreate*Something* functions take the same parameters:

```
#include <Xm/PushB.h>


Widget XmCreatePushButton(Widget parent,
     char* widget_name,
     ArgList args
     Cardinal number_args)
```

XmCreatePushButton creates a pushbutton widget. You need to pass the *parent* widget (remember that every widget—except for top-level widgets, must have a parent). The parent controls the size and location of the child widget, created by XmCreatePushButton. You also need to pass the widget's name—every widget can be identified by its name. This is important for resource-setting commands. The *args* and *number_args* parameters constitute the list of hard-coded resource values you want to set for the widget (see below for more on resources).

NOTE

The XmCreate*Something* functions create widgets, but don't manage these widgets, so you must later call XtManage-Child.

The main purpose of a pushbutton widget is to call a function (a *callback*) when activated.

Setting Up Callback Functions

The Xt function XtAddCallback registers a function as a callback for a widget:

```
void XtAddCallback(Widget widget,
```

```
String which_callback,

XtCallbackProc callback_function,

XtPointer client_data)
```

The *client_data* is a pointer to any extra data you want to pass to the callback function.

XtAddCallback adds a function of yours to the list of callbacks for a particular widget. Every widget supports a number of callbacks and each callback type is named. For the pushbutton widget, we use the activateCallback:

```
Widget  widget;
void    quitCB();


XtAddCallback(widget,
    XmNactivateCallback,
    (XtCallbackProc) quitCB,
    (XtPointer) NULL);
```

Callback Functions

All basic *callback functions* take the same parameters (exceptions include timers, event-handlers, and other callbacks, but these are not set up with XtAddCallback):

✦ The widget ID of the widget the callback was set up on.

✦ A pointer (normally, XtPointer is an alias for *caddr_t* or *void•*) to any user, that is, your data, which is termed the *client data*. This data was originally passed to XtAddCallback.

✦ A pointer to a Motif structure that includes specific information about the callback. For instance, a list widget (XmList) callback structure includes the item that the user selected from the list. For the simple case of a pushbutton widget, though, you can normally ignore the *call_data* structure. You must cast the XtPointer *call_data* to the proper structure type (these are documented in the OSF/Motif Programmer's Reference, listed in Appendix E).

✦ A common error for newcomers to Motif is to reverse the order of the *client_data* and *call_data* parameters.

Here's an example callback function:

```
void CallbackFunction(Widget widget,
    XtPointer client_data,
    XtPointer call_data)


{   /* CallbackFunction */

    /* Your code goes here... */

}   /* CallbackFunction */
```

Creating Pushbuttons

We've put together a utility function to create a pushbutton widget and set up a callback function. This CreatePushbutton function is stored in the file *m_push.c*:

```
/*
 * m_push.c
 * Routine to create a Motif pushbutton.
 */
#include "motif.h"
#include <Xm/PushB.h>


/*
```

```
 * Utility: Create a menu choice,
 * really a pushbutton.
 */


Widget CreatePushbutton(Widget parent,
      char* name,
      XtCallbackProc callback,
      XtPointer client_data)


{     /* CreatePushbutton */
      Widget   button;
      Arg      args[20];
      int      n;


      n = 0;
      button = XmCreatePushButton(parent,
              name, args, n);


      XtManageChild(button);


      XtAddCallback(button,
          XmNactivateCallback,
          callback,
          client_data);


      return button;


}     /* CreatePushbutton */


/* end of file m_push.c */
```

What Are Resources?

X *resources* are a generic means to customize X applications—without modifying the application's source code. Thus, resources form a powerful tool when building Motif and OLIT programs. You can change colors, text fonts, and sizes of windows all from resource files.

As such, this concept is questionable and has many drawbacks. Think for a moment: how much of your program internals do you want end users to have access to? Changing font sizes is one thing, but you need to be careful what you allow in resource files. And why should users be forced to edit a separate file to change aspects of a program, when other operating systems place this power within the applications themselves? Resource-setting commands are rather obtuse, and there's a confusing plethora of options, especially for the location of resource files. If that's not enough, debugging resource files is almost impossible.

What follows is a very brief introduction to X resources. If you're new to this topic, you'll want to look up more examples.

Resource Files

A *resource file* is an ASCII (ISO Latin-1, actually) text file containing resource-setting commands. When XtAppInitialize starts, it looks in a set of directories for resource files and automatically loads them. (This is one reason Motif applications take so long to start.) A common location for resource files is in /usr/lib/X11/app-defaults and in your home directory.

Resource files are a very handy way to customize your applications. For example, you could place *all* text messages for an application in resource files. If you wanted to translate your application to run in French, for instance, the majority of the work could be done by merely editing the resource file and translating the messages into French. Note that the translators could do this *without modifying the source code*. This seems to be a great advantage, but it can also be a disadvantage: if the file in which these resource-setting commands reside isn't properly set up, then the user may see a very confusing mess for the application.

Application Names and Class Names

Every Xt application has a resource class name. This name, `ProX` in our examples, is passed to `XtAppInitialize`. This then becomes the base name for application defaults resource files. The traditional grab-bag location for resources has been the `.Xdefaults` file in your home directory.

Location of Resource Files

Resources files may appear in many locations in your system. The files are searched in the order below. If the same resource is set more than once, the last value remains. In addition, resource commands that use direct names have precedence over resource class names. X resources, beyond the short introduction here, fall outside of the scope of this book.

Possibility #1:

```
/usr/lib/X11/$LANG/app-defaults/Class

/usr/lib/X11/app-defaults/Class
```

`$XFILESEARCHPATH`, if set, overrides `/usr/lib/X11/app-defaults`. $LANG is used for internationalization.

Possibility #2:

```
$XUSERFILESEARCHPATH/Class

$XAPPLRESDIR/$LANG Class

$XAPPLRESDIR Class

$HOME/$LANG/Class

$HOME/Class
```

Possibility #3:

`RESOURCE_MANAGER` property on the root window, or, it not present, `$HOME/.Xdefaults`.

Possibility #4:

$XENVIRONMENT or, if not set, $HOME/.Xdefaults-*hostname*.

Possibility #5:

Program command-line parameters, such as the -xrm parameter.

In Possibilities #1 and #2, Class is the name of an application class.

Resource-Setting Commands

When you use a *resource-setting command*, you're trying to change the behavior of a widget (or many widgets, as the case may be). Remember that widgets are named data objects. It is by these names that you can modify widgets.

The basic syntax of resource-setting commands follows the idea of name/value pairs. You specify the widgets to change, by name, then the resource to change, and, finally, the new value:

```
which-widgets . which-resource : value
```

A colon separates the name part from the value part. The *which-widgets* part is a period-separated list of widget names from the top-level parent to the actual widget you want to set. You can also use an asterisk (*) as a wild-card, as we show in the examples below.

Resource Examples

The following examples show resource-setting commands:

```
*background:     LightGray
```

Sets the background (color) of every widget to light gray.

```
*quit.background:    red
```

Sets the background color of all widgets named *quit* to red.

```
ProX.mainwindow.drawingarea.fontList: lucidasans-12
```

Sets the `fontList` resource (which names fonts) for the widget named *drawingarea* (child of *mainwindow*, child of *ProX*) to the font *lucidasans-12*. You can use the `xlsfonts` program to list the available fonts on your system.

Hard-Coding Resource Commands

In addition to using resource files, you can hard-code resource commands in your programs. There's a danger here, though, in that if you hard-code a value, users cannot set that value in resource files.

When you hard-code resource commands, you use resource-name/value pairs much like in resource files. You don't have to specify the widget names, however, because you use `Widget` pointers in your code. You do follow a very convoluted programming style, though. This style is unique to X.

The are two main steps to setting resource commands in your code. First, set the resource name and its new value into an element in an `Arg` array with `XtSetArg`. Second, pass this `Arg` array to a widget creation function or to `XtSetValues`:

```
Widget  widget;
Arg     args[20];
int     n;


n = 0;
XtSetArg(args[n], XmNwhich-resource,
     resource-value); n++;


XtSetValues(widget, args, n);
```

`XtSetArg` is a complex macro. You don't want to know what it does. In resource files, you use resource names, such as *labelString*. In your C code, you use XmN*resourceName*, such as `XmNlabelString`. Resource names normally begin with a lowercase letter. Any words following start with an uppercase letter.

The following code sets the *width*, *height*, and *allowResize* resources and passes these values on to XmCreateDrawingArea:

```
Widget   widget;
Widget   parent;
Arg      args[20];
int      n;

n = 0;
XtSetArg(args[n], XmNwidth, width); n++;
XtSetArg(args[n], XmNheight, height); n++;
XtSetArg(args[n], XmNallowResize, True); n++;

widget = XmCreateDrawingArea(parent,
              name, args, n);


XtManageChild(widget);
```

Fallback Resources

Fallback resources are a compromise between hard-coded resources that cannot be overridden by the user and resource files that may—or may not—be installed properly. Fallback resources act as a safety valve in case the resource file can't be located. Fallback resources only take effect when the user does *not* set the same resource value in a resource file.

To use fallback resources, you need to build a NULL-terminated array of type String of resource-setting commands and pass these resources to XtAppInitialize:

```
static String  fallback_resources[] = {
"*fontList:      lucidasans-12",
"*background:    lightgray",
"*foreground:    blue",
```

```
    NULL
    }; /* fallback_resources */


    /* ... */


    int main(int argc, char** argv) {


    Widget        parent;
    XtAppContext  app_context;
    Arg           args[20];
    int           n;


    parent = XtAppInitialize(&app_context,
            "ProX",
            (XrmOptionDescList) NULL,
            0,
            ARGC_PTR &argc, argv,
            fallback_resources,
            args, n);


    /* ... */


    }
```

Motif and Text Strings

Motif uses its own string format and stores strings in variables of type
XmString. All Motif widgets, except for XmText and XmTextField
widgets, use XmString data for text. Because of this, your C code will
expend a lot of effort converting back and forth to XmStrings and normal
C strings (NULL-terminated arrays of type char).

The XmPushButton widget, for example, displays a text message, stored in the *labelString* resource. The type of this is—you guessed—XmString.

To create a Motif XmString, use XmStringCreateSimple:

```
XmString XmStringCreateSimple(char* string)
```

XmStringCreateSimple creates an XmString using the default locale. This is almost always what you want. If you don't want this, however, you can use XmStringCreateLocalized, a new function in Motif 1.2:

```
XmString XmStringCreateLocalized(char* string)
```

XmStringCreateLocalized creates an XmString in the current locale.

When you're done with an XmString, you need to free the memory with XmStringFree:

```
void XmStringFree(XmString motif_string)
```

XmString Example Code

Here's some sample code to set the *labelString* resource of an XmPushButton widget from within a C program:

```
Widget    parent;
Widget    push;
Arg       args[10];
int       n;
XmString  motif_string;


/*
 * Create a Motif XmString from
 * a C string (char*).
```

```
  */
motif_string =
      XmStringCreateSimple("Push me to exit");

/*
 * Hard-code in our XmString
 * as the labelString resource.
 */
n = 0;
XtSetArg(args[n], XmNlabelString,
     motif_string); n++;

/*
 * Create a pushbutton widget.
 */
push = XmCreatePushButton(parent,
            "quit", args, n);

XtManageChild(push);

/*
 * Free the Motif string now
 * that we're done with it.
 */
XmStringFree(motif_string);
```

Container Widgets and Complex Programs

Most Motif applications have a menu bar covering the top of the application's window, with pulldown menus on the menu bar. The main part of the application goes underneath the menu bar. The widget that controls the placement of the menu bar and your main data area is considered a *container widget*. Container widgets hold other (child) widgets and control the layout of these child widgets. Motif applications make extensive use of such container widgets.

Parent and Child Relationships

Every widget has a parent widget (except for the top-level shells, such as the one returned by XtAppInitialize). This parent widget is passed to XtCreateManagedWidget or XmCreate*Something* functions.

Only certain widgets, container and shell widgets, can be parent widgets. This parent widget controls the geometry (size and location) of child widgets. Examples of container widgets include XmMainWindow and XmRowColumn (used for menus).

In every Motif program, you'll create special widgets, like row-column widgets, to control the layout of child widgets—the widgets you're really interested in. All Motif programs share this top-down hierarchical design. One such container widget is a pulldown menu.

Pulldown Menus

Pulldown menus are common in most graphical interfaces, and Motif is no exception. In Motif, though, a menu is just a row-column parent widget (with a few special resources set). The menu choices then are simple pushbutton widgets.

To create a pulldown menu, you first create the menu bar (remember the top-down design).

Menu Bars

You create a menu bar with XmCreateMenuBar:

```
#include <Xm/RowColumn.h>
```

```
Widget XmCreateMenuBar(Widget parent,
```

```
char* name,

ArgList args,

Cardinal number_args)
```

The parent is a main window widget (which we cover below, under The Main Window). We put together a simple convenience routine, CreateMenuBar, and included it in the file *m_menu.c*, below.

The menu bar is also a row-column widget, again with special resources set. This is one place where it's easier to use the Motif convenience function, XmCreateMenubar, than the generic XtCreateManagedWidget.

Menu bars hold pulldown menus.

Creating a Pulldown Menu

The parent of a pulldown menu is the menu bar. To create the actual menu, you call XmCreatePulldownMenu, but don't manage this widget:

```
#include <Xm/RowColumn.h>


Widget XmCreatePulldownMenu(Widget parent,

        char* name,

        ArgList args,

        Cardinal number_args)
```

After you create the pulldown menu, you need a widget to pull down the menu. This is a cascade-button widget, or XmCascadeButton. A cascade-button widget acts a lot like a specialized pushbutton widget. To create a cascade button, call XmCreateCascadeButton:

```
#include <Xm/CascadeB.h>


Widget XmCreateCascadeButton(Widget parent,

        char* name,

        ArgList args,

        Cardinal number_args)
```

To create a pulldown menu, then, you need both a menu widget and a cascade-button widget to pull down the menu. You also need to connect the two widgets so that the cascade button pulls down the proper menu. To do this, you set the *subMenuId* resource on the cascade button with the widget ID of the pulldown menu, which is much less confusing than it sounds.

The `CreateMenu` function below shows how to create the two and connect the cascade button to the pulldown menu:

```
#include <Xm/CascadeB.h>
#include <Xm/RowColumn.h>


Widget CreateMenu(Widget parent, char* name)


{    /* CreateMenu */
    Widget  cascade;
    Widget  menuwidget;
    Arg     args[20];
    int     n;

    /*
     * Create pulldown menu.
     */
    n = 0;
    menuwidget = XmCreatePulldownMenu(parent,
                  name, args, n);

    /*
     * Create cascade button.
     */
    n = 0;
    XtSetArg(args[n], XmNsubMenuId, menuwidget); n++;
```

```
cascade = XmCreateCascadeButton(parent,
          name, args, n);


XtManageChild(cascade);


return menuwidget;


}   /* CreateMenu */
```

We manage the cascade button, but don't manage the pulldown menu. The cascade button will automatically manage the pulldown menu when it needs to appear. The parent widget in both cases is the menu-bar widget.

Creating Menu Choices

Menu choices are simply pushbutton widgets that are children of the parent pulldown menu. The callback on the pushbutton widget executes the code for that menu choice.

The `CreateMenuChoice` convenience routine, below, calls another convenience routine, `CreatePushbutton`, which we introduced earlier, under Creating Pushbuttons. This function creates a pushbutton widget. In Motif, a pushbutton and a menu choice are essentially the same thing. But in OLIT, we need to separate the two functions. In the interest of symmetry, we built a separate function to create a pushbutton and another function to create a menu choice (which calls `CreatePushbutton` under the hood):

```
Widget CreateMenuChoice(Widget parent,
        char* name,
        XtCallbackProc callback,
        XtPointer client_data)


{   /* CreateMenuChoice */
```

```
/*
 * In OLIT, CreateMenuChoice and
 * CreatePushbutton are implemented
 * differently.
 */
return CreatePushbutton(parent, name,
        callback, client_data);


}   /* CreateMenuChoice */
```

Source Code for the Menu Convenience Functions

We placed our menu convenience functions into the file m_menu.c:

```
/*
 *  m_menu.c
 *  Motif Menu routines.
 */
#include "motif.h"
#include <Xm/CascadeB.h>
#include <Xm/PushB.h>
#include <Xm/RowColumn.h>


/* Utility: Creates a Pulldown menu. */


Widget CreateMenu(Widget parent, char* name)


{   /* CreateMenu */
    Widget  cascade;
    Widget  menuwidget;
    Arg     args[20];
```

```
    int     n;


    /*
     * Create pulldown menu.
     */
    n = 0;
    menuwidget = XmCreatePulldownMenu(parent,
                    name, args, n);


    /*
     * Create cascade button.
     */
    n = 0;
    XtSetArg(args[n], XmNsubMenuId, menuwidget); n++;


    cascade = XmCreateCascadeButton(parent,
                name, args, n);


    XtManageChild(cascade);


    return menuwidget;


}   /* CreateMenu */


/* Utility: Create a Motif menubar. */


Widget CreateMenuBar(Widget parent, char* name)


{   /* CreateMenuBar */
    Widget  menubar;
    Arg     args[20];
```

```
    int     n;


    n = 0;
    menubar = XmCreateMenuBar(parent, name, args, n);


    XtManageChild(menubar);


    return menubar;


}   /* CreateMenuBar */


/* Utility: Create a menu choice, really a pushbutton. */


Widget CreateMenuChoice(Widget parent,
        char* name,
        XtCallbackProc callback,
        XtPointer client_data)


{   /* CreateMenuChoice */


    /*
     * In OLIT, CreateMenuChoice and
     * CreatePushbutton are implemented
     * differently.
     */
    return CreatePushbutton(parent, name,
            callback, client_data);


}   /* CreateMenuChoice */


/* end of file m_menu.c */
```

A Utility Function to Exit the Program

As we stated above, the XtAppMainLoop function loops forever. To stop our program, we need to set up a callback function that calls the standard C library function exit. Normally, the first menu on the menu bar is the *File* menu. The last choice in this *File* menu is labeled *Exit*. This menu choice should stop the program.

As a convenience, we built a simple function, CreateExitChoice, to create an *Exit* choice on a pulldown menu. We stored this function in m_exit.c:

```
/*
 *  m_exit.c
 *  Motif Routines for an Exit pushbutton.
 */
#include "motif.h"

/* Simple Exit callback. */
static void exitCB(Widget widget,
    XtPointer client_data,
    XtPointer call_data)

{   /* exitCB */

    exit(0);

}   /* exitCB */

/* Creates an Exit menu choice */
Widget CreateExitChoice(Widget menu, char* name)

{   /* CreateExitChoice */
```

```
        return CreateMenuChoice(menu,
                name,
                (XtCallbackProc) exitCB,
                (XtPointer) NULL);


    }   /* CreateExitChoice */


/* end of file m_exit.c */
```

The Main Window

The Motif *main-window* widget is a special container widget designed to hold a menu bar and an application's main data area. Using the main window widget helps follow the OSF/Motif Style Guide and is very convenient. Use XmCreateMainWindow to create a main window widget. Normally, the parent widget is the top-level shell returned by XtAppInitialize.

When you've built a main-window widget and its children, you need to call a special function, XmMainWindowSetAreas. XmMainWindow-SetAreas puts the child widgets of the main window into their proper places. For example, you want the menu-bar widget to be placed at the top, like a menu bar should.

XmMainWindowSetAreas takes the main-window widget and five other widgets as parameters:

```
#include <Xm/MainW.h>


void XmMainWindowSetAreas(Widget mainwindow,
        Widget menubar,
        Widget command,
        Widget horiz_scroll,
        Widget vert_scroll,
        Widget workarea);
```

The *menubar* parameter is the menu-bar widget. The *workarea* is the main data area for your program. Most Motif applications skip the rest: the *command* area, and horizontal and vertical scroll bars (most applications with scroll bars would put them in the work area).

We placed two convenience functions for the main window widget into *m_mainw.c*:

```
/*
 *   m_mainw.c
 *   Motif main window routines.
 */
#include "motif.h"
#include <Xm/MainW.h>


/*
 * Utility: Create a main window widget
 * that holds a menu bar.
 */
Widget CreateMainWindow(Widget parent, char* name)

{   /* CreateMainWindow */
    Widget  mainwindow;
    Arg args[20];
    int n;

    /*
     * We set the parent widget to not mapped
     * when managed, so we make sure we restore
     * it here.
     */
    n = 0;
    XtSetArg(args[n], XmNmappedWhenManaged, True); n++;
```

```
        mainwindow = XmCreateMainWindow(parent,
                        name, args, n);


        /* We manage this widget in SetMainAreas. */


        return mainwindow;


}    /* CreateMainWindow */


/* Utility: Set the main window "areas." */


void SetMainAreas(Widget mainwindow,
        Widget menubar,
        Widget workarea)


{    /* SetMainAreas */


        XmMainWindowSetAreas(mainwindow,
                    menubar,
                    (Widget) NULL,  /* command window */
                    (Widget) NULL,  /* horiz scroll */
                    (Widget) NULL,  /* vert scroll */
                    workarea);      /* work area */


        XtManageChild(mainwindow);


}    /* SetMainAreas */


/* end of file m_mainw.c */
```

X Graphics From the Point of View of Motif

Finally, we arrive at a discussion of graphics under Motif. The primary widget you'll use for your own graphics in Motif is the drawing-area widget, XmDrawingArea.

The XmDrawingArea provides a raw window in which you can draw any graphics you want, using the drawing functions presented in Chapter 2 (and any other X drawing functions, e.g., the text functions presented in Chapter 14).

Creating a Drawing Area Widget

Create a drawing area widget with XmCreateDrawingArea:

```
#include <Xm/DrawingA.h>


Widget XmCreateDrawingArea(Widget parent,
          char* name,
          ArgList args,
          Cardinal number_args)
```

Before creating a drawing-area widget, it's a good idea to set up a number of resources, including the *width, height*, and *allowResize*:

```
Widget   widget;
Widget   parent;
Arg      args[20];
int      n;
int      width, height;


n = 0;
XtSetArg(args[n], XmNwidth, width); n++;
XtSetArg(args[n], XmNheight, height); n++;
XtSetArg(args[n], XmNallowResize, True); n++;
```

```
widget = XmCreateDrawingArea(parent,
                name, args, n);


XtManageChild(widget);
```

The *allowResize* resource allows the widget to be resized.

Drawing-Area Callback Functions

The *drawing-area* widget provides three main callback functions, called when a drawing-area window is resized (resizeCallback); when keyboard or mouse input goes into the window (inputCallback); and when parts of the window need to be redrawn, in response to Expose events (exposeCallback). You can also call XtAddEventHandler to add functions to handle other events, such as mouse MotionNotify events.

Each of the three standard drawing-area callbacks passes the same parameters to your callback function, an XmDrawingAreaCallbackStruct for the *call_data*:

```
typedef struct {
    int     reason;
    XEvent* event;
    Window  window;
} XmDrawingAreaCallbackStruct;
```

The *reason* field is set to XmCR_EXPOSE, XmCR_RESIZE, or XmCR_INPUT, depending on the event that caused the callback. The *event* field points at an XExposeEvent structure on Expose events, an XConfigureEvent structure on ConfigureNotify events (for resizing) and a mouse (XButtonEvent) or keyboard (XKeyEvent) event structure for input events.

When the expose callback is called, you should then redraw the necessary part of the window. A drawing-area widget effectively gives you all the benefits of an X window plus all the goodies that come from widgets, including unified event handling.

We'll continue to cover the drawing-area widget (and the corresponding OLIT `DrawArea` widget) throughout the rest of this book.

Drawing-Area Convenience Function

The `CreateDrawingArea` convenience function, in `m_draw.c`, creates a new drawing-area widget and sets up the three callback functions:

```
/*
 *  m_draw.c
 *  Routines to work with Motif drawing
 *  area widgets.
 */
#include  "motif.h"
#include  <Xm/DrawingA.h>


/* Create a drawing area widget. */
Widget CreateDrawingArea(Widget parent,
    char* name,
    int width,
    int height,
    XtCallbackProc callback,
    XtPointer client_data)


{   /* CreateDrawingArea */
    Widget  widget;
    Arg     args[20];
    int     n;

    n = 0;
    XtSetArg(args[n], XmNwidth, width); n++;
    XtSetArg(args[n], XmNheight, height); n++;
```

```
    XtSetArg(args[n], XmNallowResize, True); n++;

    widget = XmCreateDrawingArea(parent,
            name, args, n);

    XtManageChild(widget);

    /*
     * Set up callbacks.
     */
    XtAddCallback(widget,
        XmNresizeCallback,
        callback,
        client_data);

    XtAddCallback(widget,
        XmNinputCallback,
        callback,
        client_data);

    XtAddCallback(widget,
        XmNexposeCallback,
        callback,
        client_data);

    return widget;

}   /* CreateDrawingArea */

/* end of file m_draw.c */
```

Text-Editing Widgets

The Motif XmText widget provides a text editor inside a widget wrapper. You can create multiline scrolled text widgets or single-line text-entry fields. A very common case is to create a prompted text-entry field, which we'll cover below, under Prompted Test Input. XmCreateText creates an XmText widget:

```
#include <Xm/Text.h>


Widget XmCreateText(Widget parent,
            char* name,
            ArgList args,
            Cardinal number_args)
```

To make a single-line text-entry field, we need to set the editMode resource to XmSINGLE_LINE_EDIT. If we set it to XmMULTI_LINE_EDIT, we'd have a multiline text widget.

The most important callback supported by the text widget is the *valueChangedCallback* callback. This is called when the text inside the XmText widget changes.

Setting and Retrieving Text

Unlike most Motif widgets, you can set normal C strings (char*) into a Motif text widget. With Motif 1.2, you can also set multibyte and wide character strings into a text widget. You set text into a text widget with the XmTextSetString function:

```
void XmTextSetString(Widget widget, char* string)
```

You can get text from a text widget with the XmTextGetString function:

```
char* XmTextGetString(Widget widget)
```

Be sure to free the text with XtFree when done:

```
char*      string;
Widget     text;


string = XmTextGetString(text);


/* use string... */


XtFree(string);
```

Label Widgets

Label widgets are fairly simple-minded Motif widgets that display a text message or a pixmap. Create a label widget with `XmCreateLabel`:

```
#include <Xm/Label.h>


Widget XmCreateLabel(Widget parent,
            char* name,
            ArgList args,
            Cardinal number_args)
```

The main resource to set in a label widget is the *labelString* resource. This is the text to display, but remember the text is in the `XmString` format:

```
Widget      widget;
Widget      parent;
Arg         args[20];
int         n;
XmString    xmstring;


xmstring =
```

```
    XmStringCreateSimple("This is a label");


n = 0;
XtSetArg(args[n], XmNlabelString,
    xmstring); n++;


label = XmCreateLabel(parent, name, args, n);


/*
 * Free XmString when done.
 */
XmStringFree(xmstring);
```

Prompted Text Input

We can put together the text widget and the label widget to make a prompted text-entry field. To do this, we need to place both widgets into some sort
of parent widget. This simplest case (although not very efficient) is to create a parent widget for each label/text pair. In this case, we use the
XmRowColumn widget, a very simple Motif container widget. Create a row-
column widget with XmCreateRowColumn:

```
#include <Xm/RowColumn.h>


Widget XmCreateRowColumn(Widget parent,
        char* name,
        ArgList args,
        Cardinal number_args)
```

We've already used a row-column widget (under the hood) for menu bars
and pulldown menus. The main resource to set on the row-column widget
is its *orientation*: either XmHORIZONTAL or XmVERTICAL.

Once we've created the row-column widget, we create the label and then the text widget. A routine to put this all together is in the file m_prompt.c:

```
/*
 *  m_prompt.c
 *  Motif routine to create a prompted text entry.
 */
#include "motif.h"
#include <Xm/Label.h>
#include <Xm/RowColumn.h>
#include <Xm/Text.h>


/* Create prompted text entry. Returns text widget. */
Widget CreatePrompt(Widget parent, char* name,
     char* prompt,
     XtCallbackProc callback,
     XtPointer client_data)


{    /* CreatePrompt */
     Widget      row, label, text;
     Arg         args[20];
     int         n;
     XmString    xmstring;

     /*
      * Create parent row-column widget.
      */
     n = 0;
     XtSetArg(args[n], XmNorientation,
             XmHORIZONTAL); n++;
```

```
row = XmCreateRowColumn(parent, name, args, n);


/*
 * Create label child.
 */
xmstring = XmStringCreateSimple(prompt);


n = 0;
XtSetArg(args[n], XmNlabelString, xmstring); n++;


label = XmCreateLabel(row, name, args, n);


/*
 * Free XmString when done.
 */
XmStringFree(xmstring);


/*
 * Create a single-line text-editing widget.
 */
n = 0;
XtSetArg(args[n], XmNeditMode,
        XmSINGLE_LINE_EDIT); n++;


text = XmCreateText(row, name, args, n);


if (callback != (XtCallbackProc) NULL) {
    XtAddCallback(text,
        XmNvalueChangedCallback,
        callback, client_data);
```

```
    }

    XtManageChild(label);
    XtManageChild(text);
    XtManageChild(row);

    /*
     * Note special case: we return the text widget.
     */
    return text;

}   /* CreatePrompt */


/* end of file m_prompt.c */
```

Sliders or Scales

The last widget we're going to introduce in this chapter is the *scale widget*. The XmScale widget is a form of slider, where the user can move a thumb, selecting a value between the minimum and the maximum. Create a scale widget with XmCreateScale:

```
#include <Xm/Scale.h>


Widget XmCreateScale(Widget parent,
            char* name,
            ArgList args,
            Cardinal number_args)
```

The scale widget, like the XmText widget, supports a *valueChangedCallback* function as well as an XmString titleString.

We put together a convenience function, `CreateHSlider`, to create a horizontal scale widget, in `m_slider.c`:

```
/*
 *  m_slider.c
 *  Motif slider routines.
 */
#include "motif.h"
#include <Xm/Scale.h>

/* Create horizontal slider */
Widget CreateHSlider(Widget parent, char* name,
    int minimum, int maximum, char* title,
    XtCallbackProc callback,
    XtPointer client_data)

{   /* CreateHSlider */
    Widget      widget;
    Arg         args[20];
    int         n;
    XmString    xmstring;

    n = 0;
    XtSetArg(args[n], XmNorientation,
            XmHORIZONTAL); n++;
    XtSetArg(args[n], XmNprocessingDirection,
            XmMAX_ON_RIGHT); n++;

    XtSetArg(args[n], XmNmaximum, maximum); n++;
```

```
        XtSetArg(args[n], XmNminimum, minimum); n++;
        XtSetArg(args[n], XmNshowValue, True); n++;

        xmstring = XmStringCreateSimple(title);

        XtSetArg(args[n], XmNtitleString, xmstring); n++;

        widget = XmCreateScale(parent, name, args, n);

        /*
         * Free XmString when done.
         */
        XmStringFree(xmstring);

        /*
         * Set up callback.
         */
        XtAddCallback(widget,
            XmNvalueChangedCallback,
            callback, client_data);

        XtManageChild(widget);

        return widget;

    }   /* CreateHSlider */


/* end of file m_slider.c */
```

The code above sets the necessary resources to make a horizontal scale, which should be self-explanatory.

Creating More Top-Level Windows

Most X applications require more than one top-level window. Most, for example, provide dialog windows to ask users to fill in extra data (e.g., printer parameters or to specify which file to load). Motif supplies a whole number of special dialog creation functions. There are error dialogs, file selection dialogs, prompt dialogs, and many more.

For our uses, though, we don't really need dialogs. Instead, we need separate top-level windows. These windows are assumed to remain on the screen for the duration of the program and serve to unclutter our main window, which we use for drawing. (Your applications, of course, can do anything you'd like.)

To create another top-level shell widget, use `XtAppCreateShell`:

```
Widget XtAppCreateShell(const String app_name,

        const String app_class,

        WidgetClass widget_class,

        Display* display,

        ArgList args,

        Cardinal number_args)
```

You can usually use `argv[0]` (the first command-line parameter—normally the program's name) as the application name. We've been using `ProX` as the application's class name. A common widget class to use is the `topLevelShellWidgetClass`.

Example code to create a top-level shell appears in `m_shell.c`:

```
/*
 * m_shell.c
 * Motif routines to create dialogs.
 * In our case, this is another top-level
 * shell instead of a "true" dialog.
 */
#include "motif.h"
```

```
#include <X11/Shell.h>

Widget CreateShell(Widget parent,
    char* app_name,
    char* app_class)

{   /* CreateDialog */
    Widget  widget;
    Arg args[20];
    int n;

    n = 0;
    XtSetArg(args[n],
        XmNtransientFor, parent); n++;
    XtSetArg(args[n],
        XmNallowShellResize, True); n++;

    widget = XtAppCreateShell(app_name,
            app_class,
            topLevelShellWidgetClass,
            XtDisplay(parent),
            args, n);

    return widget;

}   /* CreateShell */


/* end of file m_shell.c */
```

We set the `transientFor` resource to the parent widget to tie together our new shell widget and the top-level shell widget that acts as the application's primary window.

A Sample Motif Program

After all those utility functions, it's time to start writing actual programs and drawing graphics. We've put together a sample program to make use of the techniques described in all the chapters so far.

The basic program is simple: we create a top-level shell with XtAppInitialize. Beneath this, we build a main window widget. This widget holds a menu bar and a drawing area. The menu bar holds just one menu, the *File* menu and this menu has one menu choice, which exits the program. The drawing area widget is where all the action is. We create a graphics context (GC) for this drawing area, based on code in Chapter 3. Into this drawing area, we draw a range of shapes based on the drawing functions introduced in Chapter 2 (this code is in the file drawtest.c, discussed under Drawing Graphics in a Motif Window).

From Chapter 4, which dealt with X events for graphics, we use incoming Expose events to set up a clipping region, based on the ClipToRegion function presented in that chapter. The function HandleExpose, below, handles this clipping. We call HandleExpose from the drawing-area callback function, which we set up as drawCB, also below. When all the Expose events arrive in a single batch, we set up the clipping region and then call the function DrawTest (in drawtest.c, which is discussed below) to draw some basic graphics into the window.

When you're done with this program, you have all the basic concepts down for drawing graphics with Motif programs. The code for chap5.c follows:

```
/*
 *   chap5.c
 *   Motif test program #1, for Chapter 5.
 */
#include "motif.h"

#include <X11/Xutil.h>
#include <Xm/MainW.h>
#include <Xm/RowColumn.h>
```

```
#include <stdio.h>

/*
 *  Globals
 */
Display*    global_display;
Window      global_window;
GC          global_gc;
Region      global_region = (Region) NULL;

/* Function to test drawing. */
extern void DrawTest(Display* display,
            Window window, GC gc);

/* Redraw the drawing area. */
void HandleExpose(XExposeEvent* event)

{   /* HandleExpose */
    XRectangle    rectangle;

    /*
     * Add each rectangle to the region.
     */
    if (global_region == (Region) NULL) {
        global_region = XCreateRegion();
    }

    UnionExposeWithRegion(event,
        global_region);

    /*
```

```
      * When we have all the Expose events,
      * then we need to redraw the total
      * exposed area, the area contained
      * in the region global_region.
      * So, we redraw the entire
      * contents of the window, relying
      * on the clipping to improve performance.
      */
     if (event->count == 0) {
         ClipToRegion(global_display, global_gc,
             global_region);

         XDestroyRegion(global_region);

         global_region = (Region) NULL;

         /* redraw window... */
         DrawTest(global_display,
             global_window, global_gc);

         /*
          * Restore clip mask.
          */
         XSetClipMask(global_display,
             global_gc, (Pixmap) None);
     }


}    /* HandleExpose */


void drawCB(Widget widget,
     XtPointer client_data,
```

```
        XtPointer call_data)

{   /* drawCB */
    XmDrawingAreaCallbackStruct*    ptr;

    ptr = (XmDrawingAreaCallbackStruct*) call_data;

    if (ptr->reason == XmCR_EXPOSE) {
        HandleExpose( (XExposeEvent*) ptr->event);
    }

}   /* drawCB */

/* Simple Exit callback. */
static void exitCB(Widget widget,
        XtPointer client_data,
        XtPointer call_data)

{   /* exitCB */

    exit(0);

}   /* exitCB */

int main(int argc, char** argv)

{   /* main */
    XtAppContext  app_context;
    Display*      display;
    Widget        parent;
    Widget        mainwindow;
```

```
Widget         menubar;
Widget         filemenu;
Widget         exitchoice;
Widget         drawingarea;
Arg            args[20];
int            n;
int            screen;


/* Initialize X toolkit */
n = 0;


/*
 * We need the widget's window to
 * be created, but we don't want
 * it to appear yet.
 */
XtSetArg(args[n], XmNmappedWhenManaged, False); n++;


/*
 * Allow the top-level window to be resized.
 */
XtSetArg(args[n], XmNallowResize, True); n++;
XtSetArg(args[n], XmNwidth, 500); n++;
XtSetArg(args[n], XmNheight, 360); n++;



parent = XtAppInitialize(&app_context,
        "ProX",                    /* app class */
        (XrmOptionDescList) NULL,/* options */
        0,                         /* num options */
        ARGC_PTR &argc, argv,     /* cmd line */
```

```
                    (String*) NULL,            /* fallback res. */
                    args, n);



        /*
         * Create Main Window.
         */
        n = 0;
        XtSetArg(args[n], XmNmappedWhenManaged,
            True); n++;

        mainwindow = XmCreateMainWindow(parent,
                    "main", args, n);


        /*
         * Create menu bar.
         */
        n = 0;
        menubar = XmCreateMenuBar(mainwindow,
                    "menubar", args, n);


        XtManageChild(menubar);


        /*
         * Create the file menu.
         */
        filemenu = CreateMenu(menubar, "filemenu");


        /*
         * Create a menu choice to exit the program.
         */
```

```
exitchoice = CreateMenuChoice(filemenu,
        "exitchoice",
        (XtCallbackProc) exitCB,
        (XtPointer) NULL);

drawingarea = CreateDrawingArea(mainwindow,
        "drawingarea",
        640, 480,
        (XtCallbackProc) drawCB,
        (XtPointer) NULL);

XmMainWindowSetAreas(mainwindow,
        menubar,
        (Widget) NULL,  /* command window */
        (Widget) NULL,  /* horiz scroll */
        (Widget) NULL,  /* vert scroll */
        drawingarea);   /* work area */

XtManageChild(mainwindow);

/*
 * XtRealizeWidget creates the actual
 * windows on the display.
 */
XtRealizeWidget(parent);

/*
 * Now that we have the windows, we
 * can get the window IDs.
 */
global_display = XtDisplay(drawingarea);
```

```
global_window  = XtWindow(drawingarea);
screen         = DefaultScreen(global_display);


/*
 * Create a graphics context.
 */
global_gc = XCreateGC(global_display,
        global_window,
        0L, (XGCValues*) NULL);


XSetForeground(global_display, global_gc,
    BlackPixel(global_display, screen) );


/*
 * Map parent widget to screen,
 * that is, make it visible.
 */
XtMapWidget(parent);


/*
 * Enter main application loop.
 */
XtAppMainLoop(app_context);


return 0;


}   /* main */


/* end of file chap5.c */
```

The GC for the drawing area is created after we've called
`XtRealizeWidget` to make sure the windows are created and their IDs

are valid. We also set the foreground color to the system's `BlackPixel` (the default black in the default colormap), so this program should work with monochrome and color systems alike.

Drawing Graphics in a Motif Window

The file `drawtest.c` contains test code to draw a number of shapes. We tried to provide examples of most of the drawing functions introduced in Chapter 2, as well as the filling modes covered in Chapter 3.

The `ArcTest` function fills an arc, based on the arc-filling mode you pass, whether `ArcChord` or `ArcPieSlice`:

```
/* Draw a simple arc */
void ArcTest(Display* display, Window window,
    GC gc, int x, int y, int arc_mode)


{   /* ArcTest */

    XSetArcMode(display, gc, arc_mode);

    XFillArc(display, window, gc,
        x, y,
        80, 80,
        0, 270 * 64);


}   /* ArcTest */
```

The `DrawTest` function is called from the `main` function (in `chap5.c`, shown in previous section). This function is called when `Expose` events arrive for the drawing-area widget we created. The `DrawTest` function calls `ArcTest`, above, and `PolygonTest`. The `PolygonTest` function draws a polygon using the fill rule that you pass: `EvenOddRule` or `WindingRule`. The code for `drawtest.c` follows:

```
/*
 *   drawtest.c
 *   Test Xlib drawing routines.
 */
#include  "draw.h"


/* Draw a simple arc */
void ArcTest(Display* display, Window window,
    GC gc, int x, int y, int arc_mode)


{   /* ArcTest */

    XSetArcMode(display, gc, arc_mode);

    XFillArc(display, window, gc,
        x, y,
        80, 80,
        0, 270 * 64);


}   /* ArcTest */


/* Draws a simple test polygon */
void PolygonTest(Display* display, Window window,
    GC gc, int x, int y, int fill_rule)


{   /* PolygonTest */
    XPoint  points[10];

    points[0].x = x;
    points[0].y = y;
```

```
    points[1].x = x;
    points[1].y = y + 80;


    points[2].x = x + 80;
    points[2].y = y + 80;


    points[3].x = x + 80;
    points[3].y = y + 25;


    points[4].x = x + 25;
    points[4].y = y + 25;


    points[5].x = x + 25;
    points[5].y = y + 60;


    points[6].x = x + 100;
    points[6].y = y + 60;


    points[7].x = x + 110;
    points[7].y = y;


    points[8].x = x;
    points[8].y = y;


    XSetFillRule(display, gc, fill_rule);


    XFillPolygon(display, window, gc,
        points, 9,
        Complex,
        CoordModeOrigin);
```

```
}   /* PolygonTest */

void DrawTest(Display* display, Window window, GC gc)

{   /* DrawTest */
    int i;

    /* Draw a line. */
    XDrawLine(display, window, gc,
        10, 10,
        100, 100);

    /* Draw a rectangle. */
    XDrawRectangle(display, window, gc,
        100, 10,
        100, 100);

    /* Fill a rectangle. */
    XFillRectangle(display, window, gc,
        150, 20,
        50, 50);

    /* Draw an oval. */
    DrawOval(display, window, gc,
        200, 10,
        100, 100);

    /* Fill an oval. */
    FillOval(display, window, gc,
        250, 20,
```

```
        50, 50);


    /* Draw a number of points. */
    for(i = 0; i < 20; i++) {
        XDrawPoint(display, window, gc,
            401 + (3 * i),
            101 + (3 * i) );
    }


    /* Draw polygons. */
    PolygonTest(display, window, gc,
        10, 180, EvenOddRule);
    PolygonTest(display, window, gc,
        150, 180, WindingRule);


    /* Draw arcs. */
    ArcTest(display, window, gc,
        300, 180, ArcChord);


    ArcTest(display, window, gc,
        400, 180, ArcPieSlice);


    /* Send all output to X Server. */
    XFlush(display);


}   /* DrawTest */


/* end of file drawtest.c */
```

The file `drawtest.c` includes `draw.h`, which we present in Appendix B.

A Utility Header File

We put together a Motif header file that provides function prototypes for all our Motif utility functions, `motif.h`:

```
/*
 *  motif.h
 *  Header file for Motif toolkit routines.
 */
#ifndef motif_h_
#define motif_h_    1


        /* Bug fix for HP-UX 8.0. */
#ifdef HPUX_FIX
typedef char*   caddr_t;
#endif  /* HPUX_FIX */


/* Include Motif header file. */
#include  <Xm/Xm.h>


/*
 * In X11R4, the argc pointer needs to
 * point at an unsigned int. In X11R5,
 * the pointer must point to an int.
 * We use XtSpecificationRelease to
 * tell what version of Xt we're
 * using. Note that this is not
 * always valid (a patch to X failed
 * to change this).
 */
#if XtSpecificationRelease > 4
```

```
#define ARGC_PTR     (int*)

#else   /* X11R4 */

#define ARGC_PTR     (unsigned int*)

#endif  /* X11R4 */

/*
 *  Motif utility functions.
 */

/* Create a Pulldown menu. */
extern
Widget CreateMenu(Widget parent, char* name);

/* Create a Motif menubar. */
extern
Widget CreateMenuBar(Widget parent, char* name);

/* Create a menu choice */
extern
Widget CreateMenuChoice(Widget menu,
        char* name,
        XtCallbackProc callback,
        XtPointer client_data);

/* Create a menu choice that exits the program. */
extern
Widget CreateExitChoice(Widget menu, char* name);
```

```
/* Create a main window widget. */
extern
Widget CreateMainWindow(Widget parent, char* name);


/* Set the main window "areas" */
extern
void SetMainAreas(Widget mainwindow,
    Widget menubar,
    Widget workarea);


/* Create a pushbutton/menu choice */
extern
Widget CreatePushbutton(Widget menu,
        char* name,
        XtCallbackProc callback,
        XtPointer client_data);


/* Create another top-level window */
extern
Widget CreateShell(Widget parent,
        char* app_name,
        char* app_class);


/* Create drawing area. */
extern
Widget CreateDrawingArea(Widget parent,
        char* name,
        int width,
        int height,
        XtCallbackProc callback,
        XtPointer client_data);
```

```
/* Create horizontal scale/slider. */
extern
Widget CreateHSlider(Widget parent, char* name,
        int minimum, int maximum, char* title,
        XtCallbackProc callback,
        XtPointer client_data);


/* Create prompted text entry. Returns text widget. */
extern
Widget CreatePrompt(Widget parent, char* name,
        char* prompt,
        XtCallbackProc callback,
        XtPointer client_data);


#endif  /* !motif_h_ */


/* end of file motif.h */
```

Note that we had the same problem we faced in Chapter 2 when compiling under Hewlett-Packard's HP-UX 8.0 with ANSI C. We again define the *caddr_t* data type if necessary.

Compiling and Linking Motif Programs

Motif programs require the Motif library, usually libXm.a; the Xt Intrinsics library, usually libXt.a; and the low-level X library, usually libX11.a. To compile a C file named *foo.c*, you should use a command like:

```
cc -o foo foo.c -1Xm -1Xt -1X11
```

The first rule for compiling Motif programs is simple: *read your system documentation*. Most vendor-supported versions of X and Motif come with manuals that describe how to compile X and Motif programs. We strongly advise you to use the settings recommended by your vendor. We've experienced some problems with a few systems, though, and would like to pass on our solutions and workarounds.

386/486 Systems

Some systems, particularly 386/486-based UNIX systems, require a number of other libraries, usually because networking is considered an option on those systems. SCO OpenDesktop, for instance, requires:

```
cc -Di386 -DLAI_TCP -DSYSV -o foo foo.c \
     -1Xm -1Xt -1X11 -1tlisock -1socket -1nsl_s
```

Interactive (SunSoft) SVR3.2 requires:

```
cc -o foo foo.c -1Xm -1Xt -1X11 -1nsl_s
```

Hewlett-Packard Systems

Hewlett-Packard systems place the X include files in nonstandard locations. In addition, the libraries are also placed in nonstandard locations. HP-UX 8.0 uses X11 Release 4 (X11R4) and Motif 1.1:

```
cc -I/usr/include/X11R4 -I/usr/include/Motif1.1 \
     -o foo foo.c \
     -L/usr/lib/Motif1.1 -1Xm   \
     -L/usr/lib/X11R4 -1Xt -1X11
```

HP-UX 9.0 upgrades to X11R5 and Motif 1.2 uses:

```
cc -I/usr/include/X11R5 -I/usr/include/Motif1.2 \
     -o foo foo.c \
     -L/usr/lib/Motif1.2 -1Xm   \
     -L/usr/lib/X11R5 -1Xt -1X11
```

Problems with C++ or ANSI C

C++ requires and ANSI/ISO standard C can use function prototypes. Depending on how your system is set up (and many configurations are not done properly), you may have problems compiling programs that use function prototypes. In such cases, the -DFUNCPROTO option should turn on function prototypes in the X and Motif header files, while -D_NO_PROTO should turn them off.

A Resource File for the Chap5 Program

We use X resource files, described above, to avoid a lot of coding. With these resource files, for example, we can specify the text message to display for a label widget (the *labelString* resource).

Here's an X resource file for the chap5 program:

```
!
! ProX
!
! Resource file for Chapter 5 of
! Professional Graphics
! Programming in the X Window System.
!
! Place this file in your
! home directory.
!
! Generic resources.
!
*background:            lightgray
*drawingarea.background: white


!
! Motif-specific resources.
```

```
!
*fontList: lucidasans-12

*filemenu.labelString:    File
*filemenu.mnemonic:       F

*exitchoice.labelString:  Exit
*exitchoice.mnemonic:     x

*chap5.title: Motif Test for Chapter 5

! end of file ProX
```

Name this file ProX and place it in your home directory.

Running the Chap5 Program

The main purpose of the chap5 program is to handle Expose events on a
Motif drawing area widget. The code clips to a region, so you may want to
try placing multiple windows on top of parts of the chap5 windows and
then raising the chap5 program to the top, forcing a redraw.

Use the *Exit* menu choice to quit the program.

The Long Method for XtAppInitialize

You can break up XtAppInitialize and initialize the Xt Intrinsics
using a longer method. This long method becomes important if you want to
use a nondefault visual (see Chapter 10 for more on visuals).

XtAppInitialize goes through five basic steps:

1. Calls XtToolkitInitialize to initialize the toolkit.
2. Calls XtCreateApplicationContext to create an application
   context.

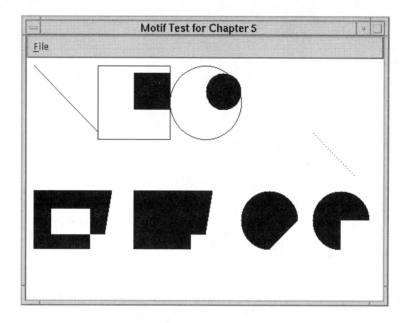

Figure 5.1 *The chap5 program in action.*

3. Makes a copy of the command-line parameters in `argc` and `argv`, using `XtMalloc`, a front-end to `malloc`.

4. Calls `XtOpenDisplay` to open a display connection to the X server.

5. Calls `XtAppCreateShell` to create a top-level shell widget.

Here's a simplified version of the code required to initialize the Xt Intrinsics manually:

```
int main(int argc, char** argv) {

XtAppContext app_context;
int          copy_of_argc;
char**       copy_of_argv;
int          argv_size;
Display*     display;
```

```
Widget       parent;
Arg          args[20];
int          n;


XtToolkitInitialize();


app_context = XtCreateApplicationContext();


/*
 * Copy command-line parameters.
 */
copy_of_argc = argc;


argv_size = argc * (sizeof(char*));


copy_of_argv = (char**) XtMalloc(argv_size);


bcopy(argv, copy_of_argv, argv_size);


display = XtOpenDisplay(app_context,
          NULL,    /* display name, use argv */
          NULL,    /* app name, use arg[0] */
          "ProX", /* app class name */
          (XrmOptionDescList) NULL,
          0,      /* number options */
          ARGC_PTR &argc, argv);


        /*
         * We assume an error opening
         * a display is a fatal error.
         */
```

```
        if (display == (Display*) NULL) {
              fprintf(stderr,
                 "Error opening display [%s].\n",
                 XDisplayName((char*) NULL) );
              exit(1);
        }


/* Determine visual here, if needed... */


/*
 * Create a top-level shell.
 */
n = 0;
XtSetArg(args[n], XmNargc, copy_of_argc); n++;
XtSetArg(args[n], XmNargv, copy_of_argv); n++;


parent = XtAppCreateShell(NULL, /* app name, use argv */
        "ProX", /* app class name */
        applicationShellWidgetClass,
        display,
        args, n);


/* the rest of your code follows... */


}
```

Summary

This chapter introduces programming graphics with the Motif toolkit. Beginning this discussion was an explanation of widgets, which are named user-interface objects, dynamically allocated via `malloc`. A widget encapsulates a user-interface element, like a menu, scroll bar, slider, or text-entry field. At the base level, each widget has an underlying X window. The basic types of Motif widgets include managers, primitives, shells and Xt-provided widgets.

Motif programs usually follow six basic steps:

✦ Initializes the Xt Intrinsics (which also sets up connection to the X server).

✦ Creates widgets.

✦ Sets up any needed callback functions.

✦ Realizes the widget hierarchy with `XtRealizeWidget`.

✦ Enters the event-handling loop.

✦ Loops forever—yes, forever.

Your code must tackle the task of managing widgets. By default, all Motif-created widgets are created unmanaged, unless you use the `XtCreateManagedWidget` function. An unmanaged widget will not be made visible when your application calls `XtRealizeWidget`, so you must manage most widgets after you create them—that is, if you want those widgets to become visible in your application's interface.

There are two main ways to create Motif widgets. First, you can use the Xt-provided functions `XtCreateWidget` (and a host of variants). Second, you can use the Motif-provided functions, one for each widget type, to create widgets. In most cases, this is all a matter of your preferred coding style.

Your Motif programming will also include the use of X resources, a generic means to customize X applications—without modifying the application's source code. As such, resources form a powerful tool when building Motif and OLIT programs. You can change colors, text fonts, and sizes of windows all from resource files. Resource files are a very handy way to customize your applications. For example, you could place *all* text messages for an application in resource files. If you wanted to translate your application to run in French, for instance, the majority of the work could be done by merely editing the resource file and translating the messages into French.

In addition to using resource files, you can hard-code resource commands in your programs. There's a danger here, though, in that if you hard-code a value, users *cannot* set that value in resource files.

Most Motif applications have a menu bar covering the top of the application's window, with pulldown menus on the menu bar. The main part of the application goes underneath the menu bar. The widget that controls the placement of the menu bar and your main data area is considered a container widget. Container widgets hold other (child) widgets and control the layout of these child widgets. Motif applications make extensive use of such container widgets.

The Motif main-window widget is a special container widget designed to hold a menu bar and an application's main data area. Using the main-window widget helps follow the OSF/Motif Style Guide and is very convenient. Use `XmCreateMainWindow` to create a main-window widget. Normally, the parent widget is the top-level shell returned by `XtAppInitialize`.

When you've built a main-window widget and its children, you need to call a special function, `XmMainWindowSetAreas`. `XmMainWindowSetAreas` puts the child widgets of the main window into their proper places.

The chapter ends with a sample (and simple) program, `chap5`. The program creates a top-level shell with `XtAppInitialize`. Beneath this, we build a main-window widget. This widget holds a menu bar and a drawing area. The menu bar holds just one menu, the *File* menu, and this menu has one menu choice, which exits the program. The drawing-area widget is where all the action is. We create a graphics context for this drawing area, based on code in Chapter 3. Into this drawing area, we draw a range of shapes based on the drawing functions introduced in Chapter 2. From Chapter 4, which dealt with events, we use incoming `Expose` events to set up a clipping region, based on the `ClipToRegion` function presented in that chapter. We call `HandleExpose` from the drawing-area callback function, which we set up as `drawCB`. When all the `Expose` events arrive in a single batch, we set up the clipping region and then call the function `DrawTest` to draw some basic graphics into the window.

X Toolkit Intrinsics Functions and Macros Introduced in This Chapter

```
XtAddCallback

XtAppCreateShell
```

```
XtAppInitialize

XtAppMainLoop

XtCreateApplicationContext

XtFree

XtMalloc

XtManageChild

XtOpenDisplay

XtRealizeWidget

XtSetArg

XtSetValues

XtToolkitInitialize
```

Motif Functions and Macros Introduced in This Chapter

```
XmCreateCascadeButton

XmCreateDrawingArea

XmCreateLabel

XmCreateMainWindow

XmCreateMenuBar

XmCreatePulldownMenu

XmCreatePushButton

XmCreateRowColumn

XmCreateScale

XmCreateText

XmMainWindowSetAreas

XmStringCreateLocalized

XmStringCreateSimple

XmStringFree

XmTextGetString

XmTextSetString
```

C h a p t e r 6

Graphics Programming with the Open Look Intrinsics Toolkit

This chapter covers:

- ✦ The Open Look Intrinsics Toolkit (OLIT) and how it works
- ✦ OLIT versions
- ✦ Initializing the toolkit
- ✦ Creating widgets
- ✦ Emulating main windows in OLIT
- ✦ Graphics with the `DrawArea` widget
- ✦ A fallback strategy with the `Stub` widget
- ✦ Pushbuttons
- ✦ Creating menus
- ✦ Text editing

199

The Open Look Intrinsics Toolkit

The *Open Look Intrinsics Toolkit*, or *OLIT*, is a lot like the Motif toolkit we covered in the last chapter. Both Motif and OLIT are based on the Xt Intrinsics, so much of our Motif code from the last chapter ports easily to OLIT.

OLIT provides an Open Look look and feel, based on the specification developed by Sun, AT&T, and Xerox.

OLIT is available mainly on SPARC-based workstations from Sun Microsystems and other SPARC vendors. OLIT and an associated toolkit named MoOLIT come with UNIX System Laboratories' UNIX System V 4.2. MoOLIT is an OLIT-based toolkit that provides a Motif look and feel or an Open Look look and feel—all with the OLIT API. You can also purchase OLIT from third parties for Hewlett-Packard and other systems.

Because OLIT is pretty much limited to Sun workstations, many users work with more widely distributed Motif applications on Sun workstations. We take no position on these interface wars, so we advise you use the toolkit you think best, be it OLIT, Motif, XView, Object Interface (OI), InterViews, or something else entirely.

In this chapter, we introduce OLIT, develop a set of OLIT utility functions that act much like our Motif utility functions presented in the last chapter, and end with an OLIT example program that, similarly, acts like the Motif program presented in the last chapter.

What is OLIT?

OLIT is an Xt-based toolkit designed to meet the Open Look Style Guide. However, you'll find OLIT applications don't look a lot like Motif applications.

Some differences are in the layout of widgets. OLIT pushbuttons (called *oblong buttons* in OLIT terminology) sport a rounded shape instead of the rectangular shape of Motif's pushbuttons. You also use the third (normally rightmost) mouse button to pull down menus. Motif and many other toolkits use the leftmost mouse button for this, which tends to be confusing if you work with both systems.

OLIT Widgets

OLIT, like Motif, uses the core widgets in the Xt Intrinsics, while adding an additional set of widgets. These widgets are divided into four categories: *action*, *container*, *popup choices*, and *text control*.

Action Widgets

The OLIT action widgets are listed in Table 6.1. This table does not include gadgets and flat widgets.

Table 6.1   *OLIT action widgets.*

Widget	Function
AbbrevMenuButton	A space-conserving widget that creates a popup menu
CheckBox	A toggle button with a check mark; can be *on* or *off*
DropTarget	Implements much of drag and drop; new in OLIT 3.0
Gauge	A read-only slider; new in OLIT 2.5
MenuButton	Used to create a popup menu
OblongButton	A rounded-corner pushbutton
RectButton	A toggle button; can be *on* or *off*
Scrollbar	Used for scroll bars
Slider	Valuator used to set a value between a minimum and a maximum
Stub	Provides a raw X window to draw into

Container Widgets

OLIT container widgets hold other widgets. Sometimes, these widgets add extra functionality, too, as listed in Table 6.2.

Table 6.2 *OLIT container widgets.*

Widget	Function
BulletinBoard	Primitive manager
Caption	Creates a label (or caption) for any child widget
ControlArea	Places child widgets into rows and columns
DrawArea	A manager that provides a raw X window to draw into; new in OLIT 3.0
Exclusives	Manages RectButton widgets; allows one choice only
FooterPanel	Puts a footer at the bottom of a window
Form	Complex manager; uses sophisticated layout rules
NonExclusives	Manages RectButton or CheckBox widgets; allows many choices
RubberTile	Manages child widgets in a single row or column; new in OLIT 3.0
ScrolledWindow	Provides a scrolled view of a child widget
ScrollingList	Presents a scrolled list of choices

Popup Choices

The popup-choice widgets provide popup windows, which (as you might guess) allow the user to make a choice. They are listed in Table 6.3.

Table 6.3 *Popup-choice widgets.*

Widget	Function
MenuShell	A menu created by XtCreatePopupShell
NoticeShell	Pops up a notice (dialog) to the user
PopupWindowShell	Used to create command and property dialogs

NOTE

In OLIT 2.x, these widgets were named `Menu`, `Notice`, and `PopupWindow`.

Text-Control Widgets

OLIT text-control widgets display text; some of them also manage the process of allowing users to type in keyboard input and take care of all the messy editing tasks. They are listed in Table 6.4.

Table 6.4 *Text-control widgets.*

Widget	Function
StaticText	Provides read-only display of text
TextEdit	Supports multiline text editing (called `Text` in OLIT 2.x)
TextField	Provides a one-line input field

The most important widget is the OLIT `DrawArea` widget. We'll use this extensively in every OLIT example program.

OLIT Versions

One of the main problems when programming with OLIT is determining what version you have. Many new, interesting, and downright essential widgets were added in the version of OLIT that comes with Sun's OpenWindows 3.

If you're still using OpenWindows 2, we advise you to upgrade. You can port many of the programs in this book to the OLIT that comes with OpenWindows 2, but you'll have a lot of problems using X visuals (which we cover in Chapter 10) with OpenWindows 2.

Wherever possible, we've tried to highlight the differences between the versions. All of the programs are written to OpenWindows 3, but we mention fallback strategies if you're still using OpenWindows 2.

204 ◆ *Professional Graphics Programming in the X Window System*

OLIT 3.0 provides a number of new widgets, including the `DrawArea`, `DropTarget`, and `RubberTile` widgets. The `DrawArea` is a key widget we need for X graphics.

One of the first differences you face, and a fundamental problem for specifying nondefault visuals, is in the way you initialize the toolkit.

Initializing the Toolkit

Like Motif, the first calls you must make with OLIT are to initialize the toolkit. OLIT, however, adds a new wrinkle.

The old way to initialize the toolkit was to use `OlInitialize`. This function predates the application contexts used by more modern versions of the Xt Intrinsics:

```
int main(int argc, char** argv) {


Widget    parent;


parent = OlInitialize(argv[0],
            "ProX",
            (XrmOptionDescList) NULL, 0,
            &argc, argv);


    /* ... */
}
```

`OlInitialize`, which is used with OpenWindows 2, corresponds roughly to the old Xt routine, `XtInitialize`. Programs written today with OpenWindows 3 should use the new method of initializing OLIT, using a combination of `OlToolkitInitialize` and `XtAppInitialize`.

`OlToolkitInitialize` takes one unused parameter:

```
Widget OlToolkitInitialize(XtPointer reserved)
```

The parameter to OlToolkitInitialize is reserved for future use, so we pass a NULL. We also ignore the return value:

```
OlToolkitInitialize( (XtPointer) NULL);
```

After calling OlToolkitInitialize, we call XtAppInitialize the same way we did in the last chapter for Motif:

```
Widget      parent;
Arg         args[20];
int         n;


n = 0;


XtSetArg(args[n], XtNmappedWhenManaged, False); n++;
XtSetArg(args[n], XtNwidth, 500); n++;
XtSetArg(args[n], XtNheight, 360); n++;


parent = XtAppInitialize(&app_context,
        "ProX",                   /* app class */
        (XrmOptionDescList) NULL,/* options */
        0,                        /* num options */
        ARGC_PTR &argc, argv,     /* cmd line */
        (String*) NULL,           /* fallback res. */
        args, n);
```

The Event Loop

Since OLIT is based on Xt, it also uses the Xt event-handling loop. Again, if you're using OpenWindows 2, you won't have an application context created in the call to XtAppInitialize. If so, you can retrieve an application context using XtWidgetToApplicationContext:

```
XtAppContext XtWidgetToApplicationContext(Widget widget)
```

If you intend to use XtAppMainLoop for handling events, you'll need to call XtWidgetToApplicationContext just before the call to XtAppMainLoop:

```
XtAppContext    app_context;
Widget          parent;


/* ... */


app_context = XtWidgetToApplicationContext(parent);


XtAppMainLoop(app_context);
```

OLIT Include Files

OLIT include files are stored in a separate directory, either under /usr/include/Xol or, on SPARC systems, /usr/openwin/include/Xol. All OLIT programs require the following include files:

```
#include <X11/Intrinsic.h>
#include <X11/StringDefs.h>
#include <Xol/OpenLook.h>
```

In all the code examples below, we assume that the above three files are included. In addition, each OLIT widget has its own include file.

OLIT Functions

Most OLIT functions start with *Ol*. Other functions, such as FreeTextBuffer and SaveTextBuffer, start with most any upper-case letter. Xt Intrinsics functions start with *Xt*, Xlib functions with *X*, and Motif functions with *Xm*.

Creating Widgets

Unlike Motif, which provides convenience functions to create every widget, OLIT uses the standard `XtCreateWidget` function (and its many variants):

```
Widget XtCreateWidget(const String name,
    WidgetClass widget_class,
    Widget parent,
    ArgList args,
    Cardinal number_args)
```

The widget class is different for each widget. Normally, any OLIT reference should provide the proper `WidgetClass` for each type of widget. We provide the `WidgetClass` for the widgets introduced below.

You can create a widget and manage it at the same time with `XtCreateManagedWidget`:

```
Widget XtCreateManagedWidget(const String name,
    WidgetClass widget_class,
    Widget parent,
    ArgList args,
    Cardinal number_args)
```

`XtCreateManagedWidget` takes the same parameters as `XtCreateWidget`. It acts the same as calling both `XtCreateWidget` and `XtManageChild`.

You can use `XtCreateWidget` and `XtCreateManagedWidget` with Motif widgets, as well as OLIT widgets.

Variable-Argument Functions for Creating Widgets

The Xt Intrinsics also provide a set of functions that take a variable number of arguments. These variable-argument functions typically start with *XtVa*. `XtVaCreateWidget` creates a widget:

```
Widget XtVaCreateWidget(const String name,
    WidgetClass widget_class,
    Widget parent,
    ...)
```

XtVaCreateManagedWidget creates and manages a widget:

```
Widget XtVaCreateManagedWidget(const String name,
    WidgetClass widget_class,
    Widget parent,
    ...)
```

The variable part of both functions are a set of resource/value pairs, such as those passed to XtSetArg. Use a NULL to terminate the list of resource/value pairs. Use a NULL alone if you have no resources to set.

When you use these functions to create widgets, you can skip the calls to the XtSetArg macro. The following code creates and manages a DrawArea widget, setting the *width* and *height* resources:

```
#include <Xol/DrawArea.h>

Widget  widget;
Widget  parent;
char*   name;
int     width, height;

widget = XtVaCreateManagedWidget(name,
            drawAreaWidgetClass,
            parent,
            XtNwidth,  width,
            XtNheight, height,
            NULL);
```

We terminate the list of resource/value pairs with a NULL.

N O T E

OLIT works with resources much like Motif does. Some of the OLIT resource names are different than the Motif names, but resources and resource files in general act the same. In OLIT code, resource names begin with *XtN*. In Motif code, we used *XmN*. The actual resource names also differ, although there is some overlap. Motif, for example, uses the `labelString` resource, while OLIT may use `label` or `string`, depending on the widget.

The above code using `XtCreateManagedWidget` would look like:

```
#include <Xol/DrawArea.h>

Widget    widget;
Widget    parent;
char*     name;
int       width, height;
Arg       args[20];
int       n;

n = 0;
XtSetArg(args[n], XtNwidth,    width); n++;
XtSetArg(args[n], XtNheight, height); n++;

widget = XtCreateManagedWidget(name,
            drawAreaWidgetClass,
            parent,
            args, n);
```

You can use the *XtVa* or the plain old Xt functions—whatever you prefer. We use a mix of both to cover the Xt Intrinsics more fully.

Now that we've covered the basics, the rest of this chapter is devoted to filling out a set of OLIT utility functions to match the Motif functions introduced in the last chapter. We also present an OLIT program that mimics the `chap5` Motif program, using OLIT.

Emulating Main Windows

OLIT has no parallel to the Motif XmMainWindow widget. We need to choose some form of geometry-manager widget in its place. We could use the RubberTile widget, but this is new with OLIT 3.0. Instead, we use the more primitive ControlArea *widget*. The main benefit of the ControlArea widget is that it is available in both OLIT 2.0 and OLIT 3.0.

The widget class of the ControlArea widget is controlAreaWidgetClass:

```
#include <Xol/ControlAre.h>


Widget  widget;

Widget  parent;

char*   name;


widget = XtVaCreateManagedWidget(name,

            controlAreaWidgetClass,

            parent,

            XtNlayoutType, OL_FIXEDCOLS,

            XtNmeasure, 1,

            NULL);
```

With a ControlArea widget, you can pick from a simple set of four layout schemes: fixed number of columns, fixed number of rows, fixed width for child widgets, and fixed height for child widgets. For a replacement of the Motif main-window widget, we use a fixed number of columns. To do this, we set the *layoutType* resource to OL_FIXEDCOLS. We use the OL_FIXEDROWS when creating a menu bar, below. The *measure* resource sets the number of columns (in this case), and we set it to one to enforce one column of child widgets.

Source Code for Main Window Emulation Functions

We named all of the OLIT utility files beginning with *o_*. We named the Motif utility files beginning with *m_*. The file o_mainw.c contains the utility functions CreateMainWindow, which creates a ControlArea widget to act as a Motif-like "main window" and hold a menu bar, and SetMainAreas, which is necessary in Motif, but only calls XtManageChild in the OLIT version. Both of these functions mimic their Motif counterparts with the OLIT equivalent.

The source code for these functions is in o_mainw.c:

```
/*
 *   o_mainw.c
 *   OLIT "main window" routines.
 */
#include "olit.h"
#include <Xol/ControlAre.h>


/*
 * Utility: Create a main window widget
 * that holds a menu bar.
 */
Widget CreateMainWindow(Widget parent, char* name)

{   /* CreateMainWindow */
    Widget  mainwindow;

    /*
     * We set the parent widget to not mapped
     * when managed, so we make sure we restore
     * it here.
     */
    mainwindow = XtVaCreateWidget(name,
```

```
                    controlAreaWidgetClass,

                    parent,

                    XtNlayoutType, OL_FIXEDCOLS,

                    XtNmeasure, 1,

                    NULL);


        /* We manage this widget in SetMainAreas */


        return mainwindow;


}   /* CreateMainWindow */


/* Utility: Set the main window "areas" */


void SetMainAreas(Widget mainwindow,

    Widget menubar,

    Widget workarea)


{   /* SetMainAreas */


    /*

     * A Motifism: Does nothing in

     * OLIT but manage main window widget.

     */

    XtManageChild(mainwindow);


}   /* SetMainAreas */


/* end of file o_mainw.c */
```

The DrawArea Widget

In the last chapter, we used a drawing-area widget to provide a raw X window in which to draw. OLIT's analog to the Motif XmDrawingArea widget is the DrawArea *widget*. Unfortunately, this widget is new with OpenWindows 3, so you'll have a lot of problems if you're still using OpenWindows 2. We provide a fallback strategy for OpenWindows 2 below.

The widget class for the DrawArea widget is drawArea-WidgetClass:

```
#include  <Xol/DrawArea.h>


Widget  widget;
Widget  parent;
char*   name;
int     width, height;


widget = XtVaCreateManagedWidget(name,
            drawAreaWidgetClass,
            parent,
            XtNwidth,  width,
            XtNheight, height,
            NULL);
```

You should set the *width* and *height* resources when you create a DrawArea widget. On later chapters, we'll work with the *visual*, *depth*, and *colormap* resources.

The DrawArea widget supports a number of callbacks.

The DrawArea Callbacks

The OLIT DrawArea widget supports an exposeCallback. This function is called whenever Expose events arrive in the DrawArea's window. The resizeCallback gets called whenever the window is resized. OLIT also adds a new callback, the `graphicsExposeCallback`, which is called when `GraphicsExpose` events arrive into the window.

All three callbacks share the same callback structure for the call-data parameter to your callback functions:

```
typedef struct {
        int             reason;
        XEvent*         event;
        Position        x;
        Position        y;
        Dimension       width;
        Dimension       height;
} OlDrawAreaCallbackStruct;
```

The *reason* field will be OL_REASON_EXPOSE for Expose events, OL_REASON_GRAPHICS_EXPOSE for GraphicsExpose events, and OL_REASON_RESIZE for resize (ConfigureNotify) events.

N O T E The SunOS 4.1.x manual pages state the *reason* field contains one of O1CR_EXPOSE, O1CR_GRAPHICS_EXPOSE, or O1CR_RESIZE. We could not find any of these symbols defined in any of the header files in the *Xol* OLIT header directory. We used the values OL_REASON_EXPOSE, OL_REASON_GRAPICS_EXPOSE, and OL_REASON_RESIZE for one simple reason: they are defined.

A sample callback function appears below:

```
void drawCB(Widget widget,
    XtPointer client_data,
    XtPointer call_data)

{   /* drawCB */
    OlDrawAreaCallbackStruct* ptr;

    ptr =
```

```
            (OlDrawAreaCallbackStruct*) call_data;


    if (ptr != NULL) {
        if (ptr->reason == OL_REASON_EXPOSE) {


            /* Redraw window... */
        }
    }


    }   /* drawCB */
```

You can set up a callback function, like the one above, with XtAddCallback:

```
Widget        widget;
XtCallbackProc callback;
XtPointer     client_data;


XtAddCallback(widget,
    XtNexposeCallback,
    callback,
    client_data);
```

Source Code for the DrawArea Utility Function

The file o_draw.c contains the utility function CreateDrawingArea, which creates an OLIT DrawArea widget and registers the callback functions:

```
/*
 *   o_draw.c
```

```
 *   Routines to work with OLIT stub
 *   or drawing area widgets.
 */
#include  "olit.h"
#include  <Xol/DrawArea.h>

/* Create a drawing area widget. */
Widget CreateDrawingArea(Widget parent,
    char* name,
    int width,
    int height,
    XtCallbackProc callback,
    XtPointer client_data)


{   /* CreateDrawingArea */
    Widget  widget;

    widget = XtVaCreateManagedWidget(name,
        drawAreaWidgetClass,
        parent,
        XtNwidth,  width,
        XtNheight, height,
        NULL);

    /*
     * Set up callbacks.
     */
    XtAddCallback(widget,
        XtNexposeCallback,
        callback,
        client_data);
```

```
        XtAddCallback(widget,

            XtNgraphicsExposeCallback,

            callback,

            client_data);


        XtAddCallback(widget,

            XtNresizeCallback,

            callback,

            client_data);


        return widget;


}    /* CreateDrawingArea */


/* end of file o_draw.c */
```

A DrawArea Fallback Strategy for OpenWindows 2

OpenWindows 2 supports the Stub widget, which we can use as a replacement for the DrawArea widget. However, the Stub widget uses nonstandard Xt callback functions and does not provide the XtNvisual resource, which is very important for sophisticated graphics.

Here's a version of the CreateDrawingArea function using the older Stub widget:

```
#include  <Xol/Stub.h>


/* Create a drawing area widget. */
Widget CreateDrawingArea(Widget parent,
    char* name,
```

```
            int width,
            int height,
            XtCallbackProc callback)


    {   /* CreateDrawingArea */
        Widget    widget;


        widget = XtVaCreateManagedWidget(name,
                    stubWidgetClass,
                    parent,
                    XtNwidth,  width,
                    XtNheight, height,
                    XtNexpose, callback,
                    NULL);


        return widget;


    }   /* CreateDrawingArea */
```

We don't set up an Xt callback with `XtAddCallback`. Instead, we set the *expose* resource with the callback function. The parameters on this function are different than the standard Xt callback:

```
void expose(Widget widget,
        XEvent* event,
        region region)
```

The `Stub` widget also provides a *resize* resource, which should be set to a pointer to a function—another pseudo-callback. The *resize* function takes just one parameter, the `Widget`:

```
void resize(Widget widget)
```

Because of this, you'll have a harder time working under OpenWindows 2. We strongly advise you to upgrade to OpenWindows 3.

OLIT Pushbuttons

OblongButton widgets act like Motif XmPushButtons, except that the OLIT widget sports rounded-corner windows.

The widget class for the OblongButton widget is oblongButtonWidgetClass:

```
#include <Xol/OblongButt.h>


Widget  widget;
Widget  parent;
char*   name;


widget = XtVaCreateManagedWidget(name,
          oblongButtonWidgetClass,
          parent,
          NULL);
```

The OblongButton widget supports a *select* callback. This acts the same as the activate callback on the Motif pushbutton widget. You can set up a callback with XtAddCallback:

```
Widget         widget;
XtCallbackProc callback;
XtPointer      client_data;


XtAddCallback(widget,
    XtNselect,
    callback,
    client_data);
```

The `CreatePushbutton` utility function, below, is stored in the file *o_push.c*:

```
/*
 *  o_push.c
 *  Routine to create an OLIT pushbutton.
 */
#include "olit.h"
#include <Xol/OblongButt.h>


/* Utility: Create a pushbutton. */
Widget CreatePushbutton(Widget parent,
    char* name,
    XtCallbackProc callback,
    XtPointer client_data)

{   /* CreatePushbutton */
    Widget  button;
    Arg     args[20];
    int     n;

    n = 0;
    button = XtCreateManagedWidget(name,
            oblongButtonWidgetClass,
            parent, args, n);

    XtAddCallback(button,
        XtNselect,
        callback,
        client_data);
```

```
        return button;


    }    /* CreatePushbutton */


    /* end of file o_push.c */
```

OLIT Menus

An OLIT menu is called up from a MenuButton widget. This widget acts
much like a cascade button in Motif. Even so, this is all you need to create
a popup menu. The MenuButton widget will take care of creating the
underlying hidden *menu pane*.

The widget class for the MenuButton widget is menuButton-
WidgetClass:

```
#include  <Xol/MenuButton.h>


Widget  widget;
Widget  parent;
char*   name;


widget = XtVaCreateManagedWidget(name,
            menuButtonWidgetClass,
            parent,
            XtNlabelJustify,  OL_LEFT,
            XtNrecomputeSize, TRUE,
            NULL);
```

The *labelJustify* resource sets the text justification to the left
(OL_LEFT). We could also set the justification to the center (OL_CENTER).
The *recomputeSize* resource allows the widget to grow or shrink as nec-
essary.

Menu Choices

In Motif, a menu choice is a simple pushbutton widget. In OLIT, this is also true, but you need some special code to get the proper parent widget. The MenuButton widget class holds another widget, the actual menu pane. This widget is the parent widget for the menu choices.

To get this parent widget, we call XtVaGetValues to get the *menuPane* resource and then call the CreatePushbutton convenience function, above, to create the menu choice—a pushbutton—but we pass the menu-pane widget as the parent.

```
Widget      menuparent;
Widget      menupane;


XtVaGetValues(menuparent,
    XtNmenuPane, &menupane,
    NULL);
```

This odd bit of code replaces the cascade button/pulldown menu code used in Motif. The CreateMenuChoice function, below, creates a menu choice from a MenuButton widget. Pass the MenuButton widget as the original *parent*:

```
Widget CreateMenuChoice(Widget parent,
        char* name,
        XtCallbackProc callback,
        XtPointer client_data)


{   /* CreateMenuChoice */
    Widget  menupane;

    /*
     * We need to get a new parent
     * from the actual menu. This odd
```

```
 * bit of code is necessary for OLIT.
 */
XtVaGetValues(parent,
    XtNmenuPane, &menupane,
    NULL);


/*
 * Now, we create a pushbutton
 * using this new parent widget.
 */
return CreatePushbutton(menupane, name,
        callback, client_data);


}   /* CreateMenuChoice */
```

Menu Bars

OLIT provides no direct analog to Motif's menu bars. We can easily build one with a `ControlArea` widget, though:

```
#include <Xol/ControlAre.h>


Widget  widget;
Widget  parent;
char*   name;


widget = XtVaCreateManagedWidget(name,
        controlAreaWidgetClass,
        parent,
        XtNlayoutType, OL_FIXEDROWS,
        XtNalignCaptions, TRUE,
        NULL);
```

This time we set the *layoutType* resource to OL_FIXEDROWS, instead of OL_FIXEDCOLS. This makes the ControlArea widget lay out horizontally. We also specify that we want the captions aligned (*alignCaptions*).

Source Code for the Menu Utility Functions

The file *o_menu.c* contains the menu convenience functions:

```
/*
 *  o_menu.c
 *  OLIT Menu routines.
 */
#include "olit.h"
#include <Xol/ControlAre.h>
#include <Xol/MenuButton.h>
#include <Xol/OblongButt.h>


/* Utility: Creates a Pulldown menu. */


Widget CreateMenu(Widget parent, char* name)


{   /* CreateMenu */
    Widget  menuwidget;

    /*
     * Create pulldown menu.
     */
    menuwidget = XtVaCreateManagedWidget(name,
            menuButtonWidgetClass,
            parent,
            XtNlabelJustify,  OL_LEFT,
```

```
                    XtNrecomputeSize, TRUE,
                    NULL);


        return menuwidget;


}   /* CreateMenu */


/* Utility: Create a Motif menubar. */


Widget CreateMenuBar(Widget parent, char* name)


{   /* CreateMenuBar */
        Widget  menubar;


        menubar = XtVaCreateManagedWidget(name,
                    controlAreaWidgetClass,
                    parent,
                    XtNlayoutType, OL_FIXEDROWS,
                    XtNalignCaptions, TRUE,
                    NULL);


        XtManageChild(menubar);


        return menubar;


}   /* CreateMenuBar */


/* Utility: Create a menu choice, really a pushbutton. */


Widget CreateMenuChoice(Widget parent,
            char* name,
```

```
                XtCallbackProc callback,
                XtPointer client_data)


   {   /* CreateMenuChoice */
       Widget   menupane;


       /*
        * We need to get a new parent,
        * from the actual menu. This odd
        * bit of code is necessary for OLIT.
        */
       XtVaGetValues(parent,
           XtNmenuPane, &menupane,
           NULL);


       /*
        * Now, we create a pushbutton,
        * using this new parent widget.
        */
       return CreatePushbutton(menupane, name,
               callback, client_data);


   }   /* CreateMenuChoice */


/* end of file o_menu.c */
```

Creating an Exit Menu Choice

The file o_exit.c contains the utility function CreateExitChoice, which creates a menu choice that exits the program:

```c
/*
 *  o_exit.c
 *  Open Look Routines for an Exit pushbutton.
 */
#include "olit.h"

/* Simple Exit callback. */
static void exitCB(Widget widget,
    XtPointer client_data,
    XtPointer call_data)

{   /* exitCB */

    exit(0);

}   /* exitCB */

/* Creates a Exit menu choice */
Widget CreateExitChoice(Widget menu,
        char* name)

{   /* CreateExitChoice */

    return CreateMenuChoice(menu,
        name,
        (XtCallbackProc) exitCB,
        (XtPointer) NULL);

}   /* CreateExitChoice */

/* end of file o_exit.c */
```

Text-Editing Widgets

TextField widgets provide a single-line text editor. The widget class for the TextField widget is textFieldWidgetClass:

```
#include  <Xol/TextField.h>


Widget  widget;
Widget  parent;
char*   name;


widget = XtVaCreateManagedWidget(name,
            textFieldWidgetClass,
            parent,
            NULL);
```

TextField widgets supply a callback (*verification*) that is called whenever the text in the widget changes value. You can set up the *verification* callback with XtAddCallback:

```
Widget        widget;
XtCallbackProc callback;
XtPointer     client_data;


XtAddCallback(widget,
    XtNverification,
    callback,
    client_data);
```

The verification callback gets an OlTextFieldVerify pointer for the *call_data* parameter:

```
typedef enum {
    OlTextFieldReturn,
```

```
        OlTextFieldPrevious,
        OlTextFieldNext
} OlTextVerifyReason;


typedef struct {
    String              string;
    Boolean             ok;
    OlTextVerifyReason  reason;
} OlTextFieldVerify, *OlTextFieldVerifyPointer;
```

Extracting the Text

You can extract the text in a `TextField` widget from the *string* resource:

```
Widget  textfield;
char*   text;


/*
 * Extract user text from text widget.
 */
XtVaGetValues(textfield,
    XtNstring, &text,
    NULL);


/* Use string... */


XtFree(text);
```

Be sure to free the text when done, using `XtFree`.

Caption Widgets

`Caption` widgets control a child widget and also place a caption—a text label—to annotate the child widget. For example, to create a prompted text entry, we can use a `Caption` widget enclosing a `TextField` widget. The two widgets together combine to make a prompted text entry.

The widget class for the `Caption` widget is `captionWidgetClass`:

```
#include   <Xol/Caption.h>


Widget   widget;
Widget   parent;
char*    name;
char*    prompt;


widget = XtVaCreateManagedWidget(name,
          captionWidgetClass,
          parent,
          XtNlabel, prompt,
          XtNposition, OL_LEFT,
          NULL);
```

The *label* resource sets the text of the caption, or label, to display. The *position* resource sets the caption to appear to the left of the child widget. We could also set the *position* resource to OL_RIGHT, OL_TOP, and OL_BOTTOM.

Putting Together a Prompted Text Entry

We then build a prompted text entry as we described above. The function `CreatePrompt` creates a `Caption` and a `TextField` as a child of the `Caption` widget. `CreatePrompt` returns the `TextField` widget. The source for `CreatePrompt` is in `o_prompt.c`:

```
/*
 *  o_prompt.c
 *  OLIT routine to create a prompted text entry.
 */
#include "olit.h"
#include <Xol/Caption.h>
#include <Xol/TextField.h>

/* Create prompted text entry. Returns text widget. */
Widget CreatePrompt(Widget parent, char* name,
    char* prompt,
    XtCallbackProc callback,
    XtPointer client_data)

{   /* CreatePrompt */
    Widget  caption, text;
    Arg     args[20];
    int     n;

    /*
     * Create parent caption widget.
     */
    caption = XtVaCreateManagedWidget(name,
            captionWidgetClass,
            parent,
            XtNlabel, prompt,
            XtNposition, OL_LEFT,
            NULL);

    /*
     * Create a single-line text-editing widget.
```

```
    */
text = XtVaCreateManagedWidget(name,
        textFieldWidgetClass,
        caption,
        NULL);

if (callback != (XtCallbackProc) NULL) {
    XtAddCallback(text,
        XtNverification,
        callback, client_data);
}

/*
 * Note special case: we return the text widget.
 */
return text;

}   /* CreatePrompt */


/* end of file o_prompt.c */
```

StaticText Widgets

StaticText widgets display a static text message. This message can span multiple lines or be a simple single word. You can use a StaticText widget whenever you need to display a text label and find that a caption widget doesn't work well.

The widget class for the StaticText widget is staticText-WidgetClass:

```
#include <Xol/StaticText.h>
```

```
Widget    widget;

Widget    parent;

char*     name;

char*     text;


widget = XtVaCreateManagedWidget(name,

          staticTextWidgetClass,

          parent,

          XtNstring, text,

          NULL);
```

The *string* resource is the text to display in the widget.

Sliders

Sliders form the OLIT equivalent of Motif XmScale widgets. Unlike the Motif scale, though, the OLIT Slider does not display the current value as text. We find this a severe limitation (and provide a workaround, below). The Slider does, however, display the minimum and maximum values as text, should you set the proper strings into the *minLabel* and *maxLabel* resources.

The widget class for the Slider widget is sliderWidgetClass:

```
#include <Xol/Slider.h>


Widget    widget;

Widget    parent;

char*     name;

int       minimum, maximum;

char      string[100];

char      string2[100];
```

```
sprintf(string, "%d", minimum);
sprintf(string2, "%d", maximum);


widget = XtVaCreateManagedWidget(name,
            sliderWidgetClass,
            parent,
            XtNorientation, OL_HORIZONTAL,
            XtNsliderValue, minimum,
            XtNsliderMin,   minimum,
            XtNsliderMax,   maximum,
            XtNminLabel,    string,
            XtNmaxLabel,    string2,
            XtNwidth,       300,
            NULL);
```

The *orientation* resource can also be set to OL_VERTICAL. The *sliderMin* and *sliderMax* resources set the minimum and maximum integer (int) or values, respectively. If you set the *sliderMin*, you should also initialize the *sliderValue* to the minimum, avoiding a common OLIT warning message in the process. We also set the *width* to 300, a purely arbitrary size for the widget. We could have, instead, placed the Slider in a Form or other container widget and let that container control the Slider's size.

Slider Callbacks

The Slider widget provides a *sliderMoved* callback, called whenever the slider moves. You can set this callback up with XtAddCallback:

```
Widget        widget;
XtCallbackProc callback;
XtPointer      client_data;


XtAddCallback(widget,
```

```
XtNsliderMoved,

callback, client_data);
```

The *call_data* parameter of your callback function will receive a pointer to an int—the current value of the slider.

Displaying the Current Slider Value

The `Slider` widget doesn't display the current value as text, and we find this to be a serious problem. To get around this, we use a simple means. Whenever we create a slider widget, we also create a `StaticText` widget to hold the value, displayed as text.

If we do this, we can set up a second function as a *sliderMoved* callback—in addition to whatever callback we need. This second callback then needs to retrieve the `Slider`'s value, which is stored in the *call_data* parameter (as a pointer to the int value).

Once we extract the `Slider`'s value, we need to convert the integer to a string and then set the `StaticText`'s *string* resource to this text string. In the code below, the `SetTextValue` function sets the string resource of the `StaticText`. The `updateSliderText` function is our secondary callback on the `Slider`. This function extracts the slider's current value and then calls `SetTextValue`. We pass the `StaticText` widget as the *client_data*.

All of this code is used by the `CreateHSlider` routine, which creates a horizontal slider. The source code is located in the file `o_slider.c`:

```
/*
 *  o_slider.c
 *  OLIT Scroll bar routines.
 */
#include "olit.h"
#include <Xol/ControlAre.h>
#include <Xol/Slider.h>
#include <Xol/StaticText.h>
#include <stdio.h>
```

```
/*
 * Updates the StaticText widget to a certain
 * number.
 */
static void SetTextValue(Widget widget, int value)

{   /* SetTextValue */
    char    string[100];

    sprintf(string, "%3.3d", value);

    XtVaSetValues(widget,
        XtNstring, string,
        NULL);

}   /* SetTextValue */

/*
 * Private callback that sets a StaticText widget to
 * hold our slider's value as text.
 */
static void updateSliderText(Widget widget,
    XtPointer client_data,
    XtPointer call_data)

{   /* updateSliderText */
    Widget  label;
    int*    value;

    label = (Widget) client_data;
```

```
    /*
     * Get slider value.
     */
    value = (int*) call_data;


    /*
     * Display as text.
     */
    SetTextValue(label, *value);


}   /* updateSliderText */


/* Create horizontal slider */
Widget CreateHSlider(Widget parent, char* name,
    int minimum, int maximum, char* title,
    XtCallbackProc callback,
    XtPointer client_data)


{   /* CreateHSlider */
    Widget  container, widget;
    Widget  label, value_label;
    Arg     args[20];
    int     n;
    char    string[100];
    char    string2[100];


    /*
     * Creates a caption and then a slider
     * as a child of the caption.
```

```
  */
sprintf(string, "%s_parent", name);

container = XtVaCreateManagedWidget(string,
        controlAreaWidgetClass,
        parent,
        XtNorientation, OL_HORIZONTAL,
        NULL);

/* come up with unique name. */
sprintf(string, "%s_label", name);

label = XtVaCreateManagedWidget(string,
        staticTextWidgetClass,
        container,
        XtNstring, title,
        NULL);

/*
 * Create a slider.
 */
sprintf(string, "%d", minimum);
sprintf(string2, "%d", maximum);

widget = XtVaCreateManagedWidget(name,
        sliderWidgetClass,
        container,
        XtNorientation, OL_HORIZONTAL,
        XtNsliderValue, minimum,
        XtNsliderMin,   minimum,
        XtNsliderMax,   maximum,
```

```
            XtNminLabel,     string,
            XtNmaxLabel,     string2,
            XtNwidth, 300,
            NULL);

/*
 * Create a StaticText label to
 * hold the slider's value as text.
 */
sprintf(string, "%s_value", name);

value_label = XtVaCreateManagedWidget(string,
        staticTextWidgetClass,
        container,
        XtNstring, string,
        NULL);

/*
 * Set up initial value.
 */
SetTextValue(value_label, minimum);

/*
 * Set up a callback.
 */
XtAddCallback(widget,
    XtNsliderMoved,
    callback, client_data);

/*
 * Set up a second callback to display the
```

```
        * slider's value as text.
        */
       XtAddCallback(widget,
           XtNsliderMoved,
           updateSliderText,
           (XtPointer) value_label);


       return widget;


}   /* CreateHSlider */


/* end of file o_slider.c */
```

Creating More Top-Level Windows

As we stated in the last chapter, most X applications require more than one top-level window. Most, for example, provide dialog windows to ask users to fill in extra data, such as printer parameters, or to specify which file to load. For our uses, though, we don't really need dialogs per se. Instead, we need separate top-level windows. These windows are assumed to remain on the screen for the duration of the program and serve to unclutter our main window, which we use for drawing.

To create another top-level shell widget, use `XtAppCreateShell`:

```
Widget XtAppCreateShell(const String app_name,
        const String app_class,
        WidgetClass widget_class,
        Display* display,
        ArgList args,
        Cardinal number_args)
```

You can usually use `argv[0]` (the first command-line parameter—normally the program's name) as the application name. We've been using `ProX` as

the application's class name. A common widget class to use is the
`topLevelShellWidgetClass`.

Example code to create a top-level shell appears in `o_shell.c`:

```
/*
 *  o_shell.c
 *  OLIT routines to create dialogs.
 *  In our case, this is another top-level
 *  shell instead of a "true" dialog.
 */
#include "olit.h"
#include <X11/Shell.h>


Widget CreateShell(Widget parent,
    char* app_name,
    char* app_class)


{   /* CreateShell */
    Widget  widget;
    Arg     args[20];
    int     n;

    n = 0;
    XtSetArg(args[n],
        XtNtransientFor, parent); n++;
    XtSetArg(args[n],
        XtNallowShellResize, True); n++;

    widget = XtAppCreateShell(app_name,
            app_class,
            topLevelShellWidgetClass,
```

```
              XtDisplay(parent),
              args, n);

      return widget;


   }   /* CreateShell */


/* end of file o_shell.c */
```

The above code is almost identical to the *m_shell.c* file introduced in the last chapter. The difference is in the include files loaded—Motif or OLIT.

A Utility Header File

We've put together a header file that provides function prototypes for all our utility functions. The header file is stored in olit.h:

```
/*
 *  olit.h
 *  Header file for OLIT routines.
 */
#ifndef olit_h_
#define olit_h_ 1

#include <X11/Intrinsic.h>
#include <X11/StringDefs.h>
#include <Xol/OpenLook.h>


/*
 *  Set up argc pointer properly.
 */
```

```
#if XtSpecificationRelease > 4

#define ARGC_PTR     (int*)

#else   /* X11R4 */

#define ARGC_PTR     (unsigned int*)

#endif  /* X11R4 */

/*
 * Function prototypes.
 */

/* Utility: Create a pushbutton. */
extern
Widget CreatePushbutton(Widget parent,
        char* name,
        XtCallbackProc callback,
        XtPointer client_data);

/* Utility: Creates a Pulldown menu. */
extern
Widget CreateMenu(Widget parent, char* name);

/* Utility: Create a Motif menubar. */
extern
Widget CreateMenuBar(Widget parent, char* name);

/* Utility: Create a menu choice, really a pushbutton. */
extern
```

```
Widget CreateMenuChoice(Widget parent,
        char* name,
        XtCallbackProc callback,
        XtPointer client_data);


/* Creates a Exit menu choice. */
extern
Widget CreateExitChoice(Widget menu, char* name);


/* Create a drawing area widget. */
extern
Widget CreateDrawingArea(Widget parent,
        char* name,
        int width,
        int height,
        XtCallbackProc callback,
        XtPointer client_data);


/* Create "main window". */
extern
Widget CreateMainWindow(Widget parent, char* name);


/* Manage main window. */
extern
void SetMainAreas(Widget mainwindow,
        Widget menubar,
        Widget workarea);


/* Create horizontal slider. */
extern
Widget CreateHSlider(Widget parent, char* name,
```

```
            int minimum, int maximum, char* title,
            XtCallbackProc callback,
            XtPointer client_data);


/* Create another top-level window. */
extern
Widget CreateShell(Widget parent,
        char* app_name,
        char* app_class);


/* Create prompted text entry. Returns text widget. */
extern
Widget CreatePrompt(Widget parent, char* name,
        char* prompt,
        XtCallbackProc callback,
        XtPointer client_data);


#endif   /* !olit_h_ */
/* end of file olit.h */
```

An OLIT Example Program

We built an OLIT version of the same program we showed in the last chapter. The file, chap6.c, appears below:

```
/*
 *  chap6.c
 *  OLIT test program #1 for Chapter 6.
 */
#include "olit.h"
```

```
#include <Xol/ControlAre.h>
#include <Xol/DrawArea.h>
#include <X11/Xutil.h>
#include <stdio.h>


/*
 *   Globals
 */
Display*    global_display;
Window      global_window;
GC          global_gc;
Region      global_region = (Region) NULL;


/* Function to test drawing. */
extern void DrawTest(Display* display,
              Window window, GC gc);


/* Redraw the drawing area. */
void HandleExpose(XExposeEvent* event)


{    /* HandleExpose */
     XRectangle    rectangle;

     /*
      * Add each rectangle to the region.
      */
     if (global_region == (Region) NULL) {
         global_region = XCreateRegion();
     }


     UnionExposeWithRegion(event,
```

```
        global_region);


    /*
      * When we have all the Expose events,
      * then we need to redraw the total
      * exposed area, the area contained
      * in the region global_region.
      * So, we redraw the entire
      * contents of the window, relying
      * on the clipping to improve performance.
      */
    if (event->count == 0) {
        ClipToRegion(global_display
            global_gc, global_region);

        XDestroyRegion(global_region);

        global_region = (Region) NULL;

        /* redraw window... */
        DrawTest(global_display,
            global_window, global_gc);

        /*
          * Restore clip mask.
          */
        XSetClipMask(global_display,
            global_gc, (Pixmap) None);
    }


}   /* HandleExpose */
```

```
/*
 * Draw callback.
 */
void drawCB(Widget widget,
    XtPointer client_data,
    XtPointer call_data)


{   /* drawCB */
    OlDrawAreaCallbackStruct* ptr;


    ptr = (OlDrawAreaCallbackStruct*) call_data;


    if (ptr != NULL) {
        if (ptr->reason == OL_REASON_EXPOSE) {
            HandleExpose( (XExposeEvent*) ptr->event);
        }
    }


}   /* drawCB */


int main(int argc, char** argv)


{   /* main */
    XtAppContext    app_context;
    Display*        display;
    Widget          parent;
    Widget          mainwindow;
    Widget          menubar;
    Widget          filemenu;
    Widget          exitchoice;
```

```
Widget          drawingarea;
Arg             args[20];
int             n;
int             screen;

/* Initialize X toolkit */
OlToolkitInitialize( (XtPointer) NULL);

n = 0;

XtSetArg(args[n], XtNmappedWhenManaged, False); n++;
XtSetArg(args[n], XtNwidth, 500); n++;
XtSetArg(args[n], XtNheight, 360); n++;

parent = XtAppInitialize(&app_context,
        "ProX",                    /* app class */
        (XrmOptionDescList) NULL,  /* options */
        0,                         /* num options */
        ARGC_PTR &argc, argv,      /* cmd line */
        (String*) NULL,            /* fallback res. */
        args, n);

/*
 * Create Main Window.
 */
mainwindow = XtVaCreateManagedWidget("main",
        controlAreaWidgetClass,
        parent,
        XtNmappedWhenManaged, True,
        XtNlayoutType, OL_FIXEDCOLS,
        XtNalignCaptions, TRUE,
```

```
        NULL);

/*
 * Create menu bar.
 */
menubar = CreateMenuBar(mainwindow, "menubar");


/*
 * Create the file menu.
 */
filemenu = CreateMenu(menubar, "filemenu");


/*
 * Create a menu choice to exit the program.
 */

exitchoice = CreateExitChoice(filemenu,
        "exitchoice");

drawingarea = CreateDrawingArea(mainwindow,
            "drawingarea",
            640, 480,
            (XtCallbackProc) drawCB,
            (XtPointer) NULL);

/*
 * XtRealizeWidget creates the actual
 * windows on the display.
 */
XtRealizeWidget(parent);
```

```
/*
 * Now that we have the windows, we
 * can get the window IDs.
 */
global_display = XtDisplay(drawingarea);
global_window  = XtWindow(drawingarea);
screen         = DefaultScreen(global_display);


/*
 * Create a graphics context.
 */
global_gc = XCreateGC(global_display,
                 global_window,
                 0L, (XGCValues*) NULL);


XSetForeground(global_display, global_gc,
    BlackPixel(global_display, screen) );


/*
 * Map parent widget to screen,
 * that is, make it visible.
 */
XtMapWidget(parent);


/*
 * Enter main application loop.
 */
XtAppMainLoop(app_context);


return 0;
```

```
}   /* main */


/* end of file chap6.c */
```

The `chap6` program uses the `DrawTest` function in the file `drawtest.c`, presented in the previous chapter under Drawing Graphics in a Motif Window. In other respects, this program is almost identical to the program created in Chapter 5.

Compiling and Linking OLIT Programs

OLIT programs require the OLIT library, `libXol.a` (or its shared equivalent); the Xt Intrinsics library, `libXt.a`; and the low-level X library, `libX11.a`. On OpenWindows systems, you'll normally find all X include files in `/usr/openwin/include` and libraries in `/usr/openwin/lib`. The following command compiles and links a program named `foo.c`:

```
acc -I/usr/openwin/include \
    -o foo foo.c \
    -L/usr/openwin/lib -lXol -lXt -lX11
```

The default Sun C compiler, `cc`, shipped with SunOS 4.1.x is not ANSI C-compliant. If you use the SunPro C compiler, `acc`, you will have better luck compiling programs that use C function prototypes.

N O T E

Resource File for the Sample Program

We use the following resource file for the `chap6` program:

```
!

! ProX

!
```

```
! Resource file for Chapter 6 of

! Professional Graphics

! Programming in the X Window System.

!

! Place this file in your

! home directory.

!

! Generic resources.

!

*background:                lightgray

*drawingarea.background: white


!

! OLIT resources.

!

*exitchoice.label: Exit

*filemenu.label:   File

*threeD:           true

*redraw.label:     Redraw


*chap6.title:      OLIT Test for Chapter 6

! end of file ProX
```

The threeD resource tells OLIT to use the 3D bevels and shading to make the interface look better. We cover this resource in depth in Chapter 9.

Name this file ProX and place it in your home directory.

Running the Chap6 Program

The chap6 program draws the same shapes as the chap5 program:

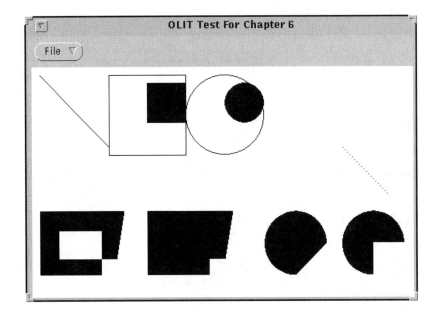

Figure 6.1   *The chap6 program in action.*

Summary

The Open Look Intrinsics Toolkit, or OLIT, borrows much of its structure and commands from the Xt Intrinsics, which is also the basis for the Motif toolkit covered in Chapter 5. This chapter discussed OLIT, where it differed from Motif, and used OLIT to create the same application that was created in Chapter 5.

OLIT, like Motif, uses the core widgets in the Xt Intrinsics, while adding an additional set of widgets. These widgets are divided into four categories: action, container, popup choices, and text control.

One of the main problems when programming with OLIT is determining what version you have. Many new, interesting, and downright essential widgets were added in the version of OLIT that comes with Sun's OpenWindows 3. If you're still using OpenWindows 2, we advise you to upgrade. You can port many of the programs in this book to the OLIT that comes with OpenWindows 2, but you'll have a lot of problems using X visuals with OpenWindows 2.

Also covered was the actual creation of an application, starting from scratch. The first calls you must make with OLIT are to initialize the toolkit. OLIT, though, adds a new wrinkle. The old way to initialize the toolkit was to use `OlInitialize`. This function predates the application contexts used by more modern versions of the Xt Intrinsics.

Unlike Motif, which provides convenience functions to create every widget, OLIT uses the standard `XtCreateWidget` function (and its many variants). Other important widgets covered included `DrawArea`, as well as tools for creating pushbuttons, scroll bars, and text-entry areas.

Most X applications require more than one top-level window. Most, for instance, provide dialog windows to ask users to fill in extra data, such as printer parameters, or to specify which file to load. For our uses, however, we don't really need dialogs per se. Instead, we need separate top-level windows. These windows are assumed to remain on the screen for the duration of the program and serve to unclutter our main window, which we use for drawing. To create another top-level shell widget, use `XtAppCreateShell`.

The chapter ended with source code for an application identical to the one created in Chapter 5.

X Toolkit Intrinsics Functions and Macros Introduced in This Chapter

```
XtCreateManagedWidget

XtCreateWidget

XtVaCreateManagedWidget

XtVaCreateWidget

XtWidgetToApplicationContext
```

OLIT Functions and Macros Introduced in This Chapter

```
OlInitialize

OlToolkitInitialize
```

Color

This section concentrates on color and X. Because there are so many types of color hardware, color in X is enormously complex. We start with the basics and delve into advanced techniques, all the while concentrating on using color in X applications. This section includes:

✦ Basic color in X, which includes allocating read-only color cells from the default colormap, and the red, green, blue (RGB) model of color.

✦ Using turtle graphics to draw L-systems in color, which allow you to model plant growth and draw space-filling curves from chaos theory.

✦ Allocating writable color cells and change the contents of colors on the fly.

✦ Choosing colors from red, green, and blue sliders.

✦ Manipulate how Motif chooses 3D bevel colors.

✦ Choosing the best visual, querying visuals, and using nondefault visuals with Open Look Intrinsincs Toolkit (OLIT) and Motif programs.

257

✦ Creating, modifying, freeing, and querying X colormaps.

✦ Working with color planes to create overlays.

✦ Using X's standard colormaps, which are often used to get an even RGB color ramp and to share colormaps between applications.

✦ Working with the X Color Management System, or Xcms, a new feature of X11 Release 5 that allows for exact colors. Xcms is useful for those who need much greater accuracy in color for applications such as prepress systems and scientific visualization.

X Color Basics

This chapter covers:

- ✦ An overview of color and X
- ✦ Visuals, colormaps, and color cells
- ✦ The RGB—red, green, blue—model of color
- ✦ Using color in X applications
- ✦ Choosing a colormap
- ✦ Read-only and read/write color cells
- ✦ Allocating read-only color cells
- ✦ Using colors with the graphics context
- ✦ Color names
- ✦ Allocating named colors
- ✦ Guidelines for using color

An Overview of Color and X

Color forms one of the most complicated topics in X. Because of this, we divided up color issues over the next six chapters. This chapter introduces color under the X Window System and shows how to allocate colors using the default method suitable for most X applications. The following chapters delve into greater detail for those applications that have more demanding control over color.

Color is complex because graphics workstations use different means for specifying color. Some have color tables, some have color planes, and all seem to be different.

X, attempting to be device-independent, has to deal with all the many color implementations. Perhaps because of this, color in X appears overly complex. The seemingly simple task of drawing a line in red leads to all sorts of contortions in initializing colors and finding visuals.

Most of these different workstations are built on an *RGB color model*: red, green, and blue phosphors within each pixel are combined to form the different hues on the screen. Electron beams excite the phosphors, which in turn provides the color. Simultaneously exciting all phosphors produces a white pixel; when all are unexcited, you're left with a black pixel.

Color displays use multiple bits within a pixel, or dot on the screen, to further specify colors. These bits are also known as planes, and the most common color display contains eight *planes* (supporting 256 different colors). You have access to many more colors, even though only a limited number of them can actually be displayed at one time.

In contrast, monochrome displays only have one plane, and the phosphor is either on or off. Gray scales are simulated by making the red, green, and blue values equal.

At the other end of the spectrum, we're starting to see more and more workstations with up to 24 planes, especially as costs dive ever downward. These are high-performance systems; you can see many more colors at a time at a greater resolution, but the trade-off is the overwhelming complexity of administering these screens.

Visuals

The main problem with color is that there are so many ways in which workstations support color. A high-end Silicon Graphics workstation looks at color differently than a 486-based PC with a SuperVGA display adapter. In addition, the high-end workstation probably provides a number of ways to view the color hardware. You may use overlay planes, or may be able to address color tables using different means.

To hide these differences, X supports a *visual*—an abstraction for color hardware subsystems. Visuals are associated with screens. The screen may support color or only scales of gray. (A monochrome screen is considered the degenerate case of a gray-scale screen.) Additionally, the colormaps on the screen may be read-only or you may be able to write to the colormaps. The colormaps may also be decomposed into separate red, green, and blue spaces.

This leads to the six visual classes X provides: `DirectColor`, `GrayScale`, `PseudoColor`, `StaticColor`, `StaticGray`, and `TrueColor`. The static visual classes and `TrueColor` are read-only, while the others are writable and readable. By having read/write classes, you can create your own colors. Table 7.1 lists the six X visual classes and their attributes (color or gray-scale, decomposed, or undecomposed colormap), and whether you can write to colormaps under that visual.

Table 7.1   *X visual classes.*

Visual Class	Color/Gray	Colormap	Writable
DirectColor	Color	Decomposed	Yes
GrayScale	Gray-scale	Undecomposed	Yes
PseudoColor	Color	Undecomposed	Yes
StaticColor	Color	Undecomposed	No
StaticGray	Gray-scale	Undecomposed	No
TrueColor	Color	Decomposed	No

Under this model, a monochrome screen would be a degenerate `StaticGray` visual with a depth of one so-called color plane. Most color workstations support 8 bit-planes of color with a `PseudoColor` visual.

Other common color systems include 4 bit-planes of color (on standard VGA systems), 16-, and 24 bit-planes. PseudoColor is also the easiest visual to work with when programming color applications. The common 8 bit-plane color workstations support only 256 simultaneous colors. This limited number of displayable colors soon becomes a problem for image-processing, visualization, or 3D rendering applications.

If you want to get technical, you could write sections of your code that would handle each visual class differently, to get the most performance out of each type. This means, however, you would essentially be duplicating your graphics code six times over with a very limited payback.

This may be necessary for complex graphics applications. In most cases, though, it is a lot easier to follow certain conventions and try to use the system defaults wherever possible, thereby making your applications work on any display monitor running X. We find that most color X servers under X11 Release 5 support multiple visuals of all six types on the same screen anyway, but generally PseudoColor visuals are the easiest to write code for. In the code examples in this chapter, we'll work with PseudoColor visuals, as they are the most common. Most of these techniques work for all visuals. In later chapters, we'll cover the other visual types in depth.

You can check which visuals are supported on your screen by using the xdpyinfo program. This program reports on many of the features support-ed by your X server. You can also query this information from within your applications. See Chapter 10 for a more detailed discussion on visuals and colormaps.

Visuals apply to screens, so a multiscreen display could support quite a few visuals. Each visual can support a number of colormaps.

Colormaps

A *colormap* is typically an index table used to look up colors. For example, color index 15 could be magenta and index 14 yellow. The colormap may be *decomposed* into separate red, green, and blue colormaps with the DirectColor and TrueColor visuals. All other visual types use *undecom-posed* colormaps. That is, the colormap acts as a large array. For each element in the array, there are the red, green, and blue components for that color.

Each window on the X display has an associated colormap. You can cre-ate a new colormap and then change the colormap attributes for a given window, if you desire. Normally, however, you can use the default colormap and have each window use its parent's colormap.

Most workstations support just one hardware colormap. For a typical system with 8 bit-planes of color, the hardware colormap will have 256 entries for 256 possible distinct colors.

In your applications, though, you may create a number of software colormaps. Each of these colormaps is associated with a given window. If the color hardware can only support one colormap at a time (which is the most common case), X must swap in and out these software colormaps. Each colormap becomes active in turn.

It is up to the window manager, such as `mwm`, `twm`, or `olwm`, to perform colormap swapping. The so-called *colormap focus* usually follows the mouse. That is, when the mouse pointer is in a window, the colormap focus follows the mouse and any colormaps for that window become active. This swapping of colormaps generates `ColormapNotify` events, which we discussed in Chapter 4.

The problem with this colormap swapping is that it creates the so-called technicolor effects so disliked by users as the mouse moves about the screen. Consequently, it is generally a good idea to use the default colormap if at all possible.

Of course, workstation hardware isn't that simple. With the dropping costs of high-end graphics systems, more and more users will run workstations that support 24 bit-planes of color. With 24 bit-planes of color, you typically have more available color cells than pixels on your display. Right now, most monitors at most provide 1280 x 1024 pixels. Within a few years, however, we expect pixel resolutions in the range of 2000 x 2000 to be common.

Each colormap is made up of color cells or colormap entries. A 256-entry colormap, then, obviously has 256 color cells.

Color Cells

To use color in X, you need to allocate color cells in a colormap. Each color cell contains a separate color, such as blue, purple, or white. The color shown is defined by the red, green, and blue components of the color, stored in the colormap at the given color index.

Each color cell is then represented by an index, an unsigned long integer (*int*) value that indexes into a colormap, either directly into one colormap or indirectly into decomposed red, green, and blue colormaps.

Your applications allocate color cells and then set graphics contexts (GCs) to draw with the colors in those cells.

The Red, Green, Blue Model of Color

All color in X is based on the RGB, or red, green, blue model. Since most monitors work this way, it makes sense. For each color, there is a red value, a green value, and a blue value. Together, the RGB values define the color. In most systems, the RGB values drive three so-called color guns in the monitor, which then display the color you desire.

This is the base for the `PseudoColor` type of visual. Each entry in the colormap then has separate red, green, and blue values. Color index 55, for instance, may have a value of 23 for red, 255 for blue, and 104 for green.

Using Color in X Applications

To put this all together, you need to use visuals, colormaps, and color cells to create color X applications. Once you've connected to an X display, there are five steps to using color in X applications:

1. First, find the desired visual; normally, a `PseudoColor` visual. If the X server's default visual is a `PseudoColor` visual, use that. We advise to always use the defaults, if possible. If not, we need to climb through the visual tree, finding a `PseudoColor` visual. See Chapter 10 for a description.

2. Normally, a new window is created using a constant of `CopyFromParent` for its visual. This means that the window takes on the same visual as its parent window. If you need to use a different visual than the default, you must create your windows under this visual. With a toolkit like Motif or OLIT, you need to set the visual resource before creating a top-level shell widget. See Chapter 10 for more on this. To use the default visual, you need perform no special actions, since by default windows are created using the default visual.

3. The next step is to get a colormap that is valid for your visual to use with your widget's associated window. If you don't use the default visual, you must create a new colormap. Otherwise, you may be able to use the default colormap for the visual. If this colormap has enough free color entries, you can use the default. If not, you still have to create your own. If possible, use the default colormap.

4. Whatever colormap you end up with, you'll then need to allocate colors from the colormap. You can use English color names, like *red* and *LimeGreen*, from the RGB color database or you can allocate colors directly from red, green, and blue values. In addition, X11 Release 5 supports other color specs, such as CIE and HVC, as part of the X Color Management System. See Chapter 13 for more on this.

5. Finally, create a graphics context for the window, and set the GC to draw in some of the colors allocated in step 4. Most widgets have an associated window. Normally, we'll allocate a GC for a Motif `XmDrawingArea` or an OLIT `DrawArea` widget.

If you can use the defaults, such as the default visual or colormap, the process of allocating color cells becomes a lot easier.

Choosing a Colormap

Before you can use a color in X, you need to allocate a color cell from a colormap. To do this, of course, you need to choose a colormap. Most X applications simply use the default colormap.

The `DefaultColormap` macro returns the default colormap ID for a given display and screen:

```
Colormap DefaultColormap(Display* display,
            int screen_number)
```

If you have a screen pointer, you can use the `DefaultColormapOfScreen` macro:

```
Colormap DefaultColormapOfScreen(Screen* screen)
```

These two macros also have associated functions that perform the same task:

```
Colormap XDefaultColormap(Display* display,
          int screen_number)
```

```
Colormap XDefaultColormapOfScreen(Screen* screen)
```

If you use the default colormap, you can access the depth, or number of color planes, with the `DefaultDepth` and `DefaultDepthOfScreen` macros:

```
int DefaultDepth(Display* display,
          int screen_number)
```

```
int DefaultDepthOfScreen(Screen* screen)
```

Determining If You Have a Color System

Because of all the layers of visual indirection, it's not easy to determine whether you have a color system from within an X program. You can get a close approximation using the `DisplayCells` and `DisplayPlanes` macros:

```
int DisplayCells(Display* display,
          int screen_number)
```

```
int DisplayPlanes(Display* display,
          int screen_number)
```

`DisplayCells` returns the number of color cells in the default colormap. `DisplayPlanes` returns the depth of the root window.

There's a problem in making assumptions from the above values, though. A terminally pathological X system might make a `StaticGray` visual with a two-entry colormap (i.e., monochrome) as the default visual.

This could even be the case on a 24 bit-plane color system. Most X vendors don't do this, but it's common for 24 bit-plane color systems to supply a default visual that is not the optimum visual. The rationale may be based on the fact that many poorly written X programs assume a `PseudoColor` visual is the default.

The bottom line is simple: the way to determine if you have a color system is to search for a visual that supports color. We cover this technique in Chapter 10.

X Color Cells

To use colors in X, you need to allocate color cells in a colormap. Color cells are normally defined by the fields in an `XColor` structure:

```
typedef struct {
    unsigned long  pixel;
    unsigned short red, green, blue;
    char           flags;
    char           pad;
} XColor;
```

The *pixel* field is the color index number in the colormap. The term *pixel* is a poor choice, because it has another common meaning: a dot on the screen. In X, each dot on the screen—pixel—has a pixel value, which is an index into a colormap.

The *red*, *green*, and *blue* fields contain the RGB values of the color, using a scale from 0 (off) to 65,535 (full on). The X server scales these values to numbers acceptable to your graphics hardware. All colors in X are specified in terms of RGB. (The X Color Management System, or Xcms, allows for other color models, such as CIE and HVC. See Chapter 13 for more on this.)

With the *flags* field, you can specify whether all three RGB values should be used or not. OR together the flags you want from the list of `DoRed`, `DoGreen`, and `DoBlue`.

The `XColor` structure is used for three main reasons. First, you can use the structure to hold an RGB definition of a color, even though that color has yet to be allocated from any colormap. In this case, the *pixel* field has no value. Only the *flags* and *red*, *green*, and *blue* fields are used.

Second, you can use the XColor structure to allocate a particular color from a colormap. In this case, the *pixel* field will be filled in from functions such as XAllocColor and XAllocNamedColor. The color is allocated with the RGB values in the *red*, *green*, and *blue* fields, based on the bit-flags in the *flags* field.

Third, you can fill in the *pixel* field and then query the colormap with XQueryColor to then retrieve the red, green, and blue values for the color.

Sometimes this distinction can be confusing because of the multiple uses of the XColor structure.

Read-Only and Read/Write Color Cells

X provides two ways to allocate color cells: *read-only* and *read/write*. If you use a read-only color cell, you can allocate any RGB values, but you cannot later change the RGB values. If you want to change the definition of your colors, you need to allocate read/write color cells. Most applications can use read-only colors.

The advantage of the read-only color cells is that with only a limited number of colors available, applications can share colors. For example, if two applications both allocate read-only color cells for red (from the same colormap—typically the default colormap—and with the same RGB values), then the X server will allocate only one color cell. This makes sense because there's no need to have two color cells both with the same red color. Both applications can then share this same color. With only 256 colors available on most workstations, sharing colors becomes an effective technique to avoid filling up your colormap. This is one reason why you want to use the default colormap if possible.

Allocating Read-Only Color Cells

XAllocColor allocates a read-only color cell. It takes in a display, colormap, and an XColor structure:

```
Status XAllocColor(Display* display,
        Colormap colormap,
        XColor* xcolor)   /* input/output */
```

You need to fill in the *red*, *green*, *blue*, and *flags* fields of the XColor structure. XAllocColor will attempt to allocate a color cell (or share an existing one) that holds the closest match the hardware supports to the RGB values passed to XAllocColor. If successful, XAllocColor will fill in the *pixel* field of the XColor structure. The *red*, *green*, and *blue* fields of the structure are filled in with the actual values used (if the color you requested couldn't be exactly matched by your workstation hardware). XAllocColor returns a nonzero value on success, zero on failure.

If XAllocColor returns a nonzero value, then the call was successful. Once the call is successful, you have a pixel value (in the XColor structure) that is an entry into the colormap where the new color is located. The pixel value may be for a new color allocated by XAllocColor. If the same RGB values were already in use in another read-only (sharable) color cell, this pixel value is then the index for the shared color.

Using the Colors Allocated by XAllocColor

Once you've allocated a color, the natural thing to do is draw with the new color. As you know by now, to draw anything in X you need a graphics context, or GC. As we showed in Chapter 3, you can set the foreground drawing color of a GC with XSetForeground. Previously, we only used only two standard pixel values, returned by the WhitePixel and BlackPixel macros. Now the colored pixel value can be used in the same way.

If you have a graphics context, you can set the foreground color from the pixel field in the XColor structure:

```
Display* display;

GC        gc;

XColor    xcolor;


XSetForeground(display, gc, xcolor.pixel);
```

The XColor structure passed to XAllocColor takes in RGB values. For some colors like red, it's easy to derive the RGB values (65535,0,0). For other colors, this process isn't so easy. Because of this, X maintains a list of named colors with their associated RGB values stored in a database.

Color Names

X provides a database of color names and RGB values. This database contains familiar colors like *red* and some less common colors like *LimeGreen* and *chartreuse*. The colors are all listed with English names and their associated RGB values. A text version of this database is normally kept in */usr/lib/X11/rgb.txt* (oftentimes, in */usr/openwin/-lib/X11/rgb.txt* on OpenWindows systems). This is compiled into `rgb.dir` and `rgb.pag` data files. An excerpt of the text file appears below:

```
 50 205  50    LimeGreen
245 245 245    white smoke
255 222 173    NavajoWhite
211 211 211    LightGray
255 255 255    white
  0   0   0    black
100 149 237    CornflowerBlue
127 255   0    chartreuse
```

For each color, the red, green, and blue values, scaled from 0 to 255, appear first, then the color name. In X, RGB values are defined on a scale from 0 to 65,535. In the `rgb.txt` file, though, the values are scaled from 0 to 255. The case of the name doesn't matter. Nor does it matter if you separate words with spaces; *NavajoWhite*, *navajo WHITE*, and *NAVajo white* are all the same as far as X is concerned. In Release 5 of the X Window System, there are over 730 color names in the default database.

You (or your hardware vendor, or your system administrator) can tune these entries to your local systems to improve the look of your X environment. Few users actually do. The point, however, is that while most of these RGB databases should have an entry for *red*, you're never sure *exactly* what shade of red you'll get. In addition, every monitor has slightly different characteristics.

If your application isn't too picky about the colors it needs, you can use a set of X convenience functions to allocate colors based on names looked up in the RGB database. Most applications, though, can use the simple convenience of specifying their colors in terms of their English names, like *red*, *orange*, and *maroon*. If you can use this color model, you'll have to write a lot less code. We'll cover both this simple use of color names as well as the more complicated use of names for far more exacting colors, to meet whatever needs you have.

Looking Up Color Names

The nice thing about this RGB database is that you can look up a color, like *red* or *LimeGreen*, on every X display and get back an RGB value for that color. XParseColor does this:

```
Status XParseColor(Display* display,

        Colormap colormap,

        const char* colorname,

        XColor* exactcolor)  /* RETURN */
```

XParseColor tries to find a match between the text name of the color, stored in *colorname*, and an entry in the system color database. If match is successful, XParseColor will return a nonzero value. XParseColor returns zero on failure.

When naming these colors, do not put any spaces in the names. Also, case does not matter, as *LimeGreen* and *LIMEGREEN* should resolve to the same color.

On return from XParseColor, *exactcolor* holds the RGB components from the color database, exactly as they are in the RGB database.

XLookupColor acts a lot like XParseColor:

```
Status XLookupColor(Display* display,

        Colormap colormap,

        const char* colorname,

        XColor* exactcolor)    /* RETURN */

        XColor* hardwarecolor) /* RETURN */
```

Like XParseColor, XLookupColor tries to find a match between the text name of the color, stored in *colorname*, and an entry in the system color database. If match is successful, XLookupColor will return a nonzero value. XLookupColor returns zero on failure.

On return from XLookupColor, *exactcolor* holds the RGB components from the color database, exactly as they are in the RGB database.

XLookupColor adds another parameter, though. The *hardware-color* parameter holds the RGB components of the closest hardware match for the requested color using the visual for the given *colormap*. Sometimes this match may not be the best match.

After a color name has been looked up in the system color database, a particular color cell must be found or allocated in the application's colormap. You can use XAllocColor, as shown above, or XAllocNamedColor.

Allocating Named Colors

You can combine XLookupColor and XAllocColor in one X library call. XAllocNamedColor will look up the English color name and allocate a colormap cell for the color:

```
Status XAllocNamedColor(Display* display,
    Colormap colormap,
    const char* color_name,
    XColor* hardwarecolor, /* RETURN */
    XColor* exactcolor)    /* RETURN */
```

Note the strangely reversed order on the *hardwarecolor* and *exact-color* from the XLookupColor function.

If you're content with basic color management, this is all you really need to know about color in X. If not—and chances are good that it's not if you bought this book, since most professional-level graphics require more elaborate color management—we cover more sophisticated color allocation schemes starting in Chapter 9.

Source Code to Allocate Color Cells

We've put together a convenience routine that allocates a named color and uses a fallback color in case of errors. In the code below, the

`AllocNamedColor` allocates a color cell by name, using
`XAllocNamedColor`, and returns either the new color index or the fallback *default_color* passed to it. The code is stored in `color.c`:

```
/       *
 *   color.c
 *   Routines to allocate color cells.
 */
#include "xlib.h"

unsigned long AllocNamedColor(Display* display,
    Colormap colormap,
    char* colorname,
    unsigned long default_color)

/*
 *   Allocates a read-only (sharable) color cell in
 *   the given colormap, using the RGB database to
 *   convert the color name to an RGB value. If the
 *   routine fails, the default_color is used instead.
 */

{   /* AllocNamedColor */
    XColor          hardwarecolor, exactcolor;
    unsigned long   color;
    int             status;

    status = XAllocNamedColor(display,
            colormap,
            colorname,
            &hardwarecolor,
```

```
                &exactcolor);


    if (status != 0) {
        color = hardwarecolor.pixel;
    } else {
        color = default_color;
    }


    return color;


}   /* AllocNamedColor */


/* end of file color.c */
```

Freeing Color Cells

When your program is done with a color cell, free it using XFreeColors. This is to return precious color cells so that other applications may allocate them, unless you're using a private colormap.

The XFreeColors function frees a number of color cells:

```
XFreeColors(Display* display,
    Colormap colormap,
    unsigned long* pixels, /* array of color cells */
    unsigned int number_pixels,
    unsigned long planes)  /* panes to free */
```

XFreeColors takes an array of pixel values and frees the cells. It can also free color planes, if you've allocated any with XAllocColorPlanes. (See Chapter 11 for more on color planes.)

X RGB Names

In addition to the names in the RGB color-name database, you can build up colors by RGB value as well. The old-style way to name such a color is #*rgb*, with the red, green, and blue values in hexadecimal. You must have an equal number of hexadecimal digits for the red, green, and blue components, as listed in Table 7.2.

Table 7.2   *The old-style RGB names, in hexadecimal.*

Numerical Specification	Red	Green	Blue
#000	0	0	0
#ff0000	ff	0	0
#112233	11	22	33

These color names can be used with functions such as XAlloc-NamedColor and XParseColor.

This old style is supported for older applications only. In X11 Release 5, you should use the new RGB numerical format: *rgb:r/g/b*, as listed in Table 7.3.

N O T E

Table 7.3   *The X11R5 RGB names, in hexadecimal.*

Numerical Specification	Red	Green	Blue
rgb:0/0/0	0	0	0
rgb:ff/00/00	ff	0	0
rgb:11/22/33	11	22	33

Other Color Naming Formats

With X11 Release 5, a number of new color formats are allowed, to go with the HVC and CIE color spaces introduced as part of the X Color Management System, as listed in Table 7.4.

Table 7.4 *X11R5 numerical color formats.*

Type	Numerical Color Format
CIE X Y Z	CIEXYZ:X/Y/Z
CIE u v Y	CIEuvY:u/v/Y
CIE x y Y	CIExyY:x/y/Y
CIE L a b	CIELab:L/a/b
CIE L u v	CIELuv:L/u/v
RGB	rgb:r/g/b
RGB intensity	rgbi:ri/gi/bi
Tektronix HVC	TekHVC:H/V/C

Using the X11R5 numerical color formats, CIEXYZ:0.234/0.32/0.288 and rgbi:0.5/0.3/0.7 are validly formatted Xcms color names. All the numbers except for *r*/*b*/*g* are floating-point numbers. The RGB numbers are hexadecimal values. The RGB intensity numbers go from 0.0 to 1.0 (full intensity).

See Chapter 13 for more on Xcms.

Getting a Colormap to Allocate Colors From

All of the above routines used a colormap to allocate or look up colors. You can use the default colormap in most cases, unless you find some need to create your own colormap (e.g., running out of color entries in the default colormap). If you work with an X toolkit, though, you should use your toolkit's means to determine what colormap is used with your windows and allocate colors from that colormap.

For example, if you use an OLIT DrawArea widget, you might want to set the colormap before creating the widget. Once created, you'll need to use the same colormap ID to allocate your colors from. Luckily, the Xt Intrinsics provides a *colormap* resource that you can query.

This resource will be valid after you've realized the widget tree using XtRealizeWidget. Once that is done and your drawing widget created, you can query the colormap. This technique works whether you've created your own colormap or used the default—in either case, the `colormap` resource will hold the proper ID.

The `XtVaGetValues` function can get any number of resource values from a widget, using a variable number of arguments (hence, the *Va* in the function name):

```
void XtVaGetValues(Widget widget, ...)
```

The argument list is a set of resource name/value pairs. In normal use, we can get the `colormap` resource from a widget:

```
Widget     widget;
Colormap   colormap;


XtVaGetValues(widget,
    XmNcolormap, &colormap,
    NULL);
```

In Motif, the C definition for the colormap resource will be `XmNcolormap`. In OLIT, use `XtNcolormap`. You can also set this resource.

When getting resource values, you need to pass the address where you want the value stored. When setting resource values, you normally use the values directly.

N O T E

Some Rules for Using Colors

Colors are precious resources on most X displays. Since most X workstations support only 256 hardware colors at a time, the default colormap is normally very limited. When such systems swap in and out colormaps, users see an ugly flashing effect as some of the colors on the screen go bad and other become good. Because of all this, if possible, your applications should use the default colormap with the default visual and allocate shared, read-only color cells. Motif and OLIT programs do this by default.

Color adds a lot to an application's interface. When designing the interface, following a few guidelines will certainly help make better, more portable applications:

✦ Not all systems support color. Many users have monochrome or gray-scale systems. If you require color, you limit the audience for your software. Some types of applications, like image processing, require color. Others don't. Think twice before requiring color. Color, of course, can certainly add meaning to displays of data. For instance, using red can highlight dangerous areas in a factory-floor application. When all is said and done, color interfaces usually look better than monochrome. One way to get around this problem is to design the original interface in monochrome (black and white). That way, you can still produce a monochrome version. One worthwhile piece of advice (from Apple Computer's Inside Macintosh series) is to color the black bits only. That way the interface will still work in black and white.

✦ A significant number of people are partially or fully color-blind—about 20 percent of U.S. males fall into this category—so be careful with the colors you display together on the screen. Users generally have a harder time differentiating between various shades of blue than between those of most other colors. A good facility to provide is the ability for end users to customize the colors in the interface. That way, a partially color-blind person could use the (potentially garish) colors that provide enough contrast to be readable.

✦ Avoid going hog-wild with colors. Unless you are attempting realistic image visualization, stick to about eight colors only. Even if you are attempting realistic image visualization, stick to about eight colors for the user interface. Use as many colors as necessary to visualize your data, but keep the interface clean and easy to read. Most color workstations support only 256 colors, so you want to keep as many colors available for your data as possible. Avoid wasting colors for the interface.

✦ Unless you need special features of a particular visual, such as `DirectColor`, design your code to be as portable as possible. Stick to the most common areas of color handling in X. This means you won't take full advantage of everyone's display, especially if it is a Silicon Graphics workstation. But your applications will be more likely to work, and work well, on different hardware. One of the prime advantages of the X Window System is that it runs on many different workstations by many different vendors. If you're writing a high-end medical imaging system, you'll need to take advantage of everything your system provides. But most application writers don't fit into this category.

Summary

Color is always a complicated subject in the computer field. And it becomes even more difficult when dealing with the X Window System. Since X is designed to be device-independent, it must deal with a wide variety of color models on many different kinds of computers. Most of these computers are built on an RGB color model: red, green, and blue phosphors within each pixel are combined to form the different hues on the screen. Electron beams excite the phosphors, which in turn provides the color. Simultaneously exciting all phosphors produces a white pixel; when all are unexcited, you're left with a black pixel. Color displays use multiple bits within a pixel, or dot on the screen, to further specify colors. These bits are also known as planes, and the most common color display contains eight planes (supporting 256 different colors). You have access to many more colors, even though only a limited number of them can actually be displayed at one time.

The main problem with color is that there are so many ways in which workstations support color. A high-end Silicon Graphics workstation looks at color differently than a 486-based PC with a SuperVGA display adapter. Additionally, the high-end workstation probably provides a number of ways to view the color hardware. You may use overlay planes, or may be able to address color tables using different means. To hide these differences, X supports a visual—an abstraction for color hardware subsystems. Visuals are associated with screens. The screen may support color or only scales of gray. (A monochrome screen is considered the degenerate case of a gray-scale screen.) In addition, the colormaps on the screen may be read-only or you may be able to write to the colormaps. The colormaps may also be decomposed into separate red, green, and blue spaces. This leads to the six visual classes X provides: `DirectColor`, `GrayScale`, `PseudoColor`, `StaticColor`, `StaticGray`, and `TrueColor`.

A colormap is typically an index table used to look up colors. For example, color index 15 could be magenta and index 14 yellow. The colormap may be decomposed into separate red, green, and blue colormaps with the `DirectColor` and `TrueColor` visuals. All other visual types use undecomposed colormaps. That is, the colormap acts as a large array. For each element in the array, there are the red, green, and blue components for that color.

To use color in X, you need to allocate color cells in a colormap. Each color cell contains a separate color, such as blue, purple, or white. The color shown is defined by the red, green, and blue components of the color, stored in the colormap at the given color index. Each color cell is then represented by an index, an unsigned long int value that indexes into a colormap, either directly into one colormap or indirectly into decomposed red, green, and blue colormaps. Your applications allocate color cells and then set graphics contexts (GCs) to draw with the colors in those cells.

Once you've connected to an X display, there are five steps to using color in X applications:

1. First, find the desired visual; normally, a `PseudoColor` visual.

2. Normally, a new window is created using a constant of `CopyFromParent` for its visual.

3. The next step is to get a colormap that is valid for your visual to use with your widget's associated window.

4. Whatever colormap you end up with, you'll then need to allocate colors from the colormap.

5. Finally, create a graphics context for the window, and set the GC to draw in some of the colors allocated in step 4.

X provides a database of color names and RGB values. This database contains familiar colors like *red* and some less common colors like *LimeGreen* and *chartreuse*. The colors are all listed with English names and their associated RGB values. A text version of this database is normally kept in */usr/lib/X11/rgb.txt* (oftentimes, in */usr/openwin/-lib/X11/rgb.txt* on OpenWindows systems). This is compiled into `rgb.dir` and `rgb.pag` data files.

In addition to the names in the RGB color-name database, you can build up colors by RGB value as well. The old-style way to name such a color is *#rgb*, with the red, green, and blue values in hexadecimal. You must have an equal number of hexadecimal digits for the red, green, and blue components.

X Library Functions and Macros Introduced in This Chapter

```
DefaultColormap

DefaultColormapOfScreen

DisplayCells

DisplayPlanes

XAllocColor

XAllocNamedColor

XDefaultColormap

XDefaultColormapOfScreen

XFreeColors

XLookupColor

XParseColor
```

X Toolkit Intrinsics Functions and Macros Introduced in This Chapter

```
XtVaGetValues
```

Turtle Graphics and X

This chapter covers:

- ✦ What turtle graphics are
- ✦ Using turtle graphics to display chaotic systems
- ✦ How to use L-systems
- ✦ Expanding L-system rules
- ✦ Modeling plants with L-systems
- ✦ OLIT and Motif programs to test turtle graphics

Introducing Turtle Graphics

Turtle graphics forms an effective way to draw space-filling curves and simulated plant growth often seen in popular books on chaotic-systems fractal geometry. Based on ideas of Seymour Papert and others, turtle graphics is very common in beginning computer languages like LOGO and BASIC. In fact, Papert's work involved teaching computer graphics to children.

The basic idea is simple: you control a *turtle* that moves about the page. The turtle's tail is a pen. As the turtle moves, the tail, or pen, can be in the down position—drawing—or in the up position—not drawing. In many respects, a turtle acts like a plotter.

Figure 8.1 *A graphics turtle.*

With something as simple as the turtle shown in Figure 8.1, you can create complex shapes, such as the Peano curve in Figure 8.2.

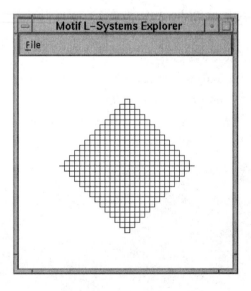

Figure 8.2 *A Peano curve.*

The Peano curve in Figure 8.2 was drawn with the sample program by setting the turn angle to 90 degrees, the start axiom to F, the expansion rule to FF+F+F+FF+F+F–F, and the number of iterations to three.

The turtle has a heading, its direction of motion. This direction is normally expressed as an angle in degrees and its position.

At any given time, the turtle's *orientation* or *heading* is expressed as an *x, y* position in the 2D plane and an angle of motion, in degrees, or compactly, as (*x, y, alpha*), where *alpha* is the angle of motion. The various turtle commands modify this heading.

Turtle Commands

You can implement a turtle-graphics system with a very small number of commands. You can move the turtle forward or turn it in place. As the turtle moves forward, if the turtle's tail or pen is down, then a line is drawn. If the tail or pen is up, then the turtle just moves to a new location without drawing a line.

Traditional turtle graphics supports only four basic commands, represented here as text characters (we'll see why in the section on L-systems below) in Table 8.1.

Table 8.1 *Basic turtle drawing commands.*

Command	Meaning
F	Draw forward
f	Move forward, but don't draw (the pen is up)
+	Turn counterclockwise
-	Turn clockwise

Table 8.5 extends the commands.

The F command moves the turtle forward, in its direction or angle of travel, one unit of distance. You can specify any unit of distance you need to make the graphics appear in a reasonable size. As the turtle moves, it draws a line from the starting position to the new position. The f command acts just like the F command, but draws no line.

The + and - commands turn the turtle in place by an angle *delta*. Picking the proper angle *delta* determines in a large part what kind of curve you will draw. For every command, the position at the end of the command is passed as the starting position for the next command.

F and f form the movement commands for the turtle.

Movement Commands

To go into a little more detail, if the turtle starts at position

   (x, y, alpha)

then an F or f command will change the turtle's position to:

   (x + (distance * cos(alpha)), y + (distance * sin(alpha)), alpha)

The new x position equals x + *(distance * cos(alpha))*. The new y position equals y + *(distance * sin(alpha))*.

For the F command, the pen is down, so a line should be drawn between the following points, where *d* is the unit of distance, as shown in Table 8.2.

Table 8.2   *Drawing the F command's line.*

Starting Point	Ending Point
(x, y)	*(x + (d * cos(alpha)), y + (d * sin(alpha)))*

The F command isn't limited to lines alone. You could draw cylinders or whatever you want. It's just easiest to draw lines.

N O T E

When you finish with a command, you keep track of the new turtle heading. This becomes the base heading against which you apply the next command. The initial heading is normally (0, 0, 0), which starts the motion going to the right.

The movement commands just change the *x* and *y* values in the turtle heading. The turning commands, + and –, change the direction angle, *alpha*.

Turning Commands

The + and – commands turn the turtle in place—just the heading changes and the turtle doesn't actually move or draw. The + command changes the angle *alpha*, to *alpha – delta*, where delta is the angle chosen for the curve you're trying to draw. Similarly, the – command changes the angle *alpha* to *alpha + delta*. These commands are explained in Table 8.3.

Table 8.3 *Commands to turn the turtle.*

Command	Old Heading	New Heading
+	*(x, y, alpha)*	*(x, y, alpha - delta)*
-	*(x, y, alpha)*	*(x, y, alpha + delta)*

We can put together the four turtle commands and summarize them in Table 8.4.

Table 8.4 *How turtle commands transform the heading.*

Command	Old Heading	New Heading
F	*(x, y, alpha)*	*(x + (d * cos(alpha)),* *y + (d * sin(alpha)), alpha)*
f	*(x, y, alpha)*	*(x + (d * cos(alpha)),* *y + (d * sin(alpha)), alpha)*
+	*(x, y, alpha)*	*(x, y, alpha - delta)*
-	*(x, y, alpha)*	*(x, y, alpha + delta)*

In Table 8.4, *d* is an arbitrary unit of distance.

With those four commands, we can draw any number of recursive space-filling curves, such as Koch curves. The key is that the commands are represented as text.

Representing Turtle Commands as Text

We represent the turtle commands as text so that we can easily generate rules. We can then feed these rules to a turtle-graphics engine for drawing, nicely separating the data to draw from the rendering engine.

For example, with the simple rule F + F – f F, we draw the picture below:

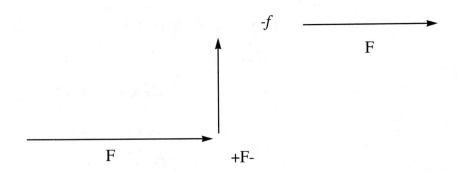

Figure 8.3   *Drawing the rule F + F - f F.*

Using a text representation makes it a lot easier to read the rules and determine if your turtle actually went to where it is supposed to go.

Data Structures for Turtle Graphics

The basic data structure we need is to hold the current heading of the turtle. The `Turtle` structure, below, holds both the heading and the necessary distance and turn angle or delta angle to manage transformations (it's just easier to cart these values around with the heading):

```
typedef struct {
    double x;
    double y;
    double alpha;
    double turn_angle;  /* delta */
    double distance;
} Turtle;
```

We store all values as doubles because we use trigonometry functions to figure the direction of motion. The C math library functions `sin` and `cos` require double values and generate values where the decimal point is significant. Hence, we use doubles to store all the values.

The function `TurtleTransform` (shown partially below) transforms the turtle heading, stored in the `Turtle` structure for one turtle-graphics command, such as F, f, +, and -. The purpose is to change the old (current) heading to the new heading.

The basic algorithm is simple. We use a `switch` statement on the *command* (an ASCII text character passed as an *int*) to determine what to do. Each command is implemented as shown in Table 8.4. The new heading is a copy of the old heading, using the convenience function `TurtleCopy`, except for whatever the *command* does to transform the heading. `TurtleTransform` uses the math library functions `sin` and `cos` to generate the sine and cosine of the angle alpha. You'll need to link with the math library when compiling—this is normally `libm.a`, so you can add on a `-lm` to your `cc` command.

We require a `Display` pointer, `Drawable`, and graphics context (GC) because the F command draws to a window or pixmap on the X display. Partial code for the `TurtleTransform` function follows (the rest of the code is in the file `turtle.c`, presented later under Source Code for Turtle.c):

```
void TurtleTransform(Display* display,
    Drawable drawable,
    GC gc,
    Turtle* turtle,  /* input/output */
    int command)


{   /* TurtleTransform */
    Turtle  new_turtle;

    /*
     * By default, the new_turtle starts at
     * the old turtle.
```

```
    */
TurtleCopy(turtle, &new_turtle);

switch(command) {
    case 'F':
        new_turtle.x = turtle->x +
            (turtle->distance * cos(turtle->alpha) );
        new_turtle.y = turtle->y +
            (turtle->distance * sin(turtle->alpha) );

        TurtleDrawLine(display, drawable, gc,
            turtle->x, turtle->y,
            new_turtle.x,
            new_turtle.y);
        break;
    case 'f':
        new_turtle.x =
            turtle->x +
            (turtle->distance * cos(turtle->alpha) );
        new_turtle.y =
            turtle->y +
            (turtle->distance * sin(turtle->alpha) );
        break;
    case '+':
        new_turtle.alpha =
            turtle->alpha - turtle->turn_angle;
        break;
    case '-':
        new_turtle.alpha =
            turtle->alpha + turtle->turn_angle;
        break;
```

```
            default:
                break;
        }


        /*
         * Now, copy the new point back to the old.
         */
        TurtleCopy(&new_turtle, turtle);


    }   /* TurtleTransform */
```

TurtleCopy is a convenience routine that copies one Turtle structure
to another:

```
    void TurtleCopy(Turtle* turtle,
        Turtle* new_turtle)


    {   /* TurtleCopy */


        new_turtle->x = turtle->x;
        new_turtle->y = turtle->y;


        new_turtle->alpha   = turtle->alpha;
        new_turtle->distance = turtle->distance;
        new_turtle->turn_angle = turtle->turn_angle;


    }   /* TurtleCopy */
```

We use TurtleCopy as a simple convenience. The TurtleDrawLine
function draws a line from the old position to the new position, as required
by the F command.

Drawing with Turtle Graphics

We need a special function to draw lines because of all the scaling that may take place. For different Koch curves or L-systems (both explained below), we may need to offset our position to appear in a window. In addition, we may want to scale each point. Finally, `TurtleDrawLine` converts each double value to an integer. This is a process that was fraught with errors, as we discovered to our chagrin.

```
void TurtleDrawLine(Display* display,

    Drawable drawable,

    GC gc,

    double x1, double y1,

    double x2, double y2)


{   /* TurtleDrawLine */

    int ix1, iy1, ix2, iy2;

    double  scale_factor;


    scale_factor = (double) global_scale_factor;


    /*

     * Convert coords to ints.

     */

    ix1 = DoubleToInt( (scale_factor * x1) ) +

                global_x_offset;

    iy1 = DoubleToInt( (scale_factor * y1) ) +

                global_y_offset;

    ix2 = DoubleToInt( (scale_factor * x2) ) +

                global_x_offset;

    iy2 = DoubleToInt( (scale_factor * y2) ) +
```

```
            global_y_offset;

   /*
    * Safety check on the coordinates.
    */
   if ((ix1 > 16000) || (ix1 < -16000) ||
       (iy1 > 16000) || (iy1 < -16000) ||
       (ix2 > 16000) || (ix2 < -16000) ||
       (iy2 > 16000) || (iy2 < -16000)) {
       return;
   }


   /*
    * Draw line.
    */
   XDrawLine(display, drawable, gc,
       ix1, iy1, ix2, iy2);


   }    /* TurtleDrawLine */
```

TurtleDrawLine uses some odd code. First, it scales each double value by a global scale factor, global_scale_factor. Then, each double coordinate value is converted to an int type using the DoubleToInt function. We next check to make sure each point is within 16,000 (a limit imposed by some X servers). Finally, TurtleDrawLine calls XDrawLine to actually draw a line. This is a lot of overhead on each and every line we draw, especially so when we draw a great many lines in the programs below. We're sure you can come up with a more efficient method.

Dealing with Inexactness in Computer Math

A little digression here. There's a lot of issues involved when you try to use mathematical functions in computer programs. Much as we'd like to just blindly use the functions, we need to be concerned about floating-point round-off errors and other concerns when representing floating-point numbers in an arbitrary format. We're not the only ones to share this concern. In fact, there's a whole group devoted to extending the ANSI C standard to better help develop numerical applications. One such problem we faced was converting double-precision (normally 8-byte) floating-point values to integers (normally 4 bytes).

The function DoubleToInt (stored in convert.c, below), converts a double value to an integer, checking against the limits, INT_MAX and INT_MIN, imposed in the header file <limits.h>:

```
int DoubleToInt(double d)


{   /* DoubleToInt */
    double rounded_value;


    rounded_value = round(d);


    if (rounded_value > (double) INT_MAX) {
        rounded_value = (double) INT_MAX;
    }


    if (rounded_value < (double) INT_MIN) {
        rounded_value = (double) INT_MIN;
    }


    return (int) rounded_value;


}   /* DoubleToInt */
```

Before casting to an int, and potentially losing data, DoubleToInt makes sure the value is within the proper range.

N O T E   All of our early attempts to draw turtle graphics failed miserably because of floating-point round-off errors. This is why we're covering all these seemingly unrelated issues here. Because of this problem, we use the following macro to round a floating-point value to its nearest `int`, using the C math library functions `ceil` and `floor`:

```
#define round(d)  (d < 0.0 ? ceil(d - 0.5) \
                   : floor(d + 0.5))
```

The `round` macro returns a double type, so you need to cast it to an `int` in actual use in your code:

```
int    i;
double d;


i = (int) round(d);
```

Sine and Cosine

The C math library functions `sin` and `cos` take input values in *radians*. Most real users are used to values in *degrees*, and in fact, most books on chaos, fractals, and L-systems represent angles in degrees. To convert from degrees to radians, we use the following function:

```
double deg2radians(double degrees)


{   /* deg2radians */


    return ((double) 0.017453293 * degrees);


}   /* deg2radians */
```

Source Code for the Conversion Functions

Both the `deg2radians` and `DoubleToInt` functions are stored in the file `convert.c`:

```c
/*
 *  convert.c
 *  Routines for converting radians and doubles.
 */
#include  "convert.h"
#include  <limits.h>
#include  <math.h>


/*
 * Converts degrees to radians used by sin() and cos().
 */
double deg2radians(double degrees)

{   /* deg2radians */

    return ((double) 0.017453293 * degrees);

}   /* deg2radians */

/*
 * Converts a double to an int.
 */
int DoubleToInt(double d)

{   /* DoubleToInt */
    double  rounded_value;
```

```
    rounded_value = round(d);

    if (rounded_value > (double) INT_MAX) {
        rounded_value = (double) INT_MAX;
    }

    if (rounded_value < (double) INT_MIN) {
        rounded_value = (double) INT_MIN;
    }

    return (int) rounded_value;

}   /* DoubleToInt */


/* end of file convert.c */
```

The header file, convert.h, provides the round macro and function prototypes:

```
/*
 *  convert.h
 *  Header file for converting radians and doubles.
 */
#ifndef convert_h_
#define convert_h_  1

/*
 * Macro to round a floating-point value
 * to its nearest int.
 */
```

```
#define round(d)    (d < 0.0 ? ceil(d - 0.5) : \
                       floor(d + 0.5))


/*
 * Conversion functions.
 */
extern double deg2radians(double degrees);


extern int DoubleToInt(double d);


#endif  /* !convert_h_ */
/* end of file convert.h */
```

This ends our diversion into the hoary details that impact even simple numerical coding. With all of the above code, we can parse—and draw—an entire text string of turtle commands using the `TurtleParse` function:

```
void TurtleParse(Display* display,
     Drawable drawable,
     GC gc,
     Turtle* turtle,       /* input/output */
     char* command_string)


{    /* TurtleParse */
     int i, length;


     length = strlen(command_string);


     for (i = 0; i < length; i++) {


          TurtleTransform(display, drawable, gc,
               turtle, (int) command_string[i]);
```

```
        }


    }    /* TurtleParse */
```

The `TurtleParse` function goes through a text string of turtle commands, and issues each command, in turn, to `TurtleTransform`, above.

Extending Turtle Commands for
Modeling Plant Growth

To draw more interesting plant-based pictures, we need to extend our set of
turtle-graphics commands. With these commands, we introduce the concept of
a *stack*. The stack holds turtle headings. The new command [pushes the current heading onto a stack. The] command then pops this heading. Together,
these commands allow us to better model branches on a plant stem or tree
trunk. In Figure 8.4, we draw the commands F[-F]F for a small turn angle
(about 20 degrees), as the bracket commands allow for a branching effect.

Figure 8.4   *Using turtle graphics to model plants branches.*

Table 8.5 summarizes our extended set of turtle-graphics commands:

Table 8.5 *Extended turtle drawing commands.*

Command	Meaning
F	Draw forward
f	Move forward, but don't draw (the pen is up)
+	Turn counterclockwise
-	Turn clockwise
[	Push heading onto stack
]	Pop heading from stack

Since both the [and] commands require a stack, we implement the stack as a simple global array of `Turtle` structures, with an integer value for the stack pointer:

```
#define MAX_STACK    200


int       turtle_stack_count = (-1);
Turtle    turtle_stack[MAX_STACK + 1];
```

Again, we're sure that you can implement a much better stack. In fact, this is a perfect task for C++.

We now need two functions to manipulate the stack: one to push entries onto the stack and one to pop entries from the stack. The `TurtlePush` function copies a heading, a `Turtle` structure, onto the stack:

```
int TurtlePush(Turtle* turtle)


{   /* TurtlePush */


    /*
     * Adjust stack pointer.
     */
```

```
        turtle_stack_count++;

        /*
         * Check stack pointer.
         */
        if (turtle_stack_count >= MAX_STACK) {
            return (-1);
        }

        /*
         * Copy from passed in turtle heading
         * to stack.
         */
        TurtleCopy(turtle,
            &turtle_stack[turtle_stack_count]);

        return 0;

    }   /* TurtlePush */
```

TurtlePush returns a nonzero value if the stack is exceeded. We find that a stack size of 200 elements is good for most basic L-systems. You can extend this by changing the value of the MAX_STACK macro. TurtlePop then pops the top Turtle structure from the stack:

```
    int TurtlePop(Turtle* turtle)    /* RETURN */

    {   /* TurtlePop */

        /*
         * Check stack.
         */
```

```
    if (turtle_stack_count < 0) {
        return (-1);
    }


    /*
     * Copy from stack to passed in parameter.
     */
    TurtleCopy(&turtle_stack[turtle_stack_count],
        turtle);


    /*
     * Adjust stack pointer.
     */
    turtle_stack_count--;


    return 0;


}   /* TurtlePop */
```

Like TurtlePush, TurtlePop returns a nonzero value when the stack underflows—that is, when you try to pop without first pushing. As you can tell, this is not a very sophisticated stack-handling system. With a little work, we're sure that you can come up with something much more robust. A word of caution, though: it's easy to mess up the stack pointer.

Source Code for Turtle.c

We placed all the functions for drawing turtle graphics into the file turtle.c:

```
    /*
     *  turtle.c
```

```
 *   Routines for drawing and transforming the turtle.
 */
#include  "turtle.h"
#include  "convert.h"
#include  <limits.h>
#include  <math.h>
#include  <stdio.h> /* NULL */


/*
 * Globals for controlling how the
 * turtle is drawn.
 */
int global_x_offset = 0;
int global_y_offset = 0;
int global_scale_factor = 1;


/*
 * Globals for the Turtle stack.
 */
#define MAX_STACK    200


static int      turtle_stack_count = (-1);
static Turtle   turtle_stack[MAX_STACK + 1];


/*
 * Copies the fields of one Turtle
 * structure to another.
 */
void TurtleCopy(Turtle* turtle,
    Turtle* new_turtle)
```

```
{   /* TurtleCopy */


    new_turtle->x = turtle->x;
    new_turtle->y = turtle->y;


    new_turtle->alpha    = turtle->alpha;
    new_turtle->distance = turtle->distance;
    new_turtle->turn_angle = turtle->turn_angle;


}   /* TurtleCopy */


/*
 * Debugging function to print out a Turtle state.
 */
static void TurtlePrint(Turtle* turtle)


{   /* TurtlePrint */


    printf("  Turtle: (%f, %f, %f)\n",
        turtle->x, turtle->y, turtle->alpha);


}   /* TurtlePrint */


/*
 * Initializes the fields in a Turtle structure.
 * The orientation is to move to the right.
 */
void TurtleInit(Turtle* turtle,
    double distance,
    double turn_angle) /* degrees */
```

```
{   /* TurtleInit */


    turtle->x = (double) 0.0;
    turtle->y = (double) 0.0;


    turtle->alpha = (double) 0.0;


    /*
     * Convert the degrees to radians.
     */
    turtle->distance   = distance;
    turtle->turn_angle = deg2radians(turn_angle);


    /*
     * Reset turtle stack.
     */
    turtle_stack_count = (-1);


}   /* TurtleInit */


/*
 * Draws a line using double coords;
 * adds offset to the line.
 */
static void TurtleDrawLine(Display* display,
    Drawable drawable,
    GC gc,
    double x1, double y1,
    double x2, double y2)


{   /* TurtleDrawLine */
```

```
int ix1, iy1, ix2, iy2;
double  scale_factor;

scale_factor = (double) global_scale_factor;

/*
 * Convert coords to ints.
 */
ix1 = DoubleToInt( (scale_factor * x1) ) +
            global_x_offset;
iy1 = DoubleToInt( (scale_factor * y1) ) +
            global_y_offset;
ix2 = DoubleToInt( (scale_factor * x2) ) +
            global_x_offset;
iy2 = DoubleToInt( (scale_factor * y2) ) +
            global_y_offset;

/*
 * Safety check on the coordinates.
 */
if ((ix1 > 16000) || (ix1 < -16000) ||
    (iy1 > 16000) || (iy1 < -16000) ||
    (ix2 > 16000) || (ix2 < -16000) ||
    (iy2 > 16000) || (iy2 < -16000)) {
    return;
}

/*
 * Draw line.
 */
XDrawLine(display, drawable, gc,
```

```
                ix1, iy1, ix2, iy2);


}    /* TurtleDrawLine */


/*
 * Transforms the turtle coordinates from the
 * original heading to a new heading based on
 * a command and a distance.
 *
 * The rules are made up of the following
 * command letters (chars cast to ints):
 *   "F" move forward distance d.
 *        x' = x + (d * cos(alpha));
 *        y' = y + (d * sin(alpha));
 *        drawline(x,y) to (x',y')
 *        x = x'
 *        y = y'
 *   "f" like "F", but don't draw, just move.
 *   "+" turn left by angle delta
 *        alpha = alpha - delta
 *   "-" turn right by angle delta
 *        alpha = alpha + delta
 *   "[" Push the current heading onto a stack.
 *   "]" Pop the current heading from the stack.
 *
 */
static void TurtleTransform(Display* display,
    Drawable drawable,
    GC gc,
    Turtle* turtle,  /* input/output */
    int command)
```

```
{   /* TurtleTransform */
    Turtle  new_turtle;

    /*
     * By default, the new_turtle starts at
     * the old turtle.
     */
    TurtleCopy(turtle, &new_turtle);

    switch(command) {
        case 'F':
            new_turtle.x =
                turtle->x +
                (turtle->distance * cos(turtle->alpha) );
            new_turtle.y =
                turtle->y +
                (turtle->distance * sin(turtle->alpha) );

            TurtleDrawLine(display, drawable, gc,
                turtle->x, turtle->y,
                new_turtle.x,
                new_turtle.y);
            break;
        case 'f':
            new_turtle.x =
                turtle->x +
                (turtle->distance * cos(turtle->alpha) );
            new_turtle.y =
                turtle->y +
                (turtle->distance * sin(turtle->alpha) );
```

```
            break;
        case '+':
            new_turtle.alpha =
                turtle->alpha - turtle->turn_angle;
            break;
        case '-':
            new_turtle.alpha =
                turtle->alpha + turtle->turn_angle;
            break;
        case '[':    /* Push */
            if (TurtlePush(&new_turtle) < 0) {
                fprintf(stderr,
                    "Error pushing to stack.\n");
                exit(1);
            }
            break;
        case ']':    /* Pop */
            if (TurtlePop(&new_turtle) < 0) {
                fprintf(stderr,
                    "Error popping from stack.\n");
                exit(1);
            }
            break;
        default:
            break;
    }

    /*
     * Now, copy the new point back to the old.
     */
    TurtleCopy(&new_turtle, turtle);
```

```
}   /* TurtleTransform */


/*
 * Parses a string of turtle-graphics commands
 * and draws the output to the given window.
 */
void TurtleParse(Display* display,
    Drawable drawable,
    GC gc,
    Turtle* turtle,        /* input/output */
    char* command_string)


{   /* TurtleParse */
    int i, length;

    length = strlen(command_string);

    for (i = 0; i < length; i++) {

        TurtleTransform(display, drawable, gc,
            turtle, (int) command_string[i]);
    }


}   /* TurtleParse */


/*
 * Pushes a turtle heading onto the stack.
 */
int TurtlePush(Turtle* turtle)
```

```
{   /* TurtlePush */

    /*
     * Adjust stack pointer.
     */
    turtle_stack_count++;

    /*
     * Check stack pointer.
     */
    if (turtle_stack_count >= MAX_STACK) {
        return (-1);
    }

    /*
     * Copy from passed in turtle heading
     * to stack.
     */
    TurtleCopy(turtle,
        &turtle_stack[turtle_stack_count]);

    return 0;

}   /* TurtlePush */

/*
 * Pops a turtle heading from the stack.
 */
int TurtlePop(Turtle* turtle)    /* RETURN */

{   /* TurtlePop */
```

```
/*
 * Check stack.
 */
if (turtle_stack_count < 0) {
    return (-1);
}


/*
 * Copy from stack to passed in parameter.
 */
TurtleCopy(&turtle_stack[turtle_stack_count],
    turtle);


/*
 * Adjust stack pointer.
 */
turtle_stack_count--;


return 0;


}   /* TurtlePop */


/* end of file turtle.c */
```

The functions in `turtle.c` work with or without a system to expand turtle-graphics rules.

The header file for the routines above is `turtle.h`:

```
/*
 *  turtle.h
 *  Structures for use with turtle graphics.
```

```
 */
#ifndef turtle_h_
#define turtle_h_    1

#include <X11/Xlib.h>

/*
 * Structure to hold the state of the L-system turtle.
 */
typedef struct {
    double  x;
    double  y;
    double alpha;
    double turn_angle;
    double distance;
} Turtle;

/*
 * Declare functions.
 */
extern
void TurtleCopy(Turtle* turtle,
        Turtle* new_turtle);

extern
void TurtleInit(Turtle* turtle,
        double distance,
        double turn_angle); /* degrees */

extern
void TurtleParse(Display* display,
```

```
        Drawable drawable,

        GC gc,

        Turtle* turtle,      /* input/output */

        char* command_string);


  #endif /* !turtle_h_ */

  /* end of file turtle.h */
```

Turtle graphics alone aren't very interesting because of the great amount of work you have to do to create a complex set of turtle-graphics commands. If you've ever worked with a set of plotter commands, such as an HPGL file, you know what we mean.

If you could build up a complex set of turtle-graphics commands from some set of rules, perhaps applied recursively, you could then draw much more complicated and interesting pictures without a lot of work. That's where L-systems come in.

L-Systems

L-systems, or *Lindenmayer systems*, come from attempts to model plant growth with mathematics. Named after Aristid Lindenmayer and explained in The Algorithmic Beauty of Plants, L-systems are also closely related to Noam Chomsky's work on formal grammars and the famous Backus-Naur form, or BNF, used for programming language syntax descriptions. Even if you're no fan of biology, L-systems provide an effective means to generate turtle commands—commands that can be used to draw realistic-looking plants or to display famous Koch, Hilbert, and Sierpinski space-filling curves.

The central concepts of L-systems include representing turtle commands as text and expanding or rewriting an initial set of commands—the axiom—with production rules.

A *rewriting system* takes a starting set of commands, or axiom, and then uses term-rewriting rules to replace parts of the initial set of commands. In L-systems, term rewriting is taken to an extreme where you start with a set of turtle commands and then recursively expand the commands using a set of production rules. In such *feedback systems*, the output of one pass or iteration of the production rules is passed as the input to the next iteration:

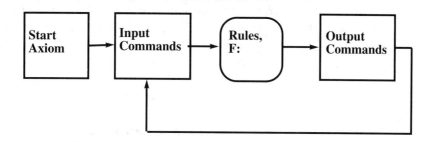

Figure 8.5 *A diagram of term-rewriting systems.*

We can stop the iteration process at any time and then draw the output commands.

An L-System Example

A classic example of an L-system (from pages 3 through 4 in The Algorithmic Beauty of Plants) presents two rules: *b* is replaced by *a* and *a* is replaced by *ab*. In L-system notation, this appears as:

b := a

a := ab

Actually, we're cheating a bit. L-system notation uses a right-pointing arrow, which looks to close to the C –> operator. Because of this, we choose the := syntax.

N O T E

Using the above rules, we can then start with a single command, *b* (called the *axiom*), and then start expanding. We expand recursively in iterations.

In the first iteration, the axiom *b* is replaced by *a*, because of the rule *b* := *a*. The second iteration starts with *a*, the output string of the first iteration, as the input string. In the second iteration, *a* is then replaced by *ab*, due to the rule *a* := *ab*. We now have the string *ab* to pass to the next iteration.

Here comes the tricky part: In the third iteration, the input string contains two commands, *ab*, both of which are *simultaneously* expanded. (Just to be clear: L-system rules are expanded simultaneously in every iteration, not just the third. In our example, this only becomes an issue starting with the third iteration.) Thus, *a* expands to *ab* and the *b* (in the input string) expands to *a*, generating *aba*. This concept is very important. If you don't get it, take a long look at Table 8.6.

Table 8.6   *Applying L-system expansion rules.*

Iteration	Expanded Commands
Start	b
1	a
2	ab
3	ab a
4	ab a ab
5	ab a ab ab a

In Table 8.6, we put in spaces to clearly show how the rules are expanded. In the computer interpretation of rules, the spaces should be ignored.

Applying L-Systems to Turtle Graphics

We can apply L-systems to turtle graphics by expanding the turtle F command as our rules. Using only F simplifies L-systems because we're using only one variable (see the section entitled Extending L-Systems, below). Even when limiting ourselves to rules with one variable, we can draw a number of interesting pictures.

For instance, if we start with an axiom of - F and an expansion rule of F := F+F-F-F+F, we can generate the following set of turtle-graphic commands. On the first iteration, - F expands to:

```
-F+F-F-F+F
```

On the second iteration, the commands expand to:

```
-F+F-F-F+F+F+F-F-F+F-F+F-F-F+F-F+F-F-F+F+F+F-F-F+F
```

We now have a quick means to generate a complex set of turtle commands to draw. One more factor, however, must be acknowledged.

Drawing L-Systems

To draw an L-system using the turtle-graphics commands in this chapter, we must choose the *delta* or *turn* angle. Otherwise, the + and - commands won't work. Choosing the proper turn angle is a key requirement in deriving the pictures you want. We also have to choose a unit distance, but this isn't that important. Basically, the unit distance just scales the picture larger or smaller. The turn angle is the key.

The expansion rule presented above, F := F+F-F-F+F, can generate the curve shown in Figure 8.6 when we set the turn angle to 90 degrees, expand the rules for four iterations, and then pass the commands to our `TurtleParse` function, presented above:

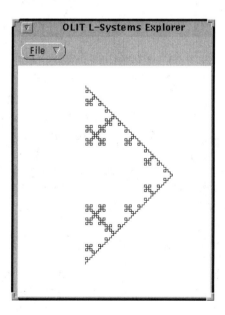

Figure 8.6 *Koch curve under OLIT using start axiom -F; expansion rule -F+F-F-F+F; four iterations; and 90-degree turn angle.*

NOTE In the above rule, we assume the F := part of the syntax. Therefore, F+F-F-F+F is really shorthand for F := F+F-F-F+F. This just makes it easier for the computer program to parse.

Koch curves work quite well in L-systems, as shown in Figure 8.7.

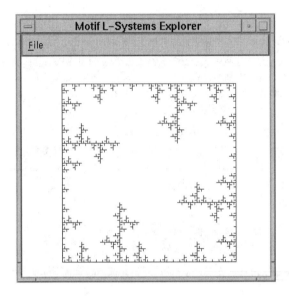

Figure 8.7 *Koch curve under Motif using start axiom F; -F-F-F; expansion rule FF-F-F+F; four iterations; and 90-degree turn angle.*

As you can tell from these pictures, we're getting ready to create a program that will draw L-systems with color. But first we need to cover some code to expand L-system rules.

Code Supporting L-Systems

The function `LSysExpandOnce`, below, expands one iteration of a rule. You pass it a rule string and a set of commands. The *cmd_string* holds both the input commands and the output commands. `LSysExpandOnce` works on an extremely simple formula: wherever an F appears in the *cmd_string*, `LSysExpandOnce` replaces that F with the contents of the *rule_string*. This forms a very simple term-rewriting system. If you ever want to allow for multiple rules and variables, you'll need to change the simplistic method in LSysExpandOnce.

The LSysExpand function expands a starting set of commands (the axiom) for a given number of iterations (number_times). The caller is expected to allocate the massive string space required to store the rules. In lsystem.h, presented after the computer code that follows, we set the LSYS_MAX_RULE_LEN to 48,000 bytes.

LSysExpandOnce, combined with LSysExpand, forms the L-system engine by which we use L-system expansion rules to generate turtle-graphics commands. This file draws no graphics: the L-system engine deals only with text-based rules and is completely separated from the graphics modules. This easy separation is one of the advantages of representing turtle-graphics commands and L-systems as text.

Both LSysExpandOnce and LSysExpand are stored in lsystem.c:

```
/*
 *  lsystem.c
 *  Routines for expanding L-System rules.
 */
#include "lsystem.h"


/*
 * Low-level function expands rule string once.
 * Basically, for every "F" in the cmd_string,
 * replace it with the contents of the rule_string.
 * This dramatically increases the size of the
 * cmd_string after just a few iterations.
 */
void LSysExpandOnce(char* rule_string,
    char* cmd_string)   /* input/output */


{   /* LSysExpandOnce */
    int    i, j, length, length_exp;
```

```c
char    string[LSYS_MAX_RULE_LEN +1];

length = strlen(cmd_string);

length_exp = strlen(rule_string);

string[0] = '\0'; /* terminate */

j = 0;
i = 0;
while((i < length) && (j < LSYS_MAX_RULE_LEN)) {

    /*
     * For this simple system,
     * we only expand on 'F'.
     */
    if (cmd_string[i] == 'F') {

        if (j + length_exp < LSYS_MAX_RULE_LEN) {
            strcat(string, rule_string);
            j += length_exp;
        }

    } else {
        /*
         * We don't expand, just copy over
         * the character.
         */
        string[j] = cmd_string[i];
        j++;
        string[j] = '\0';
```

```
        }

        i++;
    }

    string[j] = '\0';

    strcpy(cmd_string, string);

}   /* LSysExpandOnce */

/*
 * Expands cmd_string number_times.
 */
void LSysExpand(char* rule_string,
    char* cmd_string,
    int number_times)

{   /* LSysExpand */
    int i;

    for (i = 0; i < number_times; i++) {
        LSysExpandOnce(rule_string, cmd_string);
    }

}   /* LSysExpand */

/* end of file lsystem.c */
```

The header file, lsystem.h, with an ANSI C function prototype for the public function follows:

```
/*
 *  lsystem.h
 *  Header file for L-system code.
 */
#ifndef lsystem_h_
#define lsystem_h_   1


/*
 * We allow for a *very* large rule set.
 */
#define LSYS_MAX_RULE_LEN        48000


/*
 * Function to expand an L-system rule.
 */
void LSysExpand(char* start_rule,
        char* rule_string,
        int number_times);


#endif  /* !lsystem_h_ */
/* end of file lsystem.h */
```

Note that we declare a 48,000-byte rule length with the
LSYS_MAX_RULE_LEN macro. This uses up quite a lot of memory, but
you'll soon fill it up if you use five or more iterations for many of the L-systems presented below.

Using L-Systems to Model Plant Growth

L-systems were first created in an effort to model plant growth. In fact, the
[and] turtle commands are essential for this. The turtle stack commands,
[and], allow us to create branches on a tree, as shown in Figure 8.8.

Figure 8.8   *Using brackets to generate tree branches.*

Figure 8.9 represents the turtle commands F [- F] F [+F] F. Using this concept, an example of a weed-shaped plant using L-systems is shown in Figure 8.9.

Figure 8.9   *A representation of a weed: start axiom ++++F;*
expansion rule F[+F]F[-F]F; four iterations; and 25.7-degree turn angle.

We start with ++++F to change the starting direction from going to the right to going up. Most plants grow in an upward direction. A better solution would be to extend the example programs in this chapter to allow the user to specify the starting angle as well as the turn angle.

We can generate a more bushlike picture using rules shown in Figure 8.10.

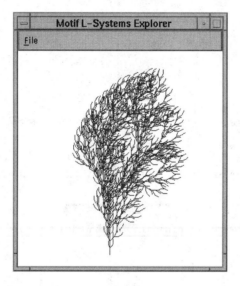

Figure 8.10 *A representation of a bush: start axiom ++++F; expansion rule FF-[-F+F+F]+[+F-F-F]; four iterations; and 22.5-degree turn angle.*

Extending L-Systems

Our examples in this chapter just expand an L-system rule based on just one variable, F. F, conveniently, also happens to be the command for drawing a line. But in the L-system expansion rules, we effectively treat F as a variable that we expand. The first step, then, in extending L-systems is to allow for multiple variables, and having an expansion rule for each one. In the end, all commands must boil down to the set of turtle commands (F, f, +, -, [, and]), or you could have the turtle ignore any unknown variables.

For instance, you might want to set up commands for left and right turns. You could create an L command, for example, that draws a detour one unit length to the left; in other words, an L command that executes a sequence of commands: +F-F-F+. A corresponding right detour could be represented as R and execute the following commands: -F+F+F-. You could also add in multiple variables, where each variable has an expansion rule. Rule expansion becomes more complex, but you get to draw neater pictures.

The next step for extending L-systems is to introduce a bit of uncertainty. Nature and plant growth certainly are not exact, especially by mathematical standards. (Yes, we know that many factors add to the growth patterns of plants: sunlight, rainfall, temperatures, the generic characteristics of the plants, other climatological factors, and soil types and condition. To someone unfamiliar with horticulture, these factors may appear to be random. But our goal isn't to abstractly illustrate how plants should grow; it's to illustrate some interesting examples of graphics programming.) You can have a set of expansion rules and choose which rule to apply at any given expansion step, using a random-number generator. For instance, you could supply four rules, each with an equal probability (one-fourth) of being executed on any attempt to expand a command. What this does is provide for a number of similar, yet different plant shapes. You can use this technique, for example, to fill in a field of weeds and bushes. All the plants would be generated from L-system models, yet each plant would be slightly different, achieving a more realistic look. Other things you might also want to do is to change the fixed step length and add new drawing commands—to fill polygons, for instance.

All in all, there's a lot more to L-systems than our brief introduction. If you're interested in more detail, we suggest you look up the following books: The Algorithmic Beauty of Plants and Chaos and Fractals: New Frontiers of Science. (See Appendix E for expanded book listings.)

A Program to Draw Turtle Graphics

The next step after viewing all this code must be to view more code, right? Actually, the next logical step is to create a program to test out L-systems and turtle graphics. As an extra bonus, we not only provide one program, but two: one using OLIT and one using Motif.

Part of the purpose is to show how easy (or how hard) it is to port between the two toolkits. First, we start with the common code, shared by both the OLIT and Motif versions.

Sharing the Common Code

The file `chap8.c` contains a number of routines, mainly to handle global variables for the current turtle state. All of the code in `chap8.c` works with both Motif and OLIT. Part of the reason for having so many global variables is to allow the user precise control over how the L-systems are drawn. The user can:

✦ Set the turn angle.

✦ Set the scale factor.

✦ Set the number of iterations.

✦ Provide *x* and *y* offsets to center the resulting picture within the drawing window.

Every time we redraw the L-system curve, with the `RedrawAll` function, we must reset the turtle. This is because the ending point of every command becomes the next command's start heading.

The code for these shared routines is stored in `chap8.c`:

```
/*
 *  chap8.c
 *  Generic turtle-drawing code for both
 *  OLIT and Motif from Chapter 8.
 */
#include "xlib.h"
#include "lsystem.h"
#include "turtle.h"


#include <X11/Xutil.h>
```

```
#include <X11/Intrinsic.h>
#include <X11/StringDefs.h>
#include <stdio.h>

/*
 *  Generic turtle globals
 */
Display*    global_display;
Window      global_window;
GC          global_gc;
Turtle      global_turtle;
char        global_command[LSYS_MAX_RULE_LEN+1];
double      global_degrees;
int         global_int_degrees = 1;
int         global_10th_degrees = 0;
int         global_iterations = 1;

/* Redraws the turtle geometry. */
void RedrawAll()

{   /* RedrawAll */

    XClearWindow(global_display, global_window);

    /*
     * Get degrees.
     */
    global_degrees = (double) global_int_degrees +
            ((double) global_10th_degrees / 10);

    /*
```

```
     * Initialize global turtle.
     */
    TurtleInit(&global_turtle,
        (double) 1.0,    /* distance */
        global_degrees);

    TurtleParse(global_display,
        global_window, global_gc,
        &global_turtle, global_command);

    XFlush(global_display);

}    /* RedrawAll */

/* Redraw the drawing area. */
void HandleExpose(XExposeEvent* event)

{   /* HandleExpose */

    if (event->count == 0) {
        RedrawAll();
    }

}    /* HandleExpose */

void ExpandRule(char* axiom, char* rule_string,
    int number_times)

{   /* ExpandRule */

    strcpy(global_command, axiom);
```

```
        LSysExpand(rule_string, global_command, number_times);


        global_iterations = number_times;


}    /* ExpandRule */


/*
 * Sets up all the global turtle parameters.
 * Used to share code between the OLIT and
 * Motif versions of the turtle code.
 *
 * NOTE: the drawingarea widget MUST
 * be realized before calling!!!!
 */


void SetUpTurtle(Widget drawingarea,
    char* colorname)


{    /* SetUpTurtle */
    int             screen;
    unsigned long   color;
    Colormap        colormap;


    /*
     * Now that we have the windows, we
     * can get the window IDs.
     */
    global_display = XtDisplay(drawingarea);
    global_window  = XtWindow(drawingarea);
    screen         = DefaultScreen(global_display);
```

```
/*
 * Create a graphics context.
 */
global_gc = XCreateGC(global_display,
                global_window,
                0L, (XGCValues*) NULL);


/*
 * Get colormap from widget.
 */
XtVaGetValues(drawingarea,
    XtNcolormap, &colormap,
    NULL);


/*
 * Allocate a color and use that for drawing.
 */
color = AllocNamedColor(global_display,
            colormap,
            colorname,
            BlackPixel(global_display, screen) );


XSetForeground(global_display, global_gc, color);

/*
 * Initialize global turtle.
 */
TurtleInit(&global_turtle,
    (double) 1.0,    /* distance */
    global_degrees);
```

```
}    /* SetUpTurtle */


/* end of file chap8.c */
```

Allocating Colors for the L-systems Program

The function `SetUpTurtle`, above, calls our utility function `AllocNamedColor` (from Chapter 7) to allocate a read-only color cell. Since this chapter appears in a section of the book that deals with color, we had better use color. And since we're drawing plant shapes, why not use the color *ForestGreen*? We use this color to draw the turtle-graphic commands. We allocate this color cell from whatever colormap our drawing area widget (`XmDrawingArea` or `DrawArea`) uses. If we change the colormap used by the drawing area widget (see Chapter 10), this routine will still work.

The trick, as shown in the last chapter, is to query the *colormap* resource using `XtVaGetValues` (note that we use the generic Xt naming scheme of `XtNcolormap` from the file `<X11/StringDefs.h>`, which works with both Motif and OLIT). Using `XtVaGetValues`, we get the ID of the colormap used by the drawing area (normally set to the default colormap, but it can be changed). From this colormap, then, we allocate a read-only color cell.

`SetUpTurtle` then sets our graphic context (GC) to draw with the newly allocated color by calling `XSetForeground`. Finally, `SetUpTurtle` calls `TurtleInit` (from `turtle.c`, above, under Source Code for Turtle.c) to set up a global `Turtle` structure, which we use to hold the current state (heading) of the turtle. We pass 1.0 for the distance to make the turtle, by default, move one pixel. The user can adjust the scaling factor to extend this.

The OLIT L-Systems Program

The turtle graphics program creates a main window, just like in Chapters 5 and 6, and another top-level shell window (using the `CreateShell` convenience function from Chapters 5 and 6). This second top-level shell window holds the controls for drawing L-systems. We create six sliders:

✦ The *x* offset, added to the *x* coordinate of all lines.

✦ The *y* offset, added to the *y* coordinate of all lines.

✦ The scale factor, which enlarges or reduces the picture.

✦ The turn angle, in whole degrees, from 1 to 90.

✦ The tenths of degrees for the turn angle. We use a separate slider because it would be impossible to select the right angle, due to the tiny slider scale.

✦ The number of iterations, from 1 to 10. Most L-systems will use three to five iterations.

We then create two prompted text-entry fields, one for the starting command (*axiom*) and the other for the expansion rule. You type in the axiom and expansion rule to draw a picture. Finally, the control window ends with a *Redraw* pushbutton. This button causes the program to expand the L-system commands from the axiom and rule, and then draws the L-system with the new parameters.

We could have initiated a redraw on every change to any of the controls, but found that some L-systems are expensive to generate. Because of this, we wait until the user makes all the desired changes and then redraw only when the *Redraw* button is pushed.

The code to create this control window resides in the `CreateControlWindow` function, below:

```
Widget CreateControlWindow(Widget parent,
        char* app_name,
        char* app_class)


{   /* CreateControlWindow */
    Widget      dialog, row;
    Widget      x_offset, y_offset;
    Widget      iterations, scale;
    Widget      redraw, degrees, tenth_degrees;
    Arg         args[20];
    int         n;
```

```
/*
 * Create a "dialog" to set the values.
 */
dialog = CreateShell(parent,
            app_name, app_class);


n = 0;
row = XtVaCreateManagedWidget("row",
      controlAreaWidgetClass,
      dialog,
      XtNlayoutType, OL_FIXEDCOLS,
      XtNmeasure, 1,
      NULL);


x_offset = CreateHSlider(row, "x_offset",
            0, 400, /* min, max */
            "X Offset",
            (XtCallbackProc) intValueCB,
            (XtPointer) &global_x_offset);


y_offset = CreateHSlider(row, "y_offset",
            0, 400, /* min, max */
            "Y Offset",
            (XtCallbackProc) intValueCB,
            (XtPointer) &global_y_offset);


scale = CreateHSlider(row, "scale",
            1, 10, /* min, max */
            "Scale Factor",
            (XtCallbackProc) intValueCB,
```

```
                            (XtPointer) &global_scale_factor);


        degrees = CreateHSlider(row, "degrees",
                    1, 90, /* min, max */
                    "Degrees",
                    (XtCallbackProc) intValueCB,
                    (XtPointer) &global_int_degrees);


        tenth_degrees = CreateHSlider(row, "tenth_degrees",
                    0, 9, /* min, max */
                    "Tenths of Degrees",
                    (XtCallbackProc) intValueCB,
                    (XtPointer) &global_10th_degrees);


        iterations = CreateHSlider(row, "iterations",
                    1, 10, /* min, max */
                    "Number Iterations",
                    (XtCallbackProc) intValueCB,
                    (XtPointer) &global_iterations);


        start_rule = CreatePrompt(row, "start_rule",
                    "Starting Commands: ",
                    (XtCallbackProc) NULL,
                    (XtPointer) NULL);


        expansion = CreatePrompt(row, }expansion",
                    "Expansion Rule: ",
                    (XtCallbackProc) NULL,
                    (XtPointer) NULL);


        redraw = CreatePushbutton(row, "redraw",
```

```
                (XtCallbackProc) redrawCB,

                (XtPointer) NULL);


      /*

       * Realize "dialog" shell.

       */

      XtRealizeWidget(dialog);


      return dialog;


   }    /* CreateControlWindow */
```

When the user presses the *Redraw* pushbutton (an OLIT OblongButton),
the L-system is redrawn. Because this may take a long time, the *Redraw*
button is ghosted, or grayed out. This means that it refuses to accept user
input. Before we draw, we set the *Redraw* pushbutton to be insensitive to
user input. Usually when this happens, the button's text appears grayed
out. We do this by calling XtSetSensitive:

```
void XtSetSensitive(Widget widget,

        Boolean sensitive_flag);
```

We set the *sensitive_flag* to False to ghost the widget and make it
insensitive to user input. After we finish drawing, we call
XtSetSensitive again, this time passing True for the
sensitive_flag. This turns the widget back on.

If you try this simple technique, you'll soon find a fatal flaw. While the
L-system expansion is going on, the display is not updated. Therefore, the
Redraw button still looks as though it will accept user input. While we
expand the L-system rules, control never returns to the XtAppMainLoop
function. It is from XtAppMainLoop that the widget is drawn grayed out.

There are two solutions for this. First, a well-behaved X program will
periodically check for user input, even in the midst of a time-consuming
operation. In fact, if the operation is really long, you should offer the user a
chance to cancel the operation. Our simple program doesn't do either.

Because of this, we fall back on the second solution. We call OlUpdateDisplay:

```
#include <Xol/OpenLook.h>

void OlUpdateDisplay(Widget widget)
```

OlUpdateDisplay causes an OLIT program to process all pending exposure events and redraw every widget. We call XtSetSensitive and then OlUpdateDisplay. This makes the *Redraw* button appear to be grayed out. Then we expand the L-system rules and redraw. Finally, we set the *Redraw* button to be sensitive to user input again, ending the whole operation.

 OlUpdateDisplay is new in OLIT 3.0.

NOTE

The redrawCB function, below, is the callback for the *Redraw* button:

```
void redrawCB(Widget widget,
    XtPointer client_data,
    XtPointer call_data)

{   /* redrawCB */

    /*
     * Disable user action until done drawing.
     */
    XtSetSensitive(widget, False);

    /* OlUpdateDisplay is new in OLIT 3.0 */
    OlUpdateDisplay(widget);

    ExtractRules();
```

```
RedrawAll();


XtSetSensitive(widget, True);


}    /* redrawCB */
```

When we need to redraw the L-system, we extract the axiom and expansion rule from the two `TextField` widgets. To get the contents of the `TextField` widgets, we query the *string* resource on each, using `XtVaGetValues`. When we're through with the text, we call `XtFree` to free the memory.

The `ExtractRules` function, below, extracts the axiom and expansion rule:

```
void ExtractRules()


{   /* ExtractRules */
    char*    expansion_text;
    char*    start_text;

    /*
     * Extract user text from text widget.
     */
    XtVaGetValues(expansion,
        XtNstring, &expansion_text,
        NULL);


    XtVaGetValues(start_rule,
        XtNstring, &start_text,
        NULL);


    if ((expansion_text != (char*) NULL) &&
```

```
            (start_text != (char*) NULL)) {

        ExpandRule(start_text, expansion_text,
            global_iterations);

        XtFree(start_text);
        XtFree(expansion_text);
    }


}    /* ExtractRules */
```

The OLIT-specific code for our sample program is in `o_chap8.c`:

```
/*
 *   o_chap8.c
 *   OLIT turtle-graphics test
 *   program for Chapter 8.
 */
#include "olit.h"
#include <X11/Xutil.h>
#include <Xol/ControlAre.h>
#include <Xol/DrawArea.h>
#include <stdio.h>


/*
 * Extern functions.
 */
extern void HandleExpose(XExposeEvent* event);

extern void RedrawAll();
```

```
extern void SetUpTurtle(Widget drawingarea,
        char* colorname);

extern void ExpandRule(char* start_rule,
        char* rule_string,
        int number_times);

/*
 * External globals.
 */
extern int  global_x_offset;
extern int  global_y_offset;
extern int  global_scale_factor;
extern int  global_iterations;
extern int  global_int_degrees;
extern int  global_10th_degrees;

/*
 * Local globals.
 */
Widget   expansion, start_rule;

/*
 * Extracts rules from text widgets.
 */
void ExtractRules()

{   /* ExtractRules */
    char*   expansion_text;
    char*   start_text;
```

```
    /*
     * Extract user text from text widget.
     */
    XtVaGetValues(expansion,
        XtNstring, &expansion_text,
        NULL);

    XtVaGetValues(start_rule,
        XtNstring, &start_text,
        NULL);

    if ((expansion_text != (char*) NULL) &&
        (start_text != (char*) NULL)) {

        ExpandRule(start_text, expansion_text,
            global_iterations);

        XtFree(start_text);
        XtFree(expansion_text);
    }

}   /* ExtractRules */

/*
 * Slider callback: changes string values for rules.
 */
void strValueCB(Widget widget,
    XtPointer client_data,
    XtPointer call_data)

{   /* strValueCB */
```

```
        ExtractRules();

}    /* strValueCB */

/*
 * Slider callback: changes an integer value.
 */
void intValueCB(Widget widget,
    XtPointer client_data,
    XtPointer call_data)

{    /* intValueCB */
    int*    value;

    value = (int*) client_data;

    /*
     * Extract slider value.
     */
    *value = *(int*) call_data;

}    /* intValueCB */

/*
 * Redraw pushbutton callback:
 * Redraw the turtle geometry
 * when this is called.
 */
void redrawCB(Widget widget,
    XtPointer client_data,
```

```
        XtPointer call_data)

{   /* redrawCB */

    /*
     * Disable user action until done drawing.
     */
    XtSetSensitive(widget, False);

    /* OlUpdateDisplay is new in OLIT 3.0 */
    OlUpdateDisplay(widget);

    ExtractRules();
    RedrawAll();

    XtSetSensitive(widget, True);

}   /* redrawCB */

void drawCB(Widget widget,
    XtPointer client_data,
    XtPointer call_data)

{   /* drawCB */
    OlDrawAreaCallbackStruct* ptr;

    ptr = (OlDrawAreaCallbackStruct*) call_data;

    if (ptr != NULL) {
        if (ptr->reason == OL_REASON_EXPOSE) {
            HandleExpose( (XExposeEvent*) ptr->event);
```

```
            }

        }


    }    /* drawCB */


/*
 * Create the window of controls
 * for the L-System display.
 */


Widget CreateControlWindow(Widget parent,
        char* app_name,
        char* app_class)


{   /* CreateControlWindow */
    Widget    dialog, row;
    Widget    x_offset, y_offset;
    Widget    iterations, scale;
    Widget    redraw, degrees, tenth_degrees;
    Arg       args[20];
    int       n;


    /*
     * Create a "dialog" to set the values.
     */
    dialog = CreateShell(parent,
                app_name, app_class);


    n = 0;
    row = XtVaCreateManagedWidget("row",
            controlAreaWidgetClass,
```

```
                    dialog,
                    XtNlayoutType, OL_FIXEDCOLS,
                    XtNmeasure, 1,
                    NULL);

x_offset = CreateHSlider(row, "x_offset",
                0, 400, /* min, max */
                "X Offset",
                (XtCallbackProc) intValueCB,
                (XtPointer) &global_x_offset);

y_offset = CreateHSlider(row, "y_offset",
                0, 400, /* min, max */
                "Y Offset",
                (XtCallbackProc) intValueCB,
                (XtPointer) &global_y_offset);

scale = CreateHSlider(row, "scale",
                1, 10, /* min, max */
                "Scale Factor",
                (XtCallbackProc) intValueCB,
                (XtPointer) &global_scale_factor);

degrees = CreateHSlider(row, "degrees",
                1, 90, /* min, max */
                "Degrees",
                (XtCallbackProc) intValueCB,
                (XtPointer) &global_int_degrees);

tenth_degrees = CreateHSlider(row, "tenth_degrees",
                0, 9, /* min, max */
```

```
                   "Tenths of Degrees",
                   (XtCallbackProc) intValueCB,
                   (XtPointer) &global_10th_degrees);


     iterations = CreateHSlider(row, "iterations",
                   1, 10, /* min, max */
                   "Number Iterations",
                   (XtCallbackProc) intValueCB,
                   (XtPointer) &global_iterations);


     start_rule = CreatePrompt(row, "start_rule",
                   "Starting Commands: ",
                   (XtCallbackProc) NULL,
                   (XtPointer) NULL);


     expansion = CreatePrompt(row, "expansion",
                   "Expansion Rule: ",
                   (XtCallbackProc) NULL,
                   (XtPointer) NULL);


     redraw = CreatePushbutton(row, "redraw",
                   (XtCallbackProc) redrawCB,
                   (XtPointer) NULL);


     /*
      * Realize "dialog" shell.
      */
     XtRealizeWidget(dialog);


     return dialog;
```

```
}    /* CreateControlWindow */


int main(int argc, char** argv)


{    /* main */
     XtAppContext  app_context;
     Display*      display;
     Widget        parent;
     Widget        mainwindow;
     Widget        menubar;
     Widget        filemenu;
     Widget        exitchoice;
     Widget        drawingarea;
     Widget        dialog;
     Arg           args[20];
     int           n;


     /* Initialize X toolkit */
     OlToolkitInitialize( (XtPointer) NULL);


     n = 0;


     XtSetArg(args[n], XtNmappedWhenManaged, False); n++;
     XtSetArg(args[n], XtNwidth, 500); n++;
     XtSetArg(args[n], XtNheight, 360); n++;


     parent = XtAppInitialize(&app_context,
             "ProX",                        /* app class */
             (XrmOptionDescList) NULL,  /* options */
             0,                             /* num options */
             ARGC_PTR &argc, argv,      /* cmd line */
```

```
                     (String*) NULL,              /* fallback res. */
                     args, n);


       /*
        * Create Main Window and menubar.
        */
       mainwindow = CreateMainWindow(parent, "main");


       menubar = CreateMenuBar(mainwindow, "menubar");


       /* Create the file menu. */
       filemenu = CreateMenu(menubar, "filemenu");


       /*
        * Create a menu choice to exit the program.
        */
       exitchoice = CreateExitChoice(filemenu, "exitchoice");


       drawingarea = CreateDrawingArea(mainwindow,
                       "drawingarea",
                       500, 500,
                       (XtCallbackProc) drawCB,
                       (XtPointer) NULL);


       SetMainAreas(mainwindow,
              menubar,
              drawingarea);   /* work area */


       /*
        * XtRealizeWidget creates the actual
        * windows on the display.
```

```
    */
  XtRealizeWidget(parent);


  /*
   * Create a "dialog" to set the values.
   */
  dialog = CreateControlWindow(parent, argv[0], "ProX");


  /*
   * Initialize the turtle.
   */
  SetUpTurtle(drawingarea, "forestgreen");


  /*
   * Map parent widget to screen,
   * that is, make it visible.
   */
  XtMapWidget(parent);
  XtAppMainLoop(app_context);


  return 0;


}   /* main */


/* end of file o_chap8.c */
```

A Combined Resource File

The following resource file contains both the OLIT and Motif resources for
our sample program this chapter. Note all the resources for the OLIT control window.

```
!
!    ProX
!
!    Resource file for Chapter 8 of
!    Professional Graphics
!    Programming in the X Window System.
!
!    Place this file in your
!    home directory.
!
!
!    Generic resources.
!
*background:              lightgray
*drawingarea.background:  white


!
! Motif resources.
!
*fontList:                lucidasans-12

*filemenu.labelString:    File
*filemenu.mnemonic:       F

*exitchoice.labelString:  Exit
*exitchoice.mnemonic:     x

*turtledialog.title:      Turtle Parameters
*redraw.labelString:      Redraw

*m_chap8.title:           Motif L-Systems Explorer

!
```

```
! OLIT Resources
!
*exitchoice.label:          Exit
*filemenu.label:            File
*threeD:                    true
*redraw.label:              Redraw


*o_chap8.title:             OLIT L-Systems Explorer


!
! Chapter 8 Control Window resources.
!
*x_offset_label.width:         200
*y_offset_label.width:         200
*scale_label.width:            200
*degrees_label.width:          200
*tenth_degrees_label.width: 200
*iterations_label.width:       200
*start_rule_label.width:       200
*expansion_label.width:        200

*x_offset_value.width:         100
*y_offset_value.width:         100
*scale_value.width:            100
*degrees_value.width:          100
*tenth_degrees_value.width: 100
*iterations_value.width:       100
*start_rule_value.width:       100
*expansion_value.width:        100


! end of file ProX
```

Name this file ProX and place it in your home directory.

Motif Source Code for the Turtle-Graphics Program

The Motif program acts just about the same as the OLIT program, above. The differences are minor. For example, we use XmTextGetString to extract the value of the expansion rule and axiom. In OLIT, we queried the *string* resource. In addition, we need to call XmUpdateDisplay, the Motif function to process all pending exposure events, instead of OlUpdateDisplay:

```
#include <Xm/Xm.h>


void XmUpdateDisplay (Widget widget)
```

The file m_chap8.c contains the Motif-specific code:

```
/*
 *  m_chap8.c
 *  Motif turtle-graphics test
 *  program for Chapter 8.
 */
#include "motif.h"

#include <X11/Xutil.h>
#include <Xm/RowColumn.h>
#include <Xm/Text.h>
#include <stdio.h>

/*
 * Extern functions.
 */
extern void HandleExpose(XExposeEvent* event);
```

```
extern void RedrawAll();

extern void SetUpTurtle(Widget drawingarea,
        char* colorname);

extern void ExpandRule(char* start_rule,
        char* rule_string,
        int number_times);

/*
 * External globals.
 */
extern int   global_x_offset;
extern int   global_y_offset;
extern int   global_scale_factor;
extern int   global_iterations;
extern int   global_int_degrees;
extern int   global_10th_degrees;


/*
 * Local globals.
 */
Widget   expansion, start_rule;


/*
 * Extracts rules from text widgets.
 */
void ExtractRules()

{   /* ExtractRules */
    char*   expansion_text;
```

```
        char*    start_text;


        /*
         * Extract user text from text widget.
         */
        expansion_text = XmTextGetString(expansion);
        start_text     = XmTextGetString(start_rule);


        if ((expansion_text != (char*) NULL) &&
            (start_text != (char*) NULL)) {


            ExpandRule(start_text, expansion_text,
                global_iterations);


            XtFree(start_text);
            XtFree(expansion_text);
        }


    }   /* ExtractRules */


/*
 * Slider callback: changes string values for rules.
 */
void strValueCB(Widget widget,
    XtPointer client_data,
    XtPointer call_data)


{   /* strValueCB */


    ExtractRules();
```

```
}   /* strValueCB */


/*
 * Slider callback: changes an integer value.
 */
void intValueCB(Widget widget,
    XtPointer client_data,
    XtPointer call_data)


{   /* intValueCB */
    XmScaleCallbackStruct*  ptr;
    int*                    value;


    ptr = (XmScaleCallbackStruct*) call_data;


    value = (int*) client_data;


    if (value != (int*) NULL) {
        *value = ptr->value;
    }


}   /* intValueCB */


/*
 * Redraw pushbutton callback:
 * Redraw the turtle geometry
 * when this is called.
 */
void redrawCB(Widget widget,
    XtPointer client_data,
    XtPointer call_data)
```

```
{   /* redrawCB */

    /*
     * Disable user action until done drawing.
     */
    XtSetSensitive(widget, False);
    XmUpdateDisplay(widget);

    ExtractRules();
    RedrawAll();

    XtSetSensitive(widget, True);

}   /* redrawCB */

void drawCB(Widget widget,
    XtPointer client_data,
    XtPointer call_data)

{   /* drawCB */
    XmDrawingAreaCallbackStruct*  ptr;

    ptr = (XmDrawingAreaCallbackStruct*) call_data;

    if (ptr->reason == XmCR_EXPOSE) {
        HandleExpose( (XExposeEvent*) ptr->event);
    }

}   /* drawCB */
```

```
/*
 * Create the window of controls
 * for the L-System display.
 */
Widget CreateControlWindow(Widget parent,
    char* app_name,
    char* app_class)

{   /* CreateControlWindow */
    Widget     dialog, row;
    Widget     x_offset, y_offset;
    Widget     iterations, scale;
    Widget     redraw, degrees, tenth_degrees;
    Arg        args[20];
    int        n;

    /*
     * Create a "dialog" to set the values.
     */
    dialog = CreateShell(parent,
                app_name, app_class);

    n = 0;
    row = XmCreateRowColumn(dialog, "row", args, n);

    x_offset = CreateHSlider(row, "x_offset",
            0, 400, /* min, max */
            "X Offset",
            (XtCallbackProc) intValueCB,
            (XtPointer) &global_x_offset);
```

```
y_offset = CreateHSlider(row, "y_offset",
            0, 400, /* min, max */
            "Y Offset",
            (XtCallbackProc) intValueCB,
            (XtPointer) &global_y_offset);


scale = CreateHSlider(row, "scale",
            1, 10, /* min, max */
            "Scale Factor",
            (XtCallbackProc) intValueCB,
            (XtPointer) &global_scale_factor);


degrees = CreateHSlider(row, "degrees",
            1, 90, /* min, max */
            "Degrees",
            (XtCallbackProc) intValueCB,
            (XtPointer) &global_int_degrees);


tenth_degrees = CreateHSlider(row, "tenth_degrees",
            0, 9, /* min, max */
            "Tenths of Degrees",
            (XtCallbackProc) intValueCB,
            (XtPointer) &global_10th_degrees);


iterations = CreateHSlider(row, "iterations",
            1, 10, /* min, max */
            "Number Iterations",
            (XtCallbackProc) intValueCB,
            (XtPointer) &global_iterations);


start_rule = CreatePrompt(row, "start_rule",
```

```
                    "Starting Commands: ",
                    (XtCallbackProc) NULL,
                    (XtPointer) NULL);


    expansion = CreatePrompt(row, "expansion",
                    "Expansion Rule: ",
                    (XtCallbackProc) NULL,
                    (XtPointer) NULL);


    redraw = CreatePushbutton(row, "redraw",
                    (XtCallbackProc) redrawCB,
                    (XtPointer) NULL);


    XtManageChild(row);


    /*
     * Realize "dialog" shell.
     */
    XtRealizeWidget(dialog);


    return dialog;


}   /* CreateControlWindow */


int main(int argc, char** argv)


{   /* main */
    XtAppContext    app_context;
    Display*        display;
    Widget          parent;
    Widget          mainwindow;
```

```
Widget          menubar;
Widget          filemenu;
Widget          exitchoice;
Widget          drawingarea;
Widget          dialog;
Arg             args[20];
int             n;

/* Initialize X toolkit */
n = 0;
XtSetArg(args[n],
    XmNmappedWhenManaged, False); n++;
XtSetArg(args[n], XmNallowResize, True); n++;
XtSetArg(args[n], XmNwidth,  500); n++;
XtSetArg(args[n], XmNheight, 500); n++;



parent = XtAppInitialize(&app_context,
        "ProX",                      /* app class */
        (XrmOptionDescList) NULL,    /* options */
        0,                           /* num options */
        ARGC_PTR &argc, argv,        /* cmd line */
        (String*) NULL,              /* fallback res. */
        args, n);



/*
 * Create Main Window and menubar.
 */
mainwindow = CreateMainWindow(parent, "main");
```

```
menubar = CreateMenuBar(mainwindow, "menubar");

/* Create the file menu. */
filemenu = CreateMenu(menubar, "filemenu");

/*
 * Create a menu choice to exit the program.
 */
exitchoice = CreateExitChoice(filemenu,
               "exitchoice");

drawingarea = CreateDrawingArea(mainwindow,
               "drawingarea",
               500, 500,
               (XtCallbackProc) drawCB,
               (XtPointer) NULL);

SetMainAreas(mainwindow,
        menubar,
        drawingarea);   /* work area */

/*
 * XtRealizeWidget creates the actual
 * windows on the display.
 */
XtRealizeWidget(parent);

/*
 * Create a dialog to set the values.
 */
dialog = CreateControlWindow(parent,
            argv[0], "ProX");
```

```
      /*
       * Initialize the turtle.
       */

      SetUpTurtle(drawingarea, "forestgreen");

      /*
       * Map parent widget to screen,
       * that is, make it visible.
       */

      XtMapWidget(parent);


      XtAppMainLoop(app_context);


      return 0;


   }    /* main */


   /* end of file m_chap8.c */
```

You can compile the Motif or OLIT version of the sample program—or both if you have access to both Motif and OLIT libraries. As you can tell from the code, the two toolkits are very similar. Both programs use the utility routines introduced in the previous chapters.

Drawing L-Systems with Turtle Graphics

We can use either the OLIT or Motif programs to draw L-systems. All of the example illustations shown so far, for example, were drawn using these programs.

To draw any of the figures in this chapter, fill in the proper values in the control window and then start the drawing with the *Redraw* button. The control or dialog window, as shown in Figure 8.11, controls all the parameters for drawing L-systems.

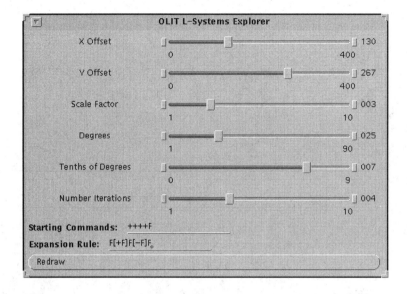

Figure 8.11   The control window.

Play with the scaling factor and *x, y* offsets to center the picture in the window. You can also make the window bigger to display larger L-system pictures. Another example L-system you can draw with this chapter's program is shown in Figure 8.12.

Summary

Turtle graphics forms an effective way to draw space-filling curves and simulated plant growth often seen in popular books on chaotic-systems fractal geometry. The basic idea is simple: you control a turtle that moves about the page. The turtle's tail is a pen. As the turtle moves, the tail, or pen, can be in the down position—drawing—or in the up position—not drawing. In many respects, a turtle acts like a plotter.

You can implement a turtle-graphics system with a very small number of commands. You can move the turtle forward or turn it in place. As the turtle moves forward, if the turtle's tail or pen is down, then a line is drawn. If the tail or pen is up, then the turtle just moves to a new location without drawing a line. The entire system can be set up based on four text commands: F, f, +, and -. We represent the turtle commands as text so that we can easily generate rules. We can then feed these rules to a turtle-graphics engine for drawing, nicely separating the data to draw from the rendering engine.

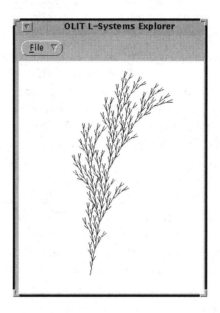

Figure 8.12 *Another representation of a weed: start axiom ++++F;*
expansion rule F[+F]F[-F][F]; four iterations; 20-degree turn angle;
230 x offset; 370 y offset; and a scaling factor of 10.

To draw interesting plantlike pictures, we need to extend our set of turtle-graphics commands. With these commands, we introduce the concept of a stack. The stack holds turtle headings. The new command [pushes the current heading onto a stack. The] command then pops this heading. Together, these commands allow us to better model branches on a plant stem or tree trunk.

Turtle graphics alone aren't very interesting because of the great amount of work you have to do to create a complex set of turtle-graphics commands. If you could build up a complex set of turtle-graphics commands from some set of rules, perhaps applied recursively, you could then draw much more complicated and interesting pictures—such as those created with L-systems. L-systems, or Lindenmayer systems, come from attempts to model plant growth with mathematics. L-systems provide an effective means to generate turtle commands—commands that can be used to draw realistic-looking plants or to display famous Koch, Hilbert, and Sierpinski space-filling curves. The central concepts of L-systems include representing turtle commands as text and expanding or rewriting an initial set of commands—the axiom—with production rules.

To draw an L-system using the turtle-graphics commands in this chapter, we must choose the delta or turn angle. Otherwise, the + and - commands won't work properly. Choosing the proper turn angle is a key requirement in deriving the pictures you want. We also have to choose a unit distance, but this isn't that important. Basically, the unit distance just scales the picture larger or smaller. The turn angle is the key.

Our examples in this chapter just expand an L-system rule based on just one variable, F. F, conveniently, also happens to be the command for drawing a line. But in the L-system expansion rules, we effectively treat F as a variable that we expand. The first step, then, in extending L-systems is to allow for multiple variables, and having an expansion rule for each one. In the end, all commands must boil down to the set of turtle commands (F, f, +, -, [, and]), or you could have the turtle ignore any unknown variables.

This chapter ends with OLIT and Motif-based implementations of the functions and theories introduced in this chapter.

OLIT Functions and Macros
Introduced in This Chapter

```
OlUpdateDisplay
```

Motif Functions and Macros
Introduced in This Chapter

```
XmUpdateDisplay
```

X Toolkit Intrinsics Functions and Macros Introduced in This Chapter

`XtSetSensitive`

Modifying Color Cells

This chapter covers:

- ✦ Allocating writable color cells
- ✦ Changing colors on the fly
- ✦ 3D bevels on widgets
- ✦ Modifying Motif 3D bevel colors
- ✦ A program to choose red, green, and blue (RGB) values with sliders

367

Read/Write Color Cells

Up to now, we've only allocated read-only sharable color cells, with the XAllocColor and XAllocNamedColor functions. Most applications can use read-only color cells to good effect. But many programs need to change the color definitions of allocated cells. This chapter describes how to do just that.

You can allocate a read-only color cell in one step with XAllocColor or XAllocNamedColor. Unlike allocating read-only colors, there's a two-step process for using writable color cells. First, you need to allocate a read/write color cell. Second, you need to store a color definition into that cell. You can later store another color definition into the same cell, changing the color on the fly.

Allocating Writable Color Cells

The two main functions for allocating read/write color cells are XAllocColorCells, covered in this chapter, and XAllocColorPlanes, covered in Chapter 11, which discusses overlay planes.

XAllocColorCells allocates a number of color cells from a given colormap:

```
Status XAllocColorCells(Display* display,
    Colormap colormap,
    Bool contiguous,
    unsigned long* plane_masks, /* RETURN */
    unsigned int   number_planes,
    unsigned long* pixels,      /* RETURN */
    unsigned int   number_pixels)
```

You allocate a number of color cells and color planes. We'll cover the planes part in Chapter 11, so for now, we request zero color planes. Set the *contiguous* parameter to True if the color planes requested must be contiguous. The *pixels* array holds the returned pixel values (unsigned long indexes into the *colormap*). You must allocate an array large enough to hold all the pixels you allocate with XAllocColorCells. The contents of the colors at those indexes are undefined. That is, you have raw cells in the colormap, but nothing has been yet written to those cells. You still have to define the colors.

XAllocColorCells returns a nonzero value on success and zero on failure. In actual code, you use XAllocColorCells like the following:

```
Display*        display;
Colormap        colormap;
int             status;
unsigned long   pixels[4];


colormap = DefaultColormap(display,
                DefaultScreen(display) );


status = XAllocColorCells(display,
            colormap,
            False,
            (unsigned long*) NULL, /* plane masks */
            0,                     /* # plane masks */
            pixels,
            3);


if (status == 0) {
    fprintf(stderr, "ERROR allocating color cells.\n");
    exit(1);
}
```

We set the *contiguous* flag to False, because we're not allocating any color planes (and we have no need for them to be contiguous). If the *status* is a nonzero value, then we have three color cells to use as we see fit, stored in the *pixels* array. It's up to our application to cache the unsigned long values in the *pixels* array.

Once you allocate the color cells, you need to fill in the cells with red, green, and blue color values.

Changing the Definition of Writable Colors

You can change the definition of writable color cells using XStoreColor, XStoreColors, and XStoreNamedColor.

XStoreColor modifies a single cell in a colormap:

```
XStoreColor(Display* display,
    Colormap colormap,
    XColor* xcolor)
```

XStoreColor uses the *pixel* field of the XColor structure to tell it which color cell to modify in the given colormap. The routine then uses the *red*, *green*, *blue*, and *flags* fields to tell it how to modify the color cell.

If you, for example, allocate a single color cell with XAlloc-ColorCells, you can then change (or set for the first time) the color definition of that cell with XStoreColor, using the code below:

```
Display*        display;
Colormap        colormap;
XColor          xcolor;
unsigned long   pixel; /* from XAllocColorCells */

xcolor.pixel = pixel;
xcolor.red   = (65535 * (long) 125) / 256;
xcolor.green = (65535 * (long) 125) / 256;
xcolor.blue  = (65535 * (long) 125) / 256;

xcolor.flags = DoRed | DoGreen | DoBlue;

XStoreColor(display, colormap, &xcolor);
```

The above code sets up a shade of gray (you can tell this because the red, green, and blue values are equal), and scales the values from a 0 to 255 scale. X defines red, green, and blue (RGB) values using a 0 to 65,535 scale. We can create a macro to perform the conversion from the 256-entry scale to the X scale. The `ConvertTo64K` macro below, performs this conversion:

```
#define ConvertTo64K(c)  ((65535 * (long) c)/256)
```

You need to call `XStoreColor` to store initial RGB values into a newly allocated color cell. You can also call `XStoreColor` at any time later to change the value of the allocated color cell. There's no difference between these calls.

With `XStoreColor`, we don't change which cell the color is stored in—the unsigned long pixel value that indexes into the colormap. That will generate an error. Instead, we change the red, green, and blue definition of the color at that cell.

Changing the Definition of Multiple Colors

If you need to store the red, green, and blue values of more than one color at a time, you can use `XStoreColors`:

```
XStoreColors(Display* display,
    Colormap colormap,
    XColor* xcolor_array,
    int number_colors)
```

`XStoreColors` works like `XStoreColor`, except `XStoreColors` takes an array of RGB definitions in the *xcolor_array*. Be sure to set the proper *pixel* field of each of the `XColor` structures in the array.

Storing a Color by Name

You can use the English color names introduced in Chapter 7 to generate an RGB color definition. `XStoreNamedColor` then takes the RGB definition of a named color and sets that definition into a given color cell, identified by the *pixel* parameter:

```
XStoreNamedColor(Display* display,
    Colormap colormap,
    const char* colorname,
    unsigned long pixel,
    int flags)
```

XStoreNamedColor is not commonly used, because most applications that want to change color cells have already determined the RGB definitions of those colors.

Utility Function to Change Color Cells

We put together a convenience function to change the definition of a writable color cell. The ChangeRGBColor function takes in an XColor structure, which is presumed to already have its *pixel* field set to the index of an allocated color cell. Red, green, and blue values are passed to the function. What's odd about these values is that we accept the values in the common scale of 0 to 255 and scale the values to X's uncommon scale of 0 to 65,535. We use the ChangeRGBColor function in the sample Motif program used to choose RGB values, below. (ChangeRGBColor is not limited to use with Motif, though, as it should work with any X application.)

The ChangeRGBColor function is stored in the file chgcolor.c:

```
/*
 * chgcolor.c
 * Routines to change colormap entries.
 */
#include "xlib.h"

/*
 * Convert an RGB value from a 0-255
```

```
 * scale to X's 0-65535 scale.
 */
#define ConvertTo64K(c)    ((65535 * (long) c)/256)


/*
 * Changes a colormap entry based on RGB values
 * that go from 0 to 255. X RGB values go from
 * 0 to 65535.
 */
void ChangeRGBColor(Display* display,
    Colormap colormap, XColor* xcolor,
    int red, int green, int blue)

{   /* ChangeRGBColor */

    xcolor->red   = ConvertTo64K(red);
    xcolor->green = ConvertTo64K(green);
    xcolor->blue  = ConvertTo64K(blue);


    xcolor->flags = DoRed | DoGreen | DoBlue;


    XStoreColor(display, colormap, xcolor);


}   /* ChangeRGBColor */


/* end of file chgcolor.c */
```

All you really need to change color cells are the XAllocColorCells and XStoreColor functions. In fact, we use these functions in a program below (under Choosing RGB Values in Depth), which is used to show the 3D bevel colors Motif would place on any base color.

3D Bevels

Most X toolkits provide a form of 3D beveling on your application's widgets. This supposedly makes the controls in the interface stand out with simulated texture and depth.

Motif programs provide a rectangularly shaped bevel around most control widgets; that is, widgets that normally accept user input. A label widget, for example, tends to be flat while a pushbutton widget, which accepts mouse (and sometimes keyboard) input, sports a 3D beveled effect.

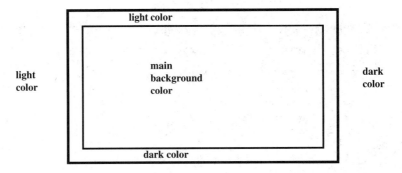

Figure 9.1 *3D bevels.*

The top and left side of the bevel usually has a lighter color, to present the illusion of a light source that is in the upper left corner. The bottom and right sides use a darker color, where as the middle uses the main background color—normally somewhere between the light and the dark colors.

OLIT 3D Bevels

The Open Look Intrinsics Toolkit (OLIT) provides a rounded 3D look on color systems and a 2D flat look on monochrome systems. You can also use a command-line parameter to use the 2D effects on a color system, or set the *threeD* resource, introduced in Chapter 6, (under Resource File for the Sample Program) to `false`. You can set the *threeD* resource in an X resource file to true to turn on the 3D bevel effects:

```
*threeD:     true
```

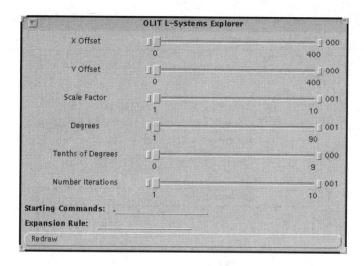

Figure 9.2   *OLIT program with 3D bevels.*

To turn off the 3D effects, use:

```
*threeD:     false
```

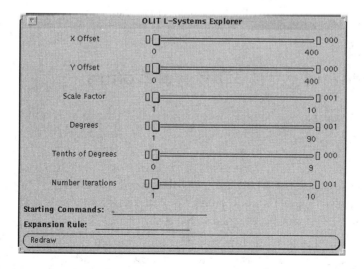

Figure 9.3   *OLIT program without 3D bevels.*

As with Motif, OLIT controls sport the 3D bevels, while display-only widgets normally look flat.

Motif 3D Bevels

Motif's bevels look a lot like OLIT's. With Motif, however, you can change the values of these bevel colors. The *topShadowColor* resource holds the color for the top part of the bevel. Similarly, the *bottomShadowColor* resource holds the color for the bottom part of the bevel.

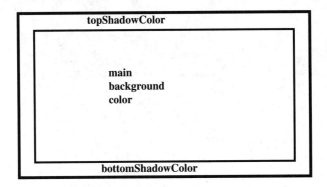

Figure 9.4 *Motif 3D bevel resources.*

Determining the 3D Bevel Colors

Motif automatically generates what the toolkit thinks are "good" 3D bevel colors for any given background color. You'll note that all this hinges on choosing a background color in the first place. The way the Motif toolkit does this is to call a *color-calculation function*. This function is called under the hood by the Motif routines that need to determine the 3D bevel colors for a widget. The color-calculation function also determines the selection and foreground colors for the widget, too.

The normal algorithm for choosing these colors is to use 85 percent of the background color for the bottom shadow and 150 percent for the top shadow. (Treat this as a rule of thumb, as the actual algorithm is a little more involved than this.) Background colors should be in the middle of the

RGB scale. Ideally, the brightest (highest) value for red, green, or blue should be greater than 155 (on a 0 to 255 scale) and less than 175.

If you don't like this algorithm, though, you can customize it by changing the Motif color-calculation function. Motif allows you to pass your own function pointer to be used in place of the default function. Actually, the default color-calculation function uses a relatively good algorithm. In most cases, if you want to customize this, it's because you need to strictly control the colors used by Motif. For example, if you have a system that supports only 256 colors and you intend to display color image files, you want as many of those 256 colors as possible for your image files. By changing the color-calculation function, you have greater control over how many colors the Motif toolkit code actually allocates. Note that this color-calculation function affects only your program. It does not change any other X or Motif program on the display.

You can change the default color-calculation function with XmSetColorCalculation:

```
#include <Xm/Xm.h>

XmColorProc
    XmSetColorCalculation(XmColorProc color_function)
```

XmSetColorCalculation takes your function pointer, *color_function*, and uses that to perform the color calculations. XmSetColorCalculation returns the previous color-calculation function.

The XmColorProc type is a function pointer for a color-calculation function. This function takes the following parameters:

```
void color_function(XColor* background_color,
    XColor* foreground_color,
    XColor* selection_color,
    XColor* top_shadow_color,
    XColor* bottom_shadow_color)
```

You can retrieve the current color-calculation function with XmGetColorCalculation:

```
XmColorProc XmGetColorCalculation(void)
```

You can test out Motif's ability to override the color-calculation function with the simple Motif test program shown just below. The `mcolor` program calls XmSetColorCalculation to set our *color_function* as the color-calculation function and then creates a simple pushbutton widget. The color-calculation function then uses a bizarre algorithm to choose the RGB values for the 3D bevel colors. We use the standard RGB definition of maroon, 143, 0, 82, as the bottom shadow color and the RGB definition of lime green, 0, 175, 20, for the top shadow color.

These colors were chosen to stand out. Why? So that we could instantly see that our color-calculation function was actually called. To also highlight this, the function prints out a message to standard output.

The file `mcolor.c`, below, contains this program:

```
/*
 *  mcolor.c
 *  Motif test program for Chapter 9,
 *  which uses Motif color calculation
 *  functions.
 */
#include "motif.h"
#include <Xm/PushB.h>
#include <stdio.h>


/*
 * Convert an RGB value from a 0-255
 * scale to X's 0-65535 scale.
 */
#define ConvertTo64K(c)   ((65535 * (long) c)/256)


/*
 * Our simple Motif color
 * calculation function.
 */
```

```
void color_function(XColor* background_color,
    XColor* foreground_color,
    XColor* selection_color,
    XColor* top_shadow_color,
    XColor* bottom_shadow_color)

{   /* color_function */

    /*
     * Print a message to show we're here.
     */
    printf("In color_function.\n");

    /* Maroon, from rgb.txt */
    foreground_color->red   = ConvertTo64K(143);
    foreground_color->green = ConvertTo64K(0);
    foreground_color->blue  = ConvertTo64K(82);
    foreground_color->flags = DoRed | DoGreen | DoBlue;

    bottom_shadow_color->red   = ConvertTo64K(143);
    bottom_shadow_color->green = ConvertTo64K(0);
    bottom_shadow_color->blue  = ConvertTo64K(82);
    bottom_shadow_color->flags = DoRed | DoGreen | DoBlue;

    /* LimeGreen, from rgb.txt */
    top_shadow_color->red   = ConvertTo64K(0);
    top_shadow_color->green = ConvertTo64K(175);
    top_shadow_color->blue  = ConvertTo64K(20);
    top_shadow_color->flags = DoRed | DoGreen | DoBlue;

    selection_color->red   = ConvertTo64K(0);
```

```
        selection_color->green = ConvertTo64K(175);
        selection_color->blue  = ConvertTo64K(20);
        selection_color->flags = DoRed | DoGreen | DoBlue;


}    /* color_function */


/* Simple Exit callback. */
static void exitCB(Widget widget,
        XtPointer client_data,
        XtPointer call_data)


{       /* exitCB */


        exit(0);


}       /* exitCB */


int main(int argc, char** argv)


{   /* main */
    XtAppContext    app_context;
    Widget          parent;
    Widget          exitchoice;
    Arg             args[20];
    int             n;


    /* Initialize X toolkit */
    n = 0;
    parent = XtAppInitialize(&app_context,
            "ProX",                     /* app class */
            (XrmOptionDescList) NULL,  /* options */
```

```
        0,                         /* num options */
        ARGC_PTR &argc, argv,      /* cmd line */
        (String*) NULL,            /* fallback res. */
        args, n);



/*
 * Set Motif color calculation.
 */
(void) XmSetColorCalculation(
        (XmColorProc) color_function);


/*
 * Now, create a pushbutton, which should
 * use the new colors.
 */
n = 0;
exitchoice = XmCreatePushButton(parent,
                "exitchoice", args, n);


XtAddCallback(exitchoice,
    XmNactivateCallback,
    (XtCallbackProc) exitCB,
    (XtPointer) NULL);


XtManageChild(exitchoice);


XtRealizeWidget(parent);


XtAppMainLoop(app_context);
```

```
    return 0;


}    /* main */


/* end of file mcolor.c */
```

When you run this program, you should see the following message:

```
In color_function.
```

WARNING

We had a lot of problems with our color-calculation function when running the program on Hewlett-Packard systems. The HP VUE environment comes with customized Motif libraries, and a lot of the HP changes have to do with specifying colors for widgets. (The VUE environment supports the concept of color schemes, where the user can choose a set of colors, and then VUE-aware applications take on those colors.)

We found, in fact, that our color-calculation function was never called in the default case. To get this color function to work, you must set up a color resource that is not a program-wide default. For instance, if you modify your ProX resource file in your home directory, this program works fine on HP systems. Change this line:

```
    *background:    lightgray
```

to this:

```
    ProX*background:    lightgray
```

By using the application class name, ProX, we use a more detailed resource command to set the color, and this keeps VUE out of the way, at least insofar as our *color_function* gets called.

If you don't make a change like this, your color-calculation function will simply never be called. (For this problem, it doesn't matter if your color-calculation function works or not, as it never gets called.)

In addition to XmSetColorCalculation and XmGetColorCalculation, there's a few more Motif-specific functions that control widget colors, including the 3D bevel colors.

Allocating the 3D Bevel Colors

The Motif function XmGetColors calls the current color-calculation function and then allocates the necessary colors using XAllocColor. XmGetColors takes the following parameters:

```
#include <Xm/Xm.h>

void XmGetColors(Screen* screen,
        Colormap color_map,
        Pixel background,
        Pixel* foreground_ret,     /* RETURN */
        Pixel* top_shadow_ret,     /* RETURN */
        Pixel* bottom_shadow_ret,  /* RETURN */
        Pixel* select_ret)         /* RETURN */
```

The Pixel type is a typedef for a unsigned long value.

Normally, your code won't need to call XmGetColors.

Changing the Color of a Widget

New in Motif 1.2, XmChangeColor changes the color of a widget. In doing so, XmChangeColor recalculates the 3D bevel colors:

```
#include <Xm/Xm.h>


void XmChangeColor(Widget widget,
        Pixel background)
```

These Motif color-calculation functions are good for two main purposes. First, we may need to exercise tight control over how Motif allocates colors. Using our own color-calculation functions allows for better control. Second, we may just want to find out what Motif will use for the 3D bevel colors, for a given background color. This information is useful when planning a user interface.

With any toolkit, we find a common problem is choosing colors that look good on the display. A common way to solve this problem is to run a color-editing application and test out different colors. These applications typically present slider widgets, one each for red, green, and blue, to change the RGB values.

A Program to Choose RGB Values

The above program, `mcolor.c`, showed how to change the way Motif allocates colors. It was mainly concerned with changing the default color-calculation function. In many cases, though, we're not concerned with overriding this function, but merely using it to generate 3D bevel colors. To help you design your application interfaces, we put together a program that shows how to change color cells and allows you to choose a good-looking color for your Motif widgets. (You could also implement a similar program using OLIT, except for the color calculation function part.)

Like the last chapter, this program uses sliders to choose a value between a minimum and a maximum. Our program below uses three sliders (Motif XmScale widgets) to choose the red, green, and blue values for a color, using the common scale of 0 to 255. You get to see the changes instantly on the display as you move about the three sliders.

In addition, we use the Motif color-calculation function to determine what Motif would use for the top and bottom shadow colors for your color. We present those colors, too, in a window that shows an enlarged 3D beveled rectangle that looks a lot like a Motif widget. The end result, as portrayed in black and white, is shown in Figure 9.5.

Our program, using the inspired name of chap9, uses the techniques introduced so far in this chapter, as well as a few new quirks. In addition to using the Motif color-calculation function, the chap9 program uses XmScale widgets in a new way as the RGB-choosing sliders and introduces a new widget, the paned window widget.

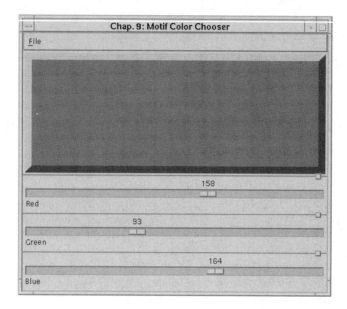

Figure 9.5 *Choosing a color using RGB sliders.*

Choosing RGB Values in Depth

The `AllocColorCells` function, below, allocates three writable color cells using `XAllocColorCells`. The first cell is for the top part of the 3D bevel, the second for the widget background, and the third for the bottom part of the bevel.

Once the colors are allocated, the program calls our utility function `ChangeRGBColor` (from `chgcolor.c` above) to store in black (RGB `0/0/0`) in the second color cell. This is for the drawing area widget's background color. Once we have a color set up, the function `DetermineBevel` calls on the current Motif color-calculation function to get the top and bottom shadow colors for the current background color. Once these colors are determined, `XStoreColor` sets up the top and bottom color cells:

```
/*
 *   Global
 */
```

```
Display*        global_display;
Colormap        global_colormap;
unsigned long   global_top, global_main, global_bottom;
XColor          global_color;


void DetermineBevel()


{   /* DetermineBevel */
    XmColorProc color_proc;
    XColor      fore_color, select_color;
    XColor      top_color, bottom_color;

    /*
     * Get Motif color procedure.
     */
    color_proc = XmGetColorCalculation();

    /*
     * Now, get what Motif thinks are
     * good RGB bevel colors.
     */
    color_proc(&global_color,
        &fore_color,
        &select_color,
        &top_color,
        &bottom_color);

    /*
     * Now, store the new color values.
     */
    top_color.pixel = global_top;
```

```
    top_color.flags = DoRed | DoGreen | DoBlue;

XStoreColor(global_display,
    global_colormap,
    &top_color);

    bottom_color.pixel = global_bottom;
    bottom_color.flags = DoRed | DoGreen | DoBlue;

XStoreColor(global_display,
    global_colormap,
    &bottom_color);


}   /* DetermineBevel */
```

The `DetermineBevel` function is called every time one of the red, green, or blue sliders changes value, because this changes the color to display and hence the top and bottom shadow colors.

Slider Callbacks

Whenever one of the three slider values changes, Motif calls our `colorCB` function, which we set up as the `valueChangedCallback` in the three calls to `CreateHSlider`.

This short callback retrieves the value of the current slider and stores it in the variable that the *client_data* points at. We use this technique to reuse the `colorCB` function for each of the three sliders. Since all the code is the same, except for the variable to store the data in, why not reuse the callback function?

After the current slider value is retrieved, the `colorCB` function changes the color definition of our main color (used as a background color). Once we have the new RGB values for this color, we call `DetermineBevel`, (see the function above) to determine the 3D bevel colors. Finally, the `colorCB` function calls `RedrawAll` to redraw the beveled widget. `RedrawAll` in turn calls `DrawBevel` (see `bevel.c` below, under Source Code for Drawing

3D Bevels) to draw a rectangle into a drawing area widget. This rectangle sports 3D bevels to look like a Motif widget.

```
static void colorCB(Widget widget,
        XtPointer client_data,
        XtPointer call_data)

{   /* colorCB */
    XmScaleCallbackStruct* ptr;
    int*                   value;

    /*
     * Get slider value.
     */
    ptr = (XmScaleCallbackStruct*) call_data;

    value = (int*) client_data;

    *value = ptr->value;

    /*
     * Translate from 0-255 to 0-65535 for X
     * and change color in colormap.
     */
    ChangeRGBColor(global_display,
        global_colormap,
        &global_color,
        red, green, blue);

    DetermineBevel();
    RedrawAll();

}   /* colorCB */
```

The normal callback we've been using for the Motif XmScale widget has been the valueChangedCallback. This callback gets executed when the value of the slider changes, obviously. But there's an odd quirk in Motif: the valueChangedCallback won't be called until the user is done moving the slider—that is, when the user lets up on the mouse button. If you think about this for a moment, this isn't what we want for a dynamic RGB chooser. We want the color displayed in the window changed to reflect the new RGB values when the user moves the slider back and forth.

Motif also supports this model as well, with the dragCallback. The dragCallback is called as the slider itself moves while the user drags the slider's thumb using the mouse. We can set up this callback using XtAddCallback. For example, the code below shows how we use the utility function CreateHSlider to create the XmScale widget. CreateHSlider also sets up the valueChangedCallback. Then we call XtAddCallback to set up the dragCallback.

```
red_slider = CreateHSlider(pane, "Red", 0, 255,
              "Red", colorCB, (XtPointer) &red);

XtAddCallback(red_slider, XmNdragCallback,
    colorCB, (XtPointer) &red);
```

The Paned Window Widget

The program below uses a simple Motif container widget, the paned window widget. This widget lays out its child widgets in a series of panes, strewn vertically down the main window. Between each pane, a sash widget allows the user to resize each individual pane's height.

We create a paned window widget with XmCreatePanedWindow:

```
#include <Xm/PanedW.h>

Widget XmCreatePanedWindow(Widget parent,
        char* widget_name,
        ArgList args
        Cardinal number_args)
```

Source Code for the Chapter 9 Program

The RGB color-chooser program for Chapter 9 is stored in the file chap9.c:

```
/*
 *   chap9.c
 *   Motif test program for Chapter 9.
 *   Edit 3D bevel colors for Motif
 *   (and other) widgets.
 */
#include "motif.h"
#include <X11/Xutil.h>


#include <Xm/PanedW.h>
#include <stdio.h>


/*
 *   Globals
 */
Display*        global_display;
Window          global_window;
GC              global_gc;
Colormap        global_colormap;
int             global_width, global_height;
unsigned long   global_top, global_main, global_bottom;
int             red, green, blue;
XColor          global_color;

/* External functions */
extern void DrawBevel(Display* display,
        Window window, GC gc,
```

```
                    int width, int height,
                    unsigned long top,      /* 3D top bevel color */
                    unsigned long main,     /* main background color */
                    unsigned long bottom);  /* 3D bottom bevel color */


extern void ChangeRGBColor(Display* display,
        Colormap colormap, XColor* color,
        int red, int green, int blue);


/*
 * Redraw all of drawing area.
 */
void RedrawAll()

{   /* RedrawAll */


    DrawBevel(global_display, global_window,
        global_gc, global_width, global_height,
        global_top, global_main, global_bottom);


    XFlush(global_display);


}   /* RedrawAll */


/*
 * Expose callback for drawing area.
 */
void drawCB(Widget widget, XtPointer client_data,
                        XtPointer call_data)


{   /* drawCB */
```

```
    XmDrawingAreaCallbackStruct* ptr;


    ptr =
        (XmDrawingAreaCallbackStruct*) call_data;


    if (ptr->reason == XmCR_EXPOSE) {
        if (ptr->event->xexpose.count == 0) {
                RedrawAll();
        }
    }


    if (ptr->reason == XmCR_RESIZE) {
        /*
         * Many versions of Motif skip the
         * event field here.
         */
        if (ptr->event != (XEvent*) NULL) {
            global_width  = ptr->event->xconfigure.width;
            global_height = ptr->event->xconfigure.height;
        } else {
            XtVaGetValues(widget,
                XmNwidth,  &global_width,
                XmNheight, &global_height,
                NULL);
        }
    }


} /* drawCB */


/*
 * Determines new bevel colors, based on
```

```
 * initial color.
 */
void DetermineBevel()

{   /* DetermineBevel */
    XmColorProc color_proc;
    XColor      fore_color, select_color;
    XColor      top_color, bottom_color;

    /*
     * Get Motif color procedure.
     */
    color_proc = XmGetColorCalculation();

    /*
     * Now, get what Motif thinks are
     * good RGB bevel colors.
     */
    color_proc(&global_color,
        &fore_color,
        &select_color,
        &top_color,
        &bottom_color);

    /*
     * Now, store the new color values.
     */
    top_color.pixel = global_top;
    top_color.flags = DoRed | DoGreen | DoBlue;

    XStoreColor(global_display,
```

```
            global_colormap,
            &top_color);


        bottom_color.pixel = global_bottom;
        bottom_color.flags = DoRed | DoGreen | DoBlue;


        XStoreColor(global_display,
            global_colormap,
            &bottom_color);


}   /* DetermineBevel */


/*
 * Callback to change RGB values.
 */
static void colorCB(Widget widget,
        XtPointer client_data,
        XtPointer call_data)


{   /* colorCB */
    XmScaleCallbackStruct* ptr;
    int*                   value;


    /*
     * Get slider value.
     */
    ptr = (XmScaleCallbackStruct*) call_data;


    value = (int*) client_data;


    *value = ptr->value;
```

```
    /*
     * Translate from 0-255 to 0-65535 for X
     * and change color in colormap.
     */
    ChangeRGBColor(global_display,
        global_colormap,
        &global_color,
        red, green, blue);

    DetermineBevel();
    RedrawAll();

}   /* colorCB */

void AllocColorCells()

{   /* AllocColorCells */
    int     status;
    unsigned long   pixels[4];

    global_colormap = DefaultColormap(global_display,
            DefaultScreen(global_display) );

    status = XAllocColorCells(global_display,
            global_colormap,
            False,  /* not contiguous */
            (unsigned long*) NULL, /* plane masks */
            0,          /* # plane masks */
            pixels,
            3);
```

```
        if (status == 0) {
            fprintf(stderr,
                "ERROR allocating color cells.\n");
            exit(1);
        }


        global_top    = pixels[0];
        global_main   = pixels[1];
        global_bottom = pixels[2];


    }   /* AllocColorCells */


int main(int argc, char** argv)


{   /* main */
    XtAppContext    app_context;
    Display*        display;
    Widget          parent;
    Widget          mainwindow;
    Widget          menubar;
    Widget          filemenu;
    Widget          exitchoice;
    Widget          pane;
    Widget          red_slider;
    Widget          green_slider, blue_slider;
    Widget          drawingarea;
    Arg             args[20];
    int             n;
    int             screen;
```

```
/* Initialize X toolkit */
n = 0;
XtSetArg(args[n], XmNmappedWhenManaged, False); n++;
XtSetArg(args[n], XmNallowResize, True); n++;
XtSetArg(args[n], XmNwidth, 520); n++;
XtSetArg(args[n], XmNheight, 430); n++;



parent = XtAppInitialize(&app_context,
        "ProX",                     /* app class */
        (XrmOptionDescList) NULL,   /* options */
        0,                          /* num options */
        ARGC_PTR &argc, argv,       /* cmd line */
        (String*) NULL,             /* fallback res. */
        args, n);



/*
 * Create Main Window with utility function.
 */
mainwindow = CreateMainWindow(parent, "main");


/*
 * Create menu bar with utility function.
 */
menubar = CreateMenuBar(mainwindow, "menubar");


/*
 * Create the file menu.
 */
filemenu = CreateMenu(menubar, "filemenu");
```

```
/* Create a menu choice to exit the program. */
exitchoice = CreateExitChoice(filemenu,
                "exitchoice");

/*
 * Create a paned window to hold the drawing
 * area and the three sliders.
 */
n = 0;
pane = XmCreatePanedWindow(mainwindow,
            "paned", args, n);

global_width = 520;
global_height = 200;
drawingarea = CreateDrawingArea(pane,
                "drawingarea",
                global_width, global_height,
                (XtCallbackProc) drawCB,
                (XtPointer) NULL);

/*
 * Create three sliders and set up
 * callbacks.
 */
red_slider = CreateHSlider(pane, "Red", 0, 255,
        "Red", colorCB, (XtPointer) &red);

XtAddCallback(red_slider, XmNdragCallback,
    colorCB, (XtPointer) &red);
```

```
green_slider = CreateHSlider(pane, "Green", 0, 255,
        "Green", colorCB, (XtPointer) &green);

XtAddCallback(green_slider, XmNdragCallback,
    colorCB, (XtPointer) &green);

blue_slider = CreateHSlider(pane, "Blue", 0, 255,
        "Blue", colorCB, (XtPointer) &blue);

XtAddCallback(blue_slider, XmNdragCallback,
    colorCB, (XtPointer) &blue);

XtManageChild(pane);

SetMainAreas(mainwindow,
        menubar,
        pane);        /* work area */

/* Create the windows. */
XtRealizeWidget(parent);

/*
 * Now that we have the windows, we
 * can get the window IDs.
 */
global_display = XtDisplayOfObject(drawingarea);
global_window  = XtWindowOfObject(drawingarea);
screen         = DefaultScreen(global_display);

/*
 * Create a graphics context.
```

```
    */
global_gc = XCreateGC(global_display, global_window,
        OL, (XGCValues*) NULL);


XSetForeground(global_display, global_gc,
    BlackPixel(global_display, screen) );

/*
 * Allocate three colors
 */
AllocColorCells();
global_color.pixel = global_main;

/*
 * Store RGB values for the 3 colors.
 */
red    = 0;
green  = 0;
blue   = 0;


ChangeRGBColor(global_display, global_colormap,
        &global_color, red, green, blue);


DetermineBevel();

/* Map parent */
XtMapWidget(parent);
XtAppMainLoop(app_context);


return 0;
```

```
}    /* main */


/* end of file chap9.c */
```

Source Code for Drawing 3D Bevels

The file bevel.c contains the DrawBevel function. This function draws a 3D beveled rectangle in the given size, using the *top*, *main*, and *bottom* colors passed to it. DrawBevel, in turn, calls DrawTopBevel and DrawBottomBevel to draw the top and bottom bevels, respectively:

```
/*
 *  bevel.c
 *  Routine for drawing a 3D beveled rectangle.
 */
#include  <X11/Xlib.h>


/*
 * Draws the top part of the 3D bevel.
 */
static void DrawTopBevel(Display* display,
    Drawable drawable,
    GC gc,
    int width, int height,
    unsigned long top,      /* 3D top bevel color */
    int bevel_width,
    int bevel_height)

{   /* DrawTopBevel */
    XPoint  points[20];
```

```
        points[0].x = 0;
        points[0].y = 0;

        points[1].x = width;
        points[1].y = 0;

        points[2].x = width - bevel_width;
        points[2].y = bevel_height;

        points[3].x = bevel_width;
        points[3].y = bevel_height;

        points[4].x = bevel_width;
        points[4].y = height - bevel_height;

        points[5].x = 0;
        points[5].y = height;

            /* close polygon */
        points[6].x = 0;
        points[6].y = 0;

        /*
         * Set top color
         */
        XSetForeground(display, gc, top);

        XFillPolygon(display, drawable, gc,
            points, 7, Complex, CoordModeOrigin);

    }    /* DrawTopBevel */
```

```
/*
 * Draws the bottom part of the 3D bevel.
 */
static void DrawBottomBevel(Display* display,
    Drawable drawable,
    GC gc,
    int width, int height,
    unsigned long bottom,  /* bottom 3D bevel color */
    int bevel_width,
    int bevel_height)

{   /* DrawBottomBevel */
    XPoint  points[20];

    points[0].x = 0;
    points[0].y = height;

    points[1].x = width;
    points[1].y = height;

    points[2].x = width;
    points[2].y = 0;

    points[3].x = width - bevel_width;
    points[3].y = bevel_height;

    points[4].x = width - bevel_width;
    points[4].y = height - bevel_height;

    points[5].x = bevel_width;
```

```
        points[5].y = height - bevel_height;


            /* close polygon */
        points[6].x = 0;
        points[6].y = height;


        /*
         * Set bottom color
         */
        XSetForeground(display, gc, bottom);


        XFillPolygon(display, drawable, gc,
            points, 7, Complex, CoordModeOrigin);


    }   /* DrawBottomBevel */


    /*
     * Draws a rectangle with a 3D bevel, a la Motif.
     */
    void DrawBevel(Display* display,
        Drawable drawable,
        GC gc,
        int width, int height,
        unsigned long top,      /* 3D top bevel color */
        unsigned long main,     /* main background color */
        unsigned long bottom)   /* 3D bottom bevel color */


    {   /* DrawBevel */
        XPoint  points[20];
        int     bevel_width, bevel_height;


        /*
```

```
 * Determine the size of our bevels.
 */
bevel_width = 12;

if (width < 30) {
    bevel_width = 2;
    }

bevel_height = 12;

if (height < 30) {
    bevel_height = 2;
}

DrawTopBevel(display, drawable, gc,
    width, height, top,
    bevel_width, bevel_height);

DrawBottomBevel(display, drawable, gc,
    width, height, bottom,
    bevel_width, bevel_height);

/*
 * Set main color
 */
XSetForeground(display, gc, main);

/*
 * Draw main area—the area between
 * the top and bottom bevels.
 */
```

```
    XFillRectangle(display, drawable, gc,
        bevel_width, bevel_height,
        width - (2 * bevel_width),
        height - (2 * bevel_height) );


}   /* DrawBevel */


/* end of file bevel.c */
```

Resource File for the Example Program

The following resource file contains the Motif resources for this chapter's
example program:

```
!
! ProX
!
! Resource file for Chapter 9 of
! Professional Graphics
! Programming in the X Window System.
!
! Generic resources.
!
*background:    #cccccc


!
! Motif resources.
!
*fontList:              lucidasans-12


*filemenu.labelString:   File
```

```
*filemenu.mnemonic:      F

*exitchoice.labelString: Exit
*exitchoice.mnemonic:    x

*chap9.title: Chap. 9: Motif Color Chooser

! end of file ProX
```

Name this file `ProX` and place it in your home directory.

Summary

To this point in the book, we've only allocated read-only sharable color cells. Most applications can use read-only color cells to good effect. But many programs need to change the color definitions of allocated cells. You can allocate a read-only color cell in one step with `XAllocColor` or `XAlloc-NamedColor`. Unlike allocating read-only colors, there's a two-step process for using writable color cells. First, you need to allocate a read/write color cell. Second, you need to store a color definition into that cell. You can later store another color definition into the same cell, changing the color on the fly. The two main functions for allocating read/write color cells are `XAllocColorCells`, covered in this chapter, and `XAllocColorPlanes`, covered in Chapter 11, which discusses overlay planes.

You can change the definition of writable color cells using `XStoreColor`, `XStoreColors`, and `XStoreNamedColor`.

The functions come in handy when dealing with 3D looks in both OLIT and Motif. Most X toolkits provide a form of 3D beveling on your application's widgets. This supposedly makes the controls in the interface stand out with simulated texture and depth. Motif programs provide a rectangularly shaped bevel around most control widgets; that is, widgets that normally accept user input. A label widget, for example, tends to be flat, while a pushbutton widget, which accepts mouse (and sometimes keyboard) input, sports a 3D beveled effect. Open Look provides a rounded 3D look on color systems and a 2D flat look on monochrome systems.

Motif automatically generates what the toolkit thinks are "good" 3D bevel colors for any given background color. You'll note that all this hinges on choosing a background color in the first place. The way the Motif toolkit does this is to call a color-calculation function. This function is called under the hood by the Motif routines that need to determine the 3D bevel colors for a widget. The color-calculation function also determines the selection and foreground colors for the widget, too. The normal algorithm for choosing these colors is to use 85 percent of the background color for the bottom shadow and 150 percent for the top shadow. (Treat this as a rule of thumb, as the actual algorithm is a little more involved than this.) Background colors should be in the middle of the red, green, blue (RGB) scale. Ideally, the brightest (highest) value for red, green, or blue should be greater than 155 (on a 0 to 255 scale) and less than 175. If you don't like this algorithm, though, you can customize it by changing the Motif color-calculation function. You can change the default color-calculation function with XmSetColorCalculation.

The chapter ends with a program that draws a 3D beveled rectangle in the given size, using the *top*, *main*, and *bottom* colors passed to it. DrawBevel, in turn, calls DrawTopBevel and DrawBottomBevel to draw the top and bottom bevels, respectively.

X Library Functions and Macros Introduced in This Chapter

XAllocColorCells

XStoreColor

XStoreColors

XStoreNamedColor

Motif Functions and Macros Introduced in This Chapter

XmChangeColor

XmCreatePanedWindow

XmGetColorCalculation

XmGetColors

XmSetColorCalculation

Colormaps and Visuals

This chapter covers:

- ✦ Creating colormaps
- ✦ Freeing colormaps
- ✦ Registering colormaps with the window manager
- ✦ Querying colormaps
- ✦ Using colormaps with X toolkits
- ✦ Notes on using colormaps
- ✦ Types of visuals
- ✦ Finding the best visual
- ✦ Using visuals with X toolkits
- ✦ Strategies for using nondefault visuals
- ✦ Working with 24 bit-planes of color

An Introduction to Colormaps and Visuals

A *visual* is a software abstraction—a way in which your applications can view color hardware. Many systems, particularly those with 24 bit-planes of color, support a number of ways in which your code can treat the color hardware, that is, these systems support a number of visuals.

Visuals, in turn, support various types of *colormaps*. The colormaps on the screen may be read-only or you may be able to write to the colormaps. The colormaps may also be decomposed into separate red, green, blue spaces. A colormap is typically an index table used to look up colors. The colormap may be *decomposed* into separate red, green, and blue colormaps with the `DirectColor` and `TrueColor` visuals. All other visual types use *undecomposed* colormaps; that is, the colormap acts as a large array. For each element in the array, there are the red, green, and blue components for that color.

This chapter covers visuals and colormaps. Because your applications are more likely to create colormaps under the default visual than use non-default visuals, we cover colormaps first, then visuals. If the default visual, normally `PseudoColor`, works fine, then you can skip over the later section on finding visuals. Of course, to be truly portable, your applications need to deal with any visual type: `DirectColor`, `GrayScale`, `PseudoColor`, `StaticColor`, `StaticGray`, and `TrueColor`.

Colormaps

Each window on the X display has an associated colormap. You can create a new colormap and then change the colormap attributes for a given window (i.e., associate the new colormap with the window, instead of the old colormap—usually the default colormap) if you desire.

In your applications, though, you may create a number of software colormaps. Each of these colormaps is associated with a given window. If the color hardware can only support one colormap at a time, which is the most common case, X must swap in and out of these software colormaps. Each colormap becomes active in turn.

It is up to the window manager, such as `mwm`, `twm`, or `olwm`, to perform colormap swapping. The window with the *colormap focus* has its colormap installed by the window manager. The colormap focus usually follows the mouse: when the mouse pointer is in a window, the colormap focus follows the mouse, and any colormap for that window becomes active. This swapping of colormaps generates `ColormapNotify` *events*, which we discussed in Chapter 4 (see the section entitled Colormap Events). `ColormapNotify` events alert your application when the window manager swaps colormaps.

The problem with this colormap swapping is that it creates the Technicolor effects so disliked by users as the mouse moves about the screen—screen colors flash and cause many distractions. Consequently, it is generally a good idea to use the default colormap if at all possible.

The Default Colormap

The X Window System uses a colormap to define the colors available to an application program. The X server associates every window with a colormap. This colormap provides an indirect method for defining colors that appear on the screen. To change color cells, you must first allocate them from a colormap. You therefore need a colormap to specify the colors you want to appear. In most cases, the standard colormap for a given workstation screen should be used, if you used the default visual for a given screen.

The easiest way to get a colormap of your own is to use the default colormap:

```
Colormap DefaultColormap(Display* display,
              int screen_number)
```

It is a good idea, and a most portable idea, to use the default colormap if at all possible. Some workstations have a hardware read-only colormap, one that you cannot modify. Other workstations have limited memory resources, and don't forget that color normally takes up a lot of random-access memory (RAM). If at all possible, try to use the default system colormap. This also avoids the Technicolor effects described above as colormaps are swapped in and out.

If you need a large number of color cells, chances are you won't be able to use the default colormap. In this case, you'll need to create your own colormap.

Creating Colormaps

XCreateColormap creates a colormap using the given visual:

```
Colormap XCreateColormap(Display* display,
    Window window,
    Visual* visual,
    int amount_alloc)
```

XCreateColormap returns the ID of the new colormap. The *window* ID passed to XCreateColormap is just used to get the screen on which the window resides. You'll find a lot of X library functions use a *window* parameter for this.

Every colormap is created under a *visual*. The *visual* parameter specifies which visual you want to use to create the colormap (visuals are discussed in more detail later in this chapter).

The *amount_alloc* should be one of the following constants: AllocNone or AllocAll. We normally find that you want to allocate zero colormap entries using AllocNone when you create the colormap—at least with PseudoColor visuals. Instead, colormap entries (color cells) are allocated later using XAllocColor, XAllocNamedColor, XAllocColorCells, or XAllocColorPlanes. AllocAll means all colormap entries are allocated at once.

N O T E

If you're using a StaticGray, StaticColor, or TrueColor visual, the allocation *must* be AllocNone, or you'll generate an error.

The following code provides a convenience function to create a colormap. Note that the CreateColormap function calls exit on errors. This code is stored in the file colormap.c:

```
/*
 *   colormap.c
 *   Routine to create a colormap.
```

```
 */
#include "xlib.h"
#include <stdio.h>

Colormap CreateColormap(Display* display,
    Window window,
    Visual* visual)

{   /* CreateColormap */
    int colormap;

    /*
     * Create a colormap.
     */
    colormap = XCreateColormap(display,
                   window,
                   visual,
                   AllocNone);

    if (colormap == (Colormap) None) {
        fprintf(stderr,
            "Error creating colormap.\n");
        exit(1);
    }


    return colormap;


}   /* CreateColormap */

/* end of file colormap.c */
```

Associating Colormaps and Windows

Once the colormap is created, you need to associate the colormap with a given window. To do this, you can pass the colormap as part of a call to XCreateWindow—that is, associating the colormap with a new window during the creation of the window. You can also call XSetWindowColormap to do this:

```
XSetWindowColormap(Display* display,

    Window window,

    Colormap colormap)
```

If you're using the Xt Intrinsics, you can set the *colormap* resource on a widget, normally a drawing area widget or a top-level shell widget (see below). Note that if you set the *colormap* resource, you must also set the *depth* resource. You should set these resources before creating the widget.

Copying Colormaps

You must create your own colormap if your application needs more color cells than there are available. The problem is that you don't always know if there are enough cells available. Usually, your application gets a failure status when trying to allocate a color cell. In this case, your application probably allocated a number of color cells from the default colormap before running out. Your application is now stuck with creating a new colormap and then reallocating all those previously allocated cells from the new colormap. This is because your application has a number of color cells still in the default colormap. To help take care of this problem, you can call the function XCopyColormapAndFree:

```
Colormap XCopyColormapAndFree(Display* display,

    Colormap old_colormap)
```

XCopyColormapAndFree creates a new colormap using an *old_colormap*. The new colormap is created with the same visual as the *old_colormap*, and all the color cells your application allocated in the *old_colormap* are reallocated in the new colormap. After allocating these cells in the new colormap, XCopyColormapAndFree frees the same cells in the *old_colormap*. XCopyColormapAndFree then returns the ID of this colormap.

If the *old_colormap* was created using an allocation of AllocAll, then the new colormap is created the same way.

When the window manager swaps colormaps, users may see a lot of flashing as previous good colors take on bizarre new colors. To minimize the flashing and Technicolor effects, you can use XCopyColormapAndFree to copy the current (usually default) colormap. The problem is that the default colormap may later change, and your application won't track these changes. Even so, XCopyColormapAndFree is a very handy routine.

Freeing Colormaps

When done with a colormap, you should call XFreeColormap to destroy the colormap and release the memory and data structures in the X server. Colormaps are precious commodities on most workstations, so if you don't need one anymore, free it:

```
XFreeColormap(Display* display, Colormap colormap)
```

Registering Colormaps with the Window Manager

If you create a colormap for a top-level window and then have all child windows inherit that colormap, then the window manager should swap in your colormap properly. If, however, you create a colormap for a subwindow of one of your application's top-level windows, you need to tell the window manager about it. Otherwise, you'll find that the window manager might not swap in your colormap properly. (We use *might* because you never know for sure what a window manager will do. It's best to program defensively around window managers.)

The WM_COLORMAP_WINDOWS property is a list of window IDs for which you have custom colormaps. This property is documented in the obscure rules for well-behaved X applications, the Inter-Client

Communications Conventions Manual, or ICCCM. The basic idea is simple: you provide the window manager with a list of window IDs for which you want the window manager to pay attention to colormaps. That is, every window with a different colormap should be in this list. You should also place the list in order, with the most important window first. The window manager should then swap in this colormap first, especially on systems that support only one colormap at a time in the hardware.

This seems confusing and it is. In most cases, your application will have one window, such as a drawing area widget, with its own colormap. You'd then pass the window ID for the drawing area first, because it's the most important colormap, and the window ID for the top-level widget second, because it has less importance. To do this, use the function XSetWMColormapWindows:

```
Status XSetWMColormapWindows(Display* display,
    Window window,
    Window* colormap_window_array,
    int number_windows)
```

The *window* parameter should be a top-level window, such as the window of an application shell widget in toolkit programs. In Xt programs, you can use XtWindow to retrieve the window ID of the top-level shell widget. Remember to call XtRealizeWidget before calling XtWindow.

If your application later changes the list of windows that have separate colormaps, or if the priority of the colormaps changes, call XSetWMColormapWindows again with the changed list.

Using the above example, if we have a drawing area widget (Motif XmDrawingArea or OLIT DrawArea) that uses its own colormap, we then need to call XSetWMColormapWindows:

```
Display*    display;
Widget      drawingarea;
Widget      topshell;
Window      window_array[2];
int         status;
```

```
window_array[0] = XtWindow(drawingarea);
window_array[1] = XtWindow(topshell);

status =  XSetWMColormapWindows(display,
            XtWindow(topshell),
            window_array,
            2);    /* two windows */
```

The code snippet above tells the window manager that our application has two colormaps, but that the drawing area's colormap is more important than the top-level shell widget's.

You need to call XSetWMColormapWindows if you have subwindows that use a different colormap than the top-level shell window. If you instead use one colormap throughout the application, you have no need to call XSetWMColormapWindows.

If you use the Xt Intrinsics, you can call XtSetWMColormapWindows:

```
#include <X11/Intrinsic.h>


void XtSetWMColormapWindows(Widget shell_widget,
    Widget* list_of_widgets,
    Cardinal number_widgets)
```

XtSetWMColormapWindows acts a lot like XSetWMColormapWindows, only the former takes a list of widgets instead of a list of windows. Again, pass a top-level shell widget, such as the widget returned by XtAppInitialize, as the *shell_widget* parameter.

You can retrieve the WM_COLORMAP_WINDOWS property using XGetWMColormapWindows:

```
Status XGetWMColormapWindows(Display* display,
    Window window,
    Window** return_windows, /* RETURN */
    int* number_windows)      /* RETURN */
```

N O T E

The X library supports functions to install and uninstall colormaps, XInstallColormap and XUninstallColormap, respectively. These functions are reserved for window managers, so never call them unless you're writing a window-manager application. On old Release 2 and 3 systems, sometimes users would avoid running a window manager, so applications had to install their colormaps manually. Ever since Release 4, installing colormaps is officially the province of the window manager.

Listing Installed Colormaps

You can get a list of the installed colormaps using XListInstalledColormaps:

```
Colormap* XListInstalledColormaps(Display* display,
    Window window,
    int* number_colormaps) /* RETURN */
```

XListInstalledColormaps returns a list of the installed colormaps for the screen containing *window* and places the number of colormaps returned in *number_colormaps*. Free the memory for the Colormap array with XFree when done.

Querying Colormaps

You can query color cells in a colormap to see what red, green, and blue (RGB) color values were allocated. XQueryColor queries one color cell:

```
XQueryColor(Display* display,
    Colormap colormap,
    XColor* xcolor)    /* input/output */
```

You fill in the *pixel* field of the XColor structure. This tells XQueryColor which color cell to query. XQueryColor then fills in the *red*, *green*, *blue*, and *flags* fields. (The *flags* field is set to all the bitmasks for DoRed, DoGreen, and DoBlue.)

If you query an undefined color cell, the results are undefined. There's no really good way to determine which color cells have been allocated. One method might be to allocate all the color cells yourself and then see which cells are left over after all color cells are allocated.

You can query multiple color cells with XQueryColors:

```
XQueryColors(Display* display,

    Colormap colormap,

    XColor* xcolor_array, /* input/output */

    int  number_colors)
```

Using Colormaps with X Toolkits

If you create private colormaps, you have two main choices for Xt-based programs.

First, you can set the whole application to use a private colormap. This makes all the colors in the application consistent, but generally creates a Technicolor flashing effect when the user moves the mouse about the screen.

Second, you can create a private colormap for a drawing widget (Motif XmDrawingArea or OLIT DrawArea) and then use the default colormap for the rest of the application's interface. The main problem with this route is again the Technicolor flashing effects mentioned above.

In addition, if you use a separate colormap for the drawing area widget, you risk making your whole application interface invisible (usually by it turning black) when the user moves the mouse into the drawing area window. Because of this, if you create a private colormap for a drawing-area window, follow this sequence:

- ✦ Create the rest of the interface (the other widgets) first, before the drawing area widget, so that the colors needed for these other widgets are allocated from the default colormap.

- ✦ Use the XCopyColormapAndFree function to copy the color cells your application has allocated into a new, private colormap. Note that most of the color allocations so far will be from within the toolkit code. By using XCopyColormapAndFree, you have a better chance of making sure that your interface widgets don't turn black when the user moves the mouse into the drawing area window.

✦ Set the `colormap` and `depth` resources to the colormap ID and depth of the new colormap. Use these resources when creating the drawing area window. Always set the `depth` resource when you set the colormap resource or you may have problems. You may also want to set the `borderColor` resource to a color cell in the colormap. This is so the drawing-area window's border matches the colormap used for inside the window.

✦ Call XSetWMColormapWindows or XtSetWMColormapWindows to tell the window manager about your private colormap. Both functions set the WM_COLORMAP_WINDOWS property on the given window. (See the section titled Registering Colormaps with the Window Manager, above.) You want to pass the drawing-area widget first, as this has the highest priority for limited colormap resources. Pass the widget for the rest of the application (which uses the default colormap) second, because its colormap is considered less important than the drawing-area widget's colormap:

```
Widget     drawingarea;
Widget     topshell;
Widget     widget_array[2];

widget_array[0] = drawingarea;
widget_array[1] = topshell;

XtSetWMColormapWindows(topshell,
    widget_array,
    2);    /* two widgets */
```

OLIT Utility Functions to Extract Colormaps

The Open Look Intrinsics Toolkit (OLIT) supports two functions to query the current colormap and depth of any object—widget, flat widget, or gadget. OlColormapOfObject returns the colormap associated with the *widget*:

```
#include <Xol/OpenLook.h>


Colormap OlColormapOfObject(Widget widget)
```

OlDepthOfObject returns the depth associated with the given *widget*:

```
#include <Xol/OpenLook.h>


int OlDepthOfObject(Widget widget)
```

Notes on Using Colormaps

For the best-looking applications, use the default visual and colormap, if at all possible. This isn't always possible, as the default colormap is shared among most X applications, so it fills up quickly on a very low-end 16-color system. This situation may force you to create your own colormap.

Most workstation hardware supports only one colormap at a time. If you create your own colormap, therefore, chances are the window manager will swap in your colormap when the mouse pointer is in your application's windows, and swap out the colormap when the pointer is in the rest of other X client windows. This colormap swapping will result in Technicolor effects.

These Technicolor effects don't look good and tend to annoy users. Unless you really need the colors, don't create your own colormap. If at all possible, use the default visual and colormap. If you write an application that analyzes Magellan space probe data, you'll probably need every available color. If you're writing a graphical electronic-mail program, you probably don't—unless you're mailing 24-bit image data, of course.

The functions described above should show you how to create your own colormaps if necessary and use these colormaps with your X toolkit programs. Many applications can simply use the default colormap or create their own colormap under the default visual. This technique works fine on most low-end systems, such as common workstations with 8 bit-planes of color. When you work with 16 or 24 bit-planes of color, your application generally needs to know more about visuals.

Using Visuals

As workstation prices drop and as technology advances, more and more X systems support 16 or 24 bit-planes of color. Usually these systems provide a default `PseudoColor` widget, and often with only 8 bit-planes of color. One of the reasons for this is that many X applications assume that any system with a depth of more than one provides a `PseudoColor` visual with 8 bit-planes of color. As hardware prices drop, this assumption is no longer valid—not that it ever was in the first place. That means to take advantage of the extra hardware, you need to code your applications to use a nondefault visual. As a result, your applications need to be aware of visual types and how to program using nondefault visuals.

Types of Visuals

X supports six types of visuals:

✦ A `PseudoColor` visual supports colormaps that act as index tables. A pixel value indexes into a colormap to produce an RGB value. These RGB values can be changed dynamically.

✦ A `GrayScale` visual is a lot like a `PseudoColor` visual, except that all colors are shades of the same color, normally gray—but not necessarily so. Thus, you should store equal values of red, green, and blue when allocating colors.

✦ A `DirectColor` visual decomposes each pixel value into separate RGB subfields. Each subfield indexes into a separate red, green, or blue colormap. The RGB values may be changed dynamically.

✦ A `TrueColor` visual is a lot like a `DirectColor` visual. The difference is that `TrueColor` visuals have read-only predefined RGB values. Normally, these predefined values provide a nearly linear ramp of colors.

✦ A `StaticColor` visual acts the same as a `PseudoColor` visual except that the RGB values in the colormap are predefined.

✦ A StaticGray visual is like a StaticColor visual. With StaticGray, the RGB values are equal, resulting in shades of gray.

The differences between the six visuals are delineated in Table 10.1.

Table 10.1 *X visual classes.*

Visual Class	Color/Gray	Colormap	Writeable
DirectColor	Color	Decomposed	Yes
GrayScale	Gray-scale	Undecomposed	Yes
PseudoColor	Color	Undecomposed	Yes
StaticColor	Color	Undecomposed	No
StaticGray	Gray-scale	Undecomposed	No
TrueColor	Color	Decomposed	No

The data that describes visuals is stored in the Visual structure.

The Visual Structure

Normally, you treat a visual pointer as a read-only structure and don't mess with its values. (In fact, the Visual structure should be treated as an opaque data type.) As we know, in the real world sometimes you need to dig into these opaque structures. If your application needs more information, you can access fields in the Visual structure. The Visual structure looks like the following (for a simplified version, see the Note below under DirectColor Visuals):

```
typedef struct {
    XExtData*      ext_data;
    VisualID       visualid;
    int            class;
    unsigned long  red_mask, green_mask, blue_mask;
    int            bits_per_rgb;
```

```
        int          map_entries;
    } Visual;
```

Going through the structure, the *ext_data* is a place where X extensions can hook in any additional data needed. The *visualid* is an ID number that identifies the visual. This is so that the entire structure doesn't have to be transmitted back and forth between your application and the X server, much the same as the reason for window IDs. You can use XVisualIDFromVisual to get the ID of a visual from a pointer to a Visual structure:

```
    VisualID XVisualIDFromVisual(Visual* visual)
```

The *class* field in the Visual structure is one of DirectColor, GrayScale, PseudoColor, StaticColor, StaticGray, and TrueColor.

The *bits_per_rgb* are the number of significant bits in red, green, and blue values. The *map_entries* indicate the number of supported colormap entries available in a colormap created for that visual type.

The various masks are only used if the visual class is DirectColor or TrueColor. If so, then the masks contain a set of bits that can be used to mask out the red, green, and blue parts of color pixel numbers.

DirectColor Visuals

As we stated above, DirectColor visuals decompose each pixel value into separate RGB subfields. Each subfield indexes into a separate red, green, or blue colormap. DirectColor visuals treat colormap cells differently than the more common PseudoColor visuals. In a DirectColor visual, there's a separate red, green, and blue table. The pixel value, or colormap index, is then made up of three parts, the red, green, and blue part.

For instance, if a DirectColor visual provided 8 bits each of red, green, and blue, then each of the separate color tables would have 256 entries. A pixel value would then look something like the following, where r is a bit that indexes the red table, g a bit that indexes the green table, and b a bit that indexes the blue table:

```
    rrrrrrrrggggggggbbbbbbbb
```

In the above example, the index in the red table can be found by the following:

```
(pixel & 0xFF0000) >> 16
```

where 0xFF0000 would be the *red_mask* of the Visual structure. Also common is the reversed case, where 0xFF is the *red_mask*, 0xFF00 the *green_mask*, and 0xFF0000 the *blue_mask*.

The green bits generate an index into the green table, using:

```
(pixel & 0x00FF00) >> 8
```

And, the index into the blue table is found by:

```
(pixel & 0x0000FF)
```

This is only an example. The order of the red, green, and blue elements may change, as well as the size of the various tables. In many cases, the tables may be of different sizes.

Using a DirectColor visual, XStoreColor then can set an entry in a single table—for example, the red table—by setting the DoRed bit in the *flags* field of the XColor structure. Or you could set the value into all three tables, using the DoRed, DoGreen, and DoBlue flags. (The value of the *red* field in the XColor structure goes into the red table, the *green* field into the green table, and so on.)

 If you use C++, you'll probably have problems with the field named *class*, as *class* is a reserved word in C++. To take care of this problem, the actual definition of the Visual structure in <X11/Xlib.h> contains compile-time directives:

N O T E

```
typedef struct {
    XExtData*       ext_data;
    VisualID        visualid;
#if defined(__cplusplus) || defined(c_plusplus)
    int             c_class;
#else
```

```
        int           class;
#endif
        unsigned long red_mask, green_mask, blue_mask;
        int           bits_per_rgb;
        int           map_entries;
    } Visual;
```

The code compiles in the name *c_class* if you have __cplusplus or c_plusplus defined. Most C++ compilers automatically define one of these symbols. If you're using C++, use the *c_class* field instead of the *class* field. Even though all of the code in this book was written with C, we included compile-time directives to access the *c_class* field in this and the XVisualInfo structures, so you won't need to modify the example code if you program with C++.

The Default Visual

In many cases, the default visual may just be what is needed—usually a class of PseudoColor. Most X color systems, in fact, make a PseudoColor visual the default. If your application just needs a PseudoColor visual, check the default first and use it, if possible. Again, color resources on the display are shared among all X applications, so the more defaults your application can use, the better-behaved X citizen it will be.

You can find the default visual with the macros DefaultVisual and DefaultVisualOfScreen:

```
Visual* DefaultVisual(Display* display,
        int screen_number)


Visual* DefaultVisualOfScreen(Screen* screen_ptr)
```

In addition to the macros, there are also X library functions to do the same thing:

```
Visual* XDefaultVisual(Display* display,
```

```
          int screen_number)
```

```
Visual* XDefaultVisualOfScreen(Screen* screen_ptr)
```

For more sophisticated X applications, however, you may require something more than the default visual. Many systems with 24 bit-planes of color, for example, provide an 8 bit-plane `PseudoColor` visual as the default. There are two main reasons for this. Many X programs are erroneously written to assume the default visual is a `PseudoColor` visual (assuming *anything* with X is generally a mistake). Second, high-end color systems often try to reserve the extra color resources for those applications that really need it. The program that tells you when you have incoming electronic mail generally doesn't need 24 bit-planes of color. Computer-aided design (CAD) packages could make good use of the extra color resources.

In such cases, you often want to find the so-called "best" visual on the display.

Finding the Best Visual

Of course, it's almost impossible to define the "best" visual. Different applications simply have different needs. Even so, we present a means to find a visual of a certain class that has the most entries in the supported colormaps. That's a good general definition of the best visual. If your application has different needs, you can then customize the code below, in visual.c (under the next heading), to meet your criteria.

Retrieving Visual Information

To find the best visual, your application needs to retrieve information on all the available visuals. The X server supports a list of visuals, and `XMatchVisualInfo` searches this list of supported visuals and finds one that provides the desired visual class and depth (number of color planes):

```
#include <X11/Xutil.h>
```

```
Status XMatchVisualInfo(Display* display,
```

```
int screen_number,
int depth,
int visual_class,
XVisualInfo* visual_info)   /* RETURN */
```

XMatchVisualInfo returns a nonzero value on success and fills in an
XVisualInfo structure with information about the visual it found. On
failure, XMatchVisualInfo returns zero.

One problem with XMatchVisualInfo is that you need to know the
depth you're looking for. The whole point of finding the best visual is to
obtain one that supports the deepest depth. And if you already knew this,
you wouldn't need to call XMatchVisualInfo.

If you don't know a desired depth as well as the visual class, you cannot
use XMatchVisualInfo. Instead, we find XGetVisualInfo works better:

```
#include <X11/Xutil.h>


XVisualInfo* XGetVisualInfo(Display* display,
    long visual_info_mask,
    XVisualInfo* visual_info_template,
    int* number_visuals)   /* RETURN */
```

You pass XGetVisualInfo a template that specifies the information
you're looking for. For example, you probably want to find the visuals on a
certain screen and perhaps with a certain class. The *visual_info_mask*
is a mask of bit-flags that tells XGetVisualInfo which fields in the
visual_info_template your application filled in. (This use of bitmasks is a lot like that of XCreateGC, presented in Chapter 3.)

The code below searches for the list of supported visuals of a certain
class (PseudoColor) that are on the default screen for the given X display:

```
#include <X11/Xutil.h>


Display*     display;
long         visual_info_mask;
```

```
int          number_visuals;
XVisualInfo* visual_array;
XVisualInfo  visual_info_template;


visual_info_template.class  = PseudoColor;
visual_info_template.screen = DefaultScreen(display);


visual_info_mask = VisualClassMask |
                       VisualScreenMask;


visual_array = XGetVisualInfo(display,
                   visual_info_mask,
                   &visual_info_template,
                   &number_visuals);
```

In our example above, we want a `PseudoColor` visual on the current screen. XGetVisualInfo then returns information on all the supported visuals that match. Since we're not asking for very much with our very general query, we may get a lot of entries back. You could, then, go through the returned XVisualInfo array and find the visual that best matches your needs.

Both XGetVisualInfo and XMatchVisualInfo provide XVisualInfo structures that describe the visuals found. The XVisualInfo structure is defined in <X11/Xutil.h>:

```
typedef struct {
  Visual*      visual;
  VisualID     visualid;
  int          screen;
  int          depth;
#if defined(__cplusplus) || defined(c_plusplus)
  int          c_class;
#else  /* C, not C++ */
```

```
    int           class;
#endif
    unsigned long red_mask;
    unsigned long green_mask;
    unsigned long blue_mask;
    int           colormap_size;
    int           bits_per_rgb;
} XVisualInfo;
```

The *class* field is named *c_class* if you compile with C++.

Included in this structure is a pointer to the actual visual information. Use this pointer as the visual when creating a window or colormap. (Usually, your X toolkit will take care of creating windows for you.)

XGetVisualInfo requires a now-familiar bitmask that tells the routine which fields in the XVisualInfo template are filled in. The constants for these bitmasks are listed in Table 10.2.

Table 10.2   *Mask bits for XGetVisualInfo.*

Mask Bits	Value
VisualNoMask	0x0
VisualIDMask	0x1
VisualScreenMask	0x2
VisualDepthMask	0x4
VisualClassMask	0x8
VisualRedMaskMask	0x10
VisualGreenMaskMask	0x20
VisualBlueMaskMask	0x40
VisualColormapSizeMask	0x80
VisualBitsPerRGBMask	0x100
VisualAllMask	0x1FF

When done with the XVisualInfo array, free it with XFree:

```
XVisualInfo*  visual_array;


XFree((void*) visual_array);
```

In the code below, we present a function that will search for the visual of the given class (*desired_class*) that supports the most colormap entries. It is up to your application to choose which class, such as DirectColor or PseudoColor, to look for. The FindDeepestVisual function returns the visual found, as well as the colormap size and depth for the visual found. Additionally, FindDeepestVisual returns a flag, *default_visual*, that is set to True if the returned visual is the default visual. The *default_visual* flag is set to False otherwise. If the default visual is the best, you might as well use it and save a lot of programming hassle. The FindDeepestVisual function is stored in the file visual.c:

```
/*
 *  visual.c
 *  Routine to get the best (deepest) visual.
 */
#include "xlib.h"
#include <X11/Xutil.h>
#include <stdio.h>  /* NULL */


Visual* FindDeepestVisual(Display* display,
    int screen,
    int desired_class,
    int* colormap_size,  /* RETURN */
    int* depth,          /* RETURN */
    int* default_visual) /* RETURN */


{   /* FindDeepestVisual */
    XVisualInfo   visual_info_template;
```

```
    XVisualInfo*   visual_array;
    int            i, number_visuals;
    Visual*        visual;


    /*
     * Initialize values.
     */
    *colormap_size = 0;
    *depth = 0;
    *default_visual = False;


    /*
     * Set up criteria for search.
     */
    visual_info_template.screen = screen;


    /*
     * In C++, class is a reserved word.
     */
#if defined(__cplusplus) || defined(c_plusplus)


    visual_info_template.c_class = desired_class;


#else    /* C */


    visual_info_template.class = desired_class;


#endif   /* C, not C++ */


    /*
     * Get info on supported Visuals.
```

```
 */
visual_array = XGetVisualInfo( display,
          VisualClassMask | VisualScreenMask,
          &visual_info_template,
          &number_visuals );

/*
 * Did we find one?
 */
if ((visual_array == (XVisualInfo*) NULL) ||
    (number_visuals < 1)) {
    return (Visual*) NULL;
}

/*
 * Go through the list of visuals
 * and find the one with the most
 * colormap entries.
 */
visual = (Visual*) NULL;

for (i = 0; i < number_visuals; i++) {
    if (visual_array[i].colormap_size >
        *colormap_size) {
        *colormap_size =
            visual_array[i].colormap_size;

        *depth = visual_array[i].depth;

        visual = visual_array[i].visual;
    }
```

```
    }


    /*

     * Free the data when done.

     */

    XFree((void*) visual_array);


    /*

     * Check if we have the default visual.

     */

    if (visual == DefaultVisual(display, screen) ) {

        *default_visual = True;

    }


    return visual;


}   /* FindDeepestVisual */


/* end of file visual.c */
```

FindDeepestVisual first retrieves information of the available visuals of the given class (*desired_class*) using XGetVisualInfo. FindDeepestVisual then goes through the list of returned visuals and finds the one with the most colormap entries. Finally, this best visual is compared against the default visual. The idea is to use the default visual if possible and avoid all the extra code required to use a nondefault visual.

The FindDeepestVisual function makes no judgments about what the best visual type is. Instead, it assumes that the calling function knows what it's looking for. This is to make FindDeepestVisual more flexible, as every X application has different needs. The most common search criteria will be to find the color visual that supports the greatest number of writable colormap entries. Normally, you look for DirectColor visuals first and then PseudoColor visuals. We've put together such a function, GetColorVisual, below. GetColorVisual calls FindDeepestVisual to first find the best `DirectColor` visual. If there are no `DirectColor` visuals available (very common on low-end color workstations), then `GetColorVisual` calls `FindDeepestVisual` again to find the best (deepest) `PseudoColor` visual. Finally, if no `PseudoColor` visuals are available, `GetColorVisual` returns the default visual.

The code for `GetColorVisual` is stored in the file `getvis.c`:

```
/*
 *   getvis.c
 *   Routine to get a color visual.
 */
#include "xlib.h"
#include <X11/Xutil.h>
#include <stdio.h>        /* NULL */


extern Visual* FindDeepestVisual(Display* display,
        int screen,
        int desired_class,
        int* colormap_size,    /* RETURN */
        int* depth,            /* RETURN */
        int* default_visual);  /* RETURN */


Visual* GetColorVisual(Display* display,
    int screen,
    int* depth,            /* RETURN */
    int* default_visual)   /* RETURN */


{   /* GetColorVisual */
    Visual* visual;
    int     colormap_size;

    /*
```

```
 * First, try for a DirectColor visual.
 */
visual = FindDeepestVisual(display,
            screen,
            DirectColor,
            &colormap_size,
            depth,
            default_visual);


/*
 * If we didn't find a visual,
 * try again with a PseudoColor visual.
 */
if (visual == (Visual*) NULL) {
    visual = FindDeepestVisual(display,
            screen,
            PseudoColor,
            &colormap_size,
            depth,
            default_visual);
}


/*
 * If we still fail, then we
 * return the default visual.
 */
if (visual == (Visual*) NULL) {
    visual = DefaultVisual(display, screen);
    *default_visual = True;
    *depth = DefaultDepth(display, screen);
}
```

```
    return visual;


}    /* GetColorVisual */


/* end of file getvis.c */
```

With the above functions for finding the best visual, we're now ready to use visuals with X toolkit applications.

Using Visuals with X Toolkits

Using nondefault visuals with X toolkit programs can be a daunting task. There are a lot of things that can go wrong and not a lot of diagnostic information to help you out.

To use a nondefault visual in an X toolkit program, set the *visual* resource on a top-level shell widget before you create the widget. The first and most important thing to remember is that only shell widgets (and the OLIT `DrawArea` widget) support the *visual* resource. All other widgets are created using their parent's visual. The second thing to remember is that you need to set a number of resources all at once to be effective (and avoid nasty X errors, such as the `BadMatch` error on window creation). These resources are listed in Table 10.3.

Table 10.3 *Resources to set when using nondefault visuals.*

Resource	Value
`backgroundPixmap`	A pixmap created for the visual
`borderPixmap`	A pixmap created for the visual
`colormap`	A colormap created for the visual
`depth`	The depth of the visual
`visual`	The visual you want to use

If you want, you can set the *background* and *borderColor* resources instead of the pixmaps, although we find setting the *backgroundPixmap* resource is generally a good idea. To use a nondefault visual in an Xt-based program, follow these five steps:

1. Initialize the Xt Intrinsics the long way, using the method presented in Chapter 5.
2. Before creating the top-level shell widget, determine the proper visual.
3. Create a colormap for that visual.
4. Create a pixmap with the same depth as the visual. This pixmap will be used for the window border.
5. Set the *colormap*, *depth*, *visual*, *backgroundPixmap*, and *borderPixmap* resources for the top-level shell widget and create the widget. You'll need to set those same resources on all other shell widgets you create.

NOTE

Be careful with the definition of shell widgets. Dialogs and menus use shell widgets (transient and override shells, respectively) under the hood. If you get a BadMatch error on window creation (X_CreateWindow), chances are you messed up the *visual* resource on a shell widget.

Setting the Visual Resource

Any shell widget you create must have the proper *visual* set. And, whenever you set the *visual* resource, you should set the following resources together: *colormap*, *depth*, *backgroundPixmap*, and *borderPixmap*. This effectively means that if you use a nondefault visual, you need to also create a colormap for that visual:

```
Display*  display;
int       screen, default_visual;
Visual*   visual;
```

```
Colormap  colormap;
int       depth,


/* Initialize toolkit and open display... */


visual = GetColorVisual(display,
            screen,
            &depth,
            &default_visual);


colormap = CreateColormap(display,
            RootWindow(display, screen),
            visual);
```

Once you find a visual and create a colormap, you can then create a top-level application shell widget:

```
Visual*   visual;
Colormap  colormap;
int       depth,
Cardinal  n;
Pixmap    pixmap;


n = 0;
XtSetArg(args[n], XtNborderPixmap, pixmap); n++;
XtSetArg(args[n], XtNbackgroundPixmap, pixmap); n++;
XtSetArg(args[n], XtNcolormap, colormap); n++;
XtSetArg(args[n], XtNdepth, depth); n++;
XtSetArg(args[n], XtNvisual, visual); n++;


/* Set other resources... */
```

```
parent = XtAppCreateShell(NULL,   /* use argv */

            "Prox",

            applicationShellWidgetClass,

            display,

            args, n);
```

Strategies for Using Nondefault Visuals

The same problem that plagues private colormaps—the Technicolor flashing effect—also plagues nondefault visuals, since you have to create your own colormap for such a visual. The problem is worse with visuals in that you're more likely to see the entire screen—except for your windows—go "bad" when the mouse is in your application's windows. Since most X workstations support multitasking, you're doing a lot to make multitasking problematic if you use nondefault visuals, especially on low-end systems. On high-end systems sporting 24 bit-planes of color, the colors on the rest of the screen aren't generally messed up when your application uses a non-default visual.

For the best effects, we found that you should use the same visual for all widgets of an entire application. Don't use a separate visual for an OLIT DrawArea widget, or for separate dialog shells. Instead, set the *visual* resource (and the other resources listed above) for all shell widgets, menus, and dialogs to use the same visual.

To show this strategy, we put together OLIT and Motif programs that try to use a nondefault visual. The programs use the GetColorVisual routine to find the deepest color visual, checking for DirectColor and then PseudoColor visuals. If your X system presents more than 8 bit-planes of color, chances are it supports a DirectColor visual.

In both cases, our program creates a simple drawing-area widget and a pulldown menu. The code that creates the menu shows how to set the proper resources on this shell widget.

N O T E Watch out for tricky bugs. We've found that since few application developers actually use nondefault visuals with the Xt Intrinsics, there are a lot of bugs. Silicon Graphics, for example, claims to have fixed many Motif bugs dealing with nondefault visuals. Be prepared to spend quite a bit of time making your programs work properly. In such a case, using an X protocol snooping program, such as `xscope` or `xmon`, can help a lot.

Visuals and OLIT

We don't use the utility function to create a menu. Instead, we call `XtCreateManagedWidget` and pass all the proper resources to set the visual for the menu. The OLIT program is stored in the file `o_chap10.c`:

```
/*
 *  o_chap10.c
 *  Open Look test program for Chapter 10
 *  finds best visual and creates a
 *  colormap.
 */
#include "olit.h"
#include <Xol/MenuButton.h>
#include <stdio.h>


/* External functions */
extern Visual* GetColorVisual(Display* display,
        int screen,
        int* depth,
        int* default_visual);

extern Colormap CreateColormap(Display* display,
        Window window,
```

```
             Visual* visual);


  extern void ChangeRGBColor(Display* display,
          Colormap colormap, XColor* color,
          int red, int green, int blue);


  /*
   * Expose callback for drawing area.
   */
  void drawCB(Widget widget, XtPointer client_data,
                              XtPointer call_data)


  {   /* drawCB */


      /* does nothing. */


  }   /* drawCB */


  int main(int argc, char** argv)


  {   /* main */
      XtAppContext    app_context;
      Display*        display;
      Widget          parent;
      Widget          mainwindow;
      Widget          menubar;
      Widget          filemenu;
      Widget          exitchoice;
      Widget          drawingarea;
      Arg             args[20];
      int             n;
```

```
int             screen;
Colormap        colormap;
Visual*         visual;
int             depth, default_visual;
int             copy_of_argc;
char**          copy_of_argv;
int             argv_size;
Pixmap          pixmap;


/* Initialize X toolkit the long way */
OlToolkitInitialize( (XtPointer) NULL);


XtToolkitInitialize();


app_context = XtCreateApplicationContext();


/*
 * Copy command-line parameters.
 */
copy_of_argc = argc;


argv_size = argc * (sizeof(char*));


copy_of_argv = (char**) XtMalloc(argv_size);


bcopy(argv, copy_of_argv, argv_size);


/*
 * Open display.
 */
display = XtOpenDisplay(app_context,
```

```
                NULL,    /* display name, use argv */
                NULL,    /* app name, use arg[0] */
                "ProX", /* class name */
                (XrmOptionDescList) NULL,
                0,       /* number options */
                ARGC_PTR &argc, argv);


    /*
     * We assume an error opening
     * display is a fatal error.
     */
    if (display == (Display*) NULL) {
        fprintf(stderr, "Error opening X display.\n");
        exit(1);
    }


    /*
     * Get a visual.
     */
    screen = DefaultScreen(display);

    visual = GetColorVisual(display,
                screen,
                &depth,
                &default_visual);


    /*
     * Now, if we got a nondefault
     * visual, we need to set up the
     * proper resources.
     */
```

```
n = 0;
XtSetArg(args[n], XtNmappedWhenManaged, False); n++;
XtSetArg(args[n], XtNwidth, 400); n++;
XtSetArg(args[n], XtNheight, 500); n++;

if (default_visual != True) {
    printf("Using nondefault visual.\n");

    XtSetArg(args[n], XtNvisual, visual); n++;
    XtSetArg(args[n], XtNdepth, depth); n++;

    /*
     * Create a colormap.
     */
    colormap = CreateColormap(display,
                    RootWindow(display, screen),
                    visual);

    XtSetArg(args[n], XtNcolormap, colormap); n++;
}

/*
 * Set up the border pixmap even if
 * using the default visual.
 */
pixmap = XCreatePixmap(display,
            RootWindow(display, screen),
            1, 1,
            depth);

XtSetArg(args[n], XtNborderPixmap, pixmap); n++;
```

```
/*
 * Set in command-line parameters.
 */
XtSetArg(args[n], XtNargc, copy_of_argc); n++;
XtSetArg(args[n], XtNargv, copy_of_argv); n++;

parent = XtAppCreateShell(NULL,  /* use argv */
        "Prox",
        applicationShellWidgetClass,
        display,
        args, n);

XtRealizeWidget(parent);

/*
 * If we used the default visual,
 * get the colormap ID.
 */
if (default_visual == True) {
    XtVaGetValues(parent,
        XtNcolormap, &colormap,
        NULL);
}

mainwindow = CreateMainWindow(parent, "main");

menubar = CreateMenuBar(mainwindow, "menubar");

/*
 * Create a pulldown menu. The menu uses an
```

```
 * override shell which requires the visual
 * resource be set.
 */
n = 0;
XtSetArg(args[n], XtNborderPixmap, pixmap); n++;
XtSetArg(args[n], XtNbackgroundPixmap, pixmap); n++;
XtSetArg(args[n], XtNcolormap, colormap); n++;
XtSetArg(args[n], XtNdepth, depth); n++;
XtSetArg(args[n], XtNvisual, visual); n++;
XtSetArg(args[n], XtNlabelJustify,  OL_LEFT); n++;
XtSetArg(args[n], XtNrecomputeSize, TRUE); n++;

filemenu = XtCreateManagedWidget("filemenu",
        menuButtonWidgetClass,
        menubar,
        args, n);

/* Create a menu choice to exit the program. */
exitchoice = CreateExitChoice(filemenu, "exitchoice");

drawingarea = CreateDrawingArea(mainwindow,
                "drawingarea",
                400, 400,
                (XtCallbackProc) drawCB,
                (XtPointer) NULL);

SetMainAreas(mainwindow,
        menubar,
        drawingarea);

/* Map parent */
```

```
        XtMapWidget(parent);
        XtAppMainLoop(app_context);

        return 0;

}    /* main */


/* end of file o_chap10.c */
```

Visuals and Motif

The code to make Motif programs work with nondefault visuals is almost exactly the same as the code for OLIT programs. The following code holds a simple Motif program.

Note the call to XmCreatePulldownMenu. We first set the proper visuals before creating the pulldown menu, because menus use shell widgets.

The Motif code is stored in the file m_chap10.c:

```
/*
 *  m_chap10.c
 *  Motif test program for Chapter 10
 *  finds best visual and creates a
 *  colormap.
 */
#include "motif.h"
#include <Xm/CascadeB.h>
#include <Xm/MainW.h>
#include <Xm/PushB.h>
#include <Xm/RowColumn.h>
#include <stdio.h>


/* External functions */
```

```
extern Visual* GetColorVisual(Display* display,
        int screen,
        int* depth,
        int* default_visual);

extern Colormap CreateColormap(Display* display,
        Window window,
        Visual* visual);

extern void ChangeRGBColor(Display* display,
        Colormap colormap, XColor* color,
        int red, int green, int blue);

/*
 * Expose callback for drawing area.
 */
void drawCB(Widget widget, XtPointer client_data,
                            XtPointer call_data)

{   /* drawCB */

    /* does nothing. */

}   /* drawCB */

int main(int argc, char** argv)

{   /* main */
    XtAppContext  app_context;
    Display*      display;
    Widget        parent;
```

```
Widget          mainwindow;
Widget          menubar;
Widget          filemenu, cascade;
Widget          exitchoice;
Widget          drawingarea;
Arg             args[20];
int             n;
int             screen;
Colormap        colormap;
Visual*         visual;
int             depth, default_visual;
int             copy_of_argc;
char**          copy_of_argv;
int             argv_size;
Pixmap          pixmap;

/* Initialize X toolkit the long way */
XtToolkitInitialize();


app_context = XtCreateApplicationContext();


/*
 * Copy command-line parameters.
 */
copy_of_argc = argc;


argv_size = argc * (sizeof(char*));


copy_of_argv = (char**) XtMalloc(argv_size);


bcopy(argv, copy_of_argv, argv_size);
```

```
/*
 * Open display.
 */
display = XtOpenDisplay(app_context,
          NULL,   /* display name, use argv */
          NULL,   /* app name, use arg[0] */
          "ProX", /* class name */
          (XrmOptionDescList) NULL,
          0,      /* number options */
          ARGC_PTR &argc, argv);


/*
 * We assume an error opening
 * display is a fatal error.
 */
if (display == (Display*) NULL) {
    fprintf(stderr, "Error opening X display.\n");
    exit(1);
}


/*
 * Get a visual.
 */
screen = DefaultScreen(display);

visual = GetColorVisual(display,
          screen,
          &depth,
          &default_visual);
```

```
/*
 * Now, if we got a nondefault
 * visual, we need to set up the
 * proper resources.
 */
n = 0;
XtSetArg(args[n], XmNmappedWhenManaged, False); n++;
XtSetArg(args[n], XmNallowResize, True); n++;
XtSetArg(args[n], XmNwidth, 400); n++;
XtSetArg(args[n], XmNheight, 500); n++;

if (default_visual != True) {
    printf("Using nondefault visual.\n");

    XtSetArg(args[n], XmNvisual, visual); n++;
    XtSetArg(args[n], XmNdepth, depth); n++;

    /*
     * Create a colormap.
     */
    colormap = CreateColormap(display,
                RootWindow(display, screen),
                visual);

    XtSetArg(args[n], XmNcolormap, colormap); n++;
}

/*
 * Set up the border pixmap even if
 * using the default visual.
 */
```

```
pixmap = XCreatePixmap(display,
          RootWindow(display, screen),
          1, 1,
          depth);


XtSetArg(args[n], XmNborderPixmap, pixmap); n++;


/*
 * Set in command-line parameters.
 */
XtSetArg(args[n], XmNargc, copy_of_argc); n++;
XtSetArg(args[n], XmNargv, copy_of_argv); n++;


parent = XtAppCreateShell(NULL,  /* use argv */
        "Prox",
        applicationShellWidgetClass,
        display,
        args, n);


XtRealizeWidget(parent);


/*
 * If we used the default visual,
 * get the colormap ID.
 */
if (default_visual == True) {
   XtVaGetValues(parent,
       XmNcolormap, &colormap,
       NULL);
}
```

```
mainwindow = CreateMainWindow(parent, "main");

menubar = CreateMenuBar(mainwindow, "menubar");

/*
 * Create a pulldown menu. The menu uses an
 * override shell which requires the visual
 * resource be set.
 */
n = 0;
XtSetArg(args[n], XmNborderPixmap, pixmap); n++;
XtSetArg(args[n], XmNbackgroundPixmap, pixmap); n++;
XtSetArg(args[n], XmNcolormap, colormap); n++;
XtSetArg(args[n], XmNdepth, depth); n++;
XtSetArg(args[n], XmNvisual, visual); n++;

filemenu = XmCreatePulldownMenu(menubar,
            "filemenu", args, n);

n = 0;
XtSetArg(args[n], XmNsubMenuId, filemenu); n++;

cascade = XmCreateCascadeButton(menubar,
            "filemenu", args, n);

XtManageChild(cascade);

/* Create a menu choice to exit the program. */
exitchoice = CreateExitChoice(filemenu, "exitchoice");

drawingarea = CreateDrawingArea(mainwindow,
                "drawingarea",
                400, 400,
```

```
                      (XtCallbackProc) drawCB,
                      (XtPointer) NULL);

     SetMainAreas(mainwindow,
                  menubar,
                  drawingarea);

     /* Map parent */
     XtMapWidget(parent);
     XtAppMainLoop(app_context);

     return 0;

}    /* main */

/* end of file m_chap10.c */
```

OLIT Utility Function to Extract Visuals

OLIT provides a function to extract the visual associated with a widget:

```
#include <Xol/OpenLook.h>

Visual* OlVisualOfObject(Widget widget)
```

This may be useful in your code.

Using 24 Bit-Planes of Color

As hardware prices drop, you can expect to pay a lot more attention to X's concept of visuals. Many systems now offer 16 or 24 bit-planes of color. When working on such systems, your users probably want to take advantage of all that extra color. (It's hard to justify an application that limits users to 16 colors on a high-end workstation that supports 24 bit-planes of color, for example.) The main problem is that the greater the sophisticated color support, the more divergent the system.

We've found a wide variety of visuals supported on a number of 24-bit color systems. Silicon Graphics systems, for instance, tend to supply `PseudoColor`, `TrueColor`, and `StaticColor`, but not `DirectColor` visuals. Hewlett-Packard systems, on the other hand, usually support `DirectColor` visuals with a depth of 24.

Working with Silicon Graphics Platforms

Silicon Graphics made a lot of changes to their X and Motif libraries to support multiple visuals. Silicon Graphics extends the normal idea of visuals to support hardware extensions, such as overlay and underlay planes.

Silicon Graphics workstations support these extra planes: *normal planes*, which act just like you'd expect; *popup planes* (with 2 bit-planes of color) that can be used for popup menus (the Silicon Graphics Toolchest program does this); and *overlay planes*, which support up to 4 bit-planes of color and are used for drawing on top of images in the other color planes. (Silicon Graphic's implementation of X does not support using visuals to draw into *underlay planes*, at least, not at this time.) Many of these extra visuals support transparent colors, a feature that is *not* supported by X. Usually, colormap index zero is transparent.

You access these extra planes to use X visuals that Silicon Graphics Inc. (SGI) Indigo workstations support. If you list all the visuals on an SGI workstation, you'll generally see more than you would on another vendor's platform—even for low-end systems with 8 bit-planes of color. Because SGI uses the concept of visuals to encapsulate the hardware add-ons, your applications can make use of these SGI-specific features. However, using these features makes your code far less portable, and the X library doesn't fully support this use of visuals.

Summary

A visual is a software abstraction—a way in which your applications can view color hardware. Many systems, particularly those with 24 bit-planes of color, support a number of ways in which your code can treat the color hardware, that is, these systems support a number of visuals. Visuals, in turn, support various types of colormaps. The colormaps on the screen may be read-only or you may be able to write to the colormaps. A colormap is typically an index table used to look up colors. The colormap may be decomposed into separate red, green, and blue colormaps with the `DirectColor` and `TrueColor` visuals. All other visual types use undecomposed colormaps; that is, the colormap acts as a large array. For each element in the array, there are the red, green, and blue components for that color.

Each window on the X display has an associated colormap. You can create a new colormap and then change the colormap attributes for a given window (i.e., associate the new colormap with the window, instead of the old colormap—usually the default colormap) if you desire. In your applications, you may create a number of software colormaps. Each of these colormaps is associated with a given window. If the color hardware can only support one colormap at a time, which is the most common case, X must swap in and out of these software colormaps. Each colormap becomes active in turn.

The X Window System uses a colormap to define the colors available to an application program. The X server associates every window with a colormap. This colormap provides an indirect method for defining colors that appear on the screen. To change color cells, you must first allocate them from a colormap. You therefore need a colormap to specify the colors you want to appear. In most cases, the standard colormap for a given workstation screen should be used, if you used the default visual for a given screen. The easiest way to get a colormap of your own is to use the default colormap.

Once the colormap is created, you need to associate the colormap with a given window. To do this, you can pass the colormap as part of a call to `XCreateWindow`—that is, associating the colormap with a new window during the creation of the window.

You must create your own colormap if your application needs more color cells than there are available. The problem is that you don't always know if there are enough cells available. Usually, your application gets a failure status when trying to allocate a color cell. In this case, your application probably allocated a number of color cells from the default colormap before running out. Your application is now stuck with creating a new colormap and then reallocating all those previously allocated cells from the new colormap. This is because your application has a number of color cells still in the default colormap. To help take care of this problem, you can call the function XCopyColormapAndFree.

If you create a colormap for a top-level window and then have all child windows inherit that colormap, then the window manager should swap in your colormap properly. If, however, you create a colormap for a subwindow of one of your application's top-level windows, you need to tell the window manager about it. Otherwise, you'll find that the window manager might not swap in your colormap properly.

If you create private colormaps, you have two main choices for Xt-based programs. First, you can set the whole application to use a private colormap. This makes all the colors in the application consistent, but generally creates a Technicolor flashing effect when the user moves the mouse about the screen. Second, you can create a private colormap for a drawing widget (Motif XmDrawingArea or OLIT DrawArea) and then use the default colormap for the rest of the application's interface.

X supports six types of visuals. Normally, you treat a visual pointer as a read-only structure and don't mess with its values.

In many cases, the default visual may just be what is needed—usually a class of PseudoColor. Most X color systems, in fact, make a PseudoColor visual the default. If your application just needs a PseudoColor visual, check the default first and use it, if possible. Color resources on the display are shared among all X applications, so the more defaults your application can use, the better-behaved X citizen it will be.

For more sophisticated X applications, you may require something more than the default visual. Many systems with 24 bit-planes of color, for example, provide an 8 bit-plane PseudoColor visual as the default. There are two main reasons for this. Many X programs are erroneously written to assume the default visual is a PseudoColor visual (assuming anything with X is generally a mistake). Second, high-end color systems often try to reserve the extra color resources for those applications that really need it. The program that tells you when you have incoming electronic mail generally doesn't need 24 bit-planes of color. Computer-aided design (CAD) packages could make good use of the extra color resources. In such cases, you often want to find the so-called "best" visual on the display. To find the best visual, your application needs to retrieve information on all the available visuals. The X server supports a list of visuals, and XMatchVisualInfo searches this list of supported visuals and finds one that provides the desired visual class and depth (number of color planes).

Using nondefault visuals with X toolkit programs can be a daunting task. There are a lot of things that can go wrong and not a lot of diagnostic information to help you out.

To use a nondefault visual in an X toolkit program, set the *visual* resource on a top-level shell widget before you create the widget. The first and most important thing to remember is that only shell widgets (and the OLIT `DrawArea` widget) support the *visual* resource. All other widgets are created using their parent's visual. The second thing to remember is that you need to set a number of resources all at once to be effective (and avoid nasty X errors, such as the `BadMatch` error on window creation).

X Library Functions and Macros Introduced in This Chapter

```
DefaultVisual

DefaultVisualOfScreen

XCopyColormapAndFree

XCreateColormap

XDefaultVisual

XDefaultVisualOfScreen

XFreeColormap

XGetVisualInfo

XGetWMColormapWindows

XListInstalledColormaps

XMatchVisualInfo

XQueryColor

XQueryColors

XSetWindowColormap

XSetWMColormapWindows

XVisualIDFromVisual
```

X Toolkit Intrinsics Functions and Macros Introduced in This Chapter

```
XtSetWMColormapWindows
```

OLIT Functions and Macros Introduced in This Chapter

```
OlColormapOfObject
OlDepthOfObject
OlVisualOfObject
```

Chapter 11

Color Overlay Planes

This chapter covers:

- ✦ The theory of overlay planes
- ✦ Allocating color planes
- ✦ Allocating colors on overlay planes
- ✦ Simple overlay planes
- ✦ Complex overlay planes
- ✦ Drawing into overlay planes
- ✦ Drawing onto the window background, or picture area
- ✦ Clearing overlay planes
- ✦ Programming with overlay planes

Overlay Planes

The main use for an *overlay plane* is when you have a very complex picture—complex in that it sucks up a lot of time and central processing unit (CPU) cycles when redrawing. If you want to annotate this picture or display any other data on top of this picture, you need to prevent the picture from being damaged or drawn upon. Otherwise, when you change the annotation you'd have to redraw the complex picture, which is a time-consuming process.

For example, if you want to annotate a computer-aided design (CAD) drawing or display a moving representation of an airplane for an air-traffic-controller display, you want to avoid redrawing the picture that sits underneath the annotation or airplane.

What you need is the ability to draw into an overlay plane. An *overlay* is a picture you want to lay over another picture in a window. Ideally, the overlay picture and the picture considered *underneath* are completely independent of each other. That is, when you draw into one plane, you don't damage the other plane or planes. To get the final image as seen by the user, each layer is "drawn" on top of the layer beneath it. Where there's overlap, items drawn in upper layers take precedence: they cover up items in lower layers.

When you implement an overlay plane, you normally use a separate color plane that you can draw into. Many systems provide hardware overlays that sit above the main picture (the main set of color planes). Some even provide *underlay planes* that sit underneath the main picture. Most of these hardware systems are proprietary, though, and any code using these planes would be inherently nonportable to other systems. As we mentioned in the last chapter, many systems implement these hardware overlays as separate X visuals. You can then access these overlays by creating a window on one of these visuals.

Instead of using nonstandard hardware-based overlay planes, we can implement something similar using a software-only solution. The solutions we describe in this chapter are general-purpose techniques that you can use and extend on most X-based workstations. In fact, just about the only requirement is that you have a visual from which you can allocate color cells and planes. The traditional `PseudoColor` visual supported on most color X servers works just fine.

The trick is allocating color planes as well as color cells, and then independently drawing into those color planes. The sum total of all the drawing generates the image seen by the user. You'll find this technique useful for sprite-based animation (see Chapter 23), annotating maps in a geographic information system (GIS), displaying airplane data for an air-traffic-controller application, and in any situation where you have a complex picture on which you want to draw other pictures without damaging the complex picture.

Working with Color Planes as Overlays

Using color planes for overlays requires a dynamic visual, such as `DirectColor`, `GrayScale`, or `PseudoColor` (at least in the general case—there's a lot of variation in X support). Since most color workstations provide a `PseudoColor` visual by default, this is usually no problem.

In Chapter 9, we introduced `XAllocColorCells`, which can ask for both color cells and planes. In that chapter, though, we asked for no color planes. In this chapter, we'll see what happens when you ask for color planes. Up to now, we've viewed a colormap as an array of color cells. You can also view a colormap as a set of color planes. A system that supports 256 simultaneous colors (the most common workstation configuration) supports 8 color planes. To implement overlays, we need to view the colormap as both an array of color indexes (pixels) and as a set of color planes.

Using color planes from a colormap is how you implement software-based overlay planes, allocating a number of the color planes as well as some color cells. The color cells are used to draw the main part of the picture. The planes are used as an overlay. If you play your cards right, drawing into the overlay planes doesn't affect the image underneath. And drawing into this image doesn't affect the color planes.

In addition to the techniques presented in this chapter, a number of systems offer hardware color-plane support for overlays. Many Silicon Graphics workstations, for instance, provide hardware overlay and underlay planes. Using those planes should be more efficient than the techniques used here, but less general. Your solution will be constrained to a single type of platform; Silicon Graphics workstations, for example, don't provide the same support for color planes on all platforms.

Using software color planes, while less efficient, will work on most UNIX workstations, from the lowliest 80386-based PC to the fastest box you have.

Definitions of Terms

In the rest of this chapter, we use the word *overlay* to refer to a color plane or planes that your application allocate from a colormap. The intention is to use these color planes as an overlay. We're *not* talking about extra hardware support available on some systems. Because we're working with general-purpose portable software, there's nothing magic that makes the color planes we allocate sit over or on top of any other planes. In fact, we just allocate whatever planes we want and don't care whether these planes sit *over* any other area. Conceptually, however, these color planes are used for an overlay, so we pretend that they sit over the picture we want to draw underneath.

Underneath the overlay, we want to draw a *picture*. In real applications, this picture tends to be rather complex, which is why we want to use an overlay plane in the first place. We call this area that is logically underneath the overlay area the *picture area*. When we draw into the picture area, we'll use a picture graphics context (GC). When we draw into an overlay area, we'll use an overlay GC. There's nothing special about these terms—we're just trying to make a difficult concept in X more understandable.

Allocating Color Planes

`XAllocColorCells`, which we introduced in Chapter 9, allocates a number of color cells and a number of color planes from a given colormap:

```
Status XAllocColorCells(Display* display,
    Colormap colormap,
    Bool contiguous,
    unsigned long* plane_masks, /* RETURN */
    unsigned int   number_planes,
    unsigned long* pixels,      /* RETURN */
    unsigned int   number_pixels)
```

When you allocate a number of color planes in addition to color cells (pixels), your application then owns all combinations of the pixel values and the plane bitmasks. That is, you're really allocating a number of colors from the colormap. You can calculate how many using the formula:

```
colors_allocated = number_pixels *  ₂(number_planes)
```

That's *number_pixels* times two raised to the *number_planes* power.

Additionally, allocating a single color plane drastically limits the amount of colors available to other applications if you're using a shared colormap. For instance, on an 8-bit color system, taking out one plane (bit) of color removes 128 colors. For this reason, you want to allocate only those color planes that your application absolutely needs.

For GrayScale and PseudoColor visuals, each mask in *plane_masks* has a single bit set to one. For DirectColor visuals, each mask has three bits set to one.

With DirectColor visuals, you can also use XAllocColorPlanes:

```
Status XAllocColorPlanes(Display* display,
    Colormap colormap,
    Bool contiguous,
    unsigned long* pixels,     /* RETURN */
    int number_colors,
    int number_reds,
    int number_greens,
    int number_blues,
    unsigned long* red_mask,   /* RETURN */
    unsigned long* green_mask, /* RETURN */
    unsigned long* blue_mask,  /* RETURN */
```

You can calculate how many color cells XAllocColorPlanes allocates using the formula below:

```
colors_allocated = number_pixels *
₂(number_reds + number_greens + number_blues)
```

Using XAllocColorCells

For now, we'll focus on XAllocColorCells because it works with more visual types, especially PseudoColor, and PseudoColor visuals are more widely available. The way XAllocColorCells works when you allocate color planes is a bit tricky.

XAllocColorCells writes into the *pixel* array and stores the colormap indexes for the allocated cells. It also writes a set of bits into the *plane_masks* array, 1 bit for each plane allocated. If you allocate 1 plane, you'll get 1 bit (your plane) written into the first entry in the *plane_masks* array. The array need only be one entry long, since in this example only one color plane was allocated.

If you allocate more than one plane, you'll get back a bit for each plane allocated (or 3 bits with a DirectColor visual). You can then treat the allocated planes as one big multiplane overlay or as separate overlays (one overlay for each plane allocated). Multiplane overlays allow you to use more colors in the overlays.

How X Color Planes Work

We can call XAllocColorCells to allocate one pixel and two color planes. XAllocColorCells will set the *pixel* array (with one element) to some valid index in the colormap, say the value 0x01. We also get back two plane masks, say 0x80 and 0x40. Using the pixel value 0x01 as an example, our application "owns" the color cells as listed in Table 11.1.

Table 11.1   Allocating two planes and one pixel.

Planes	Pixel	Color Cells
0 0 0 0 0 0 0 0	0 0 0 0 0 0 0 1	0 0 0 0 0 0 0 1
0 1 0 0 0 0 0 0	0 0 0 0 0 0 0 1	0 1 0 0 0 0 0 1
1 0 0 0 0 0 0 0	0 0 0 0 0 0 0 1	1 0 0 0 0 0 0 1
1 1 0 0 0 0 0 0	0 0 0 0 0 0 0 1	1 1 0 0 0 0 0 1

In an 8-bit PseudoColor system, both the planes and the pixel values must come from the same 8 bits of color. Thus, the color cells our application owns come from the combination of the bits in the allocated planes and the bits in the allocated pixels.

In fact, our application owns the pixel value (the colormap index) outright. This is the first line in the table above. In addition, it owns every combination of the pixel value and any of the color planes allocated. If we use XAllocColorCells and allocate two pixels (say 0x01 and 0x02— we're using arbitrary pixel values to make the examples clearer) and two planes (again, 0x80 and 0x40), the application owns the color cells listed in Table 11.2.

Table 11.2   *Allocating two planes and two pixels.*

Planes	Pixels	Color Cells
0 0 0 0 0 0 0 0	0 0 0 0 0 0 0 1	0 0 0 0 0 0 0 1
0 0 0 0 0 0 0 0	0 0 0 0 0 0 1 0	0 0 0 0 0 0 1 0
0 1 0 0 0 0 0 0	0 0 0 0 0 0 0 1	0 1 0 0 0 0 0 1
0 1 0 0 0 0 0 0	0 0 0 0 0 0 1 0	0 1 0 0 0 0 1 0
1 0 0 0 0 0 0 0	0 0 0 0 0 0 0 1	1 0 0 0 0 0 0 1
1 0 0 0 0 0 0 0	0 0 0 0 0 0 1 0	1 0 0 0 0 0 1 0
1 1 0 0 0 0 0 0	0 0 0 0 0 0 0 1	1 1 0 0 0 0 0 1
1 1 0 0 0 0 0 0	0 0 0 0 0 0 1 0	1 1 0 0 0 0 1 0

As you can tell, allocating just a few color planes quickly fills up a colormap. Wherever there's a 1 bit in the planes column in Table 11.2, we can write into that color plane. This is the overlay area. The picture area is where there's a 0 for the planes bits.

In the picture area, we can call XStoreColor as described in Chapter 9 and set a red, green, and blue (RGB) value into the allocated color cell. That is, we can store *LimeGreen* into cell 0x01 and *NavyBlue* into cell 0x02.

Storing Colors for the Overlay Planes

Storing colors for the overlay planes, though, is different. The problem is the bit-level math. The color displayed in the overlay plane is a combination of the bits in the overlay planes *and* the bits in the pixel values (color cells) we've allocated.

That is, when we draw into the overlay plane, wherever this drawing intercepts the items we draw into the picture area, we get a different value for the color index. For instance, we may draw using pixel 0x01 into the picture area. Wherever this intersects the items drawn into the overlay planes, we could get values of 0x81, 0x41, and so on. Each of these values is also an index into the colormap. Since we want items drawn into the overlay planes to maintain a consistent color, we need to allocate the same RGB values for each combination of pixel and color-plane bit. For every bit in the color plane, we need to set the same RGB value into the cell that is created by combining the color-plane bit and the pixel value. Where there's no color-plane bit, you can store RGB values normally.

This is one of the main tricks for maintaining a separation between the items drawn into the overlay area and the items drawn into the picture area. (Remember, one of our goals is to be able to clear the overlay area without damaging the picture area. As you can tell, hardware support for overlay planes takes care of a lot of nasty issues.)

Of course, you can take advantage of the differing index values if you want. To implement a traditional overlay plane, you need to set the same RGB value into each of the cells associated with the color planes and one pixel. The three cells below for the given pixel value, 0x01, are where the pixel value intercepts the color planes from our example, two color planes, 0x80 and 0x40, as shown in Table 11.3.

Table 11.3 *Where color planes and pixels intersect.*

Planes	Pixels	Color Cells
0 1 0 0 0 0 0 0	0 0 0 0 0 0 0 1	0 1 0 0 0 0 0 1
1 0 0 0 0 0 0 0	0 0 0 0 0 0 0 1	1 0 0 0 0 0 0 1
1 1 0 0 0 0 0 0	0 0 0 0 0 0 0 1	1 1 0 0 0 0 0 1

Where we have only one plane or one pixel, the problem is simple. Where we have multiple planes *and* multiple pixels, however, we have a tougher situation. We need to set the same RGB value into every combination of pixel and color plane. Ideally, if we have a single-color overlay plane, we need to set one RGB value into all the resulting combinations. The function StoreOverlayColors, below, is a start in this direction:

```
void StoreOverlayColors(Display* display,
    Colormap colormap,
    XColor* xcolor,    /* color to allocate */
```

```
        unsigned long* planes,
        unsigned int number_planes,
        unsigned long* pixels,
        unsigned int number_pixels)


{   /* StoreOverlayColors */
    int plane_count, pixel_count;


    for (plane_count = 0; plane_count < number_planes;
        plane_count++) {
        for (pixel_count = 0; pixel_count < number_pixels;
            pixel_count++) {


            xcolor->pixel = pixels[pixel_count] |
                    planes[plane_count];


            XStoreColor(display, colormap, xcolor);
        }
    }


    /*
     * Now, need to get all combinations of planes.
     * Our simple example skips this step.
     */


}   /* StoreOverlayColors */
```

StoreOverlayColors works when we just allocate one overlay plane. If you allocate more than one overlay plane, you need to store the XColor value into every combination of color plane and pixel value. StoreOverlayColors *doesn't* store the color in the cells that just contain the pixel values. Instead, it stores RGB values only where the color planes and the pixel values intersect.

Once we've stored RGB values into the color cells allocated with XStoreColor, the next step is to draw into either the color overlay or the picture area.

Drawing into Color Planes

To work with color planes, we've put together a set of utility functions that take care of much of the dirty work necessary when programming color planes. The first thing we need to do is generate the proper plane masks.

Generating Plane Masks

The plane mask for the overlay planes, when taken together, is all the bit-masks for each of the overlay planes, OR'ed together. The function OverlayMask does this:

```
unsigned long OverlayMask(unsigned long* planes,
    unsigned int number_planes)

{   /* OverlayMask */
    int             i;
    unsigned long   mask;


    mask = 0L;


    for (i = 0; i < number_planes; i++) {
        mask |= planes[i];
    }


    return mask;

}   /* OverlayMask */
```

`OverlayMask` takes in the number of planes and plane masks from the call to `XAllocColorCells`. `OverlayMask` returns the combined mask. You can then pass this mask to `XSetPlaneMask` to set up a graphics context (GC) for drawing just into the overlay planes, where `NUMBER_PLANES` is an arbitrary number of planes allocated using `XAllocColorCells`:

```
Display*        display;
GC              gc;
unsigned long planes[NUMBER_PLANES];
unsigned int   number_planes;


/* determine mask using OverlayMask */


XSetPlaneMask(display, gc,
    OverlayMask(planes, number_planes) );
```

To draw into just the rest of the picture—excluding the overlay color planes—you need to set the GC plane mask to all the bits except for the bits for the overlay planes. Using the concepts from `OverlayMask`, above, the plane mask for a GC to draw into the main picture area is just the bitwise NOT of the overlay plane mask (i.e., all the bits *except* for the bits in the overlay planes). The `PictureMask` function generates this:

```
unsigned long PictureMask(unsigned long* planes,
    unsigned int number_planes)


{   /* PictureMask */


    return ( ~ OverlayMask(planes, number_planes) );


}   /* PictureMask */
```

Once we've figured out the overlay and picture plane masks, we can create a graphics context to draw into either the overlay color plane or the picture area. Normally, when creating such a GC, we want to set the GC's drawing function (or mode) and a foreground color as well as the plane mask. The simple function `CreateOverlayGC` does this all in one step:

```
GC CreateOverlayGC(Display* display,
    Drawable drawable,
    int function,
    unsigned long plane_mask,
    unsigned long foreground)


{   /* CreateOverlayGC */
    XGCValues    xgcvalues;


    xgcvalues.plane_mask = plane_mask;
    xgcvalues.function   = function;
    xgcvalues.foreground = foreground;


    return XCreateGC(display, drawable,
            GCPlaneMask | GCFunction | GCForeground,
            &xgcvalues);


}   /* CreateOverlayGC */
```

We can also use `XSetState` (introduced in Chapter 3) to change a GC on the fly to draw into a color plane:

```
XSetState(Display* display,
    GC gc,
    unsigned long foreground,
    unsigned long background,
    int function,
    unsigned long planemask)
```

Drawing Modes for Color Planes

X provides 16 GC drawing modes or functions. (The term *function* is unfortunate, because C has another meaning for function. The GC's function is its drawing mode.) Because of this great number to choose from, there are many ways you can use to draw into color planes. We concentrate here on the clearest method. With this method, the three important drawing functions are GXcopy, which we've been using so far, GXset, and GXclear.

To draw into the picture area, we use the normal GXcopy GC mode.

To draw into a color plane, use the GXset GC drawing function or mode. The GXset mode will turn on, or set to 1, the bits in the overlay plane that we draw into. We then assume that the color cells with the overlay plane bit have a valid RGB value (you can set this up with StoreOverlayColors, above). You'll notice that this technique works best when using a single-plane overlay or when you draw the same color into all the overlay planes.

Because we use GXset to draw into the overlay planes, we use GXclear to clear the overlay planes. GXclear clears, or sets to zero, the bits drawn into. If we just draw into one color plane, then clearing the bit for the color plane should clear the overlay data. (This also works for a number of color planes as well.)

Clearing Color Planes

To clear an area in an overlay plane (or planes), we need to fill a rectangle using the GC drawing function of GXclear. The function ClearOverlay, below, does this:

```
void ClearOverlay(Display* display,
    Window window,
    GC gc,
    int x, int y,
    int width, int height)

{   /* ClearOverlay */
    XGCValues   xgcvalues;
```

```
/* Query current GC function */
XGetGCValues(display, gc,
    GCFunction,
    &xgcvalues);

/* Set to GXclear */
XSetFunction(display, gc, GXclear);

/* XFillRectangle */
XFillRectangle(display, window, gc,
    x, y, width, height);

/* Restore GC */
if (xgcvalues.function != GXclear) {
    XSetFunction(display, gc,
        xgcvalues.function);
}

}   /* ClearOverlay */
```

The GC you pass to ClearOverlay must be a GC that has the proper plane mask set up. This isn't very hard, as we intend to create the GCs and set their plane masks right away with CreateOverlayGC, above.

ClearOverlay first determines what the current GC drawing function is. This is so ClearOverlay can reset the GC when done. The idea here is to make ClearOverlay clean up after itself. Once the current GC drawing function is stored, ClearOverlay then calls XSetFunction, passing GXclear, the GC mode we need to clear out bits in color planes. ClearOverlay then calls XFillRectangle to fill (clear, actually) the bits in the given area. Finally, ClearOverlay calls XSetFunction again, restoring the GC, if necessary.

To clear the picture area, we use normal code instead of ClearOverlay. What you do is fill a rectangle with a desired background color. This "clears" the picture area. The only caveat is that the GC you use to "clear" the picture area must have its plane mask set to all planes *except* for the overlay planes. You can use `PictureMask`, above, to generate this plane mask.

You can use the following code to clear a given rectangular area of the picture planes:

```
Display*        display;
GC              picture_gc;
unsigned long   back_color;
int             x, y, width, height;


/* Clear picture planes */
XSetForeground(display,
    picture_gc, back_color);


XFillRectangle(display,
    window,
    picture_gc,
    x, y, width, height);
```

The code above looks like a normal X drawing routine to fill an area with a given color. The only tricks are that the `picture_gc` has its plane mask set to the color planes in the picture area (i.e., all color planes *except* for the overlay planes), and the `back_color` was allocated as a normal color cell (i.e., it doesn't have any of the overlay planes bits in its color index).

Clearing Both the Overlay Planes and the Picture Area

You can clear both the overlay planes and the picture area using the function below, assuming the GC plane masks are set up properly:

```
void ClearOverlayAndPicture(Display* display,
        Window window,
```

```
            GC overlay_gc,
            GC picture_gc,
            unsigned long picture_color,
            int x, int y,
            int width, int height)


{    /* ClearOverlayAndPicture */


    /* Clear overlay planes */
    ClearOverlay(display, window,
        overlay_gc,
        x, y, width, height);


    /* Clear picture planes */
    XSetForeground(display,
        picture_gc, picture_color);


    XFillRectangle(display, window,
        picture_gc,
        x, y, width, height);


}    /* ClearOverlayAndPicture */
```

Generic Overlay Routines

The code for our generic overlay routines described above is stored in the file overlay.c:

```
/*
 *   overlay.c
 *   Routines to work with software color planes.
```

```
*/
#include "xlib.h"

/*
 * Generate the mask for drawing into all
 * the overlay planes.
 */
unsigned long OverlayMask(unsigned long* planes,
    unsigned int number_planes)

{   /* OverlayMask */
    int             i;
    unsigned long   mask;

    mask = 0L;

    for (i = 0; i < number_planes; i++) {
        mask |= planes[i];
    }

    return mask;

}   /* OverlayMask */

/*
 * Generate the mask for drawing into the
 * underlying picture, without touching
 * the overlay planes.
 */
unsigned long PictureMask(unsigned long* planes,
    unsigned int number_planes)
```

```
{   /* PictureMask */

    return ( ~ OverlayMask(planes, number_planes) );

}   /* PictureMask */

/* Create GC for a given set of planes */
GC CreateOverlayGC(Display* display,
    Drawable drawable,
    int function,
    unsigned long plane_mask,
    unsigned long foreground)

{   /* CreateOverlayGC */
    XGCValues    xgcvalues;

    xgcvalues.plane_mask = plane_mask;
    xgcvalues.function   = function;
    xgcvalues.foreground = foreground;

    return XCreateGC(display, drawable,
            GCPlaneMask | GCFunction | GCForeground,
            &xgcvalues);


}   /* CreateOverlayGC */

/*
 * Allocates the same color into all
 * color planes, that is, all combinations
```

```
 * of planes and pixels you allocated.
 */


void StoreOverlayColors(Display* display,
    Colormap colormap,
    XColor* xcolor,      /* color to allocate */
    unsigned long* planes,
    unsigned int number_planes,
    unsigned long* pixels,
    unsigned int number_pixels)


{   /* StoreOverlayColors */
    int plane_count, pixel_count;


    for (plane_count = 0; plane_count < number_planes;
        plane_count++) {
        for (pixel_count = 0; pixel_count < number_pixels;
            pixel_count++) {

            xcolor->pixel = pixels[pixel_count] |
                    planes[plane_count];

            XStoreColor(display, colormap, xcolor);
        }
    }


    /*
     * Now, need to get all combinations of planes.
     * Our simple example skips this step.
     */
```

```
}    /* StoreOverlayColors */


/*
 * Clears the planes used in the
 * planemask of the given GC.
 */
void ClearOverlay(Display* display,
    Window window,
    GC gc,
    int x, int y,
    int width, int height)


{   /* ClearOverlay */
    XGCValues   xgcvalues;

    /* Query current GC function */
    XGetGCValues(display, gc,
        GCFunction,
        &xgcvalues);

    /* Set to GXclear */
    XSetFunction(display, gc, GXclear);

    /* XFillRectangle */
    XFillRectangle(display, window, gc,
        x, y, width, height);

    /* Restore GC */
    if (xgcvalues.function != GXclear) {
        XSetFunction(display, gc,
            xgcvalues.function);
```

```
    }


}   /* ClearOverlay */


/*
 * Clears both overlay planes and
 * picture area. Assumes both GCs
 * have the proper plane mask set.
 */
void ClearOverlayAndPicture(Display* display,
        Window window,
        GC overlay_gc,
        GC picture_gc,
        unsigned long picture_color,
        int x, int y,
        int width, int height)


{   /* ClearOverlayAndPicture */

    /* Clear overlay planes */
    ClearOverlay(display, window,
        overlay_gc,
        x, y, width, height);


    /* Clear picture planes */
    XSetForeground(display,
        picture_gc, picture_color);


    XFillRectangle(display, window,
        picture_gc,
        x, y, width, height);
```

```
}     /* ClearOverlayAndPicture */
```

```
/* end of file overlay.c */
```

We can then take the utility routines from the file `overlay.c` and use these routines to create a software emulation of a color overlay plane. In our example, we'll use only one color plane, but you can use how many you want (and have available, of course). We can draw into the overlay and picture areas separately, clearing one area or the other. If we clear the overlay area, the picture area is not modified (and vice versa). This technique is very useful for making annotations to images.

A Program to Demonstrate Overlay Planes

For the rest of this chapter, we'll develop a program to demonstrate the use of overlay planes. Our simple program will set up a 1-bit-deep overlay plane and allocate four extra color cells. Once set up, the program becomes menu-driven. We include menu choices to do the following:

✦ Draw a simple image into the overlay area;
✦ Clear the overlay area;
✦ Draw into the picture area; and
✦ Clear the picture area.

You can see how drawing into one area doesn't affect the other area, which is, of course, the whole purpose of using overlay color planes.

The first step in our program is to allocate a color plane and a number of color cells. The rather long `AllocColorCells` function does this:

```
#define NUMBER_PLANES    1
#define NUMBER_PIXELS    4


void AllocColorCells(Display* display,
```

```
     Window window)

{    /* AllocColorCells */
     int             status;
     unsigned long   pixels[NUMBER_PIXELS+1];
     unsigned long   planes[NUMBER_PLANES+1];
     unsigned long   overlay_mask, picture_mask;
     XColor          xcolor;
     Colormap        colormap;


     /* Allocate color cells and planes */
     colormap = DefaultColormap(display,
               DefaultScreen(display) );

     status = XAllocColorCells(display,
               colormap,
               False,  /* no need to be contiguous */
               planes,
               NUMBER_PLANES,
               pixels,
               NUMBER_PIXELS);

     if (status == 0) {
         fprintf(stderr,
             "ERROR allocating color cells.\n");
         exit(1);
     }

     /* ... */
```

We choose an arbitrary number of color planes (NUMBER_PLANES) and color cells or pixels (NUMBER_PIXELS). Once we have the color cells and plane, we need to store RGB color values to draw with. Note how we use the plane masks to generate the pixel values before calling `ChangeRGBColor` (introduced in Chapter 9):

```
/* ... */

/* Set up plane masks */
overlay_mask = OverlayMask(planes, NUMBER_PLANES);
picture_mask = PictureMask(planes, NUMBER_PLANES);

pict_color1 = pixels[0] & picture_mask;
xcolor.pixel = pict_color1;

ChangeRGBColor(display,
    colormap,
    &xcolor,
    120, 115, 160);

pict_color2 = pixels[1] & picture_mask;
xcolor.pixel = pict_color2;

ChangeRGBColor(display,
    colormap,
    &xcolor,
    64, 212, 97);

/* Picture background color */
pict_color3 = pixels[2] & picture_mask;
xcolor.pixel = pict_color3;

ChangeRGBColor(display,
```

```
        colormap,
        &xcolor,
        170, 170, 170);


    /* This last color will be used for the overlay. */
    xcolor.pixel = pixels[3] & picture_mask;

    ChangeRGBColor(display,
        colormap,
        &xcolor,
        0, 250, 0);


    /* ... */
```

Of the four colors we allocated, we devote two for drawing in the picture area. A third color will clear the picture area. The fourth color is used for the overlay plane. We call `StoreOverlayColors` to store the same RGB values into the cells where the overlay plane intercepts the pixel values:

```
    /* ... */


    StoreOverlayColors(display,
        colormap,
        &xcolor,
        planes,
        NUMBER_PLANES,
        pixels,
        NUMBER_PIXELS);


    /* ... */
```

`AllocColorCells` then creates GCs to draw into the overlay area using a GC function or mode of `GXset`. A GC for the picture area, using a mode of GXcopy, is also created at this time. Note that both GCs have their plane mask set immediately, so we don't have to worry about the plane masks any more. We just have to remember to use the `picture_gc` GC when drawing into the picture area and the `overlay_gc` GC when drawing into the overlay area. (Of course, you can create more GCs for each area. For simplicity, we're using one each.)

```
/* ... */


/* create GCs */
overlay_gc = CreateOverlayGC(display,
        window,
        GXset,
        overlay_mask,
        xcolor.pixel | overlay_mask);


picture_gc = CreateOverlayGC(display,
        window,
        GXcopy,
        picture_mask,
        pict_color1);


}    /* AllocColorCells */
```

With that, we're all set up to draw into the overlay and picture areas. The `overlayCB` callback function, below, draws into the overlay area, using the global `overlay_gc`. The `clearOverlayCB` callback clears the overlay planes. This function is called when you choose the *Clear Overlay* menu choice.

The `pictureCB` callback function draws into the picture area. The items we draw aren't that complex, as you can tell. In your applications, though, the picture area will probably have a very complex image. The `clearCB` callback clears the picture area. This function is called when you choose the *Clear Picture* menu choice.

There's a trick to handling `Expose` events. Basically, we need to clear *both* the picture area and the overlay planes for any exposed area, so we need a clean slate in the exposed area so that we maintain the independence of the overlay and picture areas. To do this, we can call the `ClearOverlayAndPicture` function from `overlay.c`, above. Once these planes are cleared, we can then draw into the exposed area. We'll need to draw both the overlay and picture images—depending on where the exposed area is. (Actually, the simple Open Look Intrinsics Toolkit [OLIT] and Motif programs below skip this step.)

Because we lack a toolkit's bias, we include both OLIT and Motif sources. Most of the code, though, is shared between the programs. This shared code is contained in the file `chap11.c`:

```
/*
 *   chap11.c
 *   Generic routines for Chapter 11.
 *   Allocate color planes.
 */
#include "xlib.h"
#include <X11/Xutil.h>
#include <X11/Intrinsic.h>
#include <X11/StringDefs.h>
#include <stdio.h>


/*
 *   Globals
 */
Display*        global_display;
Window          global_window;
GC              overlay_gc;
GC              picture_gc;
unsigned long   pict_color1, pict_color2, pict_color3;
int             global_width, global_height;


/* external functions */
```

```
extern GC CreateOverlayGC(Display* display,
        Drawable drawable,
        int function,
        unsigned long plane_mask,
        unsigned long foreground);

extern void ClearOverlayAndPicture(Display* display,
        Window window,
        GC overlay_gc,
        GC picture_gc,
        unsigned long picture_color,
        int x, int y,
        int width, int height);

extern unsigned long OverlayMask(unsigned long* planes,
        unsigned int number_planes);

extern unsigned long PictureMask(unsigned long* planes,
        unsigned int number_planes);

extern void StoreOverlayColors(Display* display,
        Colormap colormap,
        XColor* xcolor,           /* color to allocate */
        unsigned long* planes,
        unsigned int number_planes,
        unsigned long* pixels,
        unsigned int number_pixels);

/*
 * Draws a simple image into the overlay area.
 */
```

```
void overlayCB(Widget widget,
        XtPointer client_data,
        XtPointer call_data)

{   /* overlayCB */

    /* Ignores parameters on purpose. */

    XDrawRectangle(global_display,
        global_window,
        overlay_gc,
        150, 10, 200, 200);

    XDrawRectangle(global_display,
        global_window,
        overlay_gc,
        170, 20, 100, 100);

    XFlush(global_display);

}   /* overlayCB */

/*
 * Draws a simple picture "underneath"
 * the overlay planes.
 */
void pictureCB(Widget widget,
        XtPointer client_data,
        XtPointer call_data)

{   /* pictureCB */

    /* Ignores parameters on purpose. */
```

```
        XSetForeground(global_display,
            picture_gc,
            pict_color1);

        XFillRectangle(global_display,
            global_window,
            picture_gc,
            156, 6, 50, 50);

        XSetForeground(global_display,
            picture_gc,
            pict_color2);

        XFillRectangle(global_display,
            global_window,
            picture_gc,
            200, 50, 160, 160);

        XFlush(global_display);

    }    /* pictureCB */

void clearOverlayCB(Widget widget,
        XtPointer client_data,
        XtPointer call_data)

    {    /* clearOverlayCB */

        ClearOverlay(global_display,
            global_window,
```

```
                overlay_gc,
                0, 0,
                global_width, global_height);

}   /* clearOverlayCB */


void clearCB(Widget widget,
        XtPointer client_data,
        XtPointer call_data)

{   /* clearCB */

    XSetForeground(global_display,
        picture_gc, pict_color3);

    XFillRectangle(global_display,
        global_window,
        picture_gc,
        0, 0,
        global_width, global_height);

}   /* clearCB */

/*
 * On Expose events, need to clear
 * the exposed planes.
 */

void Clear(int x, int y,
    int width, int height)
```

```
{    /* Clear */

     ClearOverlayAndPicture(global_display, global_window,
          overlay_gc, picture_gc, pict_color3,
          x, y, width, height);

}    /* Clear */

#define NUMBER_PLANES    1
#define NUMBER_PIXELS    4

void AllocColorCells(Display* display,
     Window window)

{    /* AllocColorCells */
     int             status;
     unsigned long   pixels[NUMBER_PIXELS+1];
     unsigned long   planes[NUMBER_PLANES+1];
     unsigned long   overlay_mask, picture_mask;
     XColor          xcolor;
     Colormap        colormap;

     /* Store global values. */
     global_display = display;
     global_window  = window;

     /* Allocate color cells and planes */
     colormap = DefaultColormap(display,
               DefaultScreen(display) );

     status = XAllocColorCells(display,
```

```
                colormap,

                False,  /* no need to be contiguous */

                planes,

                NUMBER_PLANES,

                pixels,

                NUMBER_PIXELS);


if (status == 0) {

    fprintf(stderr,

        "ERROR allocating color cells.\n");

    exit(1);

}


/* Set up plane masks */

overlay_mask = OverlayMask(planes, NUMBER_PLANES);

picture_mask = PictureMask(planes, NUMBER_PLANES);


pict_color1 = pixels[0] & picture_mask;

xcolor.pixel = pict_color1;


ChangeRGBColor(display,

    colormap,

    &xcolor,

    120, 115, 160);


pict_color2 = pixels[1] & picture_mask;

xcolor.pixel = pict_color2;


ChangeRGBColor(display,

    colormap,

    &xcolor,
```

```
        64, 212, 97);


    /* Picture background color */
    pict_color3 = pixels[2] & picture_mask;
    xcolor.pixel = pict_color3;


    ChangeRGBColor(display,
        colormap,
        &xcolor,
        170, 170, 170);


    /* This last color will be used for the overlay. */
    xcolor.pixel = pixels[3] & picture_mask;


    ChangeRGBColor(display,
        colormap,
        &xcolor,
        0, 250, 0);


    StoreOverlayColors(display,
        colormap,
        &xcolor,
        planes,
        NUMBER_PLANES,
        pixels,
        NUMBER_PIXELS);


    /* Create GCs */
    overlay_gc = CreateOverlayGC(display,
            window,
            GXset,
```

```
            overlay_mask,
            xcolor.pixel | overlay_mask);

    picture_gc = CreateOverlayGC(display,
            window,
            GXcopy,
            picture_mask,
            pict_color1);

}   /* AllocColorCells */


/* end of file chap11.c */
```

OLIT Source for the Overlay Program

The OLIT-specific program uses all the generic routines presented so far.
This source is stored in o_chap11.c:

```
/*
 *  o_chap11.c
 *  OLIT test program for Chapter 11.
 *  Allocate color planes.
 */
#include "olit.h"
#include <Xol/DrawArea.h>


/*
 *  Globals
 */
extern int  global_width, global_height;


extern void clearCB(Widget widget,
```

```
                XtPointer client_data,
                XtPointer call_data);


extern void clearOverlayCB(Widget widget,
                XtPointer client_data,
                XtPointer call_data);


extern void overlayCB(Widget widget,
                XtPointer client_data,
                XtPointer call_data);


extern void pictureCB(Widget widget,
                XtPointer client_data,
                XtPointer call_data);


extern void Clear(int x, int y,
                int width, int height);


/*
 * Expose callback for drawing area.
 */
void drawCB(Widget widget,
                XtPointer client_data,
                XtPointer call_data)


{    /* drawCB */
     OlDrawAreaCallbackStruct* ptr;
     Dimension   width, height;


     ptr =
         (OlDrawAreaCallbackStruct*) call_data;
```

```
    if (ptr == NULL) {
        return;
    }


    if (ptr->reason == OL_REASON_EXPOSE) {

Clear(ptr->event->xexpose.x,
    ptr->event->xexpose.y,
    ptr->event->xexpose.width,
    ptr->event->xexpose.height);

        if (ptr->event->xexpose.count == 0) {
            /* Redraw picture and overlay here. */
        }


    }


    if (ptr->reason == OL_REASON_RESIZE) {
        XtVaGetValues(widget,
            XtNwidth,  &width,
            XtNheight, &height,
            NULL);

        global_width = width;
        global_height = height;
    }

}   /* drawCB */


int main(int argc, char** argv)
```

```
{   /* main */
    XtAppContext    app_context;
    Display*        display;
    Widget          parent;
    Widget          mainwindow;
    Widget          menubar;
    Widget          filemenu;
    Widget          exitchoice;
    Widget          drawingarea;
    Arg             args[20];
    int             n;

    /* Initialize X toolkit */
    OlToolkitInitialize( (XtPointer) NULL);

    n = 0;
    XtSetArg(args[n], XtNmappedWhenManaged, False); n++;
    XtSetArg(args[n], XtNwidth, 520); n++;
    XtSetArg(args[n], XtNheight, 300); n++;


    parent = XtAppInitialize(&app_context,
            "ProX",                        /* app class */
            (XrmOptionDescList) NULL,      /* options */
            0,                             /* num options */
            ARGC_PTR &argc, argv,          /* cmd line */
            (String*) NULL,                /* fallback res. */
            args, n);


    /*
```

```
 *  Create Main Window with utility function.
 */
mainwindow = CreateMainWindow(parent, "main");


/*
 * Create menu bar with utility function.
 */
menubar = CreateMenuBar(mainwindow, "menubar");


/*
 * Create the file menu.
 */
filemenu = CreateMenu(menubar, "filemenu");


(void) CreateMenuChoice(filemenu,
            "overlay",
            (XtCallbackProc) overlayCB,
            (XtPointer) NULL);


(void) CreateMenuChoice(filemenu,
            "clear_overlay",
            (XtCallbackProc) clearOverlayCB,
            (XtPointer) NULL);


(void) CreateMenuChoice(filemenu,
            "picture",
            (XtCallbackProc) pictureCB,
            (XtPointer) NULL);


(void) CreateMenuChoice(filemenu,
            "clear_picture",
```

```
                            (XtCallbackProc) clearCB,
                            (XtPointer) NULL);


        /* Create a menu choice to exit the program. */
        exitchoice = CreateExitChoice(filemenu,
                        "exitchoice");


        global_width = 520;
        global_height = 300;
        drawingarea = CreateDrawingArea(mainwindow,
                        "drawingarea",
                        global_width, global_height,
                        drawCB,
                        (XtPointer) NULL);


        SetMainAreas(mainwindow,
                    menubar,
                    drawingarea);


        /* Create the windows. */
        XtRealizeWidget(parent);


        /*
         * Allocate color planes and cells.
         */
        AllocColorCells(XtDisplay(drawingarea),
        XtWindow(drawingarea) );


        /* Map parent */
        XtMapWidget(parent);
        XtAppMainLoop(app_context);
```

```
        return 0;


    }   /* main */


    /* end of file o_chap11.c */
```

Motif Source for the Overlay Program

The Motif program is stored in `m_chap11.c`:

```
/*
 *  m_chap11.c
 *  Motif test program for Chapter 11.
 *  Allocate color planes.
 */
#include "motif.h"


/*
 *  Globals
 */
extern int    global_width, global_height;


extern void clearCB(Widget widget,
        XtPointer client_data,
        XtPointer call_data);


extern void clearOverlayCB(Widget widget,
        XtPointer client_data,
        XtPointer call_data);
```

```
extern void overlayCB(Widget widget,
        XtPointer client_data,
        XtPointer call_data);


extern void pictureCB(Widget widget,
        XtPointer client_data,
        XtPointer call_data);


extern void Clear(int x, int y,
        int width, int height);


/*
 * Expose callback for drawing area.
 */
void drawCB(Widget widget,
        XtPointer client_data,
        XtPointer call_data)


{   /* drawCB */
    XmDrawingAreaCallbackStruct* ptr;
    Dimension   width, height;


    ptr =
        (XmDrawingAreaCallbackStruct*) call_data;


    /*
     * Need to clear exposed area.
     */
    if (ptr->reason == XmCR_EXPOSE) {
    Clear(ptr->event->xexpose.x,
```

```
                ptr->event->xexpose.y,
                ptr->event->xexpose.width,
                ptr->event->xexpose.height);


            if (ptr->event->xexpose.count == 0) {
                /* Redraw picture and overlay here. */
            }
        }


        if (ptr->reason == XmCR_RESIZE) {
            XtVaGetValues(widget,
                XmNwidth,   &width,
                XmNheight,  &height,
                NULL);


            global_width = width;
            global_height = height;


        }


}   /* drawCB */


int main(int argc, char** argv)


{   /* main */
    XtAppContext    app_context;
    Display*        display;
    Widget          parent;
    Widget          mainwindow;
    Widget          menubar;
    Widget          filemenu;
```

```
Widget        exitchoice;
Widget        drawingarea;
Arg           args[20];
int           n;

/* Initialize X toolkit */
n = 0;
XtSetArg(args[n], XmNmappedWhenManaged, False); n++;
XtSetArg(args[n], XmNallowResize, True); n++;
XtSetArg(args[n], XmNwidth, 520); n++;
XtSetArg(args[n], XmNheight, 300); n++;

parent = XtAppInitialize(&app_context,
        "ProX",                    /* app class */
        (XrmOptionDescList) NULL,   /* options */
        0,                         /* num options */
        ARGC_PTR &argc, argv,      /* cmd line */
        (String*) NULL,            /* fallback res. */
        args, n);

/*
 * Create Main Window with utility function.
 */
mainwindow = CreateMainWindow(parent, "main");

/*
 * Create menu bar with utility function.
 */
menubar = CreateMenuBar(mainwindow, "menubar");
```

```
    /*
     * Create the file menu.
     */
    filemenu = CreateMenu(menubar, "filemenu");

(void) CreateMenuChoice(filemenu,
                "overlay",
                (XtCallbackProc) overlayCB,
                (XtPointer) NULL);

(void) CreateMenuChoice(filemenu,
                "clear_overlay",
                (XtCallbackProc) clearOverlayCB,
                (XtPointer) NULL);

(void) CreateMenuChoice(filemenu,
                "picture",
                (XtCallbackProc) pictureCB,
                (XtPointer) NULL);

(void) CreateMenuChoice(filemenu,
                "clear_picture",
                (XtCallbackProc) clearCB,
                (XtPointer) NULL);

    /* Create a menu choice to exit the program. */
    exitchoice = CreateExitChoice(filemenu,
                "exitchoice");

    global_width = 520;
    global_height = 300;
```

```
drawingarea = CreateDrawingArea(mainwindow,
                "drawingarea",
                global_width, global_height,
                drawCB,
                (XtPointer) NULL);

SetMainAreas(mainwindow,
            menubar,
            drawingarea);

/* Create the windows. */
XtRealizeWidget(parent);

/*
 * Allocate color planes and cells.
 */
AllocColorCells(XtDisplay(drawingarea),
XtWindow(drawingarea) );

/* Map parent */
XtMapWidget(parent);
XtAppMainLoop(app_context);

return 0;

}   /* main */


/* end of file m_chap11.c */
```

When you run one of the sample programs, choose the *Draw Picture* menu choice, then the *Draw Overlay* choice. You now have both images in the window. You can then clear one or the other, again via menu choices. This should provide a good example of how to draw into color planes and create a software overlay.

A Resource File for the Sample Program

The following resource file works with both the Motif and OLIT sample programs presented in this chapter. Name this file `ProX` and place it in your home directory:

```
!

! ProX

!

! Resource file for Chapter 11 of

! Professional Graphics

! Programming in the X Window System.

!

! Generic resources.

!

*background: #cccccc


!

! Motif resources.

!

*fontList:   lucidasans-12


*filemenu.labelString:   File
*filemenu.mnemonic:      F


*exitchoice.labelString:     Exit
*exitchoice.mnemonic:    x


*m_chap11.title:  Chap. 11: Color Overlay Planes
```

```
*overlay.labelString:        Draw Overlay
*clear_overlay.labelString: Clear Overlay

*picture.labelString:        Draw Picture
*clear_picture.labelString:  Clear Picture

! OLIT
*o_chap11.title:     Chap. 11: Color Overlay Planes

*overlay.label:          Draw Overlay
*clear_overlay.label:    Clear Overlay

*picture.label:          Draw Picture
*clear_picture.label:    Clear Picture
*filemenu.label:         File
*exitchoice.label:       Exit


*pushpin: out


! end of file ProX
```

Summary

The main use for an overlay plane is when you have a very complex picture—complex in that it sucks up a lot of time and central processing unit (CPU) cycles when redrawing. If you want to annotate this picture or display any other data on top of this picture, you need to prevent the picture from being damaged or drawn upon. Otherwise, when you change the annotation you'd have to redraw the complex picture, which is a time-consuming process.

When you implement an overlay plane, you normally use a separate color plane that you can draw into. Many systems provide hardware overlays that sit above the main picture (the main set of color planes). Some even provide underlay planes that sit underneath the main picture. Most of these hardware systems are proprietary, though, and any code using these planes would be inherently nonportable to other systems. As we mentioned in the last chapter, many systems implement these hardware overlays as separate X visuals. You can then access these overlays by creating a window on one of these visuals.

Instead of using nonstandard hardware-based overlay planes, we can implement something similar using a software-only solution. The solutions we describe in this chapter are general-purpose techniques that you can use and extend on most X-based workstations. In fact, just about the only requirement is that you have a visual from which you can allocate color cells and planes. The traditional `PseudoColor` visual supported on most color X servers works just fine.

Using color planes for overlays requires a dynamic visual, such as `DirectColor`, `GrayScale`, or `PseudoColor` (at least in the general case—there's a lot of variation in X support). Since most color workstations provide a `PseudoColor` visual by default, this is usually no problem.

The rest of the chapter covered convenience routines used in the management of overlay planes, followed by an example program in both OLIT and Motif incarnations.

X Library Functions and Macros Introduced in This Chapter

```
XAllocColorPlanes
```

Standard X Colormaps

This chapter covers:

- ✦ Standard colormaps
- ✦ Sharing colormaps between applications
- ✦ The format of standard colormaps
- ✦ Converting RGB values into colormap indexes
- ✦ Standard colormap properties
- ✦ Retrieving standard colormaps
- ✦ Creating and using standard colormaps
- ✦ Rules to follow for standard colormaps

An Introduction to Standard X Colormaps

Many X applications require most, if not all, of the available colors on a system. In addition, many image-processing applications need to have an easy way to convert a red, green, and blue (RGB) value into a colormap index, also called a *pixel*. Having such an easy conversion can improve the performance for processing images.

To aid these applications, X provides a set of so-called *standard colormaps*. These colormaps are sharable between applications and usually provide an even color ramp. This allows your applications to convert RGB values into colormap indexes with a simple calculation formula.

Up to now, we've discussed how to share color cells in a colormap, but not how to share colormaps themselves. Standard colormaps make such sharing easier. (You can also use other means to share X colormaps between applications. Just passing the colormap ID to another program usually suffices, although there are a number of associated issues to deal with.)

If you use standard colormaps, though, your application must follow a set of rules that well-behaved X programs use to ensure these colormaps act as expected. We cover these rules, part of the Inter-Client Communications Conventions Manual, or ICCCM for short, below.

To create a standard colormap, you must first allocate a structure to hold one.

Allocating Standard Colormaps

To allocate a standard colormap structure, use XAllocStandardColormap:

```
#include <X11/Xutil.h>


XStandardColormap* XAllocStandardColormap()
```

XAllocStandardColormap allocates an XStandardColormap structure and sets all the fields to zero. If XAllocStandardColormap fails, it returns NULL. Otherwise, XAllocStandardColormap returns a pointer to the new XStandardColormap structure. Free this data with XFree when done.

The `XStandardColormap` structure, defined in `<X11/Xutil.h>`, looks like:

```
typedef struct {
    Colormap        colormap;
    unsigned long   red_max;
    unsigned long   red_mult;
    unsigned long   green_max;
    unsigned long   green_mult;
    unsigned long   blue_max;
    unsigned long   blue_mult;
    unsigned long   base_pixel;
    VisualID        visualid;
    XID             killid;
} XStandardColormap;
```

The *colormap* field holds the X colormap ID used by the standard colormap. The max fields—*red_max*, *green_max*, and *blue_max*—hold the maximum number of color cells for the red, green, and blue planes. This seems confusing—and it is.

To use a common example, a frequently used standard colormap supplies 3 planes for red, 3 for green, and 2 for blue, using a notation of 3/3/2. In this example, *red_max* and *green_max* would both equal 7, while *blue_max* would equal 3. The basic idea is that with 3 planes, you have red values in the range of 0 to 7, hence a *red_max* of 7. With 2 planes, you have a range of blues of 0 to 3, hence a *blue_max* of 3.

The *visualid* field holds the ID number for the visual under which the colormap was created.

The *killid* field holds an odd flag. If set to `ReleaseByFreeingColormap`, this means that the colormap should be freed by calling `XFreeColormap`. Otherwise, to free the color data, you need to call `XKillClient` on the XID contained in the *killid* field. Normally, your applications won't have to deal with this if you just intend to create and use shared standard colormaps.

The multiplier fields, *red_mult*, *green_mult*, and *blue_mult*, are used for converting RGB values to pixels.

Converting RGB Values to Pixels

The *base_pixel* field in the XStandardColormap structure holds the base colormap index. You can use this to convert RGB values to pixels. A function to do this follows:

```
#include <X11/Xutil.h>


unsigned long
ConvertStdRGBToPixel(XStandardColormap* std_colormap,
    int red,
    int green,
    int blue)


{   /* ConvertStdRGBToPixel */
    unsigned long   pixel;


    pixel = (red   * std_colormap->red_mult) +
            (green * std_colormap->green_mult) +
            (blue  * std_colormap->blue_mult) +
            std_colormap->base_pixel;


    return pixel;


}   /* ConvertStdRGBToPixel */
```

To compute a pixel value for a GrayScale visual, use the following formula:

```
    pixel = (desired_gray * std_colormap->red_mult) +
            std_colormap->base_pixel;
```

Because of the `base_pixel` field, a standard colormap can leave blank areas in the colormap from which other applications could allocate colors. The `RGB_DEFAULT_MAP` is one such standard colormap that is usually based on the default colormap for a screen.

Standard Colormap Properties

The X Window System provides a means to store any named set of data associated with a window. This data is also typed, although the types are arbitrary. Such a collection of data associated with a window is called a *property*.

The property names are called *atoms* and start out as text strings. These text strings are converted to hash numbers by a process called *interning*. Once an atom has been interned in the X server, your application (and any other X program) can use the atom ID number in place of the string. Each property has an atom for a name. The data types also start out as text strings and—you guessed it—are interned as atoms.

Luckily, the X server starts up with a set of predefined text strings converted to atoms. If you're just using the standard colormaps, your applications won't have to intern any text strings to convert them to atom IDs.

For now, you only need to know that the standard colormaps are placed into properties, normally on the root window. Your application can then use these standard colormaps by reading the data from the property that holds the colormap you want. This is how applications share standard colormaps.

Properties Used by Standard Colormaps

The header file `<X11/Xatom.h>` defines the atoms that all X servers load up at start time. This file includes a number of predefined atoms for use with standard colormaps. You can use these atoms as the `property` parameter passed to `XGetRGBColormaps`, below.

The atoms below are numeric constants defined in `<X11/Xatom.h>`. The actual string interned for the atom is the constant without the `XA_` prefix. That is, the `XA_RGB_BEST_MAP` atom is the ID number for the string `"RGB_BEST_MAP"`.

These atoms, all of type `RGB_COLOR_MAP`, and the corresponding standard colormaps are listed in Table 12.1.

Table 12.1   *Standard colormap atoms.*

Atom
XA_RGB_BEST_MAP
XA_RGB_BLUE_MAP
XA_RGB_DEFAULT_MAP
XA_RGB_GRAY_MAP
XA_RGB_GREEN_MAP
XA_RGB_RED_MAP

The Best Map

The best standard colormap tries to provide as many perceptually distinct colors as possible. The term *perceptually distinct* is a code-phrase meaning that there are more green cells than red, and more red cells than blue. The intention is that the XA_RGB_BEST_MAP colormap be used for 3D applications and other programs that need as many distinct colors as possible. For workstations with 8 bit-planes of color, the allocation is probably 3/3/2. For those with 24 bit-planes of color, the allocation is likely 8/8/8.

The Default Map

XA_RGB_DEFAULT_MAP is a special standard colormap. It is intended to be a subset of the default colormap. Because of this, you have a better chance of avoiding the color flashing effects, as the window manager swaps colormaps if you use the XA_RGB_DEFAULT_MAP colormap. The default XA_RGB_DEFAULT_MAP provides a *red_max*, *green_max*, and *blue_max* of 5, using 216 uniformly distributed color cells and leaving 40 extra cells for other applications on a system with 256 color cells available.

The Red, Green, and Blue Maps

The XA_RGB_RED_MAP, XA_RGB_GREEN_MAP, and XA_RGB_BLUE_MAP standard colormaps all provide a colormap with shades of a single color: all-red, all-green, or all-blue, respectively. These colormaps are useful for generating color separations common with prepress applications.

The Gray Map

The XA_RGB_GRAY_MAP is a lot like the all-red, all-green, and all-blue colormaps described above. This property holds the best GrayScale colormap available on the screen. Remember to use the special GrayScale formula, above, for converting a gray value into a pixel value.

Reading Standard Colormap Properties

Even though we've barely discussed the X concept of properties, your application can read one of the properties described above through the convenience routine XGetRGBColormaps:

```
#include <X11/Xutil.h>


Status XGetRGBColormaps(Display* display,
    Window window,
    XStandardColormap** std_colormaps, /* RETURN */
    int* number_colormaps,  /* RETURN */
    Atom property)
```

XGetRGBColormaps returns a nonzero value on success, zero otherwise. Note that only the XA_RGB_DEFAULT_MAP standard colormap property should have more than one entry. All other properties should have only one entry. The *window* parameter should be the root window in most cases. You should call XFree to free the memory for the *std_colormaps*.

In most cases, some other application, such as a window manager or a special program named xstdcmap (see below under Programs That Create Standard Colormaps) will have already created the standard colormap you want. If this hasn't been done, or if your application wants to define its own standard colormap, you can store your own standard colormap properties.

Storing Your Own Standard Colormaps

You can write out a property and store your own standard colormap using the XSetRGBColormaps function:

```
void XSetRGBColormaps(Display* display,
    Window window,
    XStandardColormap* std_colormaps,
    int number_colormaps,
    Atom property)
```

All standard colormaps, except for the XA_RGB_DEFAULT_MAP, must have only one colormap in the property. There's no restriction preventing your application from violating this rule. If you want to follow the ICCCM and not mess up other applications, follow this rule. There are a few other rules as well that you need to follow to create standard colormaps.

Creating Standard Colormaps

You can use XSetRGBColormaps to store a standard colormap. Before you do so, you need to create a standard colormap. There's a set of involved conventions that describe how you do this:

1. Open a new connection to the X server. This odd requirement is because of quirks in the XSetCloseDownMode function, below. XSetCloseDownMode makes sure that all the colormaps and other X IDs created under this display connection are retained after our application quits.

2. Grab the X server, using XGrabServer.

3. Check if the standard colormap property you want to use is already created. If so, you're done.

4. If this property doesn't exist, you need to create a new colormap unless you're using the XA_RGB_DEFAULT_MAP standard colormap.

5. Determine the amount of colors available on the visual you want to use.

6. Allocate cells in the colormap using `XAllocColorCells` or `XAllocColorPlanes`.

7. Call `XStoreColor` or `XStoreColors` to store the RGB values into your allocated color cells. You should follow the conventions above. If you're creating a standard colormap that you advertise as being all green, don't store red values instead.

8. Allocate an `XStandardColormap` structure using `XAllocStandardColormap`.

9. Fill in the `XStandardColormap` structure with the proper values.

10. Call `XSetRGBColormaps` to attach the proper property on the root window.

11. Make the colormap permanent with `XSetCloseDownMode`. Because we use a separate display connection, `XSetCloseDownMode` only retains those X IDs created with the new display connection. Thus, all our windows and pixmaps won't be kept indefinitely.

12. Ungrab the X server, using `XUngrabServer`.

13. Close the new X display connection. Revert back to the old connection.

Grabbing the X Server

X allows an application to take control over the X server so that only your X requests are dealt with. The main reason to grab the X server is to avoid race conditions in the odd cases where two applications are trying to do the same thing. For instance, if two applications try to create the standard colormap properties at the same time, these definitions will conflict.

To take control of the X server, call `XGrabServer`:

```
XGrabServer(Display* display)
```

While the grab is in place, all requests from other X applications are queued up. These requests won't get dealt with by the X server until your application ungrabs the server, using `XUngrabServer`:

```
XUngrabServer(Display* display)
```

When your application closes its X connection, this function is automatically called.

Like any other function that tries to take charge in a multitasking environment, you should use XGrabServer with care. It is *not* considered good form to try to control the X server for more than a very short time.

XGrabServer also complicates debugging. If you have problems with XGrabServer, you'll need to log in with a separate terminal. Why? Because your debugger won't be able to display anything until the X server is ungrabbed. This is another good reason to minimize calls to XGrabServer.

NOTE

If you don't need to take over the whole X server, you can grab a mouse button (XGrabButton), the whole mouse pointer (XGrabPointer), a key on the keyboard (XGrabKey), or the whole keyboard (XGrabKeyboard).

Retaining X Resources after Your Program Quits

All the X resources, such as windows, pixmaps, and colormaps, associated with an application are destroyed when the application cuts its connection to the X server (using XCloseDisplay or exiting the program with exit). To change this, you can call XSetCloseDownMode:

```
XSetCloseDownMode(Display* display,
    int close_down_mode)
```

The *close_down_mode* should be one of DestroyAll, RetainPermanent, or RetainTemporary. The default is DestroyAll. If you use RetainPermanent, all these X IDs will remain until explicitly deleted with a call to XKillClient. To keep the standard colormaps from being destroyed when your application quits, you need to use RetainPermanent.

XSetCloseDownMode applies to all X IDs (windows, pixmaps, colormaps, etc.) created with a single display connection to the X server. Because of this quirk, your application must open up a separate display connection to create the standard colormaps. Otherwise, you run the danger of keeping a lot of large—unneeded—data structures active in the X server after your application quits.

Functions to Work with Standard Colormaps

The *X miscellaneous utilities library*, or *Xmu*, contains a number of routines for working with standard colormaps. This library has some interesting routines, including several that deal with standard colormaps.

All of these Xmu routines require the `<X11/Xmu/StdCmap.h>` include file.

NOTE Unfortunately, Xmu is not considered an X Consortium standard, so these routines may not be available on your system. Xmu comes with the X releases from the X Consortium, but some vendors don't ship it.

The Xmu routines start out at a very high level and then gradually go down to lower and lower levels. Each level down provides you with more control. To start at the highest level, one function, XmuAllStandardColormaps, can create all of the appropriate standard colormaps listed above:

```
Status XmuAllStandardColormaps(Display* display)
```

XmuAllStandardColormaps follows the 13 rules above for creating standard colormaps, including opening a separate display connection to the X server and making sure the colormaps are retained permanently (until the X server quits or resets). XmuAllStandardColormaps returns a nonzero value on success; zero otherwise.

The method used by XmuAllStandardColormaps is to find the most appropriate visual (an arbitrary choice) and then create all the standard colormap types for this visual. To have a little more control over the visual used, you can call XmuVisualStandardColormaps.

XmuVisualStandardColormaps creates all of the appropriate standard colormaps for a given visual on a given screen:

```
Status XmuVisualStandardColormaps(Display* display,
    int screen_number,
```

```
        VisualID  visualid,
        unsigned int depth,
        Bool replace,
        Bool retain)
```

The *replace* parameter specifies whether or not to replace any existing standard colormap properties. The *retain* parameter specifies whether or not to retain the properties and colormaps for the duration of the X-server session. Going to more and more control, we next get to XmuLookupStandardColormap.

XmuLookupStandardColormap will create one given standard colormap property if not already created. It determines whether to create a new colormap or use the default colormap with XA_RGB_DEFAULT_MAP:

```
        Status XmuLookupStandardColormap(Display* display,
            int screen_number,
            VisualID  visualid,
            unsigned int depth,
            Atom property,
            Bool replace,
            Bool retain)
```

XmuGetColormapAllocation determines the best allocation for reds, greens, and blues—that is, the values for the *red_max*, *green_max*, and *blue_max*—for the given standard colormap property:

```
        Status XmuGetColormapAllocation(XVisualInfo* visual_info,
            Atom property,
            unsigned long* red_max,    /* RETURN */
            unsigned long* green_max,  /* RETURN */
            unsigned long* blue_max)   /* RETURN */
```

Once you have the proper allocations, you can call XmuStandardColormap to allocate the XStandardColormap structure and fill in the fields with the given values:

```
XStandardColormap* XmuStandardColormap(Display* display,
    int screen_number,
    VisualID  visualid,
    unsigned int depth,
    Atom property,
    Colormap colormap,
    unsigned long red_max,
    unsigned long green_max,
    unsigned long blue_max)
```

NOTE XmuStandardColormap does not call XSetClose-DownMode to retain the properties. That's your responsibility.

Once you've filled in the XStandardColormap structure, call XmuCreateColormap to create the colormap as described in the values held in the structure:

```
Status XmuCreateColormap(Display* display,
    XStandardColormap* std_colormap)
```

NOTE According to the Xmu documentation, "No argument error checking is provided; use at your own risk." Be warned.

To delete a standard colormap property on the root window, call XmuDeleteStandardColormap:

```
void XmuDeleteStandardColormap(Display* display,
    int screen_number,
    Atom property)
```

Linking with the Xmu Library

The Xmu library uses the `Widget` type, so that it requires the Xt Intrinsics library. Therefore, if your toolkit does not use the Xt Intrinsics, you may have problems. Normally, the Xmu library is the file `libXmu.a` in the `/usr/lib` directory.

To compile a Motif program and use the Xmu routines, use the following template:

```
cc -o foo foo.c -lXm -lXmu -lXt -lX11
```

To compile an OLIT program, use the following template:

```
cc -o foo foo.c -lXol -lXmu -lXt -lX11
```

You may have problems linking with Sun shared libraries. If you experience this, you may need to link statically, using a command such as the following:

N O T E

```
cc -o foo foo.c -lXol -Bstatic -lXmu -Bdynamic
       lXt  lX11
```

A Program to List Standard Colormaps

The following simple program, `liststdc`, lists out the available standard colormaps. By available, we mean those standard colormaps that some other X application set up. You can use the `liststdc` program to verify that your application did indeed create the proper standard colormap.

The program calls `XGetRGBColormaps` in turn for each of the possible standard colormap properties. When printing out the standard colormap data, we need a way to convert the atom ID, such as XA_RGB_GRAY_MAP, to a text string suitable for printing, "RGB_GRAY_MAP" in this case. To do this, our program above uses the function `XGetAtomName` to convert the atom ID back to a text string. `XGetAtomName` takes the following parameters:

```
char* XGetAtomName(Display* display, Atom atom)
```

You need to call XFree on the text string returned.

The code for the liststdc program is stored in liststdc.c:

```
/*
 * liststdc.c
 * Program to list standard colormaps.
 */
#include "xlib.h"
#include <X11/Xutil.h>
#include <X11/Xatom.h>
#include <stdio.h>

void PrintStandardColormap(XStandardColormap* std_colormap)

{   /* PrintStandardColormap */

    printf("\t Colormap: 0x%x\n",
        std_colormap->colormap);

    printf("\t Maximum number of cells\n");
    printf("\t\t Red: %d \t green: %d \t blue: %d\n",
        std_colormap->red_max,
        std_colormap->green_max,
        std_colormap->blue_max);

    printf("\t Multipliers\n");
    printf("\t\t Red: %d \t green: %d \t blue: %d\n",
        std_colormap->red_mult,
        std_colormap->green_mult,
        std_colormap->blue_mult);

    printf("\t Base pixel %d\n",
        std_colormap->base_pixel);
```

```
        printf("\t Visual ID 0x%x,  Kill ID 0x%x\n",
            std_colormap->visualid,
            std_colormap->killid);


}   /* PrintStandardColormap */


void ListStandardColormaps(Display* display,
    int screen,
    Atom which_colormap)


{   /* ListStandardColormaps */
    XStandardColormap*  std_colormaps;
    int                 status;
    int                 number_colormaps;
    int                 i;
    char*               atom_name;


    status = XGetRGBColormaps(display,
            RootWindow(display, screen),
            &std_colormaps,
            &number_colormaps,
            which_colormap);


    if (status != 0) {
        atom_name = XGetAtomName(display, which_colormap);

        printf("\nPrinting %d standard colormaps for %s\n",
            number_colormaps, atom_name);

        XFree(atom_name);

        for (i = 0; i < number_colormaps; i++) {
```

```
            PrintStandardColormap(&std_colormaps[i]);
        }


        /*
         * Free standard colormap structures.
         */
        XFree((void*) std_colormaps);
    }


}   /* ListStandardColormaps */


int main(int argc, char** argv)

{   /* main */
    Display*  display;
    int       screen;

    /*
     * Open display connection.
     */
    display = XOpenDisplay( (char*) NULL);

    if (display != (Display*) NULL) {
        screen = DefaultScreen(display);

        ListStandardColormaps(display,
            screen, XA_RGB_DEFAULT_MAP);

        ListStandardColormaps(display,
            screen, XA_RGB_BEST_MAP);

        ListStandardColormaps(display,
```

```
                        screen, XA_RGB_RED_MAP);


            ListStandardColormaps(display,
                screen, XA_RGB_GREEN_MAP);


            ListStandardColormaps(display,
                screen, XA_RGB_BLUE_MAP);


            ListStandardColormaps(display,
                screen, XA_RGB_GRAY_MAP);


            XCloseDisplay(display);
        }


        return 0;


    }   /* main */


    /* end of file liststdc.c */
```

Using Standard Colormaps

Standard colormaps are intended to be a way to share colormaps between applications, especially 3D rendering and image-processing applications. Even so, few applications so far have used standard colormaps. The disadvantages of using standard colormaps include the fact that if you use one of the predefined standard colormaps, your application cannot specify the RGB values you desire. You have to use the RGB values in the standard colormap. Another reason for not using standard colormaps is simple lack of documentation. To help you get up to speed, you may want to look at the source code for an X application that creates standard colormaps, xstdcmap.

Programs That Create Standard Colormaps

The X Window System comes with a handy program to create and destroy standard colormaps. You can create all the documented standard colormaps using the `xstdcmap` program. (This program is not available on all systems. Hewlett-Packard, for example, doesn't ship `xstdcmap` as of this writing.)

The `-all` command-line parameter to `xstdcmap` will create all the standard colormaps, using the Xmu routines described above:

```
xstdcmap -all
```

Other command-line parameters include are listed in Table 12.2.

Table 12.2   *Parameters for xstdcmap.*

Command-Line Parameter	Standard Colormap
`-best`	`RGB_BEST_MAP`
`-blue`	`RGB_BLUE_MAP`
`-default`	`RGB_DEFAULT_MAP`
`-gray`	`RGB_GRAY_MAP`
`-green`	`RGB_GREEN_MAP`
`-red`	`RGB_RED_MAP`

Additionally, the `-delete` command-line parameter tells `xstdcmap` to delete a given standard colormap property. `Xstdcmap -delete red` will then delete the `RGB_RED_MAP`. The `-all` parameter creates all the documented standard colormaps. If we run `xstdcmap -all` and then run the `liststdc` program, above, we get the results below:

```
Printing 1 standard colormaps for RGB_DEFAULT_MAP
    Colormap: 0x20000065
    Maximum number of cells
        Red: 4     green: 4     blue: 4
    Multipliers
```

```
            Red: 25       green: 5      blue: 1
       Base pixel 10
       Visual ID 0x20000064,  Kill ID 0x2000002


   Printing 1 standard colormaps for RGB_BEST_MAP
       Colormap: 0x3400001
       Maximum number of cells
            Red: 7        green: 7      blue: 3
       Multipliers
            Red: 32       green: 4      blue: 1
       Base pixel 0
       Visual ID 0x20000064,  Kill ID 0x1


   Printing 1 standard colormaps for RGB_RED_MAP
       Colormap: 0x2800001
       Maximum number of cells
            Red: 255      green: 0      blue: 0
       Multipliers
            Red: 1        green: 0      blue: 0
       Base pixel 0
       Visual ID 0x20000064,  Kill ID 0x1


   Printing 1 standard colormaps for RGB_GREEN_MAP
       Colormap: 0x2c00001
       Maximum number of cells
            Red: 0        green: 255     blue: 0
       Multipliers
            Red: 0        green: 1      blue: 0
       Base pixel 0
       Visual ID 0x20000064,  Kill ID 0x1
```

```
Printing 1 standard colormaps for RGB_BLUE_MAP
    Colormap: 0x3000001
    Maximum number of cells
        Red: 0        green: 0      blue: 255
    Multipliers
        Red: 0        green: 0      blue: 1
    Base pixel 0
    Visual ID 0x20000064,  Kill ID 0x1


Printing 1 standard colormaps for RGB_GRAY_MAP
    Colormap: 0x2400001
    Maximum number of cells
        Red: 76       green: 151       blue: 28
    Multipliers
        Red: 1        green: 1      blue: 1
    Base pixel 0
    Visual ID 0x20000064,  Kill ID 0x1
```

Old Compatibility Routines

Two old routines from X11 Release 3 are XGetStandardColormap and
XSetStandardColormap. These routines were replaced by
XGetRGBColormaps and XSetRGBColormaps in R4. We strongly
advise you to use the new R4 routines.

If you are stuck at R3, you may have to use these routines. There are a
number of reasons to upgrade, especially since R4 and R5 improved X's performance dramatically and the C libraries had many bugs fixed.

```
Status XGetStandardColormap(Display* display,
    Window window,
    XStandardColormap* std_colormap, /* RETURN */
    Atom property)
```

`XGetStandardColormap` returns only one standard colormap.

```
void XSetStandardColormap(Display* display,
    Window window,
    XStandardColormap* std_colormap,
    Atom property)
```

`XSetStandardColormap` sets only one standard colormap.

Summary

Many X applications require most, if not all, of the available colors on a system. In addition, many image-processing applications desire to have an easy way to convert an RGB value into a colormap index, also called a pixel. Having such an easy conversion can improve the performance for processing images. To aid these applications, X provides a set of so-called standard colormaps. These colormaps are sharable between applications and usually provide an even color ramp. This allows your applications to convert RGB values to colormap indexes with a simple calculation formula.

If you use standard colormaps, though, your application must follow a set of rules that well-behaved X programs use to ensure these colormaps act as expected. We cover these rules, part of the Inter-Client Communications Conventions Manual, or ICCCM for short.

To allocate a standard colormap structure, use `XAllocStandardColormap`. `XAllocStandardColormap` allocates an `XStandardColormap` structure and sets all the fields to zero. If `XAllocStandardColormap` fails, it returns NULL. Otherwise, `XAllocStandardColormap` returns a pointer to the new `XStandardColormap` structure.

The X Window System provides a means to store any named set of data associated with a window. This data is also typed, although the types are arbitrary. Such a collection of data associated with a window is called a property. The property names are called atoms and start out as text strings. These text strings are converted to hash numbers by a process called interning. Once an atom has been interned in the X server, your application (and any other X program) can use the atom ID number in place of the string. Each property has an atom for a name. The data types also start out as text strings and—you guessed it—are interned as atoms. For now, you only need to know that the standard colormaps are placed into properties, normally on the root window. Your application can then use these standard colormaps by reading the data from the property that holds the colormap you want. This is how applications share standard colormaps.

X Library Functions and Macros Introduced in This Chapter

```
XAllocStandardColormap

XGetAtomName

XGetRGBColormaps

XGetStandardColormap

XGrabServer

XSetCloseDownMode

XSetRGBColormaps

XSetStandardColormap

XUngrabServer
```

X Miscellaneous Utilities Functions and Macros Introduced in This Chapter

```
XmuAllStandardColomaps

XmuCreateColormap

XmuDeleteStandardColormap

XmuGetColormapAllocation

XmuLookupStandardColormap

XmuStandardColormap

XmuVisualStandardColormaps
```

C h a p t e r   1 3

The X Color Management System

This chapter covers:

- ✦ The X Color Management System
- ✦ The CIE color model—going beyond RGB
- ✦ Getting exact colors
- ✦ Allocating colors with Xcms
- ✦ Xcms color names
- ✦ Converting between color spaces

Problems with the RGB Model of Color

X bases colors on RGB (red, green, blue) definitions, and these RGB values permeate the X protocol. RGB values, unfortunately, don't look the same on every monitor. The differences are apparent because of different graphics hardware that drives monitors on systems from different vendors. For example, colors on a Sun SPARCstation-2 look different than the same RGB colors on a Silicon Graphics Inc. (SGI) Indigo. In addition to the differences between the hardware that drives the monitors, each monitor may be slightly off. The displayed colors can also change because of environmental variables like nearby power lines.

Most of us simply don't care about these differences. If we allow users to specify colors in resource files or using some other user-configurable scheme, then we're free of the problem of making the right set of colors on widely different displays. (A large number of users are also partially color-blind. These users may require garish color combinations in order to provide enough contrast so they can use your application's interface. This is another reason to allow users to customize colors.) At worst, you'll want to come up with a good-looking set of default colors.

Because of the problems outlined above, X11 Release 5 introduces a device-independent way to specify exact colors. The *X Color Management System*, or *Xcms*, is a set of extra routines added to the low-level X library. Many users in the professional world require exact colors. Anyone working in the publishing industry requires exact colors. Anyone in the data-visualization world requires exact colors. Anyone in the computer-aided design field requires exact colors. If the X RGB model performs fine for you and unless TekHVC or CIE means something to you, you may want to skip ahead to the next chapter.

A Compatible Extension to the X Library

By extending the X library, the Xcms routines allow your application to demand exact coloration using a number of non-RGB color models. Even so, under the hood, the X library converts these different color formats to RGB before sending data to the X server. This is because of the unfortunate limitation of the X server and the X network protocol only supporting RGB values for color. In this case, though, the compatibility is a good thing. The Xcms routines act only on the client side—that is, in your application, so that you can use an Xcms-based application with older X servers. We've dealt with a number of incompatibilities over the years in various releases of X, so the compatibility provided by the Xcms routines is a good thing.

One problem of this model, though, is that your applications tend to grow a lot larger due to having all the color format conversion routines built into your application. Using shared libraries helps in this regard.

What's Needed to Control Colors Exactly

In order to control colors exactly, you need a color specification that is independent of any device. You must be able to specify a color and have that color repeatably appear the same on different displays. To do this, you need to *characterize* your device to define the limits of its capabilities for producing color. Xcms routines build a characterization database on each X server that is used for gamut mapping and to translate CIE XYZ values to and from RGB values. In addition to characterizing your device's capabilities, you need to measure each monitor individually to *calibrate* the process to provide the most accurate colors possible. Usually, this calibration process requires an external device to measure the display output. And, with most monitors, you still can't achieve 100 percent accuracy.

The X Color Management System

X11 Release 5 supports the following ways to define color:

- ✦ RGB (the same old way)
- ✦ RGB intensity
- ✦ CIE XYZ
- ✦ CIE u'v'Y
- ✦ CIE xyY
- ✦ CIE L*u*v*
- ✦ CIE L*a*b*
- ✦ Tektronix HVC

The X color management routines provide a way for your application to specify an exact color and then have the X library translate that color into

tines are really allocating straight RGB values. These routines act entirely on the client side of X and just translate your desired color to and from an appropriate RGB value. Sounds simple, doesn't it? It isn't.

The first caveat is that to properly translate an exact color specification to an appropriate RGB value for your screen, you'll need some form of hardware device to calibrate your monitor. Once calibrated, information on the screen must be accessible to your applications. The rules for well-behaved X applications, the Inter-Client Communications Conventions Manual, or ICCCM, describes a means to store such device color characterization data, following the XDCCC, for X Device Color Characterization Conventions, so that X applications can access it. This information includes the *device gamut*, which describes the range of colors that can be displayed on the screen. *Gamut mapping* is used to adjust colors due to differences between the *white point* assumed by the color model and the screen's white point. Gamut mapping also adjusts colors when the desired color lies outside the range of colors supported by the device. The ability of your applications (normally under the hood with the Xcms routines) to modify color specifications to fit within the screen's capability is called the *gamut compression*.

The main color model supported by Xcms is the *CIE XYZ model*. The CIE 1931 standard is used to describe perceivable colors. This XDCCC information is used to translate CIE XYZ color triplets to RGB values on the screen. The CIE XYZ format is used by all the Xcms routines to translate to RGB. All other color formats, such as TekHVC, are mapped to CIE XYZ format before the translation to RGB (You can look in Chapter 13 of Foley and van Dam's *Computer Graphics* for more on CIE color.)

The X Color Management Routines

The Xcms routines are part of the low-level X library (as of X11 Release 5) and concentrate on routines to query and set values in color cells. (They are listed in Table 13.1.) The first thing you'll notice about the Xcms routines is how closely they match the regular X color routines. For example, `XcmsLookupColor` corresponds to `XLookupColor`, and `XcmsAllocNamedColor` corresponds to `XAllocNamedColor`.

Table 13.1   *Xcms routines.*

Xcms	Corresponds to Xlib
XcmsAllocColor	XAllocColor
XcmsAllocNamedColor	XAllocNamedColor
XcmsColor structure	XColor structure
XcmsLookupColor	XLookupColor
XcmsQueryColor	XQueryColor
XcmsQueryColors	XQueryColors
XcmsStoreColor	XStoreColor
XcmsStoreColors	XStoreColors

Looking Up Color Names

XcmsLookupColor acts much like XLookupColor in that it converts a color name (formatted using the rules listed below) to two XcmsColor structures, both an exact value and the closest value supported by the hardware:

```
#include <X11/Xcms.h>

Status XcmsLookupColor(Display* display,
    Colormap colormap,
    const char* color_name,
    XcmsColor* exactcolor,    /* RETURN */
    XcmsColor* hardwarecolor, /* RETURN */
    XcmsColorFormat desired_format)
```

All the Xcms routines need the include file <X11/Xcms.h>. This file is new with X11 Release 5.

XcmsLookupColor returns a status of XcmsFailure on errors, XcmsSuccess on success, and XcmsSuccessWithCompression to indicate that while the routine succeeded, it had to convert the color specification using gamut compression.

The *color_name* must be in a special Xcms syntax described below. The *desired_format* is what type of color space the color name is defined in. You can use the constant XcmsUndefinedFormat to signify that you don't know what format the color name is in. This is useful because your application won't always know what way the color name was formatted. In your code, you can use XcmsLookupColor to look up a color name as follows:

```
#include  <X11/Xcms.h>


Display*        display;

Colormap        colormap;

char*           color_name = "rgbi:0.5/0.3/0.7";

XcmsColor       hardwarecolor, exactcolor;

unsigned long   color;

int             status;


status = XcmsLookupColor(display,

        colormap,

        color_name,

        &exactcolor,

        &hardwarecolor,

        XcmsUndefinedFormat);


if (status != XcmsFailure) {

    /* success... */

    color = hardwarecolor.pixel;

}
```

The above example uses a *color_name* in the *RGBi* or *RGB intensity* format. Because the name ("rgbi:0.5/0.3/0.7") is in this format, XcmsLookupColor knows the proper conversion, even though we passed a format identifier of XcmsUndefinedFormat. In R5, XLookupColor works with the new text format for *color_name* (see below) but the routine only returns RGB values in XColor structures.

Xcms Color Format Identifiers

The XcmsColorFormat data type is normally an unsigned int:

```
typedef unsigned int XcmsColorFormat;
```

The allowed format identifiers are listed in Table 13.2.

Table 13.2 *Xcms color format identifiers.*

Xcms Format Identifier	Color Space
XcmsUndefinedFormat	Unknown/unspecified
XcmsCIEXYZFormat	CIE XYZ
XcmsCIEuvYFormat	CIE u'v'Y
XcmsCIExyYFormat	CIE xyY
XcmsCIELabFormat	CIE L*a*b*
XcmsCIELuvFormat	CIE L*u*v*
XcmsTekHVCFormat	Tek HVC
XcmsRGBiFormat	RGBi
XcmsRGBFormat	RGB (old style)

The XcmsColor Structure

With XcmsLookupColor, both the *hardwarecolor* and the *exactcolor* are pointers to XcmsColor structures. The XcmsColor structure is a lot like the XColor structure used with XLookupColor, except that the XcmsColor structure is a union of structures for all the supported color spaces:

```
typedef struct {
```

```
union {
        XcmsRGB         RGB;
        XcmsRGBi        RGBi;
        XcmsCIEXYZ      CIEXYZ;
        XcmsCIEuvY      CIEuvY;
        XcmsCIExyY      CIExyY;
        XcmsCIELab      CIELab;
        XcmsCIELuv      CIELuv;
        XcmsTekHVC      TekHVC;
        XcmsPad         Pad;
    } spec;
    unsigned long       pixel;
    XcmsColorFormat     format;   /* which format */
} XcmsColor;
```

Each element in the *spec* union is a structure for a given type of color formatting. What follows are descriptions of more structures than you probably care to deal with. All of the Xcms structures, data types, and functions are defined in ⟨X11/Xcms.h⟩.

The old-style RGB colors are stored in a XcmsRGB structure:

```
typedef struct {
    unsigned short   red;
    unsigned short   green;
    unsigned short   blue;
} XcmsRGB;
```

The RGB values are scaled from 0x0000 to 0xFFFF.

The RGB intensity values are stored as double-precision floating-point numbers between 0.0 and 1.0, in an XcmsRGBi structure:

```
typedef struct {
        XcmsFloat    red;    /* 0.0 - 1.0 */
```

```
        XcmsFloat    green;  /* 0.0 - 1.0 */
        XcmsFloat    blue;   /* 0.0 - 1.0 */
} XcmsRGBi;
```

RGB intensity colors, like RGB colors, are *not* device-independent. The XcmsFloat data type is normally a double-precision float:

```
typedef double XcmsFloat;
```

For the CIE color space, the CIE XYZ format is stored in an XcmsCIEXYZ structure:

```
typedef struct {
        XcmsFloat    X;
        XcmsFloat    Y;
        XcmsFloat    Z;
} XcmsCIEXYZ;
```

The CIE u'v'Y values are scaled from 0.0 to 1.0 and are stored in an XcmsCIEuvY structure:

```
typedef struct {
    XcmsFloat    u_prime;  /* 0.0 - 1.0 */
    XcmsFloat    v_prime;  /* 0.0 - 1.0 */
    XcmsFloat    Y;        /* 0.0 - 1.0 */
} XcmsCIEuvY;
```

CIE xyY colors are stored in—you guessed it—an XcmsCIExyY structure:

```
typedef struct {
    XcmsFloat    x;   /* 0.0 - 1.0 */
    XcmsFloat    y;   /* 0.0 - 1.0 */
    XcmsFloat    Y;   /* 0.0 - 1.0 */
} XcmsCIExyY;
```

The CIE L*a*b* values are stored in XcmsCIELab structures:

```
typedef struct {
    XcmsFloat    L_star;    /* 0.0 - 100.0 */
    XcmsFloat    a_star;
    XcmsFloat    b_star;
} XcmsCIELab;
```

CIE L*u*v* colors use the XcmsCIELuv structure:

```
typedef struct {
    XcmsFloat    L_star;    /* 0.0 - 100.0 */
    XcmsFloat    u_star;
    XcmsFloat    v_star;
} XcmsCIELuv;
```

The Tektronix (or Tek) HVC color values are stored in an XcmsTekHVC structure:

```
typedef struct {
    XcmsFloat    H;    /* 0.0 - 360.0 */
    XcmsFloat    V;    /* 0.0 - 100.0 */
    XcmsFloat    C;    /* 0.0 - 100.0 */
} XcmsTekHVC;
```

The XcmsPad padding structure just makes sure that the *spec* union above holds at least four double-precision floating-point values:

```
typedef struct {
    XcmsFloat    pad0;
    XcmsFloat    pad1;
    XcmsFloat    pad2;
    XcmsFloat    pad3;
} XcmsPad;
```

Detecting the X Release Number

All the Xcms routines are new in X11 Release 5, or R5. Not every X vendor supports X11R5 yet, so your code must contain a method for determining the X version number

`<X11/Xlib.h>` contains a symbol, `XlibSpecificationRelease`, which you can check for the release number. `XlibSpecificationRelease` has a value of 5 with Release 5. Unfortunately, `XlibSpecificationRelease` is also new with R5. This leads to the complicated code below:

```
/*
 * Check if we are at X11R5 or higher.
 */
#ifdef XlibSpecificationRelease
#if XlibSpecificationRelease > 4
#define R5_CMS  1
#endif  /* R5 */
#endif  /* XlibSpecificationRelease */
```

We define the symbol `R5_CMS` if we are at R5 or higher and can use the Xcms routines.

Xcms Color Names

The Xcms routines expect color names to be in a certain format, as described in Table 13.3.

Table 13.3 *X11 Release 5 numerical color formats.*

Type	Xcms Format Identifier	Numerical Color Format
CIE X Y Z	`XcmsCIEXYZFormat`	`CIEXYZ:`X`/`Y`/`Z
CIE u' v' Y	`XcmsCIEuvYFormat`	`CIEuvY:`u`/`v`/`Y

CIE x y Y	XcmsCIExyYFormat	CIExyY: $x/y/Y$
CIE L* a* b*	XcmsCIELabFormat	CIELab: $L/a/b$
CIE L* u* v*	XcmsCIELuvFormat	CIELuv: $L/u/v$
RGB	XcmsRGBFormat	rgb: $r/g/b$
RGB intensity	XcmsRGBiFormat	rgbi: $ri/gi/bi$
Tektronix HVC	XcmsTekHVCFormat	TekHVC: $H/V/C$

These are not the English color names described in Chapter 7, but a way you can numerically "name" a color, using a given color model like CIE XYZ. For instance, "CIEXYZ:0.234/0.32/0.288" and "rgbi:0.5/0.3/0.7" are validly formatted Xcms color names. More examples are listed in Table 13.4.

Table 13.4 *Example color specifications.*

Example Specification	Color Format
rgbi:0.5/0.3/1.0	RGB intensity
rgb:ff/ff/00	RGB
rgb:00/ff/ff	RGB
CIEXYZ:0.2344/0.32/0.288	CIEXYZ
CIEXYZ:0.11111/0.77777/0.233333	CIEXYZ
CIEXYZ:0.2344/0.5/0.8777	CIEXYZ
CIExyY:0.399960/0.506334/0.887844	CIExyY
CIELuv:95.4938/0.061521/1.295631	CIEL*u*v*
CIELab:52.6524/0.728736/0.688501	CIEL*a*b*
TekHVC:0.0/20.0/0.0	Tektronix HVC
TekHVC:0.0/40.0/0.0	Tektronix HVC
TekHVC:0.0/60.0/0.0	Tektronix HVC

The RGB intensity numbers go from 0.0 to 1.0 (full intensity).

All the numbers except for $r/b/g$ are floating-point numbers. The RGB numbers are hexidecimal values. These RGB values can also be in the old format of #rgb, as described in Chapter 7. Table 13.5 provides some examples of the new RGB format.

Table 13.5 *The new-style (X11 Release 5) RGB names, in hexidecimal.*

Numerical Specification	Red	Green	Blue
rgb:10/cc/a0	10	cc	a0
rgb:ff/00/00	ff	0	0
rgb:11/22/33	11	22	33

Once you've converted an Xcms color name into an XcmsColor structure, you can then allocate a color cell with XcmsAllocColor.

Allocating Colors with Xcms

XcmsAllocColor acts like XAllocColor, only it supports the various Xcms color formats:

```
Status XcmsAllocColor(Display* display,
    Colormap colormap,
    XcmsColor* xcmscolor, /* input/output */
    XcmsColorFormat desired_format)
```

You can allocate a color cell with XcmsAllocColor using the following code:

```
Display*        display;
Colormap        colormap;
XcmsColor       xcmscolor;
unsigned long   color;
int             status;

status = XcmsAllocColor(display,
            colormap,
            &xcmscolor,
            XcmsUndefinedFormat);
```

```
if ( status != XcmsFailure ) {
    color = xcmscolor.pixel;
}
```

XcmsAllocNamedColor combines XcmsLookupColor with XcmsAllocColor:

```
Status XcmsAllocNamedColor(Display* display,
    Colormap colormap,
    const char* color_name,
    XcmsColor* hardwarecolor,
    XcmsColor* exactcolor,
    XcmsColorFormat desired_format)
```

Watch out. Both XcmsLookupColor, above, and XcmsAllocNamedColor take *hardwarecolor* and *exactcolor* parameters, but reverse the order.

 We found a problem with the early documentation for XcmsAllocNamedColor. The above description is correct, though your documentation may not state so. The *desired_format* parameter really does go at the end.

You can use XcmsAllocNamedColor in your code like the following:

```
Display*        display;
Colormap        colormap;
XcmsColor       cmscolor;
unsigned long   color;
int             status;
XcmsColor       hardwarecolor, exactcolor;
char*           colorname = "rgbi:0.5/0.3/0.7";

status = XcmsAllocNamedColor(display,
```

```
                colormap,

                colorname,

                &hardwarecolor,

                &exactcolor,

                XcmsUndefinedFormat);
```

A Utility Function Using XcmsAllocNamedColor

We can create a function to allocate a named read-only color cell using the Xcms color name formats. This function, CmsAllocNamedColor, acts a lot like the AllocNamedColor function in color.c from Chapter 7. Both have a function to allocate a named color, but CmsAllocNamedColor uses XcmsAllocNamedColor rather than XAllocNamedColor if you have a system that is at least upgraded to R5. If not, the CmsAllocNamedColor function, below, uses XAllocNamedColor as a fallback strategy. Even so, the fallback isn't that good in that you'll have problems with the Xcms color names if you don't have XcmsAllocNamedColor available.

The CmsAllocNamedColor function is stored in colorcms.c:

```
/*
 *   colorcms.c
 *   Device-independent color cell allocation.
 */
#include "xlib.h"
#include <X11/Xutil.h>
#include <stdio.h>


/*
 * Check if we are at X11R5 or higher.
 */
#ifdef XlibSpecificationRelease
#if XlibSpecificationRelease > 4
#define R5_CMS  1
```

```
#endif  /* R5 */
#endif  /* XlibSpecificationRelease */


#ifdef R5_CMS
#include <X11/Xcms.h>
#endif  /* R5_CMS */


/*
 * Allocates a read-only (sharable) color cell
 * in the given colormap, using the X Color
 * Management System routines to convert an
 * arbitrary color name to an RGB value.
 * This routine checks for an X release
 * at least X11R5 or higher. If we're compiling
 * on a pre-R5 system, this routine calls
 * XAllocNamedColor instead. Even so, you'll
 * have problems with the Xcms color name
 * formats if you don't have Xcms.
 */


unsigned long CmsAllocNamedColor(Display* display,
    Colormap colormap,
    char* colorname,
    unsigned long default_color)


{   /* CmsAllocNamedColor */
    unsigned long  color;
    int            status;
#ifdef R5_CMS
    XcmsColor      hardwarecolor, exactcolor;
```

```
    status = XcmsAllocNamedColor(display,
            colormap,
            colorname,
            &hardwarecolor,
            &exactcolor,
            XcmsUndefinedFormat);

    if (status != XcmsFailure) {
        color = hardwarecolor.pixel;
    } else {
        printf("XcmsFailure on [%s]\n", colorname );
        color = default_color;
    }

#else
    XColor      hardwarecolor, exactcolor;

    status = XAllocNamedColor(display,
            colormap,
            colorname,
            &hardwarecolor,
            &exactcolor);

    if (status != 0) {
        color = hardwarecolor.pixel;
    } else {
        color = default_color;
    }

#endif   /* !R5_CMS */
```

```
         return color;

     }    /* CmsAllocNamedColor */


/* end of file colorcms.c */
```

Querying Xcms Color Cells

You can query color cells using XcmsQueryColor and XcmsQueryColors. XcmsQueryColor queries one color cell:

```
Status XcmsQueryColor(Display* display,
    Colormap colormap,
    XcmsColor* xcmscolor, /* input/output */
    XcmsColorFormat desired_format)
```

XcmsQueryColor retrieves the RGB values for the given color cell (like XQueryColor) and then converts the RGB values to the desired Xcms format as passed with the *desired_format* parameter.

To query a number of color cells at a time, use XcmsQueryColors:

```
Status XcmsQueryColors(Display* display,
    Colormap colormap,
    XcmsColor* xcmscolor_array, /* input/output */
    unsigned int number_colors,
    XcmsColorFormat desired_format)
```

Changing the Value of Writable Color Cells

When using the Xcms routines, the underlying color cells haven't changed at all, as the Xcms routines just sit in your application's X library. The X protocol and the X server didn't change at all with the introduction of alternative (non-RGB) color spaces. There's a strong momentum to avoid messing with the X protocol in order to maintain compatibility with the many X applications and servers in use today. Because of this, you still use `XAllocColorCells` and `XAllocColorPlanes` to allocate writable color cells.

You can use Xcms routines, though, to change the underlying RGB values stored in the writable color cells that you allocated with `XAllocColorCells` or `XAllocColorPlanes`.

The `XcmsStoreColor` function changes the definition of a color cell:

```
Status XcmsStoreColor(Display* display,
    Colormap colormap,
    XcmsColor* xcmscolor)
```

To change the value of multiple colors, use `XcmsStoreColors`:

```
Status XcmsStoreColors(Display* display,
    Colormap colormap,
    XcmsColor* xcmscolor_array,
    unsigned int number_colors,
    Bool* is_compressed) /* RETURN */
```

The *is_compressed* array contains a flag for each color in the xcmscolor_array. For each color, the *is_compressed* is set to `True` if the color had to be compressed using the gamut compression callback and `False` if no gamut compression occurs. If you're not interested in this information, you can pass NULL for *is_compressed*.

The Color Conversion Context

The *color conversion context*, or *CCC*, is created under the hood by the X library for each colormap your application accesses. This CCC transparently follows the colormap and is used by the Xcms routines. Normally, you won't need to modify this unless you want to create your own color space or don't like the default routines supplied by the X library.

The color conversion context contains the white point assumed by Xcms (the *client white point*), the white-point adjustment callback and the gamut compression callback. To get the CCC associated with a colormap, call XcmsCCCOfColormap:

```
XcmsCCC XcmsCCCOfColormap(Display* display,

        Colormap colormap)
```

XcmsCCCOfColormap returns the CCC in the form of an XcmsCCC pointer, covered below. Each screen has a default CCC, which you can retrieve with XcmsDefaultCCC:

```
XcmsCCC XcmsDefaultCCC(Display* display,

    int screen_number)
```

This routine and XcmsCCCOfColormap, shown above, are useful for getting an XcmsCCC pointer which is needed to convert colors from one format to another.

Converting Color Formats

The CIE XYZ format is used internally by the Xcms routines as the base format. You can convert between various color formats with XcmsConvertColors:

```
Status XcmsConvertColors(XcmsCCC ccc,

    XcmsColor* color_array,  /* input/output */

    unsigned int number_colors,

    XcmsColorFormat desired_format,

    Bool* is_compressed)  /* RETURN */
```

XcmsCCCOfColormap, XcmsDefaultCCC, and XcmsConvertColors all use or return an XcmsCCC pointer.

Exploring the Color Conversion Context

The XcmsCCC data type points at the color conversion context information:

```
typedef struct _XcmsCCC {
    Display*            dpy;
    int                 screenNumber;
    Visual*             visual;
    XcmsColor           clientWhitePt;
    XcmsCompressionProc gamutCompProc;
    XPointer            gamutCompClientData;
    XcmsWhiteAdjustProc whitePtAdjProc;
    XPointer            whitePtAdjClientData;
    XcmsPerScrnInfo*    pPerScrnInfo;
} XcmsCCCRec;


typedef struct _XcmsCCC *XcmsCCC;
```

The *gamutCompProc* is the gamut compression callback function. The *whitePtAdjProc* is the white-point adjustment callback.

The XcmsPerScrnInfo structure, in turn, holds the following:

```
typedef struct _XcmsPerScrnInfo {
    XcmsColor       screenWhitePt;
    XPointer        functionSet;
    XPointer        screenData;
    unsigned char state;
    char            pad[3];
} XcmsPerScrnInfo;
```

In the XcmsPerScrnInfo structure, the *functionSet* field points to the set of functions associated with the screen color characterization. The *screenData* field points at the screen color characterization data. The *state* field can be one of XcmsInitDefault, XcmsInitNone, or XcmsInitSuccess.

The callback functions have the following formats:

```
/* Gamut Compression Proc */
typedef Status (*XcmsCompressionProc)(XcmsCCC ccc,
    XcmsColor* color_array,  /* input/output */
    unsigned int number_colors,
    unsigned int index,
    Bool* is_compressed)     /* RETURN */
```

```
/* White Point Adjust Proc */
typedef Status (*XcmsWhiteAdjustProc)(XcmsCCC ccc,
    XcmsColor* initial_white_point,
    XcmsColor* target_white_point,
    XcmsColorFormat desired_format,
    XcmsColor* color_array,  /* input/output */
    unsigned int number_colors,
    Bool* is_compressed)     /* RETURN */
```

In most cases, your code won't have to modify the gamut compression or white-point adjustment callbacks.

Querying CCC Capabilities

Even if you don't modify the gamut compression callback function, your application may need to determine the boundaries of the screen's color gamut. These values are returned by a number of routines in terms of the CIE L*u*v*, CIE L*a*b*, or TekHVC color spaces. You can query the following colors as supported by your screen with a given color conversion context:

✦ Red (full-intensity red, zero green and blue).
✦ Green (full-intensity green, zero red and blue).

✦ Blue (full-intensity blue, zero green and red).

✦ Black (zero-intensity red, green, and blue).

✦ White (full-intensity red, green, and blue).

To do so, you can call the following functions:

```
XcmsQueryRed(XcmsCCC ccc,
    XcmsColorFormat desired_format,
    XcmsColor* xcmscolor)  /* RETURN */


XcmsQueryGreen(XcmsCCC ccc,
    XcmsColorFormat desired_format,
    XcmsColor* xcmscolor)  /* RETURN */


XcmsQueryBlue(XcmsCCC ccc,
    XcmsColorFormat desired_format,
    XcmsColor* xcmscolor)  /* RETURN */


XcmsQueryBlack(XcmsCCC ccc,
    XcmsColorFormat desired_format,
    XcmsColor* xcmscolor)  /* RETURN */


XcmsQueryWhite(XcmsCCC ccc,
    XcmsColorFormat desired_format,
    XcmsColor* xcmscolor)  /* RETURN */
```

The CCC Properties

To get the color conversion context information, the Xcms routines read in the value two properties from the root window. In order to take advantage of the Xcms capabilities, you must first ensure these properties are properly loaded onto the root window. To do so, you can use the xcmsdb program, new with X11R5. Xcmsdb loads or queries screen color characterization data properties. These properties are stored on the root window for the screen and describe the exact color calibration of the screen.

You can use xcmsdb to set up the data used by the Xcms routines to convert colors to and from the CIE XYZ format.

The CCC properties include XDCC_LINEAR_RGB_CORRECTION and XDCC_LINEAR_RGB_MATRICES. The XDCC_LINEAR_RGB_MATRICES property contains the matrices to convert RGB values to CIE XYZ and back again. You can read more on these in the ICCCM.

To be effective, xcmsdb needs a data input file containing the screen color characterization information. In typical X fashion, you're left to develop this information yourself. You call xcmsdb with the following format:

```
xcmsdb < input_data_file
```

You can also pass the -query parameter to xcmsdb. This returns the values in the XDCC_LINEAR_RGB_MATRICES and XDCC_LINEAR_RGB_COR-RECTION properties if they are present on the root window. Note that the XDCC_LINEAR_RGB_CORRECTION property is *very* long. The -remove parameter causes xcmsdb to remove the XDCC_LINEAR_RGB_MATRICES and XDCC_LINEAR_RGB_CORRECTION properties.

In addition to xcmsdb, R5 comes with a demo program called xcmstest. This program is useful for testing Xcms routines.

Xcms Color Databases

Like the database of English color names described in Chapter 7, you can also set up a database of names, like *red*, with Xcms color definitions instead of RGB. The default location for this database is /usr/lib/X11/Xcms.txt, although the generic X11R5 does not ship with such a file set up, so you can't expect many sites to have this database.

Summary

X bases colors on RGB (red, green, blue) definitions, and these RGB values permeate the X protocol. RGB values, unfortunately, don't look the same on every monitor. The differences are apparent because of different graphics hardware that drives monitors on systems from different vendors. For example, colors on a Sun SPARCstation-2 look different than the same RGB colors on a Silicon Graphics Indigo. In addition to the differences between the hardware that drives the monitors, each monitor may be slightly off. The displayed colors can also change because of environmental variables like nearby power lines.

Because of the problems outlined above, X11 Release 5 introduces a device-independent way to specify exact colors. The X Color Management System, or Xcms, is a set of extra routines added to the low-level X library.

By extending the X library, the Xcms routines allow your application to demand exact coloration using a number of non-RGB color models. Even so, under the hood, the X library converts these different color formats to RGB before sending data to the X server. This is because of the unfortunate limitation of the X server and the X network protocol only supporting RGB values for color. In this case, though, the compatibility is a good thing. The Xcms routines act only on the client side—that is, in your application, so that you can use an Xcms-based application with older X servers. We've dealt with a number of incompatibilities over the years in various releases of X, so the compatibility provided by the Xcms routines is a good thing.

In order to control colors exactly, you need a color specification that is independent of any device. You must be able to specify a color and have that color repeatably appear the same on different displays. To do this, you need to *characterize* your device to define the limits of its capabilities for producing color. Xcms routines build a characterization database on each X server that is used for gamut mapping and to translate CIE XYZ values to and from RGB values. In addition to characterizing your device's capabilities, you need to measure each monitor individually to calibrate the process to provide the most accurate colors possible. Usually, this calibration process requires an external device to measure the display output.

X11 Release 5 supports the following ways to define color:

- ✦ RGB (the same old way)
- ✦ RGB intensity
- ✦ CIE XYZ
- ✦ CIE xyY

- ✦ CIE u'v'Y
- ✦ CIE L*u*v*
- ✦ CIE L*a*b*
- ✦ Tektronix HVC

The X color management routines provide a way for your application to specify an exact color and then have the X library translate that color into an RGB value for a particular screen. Under the hood, the Xcms routines are really allocating straight RGB values. These routines act entirely on the client side of X and just translate your desired color to and from an appropriate RGB value.

The Xcms routines are part of the low-level X library (as of X11 Release 5) and concentrate on routines to query and set values in color cells. (They are listed in Table 13.1.) The first thing you'll notice about the Xcms routines is how closely they match the regular X color routines. For example, `XcmsLookupColor` corresponds to `XLookupColor`, and `XcmsAllocNamedColor` corresponds to `XAllocNamedColor`.

All the Xcms routines are new in X11 Release 5, or R5. Not every X vendor supports X11R5 yet, so your code must contain a method for determining the X version number.

The color conversion context, or CCC, is created under the hood by the X library for each colormap your application accesses. This CCC transparently follows the colormap and is used by the Xcms routines. Normally, you won't need to modify this unless you want to create your own color space or don't like the default routines supplied by the X library.

X Library Functions and Macros Introduced in This Chapter

```
XcmsAllocColor

XcmsAllocNamedColor

XcmsCCCOfColormap

XcmsConvertColors

XcmsDefaultCCC
```

XcmsLookupColor

XcmsQueryBlack

XcmsQueryBlue

XcmsQueryColor

XcmsQueryColors

XcmsQueryGreen

XcmsQueryRed

XcmsQueryWhite

XcmsStoreColor

XcmsStoreColors

Section 3

Fonts and Text

The most common operation in a windowing system is drawing text. In fact, almost every application program, big or small, relies on text in one way or another. Therefore, it's mandatory for you to know how X treats text and how to use attractive text to your advantage.

The next three chapters cover fonts, from the basics of using fonts with X toolkits to all those nasty details about installing and administering fonts that never seem to be covered in X books.

Font Basics

This chapter covers:

- ✦ Fonts and characters
- ✦ Loading fonts
- ✦ Drawing text
- ✦ Drawing image text
- ✦ Drawing text items
- ✦ International text functions and font sets
- ✦ Querying font capabilities
- ✦ Unloading fonts
- ✦ Listing available fonts
- ✦ Using fonts effectively

Text and Fonts

The most common operation in a windowing system is drawing text. In fact, almost every application program, big or small, relies on text in one way or another. With an X toolkit, many of the low-level details of text handling are handled by various widgets (see Chapter 15), but even so, most applications need to work with text and fonts. The most basic text routine is drawing text.

Before you can draw text, though, you need to understand how X represents text using fonts.

Fonts

Typography is an ancient art; over the centuries, typographers have developed literally thousands of different kinds of typefaces. You won't need all of these different typefaces, of course; a few will suffice.

You gain access to these different typefaces by loading *fonts*. A complete set of characters of one size of one typeface—including upper- and lowercase letters, punctuation marks, and numerals—is called a *font*. All fonts in X are bitmaps, each character has a specific bit pattern within the font. Each face, style, and size correspond to at least one font—Times at 25 pixels high and Times at 12 pixels high are two different fonts. This is different than Adobe's Postscript-defined fonts: Postscript describes fonts by outline, which can be resized depending on the dimensions defined by the application and later filled in. The X11 Release 5 font server offers the ability to scale fonts, and many font servers support outline, scalable fonts. This font server serves fonts to the X server. (Sun's OpenWindows and other proprietary X servers also scale fonts.) Your X applications, though, still treat these fonts as bitmaps, once scaled to the proper size.

Table 14.1 Some typical fonts.

Times Roman	Helvetica	Courier
Times Roman Italic	*Helvetica Italic*	*Courier Italic*
Times Roman Bold	**Helvetica Bold**	Courier Bold

Different fonts and typefaces have distinctive characteristics:

✦ Fonts are either *serif* or *sans serif*. Serif characters have a smaller line that finishes off a large stroke, such as the strokes at the top and bottom of the letter I. Sans serif fonts do not have these finishing strokes.

✦ A font can be *proportional spaced* or *fixed width*. A fixed-width font allows the same width for each character: for instance, an *m* takes up as much space as an *i*. A fixed-width font emulates a typewriter. A proportional-spaced font emulates typeset material, such as the letters on this page, where the proportions between letters are not equal.

✦ Some fonts are better suited to some tasks than others. The serif font used in this text has been found to be easier to read than most sans-serif faces. The more elaborate serif fonts are more suited to special effects or headlines, as are all boldfaces. You want to make your text as easy to read as possible; know which fonts to use for emphasis and which to use for readability.

✦ Not all X servers support all fonts. You have to carefully design your applications to have a set of fallback fonts, in case the desired fonts are not available. Sun's OpenWindows, for example, provides a set of Open Look fonts that are not commonly available on other platforms. Watch out.

✦ In X, a font is either a single-byte (8-bit) or a 2-byte (16-bit) font. Single-byte fonts can handle up 256 characters, while the 2-byte fonts can handle up to 65,535 characters. Text in Japanese, Chinese, or Korean, for instance, requires many more than 256 characters.

Loading Fonts

Before a font can be used by your program, it must be loaded into the X server. The X server then shares the font among all programs that want to use a particular font. When all references to a font are over, the X server may free up the memory and data structures associated with the font. Thus, loading a font does not load the font into your application program—the font is loaded into the server. To load a font, use `XLoadQueryFont`:

```
XFontStruct* XLoadQueryFont(Display* display,
                    char* font_name)
```

XLoadQueryFont returns a pointer to an XFontStruct structure. This structure contains a host of information about the font; the most useful information is used to tell how large the font is. You need to pass XLoadQueryFont the name of the font you want the X server to load. Remember that the X server loads the fonts, *not* your application.

In your code, call XLoadQueryFont as follows:

```
Display*      display;
XFontStruct*  font_struct;
char*         font_name;


font_struct = XLoadQueryFont(display, font_name);

if (font_struct == (XFontStruct *) NULL ) {
    /*
     * An error occurred. Don't
     * try to use the font.
     */
} else {
    /* font loaded OK... */
}
```

The XFontStruct is defined in <X11/Xlib.h> as follows:

```
typedef struct {
    XExtData*    ext_data;
    Font         fid;
    unsigned     direction;
    unsigned     min_char_or_byte2; /* first character */
    unsigned     max_char_or_byte2; /* last character  */
```

```
      unsigned       min_byte1;        /* first row that exists */
      unsigned       max_byte1;        /* last row that exists  */
      Bool           all_chars_exist;
      unsigned       default_char;
      int            n_properties;
      XFontProp*     properties;/
      XCharStruct    min_bounds;
      XCharStruct    max_bounds;
      XCharStruct*   per_char;
      int            ascent;
      int            descent;
  } XFontStruct;
```

There are a lot of data in the XFontStruct structure, but most of these fields will be of little use, except for the fid, ascent, and descent. The *fid* holds the font ID, used by your application to refer to the font. The *ascent* is how high the font goes above the baseline. The *descent* is how far the font goes below the baseline. Together, the *ascent* and the *descent* are useful for determining how tall to make a line of text in a given font.

The *ext_data* field is a place where extensions to X can place extra data. (A typographic extension to X is in the works.) The *direction* can be either FontLeftToRight or FontRightToLeft. The *all_chars_exist* flag is True if all characters in the font have a bitmap. This includes the beginning ASCII control-sequence characters for ASCII fonts.

The *properties* array holds the font properties. The *per_char* array holds the bounding boxes for the characters, stored in XCharStruct structures.

Fonts and Characters

The XCharStruct structure contains information about the bounding box of each character:

```
    typedef struct {
```

```
    short           lbearing;
    short           rbearing;
    short           width;
    short           ascent;
    short           descent;
    unsigned short attributes;
} XCharStruct;
```

The *lbearing* field holds the left bearing, that is, the distance that the character extends to the left beyond the character origin. The *rbearing* field holds the right bearing. The *width* is the distance from the character origin to the next character's origin. The *ascent* is the height above the baseline that the character extends. The *descent* is how far below the baseline the character extends.

Any extra information may be stored in the *attributes* field of the XCharStruct structure.

Font Properties

Font properties contain any extra property information, identified by the given atom in the XFontProp structure:

```
typedef struct {
    Atom            name;
    unsigned long card32;
} XFontProp;
```

Simple Font Loading

If you don't care about the size of the font, you can use the function XLoadFont to just get a font ID:

```
Font XLoadFont(Display* display, char* font_name)
```

The font ID allows you to draw text, but does not have enough information to get the font's size, should you need to make this kind of calculation. We find you almost always need to determine the size of any fonts loaded, so we always use XLoadQueryFont. In addition, there's another reason to avoid XLoadFont and to use the function XLoadQueryFont, as XLoadFont generates an X error if the font cannot be loaded.

Setting Up the GC to Draw Text

To draw with a newly loaded font, you need to set a graphics context (GC) to use that font when drawing. To do this, use the function XSetFont:

```
XSetFont(Display* display,

    GC gc,

    Font font_id)
```

XSetFont takes the font ID, the number returned by XLoadFont, or the number in the *fid* (*font id*) field of an XFontStruct structure. When you draw with the given GC, the text will be drawn in the new font.

Drawing Text

The X library provides five types of routines to draw text. You can draw:

✦ Text characters from a character string using XDrawString.

✦ Image text (foreground and background of text character bitmaps) with XDrawImageString.

✦ Complex text items with XDrawText.

✦ Two-byte text with XDrawString16, XDrawImageString16, and XDrawText16.

✦ Internationalized routines to draw wide-character and multibyte text.

The basic function to draw a text string is XDrawString:

```
XDrawString(Display* display,
```

```
     Drawable drawable,

     GC gc,

     int x, int y,

     const char* string,

     int string_length)
```

XDrawString draws the foreground of the text in the given *string* and for *string_length* characters, which may or may not be the whole length of string. By foreground, we mean that XDrawString only draws the foreground bits of the character cells, using the GC's foreground color. Another routine, XDrawImageString, draws both the foreground of the text characters and fills in the rest of the character cell with the GC's background color:

XDrawString uses the GC's current font, which can be changed with XSetFont (as described below). To draw both the foreground image of the text as well as fill in the background of each character cell, use XDrawImageString:

```
     XDrawImageString(Display* display,

         Drawable drawable,

         GC gc,

         int x, int y,

         const char* string,

         int string_length)
```

XDrawImageString is commonly used for terminal-emulator programs, such as xterm, where each character occupies a fixed-size character cell. Writing a new character in the cell is expected to overwrite any previous character in the same cell.

Both XDrawString and XDrawImageString draw text starting at a given *baseline* origin (the x and y parameters). The text juts above and below this baseline:

X draws text starting at an x, y pixel location. The x-coordinate location is at the beginning (far left) of the text string. The y-coordinate location starts at the text baseline. Letters that drop below the baseline, such as *p*, *q*, and *j*, drop below the y-coordinate location given to XDrawString and

`XDrawImageString`. Letters will go above the *y* position and may also drop below the position.

All string-drawing routines require you to pass the length of the string. The Xlib call will assume that there are at least as many characters in the string as you tell it. In other words, don't lie to the X server.

In many cases, `XDrawString` and `XDrawImageString` will work just fine.

Drawing Complex Text Items

Some applications require more sophisticated text output. For example, you may want to draw a line of text with one word highlighted using a bold font, or with keywords in an italic font.

To draw these more complex text items, use `XDrawText`:

```
XDrawText(Display* display,

    Drawable drawable,

    GC gc,

    int x, int y,

    XTextItem* items,

    int number_items)
```

`XDrawText` draws *number_items* of `XTextItem` structures, each of which holds what is called a *text item*, starting at the given *x, y* location. A text item is a means for you to draw a number of chunks of text, each with its own font and with your own spacing requirements.

The `XTextItem` structure holds the following fields:

```
typedef struct {
    char*   chars;
    int     nchars;  /* number of characters */
    int     delta;   /* delta between strings */
    Font    font;
} XTextItem;
```

The *chars* field holds the text to draw for the given text item. XDrawText will draw *nchars* characters from the *chars* array. If the *font* field is the constant None, then XDrawText uses the given graphics context (GC), the gc parameter, to determine the font to draw with. If the *font* field holds a font ID, then XDrawText changes the GC to use this font. This is how you can draw text with multiple fonts with one X library function call. The *delta* field is any additional spacing you want to add to the x parameter passed to XDrawText.

Drawing 16-Bit Characters

To help support Asian languages and much larger fonts than a 256-character font allows, X provides a number of 16-bit character-drawing functions. These 16-bit text-drawing functions, as listed in Table 14.2, mimic the text-drawing functions introduced so far.

Table 14.2 *16-bit text drawing functions.*

8-Bit Text Function	16-Bit Text Function
XDrawImageString	XDrawImageString16
XDrawString	XDrawString16
XDrawText	XDrawText16

The parameters are almost the same, except that the 16-bit text functions take an array of XChar2b structures instead of an array of type char. The basic idea with 16-bit text is to treat a font as a two-dimensional array of character bitmaps or *glyphs*. A Latin-1 font (used by most Western European languages), holds only 256 characters and so is treated by X as a one-dimensional font (or more precisely, a two-dimensional array with one dimension NULL).

XDrawImageString16 draws the foreground and background of a 16-bit-character string:

```
XDrawImageString16(Display* display,
    Drawable drawable,
```

```
    GC gc,
    int x, int y,
    const XChar2b* string,
    int string_length)
```

The *string_length* is the number of 16-bit characters; that is, the number of entries in the XChar2b array.

XDrawString16 draws the foreground of an 16-bit-character text string:

```
XDrawString16(Display* display,
    Drawable drawable,
    GC gc,
    int x, int y,
    const XChar2b* string,
    int string_length)
```

Both XDrawImageString16 and XDrawString16 use the XChar2b structure, which holds a 16-bit character as 2 bytes:

```
typedef struct {
    unsigned char  byte1;
    unsigned char  byte2;
} XChar2b;
```

The first byte, *byte1*, is the most significant byte.

XDrawText16 is the analog to XDrawText. XDrawText16 draws an array of 16-bit text items:

```
XDrawText16(Display* display,
    Drawable drawable,
    GC gc,
    int x, int y,
    XTextItem16* items,
```

```
    int number_items)
```

The XTextItem16 structure holds the following fields:

```
typedef struct {
    XChar2b* chars;
    int      nchars;
    int      delta;
    Font     font;
} XTextItem16;
```

In real life, however, these 16-bit text functions aren't really up to snuff. What's needed are routines that draw internationalized text, using the ANSI C concepts of multibyte and wide characters.

International Text Routines

For many years, X failed miserably at providing support for Asian languages. It's true that X has a number of routines to draw 16-bit text, but support for international text really wasn't there. With X11 Release 5, though, X's support for international text exploded. These new text routines concentrate on *multibyte characters*, where each character takes up 1 or more bytes, as well as *wide characters*, where each character takes up a fixed number of bytes—usually 2 or 4 bytes. The Unicode character set is one such 16-bit wide-character text encoding.

These international routines are listed in Table 14.3.

Table 14.3   *International text-drawing routines.*

8-Bit Text Routine	Multibyte	Wide Character
XDrawImageString	XmbDrawImageString	XwcDrawImageString
XDrawString	XmbDrawString	XwcDrawString
XDrawText	XmbDrawText	XwcDrawText

Multibyte-Character Functions

As of this writing, ANSI C routines provide better support for multibyte characters, since you still use character pointers. Multibyte characters are also the default used by Motif 1.2 for international text.

```
void XmbDrawString(Display*  display,

    Drawable drawable,

    XFontSet  font_set,

    GC gc,

    int x, int y,

    const char* mb_text,

    int bytes_text)


void XmbDrawImageString(Display*  display,

    Drawable drawable,

    XFontSet  font_set,

    GC gc,

    int x, int y,

    const char* mb_text,

    int bytes_text)


void XmbDrawText(Display*  display,

    Drawable drawable,

    XFontSet  font_set,

    GC gc,

    int x, int y,

    XmbTextItem* text_items,

    int  number_items)
```

The multibyte-character text-item structure, `XmbTextItem`, then looks like:

```
typedef struct {
    char*       chars;
    int         nchars;
    int         delta;
    XFontSet    font_set;
} XmbTextItem;
```

Wide-Character Functions

The wide-character drawing functions use a special ANSI C data type, wchar_t, which holds a wide character, as defined in <stddef.h>. On most systems, this is a 16-bit value, although on some it is 32 bits long. By using the wchar_t data type, your code is insulated from most of this.

```
void XwcDrawString(Display*  display,
    Drawable drawable,
    XFontSet  font_set,
    GC gc,
    int x, int y,
    wchar_t*  wc_text,
    int    number_wchars)


void XwcDrawImageString(Display*  display,
    Drawable drawable,
    XFontSet  font_set,
    GC gc,
    int x, int y,
    wchar_t*  wc_text,
    int    number_wchars)


void XwcDrawText(Display*  display,
    Drawable drawable,
```

```
XFontSet  font_set,

GC gc,

int x, int y,

XwcTextItem* text_items,

int number_items)
```

The wide-character text-item structure, `XwcTextItem`, then looks like:

```
typedef struct {
    wchar_t*    chars;
    int         nchars;
    int         delta;
    XFontSet    font_set;
} XwcTextItem;
```

Font Sets

Both the multibyte- and wide-character drawing routines use the concept of a *font set*. Font sets are another of X's opaque data types. That is, you're not supposed to look into the internals. A font set holds a number of fonts, if necessary, to draw international text. Japanese, for example, may require a Kanji font, a Kana font, and a Latin font. To support Asian languages, therefore, the X text-drawing routines need to support text with multiple encodings in a single string. The font set ties together the fonts necessary to draw text in the various character sets.

To create a new font set, use `XCreateFontSet`:

```
XFontSet XCreateFontSet(Display* display,
    const char* base_font_name_list,
    char*** missing_charset_list,  /* RETURN */
    int* missing_charset_count,    /* RETURN */
    char** def_string)             /* RETURN */
```

The *base_font_name_list* is a comma-separated list of font names to be used for the font set. You can pass an X logical font definition format (XLFD) name using wildcards (see Chapter 16), such as:

```
-*-*-*-r-normal-*-180-100-100-*-*
```

and XCreateFontSet will load in the proper fonts for a given set. If for some reason XCreateFontSet fails to find all the necessary fonts, *missing_charset_list* contains a list of the character sets that could not be loaded. In such a case, *missing_charset_count* contains the number of charsets held in *missing_charset_list*. If *def_string* is not NULL, XCreateFontSet places a list of characters that are drawn in the case of the missing charsets.

XCreateFontSet returns NULL on errors or XFontSet on success.

When done with a font set, call XFreeFontSet:

```
void XFreeFontSet(Display* display,
    XFontSet font_set)
```

To get the list of fonts in a font set, as well as XFontStruct structures defining the fonts, use XFontsOfFontSet:

```
int XFontsOfFontSet(XFontSet  font_set,
    XFontStruct*** font_struct_list,  /* RETURN */
    char*** font_name_list)
```

XFontsOfFontSet returns the number of fonts. To get the base font named passed to XCreateFontSet, call XBaseFontNameListOfFontSet:

```
char* XBaseFontNameListOfFontSet(XFontSet font_set)
```

WARNING   Do not free the string returned by XBaseFontNameListOfFontSet. This string should be treated as a read-only string. XFreeFontSet will free the string when the font set is freed.

To get the extents or bounding size of a given font set, use
`XExtentsOfFontSet`:

```
XFontSetExtents* XExtentsOfFontSet(XFontSet font_set)
```

WARNING

Do not free the `XFontSetExtents` structure returned by
`XExtentsOfFontSet`. This structure should be treated as
read-only. `XFreeFontSet` will free the structure when the
font set is freed.

The `XFontSetExtents` structure looks like:

```
typedef struct {
    XRectangle    max_ink_extent;
    XRectangle    max_logical_extent;
} XFontSetExtents;
```

Determining Text Size

To help position a text string, it is a good idea to figure out how large the
string will appear in a given font. For a fixed-width font, like `9x15`, the
width of any text string is the number of characters times the width of one
character:

```
width = strlen(string) * width_of_one_character;
```

For proportional-width fonts, like `variable`, though, this is not the case.
In a proportional-width font, some characters, like *W* and *M*, are far wider
than other characters, such as *i*, *l*, and *t*.

In all cases, to find out the width of a text string in a given font, use the
`XTextWidth` function:

```
int XTextWidth(XFontStruct* font_struct,
    const char* string,
    int string_length)
```

To determine the width of a 16-bit text string use `XTextWidth16`:

```
int XTextWidth16(XFontStruct* font_struct,
    const XChar2b* string,
    int number_characters)
```

Determining the Height of Text

The height of a character string is a bit different. In most cases, you want the possible height necessary for one line of text, with both descending and ascending characters, rather the just the height of the string. Why? Most checks on a font height are for spacing lines of text vertically. Line 1 should not write over line 2, and so on.

You can tell how many pixels high to make a line of text using the *ascent* and the *descent* fields of the `XFontStruct` structure:

```
XFontStruct*   font_struct;
int            height;


height = font_struct->ascent +
         font_struct->descent;
```

This doesn't show how tall a given text string is. Instead, it tells you how tall a line of text in the given font would be. In most cases, this is enough information, as most Western languages display text in lines. To find out more, you can query the font extents.

Querying Font Extents

The *font extents* are the bounding area taken up by a text string when drawn with a given font. You can query the text extents for a given text string with `XTextExtents` and `XTextExtents16` for 16-bit text:

```
XTextExtents(XFontStruct* font_struct,
```

```
    const char* string,

    int number_chars,

    int* direction,        /* RETURN */

    int* font_ascent,      /* RETURN */

    int* font_descent,     /* RETURN */

    XCharStruct* overall_extents)


XTextExtents16(XFontStruct* font_struct,

    const XChar2b* string,

    int number_chars,

    int* direction,        /* RETURN */

    int* font_ascent,      /* RETURN */

    int* font_descent,     /* RETURN */

    XCharStruct* overall_extents)
```

The direction parameter is set to `FontLeftToRight` or
`FontRightToLeft`.

If you only have a font ID and don't have the full `XFontStruct` structure that describes a font, you can call `XQueryTextExtents` and
`XQueryTextExtents16`:

```
XQueryTextExtents(Display* display,

    Font font_id,

    const char*  string,

    int   number_chars,

    int* direction,        /* RETURN */

    int* font_ascent,      /* RETURN */

    int* font_descent,     /* RETURN */

    XCharStruct* overall_extents)
```

```
XQueryTextExtents16(Display* display,
    Font font_id,
    const XChar2b* string,
    int   number_chars,
    int* direction,      /* RETURN */
    int* font_ascent,    /* RETURN */
    int* font_descent,   /* RETURN */
    XCharStruct* overall_extents)
```

Both XQueryTextExtents and XQueryTextExtents16 require a round-trip to the X server to get this information, so XTextExtents and XTextExtents16 should be much more efficient.

N O T E

Freeing Fonts

When you are through with a font, tell the X server that you are done with it. This way the X server can make most efficient use of the limited resources available in the workstation, such as memory. Two functions free the font, XFreeFont and XUnloadFont:

```
XFreeFont(Display* display,
    XFontStruct* font_struct)
```

```
XUnloadFont(Display* display,
    Font font_id)
```

Use XFreeFont if you originally loaded the font into an XFontStruct structure with XLoadQueryFont. Use XUnloadFont if you originally loaded the font and just used the font ID with XLoadFont, as outlined in Table 14.4.

Table 14.4 *Font loading and freeing functions.*

Function to Load	Function to Free
XLoadFont	XUnloadFont
XLoadQueryFont	XFreeFont

As a general rule, always try to free up resources in the X server when done.

Going Beyond Text

Since the vast majority of all graphics output is text, X-server writers spend a lot of time optimizing the text-drawing routines. Because of this work, there are a number of other clever uses for X fonts and text.

The *cursor font*, for example (a font named "cursor"), holds the bitmaps or glyphs used for the basic cursor shapes. In the cursor font, you'll see xterm's I-bar cursor, the ubiquitous X cursor, and our favorite, the Gumby cursor. Each cursor is actually two characters in the cursor font: the cursor shape itself and a mask.

The XView toolkit (which supports an Open Look interface) uses glyphs in fonts to draw bitmap images like the Open Look pushpins or the scroll-bar controls. Instead of drawing a bitmap, XView draws characters in the font. Each "character" is then one of the bitmaps used in the interface. This technique results in much better performance but has a hidden problem: if the proper font isn't installed, the toolkit cannot draw the application's interface. This problem is compounded since most users simply don't know how to install X fonts—and most won't have the necessary superuser privileges to do so, even if they had the knowledge.

Listing the Available Fonts

Since each X server supports its own sets of fonts, there's no guarantee that a given font will be available to an X server. You can use the program xlsfonts as well as the XListFonts function to check on available font names:

```
char** XListFonts(Display* display,
```

```
char* pattern,
int max_names,
int* count_of_names) /* RETURN */
```

There's also an `XListFontsWithInfo` function that returns `XFontStruct`s as well as font names.

You can then free these font names with `XFreeFontNames`:

```
XFreeFontNames(char** names)
```

Using Fonts Effectively

When people inexperienced with design principles suddenly have access to many different fonts, they usually go hog-wild in their use of different faces. The end result, unfortunately, is a very unattractive design, more representing a ransom note made up of disparate letter clips from different newspapers and magazines. Aesthetically speaking, therefore, it is a good idea to avoid the use of many fonts. If the output looks like a ransom note, it probably won't look professional, unless you do this by choice and are aiming at a certain effect, like laughter, from your users. For best results, generally stick to one font per window, and two fonts maximum. Aim for an integrated look and feel to your software. Try to limit yourself to standard fonts, the most likely fonts to be available on the greatest number of systems. Use a special larger font for emphasis. When you need multiple fonts, you can often use an italic or bold version of the same font, or a different size.

For best results, let the user pick the fonts. This is generally easy with X toolkit-based programs, as the user can specify the font in a resource file. Letting the user decide the font is especially useful because X runs on very differing hardware. A color Sun SPARCstation LX, for example, comes with either a 16- or a 19-inch color monitor—both at the same pixel resolution. This means that the dots are much smaller on the 16-inch monitor. The standard X default font, `8x13`, looks tiny on a 16-inch monitor and more acceptable on the 19-inch screen. Users with the smaller screen may opt to use a larger font, such as `9x15`, just to be able to read the text. With a notebook computer, with a standard VGA (video graphics array) 640 x 480 pixel resolution, users typically want to use the smallest fonts available, due to the smaller screen resolution.

Fonts Use Memory

Some servers, especially for X terminals, simply won't have the resources (mainly random access memory, or RAM) to load a lot of different fonts.

X terminals exist mainly to provide an inexpensive hardware entry point to the X Window System. An X terminal acts much like an ASCII terminal, using another computer for the processing power and the terminal's smarts just for the display—only the X terminals have a lot more smarts than traditional ASCII terminals. Due to cost constraints, though, most X terminals have a limited amount of RAM. Fonts, like any other X resource, use up RAM. In an X-terminal environment, using the least amount of resources is a good idea.

Summary

The most common operation in a windowing system is drawing text. In fact, almost every application program, big or small, relies on text in one way or another. With an X toolkit, many of the low-level details of text handling are handled by various widgets, but even so, most applications need to work with text and fonts. The most basic text routine is drawing text. Before you can draw text, though, you need to understand how X represents text using fonts.

Before a font can be used by your program, it must be loaded into the X server. The X server then shares the font among all programs that want to use a particular font. When all references to a font are over, the X server may free up the memory and data structures associated with the font. Thus, loading a font does not load the font into your application program—the font is loaded into the server.

There is a lot of data in the XFontStruct structure, but most of these fields will be of little use, except for the *fid*, *ascent*, and *descent*. The *fid* holds the font ID, used by your application to refer to the font. The *ascent* is how high the font goes above the baseline. The *descent* is how far the font goes below the baseline. Together, the *ascent* and the *descent* are useful for determining how tall to make a line of text in a given font.

If you don't care about the size of the font, you can use the function XLoadFont to just get a font ID.

The X library provides five types of routines to draw text. You can draw:

- ✦ Text characters from a character string using XDrawString.
- ✦ Image text (foreground and background of text character bitmaps) with XDrawImageString.
- ✦ Complex text items with XDrawText.
- ✦ Two-byte text with XDrawString16, XDrawImageString16, and XDrawText16.
- ✦ Internationalized routines to draw wide-character and multibyte text.

The basic function to draw a text string is XDrawString.

For many years, X failed miserably at providing support for Asian languages. It's true that X has a number of routines to draw 16-bit text, but support for international text really wasn't there. With X11 Release 5, though, X's support for international text exploded. These new text routines concentrate on multibyte characters, where each character takes up 1 or more bytes, as well as wide characters, where each character takes up a fixed number of bytes—usually 2 or 4 bytes. The Unicode character set is one such 16-bit wide-character text encoding.

As of this writing, ANSI C routines provide better support for multibyte characters, since you still use character pointers. Multibyte characters are also the default used by Motif 1.2 for international text.

When you are through with a font, tell the X server that you are done with it. This way the X server can make most efficient use of the limited resources available in the workstation, such as memory. Two functions free the font, XFreeFont and XUnloadFont.

Since each X server supports its own sets of fonts, there's no guarantee that a given font will be available to an X server. You can use the program xlsfonts as well as the XListFonts function to check on available font names.

X Library Functions and Macros Introduced in This Chapter

```
XBaseFontNameListOfFontSet
XCreateFontSet
XDrawImageString
XDrawImageString16
XDrawString
XDrawString16
XDrawText
XDrawText16
XExtentsOfFontSet
XFontsOfFontSet
XFreeFont
XFreeFontNames
XFreeFontSet
XListFonts
XLoadFont
XLoadQueryFont
XmbDrawImageString
XmbDrawString
XmbDrawText
XQueryTextExtents
XQueryTextExtents16
XTextExtents
XTextExtents16
XTextWidth
XTextWidth16
XUnloadFont
XwcDrawImageString
XwcDrawString
XwcDrawText
```

Using Fonts with X Toolkits

This chapter covers:

- ✦ The use of fonts with X toolkits
- ✦ The OLIT `font` resource
- ✦ The Motif `fontList` resource
- ✦ Motif font lists and list entries
- ✦ Motif `XmStrings` and multiple fonts

An Introduction to Using Fonts with X Toolkits

Most X toolkits do the dirty work of basic font management with little or no interaction on your part—as a matter of fact, we haven't had to program with any fonts using any X toolkit routines up to this point of the book.

With Motif and Open Look Intrinsics Toolkit (OLIT), though, you're left with a choice. When you want to draw text in a drawing-area widget (OLIT `DrawArea` and Motif `XmDrawingArea`), you can use all the X library routines introduced in the last chapter. Or you can try to work more within the toolkit framework and use toolkit routines for font handling and drawing text.

Up to now, we've set the *font* (OLIT) or *fontList* (Motif) resources in X resource files. If you want to set these resources in your code, though, you must use the proper data types, listed in Table 15.1.

Table 15.1 Font Resources.

Toolkit	Resource	Type in Code	In Resource File
OLIT	font	XFontStruct*	Font name
Motif	fontList	XmFontList	Font name or font set names

N O T E New versions of OLIT should support XFontSet as well. OLIT also supports the *fontColor* resource, which can be set to a pixel value (a valid colormap index). If set, the *fontColor* resource controls the color of the text displayed in an OLIT widget. If not set, OLIT uses the color of the *foreground* resource to draw text.

Fonts with OLIT

Using fonts with OLIT is easier than using fonts with Motif, because OLIT uses the traditional X structures for fonts, such as `XFontStruct`, intro-

duced in the last chapter. With OLIT, you can load up a font using
XLoadQueryFont from the previous chapter and then set the *font*
resource for a widget, as the following example shows. The program below
follows these steps for drawing with text:

1. Create widgets, including a DrawArea.
2. Create a graphics context (GC).
3. Load in a font.
4. Set the GC to draw with the font.
5. Set the *font* resource for a OblongButton widget, which makes
   the *Exit* menu choice show a larger font.
6. In the DrawArea callback, draw a test string, using both XDraw-
   ImageString and XDrawString.

The code for this program is stored in the file o_chap15.c:

```
/*
 *  o_chap15.c
 *  OLIT test program for Chapter 15.
 *  Draw text.
 */
#include "olit.h"
#include <Xol/DrawArea.h>


/*
 *  Globals
 */
int        global_width, global_height;
Display*   global_display;
Window     global_window;
GC         global_gc;


/*
```

```
 * Callback for drawing area.
 */
void drawCB(Widget widget,
        XtPointer client_data,
        XtPointer call_data)


{   /* drawCB */
    OlDrawAreaCallbackStruct* ptr;
    Dimension                 width, height;

    ptr = (OlDrawAreaCallbackStruct*) call_data;

    if (ptr == NULL) {
        return;
    }

    if (ptr->reason == OL_REASON_EXPOSE) {

        if (ptr->event->xexpose.count == 0) {

#define MESSAGE "In Xanadu did Kublai Khan..."

            XDrawImageString(global_display,
                global_window, global_gc,
                50, 50,
                MESSAGE,
                strlen(MESSAGE) );

            /* Draw with only foreground bits. */
            XDrawString(global_display,
                global_window, global_gc,
```

```
                    50, 100,
                    MESSAGE,
                    strlen(MESSAGE) );
          }


     }


     if (ptr->reason == OL_REASON_RESIZE) {
          XtVaGetValues(widget,
               XtNwidth,  &width,
               XtNheight, &height,
               NULL);

          global_width  = width;
          global_height = height;
     }

}    /* drawCB */


int main(int argc, char** argv)

{    /* main */
     XtAppContext    app_context;
     Widget          parent;
     Widget          mainwindow;
     Widget          menubar;
     Widget          filemenu;
     Widget          exitchoice;
     Widget          drawingarea;
     Arg             args[20];
     int             n;
```

```
int          screen;
XFontStruct* font_struct;

/* Initialize X toolkit */
OlToolkitInitialize( (XtPointer) NULL);

n = 0;
XtSetArg(args[n], XtNmappedWhenManaged, False); n++;
XtSetArg(args[n], XtNwidth, 300); n++;
XtSetArg(args[n], XtNheight, 200); n++;


parent = XtAppInitialize(&app_context,
        "ProX",                      /* app class */
        (XrmOptionDescList) NULL,    /* options */
        0,                           /* num options */
        ARGC_PTR &argc, argv,        /* cmd line */
        (String*) NULL,              /* fallback res. */
        args, n);


/*
 * Create Main Window.
 */
mainwindow = CreateMainWindow(parent, "main");

/*
 * Create menu bar.
 */
menubar = CreateMenuBar(mainwindow, "menubar");

/*
 * Create the file menu.
```

```
     */
    filemenu = CreateMenu(menubar, "filemenu");


    /* Create a menu choice to exit the program.
*/ exitchoice = CreateExitChoice(filemenu,
                "exitchoice");


    global_width = 300;
    global_height = 200;
    drawingarea = CreateDrawingArea(mainwindow,
                "drawingarea",
                global_width, global_height,
                drawCB,
                (XtPointer) NULL);


    SetMainAreas(mainwindow,
            menubar,
            drawingarea);


    /* Create the windows. */
    XtRealizeWidget(parent);


    /*
     * Create GC.
     */
    global_display = XtDisplay(drawingarea);
    global_window  = XtWindow(drawingarea);
    screen         = DefaultScreen(global_display);


    global_gc = XCreateGC(global_display,
                global_window,
                0L, (XGCValues*) NULL);
```

```
    XSetForeground(global_display, global_gc,
        BlackPixel(global_display, screen) );


    /* Set background color, too. */
    XSetBackground(global_display, global_gc,
        WhitePixel(global_display, screen) );

/*
 * Arbitrary test font name.
 */
#define FONT_NAME \
  "-*-helvetica-medium-r-normal—*-180-75-75-*-*"


    /* Load font */
    font_struct = XLoadQueryFont(global_display,
                    FONT_NAME);


    if (font_struct == (XFontStruct*) NULL) {
        printf("Fatal error while loading font [%s]\n",
            FONT_NAME);
        exit(-1);
    }



    /* Set GC to draw with font */
    XSetFont(global_display, global_gc,
        font_struct->fid);

    /*
     * Change value of font resource
     * for exit menu choice.
     */
```

```
XtVaSetValues(exitchoice,
   XtNfont, font_struct,
   NULL);

/* Map parent */
XtMapWidget(parent);
XtAppMainLoop(app_context);

return 0;

}   /* main */


/* end of file o_chap15.c */
```

When you run this OLIT program (as shown in Figure 15.1), you'll see the difference between `XDrawImageString` and `XDrawString`, introduced in the last chapter.

Figure 15.1   *Drawing text with XDrawImageString and XDrawString.*

Fonts with Motif

Motif complicates text and fonts with the concept of Motif's compound strings and font lists. The complications added by Motif consist mainly of a new format for font sets called a *font list*, as well as the Motif string format, `XmString`. Of course, you can use the X library routines introduced in the previous chapter. These Motif-specific routines can help make your applications work better in other countries.

Motif Fonts, Font Sets, and Font Lists

In Motif terminology, a *font* is a collection of glyphs or bitmap images associated with a given character set. A *font set* is the collection of fonts needed to display text in a given language. English, for example, needs a font set with only one font. Japanese, though, needs at least three fonts in a font set. A *font list* is then a collection of font sets or fonts, each of which is in a font-list entry. Most of the font-list code was added in Motif 1.2. Each element in a font list has a *font-list tag*, an arbitrary name used to identify a font. Finally, a *font-list entry* holds either a font or a font set.

A Motif font list may support a number of font names. For instance, Japanese text may require a font for Kanji, another for Kana, and a third for Latin (that's ASCII to the rest of us). For example, you could place a number of font names in a Motif `fontList` resource:

```
*fontList:\
  -JIS-fixed-medium-r-normal—26-180-100-100-c-240,\
  -GB-fixed-medium-r-normal—26-180-100-100-c-240,\
  -adobe-courier-medium-r-normal—25-180-100-100-m-150
```

You can also provide arbitrary font-list tags:

```
*fontList:\
  -*-courier-medium-r-normal—25-180-100-100-m-150=ROMAN,\
  -*-courier-bold-r-normal—25-180-100-100-m-150=BOLD
```

In this case, *ROMAN* and *BOLD* are purely arbitrary tags. We could use them, for instance, to draw text using normal and bold fonts.

N O T E

The documentation for Motif 1.2 is very unclear over the use of a colon (:) rather than an equal sign (=) as a font-tag delimiter. The basic idea is to associate a tag with a whole set of fonts or just a single font. The actual syntax is rather complex and poorly described in the official literature. To specify a single font associated with a tag in a font list, use:

```
font_name = tag
```

To tie a whole font set to a *single* tag, use:

```
font_name ; font_name ; font_name : tag
```

We found, though, that anything with colons (:) fails miserably with Motif 1.1.

You can use as many font names as necessary. In both of the above examples, the spaces are added for clarity.

Character Sets

Much of this added complexity is because of internationalization concerns. In X, a character set is a mapping between byte-codes and characters. For example, the ISO 8859-1 character set, often called Latin-1 (a superset of US ASCII) uses the value 65 for an uppercase letter A. Most Asian languages require multiple bytes per character. Some common character sets are listed in Table 15.2.

Table 15.2 *Some character sets.*

Language	Character Set
U.S. English	ASCII, ISO 8859-1
Japan	UJIS, Shift JIS
Cyrillic Russian	ISO 8859-5

Most fonts in X are then created to a single character set. For instance, most of the X fonts use the ISO 8859-1 character set, as described in the following chapter.

604 ◆ *Professional Graphics Programming in the X Window System*

The Motif routines that convert resources from the strings in resource files to actual data types and values handle the onerous chore of converting the above character-set data to an `XmFontList` structure. In fact, you may want to avoid this problem entirely and let the user specify all fonts in resource files.

Font Lists

The basic data structure for a font list is the `XmFontList` structure. The `XmFontList` structure is considered opaque and hidden by the Motif toolkit in the include file `<Xm/Xm.h>`:

```
/* opaque to outside */
typedef struct _XmFontListRec   *XmFontList;
```

Creating Font Lists

The first thing you need to do with font lists is create one. `XmFontListCreate` creates a new font list, starting with a single font using the given *charset*:

```
XmFontList XmFontListCreate(XFontStruct* font_struct,
              XmStringCharSet charset)
```

You can pass `XmSTRING_DEFAULT_CHARSET` for the *charset*.

To add a font to a font list, use `XmFontListAdd`:

```
XmFontList XmFontListAdd(XmFontList old_fontlist,
              XFontStruct* font_struct,
              XmStringCharSet charset)
```

`XmFontListAdd` returns a new font list built from the old and the new font.

To copy a font list, use `XmFontListCopy`:

```
XmFontList XmFontListCopy(XmFontList fontlist)
```

When you're done with a font list, free it with XmFontListFree:

```
void XmFontListFree(XmFontList fontlist)
```

Font-List Entries in Motif 1.2

With Motif 1.2, you're supposed to make a font list from a set of font-list entries, instead of calling XmFontListCreate. That is, call XmFontListEntryCreate and XmFontListAppendEntry (see below) instead of XmFontListCreate.

Before you can call the new function XmFontListAppendEntry, you must create an XmFontListEntry. To create a font list entry, use XmFontListEntryCreate:

```
XmFontListEntry XmFontListEntryCreate(char* tag,

            XmFontType type,

            XtPointer font)
```

XmFontListEntryCreate creates an XmFontListEntry from a *tag* and either a font or a font set. You can use either an XFontStruct pointer or an XFontSet. If each case, you cast the XtPointer font parameter to the proper type. In addition, you have to tell XmFontListEntryCreate which type of data you're passing. The *type* parameter does this (see Table 15.3).

Table 15.3 *XmFontListEntryCreate parameters.*

Font Parameter	Type Parameter
XFontStruct*	XmFONT_IS_FONT
XFontSet	XmFONT_IS_FONTSET

The XmFontType data type holds one of XmFONT_IS_FONT or XmFONT_IS_FONTSET. The XmFontListEntry structure is another opaque data type.

If you haven't already loaded the font, or created the font set, as the case may be, you can call XmFontListEntryLoad to both load the font and create an XmFontListEntry out of it:

```
XmFontListEntry XmFontListEntryLoad(Display* display,

                 char* fontname,

                 XmFontType type,

                 char* tag)
```

Again, the *type* parameter tells whether you want a font set (XmFONT_IS_FONTSET)—and have a font-set name in the *fontname* parameter, or you just have a simple font name in the *fontname* parameter (with *type* set to XmFONT_IS_FONT).

You can append a font-list entry to a full-blown font list using XmFontListAppendEntry:

```
XmFontList XmFontListAppendEntry(XmFontList old_fontlist,

                 XmFontListEntry entry)
```

XmFontListAppendEntry returns the new combined font list. If you don't have a font list already, you can pass NULL for *old_fontlist*, and XmFontListAppendEntry will create a new font list from your XmFontListEntry.

When you're done with a font list entry, free it with XmFont-ListEntryFree:

```
void XmFontListEntryFree(XmFontListEntry* entry)
```

This frees the font-list *entry*, not a font list.

Extracting Data from Font-List Entries

You can pull the tag name from a font-list entry with XmFontListEntryGetTag:

```
char* XmFontListEntryGetTag(XmFontListEntry entry)
```

You need to call XtFree to free the text when done.

To extract the XFontStruct pointer or XFontSet from a font-list entry, use XmFontListEntryGetFont:

```
XtPointer XmFontListEntryGetFont(XmFontListEntry entry,

          XmFontType* type)  /* RETURN */
```

The *type* parameter is set to `XmFONT_IS_FONT` if `XmFontListEntryGetFont` returns an `XFontStruct` pointer. The *type* is set to `XmFONT_IS_FONTSET` if the function returns an `XFontSet`.

Motif Text Strings

Motif uses its own string format, `XmString`. `XmStrings` are specially formatted strings that Motif uses to allow for international character sets and text that goes left to right and right to left. `XmStrings` may also cross multiple lines and have multiple fonts. A number of widgets, like the label widget, and a host of Motif functions require the use of `XmStrings`, including those that draw strings to a window. You'll need a means to convert a plain old C NULL-terminated string (`char*`) to an `XmString`. All Motif widgets, except for `XmText` and `XmTextField` widgets, use `XmString` data for text.

A Motif compound string, stored in an `XmString`, holds one or more *segments*. Each segment may hold:

- ✦ Text.
- ✦ A font-list tag (which used to be called a charset).
- ✦ A direction.
- ✦ A separator (used in place of the newline character).

The font-list tag is an arbitrary name that you can use to make a text string use a particular font, like the ROMAN and BOLD tags used above, or create a string that uses multiple fonts. Additionally, there are conventions for font-list tags in countries such as Japan, which needs Kanji, Kana, and Latin fonts for everyday use. A default font-list tag is `XmFONTLIST_DEFAULT_TAG`.

You can use resource files to take care of `XmString` conversions automatically. For example, a label widget (`XmLabel`) supports a *labelString* resource of type `XmString`. In a resource file, you can place a normal string, such as the following:

```
*exitchoice.labelString:    Exit
```

In the above example, Motif will translate the text string *Exit* into an XmString.

Creating XmStrings

The main functions used to create XmStrings include XmStringCreateLocalized and XmStringCreateSimple, which we covered in Chapter 5:

```
XmString XmStringCreateSimple(char* string)
```

```
XmString XmStringCreateLocalized(char* string)
```

All the XmString creation functions allocate memory, which you should free with XmStringFree:

```
void XmStringFree(XmString xmstring)
```

XmStringCreateLtoR creates an XmString that goes from left to right, the direction of text used by most Western languages:

```
XmString XmStringCreateLtoR(char* string,
         char* tag)
```

XmStringCreateLtoR creates a left-to-right XmString. Every new line, \n, in the string is converted to an XmString separator. You should use XmStringCreateLocalized instead of XmStringCreateLtoR with Motif 1.2.

Prior to Motif 1.2, XmStringCreateLtoR took the following parameters:

```
XmString XmStringCreateLtoR(char* string,
         XmStringCharSet charset)
```

N O T E

In Motif 1.2, the *charset* becomes a *font-list tag*. The default tag is XmFONTLIST_DEFAULT_TAG. The default *charset* was XmSTRING_DEFAULT_CHARSET. Some Motif 1.2 header files still show the old XmStringCharSet parameter.

XmStringCreate creates a Motif string from a regular NULL-terminated C string, with the given font-list tag:

```
XmString XmStringCreate(char* string,
        char* tag)
```

In most cases, you'll use the default tag.

Comparing XmStrings

Motif supports a number of functions to compare XmStrings (see Table 15.4).

Table 15.4 *XmString comparison routines.*

XmStringByteCompare
XmStringCompare
XmStringEmpty

You can compare two XmStrings with XmStringCompare:

```
Boolean XmStringCompare(XmString xmstring1,
        XmString xmstring2)
```

You can compare XmStrings byte-by-byte with XmStringByte-Compare:

```
Boolean XmStringByteCompare(XmString xmstring1,
        XmString xmstring2)
```

This assumes that both XmStrings have the same font tag and direction. Also, many widgets may change the internal data of an XmString to make it more efficient. Consequently, you should use XmStringCompare instead of XmStringByteCompare where possible.

To determine if an XmString is empty, use XmStringEmpty:

```
Boolean XmStringEmpty(XmString xmstring)
```

Working with XmStrings

You can copy an XmString, that is, create a duplicate, with XmStringCopy:

```
XmString XmStringCopy(XmString xmstring)
```

XmStringConcat appends *xmstring2* onto the end of *xmstring1*. The end of *xmstring1* depends on the string order (left to right or right to left) and how many lines are in *xmstring1*:

```
XmString XmStringConcat(XmString xmstring1,
        XmString xmstring2)
```

Extracting a C String from an XmString

XmStringGetLtoR pulls a plain old C string from an XmString:

```
Boolean XmStringGetLtoR(XmString xmstring,
        XmStringCharSet charset,
        char** text)  /* RETURN */
```

In your code, you can call XmStringGetLtoR as follows:

```
XmString    xmstring;
char*       string;

XmStringGetLtoR(xmstring,
```

```
        XmSTRING_DEFAULT_CHARSET,

    &string);


printf("The string is %s\n", string);


XtFree(string);
```

XmStringGetLtoR returns True if XmStringGetLtoR found a string with the proper charset inside the XmString; False otherwise. If you use XmSTRING_DEFAULT_CHARSET, though, you should always match.

Motif Routines for Drawing XmStrings

After working with XmStrings, it's time to draw them.

Motif supports a number of routines for drawing an XmString (see Table 15.5).

Table 15.5 *XmString drawing routines.*

XmStringDraw
XmStringDrawImage
XmStringDrawUnderline

XmStringDraw draws the foreground of an XmString to the given window:

```
void XmStringDraw(Display* display,

    Window window,

    XmFontList fontlist,

    XmString xmstring,

    GC gc,  /* might be modified */

    int x, int y,

    int width,

    unsigned int alignment,
```

```
        unsigned int direction,
        XRectangle* clip_rectangle)
```

The *width* is the width of a rectangle that will hold the text output. The *alignment* should be one of XmALIGNMENT_BEGINNING, XmALIGNMENT_CENTER, or XmALIGNMENT_END. The direction controls which way the string is drawn, XmString_DIRECTION_L_TO_R, XmString_DIRECTION_R_TO_L, or XmSTRING_DIRECTION_DEFAULT if you can't tell and want the direction from the current locale. The *clip_rectangle* can be used to clip the output, or you can pass NULL for no clipping. If the XmString hasfont-list tags other than the default, the *fontlist* parameter is used to associated the proper font with the proper text segments in the XmString. Otherwise, the *gc* parameter's font is used. (The *gc* parameter may be modified and left in an undetermined state.)

XmStringDrawImage draws the foreground and background for the given XmString:

```
    void XmStringDrawImage(Display* display,
        Window window,
        XmFontList fontlist,
        XmString xmstring,
        GC gc,
        int x, int y,
        int width,
        unsigned int alignment,
        unsigned int direction,
        XRectangle* clip_rectangle)
```

XmStringDrawUnderline draws and underlines an XmString:

```
    void XmStringDrawUnderline(Display* display,
        Window window,
        XmFontList fontlist,
        XmString xmstring,
```

```
GC gc,

int x, int y,

int width,

unsigned int alignment,

unsigned int direction,

XRectangle* clip_rectangle,

XmString underline_xmstring)
```

XmStringDrawUnderline is used to draw menu names and other parts of the interface that have part of a string underlined. For instance, the Motif *File* menu usually has the *F* underlined. Because of this, you pass the *underline_xmstring*—the text in the main *xmstring* that should be underlined. In the example above, the *xmstring* would hold "File" and the *underline_xmstring* would hold "F"—both formatted as XmStrings.

Determining the Size of XmStrings

There are a number of routines you can call to get a handle on how large a given XmString is (see Table 15.6).

Table 15.6   *XmString sizing routines.*

XmStringBaseLine
XmStringExtent
XmStringHeight
XmStringLength
XmStringLineCount
XmStringWidth

Many of these routines require font-list parameters, introduced above.

XmStringBaseline returns the *baseline*, the distance between the text baseline of the first line of text in xmstring and the top of the character box:

```
Dimension XmStringBaseline(XmFontList fontlist,
            XmString xmstring)
```

XmStringExtent determines the size of the smallest rectangle that can enclose the given *xmstring* using the given *fontlist*:

```
void XmStringExtent(XmFontList fontlist,
        XmString xmstring,
        Dimension* width,
        Dimension* height)
```

To get the length (in bytes) of an XmString, use XmStringLength:

```
int XmStringLength(XmString xmstring)
```

XmStringLength includes the text, the font tags, and any separators in *xmstring*.

XmStringLineCount returns the number of separators—plus one—in the given XmString:

```
int XmStringLineCount(XmString xmstring)
```

You can determine the height and width of an XmString, using a given *fontlist*, with XmStringHeight and XmStringWidth:

```
Dimension XmStringHeight(XmFontList fontlist,
            XmString xmstring)


Dimension XmStringWidth(XmFontList fontlist,
            XmString xmstring)
```

Both routines check all the lines within the given *xmstring*. XmStringHeight totals the height of every line. XmStringWidth returns the longest width.

Motif Strings with Multiple Fonts

We can use arbitrary font tags to display text in different fonts. A common use for this is to provide bold, roman, and italic fonts for text. We can then display our text using any or all of these fonts.

One way to do this is to create XmStrings using an arbitrary font tag, in our case ROMAN, BOLD, and ITALIC.

Before we can create a program, we need to build an XmString that contains segments of text with different font tags. To do this, we can call XmStringCreate to create new XmStrings using the given tags. Then we concatenate the strings together, one at a time, using XmStringConcat. This builds a combined XmString where each segment in the string can potentially use a different font. The utility function, CombineStrings, below, handles this.

The code for the XmString concatenation routine is stored in m_string.c:

```
/*
 *  m_string.c
 *  Motif code to concatenate strings.
 */
#include "motif.h"


/*
 * Creates a new XmString from an old XmString
 * and a new text string. The tag can be used to
 * determine the font.
 */


XmString CombineStrings(XmString old_xmstring,
    char* string,
    char* tag)
```

```
{   /* CombineStrings */
    XmString    new_xmstring;
    XmString    combined_xmstring;

    /*
     * Create new string.
     */
    new_xmstring = XmStringCreate(string, tag);

    /*
     * Now, combine.
     */
    if (old_xmstring != NULL) {

        /* combine xmstrings */
        combined_xmstring =
            XmStringConcat(old_xmstring,
                new_xmstring);

        /* Free memory. */
        XmStringFree(new_xmstring);

    } else {
        combined_xmstring = new_xmstring;
    }

    return combined_xmstring;

}   /* CombineStrings */


/* end of file m_string.c */
```

Once we build together an `XmString` with multiple font tags, we then need to associate the `XmString` with a *fontList* resource. This *fontList* resource will then force our text to be displayed using the fonts from the font list.

In our case, we want to use "ROMAN" as a tag for roman or normal text, "BOLD" for bold text, and "ITALIC" for italic text. To do so, we set up a font list in a resource file as follows:

```
*font_test.fontList:\
  -*-helvetica-medium-r-normal—*-180-75-75-*-*=ROMAN,\
  -*-helvetica-bold-r-normal—*-180-75-75-*-*=BOLD,\
  -*-helvetica-medium-o-normal—*-180-75-75-*-*=ITALIC
```

All the fonts are the same size and all are the same family, Helvetica, so that the text looks good together. We use a resource file because it's a lot simpler than programming our own font list.

A Program to Display Multifont Text

A sample program that creates a Motif `XmLabel` widget and places text with multiple fonts into that widget appears below. Note the three calls to `CombineStrings` to combine strings with font tags.

The code is stored in the file `m_chap15.c`:

```
/*
 *  m_chap15.c
 *  Motif test program for Chapter 15.
 *  Test fontList resource.
 */
#include "motif.h"
#include <Xm/Label.h>


extern XmString CombineStrings(XmString old_xmstring,
    char* string,
```

```
            char* tag);


int main(int argc, char** argv)


{   /* main */
    XtAppContext   app_context;
    Widget         parent;
    Widget         mainwindow;
    Widget         menubar;
    Widget         filemenu;
    Widget         exitchoice;
    Widget         font_test;
    Arg            args[20];
    int            n;
    XmString       xmstring1, xmstring2, xmstring3;


    /* Initialize X toolkit */
    n = 0;
    parent = XtAppInitialize(&app_context,
            "ProX",                    /* app class */
            (XrmOptionDescList) NULL,   /* options */
            0,                         /* num options */
            ARGC_PTR &argc, argv,      /* cmd line */
            (String*) NULL,            /* fallback res. */
            args, n);



    /*
     * Create Main Window with utility function.
     */
    mainwindow = CreateMainWindow(parent, "main");
```

```
/*
 * Create menu bar with utility function.
 */
menubar = CreateMenuBar(mainwindow, "menubar");


/*
 * Create the file menu.
 */
filemenu = CreateMenu(menubar, "filemenu");


/* Create a menu choice to exit the program. */
exitchoice = CreateExitChoice(filemenu,
                "exitchoice");


/*
 * Create XmString components for
 * the various fonts.
 */
xmstring1 = CombineStrings((XmString) NULL,
        "This is normal text;",
        "ROMAN");


xmstring2 = CombineStrings(xmstring1,
        " this is italic text;",
        "ITALIC");


xmstring3 = CombineStrings(xmstring2,
        " this is bold text.",
        "BOLD");
```

```
    /*
     * Create a label widget to display the text.
     */
    n = 0;
    XtSetArg(args[n], XmNlabelString, xmstring3); n++;

    font_test = XmCreateLabel(mainwindow,
                    "font_test", args, n);

    XtManageChild(font_test);

    /*
     * Free XmStrings.
     */
    XmStringFree(xmstring1);
    XmStringFree(xmstring2);
    XmStringFree(xmstring3);

    SetMainAreas(mainwindow,
            menubar,
            font_test);

    /* Create the windows. */
    XtRealizeWidget(parent);
    XtAppMainLoop(app_context);

    return 0;

}   /* main */


/* end of file m_chap15.c */
```

After installing the resource file (below), you'll see a window similar to the one pictured in Figure 15.2.

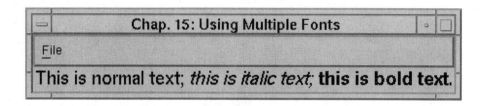

Figure 15.2   *Multiple font text with Motif.*

Note the three fonts used for the text in the window.

Resource File

Both the Motif and OLIT programs above require the following resource file:

```
! ProX
! Resource file for Chapter 15 of
! Professional Graphics
! Programming in the X Window System.
!
! Place this file in your
! home directory.
!
! Generic resources.
!
*background:        #cccccc


!
! Motif resources.
```

```
!
!
*fontList: -*-helvetica-medium-r-normal—12-120-75-75-*-*


!
! Note how to use the font-list tags
! ROMAN, BOLD, and ITALIC.
!
*font_test.fontList:\
  -*-helvetica-medium-r-normal—*-180-75-75-*-*=ROMAN,\
  -*-helvetica-bold-r-normal—*-180-75-75-*-*=BOLD,\
  -*-helvetica-medium-o-normal—*-180-75-75-*-*=ITALIC


*filemenu.labelString:    File
*filemenu.mnemonic:       F


*exitchoice.labelString:  Exit
*exitchoice.mnemonic:     x


*m_chap15.title:          Chap. 15: Using Multiple Fonts


! OLIT
*o_chap15.title:          Chap. 15: Setting Fonts


*filemenu.label:          File
*exitchoice.label:        Exit


! end of file ProX
```

Name this file ProX and place it in your home directory.

Summary

Most X toolkits do the dirty work of basic font management with little or no interaction on your part—as a matter of fact, we haven't had to program with any fonts using any X toolkit routines up to this point of the book. This chapter covers the many font-management tools included with both Motif and OLIT. When you want to draw text in a drawing-area widget (OLIT DrawArea and Motif XmDrawingArea), you can use all the X library routines introduced in the last chapter. Or you can try to work more within the toolkit framework and use toolkit routines for font handling and drawing text.

Using fonts with OLIT is easier than using fonts with Motif, because OLIT uses the traditional X structures for fonts, such as XFontStruct, introduced in the last chapter. With OLIT, you can load up a font using XLoadQueryFont from the previous chapter and then set the *font* resource for a widget.

Motif complicates text and fonts with the concept of Motif's compound strings and font lists. The complications added by Motif consist mainly of a new format for font sets called a font list, as well as the Motif string format, XmString. Of course, you can use the X library routines introduced in the previous chapter. These Motif-specific routines can help make your applications work better in other countries.

In Motif terminology, a font is a collection of glyphs or bitmap images associated with a given character set. A font set is the collection of fonts needed to display text in a given language. English, for example, needs a font set with only one font. Japanese, though, needs at least three fonts in a font set. A font-list is then a collection of font sets or fonts, each of which is in a font-list entry. Most of the font-list code was added in Motif 1.2. Each element in a font list has a font-list tag, an arbitrary name used to identify a font. Finally, a font-list entry holds either a font or a font set. A Motif font list may support a number of font names. For instance, Japanese text may require a font for Kanji, another for Kana, and a third for Latin (that's ASCII to the rest of us).

Much of this added complexity is because of internationalization concerns. In X, a character set is a mapping between byte-codes and characters. For example, the ISO 8859-1 character set, often called Latin-1 (a superset of US ASCII) uses the value 65 for an uppercase letter *A*. Most Asian languages require multiple bytes per character.

The basic data structure for a font list is the XmFontList structure. The XmFontList structure is considered opaque and hidden by the Motif toolkit in the include file <Xm/Xm.h>. All major tools in creating and manipulating a font list are reviewed.

Motif Functions and Macros
Introduced in This Chapter

XmFontListAdd

XmFontListAppendEntry

XmFontListCopy

XmFontListCreate

XmFontListEntryCreate

XmFontListEntryFree

XmFontListEntryGetFont

XmFontListEntryGetTag

XmFontListEntryLoad

XmFontListFree

XmStringBaseline

XmStringByteCompare

XmStringCompare

XmStringConcat

XmStringCopy

XmStringCreate

XmStringCreateLtoR

XmStringDraw

XmStringDrawImage

XmStringDrawUnderline

XmStringEmpty

XmStringExtent

XmStringGetLtoR

```
XmStringHeight
XmStringLength
XmStringLineCount
XmStringWidth
```

C h a p t e r 1 6

Installing, Creating, and Administrating Fonts

This chapter covers:

- ✦ Finding out what fonts are available
- ✦ Decoding the long font names
- ✦ The XLFD, the X logical font description format
- ✦ Viewing fonts
- ✦ Location of font files and directories
- ✦ The X font server and scalable fonts
- ✦ Installing fonts
- ✦ Font file formats
- ✦ Designing your own fonts

Words and Pictures

In Chapter 14, we introduced how the X Window System uses fonts, and continued that discussion in Chapter 15. In this chapter, we end our coverage of fonts by going over those niggling details about font management that always seem to fall through the cracks, including information on where fonts are usually stored in a typical X Window System installation, and the differences between the various font formats.

Tracking Down What Fonts Are Available

A standard X application program called `xlsfonts` lists the available fonts on a workstation. Running `xlsfonts` on a Release 4 or higher X server will result in pages and pages of text output. Release 5 adds a font server, which adds even more fonts to the mix.

Here's some sample output from `xlsfonts`:

```
-adobe-courier-medium-o-normal—8-80-75-75-m-50-iso8859-1
-adobe-courier-medium-r-normal—10-100-75-75-m-60-iso8859-1
-adobe-courier-medium-r-normal-11-80-100-100-m-60-iso8859-1
-adobe-courier-medium-r-normal—12-120-75-75-m-70-iso8859-1
-adobe-times-medium-r-normal—24-240-75-75-p-124-iso8859-1
-bitstream-charter-medium-r-normal—14-100-100-100-p-78-
iso8859-1
9x15
8x13
fixed
cursor
variable
olglyph-10
```

The list was grabbed from a generic X11R5 installation. There's much more to this list than we've excerpted, but it should give you an idea of how X classifies and references font names. Though there are some fonts that are available on virtually every X implementation, you need to remember that each X installation has its own set of available fonts. The fonts listed above should be available on most systems, but don't assume so. We have found that while most systems have the font files, not all systems have correctly set up all these fonts. Usually the problem is with the *font path*, specifying the directories where the X server is told to check for fonts. The font path is often set up incorrectly, so the X server will not access all the fonts. This is a problem any user can track down browsing through system subdirectories.

Another common problem involves the improper use of font aliases. An alias is akin to a macro: instead of typing out the long name of a font (who wants to type `-adobe-courier-medium-r-normal--12-120-75-75-m-70-iso8859-1` when all you want to do is change the point size to 12 point?), you can assign a shorter string to represent the long name. The `variable` font, for example, is normally an alias for another (usually Helvetica or something similar) font. The long font names are based on an X standard called the X Logical Font Description Conventions, or XLFD. A document describing the XLFD is included with the X Window System from the X Consortium.

These aliases are normally stored in files named `fonts.alias`. Each font directory, such as `/usr/lib/X11/fonts/100dpi`, should have such a file if you want to use aliases for font names. If you are having problems with font aliases, the `fonts.alias` files may very well be set up incorrectly.

In addition, each font contains a `fonts.dir` file, which maps font file names to the long XLFD-formatted font names. A standard program called `mkfontdir` generates these files. If you add a font to your system, you'll need to run `mkfontdir`.

A similar problem arises with versions of OpenWindows on SPARC machines. The X11/NeWS server provides scalable fonts, but requires a `Families.List` file in font directories, usually `/usr/openwin/lib/fonts`. When installing new programs, such as Sun's Answer Book, the default `Families.List` file may get trashed as the new font families wipe out all the old font family entries in the file. In the case of the Answer Book installation, this can prevent OpenWindows from running. The fix, which Sun does document (if obscurely), is to run the `bldfamily` program to regenerate the `Families.List` file. `Bldfamily` is usually located in `/usr/openwin/bin`.

Decoding Long Font Names

When you run a program like `xlsfonts`, you'll see that most of the X font names are extremely long and complex. The actual format of these names makes sense and is described in the XLFD. Since we hate books that promise an explanation and then refer you to another work, we'll take a few minutes and explain exactly what these font names mean. We'll first explain a portion of the font name, and then underline that portion of the font name. We'll use a rather common font name for an example:

```
-adobe-courier-bold-r-normal--11-80-100-100-m-60-iso8859-1
```

Most font names begin with a leading hyphen and then a font-company name, such as adobe (short for Adobe Systems):

```
-adobe-courier-bold-r-normal--11-80-100-100-m-60-iso8859-1
```

These names need to be registered with the X Consortium. A number of font vendors, such as Adobe and Bitstream, have donated fonts for X. Next comes the font family name field, such as courier:

```
-adobe-courier-bold-r-normal--11-80-100-100-m-60-iso8859-1
```

The weight follows, usually bold or medium:

```
-adobe-courier-bold-r-normal--11-80-100-100-m-60-iso8859-1
```

Then comes the slant field:

```
-adobe-courier-bold-r-normal--11-80-100-100-m-60-iso8859-1
```

Typographers are going to die of heart attacks when they see Table 16.1, which explains what the code field signifies. (Typographically speaking, a *true* italicized typeface should not be merely a slanted version of a roman face, but rather a face designed from scratch.)

Table 16.1 *Codes used in the slant field.*

Code	Meaning
i	Italic
o	Oblique
r	Roman
ri	Reverse italic
ro	Reverse oblique
ot	Other

The set-width name describes how wide the letters are. Some examples are condensed, semicondensed, narrow, normal, and double-wide.

```
-adobe-courier-bold-r-normal--11-80-100-100-m-60-iso8859-1
```

After the set-width name comes space for any extra information necessary to identify the font, such as sans (for sans serif). This space is not used in our example, nor for most fonts.

The pixel-size field indicates the size in dots on the screen—in our case, 11. Zero indicates a scalable font.

```
-adobe-courier-bold-r-normal--11-80-100-100-m-60-iso8859-1
```

One would assume that there would some sort of correlation between the pizel size and the point size of the font. There isn't—another cruel reminder that in the X Window System you can't take anything for granted. Instead, there's a separate point-size field, describes the size in terms of points (1/72nd of an inch). This field is 10 times the point size. The 80 means our font is an 8-point font.

```
-adobe-courier-bold-r-normal--11-80-100-100-m-60-iso8859-1
```

After the point size follows the dots per inch (dpi) in the *x* and *y* directions. Our example is 100 x 100 dpi. Most are either 75 or 100 dpi.

```
-adobe-courier-bold-r-normal--11-80-100-100-m-60-iso8859-1
```

The spacing field determines if a font is monospaced or proportional. The various settings are listed in Table 16.2.

```
-adobe-courier-bold-r-normal--11-80-100-100-m-60-iso8859-1
```

Table 16.2 *Settings in ths spacing field.*

Spacing	Meaning
p	Proportional
m	Monospaced
c	Char cell/monospaced, e.g., suitable for using with `xterm`

The average-width field provides an average size in tenths of pixels, or 6 pixels in our example:

```
-adobe-courier-bold-r-normal--11-80-100-100-m-60-iso8859-1
```

Finally, the charset registry and encoding fields tell what kind of character set we have. Most are ISO 8859-1 (Latin-1, a superset of ASCII):

```
-adobe-courier-bold-r-normal--11-80-100-100-m-60-iso8859-1
```

Viewing Fonts

After you've found the fonts, you'll probably want to preview them. There are two handy X utility programs for viewing fonts: `xfontsel` and `xfd`. The first, `xfontsel` (short for X font selecter), can help you choose fonts using the long font-name format.

You can use `xfontsel` to pick part of a long XLFD font name and then see what fonts are available. For instance, you can pick a font family name of *times* and see all the Times fonts that are installed on your system. A list of all the available options for each part of the XLFD font names are provided on `xfontsel`'s pulldown menus.

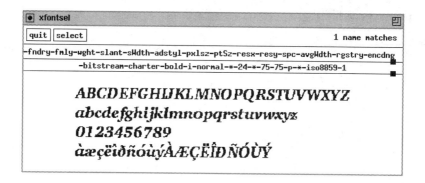

Figure 16.1   *The xfontsel program.*

The second X utility program for viewing fonts, `xfd` (short for X font displayer), will display all the characters in a font. Normally, if `xfd` cannot find the font, then your program will not either. The command below will create a window and display the characters in the font named `variable`:

```
% xfd -fn variable
```

After running this command, you'll see a window like the one shown in Figure 16.2.

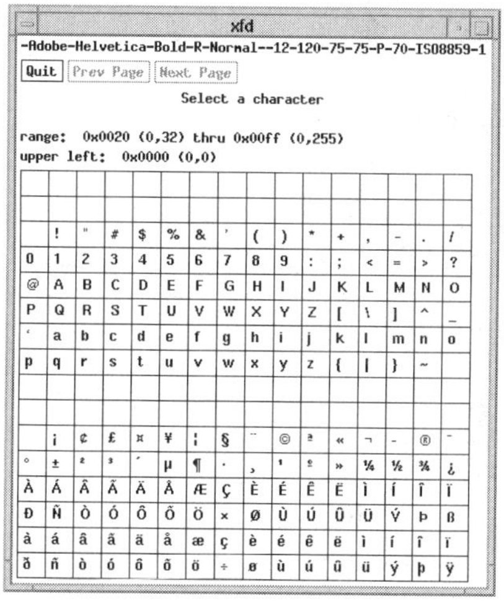

Figure 16.2   *The xfd program.*

Where Font Files Are Located

On most X systems, you'll find the font files located in subdirectories under the directory /usr/lib/X11/fonts, as listed in Table 16.3.

Table 16.3   Font directories.

Directory	Contains
/usr/lib/X11/fonts/misc	Miscellaneous bitmap fonts
/usr/lib/X11/fonts/Speedo	Bitstream's Speedo scalable fonts
/usr/lib/X11/fonts/75dpi	Fonts for 75 dots-per-inch displays
/usr/lib/X11/fonts/100dpi	Fonts for 100 dots-per-inch displays

The Speedo fonts, used by the font server, are new in X11 Release 5. Your system may have additional font directories or use nonstandard locations for fonts. OpenWindows uses /usr/openwin/lib/font, for example. In addition, you may add your own font directories using the xset command (see below, under Installing Fonts).

The X Font Server

Older (R4 and before) versions of the X Window System treated fonts with an amazing unsophistication, especially for something that claimed to provide the building blocks for a graphical-user interface. Font management meant compiling fonts in specific sizes and specific weights (hence, all the baggage attached to font names, as discussed in the previous section). The trouble is that most users of a graphical-user interface expect to have a wide variety of typefaces available in any size at all times. Since the compiled-font method didn't lend itself too well to this need (can you imagine the hard-disk real estate occupied by compiling just 10 fonts in every point size between 6 and 72 point?), and since it was logical to build the font-management capabilities into X itself (as opposed to Motif or

Open Look), the X Consortium came up with the *font server*, first introduced in X11 Release 5.

Great idea, but middling implementation. Yes, the font server makes many more fonts available, and often to all the machines on a network. But because the font server is poorly documented, it adds yet another area where users can incorrectly configure their system—and they probably will never know about it.

The lesson here is that your applications cannot depend on any X fonts. Your applications require some form of fallback strategy in case needed fonts aren't available. You may want to specify some common fonts, but then fall back on some choices that are nearly universal. We've found these universal fonts to be `fixed`; 8x13, a fixed-width font where each character fits a 8 x 13 pixel cell; 9x15; and variable, mentioned earlier.

Structurally, the font server is an add-on to the X server. If you need to change the text size, you merely ask for a new font in the desired size. The font server provides fonts to the X Server.

Unfortunately, the true goal of scalable text is only partially met. The font server serves up bitmap fonts to the X server, scaling these bitmaps to the desired sizes. Your application cannot use the font server to output dynamically scaled text, but instead asks the X server for a particular font in a particular size.

The font server is included in the general release of X11 Release 5, and it contains a number of scalable fonts provided by Bitstream, using the Speedo font format. As Release 5 proliferates, you'll no doubt be able to get scalable fonts from a number of vendors, and we expect to see a good number of public-domain fonts. (Release 6 should contain a PostScript Type 1 font renderizer as well.)

The font server causes problems in a number of environments, especially where users run X under another windowing system, such as NextStep, Microsoft Windows, DESQview/X, or the Macintosh. Users on those systems may well want to use their native fonts with X, since supporting fonts period in such an environment has proven difficult.

Why cover a user-configuration issue like the font server in a programming book? The Release 5 sorely needs a font-server overview document, because nothing really describes how to put all the parts together and actually use the font server. If you're going to program in the X environment and use all of the available tools—including a font server—you've got to be using the font server yourself.

We've found the five following steps work on our system:

1. Configure the font server using a configuration file.
2. Choose a TCP/IP port number for the font server.
3. Start the font server.
4. Configure the X server to recognize the font server.
5. Verify that scalable fonts are available and start using the fonts.

Configuring the Font Server

The font server requires a rigidly formatted configuration file, as any deviations result in program death. The only correct, or nearly correct, example configuration file is in the font server (`fs`) man page. All other example configuration files, including an example file that came with the X11R5 sources, cause system crashes. Skip the `doc` directories in the X11R5 source tree. They're all wrong.

Here is a proper `config` file, or at least one that works for us:

```
clone-self = on
use-syslog = off
catalogue = /usr/local/X11R5/lib/X11/fonts/Speedo
error-file = FSERRORS
default-point-size = 120
default-resolutions = 75,75,100,100
```

The catalogue path is where your scalable fonts are located. In our case, we stored the Speedo fonts in the directory `/usr/local/X11R5/-lib/X11/fonts/Speedo`.

The Speedo directory contains some example scalable fonts. Usually, these will be in `/usr/lib/X11/fonts/Speedo`. Note that many example catalogues use *speedo* with a lowercase *s*. Our directory had an uppercase *S*. (Remember—in UNIX, the case of the directory name makes a difference.)

The font server communicates to the X server using a TCP/IP port, for which you have to choose a port number; the same number must be used consistently. All examples use port 7000, and we suggest sticking with 7000 unless you have a compelling reason to change.

Starting the Font Server

Once you get a good configuration file and choose a port number, you can start the font server. Start it in the background.

The `fs` program is the actual font server. You can start it with the following command:

```
fs -config ./config -port 7000 &
```

This tells the font server (`fs`) to use the configuration file named `config` in the current directory and the TCP/IP port number of `7000`. If the font server detects any problems, especially with your configuration file, it will crash.

As it did several times for us, as we relied perhaps too heavily on the documentation. Every piece of documentation describing the configuration file, in particular, contradicted other documents. For instance, the catalogue command, above, does not have a leading name for the type of fonts. One example used:

```
catalogue =
pcf:/usr/lib/X11/fonts/misc,speedo:/usr/lib/fonts/speedo
```

This fails. Not only does the Speedo directory start with an uppercase name, the leading `pcf:` or `speedo:` caused the font server to die a flaming death.

After starting the font server, you need to configure the X server to recognize the font server and use the scalable fonts.

Configuring the X Server

To configure the X server for the font server, tell the X server to include the font server in its font path. This requires an X server from Release 5.

Using the font path is a clever way to extend the X server without breaking X application software. Since the font server communicates only with the X server, the programmer can essentially ignore it. The font server provides more fonts, so it fits naturally as part of the X server's font path—just another path for more fonts. This is probably the best part of the font-server design.

To configure the X server, we use a syntax much like that for current font paths. Use the `xset` command to add (extend) the font path:

```
xset +fp tcp/hostname:7000
```

The `+fp` tells `xset` to add to the font path, and the new font path is `tcp/hostname:7000`, where *hostname* is the computer network name where the font server computes. The `7000` is the TCP/IP port number, used in the `fs` command line.

If you don't replace the word `hostname` above with the proper hostname where the font server computes, you'll get a very strange X error from `xset`:

```
X Error of failed request: BadValue (integer parameter out of
range for operation)
   Major opcode of failed request: 51 (X_SetFontPath)
   Value in failed request: 0x0
   Serial number of failed request: 4
   Current serial number in output stream: 6
```

A proper command for a computer with a hostname of `nicollet` is:

```
xset +fp tcp/nicollet:7000
```

Working with Scalable Fonts

Once you get the font server running and the X server to recognize the font server as part of its font path, you can try using some scalable fonts. First, try the `xlsfonts` command to see the available fonts. Look for fonts with zeros in the size fields.

You'll see a lot of fonts with something like:

```
-adobe-courier-bold-r-normal--0-0-75-75-m-0-iso8859-1
-adobe-courier-medium-o-normal--0-0-75-75-m-0-iso8859-1
-adobe-helvetica-bold-r-normal--0-0-75-75-p-0-iso8859-1
-adobe-times-medium-i-normal--0-0-75-75-p-0-iso8859-1
-bitstream-charter-bold-i-normal--0-0-0-0-p-0-iso8859-1
-bitstream-charter-bold-i-normal--0-0-75-75-p-0-iso8859-1
-daewoo-mincho-medium-r-normal--0-0-100-100-c-0-ksc
      5601.1987-0
-dec-terminal-bold-r-normal--0-0-75-75-c-0-dec-dectech
```

These are fonts that are explicitly scalable by the font server.

The font server itself comes with a number of utility programs, including `fsinfo`, which provides information about the font server. We use `fsinfo` to help verify that the font server is actually running:

```
fsinfo -server hostname:7000
```

Again, replace `hostname` with the name of the machine containing the font server. Here's some sample output of `fsinfo`:

```
name of server: nicollet:7000
version number: 1
vendor string: MIT X Consortium
vendor release number: 5000
maximum request size: 16384 longwords (65536 bytes)
number of catalogues: 1
        all
Number of alternate servers: 0
number of extensions: 0
```

You can replace `-server hostname:7000` if you properly set up the FONTSERVER environment variable. Set FONTSERVER to the hostname and TCP/IP port number used for the font server, such as `hostname:7000`. For a hostname of `nicollet` and a TCP/IP port of 7000, use:

```
setenv FONTSERVER nicollet:7000
```

Using a description of the long font names (from the X Logical Font Description or XLFD, mentioned earlier), you can try the X font displayer program, `xfd`, with a rather large font. First, we take an XLFD name with zeros:

```
-bitstream-courier-medium-r-normal--0-0-0-0-m-0-iso8859-1
```

Then we build a proper name in the size we want, in this case, 39 point:

```
-bitstream-courier-bold-r-normal--39-390-75-75-m-39-iso8859-1
```

We have found that 39 point seems to be the largest-sized scalable font. Trying a 40-point font, such as the font below, fails:

```
-bitstream-courier-bold-r-normal--40-400-75-75-m-40-iso8859-1
```

With the same font, 39 point works. You may want to play with the configurations to get around this limitation.

Typing in these long XLFD font names is a real chore, but the cut and paste offered in `xterm` windows really helps here. Beware of making a mistake, though. You must build a proper name or you'll get an error—as we've seen, the X font server is not forgiving. You can try the `xfd`, or X font displayer, program to display a scaled font. The following command displays a 37-point scalable font:

```
xfd -fn "-bitstream-courier-bold-r-normal--37-370-75-75-m-37-
    iso8859-1"
```

Another program that comes with the font server is `fslsfonts`, which lists the fonts supported by the font server:

```
fslsfonts -server hostname:7000
```

Note that the resulting list is much smaller than the list of scalable fonts reported by `xlsfonts`:

```
-bitstream-charter-bold-i-normal--0-0-0-0-p-0-iso8859-1
-bitstream-charter-bold-r-normal--0-0-0-0-p-0-iso8859-1
-bitstream-charter-medium-i-normal--0-0-0-0-p-0-iso8859-1
```

```
-bitstream-charter-medium-r-normal--0-0-0-0-p-0-iso8859-1

-bitstream-courier-bold-i-normal--0-0-0-0-m-0-iso8859-1

-bitstream-courier-bold-r-normal--0-0-0-0-m-0-iso8859-1

-bitstream-courier-medium-i-normal--0-0-0-0-m-0-iso8859-1

-bitstream-courier-medium-r-normal--0-0-0-0-m-0-iso8859-1
```

The program showfont outputs a text description of a whole font. These text descriptions tend to be long. Here's just one letter, the right bracket, }, from the following command:

```
showfont -fn "-bitstream-charter-bold-i-normal--0-0-0-0-p-0-
iso8859-1"

char #125 ('}')

Right: 6    Left: 1    Descent: 3    Ascent: 8    Width: 6

##---

-##--

-##--

-##--

-##--

---##

-##--

-##--

-##--

-##--

##---
```

Font File Formats

X includes a number of special font formats:

- ✦ **PCF** (*Portable Compiled Font*)—an enhanced version of the SNF format introduced in Release 5. These fonts are portable, which means they can be shared between machines of disparate types.

This is especially useful if you have a UNIX host supporting a number of X terminals (probably an entirely different processor architecture than your UNIX host). Note that a number of vendors have used the PCF moniker in the past for proprietary font formats.

If your X11R5 vendor supports a font server, the vendor should also include a compiler to generate fonts for your particular system. If you're lucky, the vendor will also supply a few precompiled fonts to get you up and running immediately.

✦ **BDF** (*Bitmap Distribution Format*)—a portable format based on the ASCII bitmap format. A font file in this format must usually be converted to another (binary) format for use by X, but this is the format you use to exchange fonts between systems, since the files are ASCII text.

✦ **SNF** (*Server Normal Format*)—a BDF font compiled into the format best suited for your particular X server. Inherently nonportable, these fonts must be converted back to the BDF format to exchange fonts with other architectures and systems.

   The SNF format was replaced by PCF in Release 5.

✦ **Speedo**—Bitstream donated a number of Speedo scalable fonts with X11 Release 5. These fonts use the font server, described below.

✦ **Folio** (also called *F3* or *OpenFonts*) **fonts**—a scalable format used under OpenWindows. A program called `convertfont` converts to and from this format.

Managing these different font formats represents some work for the system administrator, who should maintain a separate directory on a network for every type of server on a network. Not every type of server needs a separate format; for instance, in the past, NCD X terminals and Sun workstations used the same font format.

Prior to Release 5, most X implementations included a program called `bdftosnf` to convert ASCII BDF font files to binary SNF files. Release 5 replaces `bdftosnf` with `bdftopcf`, which converts BDF files to the portable binary PCF format.

The contributed software with X often includes a `snftobdf` to reverse the process and create an ASCII bitmap BDF file from a binary X font. This is useful for exchanging fonts between systems.

The BDF File Format

The BDF file format is described in a document entitled Bitmap Distribution Format that comes with the X releases from the X Consortium. If you intend to create your own fonts, you should be familiar with this document as well as the X Logical Font Description Conventions, because your fonts must meet the requirements in both documents.

BDF files are ASCII bitmap files that hold information about a font and each of its characters. One BDF file holds one X font, that is, only one font family and face at one size and orientation (bold, italic, roman, and so on).

The BDF files begin with a STARTFONT command. Each command is stored on a single line of text. A STARTPROPERTIES command begins the description of the font's properties. A FONT comand provides the full XLFD name. The font properties section goes to the ENDPROPERTIES command.

Here's an abbreviated (we removed most of the comments) BDF file header for a simple Times font from Adobe. We end after the first two characters, a space, and the exclamation mark:

```
STARTFONT 2.1

COMMENT  Copyright 1984, 1987 Adobe Systems, Inc.

FONT -Adobe-Times-Medium-R-Normal--11-80-100-100-P-54-
    ISO8859-1

SIZE 8 100 100

FONTBOUNDINGBOX 11 12 -1 -3

STARTPROPERTIES 22

FONTNAME_REGISTRY ""

FAMILY_NAME "Times"

FOUNDRY "Adobe"

WEIGHT_NAME "Medium"

SETWIDTH_NAME "Normal"

SLANT "R"

ADD_STYLE_NAME ""

PIXEL_SIZE 11

POINT_SIZE 80
```

```
RESOLUTION_X 100
RESOLUTION_Y 100
SPACING "P"
AVERAGE_WIDTH 54
CHARSET_REGISTRY "ISO8859"
CHARSET_ENCODING "1"
COMMENT END LogicalFontDescription
CHARSET_COLLECTIONS "ASCII ISO8859-1 ADOBE-STANDARD"
FULL_NAME "Times Roman"
COPYRIGHT "Copyright (c) 1987 Adobe Systems, Inc., Portions
Copyright 1988 Digital Equipment Corp."
COMMENT ***** end of inserted font properties
FONT_ASCENT 8
FONT_ASCENT 8
FONT_DESCENT 3
CAP_HEIGHT 7
X_HEIGHT 5
ENDPROPERTIES
CHARS 194
STARTCHAR space
ENCODING 32
SWIDTH 250 0
DWIDTH 2 0
BBX 1 1 0 0
BITMAP
00
ENDCHAR
STARTCHAR exclam
ENCODING 33
SWIDTH 333 0
DWIDTH 3 0
BBX 1 7 1 0
```

```
BITMAP

80

80

80

80

80

00

80

ENDCHAR


...


ENDFONT
```

The font begins with the space character, ASCII 32. This means that the characters before 32 have no bitmap glyphs.

Installing Fonts

If you get a new set of BDF fonts and want to add them to your system, there are a number of steps you must take.

Start by choosing the directory where the font should go. A good general choice is /usr/lib/X11/fonts/misc, a sort of catchall font directory available on most systems. You can also make you own font directory, especially if you don't have permission to change /usr/lib/X11/fonts/misc.

The next step is to convert your font to the PCF format required by the X server, or the SNF format used by older X servers. The programs bdftopcf and bdftosnf take care of this:

```
bdftopcf fontfile.bdf > fontfile.pcf
```

or

```
bdftosnf fontfile.bdf > fontfile.snf
```

Place the resulting file in your font directory. Then run `mkfontdir` on that directory, so that your new font is in the `fonts.dir` file. (This file maps between file names and XLFD long font names.) Change to the font directory and run `mkfontdir`:

```
mkfontdir
```

If you're using your own font directory, you need to inform the X server about this directory, using the `xset` program, where *mydirectory* is the name of your font directory:

```
xset +fp mydirectory
```

Finally, tell the X server to rebuild its internal list of available fonts, also with `xset`:

```
xset fp rehash
```

Your new font should now be available. Run `xlsfonts` to check.

Designing Your Own Fonts

While X provides a large number of fonts, you may want to create one of your own. You might want a distinctive style for your user interface, or you may want to use a font for something other than text. Many X mah-jongg game programs, for example, use an X font for the mah-jongg tile game pieces. The XView toolkit uses X fonts for small bitmaps used in the interface. The XView scroll-bar elevator, for instance, is drawn using a specialized font.

If you want to make a new font, there are two basic routes you can take. You can convert an existing font from another format to an X format, or you can create your own font.

Since X fonts start out as bitmaps (except for the scalable fonts provided by the font server), all you need to create your own fonts is a specialized bitmap editor. (You could actually use a text editor, since the BDF format is ASCII text, but we don't consider that route too convenient.) And yes, we advise using the BDF format for fonts you create. Because BDF is the generic format for exchanging fonts, you'll have the most luck porting your fonts to other systems if you use BDF.

What you really need is a font editor. Unfortunately, we've seen few freely available font editors. (Or commercial X font editors, for that matter. We wonder how the original X fonts were created.) Luckily, there's an X font editor available with the contributed software as part of the X Consortium's release of the X Window System.

Klaus Gittinger of Siemens in Munich wrote a free font editor named `xfed`, which allows you to edit BDF font files one character at a time. It presents a magnified view of each character in a font, as shown in Figure 16.3.

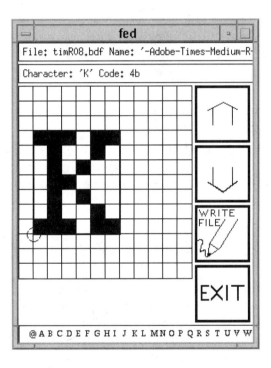

Figure 16.3   *Editing BDF fonts with xfed.*

Editing BDF Files with xfed

With `xfed`, you can change the bits in each character in the font.

The user interface of `xfed` is very simple. Pressing the left mouse button turns a bit black. Pressing the right mouse button turns a bit white.

The middle mouse button (assuming you have a three-button mouse) toggles the color of the pixel. If the color was white, it becomes black, and vice versa. You can click on icons to move forward to the next character in the font or backward to the previous character. That's all there is to it.

The easiest way to create your own font is to start out with a preexisting font and then edit that font to make your new font. Of course, there's the small issue of intellectual property rights. Before you claim someone else's work, you should check up on the legality of your new font.

WARNING

If you do intend to edit your own fonts, be sure they follow the rules listed in the X Logical Font Description Conventions, part of the documentation that comes with the X releases from the X Consortium. (See Appendix E for more information.)

Besides `xfed`, there's another free font editor called `xfedor`. We haven't seen any commercial font editors.

If you can't find a font editor, you could write a conversion program to translate an existing font for another windowing system (e.g., Microsoft Windows or the Macintosh), into an X BDF font. Again, be sure to check up on the legality of this process.

Summary

As with any graphical software, using X means using fonts. A font is a complete set of characters of one size of one typeface—including upper- and lowercase letters, punctuation marks, and numerals. All fonts in X are bitmaps; each character has a specific bit pattern within the font. We discuss the characteristics that distinguish fonts.

X includes a number of special font formats: PCF (portable compiled font), BDF (bitmap distribution format), and SNF (server normal format). You'll need to create your own fonts from these formats. Prior to Release 5, most X implementations included a program called `bdftosnf` to convert ASCII BDF font files to SNF files. Release 5 replaces `bdftosnf` with `bdftopcf`, which converts BDF files to the portable binary PCF format. The `snftobdf` program reverses the process and creates an ASCII bitmap BDF file from a binary X font.

A standard X application program called `xlsfonts` lists the available fonts on a workstation. Running `xlsfonts` on a Release 4 or higher X server will result in pages and pages of text output. When you run a program like `xlsfonts`, you'll see that most of the X font names are extremely long and complex. The actual format of these names makes sense and is described in the XLFD standard, mentioned earlier. Most names begin with a leading hyphen and then a font-company name, such as `adobe`.

Most systems will include fonts with the names of `fixed` and `variable`, which are called aliases. Instead of entering font names in the long format, applications can enter aliases that reference the real font name.

A program called `xfontsel` can help you choose fonts using the long font name format. Another X application called `xfd` (X font displayer) will display the characters in a font. Normally, if `xfd` cannot find the font, then your program will not, either.

With X11 Release 5, the X Consortium introduced a new font server, promising a modern world of scalable fonts and greatly improved text options. Structurally, the font server is an add-on to the X server. If you need to change the text size, you merely ask for a new font in the desired size. The font server provides fonts to the X Server.

The font server requires a rigidly formatted configuration file, as any deviations result in program death. The only correct, or nearly correct, example configuration file is in the font server (`fs`) man page. All other example configuration files, including an example file that came with the X11R5 sources, cause system crashes. We provide a `config` file that actually works.

To configure the X server for the font server, tell the X server to include the font server in its font path. This requires an X server from Release 5.

Once you get the font server running and the X server to recognize the font server as part of its font path, you can try using some scalable fonts. First, try the `xlsfonts` command to see the available fonts. Look for fonts with zeros in the size fields.

Finally, you can create your own fonts using a free font editor named `xfed`, which allows you to edit BDF font files one character at a time. It presents a magnified view of each character in a font, from which you can then edit the font.

Bitmaps

This section covers bitmaps and pixmaps—the X Window System's off screen drawing areas. These chapters:

- ✦ Introduce bitmaps and pixmaps.
- ✦ Describe X's method of storing bitmaps in ASCII text files.
- ✦ Introduce a free library for working with color pixmap files
- ✦ Show how to create cursors and make a busy-cursor routine.
- ✦ Introduce X icons and shows how to create a color, dynamic icon.
- ✦ Show how to capture screen images with `XImage`s and draw fractal images.
- ✦ Provide shared-memory techniques for large images.
- ✦ Introduce XIE, the X Image Extension.

651

C h a p t e r   1 7

Pixmaps, Bitmaps, and Bitmap Files

This chapter covers:

✦ Drawing into bitmaps and pixmaps
✦ Clearing pixmaps
✦ Copying pixmaps to windows
✦ Using backing pixmaps to handle Expose events
✦ Using the monochrome bitmap file format
✦ Loading bitmap files
✦ Saving a bitmap to disk
✦ Creating pixmaps from bitmap data
✦ Creating a program to view bitmaps
✦ Using the standard X bitmap program to edit bitmaps

653

Bitmaps and Pixmaps

All of our drawing so far has gone into widgets—windows on the display. But sometimes you want to draw into an offscreen area, later copying part (or all) of that area to a window on the screen. The X Window System provides *pixmaps* for this purpose. Pixmaps work well for bitmap image files, icons, and backing store for complex drawings.

Pixmaps are X Window offscreen drawing areas. Pixmaps are drawables, just like windows. Pixmaps reside in the X server, and you can draw into them just like drawing into windows. Pixmaps have a width and height, but no *x, y* location on the screen. And pixmaps have depth, or color planes, just like windows. Pixmaps are important for clipping, tiling, and stippling with graphics contexts (GC), as we introduced in Chapter 3.

Creating Pixmaps

You can create pixmaps with `XCreatePixmap`:

```
Pixmap XCreatePixmap(Display* display,
    Drawable drawable,
    unsigned int width,
    unsigned int height,
    unsigned int depth)
```

The `drawable` parameter is used to determine which screen to place the pixmap on. When you create a pixmap, you specify the desired `depth`. A large pixmap at a large `depth` obviously uses a lot of X server memory. A `depth` of 1 generates a monochrome pixmap, also called a *bitmap*. Bitmaps are very important, especially since program icons are bitmaps.

 If you intend to use a pixmap in a Motif or Open Look Intrinsics Toolkit (OLIT) widget, you must be careful to match the depths between the pixmap and the widget's window.

N O T E

Errors and Pixmaps

The call to `XCreatePixmap` can generate a `BadAlloc` X error. These X errors arrive at some later time (another problem due to X's asynchronous nature). To check that a pixmap is actually created, you can call XGetGeometry (see the next chapter for a description of XGetGeometry under the section entitled Matching Depths) right after you call XCreatePixmap. XGetGeometry should return 0 if it fails to get the geometry for a given pixmap.

This handy technique doesn't work on operating systems that use a *lazy method* for memory allocation. On these systems, XCreatePixmap will not generate a BadAlloc X error if the X server fails to allocate the memory. Instead, these lazy memory allocation systems will generate an error later when the memory is accessed. This can cause you lots of grief. If you attempt to create very large pixmaps, you may need to perform some experiments on your systems to ensure your programs operate the way you want.

Bitmaps: Single-Plane Pixmaps

Bitmaps are single-plane pixmaps. In fact, in X there is no Bitmap data type. The term *bitmap* is just used as a convenience to signify a very common type of pixmap: a pixmap with a depth of 1.

Bitmaps are important when we discuss icons (see Chapter 20) and bitmap files (see below). For now, though, a bitmap is just a single-plane pixmap. Bitmaps are also used for stippling, as described in Chapter 3. You can then create bitmaps using XCreatePixmap, passing a *depth* of 1.

Freeing Pixmaps

Pixmaps tend to use a lot of memory in the X server, so whenever you are done with a pixmap, free it with XFreePixmap:

```
XFreePixmap(Display* display,
    Pixmap pixmap)
```

Clearing Pixmaps

When pixmaps are created, their contents are undefined. The memory used by a pixmap is not cleared, so if you try to copy a new pixmap to a window, you'll see some odd effects. Always clear any pixmaps you create.

You clear pixmaps by filling a rectangle the size of the pixmap, using whatever color you want, with `XFillRectangle`. Pixmaps have no concept of a window background color, and you cannot call `XClearWindow` or `XClearArea` on a pixmap.

Drawing into Bitmaps and Pixmaps

You can draw into pixmaps just like you draw into windows. Pixmaps and windows are both drawables, so most drawing routines work on both windows and pixmaps. And yes, you do need a graphics context (GC) to draw into a pixmap. In fact, pixmaps act like windows in most respects.

You can draw into pixmaps just like drawing into windows, but since pixmaps are offscreen, you won't see the results of the drawing. To see the results, you need to copy data from the pixmap to a window.

Copying Areas

Two functions copy data from a pixmap to a window (or to another pixmap, for that matter): `XCopyArea` and `XCopyPlane`.

`XCopyArea` copies a rectangular area—all the dots, or pixels—from one drawable to another. These drawables can be pixmaps or windows. Watch out, though, as both drawables must have the same depth and the same root window (i.e., be on the same screen):

```
XCopyArea(Display* display,
    Drawable src_drawable,
    Drawable dest_drawable,
    GC gc,
    int src_x,
    int  src_y,
    unsigned int width,
    unsigned int height,
    int dest_x,
    int dest_y)
```

XCopyPlane copies one bit-plane of one drawable to another (usually a pixmap to a window, but not always):

```
XCopyPlane(Display* display,
    Drawable src_drawable,
    Drawable dest_drawable,
    GC gc,
    int src_x,
    int src_y,
    unsigned int width,
    unsigned int height,
    int dest_x,
    int dest_y,
    unsigned long which_plane)
```

The bit plane to copy, *which_plane*, is normally 0x01, which copies the first (and only) plane of a one-plane bitmap to another drawable. If you're using color planes though, you may want to copy a different plane than 0x01.

The nice thing about XCopyPlane is that the two drawables, the source and destination, don't need to have the same depth. You can then use XCopyPlane to copy between disparate drawables. In fact, we use XCopyPlane quite a lot for copying a bitmap (a single-plane pixmap) to a window, setting the *which_plane* parameter to 0x01.

Graphics Exposures

When using XCopyPlane or XCopyArea, always make sure that the rectangle of the source, *src_x*, *src_y*, *width*, and *height* are within the source drawable. In other words, if a pixmap has a width of 100 pixels and a height of 100, then you cannot pass a width and height of 200 when copying from this drawable.

If you try to copy an area that doesn't exist, or is obscured (if the *src_drawable* is a window), then your application may receive GraphicsExpose events for each rectangular area that could not be copied. If the GC's graphics exposures flag is set to True (see Chapter 3), then your application will receive a series of GraphicsExpose events for any area that could not be copied. Otherwise, your application receives a NoExpose event.

If the GC's graphics exposures flag is False, then no GraphicsExpose or NoExpose events will arrive.

 If your code makes a lot of calls to XCopyPlane or XCopyArea, you may want to set the GC's graphics exposures flag to False. Why? Because even in the best case, your application may get deluged with NoExpose events. Handling these
N O T E events slows your program down. Before you set the GC's graphics exposures flag to False, you probably want to ensure that both the source and destination areas are valid and that neither is obscured.

The bottom line is to check that you're copying data that is physically inside the window or pixmap and that if you use a window as the *src_drawable*, make sure the window is visible.

Using Backing Pixmaps to Handle Expose Events

XCopyArea is very effective for providing your own backing store. Using XCopyArea, you could create a pixmap with the same size and depth of your application's window. Then you could use the pixmap as backing store for the window. If you do this, you need to draw all graphics output twice, to *both* the pixmap and the window. That way, the pixmap is always an exact copy of the window.

When Expose events arrive, use XCopyArea to copy parts of the pixmap to the window (use the *x*, *y*, *width*, and *height* fields of the XExposeEvent structure as the source and destination *x*, *y*, *width*, and *height* to pass to XCopyArea).

This is great in concept, because it frees your code from having to worry about Expose events. But this technique can use a lot of memory if your application window is large. Your application also has the problem of figuring out what to do if the window is enlarged or shrunk.

Pixmaps and Windows

Each window on the display has a border (which may be 0 pixels wide) and a background. Both the border and the background can be set to a solid color (a pixel value) or to a pixmap. XSetWindowBackgroundPixmap sets the window background to a pixmap:

```
XSetWindowBackgroundPixmap(Display* display,

    Window window,

    Pixmap background_pixmap)
```

XSetWindowBorderPixmap sets the window border to a pixmap:

```
XSetWindowBorderPixmap(Display* display,

    Window window,

    Pixmap border_pixmap)
```

Window managers and your toolkit may decide to modify the size of a window's border, which limits the effectiveness of XSetWindow-BorderPixmap.

For Xt-based programs, you can also set the *borderPixmap* or *backgroundPixmap* resources.

Bitmaps

X places a lot of emphasis on single-plane pixmaps, or bitmaps. Bitmaps are used as icons (see Chapter 20) and to create cursors (see Chapter 19). X fonts are described in terms of bitmaps. X even defines a portable means of storing bitmaps to disk. The X bitmap file format is an ASCII text format, used to avoid byte-ordering problems on many different architectures. This format doesn't store the pixmap per se, but instead stores the raw data used to generate the bitmap.

The odd thing about the X bitmap file format is that the format actually creates snippets of valid C code. (This is a monochrome format. We cover a similar color format, called *xpm*, for *X Pixmap*, in the next chapter.)

The Monochrome Bitmap File Format

The following code is in the X monochrome bitmap file format. Notice that it really is a C code fragment:

```
#define circle1_width 16
#define circle1_height 16
#define circle1_x_hot 7
#define circle1_y_hot 8
static char circle1_bits[] = {
    0x00, 0x00, 0xf0, 0x07, 0x08, 0x08,
    0x04, 0x10, 0x0e, 0x38, 0x1f, 0x7c,
    0x3f, 0x7e, 0x7f, 0x7f, 0xff, 0x7f,
    0x7f, 0x7f, 0x3f, 0x7e, 0x1f, 0x7c,
    0x0e, 0x38, 0x04, 0x10, 0x08, 0x08,
    0xf0, 0x07};
```

The subsequent bitmap is shown in Figure 17.1.

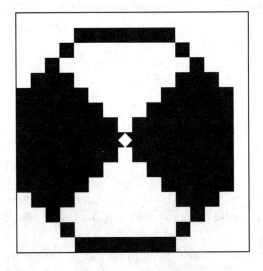

Figure 17.1   *A sample bitmap.*

Loading in Bitmap Files

You can read in an ASCII bitmap file from disk with XReadBitmapFile:

```
int XReadBitmapFile(Display* display,
    Drawable drawable,
    const char* filename,
    unsigned int* width,    /* RETURN */
    unsigned int* height,   /* RETURN */
    Pixmap* bitmap,         /* RETURN */
    int* x_hotspot          /* RETURN */
    int* y_hotspot)         /* RETURN */
```

XReadBitmapFile loads up the given *filename* and tries to convert the contents to an X bitmap. It is assumed that the contents of the file are really an X bitmap file, or else XReadBitmapFile will return BitmapFileInvalid. XReadBitmapFile returns the *width* and *height* of the new bitmap. In addition, cursor bitmaps (see Chapter 19) have hot spots. XReadBitmapFile also returns these hot spots. XReadBitmapFile returns a status of BitmapSuccess on success and BitmapOpenFailed, BitmapFileInvalid, or BitmapNoMemory on errors.

In many cases, you won't be concerned with the hot spot for the bitmap, because you normally won't be creating cursors. Moreover, most bitmaps can be loaded from the root window, since XReadBitmapFile just uses the *drawable* parameter to get the screen. With this in mind, we can put together a simple utility routine that eliminates the unnecessary parameters. The function ReadBitmapFile, below, reads in an X bitmap file and ignores the hot spots:

```
Pixmap ReadBitmapFile(Display* display,
    char* filename,
    int* width,     /* RETURN */
    int* height)    /* RETURN */


{   /* ReadBitmapFile */
```

```
Pixmap   bitmap;
Window   root;
int      x_hotspot, y_hotspot;
int      status;

root = RootWindow(display,
          DefaultScreen(display) );

status = XReadBitmapFile(display,
            root,
            filename,
            (unsigned int*) width,
            (unsigned int*) height,
            &bitmap,
            &x_hotspot, &y_hotspot);

if (status != BitmapSuccess) {
    return (Pixmap) None;
}

return bitmap;

}   /* ReadBitmapFile */
```

When you're done with the *bitmap*, be sure to free it with XFreePixmap (remember bitmaps are pixmaps).

Saving a Bitmap to Disk

You can save a bitmap to an ASCII file in the format described above using the XWriteBitmapFile function:

```
int XWriteBitmapFile(Display* display,
    const char* filename,
```

```
Pixmap bitmap,

unsigned int width,

unsigned int height,

int x_hotspot,

int y_hotspot)
```

If the status returned is not `BitmapSuccess`, you have not saved the
bitmap to a file. A status of `BitmapNoMemory` means that the routine failed
in some way. The hot spots are for cursors, so if you have an icon (or other
noncursor bitmap), simply set the *x_hotspot* and *y_hotspot* to *-1*.

Creating Pixmaps from Bitmap Data

Since the X bitmap file format is really made up of C code fragments, you
can include such a file in a C program with #include, or simply use a
text editor to stick the code into a C file. The data is really a character
pointer.

You can then call two X functions to create pixmaps from that raw
character data. `XCreatePixmapFromBitmapData` creates a pixmap (one
to many planes) from the raw bitmap data:

```
Pixmap XCreatePixmapFromBitmapData(Display* display,

    Drawable drawable,

    char* bitmap_data,

    unsigned int width,

    unsigned int height,

    unsigned long foreground,

    unsigned long background,

    unsigned int depth)
```

`XCreateBitmapFromData` creates a single-plane pixmap from the raw
data:

```
Pixmap XCreateBitmapFromData(Display* display,
```

```
Drawable drawable,
const char* bitmap_data,
unsigned int width,
unsigned int height)
```

Clearing Bitmaps

As we mentioned above, you need to clear all pixmaps at creation time. Bitmaps, as single-plane pixmaps, use special values for colors. All one bits within a bitmap indicate the foreground color and all zeros indicate the background color, since bitmaps are monochrome. To clear a bitmap, use a foreground color of 0L, as shown in the following code:

```
Display*        display;
Pixmap          bitmap;
GC              gc;
unsigned int    width, height;


pix_gc = CreateGC(display, bitmap,
           0L,(XGCValues*) NULL);


/*
 * Clear the pixmap
 */
XSetForeground(display, pix_gc, 0L);


XFillRectangle(display, bitmap, pix_gc,
    0, 0, width, height);
```

When drawing into a bitmap, though, you normally want to use a color of 1L, to set ones into the bitmap:

```
XSetForeground(display, pix_gc, 1L);
```

Creating Pixmaps from Bitmaps

When working with X toolkits, you commonly must convert a bitmap created by reading an ASCII bitmap file into a pixmap. Why? Because you want to display the bitmap in a window and you need to make the depths of the bitmap and the window match. Since you cannot make a bitmap deeper, you need to convert a single-plane pixmap (the bitmap) to a multi-plane pixmap.

To do this, follow these steps:

1. Load in your bitmap file with `XReadBitmapFile`. This creates a single-plane pixmap or bitmap, which we will call the *bitmap*.

2. Determine the depth of the window you need to match. With an X toolkit program, you can query the `depth` resource.

3. Create a pixmap using the width and height of the bitmap and the depth of the window. We'll call this the *pixmap*.

4. Create a GC (graphics context) for the *pixmap*.

5. Set the GC's foreground and background colors to the colors you want for the window. (With an X toolkit program, you can query the `foreground` and `background` resources.)

6. Call `XCopyPlane` to copy the *bitmap* data to the *pixmap*, using the new GC.

7. Free the GC as you no longer need it.

We can use the utility function `ReadBitmapFile`, above, to handle step 1. The function `CreatePixmapFromBitmap`, below, performs steps 3 through 7. (The widget-based code in `pixwidgt.c`, shown later in the chapter under the section Loading in Bitmaps for Widgets, performs step 2 and ties all these routines together for Xt Instrinsics-based programs.) The code for `CreatePixmapFromBitmap` follows:

```
Pixmap CreatePixmapFromBitmap(Display* display,

    Pixmap bitmap,

    int width, int height,

    int depth,
```

```
        unsigned long fore,
        unsigned long back)

{   /* CreatePixmapFromBitmap */
    Pixmap   pixmap;

    /*
     * Create pixmap.
     */
    pixmap = XCreatePixmap(display, bitmap,
                width, height, depth);

    if (pixmap == (Pixmap) None) {
        return pixmap;
    }

    /*
     * Copy bitmap to pixmap.
     */
    BitmapToPixmap(display,
        bitmap,
        pixmap,
        width, height,
        fore, back);

    return pixmap;

}   /* CreatePixmapFromBitmap */
```

CreatePixmapFromBitmap calls another utility function, BitmapToPixmap, to copy the contents of the bitmap to the pixmap. This function follows:

```
void BitmapToPixmap(Display* display,
    Pixmap bitmap,        /* input */
    Pixmap pixmap,        /* output */
    int width, int height,
    unsigned long fore,
    unsigned long back)


{    /* BitmapToPixmap */
    GC  gc;

    /*
     * Create GC for copying.
     */
    gc = XCreateGC(display, pixmap,
            0L, (XGCValues*) NULL);


    XSetForeground(display, gc, fore);
    XSetBackground(display, gc, back);

    /*
     * Copy bitmap to pixmap.
     */
    XCopyPlane(display,
        bitmap, /* source */
        pixmap, /* destination */
        gc,
        0, 0,   /* source x, y */
        width, height,
        0, 0,   /* destination x, y */
        0x01);  /* which plane */

    /* Free GC */
```

```
        XFreeGC(display, gc);


}    /* BitmapToPixmap */
```

We store all these functions in the file `pixmap.c`, below:

```
/*
 *  pixmap.c
 *  Routines to work with pixmaps
 *  and bitmaps.
 */
#include "xlib.h"
#include <stdio.h>


/*
 * Reads in an X bitmap file and
 * ignores the hotspot.
 */


Pixmap ReadBitmapFile(Display* display,
     char* filename,
     int* width,       /* RETURN */
     int* height)      /* RETURN */


{    /* ReadBitmapFile */
     Pixmap  bitmap;
     Window  root;
     int     x_hotspot, y_hotspot;
     int     status;


     root = RootWindow(display,
             DefaultScreen(display) );
```

```
status = XReadBitmapFile(display,
            root,
            filename,
            (unsigned int*) width,
            (unsigned int*) height,
            &bitmap,
            &x_hotspot, &y_hotspot);

    if (status != BitmapSuccess) {
        return (Pixmap) None;
    }

    return bitmap;

}   /* ReadBitmapFile */

/*
 * Copies a bitmap to a pixmap.
 */

void BitmapToPixmap(Display* display,
    Pixmap bitmap,      /* input */
    Pixmap pixmap,      /* output */
    int width, int height,
    unsigned long fore,
    unsigned long back)

{   /* BitmapToPixmap */
    GC  gc;

    /*
```

```
 * Create GC for copying.
 */
gc = XCreateGC(display, pixmap,
        0L, (XGCValues*) NULL);

XSetForeground(display, gc, fore);
XSetBackground(display, gc, back);

/*
 * Copy bitmap to pixmap.
 */
XCopyPlane(display,
    bitmap, /* source */
    pixmap, /* destination */
    gc,
    0, 0,   /* source x, y */
    width, height,
    0, 0,   /* destination x, y */
    0x01);  /* which plane */

/* Free GC */
XFreeGC(display, gc);

}   /* BitmapToPixmap */


/*
 * 1. Creates a pixmap to the proper depth.
 * 2. Copies the bitmap to the pixmap.
 * 3. Returns the new pixmap.
 */
Pixmap CreatePixmapFromBitmap(Display* display,
```

```
    Pixmap bitmap,
    int width, int height,
    int depth,
    unsigned long fore,
    unsigned long back)


{   /* CreatePixmapFromBitmap */
    Pixmap  pixmap;

    /*
     * Create pixmap.
     */
    pixmap = XCreatePixmap(display, bitmap,
            width, height, depth);

    if (pixmap == (Pixmap) None) {
        return pixmap;
    }

    /*
     * Copy bitmap to pixmap.
     */
    BitmapToPixmap(display,
        bitmap,
        pixmap,
        width, height,
        fore, back);

    return pixmap;

}   /* CreatePixmapFromBitmap */

/* end of file pixmap.c */
```

Bitmaps, Pixmaps, and X Toolkits

With your X toolkit code, you can use most of these functions directly, as you can with most X library functions. The key is to draw into a drawing-area widget. Furthermore, most X toolkits offer a number of specialized functions for working with the toolkit's particular widgets.

Loading in Bitmaps for Widgets

The utility function `CreateBitmapForWidget`, below, performs all the seven steps listed earlier (under Creating Pixmaps from Bitmaps) for loading in a bitmap and converting it to a pixmap suitable for use in a widget. The code for `CreateBitmapForWidget` appears below, in the file `pixwidgt.c`:

```
/*
 *  pixwidgt.c
 *  Pixmap/Widget routine.
 */
#include "xlib.h"
#include <X11/Intrinsic.h>
#include <X11/StringDefs.h>
#include <stdio.h>


extern Pixmap CreatePixmapFromBitmap(Display* display,
            Pixmap bitmap,
            int width, int height,
            int depth,
            unsigned long fore,
            unsigned long back);


extern Pixmap ReadBitmapFile(Display* display,
        char* filename,
        int* width,      /* RETURN */
```

```
        int* height);     /* RETURN */



/*
 * This routine loads in a bitmap
 * file and creates a pixmap with
 * the proper depth, foreground and
 * background colors. It works with
 * both OLIT and Motif.
 */
Pixmap CreateBitmapForWidget(Widget parent,
        char* filename)

{   /* CreateBitmapForWidget */
    Pixmap          bitmap, pixmap;
    int             depth;
    Display*        display;
    int             width, height;
    unsigned long   back, fore;

    /*
     * Get widget's depth,
     * and background color.
     */
    XtVaGetValues(parent,
        XtNbackground, &back,
        XtNforeground, &fore,
        XtNdepth,       &depth,
        NULL);

    /*
```

```
     * We need to match the depth
     * when we create our pixmap.
     */
    display = XtDisplay(parent);

    bitmap = ReadBitmapFile(display,
                filename,
                &width, &height);


    if (bitmap == (Pixmap) None) {
        return (Pixmap) None;
    }

    /*
     * Now, we have a one-plane Pixmap.
     * We need to expand to the full
     * depth and copy the bitmap to
     * a pixmap.
     */
    pixmap = CreatePixmapFromBitmap(display,
                bitmap,
                width, height,
                depth,
                fore, back);

    XFreePixmap(display, bitmap);

    return pixmap;

}   /* CreateBitmapForWidget */

/* end of file pixwidgt.c */
```

Note the call to XtVaGetValues to query the *foreground, background*, and *depth* resources. This is to make the newly created pixmap match the colors and depth of the associated widget.

Pixmaps and OLIT

Oddly enough, most of the OLIT image functions and resources use the XImage data type instead of pixmaps. Even so, we can set the *backgroundPixmap* resource for the StaticText widget and see a bitmap image. The program below, stored in the file o_chap17.c, does just this:

```
/*
 *  o_chap17.c
 *  OLIT test program for Chapter 17.
 */
#include "olit.h"
#include <Xol/StaticText.h>
#include <stdio.h>


extern Pixmap CreateBitmapForWidget(Widget parent,
                  char* filename);


int main(int argc, char** argv)


{   /* main */
    XtAppContext   app_context;
    Display*       display;
    Widget         parent;
    Widget         text;
    Arg            args[20];
    int            n;
    int            screen;
```

```
Pixmap          pixmap;
Dimension       width, height;


/* Initialize X toolkit */
OlToolkitInitialize( (XtPointer) NULL);


n = 0;


XtSetArg(args[n], XtNmappedWhenManaged, False); n++;
XtSetArg(args[n], XtNwidth, 100); n++;
XtSetArg(args[n], XtNheight, 100); n++;


parent = XtAppInitialize(&app_context,
        "ProX",                     /* app class */
        (XrmOptionDescList) NULL,   /* options */
        0,                          /* num options */
        ARGC_PTR &argc, argv,       /* cmd line */
        (String*) NULL,             /* fallback res. */
        args, n);



XtRealizeWidget(parent);


/*
 * Create a pixmap.
 */
pixmap = CreateBitmapForWidget(parent,
            "test.xbm");


/*
 * Create static text widget.
```

```
    */
    text = XtVaCreateManagedWidget("text",
            staticTextWidgetClass,
            parent,
            XtNbackgroundPixmap, pixmap,
            XtNstring, "Test Message",
            NULL);

    /*
     * Set proper size.
     */
    XtVaGetValues(text,
        XtNwidth,   &width,
        XtNheight, &height,
        NULL);

    XtVaSetValues(parent,
        XtNwidth,   width,
        XtNheight, height);

    XtMapWidget(parent);
    XtAppMainLoop(app_context);

    return 0;

}   /* main */


/* end of file o_chap17.c */
```

When you run this program, you'll see a test bitmap tiled in the background of the StaticText widget, along with the "Test Message" text string—something like what's shown in Figure 17.2.

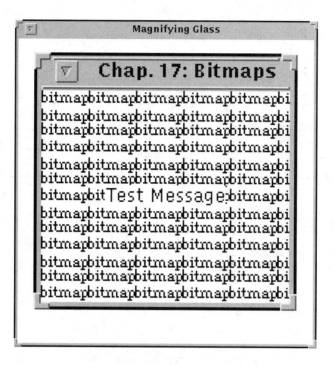

Figure 17.2   *The test bitmap.*

This bitmap is stored in the file `test.xbm`:

```
#define test.xbm_width 32
#define test.xbm_height 32
static unsigned char test.xbm_bits[] = {
    0x01, 0x00, 0x00, 0x00, 0x41, 0x02,
    0x00, 0x00, 0x01, 0x02, 0x00, 0x00,
    0x67, 0xd7, 0x86, 0x69, 0x49, 0x22,
    0x49, 0x92, 0x49, 0x22, 0x89, 0x93,
    0x49, 0x22, 0x49, 0x92, 0xe7, 0x7c,
    0xdb, 0x77, 0x00, 0x00, 0x00, 0x10,
    0x00, 0x00, 0x00, 0x38, 0x00, 0x00,
    0x00, 0x00, 0x00, 0x00, 0x00, 0x00,
```

```
0x01, 0x00, 0x00, 0x00, 0x41, 0x02,
0x00, 0x00, 0x01, 0x02, 0x00, 0x00,
0x67, 0xd7, 0x86, 0x69, 0x49, 0x22,
0x49, 0x92, 0x49, 0x22, 0x89, 0x93,
0x49, 0x22, 0x49, 0x92, 0xe7, 0x7c,
0xdb, 0x77, 0x00, 0x00, 0x00, 0x10,
0x01, 0x00, 0x00, 0x38, 0x41, 0x02,
0x00, 0x00, 0x01, 0x02, 0x00, 0x00,
0x67, 0xd7, 0x86, 0x69, 0x49, 0x22,
0x49, 0x92, 0x49, 0x22, 0x89, 0x93,
0x49, 0x22, 0x49, 0x92, 0xe7, 0x7c,
0xdb, 0x77, 0x00, 0x00, 0x00, 0x10,
0x00, 0x00, 0x00, 0x38, 0x00, 0x00,
0x00, 0x00};
```

You can create this bitmap using the `bitmap` or `iconedit` programs (see the section entitled Editing Bitmaps, just before the chapter summary). You probably don't want to type in the numbers above.

OLIT Gray-Scale Pixmaps

OLIT provides two functions to get generic pixmaps for use with gray scales. `OlGet50PercentGrey` returns a pixmap that is 50 percent gray:

```
#include <Xol/OlCursors.h>


Pixmap OlGet50PercentGrey(Screen* screen)
```

`OlGet50PercentGrey` returns a 2 x 2 pixel pixmap with a depth of 1 (a bitmap, that is). `OlGet75PercentGrey` returns a 75-percent gray pixmap:

```
#include <Xol/OlCursors.h>


Pixmap OlGet75PercentGrey(Screen* screen)
```

OlGet75PercentGrey returns a 4 x 2 pixel pixmap with a depth of 1. These pixmaps are useful for tiling. Be sure to include the file <Xol/OlCursors.h>.

Pixmaps and Motif

With Motif, you can set a label widget (XmLabel) to hold either a pixmap or a text message (in XmString format). The same goes for most widgets derived from XmLabel, including pushbuttons and toggle buttons. To do so, you need to set both the *labelType* and *labelPixmap* resources:

```
Widget     widget;
Pixmap     pixmap;

XtVaSetValues(widget,
    XmNlabelType,   XmPIXMAP,
    XmNlabelPixmap, pixmap,
    NULL);
```

You need to make sure that the pixmap has the same depth as the widget and uses the same colormap. To change such a widget back to displaying a text message, use the following code:

```
Widget     widget;
XmString   xmstring;

XtVaSetValues(widget,
    XmNlabelType,   XmSTRING,
    XmNlabelString, xmstring,
    NULL);
```

Creating Label Widgets with Pixmaps

We can then put together a utility function to create a Motif label widget with a pixmap instead of a text message. The function CreatePixmapLabel, following, does this:

```
Widget CreatePixmapLabel(Widget parent,

    char* name,

    Pixmap pixmap)


{   /* CreatePixmapLabel */

    Widget  widget;

    Arg     args[20];

    int     n;


    n = 0;

    XtSetArg(args[n], XmNlabelType, XmPIXMAP); n++;

    XtSetArg(args[n], XmNlabelPixmap, pixmap); n++;


    widget = XmCreateLabel(parent, name, args, n);


    XtManageChild(widget);


    return widget;


}   /* CreatePixmapLabel */
```

If we want to create a label widget that holds a pixmap, we need to make sure that the pixmap and the widget share the same depth, or we'll see an X error. In addition, if we're starting with a monochrome bitmap, we probably want to draw the bitmap using the widget's foreground and background colors instead of plain old black and white.

To pull all this together, the function CreateBitmapLabel, below, reads in a bitmap file with XReadBitmapFile and then creates a pixmap with the proper depth from the bitmap with a depth of 1. Finally, CreateBitmapLabel creates a label widget with the new pixmap, using the utility function CreatePixmapLabel, presented above. The code for CreateBitmapLabel follows:

```
Widget CreateBitmapLabel(Widget parent,
        char* name,
        char* filename)


{   /* CreateBitmapLabel */
    Widget    widget;
    Pixmap    pixmap;


    pixmap = CreateBitmapForWidget(parent,
               filename);


    widget = CreatePixmapLabel(parent, name,
               pixmap);


    return widget;


}   /* CreateBitmapLabel */
```

The code for both `CreatePixmapLabel` and `CreateBitmapLabel` is stored in the file `m_pixmap.c`:

```
/*
 *   m_pixmap.c
 *   Motif pixmap/label routines.
 */
#include "motif.h"
#include <Xm/Label.h>
#include <stdio.h>


extern Pixmap CreateBitmapForWidget(Widget parent,
        char* filename);


/*
```

```
 * Creates a label widget and
 * loads in a pixmap.
 */
Widget CreatePixmapLabel(Widget parent,
    char* name,
    Pixmap pixmap)

{   /* CreatePixmapLabel */
    Widget  widget;
    Arg     args[20];
    int     n;

    /*
     * Create label widget.
     */
    n = 0;
    XtSetArg(args[n], XmNlabelType, XmPIXMAP); n++;
    XtSetArg(args[n], XmNlabelPixmap, pixmap); n++;

    widget = XmCreateLabel(parent, name, args, n);

    XtManageChild(widget);

    return widget;

}   /* CreatePixmapLabel */


Widget CreateBitmapLabel(Widget parent,
        char* name,
        char* filename)

{   /* CreateBitmapLabel */
```

```
    Widget      widget;
    Pixmap      pixmap;


    pixmap = CreateBitmapForWidget(parent,
                filename);


    widget = CreatePixmapLabel(parent, name,
                pixmap);


    return widget;


}    /* CreateBitmapLabel */


/* end of file m_pixmap.c */
```

A Program to View Bitmaps

We've put together a short Motif program to view bitmaps. The program loads bitmap files with XReadBitmapFile. We then use the CreatePixmapFromBitmap convenience routine to convert the bitmap data created by XReadBitmapFile to a pixmap of the proper depth. The code for this program is stored in the file m_chap17.c:

```
/*
 *  m_chap17.c
 *  Motif test program for Chapter 17.
 *  Load in bitmap files.
 */
#include "motif.h"
#include <Xm/RowColumn.h>
#include <stdio.h>


extern Widget CreateBitmapLabel(Widget parent,
```

```
                            char* name,
                            char* filename);

int main(int argc, char** argv)

{    /* main */
     XtAppContext    app_context;
     Widget          parent;
     Widget          mainwindow;
     Widget          menubar;
     Widget          filemenu;
     Widget          exitchoice;
     Widget          row;
     Arg             args[20];
     int             n, i;


     /* Initialize X toolkit */
     n = 0;
     XtSetArg(args[n], XmNallowResize, True); n++;


     parent = XtAppInitialize(&app_context,
             "ProX",                      /* app class */
             (XrmOptionDescList) NULL,    /* options */
             0,                           /* num options */
             ARGC_PTR &argc, argv,        /* cmd line */
             (String*) NULL,              /* fallback res. */
             args, n);



     /* Create Main Window. */
     mainwindow = CreateMainWindow(parent, "main");


     /* Create menu bar. */
```

```
menubar = CreateMenuBar(mainwindow, "menubar");

/* Create the file menu. */
filemenu = CreateMenu(menubar, "filemenu");

/* Create a menu choice to exit the program. */
exitchoice = CreateExitChoice(filemenu,
                "exitchoice");

/* Create row column to hold bitmaps. */
n = 0;

row = XmCreateRowColumn(mainwindow,
        "row", args, n);

XtManageChild(row);
SetMainAreas(mainwindow, menubar, row);

/*
 * Create bitmaps for display.
 * This really should be in
 * a scrolled window.
 */
for (i = 1; i < argc; i++ ) {

    (void) CreateBitmapLabel(row,
                "bitmap", argv[i]);
}

XtRealizeWidget(parent);
XtAppMainLoop(app_context);

return 0;
```

```
}    /* main */


/* end of file m_chap17.c */
```

When you run the program above, it takes every command-line parameter as a bitmap file. The program creates a label widget for each bitmap file and places all the label widgets in a row column container widget. In a real bitmap-viewing application, you'd need to check the size of these bitmaps. If you load up a large number of bitmaps, you'd need to place the row column widget inside a scrolled window widget, so that the user could scroll the much larger area. If you wish to extend the above program, that would be the first place to start.

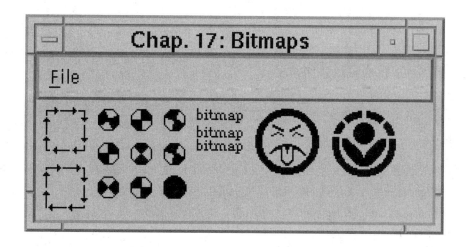

Figure 17.3   *Viewing bitmaps.*

Resource File for the Example Programs

Use the following resource file for both the OLIT and Motif example programs for this chapter. name this file ProX and place it in your home directory:

```
! ProX
! Resource file for chapter 17 of
! Professional Graphics
! Programming in the X Window System.
!
! Place this file in your
! home directory.
!
! Generic resources.
!
*background:     #cccccc


*title:    Chap. 17: Bitmaps


!
! Motif resources.
!
*fontList: lucidasans-12


*filemenu.labelString:      File
*filemenu.mnemonic:         F


*exitchoice.labelString:  Exit
*exitchoice.mnemonic:     x
! end of file ProX
```

Creating Motif Pixmaps from Bitmap Files

In addition to XCreatePixmap, you can use Motif's pixmap cache. The
function XmGetPixmap converts a image name to a Pixmap:

```
Pixmap XmGetPixmap(Screen* screen_ptr,
          char* image_name,
```

```
    Pixel foreground,

    Pixel background)
```

The *image_name* is used to look up a preexisting pixmap in the Motif pixmap cache. If a match is found, then XmGetPixmap returns that pixmap—allowing your application to share pixmaps. If a match is not found, XmGetPixmap tries to find a match in the Motif image cache (a cache of XImages; see Chapter 21). If a match is found, then XmGetPixmap converts the image to a pixmap and returns this pixmap. Finally, if no image matches, then XmGetPixmap treats the *image_name* as a bitmap file name. File names that begin with a slash (/) are treated as a full path. Otherwise, XmGetPixmap uses the XBMLANGPATH environment variable (which holds the path to look for bitmap files) or the current directory.

If you need to specify the pixmap's depth, then call XmGetPixmapByDepth:

```
Pixmap XmGetPixmapByDepth(Screen* screen_ptr,

        char* image_name,

        Pixel foreground,

        Pixel background,

        int depth)
```

XmGetPixmapByDepth is new in Motif 1.2.

If you create a pixmap with XmGetPixmap or XmGetPixmapByDepth, you should free it with XmDestroyPixmap:

```
Boolean XmDestroyPixmap(Screen* screen_ptr,

        Pixmap pixmap)
```

Pixmaps and Motif Dialogs

Many Motif dialogs, such as the error or warning dialogs, provide a pixmap symbol; for example, the question dialog sports a question-mark pixmap. If you set the *background* resource before creating such a dialog, then the pixmap's background color should be correct. If you call XtSetValues or

XtVaSetValues to change the background color later, you may find the pixmap has the wrong background color.

You can also call XmGetPixmap and pass in the new foreground and background colors to get a pixmap suitable for your dialogs.

Editing Bitmaps

The bitmap program allows you to edit bitmaps, as pictured in Figure 17.4.

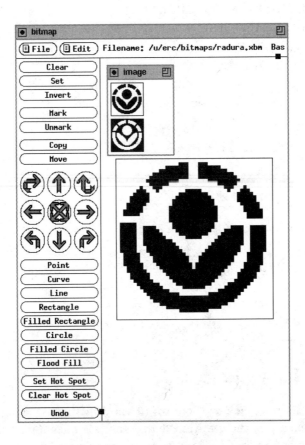

Figure 17.4   *The bitmap program.*

Most X systems include the `bitmap` program. You can read in and edit files in the format described above. You can then save the bitmaps you edit with the `bitmap` program into files that you can read in with `XReadBitmapFile`. You can also use the OpenWindows program `iconedit` to edit X bitmap files.

Summary

Pixmaps are X Window offscreen drawing areas. Pixmaps reside in the X server, and you can draw into them just like drawing into windows. Pixmaps have a width and height, but no *x, y* location on the screen. And pixmaps have depth, or color planes, just like windows.

Pixmaps and windows are both drawables, so most drawing routines work on both windows and pixmaps. You can draw into pixmaps just like drawing into windows, but since pixmaps are offscreen, you won't see the results of the drawing. To see the results of drawing, you copy data from the pixmap to a window. Two functions copy data from a pixmap to a window (or to another pixmap, for that matter), `XCopyArea` and `XCopyPlane`.

Using `XCopyArea`, you could create a pixmap just the size and depth of your application's window. Then you could use the pixmap as backing store for the window. When `Expose` events arrive, use `XCopyArea` to copy parts of the pixmap to the window (use the *x, y*, `width`, and `height` fields of the `XExposeEvent` structure as the source and destination *x, y*, `width` and `height` to pass to `XCopyArea`).

When pixmaps are created, their contents are undefined. Always clear any pixmaps you create.

X places a lot of emphasis on single-plane pixmaps, also called bitmaps. Bitmaps are used as icons and to create cursors. X fonts are described in terms of bitmaps. X even defines a portable means of storing bitmaps to disk. The X bitmap file format is an ASCII text format, used to avoid byte-ordering problems on many different architectures. This format doesn't store the pixmap per se, but instead stores the raw data used to generate the bitmap.

X Library Functions and Macros Introduced in This Chapter

```
XCopyArea
XCopyPlane
XCreateBitmapFromData
XCreatePixmap
XCreatePixmapFromBitmapData
XFreePixmap
XReadBitmapFile
XSetWindowBackgroundPixmap
XSetWindowBorderPixmap
XWriteBitmapFile
```

Motif Functions and Macros Introduced in This Chapter

```
XmDestroyPixmap
XmGetPixmap
XmGetPixmapByDepth
```

OLIT Functions and Macros Introduced in This Chapter

```
OlGet50PercentGrey
OlGet75PercentGrey
```

Color Bitmap Files

This chapter covers:

- ✦ Using the Xpm color pixmap file format
- ✦ Obtaining the Xpm or X Pixmap library
- ✦ Creating Xpm pixmaps
- ✦ Reading in Xpm files
- ✦ Writing Xpm files to disk

693

An Introduction to Color Bitmap Files

X defines a standard file format for monochrome bitmaps. For all the effort and complexity X spends on color, it's surprising that there is no standard X file format for color images. Microsoft Windows has a bitmap format (BMP), but X so far has only standardized on monochrome bitmap files.

These files, often used for program icons, are stored in a standard ASCII format, described in the last chapter.

Yet the world is not limited to only black and white, although X program icons are only officially supported as monochrome bitmaps as well. The real world is in color, and real-world applications need colored images.

Application developers can choose some standard graphic file format, such as GIF or PC Paintbrush (PCX) images, but most graphic formats require a lot of overhead and are mainly intended for large images. These formats don't handle the small pictures used in an application's interface very well.

What is needed is a colored X analog to monochrome bitmaps. And that's where the free *X Pixmap library*, or *Xpm*, comes in.

X uses the term pixmap, introduced in the last chapter, to describe a potentially colored image. Technically, a pixmap is an offscreen drawing area, which acts much like a window, except that it isn't visible. Both windows and pixmaps are considered drawables in X.

Bitmaps in X really fall under the pixmap rubric, and are considered pixmaps with a depth of 1. That is, bitmaps have only one color plane, and have *on* or *off* pixels.

X provides standard functions, such as `XReadBitmapFile` and `XWriteBitmapFile`, covered in the last chapter, to read and write disk files with monochrome images. The Xpm library extends this concept to provide functions, such as `XpmReadFileToPixmap` and `XpmWriteFileFromPixmap`, to do the same for colored images.

You can get the latest Xpm version with the X contributed sources, available on tape or CD-ROM from a variety of sources. We wrote the examples in this book with Xpm 3. Furthermore, you can FTP the sources from `export.lcs.mit.edu` in the United States and `avahi.inria.fr` in France. Be sure to check local archive sites before making cross-ocean or cross-continent network hops.

Unfortunately, the Xpm library is not standardized as part of X. This is ironic, as both the Motif and Open Look interfaces support colored images in the form of pixmaps. In Motif, for example, you can set a label widget or a pushbutton to display a text message with the *labelString* resource or a pixmap image with the *labelPixmap* resource, as described in the last chapter.

Even though it's not officially blessed, the Xpm library works just fine for small colored pictures that you may want to place in your application interface. Xpm is also used in many software packages, such as OpenWindows from Sun. Developed in France by Arnaud Le Hors of Groupe Bull, the Xpm library provides only 10 functions—a marked change from the more than 400 provided by Xlib.

Like the ASCII-based X bitmap format, Xpm files are also ASCII (Latin-1, really) text and are made up of C code. You can include an Xpm file into your code and compile in colored pixmaps. But the drawback to the ASCII format is that Xpm files don't store data very efficiently.

Xpm Files

Here's an example Xpm file:

```
/* XPM */
static char * bluepyramid[] = {
/* Eric's pixmap
 * width height ncolors chars_per_pixel */
"24 24 6 1 ",
/* colors */
"x   c white             m white   s light_color ",
"Y   c lightslateblue    m black   s lines_in_mix ",
"+   c slateblue         m white   s lines_in_dark ",
"b   c mediumslateblue   m white   s lines_in_dark ",
"    c darkslateblue     m black   s dark_color ",
"z                       m black   s dark_color ",
/* pixels */
```

```
"xxxxxxxxxxxxxxxxxxxxxxxx",
"xxYYYYYYYYYYYYYYYYYYYYx+",
"xbxYYYYYYYYYYYYYYYYYYx++",
"xbbxYYYYYYYYYYYYYYYYYx+++",
"xbbbxYYYYYYYYYYYYYYYx++++",
"xbbbbxYYYYYYYYYYYYYx+++++",
"xbbbbbxYYYYYYYYYYYx++++++",
"xbbbbbbxYYYYYYYYYx+++++++",
"xbbbbbbbxYYYYYYx++++++++",
"xbbbbbbbbxYYYYx+++++++++",
"xbbbbbbbbbxYYx++++++++++",
"xbbbbbbbbbbxx+++++++++++",
"xbbbbbbbbbbxb+++++++++++",
"xbbbbbbbbbx   b+++++++++++",
"xbbbbbbbbx    b++++++++++",
"xbbbbbbbx     b+++++++++",
"xbbbbbbx      b++++++++",
"xbbbbbx       b+++++++",
"xbbbbx        b++++++",
"xbbbx         b+++++",
"xbbx          b++++",
"xbx           b+++",
"xx            b++",
"xzzzzzzzzzzzzzzzzzzzzzzz"
};
```

As you can tell, this file forms valid C syntax and can be included in your program files, just like the monochrome X bitmap files. The first part of the file provides the width and height (24x24), the number of colors (6), and the characters per pixel. Most Xpm files use two characters per pixel instead of the one used here to make a more readable file. The extra characters are just spaces padded between each of the characters in the bitmap area above. The comment at the beginning, / * XPM * /, identifies the file as an Xpm file.

The colors section provides an ASCII character for each of the six colors used in the pixmap. The pixmap uses *x*, for instance, to indicate white pixels. After each color is a monochrome section and a means to reduce the number of colors used, if necessary. In most cases, though, your Xpm file will load in with the proper colors.

N O T E   IXI's X.desktop uses a modified version of Xpm files. IXI extended Xpm to allow a color named *none*. (Older versions of X.desktop used a color named *transparent*.) The *none* color is transparent, so that you can display a given bitmap on any color background. This is especially useful if you have a set of iconic shapes that represent files in a current directory. Xpm version 3 supports the color *none* as well.

Matching Depths

One problem you'll find with X pixmaps is that you must match the color-plane depths between the pixmap and any windows you want to use the pixmap with.

The example Xpm file above uses six X colors, which require at least three color planes. Most graphics systems, though, offer 1 (monochrome), 4, 8, 12, 16, 24, or 32 color planes. The best advice in this regard is to find out the depth of the window you're working with, and then create the pixmap to match that depth.

The following X toolkit-based code gets the default depth for the screen on which a given toolkit widget resides:

```
unsigned int   depth;
Widget         widget;
Screen*        screenptr;


screenptr = XtScreen(widget);


depth = DefaultDepthOfScreen(screenptr);
```

This technique, of course, won't work if your application uses color-plane depths other than the default. To handle this case, use XGetGeometry. The Xlib function XGetGeometry will return the depth for a given window or pixmap:

```
Status XGetGeometry(Display* display,
          Drawable drawable,
          Window* rootwindow,
          int* x, int* y,
          unsigned int* width,
          unsigned int* height,
          unsigned int* border_width,
          unsigned int* depth)
```

XGetGeometry returns a nonzero value on success; 0 otherwise. Pixmaps have no *x*, *y* location nor a *border_width*, so these values will be 0 for pixmaps.

You can also retrieve the *depth* resource for the given widget in Xt-based programs:

```
Widget    widget;
int       depth;

XtVaGetValues(widget,
    XtNdepth, &depth,
    NULL);
```

Coding with Xpm

The Xpm function XpmCreatePixmapFromData creates a pixmap from Xpm data compiled in your program, either from an include file or directly in your program's source. The closest Xlib analog to XpmCreate-PixmapFromData is XCreatePixmapFromBitmapData.

```
#include "xpm.h"


int XpmCreatePixmapFromData(Display* display,
    Drawable drawable,
    char**  xpmdata,
    Pixmap* pixmap,    /* RETURN */
    Pixmap* shapemask, /* RETURN */
    XpmAttributes* xpmattributes)
```

All Xpm routines require the include file `xpm.h`. Since Xpm is contributed software, there's no standard location for the `xpm.h` include file or the Xpm library, `libXpm.a`.

`XpmCreatePixmapFromData` returns a status code of `XpmOpenFailed`, `XpmFileInvalid`, `XpmNoMemory`, `XpmColor-Error`, or `XpmColorFailed` on failure, and `XpmSuccess` on success.

The function returns two pixmaps, a shape mask (if nonnull) and a regular pixmap. Your application must free both pixmaps, using `XFreePixmap`, if they were successfully created. The *shapemask*, for example, is often passed as a NULL.

In your code, you can call `XpmCreatePixmapFromData`, as the example function `CreateXpmPixmap` shows:

```
Pixmap CreateXpmPixmap(Widget widget,
    char** xpmdata)


{   /* CreateXpmPixmap */
    Pixmap          pixmap, shapemask;
    int             status;
    XpmAttributes   xpmattributes;
    Display*        display;

    /*
     * Get proper depth
     */
```

```
XtVaGetValues(widget,
    XtNdepth, &xpmattributes.depth,
    NULL);

xpmattributes.valuemask = XpmDepth;

/*
 * Create pixmap from Xpm data
 */
display = XtDisplay(widget);

status = XpmCreatePixmapFromData(display,
        RootWindowOfScreen(XtScreen(widget) ),
        xpmdata,
        &pixmap,
        &shapemask,
        &xpmattributes);

if (status == XpmSuccess) {

    if (shapemask != (Pixmap) None) {
        XFreePixmap(display, shapemask);
    }

} else {
    printf("Xpm failure %d\n", status);

    pixmap = (Pixmap) None;
}


    return pixmap;


}   /* CreateXpmPixmap */
```

You can pass in a number of values into XpmCreatePixmapFromData with the XpmAttributes structure, including the desired colormap, visual, depth, and size. In the above code, we passed in just the depth, but your applications may need more control over the way XpmCreate-PixmapFromData creates the pixmap. These control options are necessary because of the complex way X handles color. Most Xpm routines take an XpmAttributes parameter for this purpose.

Once successfully created with XpmCreatePixmapFromData, you can get the *width* and *height* of the pixmap by checking the width and height fields of the XpmAttributes structure.

The XpmAttributes structure is intended so that you can customize how the Xpm routines create and store pixmaps. The XpmAttributes structure looks like:

```
typedef struct {
    unsigned long    valuemask;
    Visual*          visual;
    Colormap         colormap;
    unsigned int     depth;
    unsigned int     width;      /* RETURN */
    unsigned int     height;     /* RETURN *
    unsigned int     x_hotspot; /* RETURN */
    unsigned int     y_hotspot; /* RETURN */
    unsigned int     cpp;
    Pixel*           pixels;
    unsigned int     npixels;
    XpmColorSymbol* colorsymbols;
    unsigned int     numsymbols;
    char*            rgb_fname;

    /* Infos */
    unsigned int     ncolors;
    char***          colorTable;
```

```
    char*           hints_cmt;  /* Comment */

    char*           colors_cmt; /* Comment */

    char*           pixels_cmt; /* Comment */

    unsigned int    mask_pixel;

} XpmAttributes;
```

The *valuemask* is a set of bit-flags that tell the Xpm routines which of the fields are filled in, or which you want filled in for the return values. Just like the XGCValues structure introduced in Chapter 3, you need to pass a mask of bit-flags for the fields you fill in an XpmAttributes structure. The available masks are listed in Table 18.1.

Table 18.1   *XpmAttributes masks.*

Mask	XpmAttributes Field
XpmVisual	visual
XpmColormap	colormap
XpmDepth	depth
XpmSize	width, height
XpmHotspot	x_hotspot, y_hotspot
XpmCharsPerPixel	cpp
XpmColorSymbols	colorsymbols, numsymbols
XpmRgbFilename	rgb_fname
XpmInfos	ncolors, colorTable, hints_cmt, colors_cmt, pixels_cmt, mask_pixel

You can also ask the Xpm routines to return the "Infos" values, using a flag of XpmReturnInfos. If you want the pixels, then ask for them with a flag of XpmReturnPixels.

In the XpmAttributes structure, you can specify the *depth*, *colormap*, and *visual* to use when creating pixmaps from the data. The *cpp* field holds the number of characters per pixel. In the example Xpm file, above, there is one character per pixel.

The section marked *Infos* holds comments that you can read in with XpmReadFileToPixmap and write out with XpmWriteFileFromPixmap. The basic idea is that if you read in an Xpm file, you don't lose the comments associated with the pixmap data in the file.

Overriding Color Selection

If you want to override the colors chosen at load time, you can fill in the *colorsymbols* and *numsymbols* fields. The *numsymbols* field indicates how many XpmColorSymbol structures are stored in the colorsymbols array. The XpmColorSymbol structure looks like:

```
typedef struct {
    char*   name;    /* Symbolic color name */
    char*   value;   /* Color value */
    Pixel   pixel;   /* Color pixel */
} XpmColorSymbol;
```

The *name* is the symbolic color name, such as "red." This is the name to look for. You can then specify the color to use either by its color name in the *value* field or by pixel (colormap index) in the *pixel* field.

Converting a Pixmap to Xpm Data

To reverse the process used by XpmCreatePixmapFromData, call XpmCreateDataFromPixmap:

```
int XpmCreateDataFromPixmap(Display* display,
    char*** xpmdata,   /* RETURN */
    Pixmap pixmap,
    Pixmap shapemask,
    XpmAttributes* xpmattributes) /* input/output */
```

You must free the *xpmdata* when done. XpmCreateDataFromPixmap returns a status of XpmNoMemory or XpmSuccess.

Loading a Pixmap File

The XpmReadFileToPixmap function reads in an ASCII file in Xpm format and converts the Xpm data to an X pixmap:

```
int XpmReadFileToPixmap(Display* display,
        Drawable drawable,
        char* filename,
        Pixmap* pixmap,     /* RETURN */
        Pixmap* shapemask,  /* RETURN */
        XpmAttributes* xpmattributes) /* input/output */
```

Since the *drawable* ID passed to the Xpm routines is just used to determine which screen the window is on, you can use the root window for the current screen. (This anachronism follows the model used by the Xlib routines XReadBitmapFile and XWriteBitmapFile.) XpmRead-FileToPixmap creates both a *pixmap* and a *shapemask* pixmap. Normally, your routines won't need this *shapemask* (see the code in *xpm.c*, below, under Coding with Xpm Functions, for more on this topic). You can modify how XpmReadFileToPixmap works, or extract more information with the XpmAttributes structure.

The returned status code will be one of XpmOpenFailed, XpmFileInvalid, XpmNoMemory, XpmColorError, XpmColor-Failed, or XpmSuccess.

The following function, LoadXpmPixmap, shows how to call XpmReadFileToPixmap:

```
Pixmap LoadXpmPixmap(Widget widget,
    char* filename)


{   /* LoadXpmPixmap */
    Pixmap          pixmap, shapemask;
    int             status;
    XpmAttributes   xpmattributes;
```

```
Display*        display;

/*
 * Get proper depth
 */
XtVaGetValues(widget,
    XtNdepth, &xpmattributes.depth,
    NULL);


xpmattributes.valuemask = XpmDepth;


display = XtDisplay(widget);


status = XpmReadFileToPixmap(display,
            RootWindowOfScreen(XtScreen(widget) ),
            filename,
            &pixmap, &shapemask,
            &xpmattributes);


if (status != XpmSuccess) {

    printf("Xpm failure %d\n", status);
    pixmap = (Pixmap) None;


} else {

    if (shapemask != (Pixmap) None) {
        XFreePixmap(display, shapemask);
    }
}
```

```
    return pixmap;


}   /* LoadXpmPixmap */
```

Writing Xpm Data to Disk

The last Xpm function you'll probably need is `XpmWriteFile-FromPixmap`, which writes out a pixmap to an Xpm file on disk:

```
int XpmWriteFileFromPixmap(Display* display,
        char* filename,
        Pixmap pixmap,
        Pixmap shapemask,
        XpmAttributes* xpmattributes)
```

`XpmWriteFileFromPixmap` returns a status code of `XpmOpenFailed`, `XpmNoMemory`, or `XpmSuccess`.

Coding with Xpm Functions

The example functions, `CreateXpmPixmap` and `LoadXpmPixmap`, are stored in the file `xpm.c`:

```
/*
 *  xpm.c
 *  Routines that work with Xpm pixmaps.
 */
#include "xlib.h"
#include "xpm.h"
#include <X11/Intrinsic.h>
#include <X11/StringDefs.h>


/*
```

```
 * Creates a pixmap from the given
 * Xpm-formatted data.
 */
Pixmap CreateXpmPixmap(Widget widget,
    char** xpmdata)

{   /* CreateXpmPixmap */
    Pixmap          pixmap, shapemask;
    int             status;
    XpmAttributes   xpmattributes;
    Display*        display;

    /*
     * Get proper depth
     */
    XtVaGetValues(widget,
        XtNdepth, &xpmattributes.depth,
        NULL);

    xpmattributes.valuemask = XpmDepth;

    /*
     * Create pixmap from Xpm data
     */
    display = XtDisplay(widget);

    status = XpmCreatePixmapFromData(display,
            RootWindowOfScreen(XtScreen(widget) ),
            xpmdata,
            &pixmap,
            &shapemask,
```

```
                          &xpmattributes);

        if (status == XpmSuccess) {

            if (shapemask != (Pixmap) None) {
                XFreePixmap(display, shapemask);
            }

        } else {
            printf("Xpm failure %d\n", status);

            pixmap = (Pixmap) None;
        }


        return pixmap;

}   /* CreateXpmPixmap */

/*
 * Loads in an Xpm file.
 */
Pixmap LoadXpmPixmap(Widget widget,
    char* filename)

{   /* LoadXpmPixmap */
    Pixmap          pixmap, shapemask;
    int             status;
    XpmAttributes   xpmattributes;
    Display*        display;


    /*
```

```
     * Get proper depth
     */
    XtVaGetValues(widget,
        XtNdepth, &xpmattributes.depth,
        NULL);


    xpmattributes.valuemask = XpmDepth;


    display = XtDisplay(widget);


    status = XpmReadFileToPixmap(display,
                RootWindowOfScreen(XtScreen(widget) ),
                filename,
                &pixmap, &shapemask,
                &xpmattributes);


    if (status != XpmSuccess) {

        printf("Xpm failure %d\n", status);
        pixmap = (Pixmap) None;

    } else {

        if (shapemask != (Pixmap) None) {
            XFreePixmap(display, shapemask);
        }
    }


    return pixmap;

}   /* LoadXpmPixmap */


/* end of file xpm.c */
```

The functions work with Open Look Intrinsics Toolkit (OLIT) and Motif programs, as long as you have the Xpm library.

Editing Xpm Files

One nice aspect to a text-based format is that you can use a text editor, such as emacs or vi, to edit the pixmap. This process is very tedious, though. A better answer is to get a pixmap editor. The X contributed sources also contain an Xpm pixmap editor, called, appropriately enough, pixmap. The pixmap program requires, obviously, the Xpm library.

You can also edit Xpm files with the iconedit program, mentioned in the last chapter, under Sun's OpenWindows. Unfortunately, the iconedit with OpenWindows 3.1 saves files to an older Xpm format (version 2). Here's an example of this older file format:

```
! XPM2
48 48 5 1
   c #FFFFFFFFFFFF
.  c #000000000000
X  c #8989A0A0E5E5
o  c #5B5B7E7EE5E5
O  c #2D2D5B5BE5E5
```

```
.............................
..XXXXXXXXXXXXXXXXXXXXXXXXXXX..
.o.XXXXXXXXXXXXXXXXXXXXXXXXX.o.
.oo..XXXXXXXXXXXXXXXXXXXX..oo.
.oooo.XXXXXXXXXXXXXXXXXX.0000.
.ooooo.XXXXXXXXXXXXXXXX.00000.
.oooooo.XXXXXXXXXXXXXX.000000.
.ooooooo.XXXXXXXXXXXX.0000000.
.oooooooo.XXXXXXXXXX.00000000.
```

```
.ooooooooo.XXXXXXXXXX.ooooooooo.
.oooooooooo..XXXXXX..Ooooooooo.
.oooooooooooo.XXXX.ooooooooooo.
.ooooooooooooo.XX.Ooooooooooooo.
.ooooooooooooooo..Ooooooooooooo.
.ooooooooooooooo..Ooooooooooooo.
.ooooooooooooooo.OO.Ooooooooooo.
.oooooooooooo.OOoo.ooooooooooo.
.ooooooooooo..oooooo..oooooooooo.
.ooooooooo.Oooooooooo.Ooooooooo.
.oooooooo.OOooooooooooo.Oooooooo.
.ooooooo.Ooooooooooooooo.ooooooo.
.oooooo.Oooooooooooooooooo.oooooo.
.ooooo.Ooooooooooooooooooooo.ooooo.
.oooo.Ooooooooooooooooooooooo.oooo.
.oo..ooooooooooooooooooooooo..oo.
.o.ooooooooooooooooooooooooooo.o.
..ooooooooooooooooooooooooooooo..
..............................
```

```
...      ..
..      ..
......
    ....      ......    .....  ...
    ..      ..    ..  ..  ..  ..
    ....    ..    ..  ..    ..  ..
    ......  ..      ..  ..  ..  ..
    ..  ..  ..    ......    ..  ..
    ...    ..  ......    ..    ..  ..
              ..
              ..
```

As you can tell, this is not valid C code, like the Xpm version 3 files are. Even so, the Xpm version 3 routines should be able to read in version 2 pixmap files, especially those files created with Sun's `iconedit`.

Compiling with Xpm

Programs using the Xpm routines require the Xpm library, normally stored in `libXpm.a`. You can compile and link a Motif program with the following command:

```
cc -o foo foo.c -lXpm -lXm -lXt -lX11
```

The following command works with OLIT:

```
cc -o foo foo.c -lXpm -lXol -lXt -lX11
```

You'll also need the include file, `xpm.h`.

Summary

There's no such thing as colored bitmaps in the X Window System—which is too bad for developers who want to add splashes of color to their interfaces. However, there's consensus in the X Window System programming community to support the X Pixmap (Xpm) library.

Technically, Xpm is not part of X, though it appears with the X contributed sources. Furthermore, you can FTP the sources from `export.lcs.mit.edu` in the United States and `avahi.inria.fr` in France.

Even though it's not officially blessed, the Xpm library works just fine for small colored pictures that you may want to place in your application interface. Xpm is also used in many software packages, such as OpenWindows from Sun. Developed in France by Arnaud Le Hors of Groupe Bull, the Xpm library provides only 10 functions—a marked change from the more than 400 provided by Xlib.

Like the ASCII-based X bitmap format, Xpm files are also ASCII (Latin-1, really) text and are made up of C code. You can include an Xpm file into your code and compile in colored pixmaps. But the drawback to the ASCII format is that Xpm files don't store data very efficiently.

Covered in this chapter were several tools that enabled programming with Xpm.

X Library Functions and Macros Introduced in This Chapter

```
XGetGeometry
```

Xpm Functions and Macros Introduced in This Chapter

```
XpmCreateDataFromPixmap
XpmCreatePixmapFromData
XpmReadFileToPixmap
XpmWriteFileFromPixmap
```

Chapter 19

Bitmap Cursors

This chapter covers:

- ✦ Creating cursors
- ✦ Creating cursors from bitmaps
- ✦ Changing cursors
- ✦ Making a busy cursor
- ✦ Animating a busy cursor

Bitmap Cursors

X supports many different cursor shapes, such as the ubiquitous left-pointing arrow, the watch (letting you know the system is busy), and the pointing hand. Our favorite, though, is the waving Gumby cursor.

As mentioned in Chapter 14, X follows the clever notion that cursors are characters in a font. Since each character in a font is really a symbolic picture or *glyph*, why can't a cursor be the same thing? This may seem weird, but the designers of X spent a lot of time optimizing text output. At one level, text characters are merely bitmap images or glyphs that need to be drawn in sequence very quickly. Even in a graphical environment, 80 percent of what you display is still text. Why not take advantage of the optimized text output routines to draw cursors?

Actually, cursors are two characters in a font. The first character is the outline of the cursor; the second character of the pair is the *mask*, which defines the shape of the cursor. A whole font, the font named cursor, contains a standard set of X cursors. If you don't like the shapes in the cursor font, you can still create your own (see below), but it is easiest to use the standard.

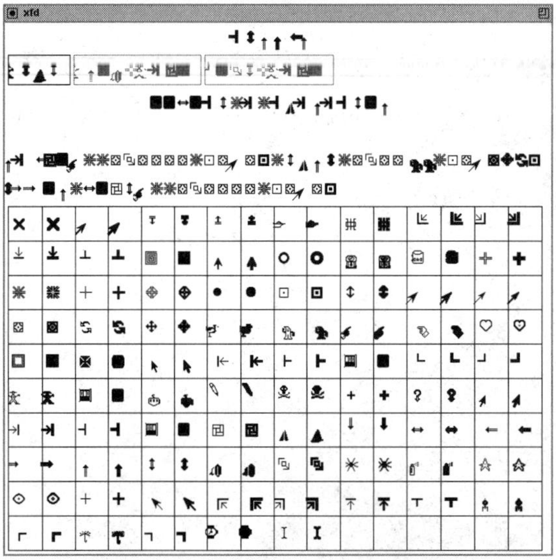

Figure 19.1 *The X cursor font.*

To get a good look at the available cursors in the cursor font, use the X program that displays fonts, `xfd`. Simply type:

```
xfd -font cursor
```

at the command prompt (on a UNIX workstation) and the `xfd` client program will pop up a window with the cursor shapes and their masks.

To use one of the cursor font cursors for your application's window, the cursor must first be created. Use `XCreateFontCursor` to create a cursor from the standard cursor font:

```
Cursor XCreateFontCursor(Display* display,

    unsigned int cursor_number)
```

`XCreateFontCursor` returns a cursor ID of the new cursor. The *cursor_number* must be a valid cursor from the cursor font. The include file `<X11/cursorfont.h>` contains all the valid cursor numbers, 77 different cursors in all. Each of the cursor IDs in `<X11/cursorfont.h>` corresponds to an even-numbered character in the cursor font (the odd-numbered characters are the masks). The available cursors are listed in Table 19.1.

Table 19.1   *The X cursor font.*

Cursor	Number
XC_XCursor	0
XC_arrow	2
XC_based_arrow_down	4
XC_based_arrow_up	6
XC_boat	8
XC_bogosity	10
XC_bottom_left_corner	12
XC_bottom_right_corner	14
XC_bottom_side	16
XC_bottom_tee	18

```
XC_box_spiral              20
XC_center_ptr              22
XC_circle                  24
XC_clock                   26
XC_coffee_mug              28
XC_cross                   30
XC_cross_reverse           32
XC_crosshair               34
XC_diamond_cross           36
XC_dot                     38
XC_dotbox                  40
XC_double_arrow            42
XC_draft_large             44
XC_draft_small             46
XC_draped_box              48
XC_exchange                50
XC_fleur                   52
XC_gobbler                 54
XC_gumby                   56
XC_hand1                   58
XC_hand2                   60
XC_heart                   62
XC_icon                    64
XC_iron_cross              66
XC_left_ptr                68
XC_left_side               70
XC_left_tee                72
XC_leftbutton              74
XC_ll_angle                76
XC_lr_angle                78
XC_man                     80
```

XC_ul_angle	144
XC_umbrella	146
XC_ur_angle	148
XC_watch	150
XC_xterm	152

To create a Gumby cursor (our favorite), identified by XC_Gumby, you can call XCreateFontCursor, as shown in the following code:

```
#include <X11/cursorfont.h>

Display* display;
Cursor   cursor;

cursor = XCreateFontCursor(display,
          XC_Gumby);

if (cursor != (Cursor) None) {
    /* we have success... */
}
```

Cursor Masks

Cursors in X use two colors, a foreground and a background. A single-color cursor is simply not workable, as you can imagine with an all-black cursor over a window with a black background. You also don't want all your cursors to have a rectangular shape. A text I-beam cursor, for instance, should be very thin and tall so it doesn't obscure the text that lies underneath. So, to make for odd-shaped cursors, X provides the concept of an optional *cursor mask*.

The cursor mask is another bitmap that describes the outline of the cursor. The mask and the cursor pixmaps must both have a depth of 1 and be the same size. Whatever underlies the cursor will show through wherever there are zero bits in the mask bitmap. The cursor itself appears where there are ones in the mask. And yes, you can have a cursor with holes in it. An example cursor and a cursor mask are shown in Figure 19.2.

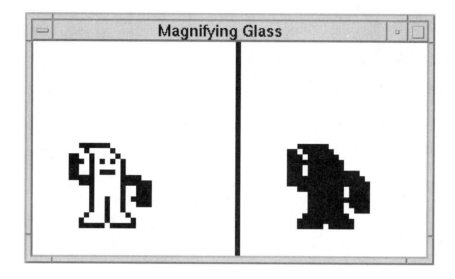

Figure 19.2   *A cursor with a mask.*

Every pixel outside of the mask is outside of the cursor. Some hardware, though, may not be able to implement cursor masks.

Creating Cursors from Pixmaps

You can create your own cursors out of bitmaps (single-plane pixmaps, remember) or other fonts. Use one font character or bitmap for the cursor mask and one font character or bitmap for the cursor itself.

Each cursor created in this manner needs a *hot spot*, the point that is considered the *x, y* location of the cursor. With an arrow cursor, for example, you want the hot spot to be at the tip of the arrow. With a watch cursor, a good hot spot is the center of the watch. You also specify the foreground and background color of the cursor.

Since you can create cursors from bitmaps, the X bitmap file format can also optionally hold the hot spot for the cursor. The bitmap file below has a hot spot of 7, 8 within a 16 x 16 pixel bitmap:

```
#define circle1_width 16
#define circle1_height 16
#define circle1_x_hot 7
#define circle1_y_hot 8
static char circle1_bits[] = {
    0x00, 0x00, 0xf0, 0x07, 0x08, 0x08,
    0x04, 0x10, 0x0e, 0x38, 0x1f, 0x7c,
    0x3f, 0x7e, 0x7f, 0x7f, 0xff, 0x7f,
    0x7f, 0x7f, 0x3f, 0x7e, 0x1f, 0x7c,
    0x0e, 0x38, 0x04, 0x10, 0x08, 0x08,
    0xf0, 0x07};
```

The `circle1_x_hot` and `circle1_y_hot` defines list the hot spot.

Use `XCreatePixmapCursor` to create a cursor from two pixmaps:

```
Cursor XCreatePixmapCursor(Display* display,
    Pixmap    cursor_pixmap,
    Pixmap    mask_pixmap,
    XColor*   foreground_color,
    XColor*   background_color,
    unsigned int x_hotspot,
    unsigned int y_hotspot)
```

Both the cursor and the mask pixmaps must have a depth of one plane. In other words, both must be bitmaps. Normally, cursors fit in a 16 x 16 pixel cell. You can make larger cursors, though not all systems support this. To determine what cursor sizes are supported, you can call `XQueryBestCursor`:

```
Status XQueryBestCursor(Display* display,
        Drawable drawable,
        unsigned int preferred_width,
        unsigned int preferred_height,
```

```
    unsigned int* closest_width,   /* RETURN */
    unsigned int* closest_height)  /* RETURN */
```

You pass the desired size for your cursor in the *preferred_width* and *preferred_height* parameters. XQueryBestCursor then fills in the *closest_width* and *closest_height* with the closest size supported. The *drawable* is just used to get the screen, as different screens may support different cursor sizes (some systems provide a hardware cursor). If XQueryBestCursor succeeds, it returns a nonzero value. It returns 0 on errors.

Creating Cursors from Font Glyphs

To create a cursor from a character in a font, use the XCreateGlyphCursor function:

```
Cursor XCreateGlyphCursor(Display* display,
    Font cursor_font_id,
    Font mask_font_id,
    unsigned int cursor_char,
    unsigned int mask_char,
    XColor* foreground_color,
    XColor* background_color)
```

In this case, the hot spot is formed by the origins of the characters. These origins are placed at the same position in the new cursor.

The values for *cursor_char* and *mask_char* define the characters in the respective fonts used for creating the cursor. In most cases, the *cursor_font_id* and *mask_font_id* fonts will be the same.

Freeing Cursors

Like everything else, cursors take up random-access memory (RAM) in the X server, so it is a good idea to free them up when you are finished with the cursor. Use XFreeCursor to free a cursor:

```
XFreeCursor(Display* display, Cursor cursor)
```

Cursors and Windows

Cursors and windows are tied together. In X, each window can be associated with one cursor shape. Whenever the mouse pointer is in the window, the pointer shape is set to the shape of the cursor defined for that window. (This is done automatically by the X server.)

Since the X server automatically changes the cursor for you, you can create special cursors as part of your application's user interface. The Motif window manager, for example, uses cursors to show how you can change the window's size. As you move the mouse over the mwm window title bar and decorations, the cursor shape changes to provide some indication of the function you can perform with the mouse over that area. This is a very useful technique for your programs. The only constraint is that you can only have one cursor at a time for each window. Thus, you may need to create a number of small subwindows, as mwm does, to allow for all the different cursors you want.

If you do not define a cursor for a window, the window's cursor will be inherited from the window's parent. The root window's default cursor is a big *X*. If you do not define a cursor for your window, it will inherit the big *X* cursor, or whatever is defined for the root window.

You can set the cursor you want for a window when you first create the window with the XCreateWindow function. The *cursor* is part of the XSetWindowAttributes structure. The following code stores a *cursor* in the cursor field of the XSetWindowAttributes structure:

```
XSetWindowAttributes attributes;
Cursor               cursor;
unsigned long        attr_mask;


/* Create cursor first... */


/* Fill cursor ID into attributes struct */
attributes.cursor = cursor;


attr_mask |= CWCursor;
```

```
/* call XCreateWindow... */
```

You can also define a cursor for an already-created window with the XDefineCursor function:

```
XDefineCursor(Display* display,

    Window window,

    Cursor cursor)
```

The window will now use the new *cursor*. If you're using an X toolkit, most of this will be taken care of for you, so long as you want to use the toolkit's default cursors.

You can undo the cursor definition with the XUndefineCursor function:

```
XUndefineCursor(Display* display,

    Window window)
```

Calling XUndefineCursor means the window will now use the cursor of its parent. There's no way to restore a previous cursor for a particular window. You can also call XDefineCursor and pass None for the *cursor* parameter. There's essentially no difference between the two.

Changing Cursor Colors

You can change the foreground and background colors of a cursor with XRecolorCursor:

```
XRecolorCursor(Display* display,

    Cursor cursor,

    XColor* foreground_color,

    XColor* background_color)
```

For instance, you can make the Gumby cursor green.

Busy Cursors

When your application performs a task that requires processing for a long time, it's a good idea to let the user know what's going on. You may also want to give the user some means for terminating this time-consuming task. For example, if the task is taking a long time or if the user made a mistake in setting up the task, a friendly interface will allow the user a chance to cancel this process. There's no sense in making the user wait a long time. With Motif, the *working dialog* is intended for this purpose. In addition, many applications display a *busy cursor* while this time-consuming task computes. Most busy cursors have clock, stopwatch, coffee-cup (telling you to take a coffee break while waiting for the task to complete) or hourglass shapes (something related to time). This concept is fairly standard across most user interfaces.

The busy cursor helps let users know the application is busy doing something. We strongly advise providing feedback to users, so that they have a better idea of what is going on. This is all part of event-driven programming, where users control applications, and not vice versa.

One way to implement a busy cursor would be to create a clock-shaped cursor (e.g., XC_watch in the cursor font) and then call XDefineCursor to set this cursor on all your application windows. This means, however, that your application must remember all the original window cursors, so they can be restored when the busy task finishes.

Another technique involves creating an InputOnly (transparent) window covering your entire application (all your application windows). Set the cursor for this InputOnly window to the busy clock shape. When the busy task is finished, merely unmap or destroy the busy InputOnly window.

Developing a Busy Cursor by Cheating

Another way to do this is to choose some nearly top-level widget, such as a Motif main window widget, and then change the cursor for that widget to the busy cursor using XDefineCursor. When you're done with the busy cursor—that is, when you're done with the time-consuming task that you needed the busy cursor for—you can then pass None to XDefineCursor to use the parent's cursor. In this case, the parent is also a toolkit widget (the top-level shell), so that the cursor should be restored just fine.

The cheating part is that we assume the top-level shell widget properly sets up a cursor and this cursor is the cursor you want back when you're done with the time-consuming task and need to get rid of the busy cursor. If this isn't the case, then you simply need to restore the proper cursor your application needs.

Animated Busy Cursors

In addition to a busy cursor, you ought to provide some feedback to the user that the time-consuming process isn't stalled. One way to do so is to animate the busy cursor. For instance, you can animate the hands on a watch cursor. As the user sees the watch cursor changing, the user feels that the program hasn't crashed and is still processing.

Another good technique is to show a gauge or bar chart indicating the percentage of work completed, so that the user can get a grip on how long it will take to finish the task at hand. Such a gauge is beyond the scope of this chapter, so we'll just concentrate on making a busy cursor.

How can we "animate" a busy cursor? Well, the easiest method is to simply change the shape of the busy cursor at periodic intervals. That is, we can call XDefineCursor every now and then to set a new cursor shape. The trick is to make all the busy cursor shapes related and to make the changes in shape provide a realistic motion. For example, a set of watch-shaped busy cursors would look almost the same except that the hands would be in different positions. These different positions should change in a clockwise manner, or the user will think that time is flowing backward. (If they are extremely gullible, anyway.) As with all animation, the key is making believable output.

The algorithm we use for these busy cursors is as follows. First, we need to create a set of cursor shapes. All these shapes should be related and all should share the same mask. We store these busy cursors in an array of type Cursor. When it comes time to display the busy cursors, we call XDefineCursor with the first cursor in the array.

Second, at periodic intervals, we need to animate the cursor shapes to provide feedback to the user that the program hasn't crashed. To animate the next cursor, we simply call XDefineCursor again, with the next cursor in the array. We continue to do this at periodic intervals. In Chapter 24, we'll show how to use an Xt timer procedure for general animation. For now, though, we'll simply use a dumb busy-wait loop with the sleep function to simulate a time-consuming task.

Third, when we're all done with the time-consuming task, we need to restore the original cursor. The cheating method we use here is to call XDefineCursor with a cursor of None or to call XUndefineCursor, instead of restoring the original cursors.

Creating the Busy Cursors

A utility function, CreateBusyCursors, creates the busy cursors used by this simple package. CreateBusyCursors uses an array of pixmaps and converts a set of bitmap data to pixmaps using XCreateBitmapFromData. We create the mask bitmap in the same manner. We could also have loaded in the cursor files from disk using XReadBitmapFile, but it's just easier to store all the cursor bitmap data in one file.

Once all the bitmaps are created, we can use XCreatePixmapCursor to create a cursor from a cursor bitmap and a mask bitmap. These cursors are stored in a global array of type Cursor, *busy_cursors*.

In order to call XCreatePixmapCursor, we need XColor structures for the new cursor's foreground and background colors. Since most X programs deal with just unsigned long pixel values, we convert the foreground and background colors to XColor structures by calling XQueryColor.

Finally, CreateBusyCursors frees the bitmaps created with XCreateBitmapFromData, using XFreePixmap, since we don't need them anymore. The code for CreateBusyCursors follows:

```
/*
 * Globals
 */
#define NUMBER_CURSORS   8

static Cursor    busy_cursors[NUMBER_CURSORS+1];
static int       busy_init     = False;


void CreateBusyCursors(Display* display,
```

```
        Window window,
        Colormap colormap,
        unsigned long fore,
        unsigned long back)


{       /* CreateBusyCursors */
        XColor  fcolor, bcolor;
        Pixmap  bitmap[NUMBER_CURSORS];
        Pixmap  mask;
        int     i;

        /*
         * Get the full XColor structures
         * for the foreground and
         * background colors.
         */
        fcolor.pixel = fore;

        XQueryColor(display, colormap, &fcolor);

        bcolor.pixel = back;

        XQueryColor(display, colormap, &bcolor);

        /*
         * Create bitmaps from the cursor data.
         */
        bitmap[0] = XCreateBitmapFromData(display,
                     window, circle1_bits,
                     circle1_width, circle1_height);

        bitmap[1] = XCreateBitmapFromData(display,
```

```
                    window, circle2_bits,
                    circle2_width, circle2_height);

    bitmap[2] = XCreateBitmapFromData(display,
                    window, circle3_bits,
                    circle3_width, circle3_height);

    bitmap[3] = XCreateBitmapFromData(display,
                    window, circle4_bits,
                    circle4_width, circle4_height);

    bitmap[4] = XCreateBitmapFromData(display,
                    window, circle5_bits,
                    circle5_width, circle5_height);

    bitmap[5] = XCreateBitmapFromData(display,
                    window, circle6_bits,
                    circle6_width, circle6_height);

    bitmap[6] = XCreateBitmapFromData(display,
                    window, circle7_bits,
                    circle7_width, circle7_height);

    bitmap[7] = XCreateBitmapFromData(display,
                    window, circle8_bits,
                    circle8_width, circle8_height);

    mask = XCreateBitmapFromData(display,
                    window, circlem_bits,
                    circlem_width, circlem_height);

    /*
     * Create cursors from the bitmaps
```

```
*/
for (i = 0; i < NUMBER_CURSORS; i++) {
    busy_cursors[i] =
        XCreatePixmapCursor(display,
            bitmap[i],
            mask,
            &fcolor, &bcolor,
            circle1_x_hot,
            circle1_y_hot);
}


/*
 * Free all the bitmaps.
 */
for (i = 0; i < NUMBER_CURSORS; i++) {
    XFreePixmap(display, bitmap[i]);
}


XFreePixmap(display, mask);


busy_init = True;


}   /* CreateBusyCursors */
```

Once we've created the busy cursors, the next step is to display them.

Setting Up the Busy Cursors

We need to display the first busy cursor just before the application starts a time-consuming task. The function `SetBusy` sets up the first busy cursor and stores a `Display` pointer and `Window` ID in global values. The code for `SetBusy` follows:

```
void SetBusy(Display* display, Window window)


{   /* SetBusy */


    /*
     * Check that we have called
     * CreateBusyCursors.
     */
    if (!busy_init) {

        return;

    }



    /*
     * Set the first busy cursor to
     * the first cursor in the sequence.
     */
    busy_display   = display;
    busy_window    = window;
    current_cursor = 0;


    SetBusyCursor(current_cursor);


}   /* SetBusy */
```

The SetBusy function basically just caches the display and window, sets
the first cursor up, and then stores a zero in *current_cursor*. This integer variable just holds the current index into the *busy_cursors* Cursor
array. To actually set up the first cursor, SetBusy calls SetBusyCursor:

```
void SetBusyCursor(int which_cursor)
```

```
{   /* SetBusyCursor */


    if ((which_cursor >= 0) &&
        (which_cursor < NUMBER_CURSORS)) {


        XDefineCursor(busy_display, busy_window,
            busy_cursors[which_cursor]);
    }


}   /* SetBusyCursor */
```

Changing to the Next Busy Cursor

At periodic intervals, we need to change from one busy cursor to the next, providing the user feedback and giving a sense of animation to the busy cursors. Your application will probably be in a callback function when you want to do this, so the busyCB function, below, takes no parameters:

```
void busyCB()


{   /* busyCB */

    /*
     * Increment to the next cursor.
     */
    current_cursor++;


    if (current_cursor >= NUMBER_CURSORS) {
        current_cursor = 0;
    }
```

```
/*
 * Set the new busy cursor.
 */
SetBusyCursor(current_cursor);


}   /* busyCB */
```

The busyCB function merely increments the *current_cursor* index to the next cursor and calls SetBusyCursor to change the window's cursor.

When the application is all done with the time-consuming task, you need to restore the original cursors.

Restoring the Original Cursor

The function RestoreCursor uses the cheating method described above to restore the window's cursor:

```
void RestoreCursor()


{   /* RestoreCursor */


    XUndefineCursor(busy_display, busy_window);


}   /* RestoreCursor */
```

Creating the Cursor Bitmaps

A key part of animated busy cursors is getting the cursor images to look like they follow a sequence. You can create the bitmap images using the bitmap or iconedit program, or, if you really like typing, you can type in the values listed in the file busy.c, below.

The cursor shapes follow a primitive sequence that should provide the illusion of motion when animated using the techniques described above.

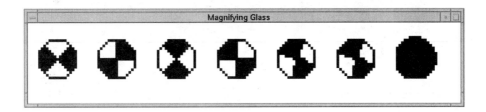

Figure 19.3 *The busy cursors.*

Source Code To Implement Animated Busy Cursors

The code for our simple busy cursor package is stored in the file busy.c:

```
/*
 *  busy.c
 *  Routines for a busy cursor.
 */
#include "xlib.h"
#include <stdio.h>


/*
 * Define eight circles for the busy cursor.
 * You can try your own bitmaps instead.
 */
#define circle1_width 16
#define circle1_height 16
#define circle1_x_hot 7
#define circle1_y_hot 8
static char circle1_bits[] = {
    0x00, 0x00, 0xf0, 0x07, 0x08, 0x08,
    0x04, 0x10, 0x0e, 0x38, 0x1f, 0x7c,
    0x3f, 0x7e, 0x7f, 0x7f, 0xff, 0x7f,
```

```
    0x7f, 0x7f, 0x3f, 0x7e, 0x1f, 0x7c,
    0x0e, 0x38, 0x04, 0x10, 0x08, 0x08,
    0xf0, 0x07};


#define circle2_width 16
#define circle2_height 16
#define circle2_x_hot 7
#define circle2_y_hot 8
static char circle2_bits[] = {
    0x00, 0x00, 0xf0, 0x07, 0x18, 0x08,
    0x3c, 0x10, 0x3e, 0x20, 0x7f, 0x60,
    0x7f, 0x78, 0xff, 0x7f, 0xff, 0x7f,
    0xff, 0x7f, 0x1f, 0x7f, 0x0f, 0x7f,
    0x02, 0x3e, 0x04, 0x1e, 0x08, 0x0c,
    0xf0, 0x07};


#define circle3_width 16
#define circle3_height 16
#define circle3_x_hot 7
#define circle3_y_hot 8
static char circle3_bits[] = {
    0x00, 0x00, 0xf0, 0x07, 0xf8, 0x08,
    0xfc, 0x10, 0xfe, 0x20, 0xff, 0x40,
    0xff, 0x40, 0xff, 0x40, 0xff, 0x7f,
    0x81, 0x7f, 0x81, 0x7f, 0x81, 0x7f,
    0x82, 0x3f, 0x84, 0x1f, 0x88, 0x0f,
    0xf0, 0x07};


#define circle4_width 16
#define circle4_height 16
#define circle4_x_hot 7
```

```
#define circle4_y_hot 8
static char circle4_bits[] = {
    0x00, 0x00, 0xf0, 0x07, 0xf8, 0x0f,
    0xfc, 0x13, 0xfe, 0x23, 0xff, 0x41,
    0xff, 0x41, 0xf9, 0x41, 0xc1, 0x47,
    0x81, 0x4f, 0x81, 0x7f, 0xc1, 0x7f,
    0xc2, 0x3f, 0xc4, 0x1f, 0xc8, 0x0f,
    0xf0, 0x07};


#define circle5_width 16
#define circle5_height 16
#define circle5_x_hot 7
#define circle5_y_hot 8
static char circle5_bits[] = {
    0x00, 0x00, 0xf0, 0x07, 0xf8, 0x0f,
    0xfc, 0x1f, 0xfa, 0x2f, 0xf1, 0x47,
    0xe1, 0x43, 0xc1, 0x41, 0x81, 0x40,
    0xc1, 0x41, 0xe1, 0x43, 0xf1, 0x47,
    0xfa, 0x2f, 0xfc, 0x1f, 0xf8, 0x0f,
    0xf0, 0x07};


#define circle6_width 16
#define circle6_height 16
#define circle6_x_hot 7
#define circle6_y_hot 8
static char circle6_bits[] = {
    0x00, 0x00, 0xf0, 0x07, 0xf8, 0x0f,
    0xf4, 0x1f, 0xe2, 0x3f, 0xe1, 0x7f,
    0xc1, 0x5f, 0xc1, 0x47, 0x81, 0x41,
    0xe1, 0x40, 0xf9, 0x41, 0xff, 0x41,
    0xfe, 0x23, 0xfc, 0x17, 0xf8, 0x0f,
```

```
    0xf0, 0x07};


#define circle7_width 16
#define circle7_height 16
#define circle7_x_hot 7
#define circle7_y_hot 8
static char circle7_bits[] = {
    0x00, 0x00, 0xf0, 0x07, 0x88, 0x0f,
    0x84, 0x1f, 0x82, 0x3f, 0x81, 0x7f,
    0x81, 0x7f, 0x81, 0x7f, 0xff, 0x7f,
    0xff, 0x40, 0xff, 0x40, 0xff, 0x40,
    0xfe, 0x20, 0xfc, 0x10, 0xf8, 0x08,
    0xf0, 0x07};


#define circle8_width 16
#define circle8_height 16
#define circle8_x_hot 7
#define circle8_y_hot 8
static char circle8_bits[] = {
    0x00, 0x00, 0xf0, 0x07, 0x08, 0x0e,
    0x04, 0x1e, 0x02, 0x3e, 0x01, 0x7e,
    0x03, 0x7f, 0x3f, 0x7f, 0xff, 0x7f,
    0x7f, 0x7f, 0x7f, 0x78, 0x3f, 0x60,
    0x3e, 0x20, 0x3c, 0x10, 0x38, 0x08,
    0xf0, 0x07};


/*
 * Cursor mask.
 */
#define circlem_width 16
#define circlem_height 16
```

```
static char circlem_bits[] = {
   0xe0, 0x03, 0xf8, 0x0f, 0xfc, 0x1f,
   0xfe, 0x3f, 0xff, 0x7f, 0xff, 0x7f,
   0xff, 0xff, 0xff, 0xff, 0xff, 0xff,
   0xff, 0xff, 0xff, 0xff, 0xff, 0x7f,
   0xff, 0x7f, 0xfe, 0x3f, 0xfc, 0x1f,
   0xf8, 0x0f};

/*
 * Global variables for the 8 cursors.
 */
#define NUMBER_CURSORS  8

static Cursor   busy_cursors[NUMBER_CURSORS+1];
static int      current_cursor = 0;
static Display* busy_display = NULL;
static Window   busy_window  = None;
static int      busy_init    = False;

/*
 * Convenience function: Sets the numbered
 * cursor to the global busy_window.
 */
void SetBusyCursor(int which_cursor)

{   /* SetBusyCursor */

    if ((which_cursor >= 0) &&
        (which_cursor < NUMBER_CURSORS)) {

        XDefineCursor(busy_display, busy_window,
```

```
                    busy_cursors[which_cursor]);
    }


}   /* SetBusyCursor */


void RestoreCursor()


{   /* RestoreCursor */


    XUndefineCursor(busy_display, busy_window);


}   /* RestoreCursor */


/*
 * Callback to change the cursor. You can call
 * this from a timer.
 */
void busyCB()


{   /* busyCB */


    /*
     * Increment to the next cursor.
     */
    current_cursor++;


    if (current_cursor >= NUMBER_CURSORS) {
        current_cursor = 0;
    }


    /*
```

```
 * Set the new busy cursor.
 */

SetBusyCursor(current_cursor);


}   /* busyCB */


/*
 * Sets the first busy cursor.
 */


void SetBusy(Display* display, Window window)


{   /* SetBusy */

    /*
     * Check that we have called
     * CreateBusyCursors.
     */
    if (!busy_init) {
        return;
    }


    /*
     * Set the first busy cursor to
     * the first cursor in the sequence.
     */
    busy_display   = display;
    busy_window    = window;
    current_cursor = 0;


    SetBusyCursor(current_cursor);
```

```
}   /* SetBusy */


/*
 *  Creates the busy cursors.
 */
void CreateBusyCursors(Display* display,
    Window window,
    Colormap colormap,
    unsigned long fore,
    unsigned long back)


{   /* CreateBusyCursors */
    XColor   fcolor, bcolor;
    Pixmap   bitmap[NUMBER_CURSORS];
    Pixmap   mask;
    int      i;


    /*
     * Get the full XColor structures
     * for the foreground and
     * background colors.
     */
    fcolor.pixel = fore;

    XQueryColor(display, colormap, &fcolor);

    bcolor.pixel = back;

    XQueryColor(display, colormap, &bcolor);
```

```
/*
 * Create bitmaps from the cursor data.
 */
bitmap[0] = XCreateBitmapFromData(display,
            window, circle1_bits,
            circle1_width, circle1_height);

bitmap[1] = XCreateBitmapFromData(display,
            window, circle2_bits,
            circle2_width, circle2_height);

bitmap[2] = XCreateBitmapFromData(display,
            window, circle3_bits,
            circle3_width, circle3_height);

bitmap[3] = XCreateBitmapFromData(display,
            window, circle4_bits,
            circle4_width, circle4_height);

bitmap[4] = XCreateBitmapFromData(display,
            window, circle5_bits,
            circle5_width, circle5_height);

bitmap[5] = XCreateBitmapFromData(display,
            window, circle6_bits,
            circle6_width, circle6_height);

bitmap[6] = XCreateBitmapFromData(display,
            window, circle7_bits,
            circle7_width, circle7_height);
```

```
bitmap[7] = XCreateBitmapFromData(display,
            window, circle8_bits,
            circle8_width, circle8_height);

mask = XCreateBitmapFromData(display,
            window, circlem_bits,
            circlem_width, circlem_height);



/*
 * Create cursors from the bitmaps
 */
for (i = 0; i < NUMBER_CURSORS; i++) {
    busy_cursors[i] =
        XCreatePixmapCursor(display,
            bitmap[i],
            mask,
            &fcolor, &bcolor,
            circle1_x_hot,
            circle1_y_hot);
}


/*
 * Free all the bitmaps.
 */
for (i = 0; i < NUMBER_CURSORS; i++) {
    XFreePixmap(display, bitmap[i]);
}

XFreePixmap(display, mask);
```

```
       busy_init = True;


}    /* CreateBusyCursors */


/* end of file busy.c */
```

Limitations of the Busy Cursors

There are a number of limitations using this model to implement animated busy cursors. First off, we cheat when restoring the original cursor. This technique may not work on your system. In such a case, you can either keep track of the original cursors, or create an `InputOnly` window over the application's shell widgets.

Second, we use global values for the window ID and display pointer. The display pointer isn't that big an issue, but with one global for a window ID, we're limited to one application shell widget. Most sophisticated applications require more than one shell widget.

A Program to Show Busy Cursors

We've developed a simple program to show our animated busy cursors in action. You'll find the Motif and Open Look Intrinsics Toolkit (OLIT) code is almost exactly the same.

Motif Source for the Busy Cursor Program

The Motif source code for the busy cursor program is stored in the file `m_chap19.c`, below. This program uses `sleep` to simulate a time-consuming task.

```
/*
 *  m_chap19.c
 *  Motif test program for Chapter 19.
 *  Animate a busy cursor.
```

```
 */
#include "motif.h"
#include <stdio.h>

/*
 * Callback to start busy cursor.
 */
void busyCursorCB(Widget widget,
        XtPointer client_data,
        XtPointer call_data)

{   /* busyCursorCB */
    Widget    mainwindow;
    int       i;
    Display*  display;

    mainwindow = (Widget) client_data;

    /*
     * Set up busy cursor.
     */
    display = XtDisplay(mainwindow);

    SetBusy(display, XtWindow(mainwindow) );

    /*
     * Now, animate this cursor.
     * Note that a Xt timer proc
     * would be better.
     */
    XmUpdateDisplay(mainwindow);
```

```
for (i = 0; i < 20; i++) {

    /*
     * Change to the next busy cursor.
     */
    busyCB();

    /*
     * Make sure the user sees
     * the new cursor.
     */
    XFlush(display);

    /* Busy-wait to simulate a long
     * process. Note that this really
     * should be in a work proc or timer
     * proc instead of a tight CPU loop.
     * You may need to adjust the value
     * passed to sleep().
     */
    sleep(1);
}

RestoreCursor();

}   /* busyCursorCB */

int main(int argc, char** argv)

{   /* main */
```

```
XtAppContext   app_context;
Widget         parent;
Widget         mainwindow;
Widget         menubar;
Widget         filemenu;
Widget         exitchoice;
Arg            args[20];
int            n;
Display*       display;
Colormap       colormap;
unsigned long yellow, blue;
int            screen;

/* Initialize X toolkit */
n = 0;
XtSetArg(args[n], XmNmappedWhenManaged, False); n++;
XtSetArg(args[n], XmNallowResize, True); n++;
XtSetArg(args[n], XmNwidth, 200); n++;
XtSetArg(args[n], XmNheight, 200); n++;

parent = XtAppInitialize(&app_context,
        "ProX",                     /* app class */
        (XrmOptionDescList) NULL,    /* options */
        0,                          /* num options */
        ARGC_PTR &argc, argv,       /* cmd line */
        (String*) NULL,             /* fallback res. */
        args, n);


/*
 * Create Main Window with utility function.
```

```
 */
mainwindow = CreateMainWindow(parent, "main");


/*
 * Create menu bar with utility function.
 */
menubar = CreateMenuBar(mainwindow, "menubar");


/*
 * Create the file menu.
 */
filemenu = CreateMenu(menubar, "filemenu");

(void) CreateMenuChoice(filemenu,
                "busy",
                (XtCallbackProc) busyCursorCB,
                (XtPointer) mainwindow);


/* Create a menu choice to exit the program. */
exitchoice = CreateExitChoice(filemenu,
                "exitchoice");


SetMainAreas(mainwindow,
            menubar,
            (Widget) NULL);


/* Create the windows. */
XtRealizeWidget(parent);
```

```
      /*
       * Allocate color cells.
       */
      display  = XtDisplay(mainwindow);
      screen   = DefaultScreen(display);


      colormap = DefaultColormap(display, screen);


      yellow = AllocNamedColor(display, colormap,
                  "Yellow",
                  BlackPixel(display, screen) );


      blue = AllocNamedColor(display, colormap,
                  "Blue",
                  WhitePixel(display, screen) );


      /* Create busy cursors. */
      CreateBusyCursors(display,
          XtWindow(mainwindow),
          colormap, yellow, blue);


      /* Map parent */
      XtMapWidget(parent);
      XtAppMainLoop(app_context);


      return 0;


}    /* main */


/* end of file m_chap19.c */
```

OLIT Source for the Busy Cursor Program

The OLIT source code for the busy cursor program is stored in the file
o_chap19.c, below:

```
/*
 *  o_chap19.c
 *  OLIT test program for Chapter 19.
 *  Animate a busy cursor.
 */
#include "olit.h"
#include <stdio.h>


/*
 * Callback to start busy cursor.
 */
void busyCursorCB(Widget widget,
        XtPointer client_data,
        XtPointer call_data)


{   /* busyCursorCB */
    Widget    mainwindow;
    int       i;
    Display*  display;

    mainwindow = (Widget) client_data;

    /*
     * Set up busy cursor.
     */
    display = XtDisplay(mainwindow);
```

```
SetBusy(display, XtWindow(mainwindow) );

/*
 * Now, animate this cursor.
 * Note that a Xt timer proc
 * would be better.
 */
OlUpdateDisplay(mainwindow);

for (i = 0; i < 20; i++) {

    /*
     * Change to the next busy cursor.
     */
    busyCB();

    /*
     * Make sure the user sees
     * the new cursor.
     */
    XFlush(display);

    /* Busy-wait to simulate a long
     * process. Note that this really
     * should be in a work proc or timer
     * proc instead of a tight CPU loop.
     * You may need to adjust the value
     * passed to sleep().
     */
    sleep(1);
```

```
        }

    RestoreCursor();

}   /* busyCursorCB */


int main(int argc, char** argv)

{   /* main */
    XtAppContext    app_context;
    Widget          parent;
    Widget          mainwindow;
    Widget          menubar;
    Widget          filemenu;
    Widget          exitchoice;
    Arg             args[20];
    int             n;
    Display*        display;
    Colormap        colormap;
    unsigned long yellow, blue;
    int             screen;

    /* Initialize X toolkit */
    n = 0;
    XtSetArg(args[n], XtNmappedWhenManaged, False); n++;
    XtSetArg(args[n], XtNwidth, 200); n++;
    XtSetArg(args[n], XtNheight, 200); n++;

    parent = XtAppInitialize(&app_context,
            "ProX",                     /* app class */
            (XrmOptionDescList) NULL,   /* options */
```

```
                    0,                       /* num options */
                    ARGC_PTR &argc, argv,    /* cmd line */
                    (String*) NULL,          /* fallback res. */
                    args, n);




    /*
     * Create Main Window with utility function.
     */
    mainwindow = CreateMainWindow(parent, "main");


    /*
     * Create menu bar with utility function.
     */
    menubar = CreateMenuBar(mainwindow, "menubar");


    /*
     * Create the file menu.
     */
    filemenu = CreateMenu(menubar, "filemenu");


(void) CreateMenuChoice(filemenu,
                "busy",
                (XtCallbackProc) busyCursorCB,
                (XtPointer) mainwindow);


    /* Create a menu choice to exit the program. */
    exitchoice = CreateExitChoice(filemenu,
                "exitchoice");


    SetMainAreas(mainwindow,
```

```
                menubar,
                (Widget) NULL);


/* Create the windows. */
XtRealizeWidget(parent);


/*
 * Allocate color cells.
 */
display  = XtDisplay(mainwindow);
screen   = DefaultScreen(display);


colormap = DefaultColormap(display, screen);


yellow = AllocNamedColor(display, colormap,
            "Yellow",
            BlackPixel(display, screen) );


blue = AllocNamedColor(display, colormap,
            "Blue",
            WhitePixel(display, screen) );


/* Create busy cursors. */
CreateBusyCursors(display,
    XtWindow(mainwindow),
    colormap, yellow, blue);


/* Map parent */
XtMapWidget(parent);
```

```
    XtAppMainLoop(app_context);

    return 0;

}   /* main */


/* end of file o_chap19.c */
```

Resource File for the Busy Cursor Programs

Name the following resource file ProX and place it in your home directory:

```
! ProX
! Resource file for Chapter 19 of
! Professional Graphics
! Programming in the X Window System.
!
! Place this file in your
! home directory.
!
! Generic resources.
!
*background:    #cccccc
*title:         Chap. 19: Busy Cursors


!
! Motif resources.
!
!
*fontList: lucidasans-12
```

```
*filemenu.labelString:      File

*filemenu.mnemonic:         F


*exitchoice.labelString:    Exit

*exitchoice.mnemonic:       x


*busy.labelString:          Set busy cursor


! OLIT

*filemenu.label:            File

*exitchoice.label:          Exit

*busy.label:                Set busy cursor

! end of file ProX
```

Motif Cursor Functions

Motif provides two cursor routines for setting and getting the cursor used for menu widgets. XmGetMenuCursor returns the current menu cursor:

```
Cursor XmGetMenuCursor(Display *display)
```

XmSetMenuCursor sets the menu cursor:

```
void XmSetMenuCursor(Display *display,
    Cursor cursor_id)
```

N O T E

As of Motif 1.2, both XmGetMenuCursor and XmSetMenuCursor are considered obsolete. You should query and set the *menuCursor* resource on the XmScreen object instead. You can call XmGetXmScreen to get the widget ID for the XmScreen object associated with a given screen:

```
Widget XmGetXmScreen(Screen* screen_ptr)
```

OLIT Cursor Functions

OLIT provides zillions and zillions of functions to get at OLIT-specific cursors. Basically, there are two types of routines to get these cursors. The older *GetOl* functions take in a `Screen` pointer and return an OLIT cursor. The newer routines (new in OLIT 3.0), start with *OlGet*. These routines take in a `Widget` and return an OLIT cursor. Most of these new routines are devoted to drag and drop cursors.

For example, an OLIT version 3.0 function to get the OLIT-defined busy cursor is `OlGetBusyCursor`:

```
#include <Xol/OlCursors.h>


Cursor OlGetBusyCursor(Widget widget)
```

The older routine takes the following parameter:

```
#include <Xol/OlCursors.h>


Cursor GetOlBusyCursor(Screen* screen)
```

There are zillions of these cursor functions, which you can look up in an OLIT manual.

Summary

With X, cursors are not special drawings, but are merely two characters in a font. The first character is the outline of the cursor; the second character of the pair is the mask, which defines the shape of the cursor. A whole font, the font named *cursor*, contains a standard set of X cursors.

In X, each window can be associated with a cursor shape. Whenever the mouse pointer is in the window, the pointer shape is set to the shape of the cursor defined for that window.

You can create your own cursors out of bitmaps or other fonts. Make sure that you assign a hot spot to the cursor. You can also specify the color of the cursor foreground and background, should you desired a colored cursor.

X Library Functions and Macros Introduced in This Chapter

```
XCreateFontCursor

XCreateGlyphCursor

XCreatePixmapCursor

XDefineCursor

XFreeCursor

XQueryBestCursor

XUndefineCursor
```

Motif Functions and Macros Introduced in This Chapter

```
XmGetMenuCursor

XmGetXmScreen

XmSetMenuCursor
```

OLIT Functions and Macros Introduced in This Chapter

```
GetOlBusyCursor

OlGetBusyCursor
```

C h a p t e r   2 0

X Icons

This chapter covers:

- ✦ Using icons in X
- ✦ Working with the window manager
- ✦ Finding out the supported icon sizes
- ✦ Installing your icons
- ✦ The window manager hints structure
- ✦ Starting in iconic state
- ✦ Setting icon names
- ✦ Creating icon windows—dynamic icons
- ✦ Shell widgets as icon windows
- ✦ Iconifying windows
- ✦ Deiconifying windows
- ✦ Tracking a window's iconic status

761

Icons in X

An *icon* is a small window displaying a bitmap image that represents an application's top-level window. Most window managers allow users to *iconify* windows, that is, turn windows into small icons in a space-saving measure. These icons are then either a default bitmap supplied by the window manager or a bitmap supplied by your application.

Icons in X are bitmaps, which eliminates the possibility for color icons in the default case. You can also set up an *icon window*, as we discuss below, and provide your own color icon, although this is not always supported.

The first and foremost thing you must note about icons is that the window manager controls the whole process. Some window managers don't even support icons, though most do. Some window managers place icons into an *icon box*. (With many window managers, such as mwm or twm, the user may configure this.) Sometimes, your application can control where the window manager places the icons on the screen. Other times, you have no control over it.

Working with the Window Manager

Working with window managers forces you into a series of compromises. You never really seem to get everything you want, even though most user requests are perfectly reasonable. The problem is that the rules that describe how well-behaved applications communicate with the window manager, the Inter-Client Communications Conventions Manual, or ICCCM, leave a lot of areas open—on purpose—as part of X's oft-stated mantra of mechanism, not policy.

Wherever there was a user-interface decision, the designers of X left that matter for individual applications and window managers. While that may be a nice-sounding policy, application developers are left with a lot of gaping holes.

According to the theory, the user can choose any desired window manager. If you don't like the user-interface policies of one window manager, simply change to a new one. However, few users even know what a window manager is, let alone know the complex system-dependent means to change the configured window manager.

In real life, there are basically four types of window managers:

1. The *Motif window manager*, mwm, and its variants (e.g., Silicon Graphics' 4Dwm and Hewlett Packard's vuewm), which come with most non-Sun systems.

2. The *Open Look window manager*, olwm, which comes with Sun's OpenWindows.

3. The *Tab window manager*, twm, the freely available window manager that is part of the X releases from the X Consortium.

4. Twm variants that provide a virtual screen. These virtual screen window managers, such as tvtwm, vtwm (variants on twm), and olvwm (a variant on olwm), allow you to use an area larger than your physical screen size. The reason these window managers are significant for application developers is that they place a very large window as a child of the root window, obscuring the normal screen background.

The vast majority of X users run mwm or olwm (or a close variant). Your applications, though, should be able to run under any window manager.

The problem is that these window managers sometimes act in odd ways. For example, some window managers will iconify all your application's top-level windows together as a group. Some don't. Some enforce a rule that dialog windows must always appear on top of application windows. Some don't. (And so on.)

After a while, you begin to get frustrated when you want to do what should be a very simple thing, like determine the height of the window manager's title bar.

Anyway, the ICCCM officially supports only monochrome icons, so you may not be able to get the example programs in this chapter to really display an icon in color.

The basic way your application communicates to the window manager is by hinting. That is, your application hints that it wants the window manager to do something. The window manager may then follow your hint, or do its own thing entirely.

Determining the Supported Icon Sizes

Since icons are the domain of the window manager, the manager may desire icons to be a certain size and shape. Officially, your program should keep a selection of potential icons at various sizes or be able to generate icons at various supported sizes on cue. In most cases, a few sizes, such as 32 x 32 and 48 x 48 pixels, seem nearly universal. It's generally not worth keeping a set of icon bitmaps around for the infinite set of possible sizes.

If, however, you set up an icon window, you can create that window to be any size. In that case, you might want to know how big an icon you can make. To get the list of icon sizes supported by the window manager, call XGetIconSizes:

```
#include <X11/Xutil.h>


Status XGetIconSizes(Display* display,

        Window window,

        XIconSize** size_list,   /* RETURN */

        int* number_items)       /* RETURN */
```

XGetIconSizes reads the WM_ICON_SIZE property on the given window. (Only window managers may call the corresponding XSetIconSizes.) Normally, you pass the root window ID as the *window* parameter. XGetIconSizes returns a nonzero value on success; 0 otherwise. On success, use XFree to free the memory for the *size_list*. When you then call XSetWMHints, introduced in the next section, you should only pass an icon of a supported size.

The XIconSize structure, defined in <X11/Xutil.h>, looks like:

```
typedef struct {
    int     min_width, min_height;
    int     max_width, max_height;
    int     width_inc, height_inc;
} XIconSize;
```

For a given XIconSize, you can determine the minimum and maximum sizes and the increments (*width_inc*, *height_inc*) that are allowed between the minimum and maximum sizes.

Setting Up Your Own Icons

You create an icon like you do any pixmap. Since X only officially supports monochrome icons, the pixmap you create should have a depth of 1. Once the icon is created as a pixmap with a depth of 1, it is passed to the window manager through the XSetWMHints (for X Set Window Manager Hints) Xlib function:

```
#include <X11/Xutil.h>


XSetWMHints(Display* display,
    Window window,
    XWMHints* wmhints)
```

You can extract the window-manager hints from a window using XCctWMHints:

```
#include <X11/Xutil.h>


XWMHints* XGetWMHints(Display* display,
            Window window)
```

Free the returned XWMHints pointer with XFree. XGetWMHints returns NULL on errors.

The XWMHints Structure

The window manager hints are stored in the XWMHints structure, which is defined in the file <X11/Xutil.h>:

```
typedef struct {
```

```
    long        flags;

    Bool        input;

    int         initial_state;

    Pixmap      icon_pixmap;

    Window      icon_window;

    int         icon_x, icon_y;

    Pixmap      icon_mask;

    XID         window_group;

} XWMHints;
```

The *input* field holds a flag that tells the window manager whether the window desires keyboard input or not. Most X toolkits set this to True by default. The *initial_state* field tells the window manager whether the window should start as an icon or as a window (see below). To set an icon, fill in the *icon_pixmap* field with the icon's pixmap ID. You also need to set the *flags* field, as we show in the code examples, below.

Instead of an icon pixmap (really a bitmap), you can set up an *icon_window*. Regardless of what kind of icon you have, you can ask the window manager to place it at a certain location with the *icon_x* and *icon_y* fields. Some window managers allow you to provide a mask for the icon, which is used for special effects or when drawing the icon on a particular background. The mask bitmap is stored in the *icon_mask* field. The *icon_mask* determines which pixels of the *icon_pixmap* should be used for the icon, which allows for nonrectangular icons. Not all applications provide an *icon_mask*, though. Some window managers can deal with windows in a group. For example, some window managers iconify all the windows in a group together. The *window_group* field holds a window ID of the window group leader (an arbitrary window, but all windows in the same group must choose the same leader).

Again, the *flags* field indicates which of the other fields are actually filled in. The flag constants are listed in Table 20.1.

Table 20.1 *The XWMHints Flags*

Mask	Value	Field in XWMHints
InputHint	(IL << 0)	input
StateHint	(IL << 1)	initial_state
IconPixmapHint	(IL << 2)	icon_pixmap
IconWindowHint	(IL << 3)	icon_window
IconPositionHint	(IL << 4)	icon_x, icon_y
IconMaskHint	(IL << 5)	icon_mask
WindowGroupHint	(IL << 6)	window_group

Adding an Icon to the Window Manager Hints

To set up an icon, we need to fill in the *icon_pixmap* and *flags* fields of the XWMHints structure. There's a potential problem, though. If XSetWMHints was already called, then we don't want to overwrite any other window-manager hints.

If XSetWMHints was already called, you can use XGetWMHints to retrieve the current WM hints values and then add in the IconPixmapHint, as shown in the following code:

```
Display*    display;
Window      window;
Pixmap      icon;
XWMHints*   wmhints;
/*
 * Get current WM hints,
 * because we want to add
 * to what is already there.
 */
wmhints = XGetWMHints(display, window);
```

```
if (wmhints == (XWMHints*) NULL) {

    /*
     * Allocate a new XWMHints if
     * one hasn't been set yet.
     */
    wmhints = (XWMHints*) malloc( sizeof(XWMHints) );

    if (wmhints == (XWMHints*) NULL) {
        /* deal with the error... */
    }

    wmhints->flags = 0;
}

/*
 * Set up our icon
 */
wmhints->flags |= IconPixmapHint;

wmhints->icon_pixmap = icon;

/*
 * Set extended hints.
 */
XSetWMHints(display, window, wmhints);

XFree(wmhints);
```

Making Windows Start Out as Icons

The *initial_state* field of the XWMHints structure tells the window manager what state you want the window to start in. The *initial_state* can be one of the states listed in Table 20.2.

Table 20.2 *Window States*

State	Value	Meaning
WithdrawnState	0	Window is not visible
NormalState	I	Window is visible
IconicState	3	Window is replaced by an icon

The bitmask to set in the XWMHints flags field is StateHint. To make a window start out as an icon, you can set the *initial_state* field to IconicState. You should set this up before mapping the window.

Icon Names

Icons can also have names. These names are usually displayed along with the icon bitmap when your program is iconified. Not all window managers support icon names, so you don't have a lot of choice in the matter, but since most window managers do support both icons and icon names, it's a good idea to set an icon name for your application's windows.

The icon name is technically stored in the WM_ICON_NAME property. You can set this property, thereby setting the icon name with XSetWMIconName:

```
void XSetWMIconName(Display* display,
        Window window,
        XTextProperty* text_property)
```

XSetWMIconName sets the icon name to the value in the text_property, which is used to hold most any international name, so it cannot be a simple character pointer. Icon names should be short, since there normally isn't a lot of room to display the icon. Most X applications just use the program name in argv[0], such as xterm. Your window's title can extend a lot longer than the icon name. You can also use the simple, old function, XSetIconName:

```
XSetIconName(Display* display,
    Window window,
    char* icon_name)
```

XSetIconName uses a traditional C string and supports only 8-bit text for the icon name. XSetWMIconName supersedes XSetIconName.

You can retrieve an icon name with XGetWMIconName:

```
Status XGetWMIconName(Display* display,
        Window window,
        XTextProperty* text_property)  /* RETURN */
```

XGetWMIconName returns a nonzero value on success; 0 otherwise. On success, the *value* field of the XTextProperty structure will hold allocated memory. Both XGetWMIconName and XSetWMIconName use text properties.

Text Properties

Your application probably starts with an icon name stored in a text string. You must convert that string to an XTextProperty structure before calling XSetWMIconName.

The XTextProperty structure holds the following fields:

```
typedef struct {
  unsigned char* value;
  Atom           encoding;
  int            format;
  unsigned long  nitems;
} XTextProperty;
```

The *value* field holds the actual text. The *encoding* field holds an atom that describes the encoding used for the text. The *format* holds 8, 16, or 32, depending on whether the text is formatted in 8-bit, 16-bit, or 32-bit characters. The *nitems* field holds the number of items in the *value*.

The XStringListToTextProperty function converts a list of strings to an XTextProperty structure:

```
Status XStringListToTextProperty(char** string_list,
        int number_strings,
        XTextProperty* text_property) /* RETURN */
```

XStringListToTextProperty returns a nonzero value on success, and 0 on failure. Call XFree to free the *text_property* when done.

You can convert a text property back to a string list with XTextPropertyToStringList:

```
Status
XTextPropertyToStringList(XTextProperty* text_property,
        char*** string_list,    /* RETURN */
        int* number_strings)    /* RETURN */
```

XTextPropertyToStringList also returns a nonzero value on success, and 0 on failure. Both of these functions are new in Release 4.

Use XFreeStringList to free the list of strings when done:

```
void XFreeStringList(char** string_list)
```

Icons and X Toolkits

If you use an Xt-based toolkit like Motif or Open Look Intrinsics Toolkit (OLIT), you're spared much of the hassle of the low-level X library functions. To set an icon on a top-level shell widget, set the *iconPixmap* resource. For toolkit programs, you can set the icon-related resources listed in Table 20.3.

Table 20.3 *Icon resources.*

Resource	Type	Default Value
iconic	Boolean	False
iconName	String	NULL
iconNameEncoding	Atom	STRING
iconPixmap	Pixmap	NULL
iconWindow	Window	NULL
iconX	int	-1
iconY	int	-1
initialState	int	NormalState

As you can tell, setting resources in this way cuts down on a lot of code on your part. If set to True, the *iconic* resource overrides the *initialState*.

Color Icons

X basically supports two types of icons: either a monochrome bitmap or an icon window. Some window managers will also support a color pixmap. We've already shown how to set a bitmap for an icon. The ICCCM doesn't support color icons, although some window managers do. If so, you can set the icon pixmap, or the *iconPixmap* resource, to a multiplane pixmap rendered in full color. Unfortunately, you cannot depend on this. In this next section, we'll cover how to create an icon window. An icon window takes more effort to set up, so you need to decide whether the added complexity is worth it.

Icon Windows: Dynamic Icons

An *icon window* is a window your application creates instead of an icon pixmap. With icon pixmaps, the window manager creates the underlying window on the screen for you and paints the pixmap into this window. Thus, using an icon window is a more manual process than using icon pixmaps. By going to a lower level, you get more control over the process.

The icon window gives you three advantages over a bitmap. First, you can change the contents of the icon window to reflect a changing program state—like turning the window green on successful completion of a time-consuming operation, or red if an error occurs. Second, as you guessed, you can display color in the icon window. X only supports monochrome bitmaps should you use an icon bitmap. Some window managers already provide for colored icons, but this is not portable. Third, you can place widgets inside an icon window, although there are some problems.

What does an icon window give you? You get a raw X window, with some limitations. The main limitations are the size—typically very small—and the lack of input.

Icon windows are only supported at the same sizes that X supports icon bitmaps, as we covered above. A good, portable size is 48 x 48 pixels. Your icon windows also will not normally receive keyboard or mouse input from the window manager. While you can put a pushbutton within an icon window, that push button will never get pushed.

The basic idea is simple: you create a window as a child of the root window. This window should be one of the supported icon sizes. You do *not* map this window, as the window manager will take care of this for you. At the appropriate time, that is, when the user iconifies a window, the window manager will automatically unmap your application's top-level window and map the icon window.

When an `Expose` event arrives on the icon window, you should redraw its contents. If you draw colored graphics, you then have a colored icon. Don't expect to get any input to the icon window.

If you don't want to handle `Expose` events on the icon window, you can set the icon window's background pixmap to a colored pixmap.

To create an icon window, you can either create a raw X window, or a popup transient shell widget.

Raw Windows as Icon Windows

The simplest type of icon window can be made by merely creating a raw X window on the display. Make this window a child of the root window and create it with `XCreateWindow`:

```
Display*  display;
```

```
Window    icon;


icon = XCreateWindow(display,
            RootWindow(display,
                DefaultScreen(display) ),
            0, 0, width, height,
            (int) CopyFromParent,        /* depth */
            (unsigned int) InputOutput, /* class */
            (Visual*) CopyFromParent,    /* visual */
            (unsigned long) 0,           /* event mask */
            (XSetWindowAttributes*) NULL);
```

Don't map this window. More formally, XCreateWindow takes the following parameters:

```
Window XCreateWindow(Display* display,
            Window parent,
            int x, int y,
            unsigned int width, unsigned int height,
            unsigned int border_width,
            int depth,
            unsigned int class,
            Visual* visual,
            unsigned long valuemask,
            XSetWindowAttributes *xattributes)
```

Once the window is created, you need to register that window as an icon window. If you use Motif, OLIT, or another toolkit based on the Xt Intrinsics, you can set the *iconWindow* resource on your application's top-level widget, as shown in the following code:

```
Widget  parent;
Window  icon;
```

```
XtVaSetValues(parent,

    XtNiconWindow, icon,

    NULL);
```

N O T E   XtNiconWindow is an Xt constant defined in
<X11/Shell.h>. Motif also defines the constant
XmNiconWindow. Both constants define the string
"iconWindow".

A Function to Create an Icon Window

Here's a C function to create a raw icon window from a widget parent. This
should work with both OLIT and Motif:

```
Window CreateIconWindow(Widget parent,

        int width, int height)


{   /* CreateIconWindow */

    Display*    display;

    Window      window;


    display = XtDisplay(parent);


    window = XCreateWindow(display,

        RootWindow(display,

            DefaultScreen(display) ),

        0, 0, width, height,

        0,                          /* border width */

        (int) CopyFromParent,       /* depth */

        (unsigned int) InputOutput, /* window class */
```

```
            (Visual*) CopyFromParent,    /* visual */

            (unsigned long) 0,           /* event mask */

            (XSetWindowAttributes*) NULL);


    /*
     * Now, set up icon.
     */
    XtVaSetValues(parent,
        XtNiconWindow, window,
        NULL);


    return window;


}    /* CreateIconWindow */
```

What can you do with a raw icon window? Not much, unless you can manage to get events for this window. Most X toolkits, like Motif and OLIT, want you to go through the toolkit's mechanisms to get X events. You probably won't get Expose events that tell you when to draw into the icon window.

Because of this, the easiest thing to do is to set the background pixmap of the window to your desired pixmap, using the XSetWindow-BackgroundPixmap function described in Chapter 17. You can use a colored pixmap. You can also change this pixmap at any time by calling XSetWindowBackgroundPixmap with a new or changed pixmap. Because you probably won't get Expose or other events on this window, you won't know when the window is visible or not. So, just change the pixmap whenever you want and don't depend on it being visible.

The most natural way to create a window and have it be a full part of your toolkit's event loop is to create a window using only toolkit functions. For Motif and OLIT, you can create a transient shell widget.

Icon Windows and Xt

With Xt-based toolkits, you should create a *popup transient shell*. The window that underlies this widget will be the icon window. With a shell widget, we can set the widget's *backgroundPixmap* resource if we want. In this case, we don't have to worry about redrawing any part of the icon window, as the Xt Intrinsics will take care of everything for us.

If you want more control over the icon, you can create a child widget of the transient shell. If you create a transient-shell widget as the icon window, you can then place a child widget into this shell widget, just like for any other shell widget. Of course, the shell widget will be very small, such as 48 x 48 pixels, but you can still place a label widget or a drawing-area widget inside the shell widget. You could create a Motif XmLabel or OLIT StaticText widget to display a text message or colored pixmap (Motif) or XImage (OLIT). If you really went all out, you could create a form widget or other container widget and have thousands of child widgets. Because of the small size of icons, though, this isn't very practical.

We found the best results by creating a drawing-area widget (Motif XmDrawingArea, OLIT DrawArea) child of the transient shell. With this drawing-area widget, we can draw into the window just like we've done in a number of example programs in this book. You could draw a thumbnail reduction of an image file, or your company's logo in its multicolor glory, or whatever you want. This way you can get a simple colored icon and have the displayed icon be part of the toolkit's normal event processing.

Dynamic Icons

Using an icon window also allows you to create dynamic icons. For instance, if the user iconifies a spreadsheet window, the icon could change color when it finished recalculating all the spreadsheet cells. Or the icon could change to a red picture to signal to the user that an error occurred. There are a lot of things you can do to give the user feedback from an icon using a drawing-area widget as part of an icon window.

We've developed a small routine to create a popup transient shell as an icon window, in the function CreateIconWidget, stored in the file iconwid.c, below:

```
/*
 *   iconwid.c
 *   Routine to create an icon window widget.
 */
```

```
#include "xlib.h"
#include <X11/Xutil.h>
#include <X11/Intrinsic.h>
#include <X11/StringDefs.h>
#include <X11/Shell.h>
#include <stdio.h>


/*
 * Note: parent must be realized before calling!
 */
Widget CreateIconWidget(Widget parent,
        int width, int height)


{   /* CreateIconWidget */
    Widget  iconwidget;

    iconwidget = XtVaCreatePopupShell("iconwindow",
                transientShellWidgetClass,
                parent,
                XtNwidth,  (Dimension) width,
                XtNheight, (Dimension) height,
                NULL);


    XtRealizeWidget(iconwidget);

    /*
     * Set up parent's
     * iconWindow resource.
     */
    XtVaSetValues(parent,
        XtNiconWindow, XtWindow(iconwidget),
```

```
        NULL);

    return iconwidget;

}   /* CreateIconWidget */

/* end of file iconwid.c */
```

To create the top-level shell widget, we call `XtVaCreatePopupShell` with a widget class of `transientShellWidgetClass`:

```
Widget XtVaCreatePopupShell(String name,
        WidgetClass widget_class,
        Widget parent,
        ...)
```

End the set of resource/value pairs to `XtVaCreatePopupShell` with a NULL.

The `CreateIconWidget` function is passed the desired icon *width* and *height*. We realize this widget, but don't manage it. Finally, `CreateIconWidget` calls `XtVaSetValues` to change the *iconWindow* resource on the top-level parent widget to be the window associated with the new popup transient-shell widget. This code should work with both Motif and OLIT programs.

You can now create a child of the icon widget and then use that widget to draw whatever you want for the icon. For example, you can create a drawing-area widget child of the icon widget and then draw into the drawing-area widget as we have done in most of the programs so far. Or you could create a label widget or other widget and then display text or a pixmap. You can expect none of these widgets will get mouse or keyboard input.

Turning Windows into Icons

You can turn a window into an icon—if the window manager agrees—with `XIconifyWindow`:

```
Status XIconifyWindow(Display* display,

        Window window,

        int screen_number)
```

`XIconifyWindow` sends a `ClientMessage` event with a `WM_CHANGE_STATE` atom to ask the window manager to turn the window into an icon. `XIconifyWindow` returns a nonzero value if the message was successfully sent to the window manager, and 0 otherwise. Even if the message is sent to the window manager, the window manager has the option of refusing.

Deiconifying a Window

You can forcibly deiconify a window with `XMapRaised`, which we discussed in Chapter 1. With Xt-based programs, you can also call `XtMapWidget` on a widget ID.

Detecting When Windows Are Icons

There's no absolutely certain method for detecting when an application's window has been iconified. There are three main ways you can use to try to track this, though. First, if you use an icon window, you can track `Expose` events on the icon window. Second, you can track the `WM_STATE` property on top-level windows. And third, you can check for `MapNotify` and `UnmapNotify` events.

The last two methods can also be used to detect deiconification as well. If you use an Xt-based toolkit, both of these methods require the use of Xt event-handling functions.

Adding Xt Event Handlers

You can add an Xt event-handling callback function with `XtAddEventHandler`, introduced in Chapter 4:

```
void XtAddEventHandler(Widget widget,

        EventMask eventmask,
```

```
        Boolean nonmaskable,
        XtEventHandler callback;
        XtPointer client_data)
```

The *eventmask* specifies which events your callback is interested in. Some events have no mask, including `ClientMessage`, `GraphicsExpose`, `MappingNotify`, `NoExpose`, `SelectionClear`, `SelectionNotify`, and `SelectionRequest`. If you set the nonmaskable parameter to `True`, your event-handling callback will be called for these events as well.

When one of the events you've registered an interest in happens, your callback function is called with the following parameters:

```
    void callback(Widget widget,
        XtPointer client_data
        XEvent* event,
        Boolean* continue_to_dispatch)
```

Generally, don't mess with the *continue_to_dispatch* parameter.

Detecting Iconification—Method 1

The first method for tracking iconification is to track `Expose` events on the icon window. Every time an `Expose` event arrives on an icon window, you know that the top-level window has been iconified. This sounds easy, especially if you use a drawing-area widget for the icon, because the drawing-area callbacks help you track the events.

The main problem with this approach is that you cannot ever be sure. For example, if your window is iconified but the icon is obscured, your application will not receive an `Expose` event. This method is not reliable.

Detecting Iconification—Method 2

The second method involves tracking `PropertyNotify` events. What we want to do is check for when the `WM_STATE` property on our top-level window is modified. The problem with this approach is that the `WM_STATE` property is intended entirely for window-manager-to-session-manager communication. (Session managers control a user's session and may allow you to restart the session later, restoring the windows to their proper sizes and locations.)

The WM_STATE property holds the window state, one of IconicState, NormalState, or WithdrawnState. This process can fail if the window manager fails to update the WM_STATE property. If you set up an event-handler for this method, you need to pass the PropertyChangeMask event mask to XtAddEventHandler.

Detecting Iconification—Method 3

The third and most effective method is to track UnmapNotify and MapNotify events for top-level shells. When a window is iconified, the application will receive an UnmapNotify event. When the window is later deiconified, the application will receive a MapNotify event.

WARNING

When using this technique, you must keep track of the first time you map a window. Why? Because otherwise you'll erroneously detect the window first coming up with a change from iconic to noniconic state.

To select for MapNotify and UnmapNotify events, you should pass an *eventmask* of StructureNotifyMask:

```
Widget    shell_widget;


XtAddEventHandler(shell_widget,
        StructureNotifyMask,
        False,
        (XtEventHandler) track_icon_status,
        client_data);
```

In the code snippet above, the track_icon_status is the callback function:

```
void track_icon_status(Widget widget,
        XtPointer client_data,
```

```
        XEvent* event,
        Boolean* continue_to_dispatch)


{   /* track_icon_status */


    /* Remove cc warning. */
    if (continue_to_dispatch) {
        /* do nothing... */
    }


    /*
     * We assume the client_data
     * points to any extra data you need.
     */
    if (client_data != (XtPointer) NULL) {
        /* extract data... */
    }


    /*
     * Print out message.
     */
    switch(event->xany.type) {
        case MapNotify:
            printf("Widget %s is Mapped %s\n",
                XtName(widget),
                "(probably deiconified)" );
            break;


        case UnmapNotify:
            printf("Widget %s is Unmapped %s\n",
                XtName(widget),
```

```
                    "(probably iconified)" );
               break;


          default: ; /* ignore the other event types */
     }


}    /* track_icon_status */
```

In the above code, we call the function XtName to get the name of a widget:

```
String XtName(Widget widget)
```

Do *not* free the returned string, as this is owned by the Xt Intrinsics.

We can put together a function, TrackIconStatus, that will track the iconification status of a shell widget. This code is stored in the file iconchk.c:

```
/*
 *   iconchk.c
 *   Tracks iconic status.
 */
#include "xlib.h"
#include <X11/Intrinsic.h>
#include <stdio.h>

/*
 * This function is called to track
 * the change in status for a shell
 * widget. Modify it for whatever
 * you need accomplished when a shell
 * is iconified or deiconified.
 */
```

```
static
void track_icon_status(Widget widget,
      XtPointer client_data,
      XEvent* event,
      Boolean* continue_to_dispatch)


{    /* track_icon_status */

    /* Remove cc warning. */
    if (continue_to_dispatch) {
        /* do nothing... */
    }

    /*
     * We assume the client_data
     * points to any extra data you need.
     */
    if (client_data != (XtPointer) NULL) {
        /* extract data... */
    }

    /*
     * Print out message.
     */
    switch(event->xany.type) {
        case MapNotify:
            printf("Widget %s is Mapped %s\n",
                XtName(widget),
                "(probably deiconified)" );
            break;

        case UnmapNotify:
            printf("Widget %s is Unmapped %s\n",
```

```
                          XtName(widget),
                          "(probably iconified)" );
                  break;


              default: ; /* ignore the other event types */
        }


}    /* track_icon_status */


/*
 * Call this function to set up
 * tracking of iconic status.
 */
void TrackIconStatus(Widget shell_widget,
      XtPointer client_data)


{    /* TrackIconStatus */


      XtAddEventHandler(shell_widget,
          StructureNotifyMask,
          False,
          (XtEventHandler) track_icon_status,
          client_data);


}    /* TrackIconStatus */


/* end of file iconchk.c */
```

For our simple example, we just print out a status change message. Your code, though, could withdraw all other top-level shell widgets when one widget is iconified.

Iconifying a Number of Windows Together

Once you can detect when a window is turned into an icon and you can iconify a window on demand, then you can implement a policy whereby all your application's windows disappear when the main window is iconified. If you attempt this, you're entering a gray area that ought to be under the purview of the window manager. The problem arises when you iconify an application's main window: some window managers will unmap all the application's other top-level windows, such as dialogs. Other window managers don't do this. In addition, dialog windows, with the WM_TRANSIENT_FOR property set (or the *transientFor* resource) are often treated differently from full-fledged top-level shell windows.

You may want to hide all your other application windows when the original top-level application window is iconified. To hide a dialog window, you can call XtUnmanageChild as normal. For a top-level application window, though, you should call XWithdrawWindow:

```
Status XWithdrawWindow(Display* display,
        Window window,
        int screen_number)
```

XWithdrawWindow unmaps the given window and sends a synthetic UnmapNotify event to the window manager. (Actually, the event is sent to the root window, where the window manager presumably picks it up.) This UnmapNotify event informs the window manager about what your application wants.

You can call XWithdrawWindow for each of the windows you want withdrawn from the screen.

A Program to Create a Color Icon

We developed a Motif and OLIT program to show icon windows in action. Each program calls CreateIconWidget, shown earlier under Dynamic Icons, to create an icon window. Both programs also create a drawing-area widget as a child of the icon window widget.

In the drawing-area-widget callback function, we can draw whatever we want, in as many colors as are supported by the system. (Be warned that some window managers may prevent colored icons, but this usually isn't a problem.) In our simple example programs, we just draw a small colored rectangle to show a color icon. The rest, as they say, is up to you.

OLIT Source Code For Color Icons

The OLIT source for the example program is stored in the file o_chap20.c:

```
/*
 *  o_chap20.c
 *  OLIT test program for Chapter 20,
 *  which creates an icon window.
 *
 */
#include "olit.h"
#include <X11/Xutil.h>
#include <X11/Intrinsic.h>
#include <X11/StringDefs.h>
#include <Xol/DrawArea.h>
#include <stdio.h>


/*
 *  Globals
 */
Display*  global_display;
Window    global_window;
GC        global_gc;

extern Widget CreateIconWidget(Widget parent,
        int width, int height);


extern unsigned long AllocNamedColor(Display* display,
```

```
        Colormap colormap,
        char* colorname,
        unsigned long default_color);



extern void TrackIconStatus(Widget shell_widget,
        XtPointer client_data);

void exitCB(Widget widget,
    XtPointer client_data,
    XtPointer call_data)

{   /* exitCB */


    exit(0);


}   /* exitCB */


void drawCB(Widget widget,
    XtPointer client_data,
    XtPointer call_data)

{   /* drawCB */
    OlDrawAreaCallbackStruct*   ptr;


    ptr = (OlDrawAreaCallbackStruct*) call_data;


    if (ptr != NULL) {
        if (ptr->reason == OL_REASON_EXPOSE) {
                if (ptr->event->xexpose.count == 0) {
                    XDrawRectangle(global_display,
```

```
                              global_window, global_gc,
                              10, 10, 10, 10);

                }

            }

        }


    } /* drawCB */


int main(int argc, char** argv)


{   /* main */
    XtAppContext    app_context;
    Display*        display;
    Widget          parent, icon, drawingarea;
    Widget          exitchoice;
    Arg             args[20];
    int             n;
    int             screen;
    unsigned long   fore;


    /* Initialize X toolkit */
    n = 0;


    XtSetArg(args[n], XtNmappedWhenManaged, False); n++;
    XtSetArg(args[n], XtNwidth, 100); n++;
    XtSetArg(args[n], XtNheight, 100); n++;


        parent = XtAppInitialize(&app_context,
            "ProX",                     /* app class */
            (XrmOptionDescList) NULL,    /* options */
            0,                          /* num options */
```

```
                ARGC_PTR &argc, argv,     /* cmd line */
                (String*) NULL,           /* fallback res. */
                args, n);

    /*
     * Create a menu choice to exit the program.
     */
    exitchoice = CreatePushbutton(parent,
                    "exitchoice",
                    (XtCallbackProc) exitCB,
                    (XtPointer) NULL);


    XtRealizeWidget(parent);

    /*
     * A good, portable icon size is 48x48.
     */
    icon = CreateIconWidget(parent, 48, 48);

    /*
     * Create a drawing area
     * into the icon window.
     */
    drawingarea = CreateDrawingArea(icon,
                    "drawingarea",
                    48, 48,
                    (XtCallbackProc) drawCB,
                    (XtPointer) NULL);

    /*
     * Now that we have the windows, we
```

```
 * can get the window IDs.
 */

global_display = XtDisplayOfObject(drawingarea);
global_window  = XtWindowOfObject(drawingarea);
screen         = DefaultScreen(global_display);


/*
 * Create a graphics context.
 */
global_gc = XCreateGC(global_display,
                global_window,
                0L, (XGCValues*) NULL);


fore = AllocNamedColor(global_display,
            DefaultColormap(global_display, screen),
            "red",
            BlackPixel(global_display, screen) );


XSetForeground(global_display, global_gc, fore);

/* Track iconic status. */
TrackIconStatus(parent, (XtPointer) NULL);

/* Map parent */
XtMapWidget(parent);
XtAppMainLoop(app_context);

return 0;

}   /* main */


/* end of file o_chap20.c */
```

Motif Source Code for Color Icons

The Motif source for the example program is stored in the file
`m_chap20.c`:

```
/*
 *   m_chap20.c
 *   Motif test program for Chapter 20,
 *   which creates an icon window.
 */
#include "motif.h"
#include <X11/Xutil.h>
#include <X11/Intrinsic.h>
#include <X11/StringDefs.h>
#include <stdio.h>


/*
 *   Globals
 */
Display*  global_display;
Window    global_window;
GC        global_gc;


extern Widget CreateIconWidget(Widget parent,
        int width, int height);


extern unsigned long AllocNamedColor(Display* display,
    Colormap colormap,
    char* colorname,
    unsigned long default_color);


extern void TrackIconStatus(Widget shell_widget,
```

```
           XtPointer client_data);

void exitCB(Widget widget,
            XtPointer client_data,
            XtPointer call_data)


{       /* exitCB */


        exit(0);


}       /* exitCB */




void drawCB(Widget widget, XtPointer client_data,
            XtPointer call_data)


{   /* drawCB */
    XmDrawingAreaCallbackStruct*     ptr;


    ptr = (XmDrawingAreaCallbackStruct*) call_data;


    if (ptr->reason == XmCR_EXPOSE) {
           if (ptr->event->xexpose.count == 0) {
                XDrawRectangle(global_display,
                        global_window, global_gc,
                        10, 10, 10, 10);
           }
    }


}   /* drawCB */
```

```
int main(int argc, char** argv)

{   /* main */
    XtAppContext    app_context;
    Display*        display;
    Widget          parent, icon, drawingarea;
    Widget          exitchoice;
    Arg             args[20];
    int             n;
    int             screen;
    unsigned long   fore;


    /* Initialize X toolkit */
    n = 0;


    XtSetArg(args[n], XmNmappedWhenManaged, False); n++;
    XtSetArg(args[n], XmNallowResize, True); n++;
    XtSetArg(args[n], XmNwidth, 100); n++;
    XtSetArg(args[n], XmNheight, 100); n++;



    parent = XtAppInitialize(&app_context,
            "ProX",                         /* app class */
            (XrmOptionDescList) NULL,    /* options */
            0,                              /* num options */
            ARGC_PTR &argc, argv,        /* cmd line */
            (String*) NULL,              /* fallback res. */
            args, n);


    /*
     * Create a menu choice to exit the program.
```

```
       */
   exitchoice = CreatePushbutton(parent,
                   "exitchoice",
                   (XtCallbackProc) exitCB,
                   (XtPointer) NULL);


   XtRealizeWidget(parent);

   /*
    * A good, portable icon size is 48x48.
    */
   icon = CreateIconWidget(parent, 48, 48);


   /*
    * Create a drawing area widget
    * as a child of the icon window.
    */
   drawingarea = CreateDrawingArea(icon,
                   "drawingarea",
                   48, 48,
                   (XtCallbackProc) drawCB,
                   (XtPointer) NULL);


   /*
    * Now that we have the windows, we
    * can get the window IDs.
    */

   global_display = XtDisplayOfObject(drawingarea);
   global_window  = XtWindowOfObject(drawingarea);
   screen         = DefaultScreen(global_display);
```

```
/*
 * Create a graphics context.
 */
global_gc = XCreateGC(global_display, global_window,
              0L, (XGCValues*) NULL);


fore = AllocNamedColor(global_display,
          DefaultColormap(global_display, screen),
          "red",
          BlackPixel(global_display, screen) );


XSetForeground(global_display, global_gc, fore);


/* Track iconic status. */
TrackIconStatus(parent, (XtPointer) NULL);


/* Map parent */
XtMapWidget(parent);
XtAppMainLoop(app_context);


return 0;


}   /* main */


/* end of file m_chap20.c */
```

Resource File for the Example Programs

The following resource file works with both the Motif and OLIT example programs. Name this file ProX and place it in your home directory:

```
! ProX

! Resource file for Chapter 20 of

! Professional Graphics

! Programming in the X Window System.

!

! Place this file in your

! home directory.

!

! Generic resources.

!

*background:      #cccccc

*title:           Chap. 20: Icon Windows


!

! Motif resources.

!

!

*fontList: lucidasans-12


*filemenu.labelString:    File

*filemenu.mnemonic:       F


*exitchoice.labelString:  Exit

*exitchoice.mnemonic:     x


! OLIT

*filemenu.label:          File

*exitchoice.label:        Exit


! end of file ProX
```

Running the Example Programs

When you run either of the two example programs and turn the application's window into an icon, you'll see the icon shown in Figure 20.1.

Figure 20.1 *An icon window.*

The program should also print out a message when you iconify or deiconify the top-level window.

Some versions of mwm won't support icon windows on top-level application shell widgets. Other versions of mwm present problems with transient shells and icon windows. The latest versions of mwm should work fine, though.

With olwm, the Open Look window manager, we found that icon windows didn't work as well as under twm or mwm. This is because of the way olwm borders icons.

Summary

An icon is a small window displaying a bitmap image that represents an application's top-level window. Most window managers allow users to iconify windows, that is, turn windows into small icons in a space-saving measure. These icons are then either a default bitmap supplied by the window manager or a bitmap supplied by your application. This chapter covers the process of creating and managing icons.

X Library Functions and Macros Introduced in This Chapter

```
XFreeStringList

XGetIconSizes

XGetWMHints

XGetWMIconName

XIconifyWindow

XSetIconName

XSetWMHints

XSetWMIconName

XStringListToTextProperty

XTextPropertyToStringList

XWithdrawWindow
```

X Toolkit Intrinsics Functions and Macros Introduced in This Chapter

```
XtName
```

Chapter 21

X Images

This chapter covers:

- ✦ Capturing screen images
- ✦ Dealing with problems with obscured areas
- ✦ Using the `XImage` structure
- ✦ Pulling pixels out of an `XImage`
- ✦ Writing an `XImage` back to the screen
- ✦ Creating an `XImage`
- ✦ Manipulating an `XImage`
- ✦ Resizing an `XImage`
- ✦ Strategies for using an `XImage`
- ✦ Drawing fractals to an `XImage`
- ✦ A program that draws fractals using an `XImage`

Images in **X**

Pixmaps, which we've been covering in the last few chapters, can be used for image-processing applications. You can draw to individual dots and you can copy areas of a pixmap to another drawable. Unfortunately, using pixmaps requires you to send every drawing request over the network link to the X server. Since images demand a *large* number of data bytes, this usually results in a far too poor performance to be usable. This is especially true because images often require drawing dot by dot, instead of using the higher-level line, rectangle, arc, and polygon drawing routines. What's needed is a means to create and manipulate images entirely on the client, or application, side. Only when the image is complete do you need to send the image to the X server.

These client-side images are stored in an *XImage structure*, which you can manipulate entirely within your application. The `XImage` structure also largely frees your application from differences in byte ordering between the X server and your application program (remember with X, your applications can compute on a different machine). Even so, the X Window System provides only a primitive means for handling client-side images. And while using pixmaps for all image-handling results in poor performance, most X programmers also feel that an `XImage` provides poor performance as well.

The main use for an `XImage` is to capture images of the screen.

Capturing Screen Images

X allows your application to capture images of the screen, to make *screen dumps*. To capture an area of the screen, call `XGetImage`:

```
XImage* XGetImage(Display* display,
    Drawable drawable,
    int x,
    int y,
    unsigned int width,
    unsigned int height,
    unsigned long planemask,
    int format)
```

According to the designers of X, XGetImage supports only rudimentary screen dumps. XGetImage captures the pixels within a given area of the given *drawable*. The format can be XYPixmap or ZPixmap.

If the format is XYPixmap, then XGetImage only captures the planes stored in the *planemask*. The depth of this image, stored in the XImage structure (presented below under The XImage Structure), will only be the number of requested planes, the number of one bits in the *planemask*. If you pass too many one bits in the *planemask*, then the extra bits are ignored.

If the format is ZPixmap, then XGetImage zeros out the planes that are not in the *planemask*. The depth in this case is the depth of the *drawable*.

XGetImage can generate a BadMatch error if the requested rectangle (bounded by *x*, *y*, *width*, *height*) is not within the given *drawable*. If the *drawable* is a window, then part of the image may be obscured. These areas are undefined in the returned XImage. If you capture the image of a window that encloses other windows, such as the root window, you also capture the pixels of any child window within the area you're capturing. This is to be expected when making screen dumps.

If there's any problem in the call, XGetImage returns NULL. Otherwise, XGetImage returns a pointer to the new XImage. However, if the *drawable* is a window and that window is using backing store, then XGetImage may be able to retrieve the contents of obscured areas of the window.

N O T E There are no X library functions for writing an XImage to disk nor for reading one back in. If you need to do this, we suggest you convert the XImage data to a more common image format, such as TIFF, GIF, or PCX. If this won't work and you still need to write XImage files to disk, take a look at the sources for the xwd (*X window dump*) program that captures screen images and can write the XImage data to disk. The xpr (*X print*) and xwud (*X window undump*) programs can load up XImage data from disk. Both of these programs come with the X release from the X Consortium.

Capturing More Images

Since creating an XImage is a fairly expensive operation, which involves allocating memory dynamically and setting up six function pointers, you may want to reuse an XImage pointer to capture a new part of the screen. To do so, you can call XGetSubImage:

```
XImage* XGetSubImage(Display* display,
    Drawable drawable,
    int x,
    int y,
    unsigned int width,
    unsigned int height,
    unsigned long plane_mask,
    int format,
    XImage* original_image,
    int dest_x,
    int dest_y)
```

You pass your original XImage pointer as the *original_image* parameter. XGetSubImage then returns this same image, but updates the image for the contents of the new area (*x*, *y*, *width*, *height*). The *dest_x* and *dest_y* parameters indicate where in the *original_image* the new pixels should go. The *original_image* must be large enough for the new rectangle or the area will be clipped. XGetSubImage can therefore be used to fill in parts of an XImage with new image data, captured from a *drawable*. You can use XSubImage, covered later (under Extracting an XImage from an XImage), to extract an XImage from an XImage.

Pulling Pixels Out of an XImage

Once you've captured an image with XGetImage or XGetSubImage, you can then extract individual pixel values with XGetPixel, typically defined as a macro in the include file <X11/Xutil.h>:

```
#include <X11/Xutil.h>


unsigned long XGetPixel(XImage* ximage,
                int x, int y)
```

The pixel value returned is a raw colormap index. Since you're not told which colormap the pixel values come from, you have a problem. The general way around this problem is to either query the target drawable's colormap or to capture images only from drawables with a known colormap. Both techniques have drawbacks.

XGetPixel is one of the few X library routines that does not take a Display pointer as a parameter, as XGetPixel operates entirely on data in your application's memory.

N O T E

The XImage Structure

An XImage, obviously enough, is stored in an XImage structure:

```
typedef struct _XImage {
    int             width, height;
    int             xoffset;
    int             format;
    char*           data;
    int             byte_order;
    int             bitmap_unit;
    int             bitmap_bit_order;
    int             bitmap_pad;
    int             depth;
    int             bytes_per_line;
    int             bits_per_pixel;
    unsigned long   red_mask;
    unsigned long   green_mask;
    unsigned long   blue_mask;
    char*           obdata;
    struct funcs {
        struct _XImage *(*create_image)();
```

```
#if NeedFunctionPrototypes
        int (*destroy_image)
            (struct _XImage *);
        unsigned long (*get_pixel)
            (struct _XImage *, int, int);
        int (*put_pixel)
            (struct _XImage *, int, int,
             unsigned long);
        struct _XImage *(*sub_image)
            (struct _XImage *, int, int,
             unsigned int, unsigned int);
        int (*add_pixel)
            (struct _XImage *, long);
#else
        int (*destroy_image)();
        unsigned long (*get_pixel)();
        int (*put_pixel)();
        struct _XImage *(*sub_image)();
        int (*add_pixel)();
#endif
        } f;
} XImage;
```

The XImage structure is intended to hide the details of numerous hardware image formats. The *width* and *height* are, obviously, the size of the image. The *xoffset* field holds the number of pixels to skip at the beginning of each scan line. The *xoffset* field doesn't apply to ZPixmap-formatted images.

The *format* can be one of XYBitmap, XYPixmap, or ZPixmap. This value determines how the data field is interpreted. The *data* field points at the image data. If the *format* is XYBitmap, then the image *data* has one bit per pixel and the *depth* must be one. If the *format* is XYPixmap, then the image *data* is treated as an array of bit-planes. Each bit on a bit-plane is stored in one bit of the image *data*. The color to display is then the pixel value created from all the bits. If the *format* is ZPixmap, then the image data is stored in pixel order. That is, the image *data* holds an array of pixel values.

The *byte_order* is either LSBFirst, least significant byte first, or MSBFirst, most significant byte first. LSBFirst is the format used on the popular Intel 486 architecture. MSBFirst is generally used for most RISC processors, like SPARC.

To determine the image byte order, you can call XImageByteOrder or the macro ImageByteOrder:

```
int ImageByteOrder(Display* display)
```

```
int XImageByteOrder(Display* display)
```

Each returns LSBFirst or MSBFirst.

The *bitmap_bit_order* is also LSBFirst or MSBFirst, here interpreted to mean least or most significant *bit* first. This is the order of bits in each byte. The *bitmap_bit_order* is not applicable to ZPixmap format images. You can call BitmapBitOrder to get the X server's bitmap bit order:

```
int BitmapBitOrder(Display* display)
```

```
int XBitmapBitOrder(Display* display)
```

Both return LSBFirst or MSBFirst.

The *bitmap_unit* defines the number of bits in each section of scanline memory, and can be 8, 16, or 32. There's a macro and function to determine the X server's bitmap unit:

```
int BitmapUnit(Display* display)
```

```
int XBitmapUnit(Display* display)
```

BitmapUnit and XBitmapUnit return 8, 16, or 32.

The `bitmap_pad` defines the needed alignment for the end of each scanline. That is, does each scanline need to be aligned on a 8-bit, 16-bit, or 32-bit boundary? The macro `BitmapPad` and function `XBitmapPad` both return the X server's bitmap pad value:

```
int BitmapPad(Display* display)
```

```
int XBitmapPad(Display* display)
```

For `ZPixmap` images, the `bits_per_pixel` tells you how many bits are required for a given pixel, and can have a value of 1, 4, 8, 16, or 32 (not 2, for some reason).

The `red_mask`, `green_mask`, `blue_mask` come from the visual used to create the image. These fields only have meaning for `DirectColor` or `TrueColor` visuals.

The `depth` field holds the depth of the `XImage`. The `bytes_per_line` field tells you how many bytes to go to get to the next line.

Don't mess with the `obdata` field, nor with any of the function pointers. These function pointers are set up by `XCreateImage` and other `XImage` creation routines to be a set of private functions that manipulate the `XImage`.

Destroying an XImage

When you're done with an `XImage`, free it using the `XDestroyImage` macro:

```
#include <X11/Xutil.h>
```

```
int XDestroyImage(XImage* ximage)
```

`XDestroyImage` calls the `destroy_image` function pointer stored in the `XImage` structure. The return value is supposed to be an int (integer), but is not documented.

WARNING
XDestroyImage frees *both* the XImage pointer and the *data* held within the XImage. If the *data* field of the XImage structure is statically allocated, you need to set the *data* pointer to NULL before calling XDestroyImage.

Writing an XImage Back to the Screen

You can write an XImage back to the screen with XPutImage:

```
XPutImage(Display* display,
    Drawable drawable,
    GC gc,
    XImage* ximage,
    int src_x,
    int src_y,
    int dest_x,
    int dest_y,
    unsigned int width,
    unsigned int height)
```

With XPutImage, you can blast an XImage to any *drawable*, either a pixmap or a window. Normally, your application will create an XImage—either by capturing the bits with XGetImage or XGetSubImage or creating an XImage from scratch with XCreateImage, manipulate the XImage data, and then blast the XImage over the wire to the X server.

Creating an XImage

You can create an XImage from scratch using the tricky function XCreateImage:

```
XImage* XCreateImage(Display* display,
    Visual* visual,
```

```
    unsigned int depth,
    int format,
    int offset,
    char* data,
    unsigned int width,
    unsigned int height,
    int bitmap_pad,
    int bytes_per_line)
```

We say XCreateImage is tricky because of the host of things that can go
wrong when you try to create an XImage from scratch. First of all,
XCreateImage allocates memory for the XImage structure, but not for
the image data. You must allocate the memory for this data yourself. (Even
so, XDestroyImage frees both the XImage structure and the image data.
Go figure.)

XCreateImage creates an XImage under the given *visual*. If you
intend to write this image to a window or pixmap, then you should make
sure this *visual* matches that of the window or pixmap. The *depth*
should also match.

The *format* can be one of XYBitmap, XYPixmap, or ZPixmap. Each
of these formats determines how XCreateImage interprets the image
data stored in the data parameter. The *offset* is the number of pixels to
ignore at the beginning of each scan line. The *height* is the number of
scanlines, while the *width* is the number of pixels across in each image
scanline. The *bitmap_pad* is the required alignment between the bytes in
each scanline; that is, does the image require each scanline to be aligned on
an 8-, 16-, or 32-bit boundary? The *bytes_per_line* is the number of
bytes in a given scanline.

If successful, XCreateImage returns a pointer to the newly allocated
XImage structure. If not successful, XCreateImage returns NULL.

Creating an XImage in Depth

Many of the values required by XCreateImage are hard to determine,
because they're based on central processing unit (CPU) architectures and
what the X server prefers. In a few cases, we can pass 0 or NULL to ask

XCreateImage to figure out the value for itself. In the code below, we show how you can create an XImage:

```
XImage* CreateXImage(Display* display,
    Visual* visual,
    unsigned int depth,
    int width, int height)

{   /* CreateXImage */
    int       format;
    long      number_bytes;
    XImage*   ximage;

    /*
     * Choose format.
     */
    if (depth == 1) {
        format = XYBitmap;
    } else {
        format = ZPixmap;
    }

    /*
     * Create the XImage.
     */
    ximage = XCreateImage(display,
            visual,
            depth,
            format,
            0,                    /* offset */
            (char*) NULL,         /* image data */
```

```
            width, height,
            XBitmapPad(display), /* bitmap pad */
            0);                  /* bytes per line */


    /*
     * Was the image created?
     */
    if (ximage == (XImage *) NULL) {
        return ximage;
    }


    /*
     * Now, we need to allocate the
     * data to hold in the image.
     * XDestroyImage will free this.
     */
    number_bytes = ximage->bytes_per_line *
                    ximage->height;


    ximage->data=(char *) malloc(number_bytes);


    return ximage;


}   /* CreateXImage */
```

The first part of CreateXImage chooses the *format* to use. We've had the best luck with the XYBitmap for depth-1 images and ZPixmap for deeper (color) images.

Once we choose the format, we call XCreateImage. Note how many of the parameters to XCreateImage are passed as 0 or NULL. This is because it's hard to determine the image offset, bytes per line, and bitmap pad. Since we don't need an image offset, we pass 0. We'll let the XImage routines determine the bytes per line, which are necessary when we later allocate memory to hold the image data. For the bitmap pad, we call XBitmapPad.

Determining the Size of the XImage Data

We've had the best luck with the ZPixmap format for color images. The XYBitmap, obviously, works for single-plane bitmaps. To determine the number of bytes to allocate for the XImage data, use the following formula:

```
int     number_bytes;

XImage* ximage;


number_bytes = ximage->bytes_per_line *
               ximage->height;
```

In this manner, you can determine how many bytes to allocate for the XImage data field. We let CreateXImage determine the *bytes_per_line*, because this value depends on the *bitmap_unit*, *bitmap_pad*, *format*, *depth*, and *width*.

Creating an XImage for Widgets

If you're starting out with a widget, you need to query the widget's depth and visual to ensure the image suitably matches the widget. Remember that the *visual* resource normally applies only to shell widgets. Consequently, we can create a wrapper around CreateXImage, above (which is, in turn, a wrapper around XCreateImage), for use with shell widgets. The function CreateXImageFromWidget, below, creates an XImage with the given *width* and *height*, suitable for use with the given shell widget:

```
XImage* CreateXImageFromWidget(Widget shell_widget,
    int width, int height)


{   /* CreateXImageFromWidget */
```

```
Visual*     visual;
int         depth;
XImage*     ximage;
Display*    display;

/*
 * Query depth and visual.
 */
XtVaGetValues(shell_widget,
    XtNdepth,   &depth,
    XtNvisual,  &visual,
    NULL);

/*
 * Create the image.
 */
display = XtDisplay(shell_widget);

ximage = CreateXImage(display,
            visual,
            depth,
            width, height);

/* Debugging info */
PrintImage(ximage);

return ximage;

}   /* CreateXImageFromWidget */
```

We pass a shell widget to `CreateXImageFromWidget` to ensure you get
the proper *visual* resource, although this resource should be inherited by
all child widgets.

Extracting an XImage from an XImage

To extract a smaller part of an existing `XImage`, call the `XSubImage` macro:

```
#include <X11/Xutil.h>


XImage* XSubImage(XImage* ximage,
        int x, int y,
        unsigned int width,
        unsigned int height)
```

`XSubImage` returns a pointer to a new `XImage` structure, allocated dynamically.

Manipulating an XImage

You can manipulate an `XImage` with `XPutPixel` and `XAddPixel`. We know it's very tempting to try to manipulate the *data* field of the `XImage` structure directly, but you really shouldn't. The performance of `XPutPixel` leaves a lot to be desired, as you'll soon discover if you do a lot of image processing using an `XImage`, but the only truly portable way to manipulate an `XImage` is to go through `XPutPixel` and `XAddPixel`.

`XPutPixel` stores a given *color_pixel* value at the given *x, y* location within the `XImage`. An `XImage`, like a window, has its origin in the upper left corner:

```
#include <X11/Xutil.h>


int XPutPixel(XImage* ximage,
      int x, int y,
      unsigned long color_pixel)
```

`XAddPixel` adds the constant value to every pixel in the given `XImage`:

```
#include <X11/Xutil.h>

int XAddPixel(XImage* ximage,
        unsigned long value)
```

XAddPixel is useful if you want to lighten or darken an XImage.

Resizing an XImage

If you're writing an image-processing application, you may want to use an XImage to hold an image while your program generates the full picture. Once the picture is complete, you can then send the XImage to a window or pixmap in the X server with XPutImage. If you follow this model, though, you need to deal with unexpected window resizes. Since the user should be able to resize application windows at any time, your applications must stand ready to deal with a new window size. One way to deal with a new size is to create a new XImage with the new size. You're then left with the problem of copying over the old XImage data and destroying the old XImage.

Because this is a common situation, we created the following routine, CopyImage. CopyImage creates a new XImage to the proper size and depth and then copies over all the old data into the new XImage. Finally, it's up to your application to free the old XImage. The code for CopyImage follows:

```
XImage* CopyImage(Display* display,
    Visual* visual,
    XImage* src_image,
    int new_width,
    int new_height)

{   /* CopyImage */
    XImage*        ximage;
    int            x, y;
```

```
int            x_max, y_max;
unsigned long  color;


/*
 * Create new image.
 */
ximage = CreateXImage(display,
           visual,
           src_image->depth,
           new_width, new_height);


/*
 * Copy over old pixels.
 */
y_max = src_image->height;


if (y_max > new_height) {
    y_max = new_height;
}


x_max = src_image->width;


if (x_max > new_width) {
    x_max = new_width;
}


for (y = 0; y < y_max; y++) {
    for (x = 0; x < x_max; x++) {

        color = XGetPixel(src_image, x, y);
```

```
            XPutPixel(ximage, x, y, color);

        }

    }


    return ximage;


}   /* CopyImage */
```

Source Code for XImage Utility Functions

The XImage utility functions described above, as well as the debugging
routine PrintImage, are stored in the file ximage.c:

```
/*
 *  ximage.c
 *  XImage routines.
 */
#include "xlib.h"
#include <X11/Intrinsic.h>
#include <X11/StringDefs.h>
#include <X11/Shell.h>
#include <stdio.h>


/*
 * Debugging/query routine.
 */
void PrintImage(XImage* ximage)


{   /* PrintImage */


    printf("\nXImage size is %d by %d pixels, depth %d.\n",
```

```
            ximage->width, ximage->height,
            ximage->depth);

    printf("  Bytes per line:  \t %d.\n",
            ximage->bytes_per_line);

    printf("  Bits per pixel:  \t %d (ZPixmap).\n",
            ximage->bits_per_pixel);

    printf("  Offset: \t\t %d\n", ximage->xoffset);

    printf("  Bitmap unit:\t\t %d\n",
            ximage->bitmap_unit);

    if (ximage->bitmap_bit_order == MSBFirst) {
        printf("  Bitmap bit order is \t MSBFirst.\n");
    } else {
        printf("  Bitmap bit order is \t LSBFirst.\n");
    }

    if (ximage->byte_order == MSBFirst) {
        printf("  Byte order is \t MSBFirst.\n");
    } else {
        printf("  Byte order is \t LSBFirst.\n");
    }

    printf("  Format:\t ");

    switch (ximage->format) {
        case XYBitmap:
            printf("\t XYBitmap.\n"); break;
```

```
        case XYPixmap:
            printf(" \t XYPixmap.\n"); break;
        case ZPixmap:
            printf(" \t ZPixmap.\n"); break;
        default:
            printf(" \t Unknown.\n");
    }


    printf("  Masks: \t\t red 0x%x, ",
        ximage->red_mask);

    printf("green 0x%x, blue 0x%x.\n\n",
        ximage->green_mask,
        ximage->blue_mask);

}   /* PrintImage */


/*
 * Creates an XImage from
 * scratch and allocates
 * the data field.
 */
XImage* CreateXImage(Display* display,
    Visual* visual,
    unsigned int depth,
    int width, int height)


{   /* CreateXImage */
    int      format;
    long     number_bytes;
    XImage*  ximage;
```

```
/*
 * Choose format.
 */
if (depth == 1) {
    format = XYBitmap;
} else {
    format = ZPixmap;
}


/*
 * Create the XImage.
 */
ximage = XCreateImage(display,
        visual,
        depth,
        format,
        0,                      /* offset */
        (char*) NULL,           /* image data */
        width, height,
        XBitmapPad(display),    /* bitmap pad */
        0);                     /* bytes per line */

/*
 * Was the image created?
 */
if (ximage == (XImage *) NULL) {
    return ximage;
}


/*
```

```
         * Now, we need to allocate the
         * data to hold in the image.
         * XDestroyImage will free this.
         */
        number_bytes = ximage->bytes_per_line *
                       ximage->height;

        ximage->data=(char *) malloc(number_bytes);

        return ximage;

}   /* CreateXImage */


/*
 * Utility function, eases means to
 * create XImage.
 */
XImage* CreateXImageFromWidget(Widget shell_widget,
     int width, int height)

{   /* CreateXImageFromWidget */
    Visual*     visual;
    int         depth;
    XImage*     ximage;
    Display*    display;

    /*
     * Query depth and visual.
     */
    XtVaGetValues(shell_widget,
        XtNdepth,   &depth,
```

```
        XtNvisual, &visual,
        NULL);

    /*
     * Create the image.
     */
    display = XtDisplay(shell_widget);

    ximage = CreateXImage(display,
            visual,
            depth,
            width, height);

    /* Debugging info */
    PrintImage(ximage);

    return ximage;

}    /* CreateXImageFromWidget */

/*
 * Creates an image of a new size and
 * copies the necessary pixels from the
 * old image to the new one.
 */

XImage* CopyImage(Display* display,
    Visual* visual,
    XImage* src_image,
    int new_width,
    int new_height)
```

```
{   /* CopyImage */
    XImage*         ximage;
    int             x, y;
    int             x_max, y_max;
    unsigned long   color;

    /*
     * Create new image.
     */
    ximage = CreateXImage(display,
                visual,
                src_image->depth,
                new_width, new_height);

    /*
     * Copy over old pixels.
     */
    y_max = src_image->height;

    if (y_max > new_height) {
        y_max = new_height;
    }

    x_max = src_image->width;

    if (x_max > new_width) {
        x_max = new_width;
    }

    for (y = 0; y < y_max; y++) {
```

```
    for (x = 0; x < x_max; x++) {

        color = XGetPixel(src_image, x, y);

        XPutPixel(ximage, x, y, color);
    }
  }

  return ximage;

}   /* CopyImage */


/* end of file ximage.c */
```

Strategies for Using an XImage

There are two main reasons you may want to use an `XImage`. The first is that you may need to capture the pixels in a window and export them for another use—create a screen dump, for instance. Second, you can use an `XImage` as a client-side image format, where you can write data into the image and then blast it to a drawable with one X operation.

For example, if you want to draw a complex image, like that of the *Mandelbrot set* (named after Benoit Mandelbrot and commonly used in fractal software), you could draw the Mandelbrot set to an `XImage`. Once completed with this expensive operation, you can display the `XImage` using `XPutImage`.

Most real applications don't draw fractal images, but the concepts are the same for geographic information systems or with the mythical paper-less office, which uses imaging software to reproduce documents that were formerly on paper. The Mandelbrot set requires that you build an image dot by dot, which is the worst case for most image processing. To show how to use an `XImage`, though, we present a simple and fun example using the Mandelbrot set.

Using an XImage to Draw Fractal Images

We can draw the Mandelbrot set dot by dot using `XPutPixel` with an `XImage` created via `XCreateImage`. Before we draw anything, though, we should explain what fractals are. Fractals deal with objects in fractional dimensions (shortened to fractal dimensions) between two and three dimensions. These objects are usually self-reflective (although the Mandelbrot set isn't) and you can model objects in fractal space using iterative equations where the output of one iteration is fed back as the input to the next iteration. This is a *feedback loop*.

The famous Mandelbrot set is based in the *imaginary plane*. The Mandelbrot set uses imaginary or *complex numbers*, each of which has two components: a real part and an imaginary part. The imaginary part is multiplied by the square root of –1, the imaginary number. Thus, a complex or imaginary number has the format:

a + bi

where *a* is the real component, *b* is the imaginary component, and *i* is the square root of –1. To draw such a number in 2-dimensional space (like your computer screen), we can tie the real component to the x axis and the imaginary component to the y axis. Our basic complex or imaginary number can now be treated as having the format:

x + yi

To plot 5.0 + 6.0*i*, we'd place a point at *x* = 5.0 and *y* = 6.0. Note that *x* and *y* are both floating-point numbers. When graphing, we ignore *i* itself.

Fractal Math

We need imaginary numbers to generate the Mandelbrot set. The key to the Mandelbrot set and fractals in general is the concept of a feedback loop. You start with an equation. The result of the equation, the output, is fed to the next iteration of the equation as input. For the examples in this chapter, we generate the Mandelbrot set using the following equation:

$z = z^2 + c$

(Doug Young uses the equation $z = (z + c) * (z + c)$ in The X Window System: Programming and Applications with Xt. There are a number of other equations to view fractal images.)

Values z and c are complex numbers. We can rewrite the equation in a more C-oriented format as follows:

```
new_z = (z * z) + c
```

where *new_z, z,* and *c* are all complex numbers. The right-hand side of the equation expands out when we take into account the fact that each element is a complex number. We use *new_zx* for the x-axis component of *new_z,* and *new_zy* for the y-axis component (the imaginary part) of new_z. We use x and y for the components because of the implied connection to computer graphics. Similarly, we split up *c* into *cx* and *cy* and *z* (the old *z*) into *zx* and *zy*. With all this expansion, our equations become:

```
float      new_x, new_y;
float      zx, zy;
float      cx, cy;


new_zx = zx * zx - zy * zy + cx;


new_zy = zx * zy + zy * zx + cy;
```

We can generate a new x and y component (real and imaginary, respectively) of *z* with each iteration of the above equation.

Iterating the Fractal Equation

Each iteration of the equation generates a new value for *z*. The value *z* starts at zero (0.0, 0.0). It starts at (0.0, 0.0) because this is the *critical point* for our fractal equation. Different equations require different critical points. In addition, to optimize performance, you can start by setting $z = c$, instead of $z = 0$. Why? Because if we set *zx* and *zy* to 0.0, our equations become the following:

```
new_x = 0.0 * 0.0 - 0.0 * 0.0 + cx;
```

```
new_y = 0.0 * 0.0 + 0.0 * 0.0 + cy;
```

This is the same as:

```
new_x = cx;
```

```
new_y = cy;
```

The value *c* remains constant through all the iterations. You set *c* to the *x*, *y* location normalized to the location within the complex plane:

```
float     cx, cy;
float     start_x;
float     start_y;
float     x_width;
float     x_height;
int       px, py;

cx = start_x + (float) px /
       (float) pixel_width * x_width;

cy = start_y + (float) py /
       (float) pixel_height * y_height;
```

In the above code, the *px, py* is your *x, y* location in traditional pixels, that is, a location within a window or XImage. We need to normalize this location onto some area of the complex plane that we consider interesting.

NOTE

We consider the area bounded by –1.5, –1.2, 0.5, 1.2 to be interesting. You can later zoom in or zoom out by adjusting this area. The *start_x* is set to –1.5 and is the starting *x* coordinate in the complex plane. The *start_y* is similarly set to –1.2 and is the starting *y* coordinate in the complex plane. The *x_width* is the width of the area in the complex plane that we're interested in, 2.0 in this case. The *y_height* is the height of the area in the complex plane that we're interested in, 2.4 in this case.

Once we calculate *cx* and *cy*, these values remain constant for all iterations of the fractal equation for a given location *px*, *py*.

Generating the Mandelbrot Set

To generate the Mandelbrot set, you apply the above equation to every *x*, *y* location in the window (or XImage or area for which you are generating the set). For each *x*, *y* point, you first calculate the normalized coordinates in the complex plane, as we described above. This is the value of *c* (really *cx*, *cy*). Then, you iterate through the above fractal equation, starting *z* at (0.0, 0.0), or setting *z* to *c* with our performance improvement, until you come to a stopping point.

The idea is to iterate the fractal equation until it is either known to be in the Mandelbrot set or is known to leave the allowed values for the Mandelbrot set. That is, iterate until we're certain of where the point lands. If the given point is within the Mandelbrot set, we color the *x*, *y* location with a given color. If the point goes out of the Mandelbrot set, we can choose a color based on the number of iterations it took for the point to leave the Mandelbrot set.

How do we know when to stop iterating? Well, we cheat. For the above fractal equation, we found that about 20 iterations is fine for telling whether the given point will remain within the Mandelbrot set. We also know that if *z* stays within the proper region, it will stay within the Mandelbrot set. If *z* strays from this region, (–2.0, –2.0, 2.0, 2.0), then the point has strayed from the Mandelbrot set. If *z* leaves the region of (–2.0, –2.0, 2.0, 2.0), then *z* will shoot off into infinity, given enough iterations. We can square *zx* and *zy* and then simply compare if the sum of the two is larger than 4.0. For finer detail, but slower performance, you can try 100 iterations. Go to as many iterations as you prefer.

Julia Sets

Julia sets are closely related to the Mandelbrot sets. To generate a Julia set, you keep *z* constant and modify *c*, while iterating through the equation. The Mandelbrot set, on the other hand, keeps *c* constant and modifies *z*. Both sets use the same equation:

$$z = z^2 + c$$

Graphing the Mandelbrot Set

How do you apply this to the X Window System? With graphics, we're not concerned so much whether the point is within the Mandelbrot set. Instead, we want to know what color to draw the point with. We take in an array of colors and then use color zero for the Mandelbrot set color. We can use modula division to determine the color for the points that leave the Mandelbrot set.

The following function, `ComputeMandelPoint`, shows how to generate the proper color for a given *px, py,* pixel location:

```
/*
 * Interested location in
 * the complex plane.
 */
float   start_x  = -1.5;
float   start_y  = -1.2;
float   x_width  = 2.0;
float   y_height = 2.4;


/*
 * Escape value to check against.
 */
#define MAX_VALUE    4.0


#define MAX_ITERATIONS   20


/*
 * Returns the color to shade the
 * given point, using the Mandelbrot
 * set computations.
 */
unsigned long ComputeMandelPoint(int px, int py,
```

```
        int max_iterations,
        unsigned long* colors,
        int number_colors,
        int width, int height)


{       /* ComputeMandelPoint */
        int     i;
        int     color_index;
        float   new_x, new_y;
        float   zx, zy, cx, cy;


        /*
         * X is the real axis.
         * Y is the imaginary axis.
         */
        cx = start_x + (float) px / (float) width  * x_width;
        cy = start_y + (float) py / (float) height * y_height;


        /* Start at Z at X, Y (0.0, 0.0) */
        zx = 0.0;
        zy = 0.0;


        /* Or, we can cheat and start with z = c. */
        zx = cx;
        zy = cy;


        /*
         * Compute z = z * z + c
         * for the given number of iterations.
         */
        for (i = 0; i < max_iterations; i++) {
```

```
        new_x = zx * zx - zy * zy + cx;
        new_y = zx * zy + zy * zx + cy;


        zx = new_x;
        zy = new_y;


        /*
         * Check if we've gone out
         * of the Mandelbrot set.
         */
        if ((zx * zx + zy * zy) > MAX_VALUE) {

            color_index = i % number_colors;

            return colors[color_index];
        }
    }


    /*
     * If you get to here, then we have
     * a point in the Mandelbrot set.
     */
    return colors[0];


}    /* ComputeMandelPoint */
```

Note how ComputeMandelPoint determines the color for a given pixel location. If the point is within the Mandelbrot set, ComputeMandelPoint uses *colors[0]*. If the point strays from the Mandelbrot set, ComputeMandelPoint uses (*i % number_colors*), where *i* is the number of iterations it took to stray from the Mandelbrot set, and *number_colors* is, obviously, the number of colors in the colors array. This leads to a pleasing picture with alternating bands of color.

The `ComputeMandelPoint` code is really very simple. The main problem is that we must call the `ComputeMandelPoint` function for every point we want to draw. This may take a long time, especially for larger images. We do this from the `ComputeMandel` function, below:

```
void ComputeMandel(XImage* ximage,
    unsigned long* colors,
    int number_colors)


{   /* ComputeMandel */
    int           x, y;
    unsigned long color;

    if (ximage == (XImage*) NULL) {
        return;
    }

    if ((ximage->width < 2) || (ximage->height < 2)) {
        return;
    }

    for (y = 0; y < ximage->height; y++) {
        for (x = 0; x < ximage->width; x++) {

            color = ComputeMandelPoint(x, y,
                    MAX_ITERATIONS,
                    colors, number_colors,
                    ximage->width, ximage->height);

            (void) XPutPixel(ximage, x, y, color);
```

```
        }

        /*
         * Print out info to tell the user
         * the program hasn't stopped.
         */
        if ((y % 20) == 0) {
            printf("Finished row %d.\n", y);
        }

    }


}   /* ComputeMandel */
```

ComputeMandel takes in an XImage pointer. The fractal image will be drawn into this XImagee, one pixel at a time, using XPutPixel. ComputeMandel prints out a message every 20 scanline rows. This is to provide some feedback to the user that the program is still working. In your programs, you could use the busy cursors introduced in Chapter 19 or some other means to let the user know that the program is still on track. Using this algorithm is painfully slow on a low end system, such as a 486 ISA workstation. If you use numbers of type double instead of float, you'll also see a further performance degradation.

ComputeMandel just fills in an XImage. It's up to another routine (see the file chap21.c, below, under Generic Code for the Fractal Program) to blast the completed image to a window, using XPutImage.

Drawing Fractal Pictures into an XImage

The code for the ComputeMandelPoint and ComputeMandel routines is stored in the file fractal.c:

```
/*
 *  fractal.c
 *  mandelbrot set routines.
 */
```

```
#include "xlib.h"
#include <stdio.h>

/*
 * Globals for bounding area
 * in the complex plane. A good
 * overall area is
 * (-1.5, -1.0) with a width
 * and height of 2.0.
 */
float  start_x  = -1.5;
float  start_y  = -1.2;
float  x_width  = 2.0;
float  y_height = 2.4;


/*
 * Escape value to check against.
 */
#define MAX_VALUE   4.0


#define MAX_ITERATIONS  20


/*
 * Returns the color to shade the
 * given point, using the Mandelbrot
 * set computations.
 */
unsigned long ComputeMandelPoint(int px, int py,
    int max_iterations,
    unsigned long* colors,
    int number_colors,
```

```
                int width, int height)


{      /* ComputeMandelPoint */
       int    i;
       int    color_index;
       float  new_x, new_y;
       float  zx, zy, cx, cy;


       /*
        * X is the real axis.
        * Y is the imaginary axis.
        */
       cx = start_x + (float) px / (float) width  * x_width;
       cy = start_y + (float) py / (float) height * y_height;


       /* Start at Z at X, Y (0.0, 0.0) */
       zx = 0.0;
       zy = 0.0;


       /* Or, we can cheat and start with z = c. */
       zx = cx;
       zy = cy;


       /*
        * Compute z = z * z + c
        * for the given number of iterations.
        */
       for (i = 0; i < max_iterations; i++) {

           new_x = zx * zx - zy * zy + cx;
           new_y = zx * zy + zy * zx + cy;
```

```
        zx = new_x;
        zy = new_y;

        /*
         * Check if we've gone out
         * of the Mandelbrot set.
         */
        if ((zx * zx + zy * zy) > MAX_VALUE) {

            color_index = i % number_colors;

            return colors[color_index];
        }
    }

    /*
     * If you get to here, then we have
     * a point in the Mandelbrot set.
     */
    return colors[0];

}   /* ComputeMandelPoint */

/*
 * Fills an XImage with the
 * contents of a Mandelbrot set.
 */
void ComputeMandel(XImage* ximage,
    unsigned long* colors,
    int number_colors)
```

```
{   /* ComputeMandel */
    int           x, y;
    unsigned long color;

    if (ximage == (XImage*) NULL) {
        return;
    }

    if ((ximage->width < 2) || (ximage->height < 2)) {
        return;
    }

    for (y = 0; y < ximage->height; y++) {
        for (x = 0; x < ximage->width; x++) {

            color = ComputeMandelPoint(x, y,
                    MAX_ITERATIONS,
                    colors, number_colors,
                    ximage->width, ximage->height);

            (void) XPutPixel(ximage, x, y, color);
        }

        /*
         * Print out info to tell the user
         * the program hasn't stopped.
         */
        if ((y % 20) == 0) {
            printf("Finished row %d.\n", y);
        }
```

```
    }


}    /* ComputeMandel */


/* end of file fractal.c */
```

A Program to Draws Fractals Using an XImage

Bringing us back to this chapter's main topic, the XImage, we can create a program to draw the Mandelbrot set into an XImage using the code from fractal.c, as well as ximage.c, both presented above.

Our simple program places a fractal image into an XImage and then displays that XImage into a drawing area widget. When the widget changes size, we create a new XImage and copy the old fractal data over from the old image.

While there are many areas where you can enhance our example program, the basic idea is to show how to use an XImage in your code.

Generic Code for the Fractal Program

The MakeImage function, below, creates the proper XImage for a shell widget's visual. MakeImage also allocates a number of colors for use with the fractal image. The static array of text strings, *color_names*, holds some arbitrary color names for drawing the fractal image. You can change these color names to colors you like better. The calling program must allocate an array, *colors*, to color the color values, and also pass the number of elements in this array in the *num_colors* parameter.

The MakeImage function, generic to most Xt-based toolkits, is stored in the file chap21.c:

```
/*
 *    chap21.c
 *    Generic code for Chapter 21.
```

```
    */
#include "xlib.h"
#include <X11/Intrinsic.h>
#include <X11/StringDefs.h>

extern unsigned long AllocNamedColor(Display* display,
    Colormap colormap,
    char* colorname,
    unsigned long default_color);

extern XImage* CreateXImageFromWidget(Widget shell_widget,
        int width, int height);

extern void ComputeMandel(XImage* ximage,
        unsigned long* colors,
        int number_colors);

/*
 * Global color name array.
 */
#define MAX_COLORS   17

static char* color_names[MAX_COLORS] = {
    "black",
    "orchid",
    "white",
    "seagreen",
    "thistle",
    "tan",
    "red",
    "blue",
```

```
        "beige",
        "palegreen",
        "thistle",
        "orangered",
        "lightgray",
        "wheat",
        "darkorange",
        "tomato",
        "slateblue"
};


/*
 * Returns XImage filled with
 * a fractal picture.
 */


XImage* MakeImage(Widget widget,
        int width, int height,
        unsigned long* colors,
        int num_colors)


{    /* MakeImage */
    Colormap        colormap;
    unsigned long   black;
    Display*        display;
    XImage*         ximage;
    int             i, max;

    /*
     * Allocate colors
     */
```

```
XtVaGetValues(widget,
    XtNcolormap, &colormap,
    NULL);


display = XtDisplay(widget);


black = BlackPixel(display,
        DefaultScreen(display) );


max = num_colors;


if (max > MAX_COLORS) {
    max = MAX_COLORS;
}


for (i = 0; i < max; i++) {
    colors[i] = AllocNamedColor(display,
                colormap,
                color_names[i],
                black);
}


/*
 * Create XImage.
 */
ximage = CreateXImageFromWidget(widget,
        width, height);


/*
 * Compute Mandelbrot image.
 */
```

```
    if (ximage != (XImage*) NULL) {

        ComputeMandel(ximage,
            colors,
            num_colors);

    }

    return ximage;

}   /* MakeImage */


/* end of file chap21.c */
```

A Motif Program for Drawing Fractal Images

The important part of the Motif program below is in the drawing-area call-back function, drawCB. The drawCB function handles two tasks: redrawing the drawing-area widget and dealing with a new window size.

To redraw the widget, drawCB calls XPutImage with each Expose event, passing the exposed area as the area from which to paint the XImage.

To handle a new window size, drawCB calls CopyImage—but only if necessary. If our window shrinks, there's no need to allocate a new XImage. If the window grows, though, we have to create a new XImage, which is handled by the utility function CopyImage. Note that our callback, drawCB, may get executed before the widget's window is actually created. Because of this, we check if the global_ximage XImage pointer is NULL before making any calls with the XImage.

The Motif code for the fractal program is stored in the file m_chap21.c:

```
/*
 *  m_chap21.c
```

```
*    Motif test program for Chapter 21,
*    which creates an XImage.
*/
#include "motif.h"
#include <X11/Xutil.h>
#include <stdio.h>


/*
 *   Globals
 */
#define NUM_COLORS   12

Display*       global_display;
Window         global_window;
GC             global_gc;
int            global_width, global_height;
XImage*        global_ximage;
unsigned long global_colors[NUM_COLORS+1];

extern void ComputeMandel(XImage* ximage,
          unsigned long* colors,
          int number_colors);

extern XImage* MakeImage(Widget widget,
      int width, int height,
      unsigned long* colors,
      int num_colors);

extern XImage* CopyImage(Display* display,
      Visual* visual,
      XImage* src_image,
```

```
        int new_width,
        int new_height);

void drawCB(Widget widget,
    XtPointer client_data,
    XtPointer call_data)

{   /* drawCB */
    XmDrawingAreaCallbackStruct*  ptr;
    Dimension                     width, height;
    XImage*                       new_ximage;

    ptr = (XmDrawingAreaCallbackStruct*) call_data;

    if (ptr->reason == XmCR_EXPOSE) {
            if (global_ximage != (XImage*) NULL) {
                XPutImage(global_display,
                    global_window,
                    global_gc,
                    global_ximage,
                    ptr->event->xexpose.x,  /* src */
                    ptr->event->xexpose.y,  /* src */
                    ptr->event->xexpose.x,  /* dest */
                    ptr->event->xexpose.y,  /* dest */
                    ptr->event->xexpose.width,
                    ptr->event->xexpose.height);
        }
    }

    if (ptr->reason == XmCR_RESIZE) {
        /*
```

```
 * Ignore all resize events that
 * arrive before we create the
 * original XImage.
 */
if (global_ximage == (XImage*) NULL) {
    return;
}


/*
 * Get new width and height.
 */
XtVaGetValues(widget,
    XmNwidth,  &width,
    XmNheight, &height,
    NULL);


/*
 * Only make a new image if
 * the window is larger.
 */
if (( (int) width  <= global_width) &&
    ( (int) height <= global_height)) {
    /* Store new sizes */
    global_width  = width;
    global_height = height;

    return;
}

/* Store new sizes */
global_width  = width;
```

```
global_height = height;

/*
 * Make new image. We cheat. We should
 * either query the visual resource or
 * pass a nondefault visual as the
 * client_data.
 */
new_ximage = CopyImage(global_display,
                 DefaultVisual(global_display,
                    DefaultScreen(global_display) ),
                 global_ximage,
                 global_width,
                 global_height);

if (new_ximage != (XImage*) NULL) {

    /* Free old XImage */
    XDestroyImage(global_ximage);

    global_ximage = new_ximage;

    ComputeMandel(global_ximage,
        global_colors, NUM_COLORS);

    XClearWindow(global_display,
        global_window);

    XPutImage(global_display,
        global_window,
        global_gc,
```

```
                        global_ximage,
                        0, 0,
                        0, 0,
                        global_width,
                        global_height);
            }
        }

    }   /* drawCB */


int main(int argc, char** argv)

{   /* main */
    XtAppContext    app_context;
    Display*        display;
    Widget          parent, drawingarea;
    Widget          mainwindow;
    Widget          menubar;
    Widget          filemenu;
    Widget          exitchoice;
    Arg             args[20];
    int             n;

    /* Set size of our image. */
    global_width  = 350;
    global_height = 300;

    /* Initialize X toolkit */
    n = 0;

    XtSetArg(args[n], XmNmappedWhenManaged, False); n++;
```

```
XtSetArg(args[n], XmNallowResize, True); n++;
XtSetArg(args[n], XmNwidth, global_width); n++;
XtSetArg(args[n], XmNheight, global_height + 40); n++;


parent = XtAppInitialize(&app_context,
        "ProX",                        /* app class */
        (XrmOptionDescList) NULL,      /* options */
        0,                             /* num options */
        ARGC_PTR &argc, argv,          /* cmd line */
        (String*) NULL,                /* fallback res. */
        args, n);

/* Create Main Window. */
mainwindow = CreateMainWindow(parent, "main");

/* Create menu bar. */
menubar = CreateMenuBar(mainwindow, "menubar");

/* Create the file menu. */
filemenu = CreateMenu(menubar, "filemenu");

/* Create a menu choice to exit program. */
exitchoice = CreateExitChoice(filemenu,
                "exitchoice");

/* Create a drawing area widget. */
drawingarea = CreateDrawingArea(mainwindow,
                "drawingarea",
                global_width, global_height,
                (XtCallbackProc) drawCB,
```

```
                (XtPointer) NULL);


SetMainAreas(mainwindow,
            menubar,
            drawingarea);


XtRealizeWidget(parent);


/*
 * Now that we have the windows, we
 * can get the window IDs.
 */


global_display = XtDisplay(drawingarea);
global_window  = XtWindow(drawingarea);


/*
 * Create a graphics context.
 */
global_gc = XCreateGC(global_display,
               global_window,
               OL, (XGCValues*) NULL);


/*
 * Create an XImage.
 */
global_ximage = MakeImage(parent,
               global_width,
               global_height,
               global_colors,
               NUM_COLORS);
```

```
      /* Map parent */
      XtMapWidget(parent);
      XtAppMainLoop(app_context);


      return 0;


}    /* main */


/* end of file m_chap21.c */
```

An OLIT Program for Drawing Fractal Images

The Open Look Intrinsics Toolkit (OLIT) program acts just like the Motif program, above. Like the Motif program, it also performs most of the work in the drawCB function. The OLIT-specific code is stored in the file o_chap21.c:

```
/*
 *  o_chap21.c
 *  OLIT test program for Chapter 21,
 *  which creates an XImage.
 */
#include "olit.h"
#include <X11/Xutil.h>
#include <Xol/DrawArea.h>
#include <stdio.h>


/*
 *  Globals
 */
#define NUM_COLORS  12
```

```
Display*        global_display;
Window          global_window;
GC              global_gc;
int             global_width, global_height;
XImage*         global_ximage;
unsigned long global_colors[NUM_COLORS+1];

extern void ComputeMandel(XImage* ximage,
        unsigned long* colors,
        int number_colors);

extern XImage* MakeImage(Widget widget,
    int width, int height,
    unsigned long* colors,
    int num_colors);

extern XImage* CopyImage(Display* display,
        Visual* visual,
        XImage* src_image,
        int new_width,
        int new_height);

void drawCB(Widget widget,
    XtPointer client_data,
    XtPointer call_data)

{   /* drawCB */
    OlDrawAreaCallbackStruct* ptr;
    XImage*                   new_ximage;
    Dimension                 width, height;
```

```
ptr = (OlDrawAreaCallbackStruct*) call_data;

if (ptr->reason == OL_REASON_EXPOSE) {
        if (global_ximage != (XImage*) NULL) {
            XPutImage(global_display,
                global_window,
                global_gc,
                global_ximage,
                ptr->event->xexpose.x,    /* src */
                ptr->event->xexpose.y,    /* src */
                ptr->event->xexpose.x,    /* dest */
                ptr->event->xexpose.y,    /* dest */
                ptr->event->xexpose.width,
                ptr->event->xexpose.height);
    }
}


if (ptr->reason == OL_REASON_RESIZE) {
    /*
     * Ignore all resize events that
     * arrive before we create the
     * original XImage.
     */
    if (global_ximage == (XImage*) NULL) {
        return;
    }

    /*
     * Get new width and height.
     */
```

```
XtVaGetValues(widget,
    XtNwidth,  &width,
    XtNheight, &height,
    NULL);

/*
 * Only make a new image if
 * the window is larger.
 */
if (( (int) width  <= global_width) &&
    ( (int) height <= global_height)) {
    /* Store new sizes */
    global_width  = width;
    global_height = height;

    return;
}


/* Store new sizes */
global_width  = (int) width;
global_height = (int) height;


/*
 * Make new image.
 */
new_ximage = CopyImage(global_display,
               OlVisualOfObject(widget),
               global_ximage,
               global_width,
               global_height);
```

```
        if (new_ximage != (XImage*) NULL) {

            /* Free old XImage */
            XDestroyImage(global_ximage);

            global_ximage = new_ximage;

            ComputeMandel(global_ximage,
                global_colors, NUM_COLORS);

            XClearWindow(global_display,
                global_window);

            XPutImage(global_display,
                global_window,
                global_gc,
                global_ximage,
                0, 0,
                0, 0,
                global_width,
                global_height);
        }
    }

}   /* drawCB */


int main(int argc, char** argv)

{   /* main */
    XtAppContext    app_context;
    Display*        display;
```

```
Widget          parent, drawingarea;
Widget          mainwindow;
Widget          menubar;
Widget          filemenu;
Widget          exitchoice;
Arg             args[20];
int             n;

/* Set size of our image. */
global_width  = 350;
global_height = 300;

/* Initialize X toolkit */
OlToolkitInitialize( (XtPointer) NULL);

n = 0;

XtSetArg(args[n], XtNmappedWhenManaged, False); n++;
XtSetArg(args[n], XtNwidth,  global_width); n++;
XtSetArg(args[n], XtNheight, global_height + 40); n++;


parent = XtAppInitialize(&app_context,
        "ProX",                      /* app class */
        (XrmOptionDescList) NULL,    /* options */
        0,                           /* num options */
        ARGC_PTR &argc, argv,        /* cmd line */
        (String*) NULL,              /* fallback res. */
        args, n);


/* Create Main Window. */
```

```
mainwindow = CreateMainWindow(parent, "main");

/* Create menu bar. */
menubar = CreateMenuBar(mainwindow, "menubar");

/* Create the file menu. */
filemenu = CreateMenu(menubar, "filemenu");

/* Create a menu choice to exit program. */
exitchoice = CreateExitChoice(filemenu,
                "exitchoice");

/* Create a drawing area widget. */
drawingarea = CreateDrawingArea(mainwindow,
                "drawingarea",
                global_width, global_height,
                (XtCallbackProc) drawCB,
                (XtPointer) NULL);

SetMainAreas(mainwindow,
            menubar,
            drawingarea);

XtRealizeWidget(parent);

/*
 * Now that we have the windows, we
 * can get the window IDs.
 */

global_display = XtDisplay(drawingarea);
global_window  = XtWindow(drawingarea);
```

```
/*
 * Create a graphics context.
 */
global_gc = XCreateGC(global_display,
              global_window,
              OL, (XGCValues*) NULL);


/*
 * Create an XImage.
 */
global_ximage = MakeImage(parent,
              global_width,
              global_height,
              global_colors,
              NUM_COLORS);


/* Map parent */
XtMapWidget(parent);
XtAppMainLoop(app_context);


return 0;

}   /* main */


/* end of file o_chap21.c */
```

N O T E

You may get C-compiler warnings for the call to XDestroyImage from the following snippet of code:

```
/* Free old XImage */
XDestroyImage(global_ximage);
```

The warnings will be something like the following:

```
cc: "m_chap21.c", line 138: warning 604:
    Pointers are not assignment-compatible.
cc: "m_chap21.c", line 138: warning 563:
    Argument #1 is not the correct type.
```

Why does the C compiler generate this warning? Well, the
XDestroyImage macro is defined in <X11/Xutil.h> as the
following:

```
#define XDestroyImage(ximage) \
        ((*((ximage)->f.destroy_image))((ximage)))
```

XDestroyImage calls the *destroy_image* function in the
XImage structure, which is defined in turn, in
<X11/Xlib.h>, as:

```
int (*destroy_image)(struct _XImage *);
```

Note the difference between struct _XImage* and
XImage*. Your C compiler may generate a similar warning
message when compiling the file fractal.c with the
XPutPixel macro. We experienced this warning only under
Hewlett-Packard's HP-UX 8.07.

Resource File for the Example Programs

Name this resource file ProX and place it in your home directory:

```
! ProX
! Resource file for chapter 21 of
! Professional Graphics
! Programming in the X Window System.
!
! Place this file in your
```

```
! home directory.
!
! Generic resources.
*background:      #cccccc
*title:           Chap. 21: Mandelbrot


! Motif resources.
*fontList: lucidasans-12


*filemenu.labelString:    File
*filemenu.mnemonic:       F


*exitchoice.labelString:  Exit
*exitchoice.mnemonic:     x


! OLIT
*filemenu.label:          File
*exitchoice.label:        Exit


! end of file ProX
```

Running the Fractal Program

When you run the fractal program, you'll see the program print out a number of messages, one for each set of 20 scanline rows completed. When all the rows are done, the program will display the fractal image in a window, like the one from Figure 21.1.

You can modify the *start_x*, *start_y*, *x_width*, and *y_height* values in `fractal.c` to change the magnification of the fractal image and to zoom in on interesting areas.

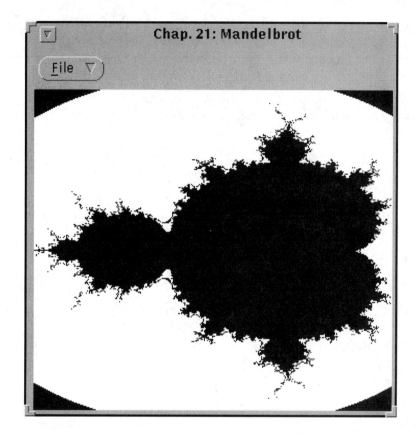

Figure 21.1   *Drawing a fractal image.*

Motif Image Functions

Motif provides an *image cache* of commonly used XImages, usually made from bitmap files. XmInstallImage stores an XImage with an associated name in Motif's image cache:

```
#include <Xm/Xm.h>


Boolean XmInstallImage(XImage* image,
          char* image_name)
```

This cache is also used by XmGetPixmap, as described in Chapter 17. The basic idea is that you can later retrieve the XImage by name. XmInstallImage returns True on success; False otherwise. Do *not* destroy this XImage, as the Motif toolkit routine won't make a copy of it.

Motif includes a number of built-in images. Some of these built-in XImage types are listed in Table 21.1.

Table 21.1   *Built-in Motif images.*

Image Name	Content
25_foreground	25% foreground, 75% background
50_foreground	50% foreground, 50% background
75_foreground	75% foreground, 25% background
background	Solid background
horizontal	Horizontal lines of the foreground and background
slant_left	Slanting lines of the foreground and background
slant_right	Slanting lines of the foreground and background
vertical	Vertical lines of the foreground and background

To remove an XImage from Motif's image cache, call XmUninstallImage:

```
#include <Xm/Xm.h>


Boolean XmUninstallImage(XImage* image)
```

Working with XImages and OLIT

While Motif seems to prefer pixmaps for use with widgets, OLIT tends toward using an XImage. The OLIT analog to Motif's labelPixmap resource is the `labelImage` resource, supported by the OLIT widgets listed in Table 21.2.

Table 21.2   *OLIT widget types supporting the labelImage resource.*

`CheckBox`
`FlatCheckBox`
`FlatExclusives`
`FlatNonexclusives`
`OblongButton`
`RectButton`

The three resources used to set the label string or image are listed in Table 21.3.

Table 21.3   *OLIT label resources.*

Resource	Type
`label`	`String`
`labelImage`	`XImage*`
`labelType`	`OlDefine`

The *labelType* resource should be set to OL_STRING or OL_IMAGE. If the *labelType* resource is not set to OL_IMAGE, then the *labelImage* resource is ignored. For `OblongButton` widgets, you can also set the *labelType* resource to OL_POPUP to place an ellipsis after the text, which signals to the user that the `OblongButton` widget calls up something more.

Summary

Pixmaps, which we've been covering in the last few chapters, can be used for image-processing applications. You can draw to individual dots and you can copy areas of a pixmap to another drawable. Unfortunately, using pixmaps requires you to send every drawing request over the network link to the X server. Since images demand a *large* number of data bytes, this usually results in a far too poor performance to be usable. This is especially true because images often require drawing dot by dot, instead of using the higher-level line, rectangle, arc, and polygon drawing routines. What's needed is a means to create and manipulate images entirely on the client, or application, side. Only when the image is complete do you need to send the image to the X server.

These client-side images are stored in an `XImage` structure, which you can manipulate entirely within your application. The `XImage` structure also largely frees your application from differences in byte ordering between the X server and your application program (remember with X, your applications can compute on a different machine). Even so, the X Window System provides only a primitive means for handling client-side images. And while using pixmaps for all image-handling results in poor performance, most X programmers also feel that an `XImage` provides poor performance as well.

X allows your application to capture images of the screen, to make screen dumps. To capture an area of the screen, call `XGetImage`.

Since creating an `XImage` is a fairly time-consuming operation, which involves allocating memory dynamically and setting up six function pointers, you may want to reuse an `XImage` pointer to capture a new part of the screen. To do so, you can call `XGetSubImage`.

Once you've captured an image with `XGetImage` or `XGetSubImage`, you can then extract individual pixel values with `XGetPixel`, typically defined as a macro in the include file `<X11/Xutil.h>`.

When you're done with an `XImage`, free it using the `XDestroyImage` macro.

You can manipulate an `XImage` with `XPutPixel` and `XAddPixel`. We know it's very tempting to try to manipulate the *data* field of the `XImage` structure directly, but you really shouldn't. The performance of `XPutPixel` leaves a lot to be desired, as you'll soon discover if you do a lot of image processing using an `XImage`, but the only truly portable way to manipulate an `XImage` is to go through `XPutPixel` and `XAddPixel`.

If you're writing an image-processing application, you may want to use an `XImage` to hold an image while your program generates the full picture. Once the picture is complete, you can then send the `XImage` to a window or pixmap in the X server with `XPutImage`. If you follow this model, though, you need to deal with unexpected window resizes. Since the user should be able to resize application windows at any time, your applications must stand ready to deal with a new window size. One way to deal with a new size is to create a new XImage with the new size. You're then left with the problem of copying over the old XImage data and destroying the old XImage.

There are two main reasons you may want to use an XImage. The first is that you may need to capture the pixels in a window and export them for another use—create a screen dump, for instance. Second, you can use an XImage as a client-side image format, where you can write data into the image and then blast it to a drawable with one X operation.

For example, if you want to draw a complex image, like that of the Mandelbrot set, you could draw the Mandelbrot set to an XImage. Once completed with this expensive operation, you can display the XImage using XPutImage.

Most real applications don't draw fractal images, but the concepts are the same for geographic information systems (GISs) or with the mythical paperless office, which uses imaging software to reproduce documents that were formerly on paper. The Mandelbrot set requires that you build an image dot by dot, which is the worst case for most image processing. To show how to use an XImage, though, we present a simple and fun example using the Mandelbrot set.

X Library Functions and Macros Introduced in This Chapter

```
BitmapBitOrder

BitmapPad

BitmapUnit

ImageByteOrder

XAddPixel

XBitmapBitOrder

XBitmapPad

XBitmapUnit
```

XCreateImage

XDestroyImage

XGetImage

XGetPixel

XGetSubImage

XImageByteOrder

XPutImage

XPutPixel

XSubImage

Motif Functions and Macros Introduced in This Chapter

XmInstallImage

XmUninstallImage

Chapter 22

Shared Memory and Image Extensions

This chapter covers:

- ✦ Extensions to the base X Window System
- ✦ Determining which extensions are available
- ✦ Common X extensions
- ✦ The MIT-SHM (shared-memory) extension
- ✦ Using shared memory for large images
- ✦ Detecting the MIT-SHM extension
- ✦ Shared-memory `XImages`
- ✦ Shared-memory X pixmaps
- ✦ The X Image Extension (XIE)

Extensions to the Base X Window System

To avoid having to change the core X11 protocol, the X Window System defines a way for adding extensions to the base protocol. These extensions, especially the *SHAPE extension* for nonrectangular windows, such as round analog clocks, have proven very popular. Two X extensions, in particular, support extra image-processing options. The *MIT-SHM (shared-memory) extension* allows you to store images into segments of memory shared between the client application and X server. This eliminates a number of expensive transmissions of data between your application and the X server. The proposed *X Image Extension*, or *XIE*, provides for a number of image-processing routines to reside in the X server, freeing your application from these tasks.

Common X Extensions

Chances are your X server supports a number of common extensions, as listed in Table 22.1.

Table 22.1 *Common X extensions.*

Extension	Description
SHAPE	Nonrectangular windows
MIT-SHM	MIT shared-memory `XImage` extension
XTestExtension1	For testing
XInputExtension	For adding new input devices, like digitizing tablets
X3D-PEX	PHIGS 3D extension to X
XIE	X Image Extension
SIE	Simple Image Extension
XVideo	Video extension

You can determine what extensions your X server offers by running the `xdpyinfo` program. This program will print out, among other things, a list of the supported X extensions. Some vendors, though, don't provide xdpyinfo, although we cannot figure out why, as this is a *very* simple program. (Some vendors, like Hewlett-Packard, provide xdpyinfo in a nontraditional location, e.g., /usr/contrib/bin/X11 on HP-UX 9.0.) You can get around the lack of xdpyinfo with two methods. First, just about every extension to X provides a set of functions for querying whether the extension is supported. We'll cover a few of these functions when we get into the MIT-SHM extension, below.

Second, you can use XListExtensions from the X library to list the names of the supported extensions:

```
char** XListExtensions(Display* display,
        int* number_extensions) /* RETURN */
```

XListExtensions returns a list of the names of the supported extensions:

```
Display*    display;
int         number_extensions;
int         i;
char**      extension_list;


extension_list = XListExtensions(display,
                    &number_extensions);


if ((extension_list != (char**) NULL) &&
    (number_extensions > 0)) {

    printf("\nX Server extensions include:\n\n");

    for (i = 0; i < number_extensions; i++) {
        printf("\t %s\n", extension_list[i]);
    }

    XFreeExtensionList(extension_list);
}
```

After you call `XListExtensions`, assuming you get a non-NULL list of extensions, you should call `XFreeExtensionList` to free the memory associated with the list of extensions:

```
XFreeExtensionList(char** extension_list)
```

To show `XListExtensions` in action, we've built a simple program to list the available X extensions. The `xext` program, listed in the next section, prints out the list of extensions provided by `XListExtensions`, as well as further descriptions of the extensions.

`Xext` uses only the low-level X library and consequently, uses the `XOpenDisplay` function, introduced way back in Chapter 1, to open the connection to the X server:

```
Display* XOpenDisplay(char* display_name)
```

Normally, your toolkit initialization function, such as `XtApp-Initialize`, takes care of this for you. `XOpenDisplay` returns the `Display` pointer for an open connection to the X server. You need to pass a display name to `XOpenDisplay`, or NULL. If you pass NULL, `XOpenDisplay` will look for the `DISPLAY` environment variable and use that value for the display name.

When you're done with X, use `XCloseDisplay` to close the display connection to the X server:

```
XCloseDisplay(Display* display)
```

A Program to List X Extensions

The `xext` program lists the extensions supported by your X server. The code for this program is stored in the file `xext.c`:

```
/*
 *  xext.c
 *  Program to list X extensions.
 */
```

```c
#include <X11/Xlib.h>
#include <stdio.h>

void PrintExtension(char* extension)

{   /* PrintExtension */

    printf("   %25s", extension);

    if (strcmp(extension, "SHAPE") == 0) {
        printf("\t For nonrectangular windows.");
    }

    if (strcmp(extension, "X3D-PEX") == 0) {
        printf("\t PHIGS 3D Extension to X.");
    }

    if (strcmp(extension, "MIT-SHM") == 0) {
        printf("\t MIT shared-memory XImage extension.");
    }

    if (strcmp(extension, "Multi-Buffering") == 0) {
        printf(
            "\t Multi-buffering extension for animation.");
    }

    if (strcmp(extension, "XInputExtension") == 0) {
        printf("\t Extension for input devices.");
    }

    if (strcmp(extension, "HPExtension") == 0) {
```

```
            printf("\t Hewlett-Packard extension.");
    }


    if (strcmp(extension, "XTestExtension1") == 0) {
        printf("\t XTest testing extension.");
    }


    if (strcmp(extension, "MIT-SUNDRY-NONSTANDARD") == 0) {
        printf("\t X Consortium misc. extension.");
    }


    printf("\n");   /* ending newline */


}   /* PrintExtension */


void ListExtensions(Display* display)


{   /* ListExtensions */
    int     number_extensions;
    int     i;
    char**  extension_list;


    extension_list = XListExtensions(display,
                        &number_extensions);


    if ((extension_list != (char**) NULL) &&
        (number_extensions > 0)) {


        printf("\nX Server extensions include:\n\n");


        for (i = 0; i < number_extensions; i++) {
```

```
            PrintExtension(extension_list[i]);
        }


        XFreeExtensionList(extension_list);
    }


}   /* ListExtensions */


int main(int argc, char** argv)


{   /* main */
    Display*    display;


    /*
     * Open display connection.
     */
    display = XOpenDisplay( (char*) NULL);


    if (display != (Display*) NULL) {
        ListExtensions(display);


        XCloseDisplay(display);
    } else {
        printf("Unable to connect to X server.\n");
    }


    return 0;


}   /* main */


/* end of file xext.c */
```

Compiling the Xext Program

All you need to compile the xext program is the X11 library, libX11.a, as the following command shows:

```
cc -o xext xext.c -lX11
```

Here's the output of this program, slightly formatted, on a number of X servers:

Hewlett-Packard HP-UX 9.01, X11 Release 5

X-server extensions include:

HPExtension	Hewlett-Packard extension
XTestExtension1	XTest testing extension
SHAPE	For nonrectangular windows
MIT-SHM	MIT shared-memory XImage extension
Multi-Buffering	Multibuffering extension for animation
XInputExtension	Extension for input devices
XTEST	
MIT-SUNDRY-NONSTANDARD	X Consortium miscellaneous extension
stellar-shmLink	
shmLink	
XVideo	

Silicon Graphics IRIX 4.0.5, X11 Release 4

X-server extensions include:

SHAPE	For nonrectangular windows
MIT-SHM	MIT shared-memory XImage extension

Multi-Buffering	Multibuffering extension for animation
XInputExtension	Extension for input devices
MIT-SUNDRY-NONSTANDARD	X Consortium miscellaneous extension
SGI-SUNDRY-NONSTANDARD	
SCREEN-SAVER	
READDISPLAY	

Solaris 2.1, OpenWindows 3.1, X11 Release 4

X-server extensions include:

SUN_DGA	
SunWindowGrabber	
XInputDeviceEvents	
Multi-Buffering	Multibuffering extension for animation
SHAPE	For nonrectangular windows
SUN_ALLPLANES	
MIT-SHM	MIT shared-memory `XImage` extension

MIT X Consortium, X11 Release 5

X-server extensions include:

XTestExtension1	XTest testing extension
SHAPE	For nonrectangular windows
MIT-SHM	MIT shared-memory `XImage` extension
X3D-PEX	PHIGS 3D Extension to X
Multi-Buffering	Multibuffering extension for animation

MIT-SUNDRY-NONSTANDARD	X Consortium miscellaneous extension

Once we've checked what extensions are available, we note that the handy MIT-SHM extension is supported on a number of systems.

The MIT-SHM (Shared-Memory) Extension

The *MIT-SHM (shared-memory) extension* provides a means to place an XImage or pixmaps into memory shared between your application and the X server, avoiding the potentially large overhead of sending huge XImages over the wire to the X server. Additionally, if the X server supports shared-memory pixmaps, you can write directly into the pixmap data without the overhead of the X library function calls that send drawing-request packets over the wire to the X server.

To do so, the MIT-SHM extension uses the System V UNIX notion of shared memory, using routines such as shmget and shmat. This does not include the alternative UNIX style of shared memory, based on mmap. The System V UNIX style of shared memory, based on shmget, is also supported by the X/Open Portability Guide, or XPG.

Your system must have the MIT-SHM extension to the X server *and* it must support System V shared memory. These requirements eliminate a number of other operating systems, such as DOS, right away. You also must run your X application program on the same machine as the X server, or the shared memory won't work. While there is some support in X11 Release 4, you pretty much need Release 5 to use the MIT-SHM extension.

On Sun systems, you may need to rebuild the kernel to support shared memory.

The default sizes for shared memory on Sun and Digital Equipment systems are generally too small for working with large images. You'll probably need to increase the maximum shared-memory size on these platforms.

MIT-SHM Include Files

If you program with the shared-memory extension, you must include the following include files:

```
#include <X11/Xlib.h>
#include <sys/ipc.h>
#include <sys/shm.h>
#include <X11/extensions/XShm.h>
```

All routines that begin with *XShm* require these header files.

WARNING

On older systems, you may not have the *extensions* subdirectory under the X11 include directory.

Detecting the MIT-SHM Extension

To detect whether the shared-memory extension is available, you can run the `xdpyinfo` program or the `xext` program. Examine the output of `xdpyinfo` for the section that covers supported extensions, for instance:

```
number of extensions:    10

   ...

     MIT-SHM
```

The key here is the *MIT-SHM*

From within your programs, you can call `XListExtensions`, as we described above, as well as two functions specific to the shared-memory extension, `XShmQueryExtension` and `XShmQueryVersion`. Both of these functions require the X extension library, but if you don't have that, you won't get very far using the shared-memory extension anyway.

`XShmQueryExtension` returns a nonzero value (usually `True`) if the MIT-SHM extension is available:

```
Status XShmQueryExtension(Display* display)
```

You can get more information with XShmQueryVersion:

```
Status XShmQueryVersion(Display* display,
        int* major,              /* RETURN */
        int* minor,              /* RETURN */
        Bool* pixmaps_supported) /* RETURN */
```

Like XShmQueryExtension, XShmQueryVersion returns a nonzero value to indicate that the extension is available. Unlike XShmQueryExtension, though, XShmQueryVersion provides the *major* and *minor* version numbers of the extension, as well as a flag that tells you whether shared-memory pixmaps are supported. Many systems simply don't provide this support, even though the shared-memory extension is available. We can determine if the MIT-SHM extension is supported by the X server and whether it supports shared-memory pixmaps with the following utility function:

```
int QueryShm(Display* display,
     int* major_ver,       /* major_ver version number */
     int* minor_ver,       /* minor_ver version number */
     Bool* pixmaps)        /* Supports shared Pixmaps? */

{    /* QueryShm */
     int status = False;

     /*
      * Set up default values.
      */
     *major_ver = 0;
     *minor_ver = 0;
     *pixmaps   = False;

#ifdef MITSHM

     status = (int) XShmQueryVersion(display,
```

```
            major_ver, minor_ver, pixmaps);


#endif /* MITSHM */


    return status;



}    /* QueryShm */
```

Note the use of the #ifdef MITSHM. This allows us to compile a bare-bones routine if the shared-memory extension library, which holds the application routines, is not available. The key is that you need *both* the MIT-SHM library routines (in the X extension library) for your application and the X server to support the MIT-SHM extension.

 We originally named the parameters to QueryShm *major* and *minor*, but this generated problems on a SPARC-10 running Solaris 2.1, with Sun's C compiler. With the GNU C compiler under Solaris 2.1, we didn't experience this problem. To make life easier, we changed *major* to *major_ver* and *minor* to *minor_ver*.

N O T E

If the shared-memory extension is supported, though, you should at least have the ability to share XImages.

With the generic function QueryShm, above, we can print out more information:

```
int QueryAndPrintShm(Display* display)


{    /* QueryAndPrintShm */
    int    major_ver, minor_ver;
    Bool   pixmaps;
    int    status;


    status = QueryShm(display,
```

```
                    &major_ver, &minor_ver, &pixmaps);


    if (status == True) {
        printf(
            "Supports the MIT-SHM extension ver. %d.%d\n",
            major_ver, minor_ver);


        if (pixmaps == True) {
            printf(
                "Supports shared-memory Pixmaps, too.\n");
        } else {
            printf(
                "Does not support shared-memory Pixmaps.\n");
        }
    } else {
        printf(
            "Does not support the MIT-SHM extension.\n");
    }


    return status;


}   /* QueryAndPrintShm */
```

Creating Shared-Memory XImages

By sharing XImage data between the client application and the X server, you can save a lot of data transfers. Therefore, the shared-memory extension provides a special means to create a sharable XImage. To do so, follow these six steps:

1. Allocate an XShmSegmentInfo structure for use with the XImage.
2. Create the shared XImage with XShmCreateImage.

3. Create a shared-memory segment for the `XImage` data using `shmget`.

4. Attach this shared-memory segment with `shmat`.

5. Decide whether the X server can write to the `XImage` data.

6. Tell the X server to attach your shared-memory segment with `XShmAttach`.

The first step is to allocate an `XShmSegmentInfo` structure:

```
XShmSegmentInfo      shminfo;


shminfo = (XShmSegmentInfo*)
          malloc( sizeof(XShmSegmentInfo) );
```

You really don't have to dynamically allocate the `XShmSegmentInfo` structure. There is a key requirement: the `XShmSegmentInfo` structure must remain as long as the shared `XImage` we create. If you're creating a shared `XImage` from within a C function (outside of `main`), then you need to either use a global variable or allocate the `XShmSegmentInfo` structure dynamically, as we showed above. The `XShmSegmentInfo` structure is used in the call to create a shared `XImage`.

The second step is to create the shared `XImage` with `XShmCreateImage`:

```
XImage* XShmCreateImage(Display* display,
        Visual* visual,
        unsigned int depth,
        int format,
        char* data,
        XShmSegmentInfo* shminfo,
        unsigned int width,
        unsigned int height)
```

`XShmCreateImage` acts a lot like `XCreateImage`, described in the last chapter. Most of the parameters are the same, except that you're forced to use what the X server wants for the offset, bitmap pad, and bytes per line. The *visual* parameter should be set to the visual you intend to use for the image, which most likely should match that used for your windows. The *format* is again one of XYBitmap, XYPixmap, or ZPixmap. We've had best luck with the ZPixmap format for colored images.

The *data* parameter can be set to NULL, just like the call to XCreateImage. In fact, we strongly advise you to pass NULL as the data to XShmCreateImage. Why? Because we allocate the *data* from a shared-memory segment in the next step. For the *shminfo* parameter, you must use an XShmSegmentInfo structure that remains as long as you want the XImage to. That is, the shminfo parameter should be a global variable or be dynamically allocated.

The XShmSegmentInfo Structure

The XShmSegmentInfo structure holds the following fields:

```
typedef struct {
    ShmSeg   shmseg;
    int      ohmid;
    char*    shmaddr;
    Bool     readOnly;
} XShmSegmentInfo;
```

The *shmseg* is a resource ID, used later in the completion event. The *shmid*, or shared-memory ID, is returned from the call to shmget, below. Similarly, the *shmaddr*, or shared-memory address, is returned from the call to shmat. The *readOnly* flag indicates whether the X server can write to the XImage (False) or not (True). This value is also set below.

The third step is to create the shared-memory segment with shmget.

Creating the Shared-Memory Segment

We need to get, or create, a shared-memory memory segment, using the System V UNIX call to shmget:

```
#include <sys/shm.h>

int shmget(key_t key,
       size_t size,
       int shmflg)
```

The *size* parameter is the number of bytes to make the shared-memory segment. If this number is too large, that is, if it exceeds your system's maximum value, then shmget will fail. The *key* can be an arbitrary key number or the constant IPC_PRIVATE, which indicates that shmget should create a new shared-memory identifier. The shmflg is the creation bit-flags, which specify the mode used for the shared memory, much like file permissions. The *shmflg* allows you to have control over what other processes can access this shared memory. The allowable *shmflg* bit-flag values are listed in Table 22.2.

Table 22.2 *Flag values for shared-memory segments.*

Constant	Value	Meaning
SHM R	0400	Read permission for the owner
(SHM_R >> 3)	0040	Read for group
(SHM_R >> 6)	0004	Read for world
SHM_W	0200	Write permission for the owner
(SHM_W >> 3)	0020	Write for group
(SHM_W >> 6)	0002	Write for world
IPC_CREAT	0001000	Create segment if it doesn't exist, otherwise return existing segment
IPC_EXCL	0002000	If IPC_CREAT is also set, then succeed only if segment didn't already exist

Note that you should never use the values of IPC_CREAT, 0001000, and IPC_EXCL, 0002000, directly. Always use the symbolic constant.

The return value of `shmget` is the shared-memory identifier that you need to pass to the X server. A return value of –1 indicates a failure. In your code, you can call `shmget` as follows:

```
XShmSegmentInfo     shminfo;
Ximage*             shared_image;
int                 number_bytes;


number_bytes = shared_image->bytes_per_line *
                  shared_image->height;


shminfo.shmid = shmget(IPC_PRIVATE,
                  number_bytes,
                  IPC_CREAT | 0777);
```

In your code, you should check for errors from `shmget`. The fourth step is to attach the shared-memory segment.

Attaching the Shared-Memory Segment

We use the function `shmat` to attach the shared-memory segment to our program's process address space:

```
#include <sys/shm.h>


char* shmat(int shmid,
        void* shmaddr,
        int shmflg)
```

The *shmid* parameter holds the shared-memory ID returned by `shmget`. The *shmaddr* is the address at which to attach the segment. If successful, shmat returns the address where the shared-memory is attached. The *shmflg* value determines how the *shmaddr* is treated. If *shmflg* is SHM_RND and the *shmaddr* is non-NULL, the shared memory is attached at the given address, *shmaddr*, rounded down by the constant SHMLBA, the so-called lower boundary address. If *shmflg* is not SHM_RND, then the given address is used. If the *shmaddr* is NULL, then shmget chooses the address.

WARNING

On many systems, such as Hewlett-Packard's HP-UX, you must pass 0 for *shmaddr* if the shared-memory segment has yet to be attached. Because our program created the segment, we know it is not yet attached. By passing 0, we signify that the system can choose the address.

In your code, you can call shmat as follows:

```
XShmSegmentInfo     shminfo;
Ximage*             shared_image;


shminfo.shmaddr    = shmat(shminfo.shmid,
                           (void*) 0, 0);


shared_image->data = shminfo.shmaddr;
```

WARNING

We set *both* the *shmaddr* field in the XShmSegmentInfo structure as well as the XImage *data* field to hold the address returned by shmat. This is essential.

The fifth step is to decide whether the X server can write to the XImage data. We've already introduced the *readOnly* field in the XShmSegment-Info structure. Normally, you set this to False, which allows the X server to write into the XImage:

```
XShmSegmentInfo     shminfo;


shminfo.readOnly = False;
```

Our final step toward creating a shared-memory XImage is to tell the X server to attach the shared-memory segment with XShmAttach:

```
Status XShmAttach(Display* display,
        XShmSegmentInfo* shminfo)
```

XShmAttach returns a nonzero value on success. If this happens, we are now ready to use the shared XImage just like we use normal XImages.

A Utility Function for Creating Shared-Memory XImages

We can then create a utility function that shows how to create a shared-memory XImage. This function, CreateShmImage, performs all the six steps described above:

```
XImage* CreateShmImage(Display* display,
    Visual* visual,
    unsigned int depth,
    int width, int height,
    XShmSegmentInfo** shminfo)   /* RETURN */


{   /* CreateShmImage */
    XImage*          ximage;
    int              number_bytes;
    XShmSegmentInfo* local_shminfo;

    /*
     * Allocate memory for the
     * XShmSegmentInfo structure.
     */
    local_shminfo = (XShmSegmentInfo*)
            malloc( sizeof(XShmSegmentInfo) );

    /*
     * Create the shared XImage.
```

```
    */
ximage = XShmCreateImage(display,
            visual,
            depth,
            ZPixmap,
            (char*) NULL,
            local_shminfo,
            width, height);

if (ximage == (XImage*) NULL) {
    return ximage;
}


/*
 * Create a shared-memory segment.
 */
number_bytes = ximage->bytes_per_line *
                ximage->height;

local_shminfo->shmid = shmget(IPC_PRIVATE,
                    number_bytes,
                    IPC_CREAT | 0777);

if (local_shminfo->shmid < 0) {
    XDestroyImage(ximage);

    return (XImage*) NULL;
}

/*
 * Attach the shared-memory segment.
```

```
 */
local_shminfo->shmaddr =
          (char*) shmat(local_shminfo->shmid,
                        (void*) 0, 0);


ximage->data = local_shminfo->shmaddr;


if (local_shminfo->shmaddr == (char*) -1) {


    shmctl(local_shminfo->shmid, IPC_RMID, 0);


    XDestroyImage(ximage);


    return (XImage*) NULL;
}


/*
 * Allow the X server to
 * modify the shared data.
 */
local_shminfo->readOnly = False;


/*
 * Tell the X server to attach
 * the shared-memory segment.
 */
XShmAttach(display, local_shminfo);


*shminfo = local_shminfo;


return ximage;
```

```
}    /* CreateShmImage */
```

CreateShmImage returns the new shared XImage on success, or NULL on failure. Note how the XShmSegmentInfo structure is allocated.

Creating Shared XImages for Widgets

If you're starting out with a widget, you need to query the widget's depth and *visual* to ensure the image suitably matches the widget. Remember that the visual resource normally applies only to shell widgets. Consequently, we can create a wrapper around CreateShmImage, above (which is, in turn, a wrapper around XShmCreateImage and a host of shared-memory routines), for use with shell widgets. The function CreateShmImageFromWidget, below creates a shared XImage with the given *width* and *height*, suitable for use with the given shell widget:

```
XImage* CreateShmImageFromWidget(Widget shell_widget,
    int width, int height,
    XShmSegmentInfo** shminfo)   /* RETURN */


{    /* CreateShmImageFromWidget */
    Visual*    visual;
    int        depth;
    XImage*    ximage;
    Display*   display;

    /*
     * Query depth and visual.
     */
    XtVaGetValues(shell_widget,
        XtNdepth,   &depth,
        XtNvisual, &visual,
        NULL);
```

```
    /*
     * Create the image.
     */
    display = XtDisplay(shell_widget);

    ximage = CreateShmImage(display,
                visual,
                depth,
                width, height,
                shminfo);


    return ximage;


}   /* CreateShmImageFromWidget */
```

As in the last chapter, we pass a shell widget to CreateShmImageFromWidget to ensure you get the proper *visual* resource, although this resource should be inherited by all child widgets.

Once we create the shared-memory XImage, we can use it like most other XImages. There are a few differences, though. For example, you need to do some extra work when destroying a shared-memory XImage.

Destroying a Shared-Memory XImage

There are four steps needed to destroy a shared-memory XImage:

1. Tell the X server to detach the XImage with XShmDetach.
2. Destroy the XImage with XDestroyImage.
3. Detach the shared-memory segment from our process with shmdt.
4. Destroy the shared-memory segment with shmctl.
5. Free the XShmSegmentInfo structure, if you've allocated it with malloc.

The code for the necessary steps needed to destroy a shared XImage follows:

```
Display*          display;
XShmSegmentInfo*  shminfo;
XImage*           ximage;


XShmDetach(display, shminfo);


XDestroyImage(ximage);


shmdt(shminfo->shmaddr);


shmctl(shminfo->shmid, IPC_RMID, 0);
```

If you've allocated the XShmSegmentInfo structure with malloc, then you should free it:

```
free(shminfo);
```

Destroying a Shared-Memory XImage in Depth

In more depth, the first step is to tell the X server to detach its use of the shared memory, with XShmDetach:

```
Status XShmDetach(Display* display,
        XShmSegmentInfo* shminfo)
```

The second step is handled by XDestroyImage, introduced in the last chapter on XImage structures. In the third step, shmdt then detaches the given shared-memory segment from a process:

```
#include <sys/shm.h>


int shmdt(void* shmaddr)
```

The *shmaddr* parameter is the address of the shared-memory segment returned by shmat. You can check the return value: 0 means success and –1 means an error occurred.

The shared-memory equivalent of ioctl is shmctl:

```
#include <sys/shm.h>

int shmctl(int shmid,
        int command,
        struct shmid_ds* buffer)
```

The shmctl function handles the fourth step in destroying a shared XImage. The shmid parameter is the shared-memory ID, which we originally got from shmget, above. The possible commands are listed in Table 22.3.

Table 22.3   Shmctl Commands.

Command	Meaning
IPC_STAT	Query the shared-memory values and place them into the shmid_ds *buffer*
IPC_SET	Set the values from the shmid_ds *buffer* to the segment
IPC_RMID	Remove the shared-memory identifier *shmid* and destroy the shared-memory segment
SHM_LOCK	Lock the *shmid* segment
SHM_UNLOCK	Unlock the *shmid* segment

The shmctl function returns 0 on success; –1 on errors. You can pass 0 or NULL as the *buffer* parameter for most values of command, including IPC_RMID, which we use to remove the shared-memory segment.

To put all this together, you can use the DestroyShmImage function, below:

```
void DestroyShmImage(Display* display,
    XImage* ximage,
```

```
        XShmSegmentInfo** shminfo)

{   /* DestroyShmImage */
    XShmSegmentInfo* local_shminfo;

    local_shminfo = *shminfo;

    XShmDetach(display, local_shminfo);

    XDestroyImage(ximage);

    shmdt(local_shminfo->shmaddr);

    shmctl(local_shminfo->shmid, IPC_RMID, 0);

    /*
     * We assume shminfo was
     * allocated in CreateShmImage,
     * above.
     */
    free( *shminfo );

}   /* DestroyShmImage */
```

Note how we treat the XShmSegmentInfo structure. This is an artifact of the way we allocate it in CreateShmImage, above.

Writing a Shared XImage to a Drawable

You can write a shared XImage into a drawable with XShmPutImage:

```
    Status XShmPutImage(Display* display,
```

```
Drawable drawable,
GC gc,
XImage* ximage,
int src_x, int src_y,
int dest_x, int dest_y,
unsigned int width,
unsigned int height,
bool send_event)
```

Since you have a valid XImage pointer, you could also use XPutImage—but this defeats the whole purpose of using shared memory. XShmPutImage avoids sending all the data over the wire to the X server, as is required by XPutImage.

The *src_x* and *src_y* refer to the XImage. The *dest_x* and *dest_y* are the locations in the destination drawable. The boolean *send_event* parameter tells the X server whether to send a shared-memory *completion event* when finished. Because we assume this XImage is shared, your application might want to know when it is free to write to the XImage. This completion event provides that notification. Don't modify the shared image until this event arrives. Set the *send_event* parameter to True if you want the completion event, False otherwise.

The XShmCompletionEvent

X extensions can define their own event types. In this case, the MIT-SHM extension defines an XShmCompletionEvent type:

```
typedef struct {
    int           type;
    unsigned long serial;
    Bool          send_event;
    Display*      display;
    Drawable      drawable;
    int           major_code;
    int           minor_code;
```

```
    ShmSeg          shmseg;
    unsigned long   offset;
} XShmCompletionEvent;
```

In the case of the completion event from XShmPutImage, the *minor_code* will be X_ShmPutImage. Unlike most X events, the *type* parameter is not fixed. The base set of X events all have constant numbers for the event *type*. With X extensions, though, there's no way to tell in advance whether the extension is available on a given X server. The extension event *type* (or event number) is based on all the other X extensions and how many events they provide. You need to dynamically determine the *type* of the shared-memory extension completion, using XShmGetEventBase:

```
Display* display;
int      completion_type;


completion_type = XShmGetEventBase(display)
                  + ShmCompletion;
```

The constant ShmCompletion (defined as 0) is the event number offset within the shared-memory extension. The XShmGetEventBase function returns the base event for the shared-memory extension:

```
int XShmGetEventBase(Display* display)
```

Problems with XShmPutImage

If you have an image larger than 32 kilobytes, you may have problems with XShmPutImage. The problem manifests itself when transferring the last pixel of the large image. This problem is due to bugs in the X server. While it hasn't hit us, we've seen reports of the X server crashing.

If you experience this, try sending out all but the last few pixels of your image with XShmPutImage (adjust the *src_x*, *src_y*, *width*, and *height* parameters). Then fill out your image using the conventional and slow XPutImage for the last few pixels. XPutImage is much slower than XShmPutImage, but working slowly is better than not working at all.

Another potential solution is to allocate extra image data, say 100 bytes, when you create the shared XImage. In this case, just ignore the extra data when using the image.

In all cases, check to see if you actually face this problem before spending time taking corrective action.

Grabbing Pixels on the Screen into a Shared XImage

The opposite of XShmPutImage is XShmGetImage, which retrieves pixels from the screen and places those into a given *shared_ximage*:

```
Status XShmGetImage(Display* display,
         Display *display;
         Drawable drawable,
         XImage* shared_ximage; /* input/output */
         int x, int y,
         unsigned long plane_mask)
```

Unlike XGetImage, XShmGetImage does not return the XImage pointer. Instead, you must have already created this image in shared memory using the code presented above.

NOTE

You don't provide XShmGetImage with *width* and *height* parameters. Instead, XShmGetImage uses the XImage's internal width and height.

Error-Checking XShmGetImage

You need to make sure that the area you pass to XShmGetImage, the *x* and *y* location in conjunction with the XImage's internal width and height, is within the screen. Otherwise, you'll generate an X error like the following:

```
X Error of failed request:  BadMatch (invalid parameter
      attributes)
   Major opcode of failed request:  133 (MIT-SHM)
   Minor opcode of failed request:  4 (X_ShmGetImage)
   Serial number of failed request:  438
   Current serial number in output stream:  438
```

Utility Code for Shared-Memory Images

We placed all the shared XImage utility code in the file mitshm.c:

```c
/*
 *  mitshm.c
 *  Routines to use the MIT-SHM (shared-memory)
 *  extension to X.
 *
 *  Note: You must define MITSHM to use the
 *  functions in this file.
 */
#include "xlib.h"
#include "mitshm.h"
#include <stdio.h>


int QueryShm(Display* display,
    int* major_ver,      /* major version number */
    int* minor_ver,      /* minor version number */
    Bool* pixmaps)       /* Supports shared Pixmaps? */


{   /* QueryShm */
    int status = False;

    /*
```

```
 * Set up default values.
 */
*major_ver = 0;
*minor_ver = 0;
*pixmaps   = False;

#ifdef MITSHM

    status = (int) XShmQueryVersion(display,
            major_ver, minor_ver, pixmaps);

#endif /* MITSHM */

    return status;

}    /* QueryShm */

int QueryAndPrintShm(Display* display)

{    /* QueryAndPrintShm */
    int    major_ver, minor_ver;
    Bool   pixmaps;
    int    status;

    status = QueryShm(display,
            &major_ver, &minor_ver, &pixmaps);

    if (status == True) {
        printf(
            "Supports the MIT-SHM extension ver. %d.%d\n",
            major_ver, minor_ver);
```

```
        if (pixmaps == True) {
            printf(
              "Supports shared-memory Pixmaps, too.\n");
        } else {
            printf(
              "Does not support shared-memory Pixmaps.\n");
        }
    } else {
        printf("Does not support the MIT-SHM extension.\n");
    }

    return status;

}   /* QueryAndPrintShm */


/*
 * Without the MIT-SHM headers,
 * you won't be able to define
 * the XShmSegmentInfo structure,
 * so you won't be able to use
 * the following functions at all.
 */


#ifdef MITSHM

XImage* CreateShmImage(Display* display,
    Visual* visual,
    unsigned int depth,
    int width, int height,
    XShmSegmentInfo** shminfo)    /* RETURN */
```

```
{   /* CreateShmImage */
    XImage*          ximage;
    int              number_bytes;
    XShmSegmentInfo* local_shminfo;


    /*
     * Allocate memory for the
     * XShmSegmentInfo structure.
     */
    local_shminfo = (XShmSegmentInfo*)
            malloc( sizeof(XShmSegmentInfo) );


    /*
     * Create the shared XImage.
     */
    ximage = XShmCreateImage(display,
                visual,
                depth,
                ZPixmap,
                (char*) NULL,
                local_shminfo,
                width, height);


    if (ximage == (XImage*) NULL) {
        return ximage;
    }


    /*
     * Create a shared-memory segment.
     */
```

```
number_bytes = ximage->bytes_per_line *
               ximage->height;

local_shminfo->shmid = shmget(IPC_PRIVATE,
                       number_bytes,
                       IPC_CREAT | 0777);

if (local_shminfo->shmid < 0) {

    XDestroyImage(ximage);

    return (XImage*) NULL;
}


/*
 * Attach the shared-memory segment.
 */
local_shminfo->shmaddr =
        (char*) shmat(local_shminfo->shmid,
                      (void*) 0, 0);

ximage->data = local_shminfo->shmaddr;

if (local_shminfo->shmaddr == (char*) -1) {

    shmctl(local_shminfo->shmid, IPC_RMID, 0);

    XDestroyImage(ximage);

    return (XImage*) NULL;
}
```

```
    /*
     * Allow the X server to
     * modify the shared data.
     */
    local_shminfo->readOnly = False;


    /*
     * Tell the X server to attach
     * the shared-memory segment.
     */
    XShmAttach(display, local_shminfo);


    *shminfo = local_shminfo;


    return ximage;


}   /* CreateShmImage */


XImage* CreateShmImageFromWidget(Widget shell_widget,
    int width, int height,
    XShmSegmentInfo** shminfo)   /* RETURN */


{   /* CreateShmImageFromWidget */
    Visual*     visual;
    int         depth;
    XImage*     ximage;
    Display*    display;


    /*
     * Query depth and visual.
     */
```

```
    XtVaGetValues(shell_widget,
        XtNdepth,   &depth,
        XtNvisual, &visual,
        NULL);


    /*
     * Create the image.
     */
    display = XtDisplay(shell_widget);


    ximage = CreateShmImage(display,
            visual,
            depth,
            width, height,
            shminfo);


    return ximage;


}   /* CreateShmImageFromWidget */


void DestroyShmImage(Display* display,
    XImage* ximage,
    XShmSegmentInfo** shminfo)


{   /* DestroyShmImage */
    XShmSegmentInfo* local_shminfo;


    local_shminfo = *shminfo;


    XShmDetach(display, local_shminfo);
```

```
        XDestroyImage(ximage);

        shmdt(local_shminfo->shmaddr);

        shmctl(local_shminfo->shmid, IPC_RMID, 0);

        /*
         * We assume shminfo was
         * allocated in CreateShmImage,
         * above.
         */
        free( *shminfo );

    }   /* DestroyShmImage */


#endif /* MITSHM */


/* end of file mitshm.c */
```

The liberal use of #ifdef MITSHM protects our code should the MIT-SHM extension headers not be available when compiling. The function prototypes and header information are stored in the file mitshm.h:

```
/*
 *   mitshm.h
 *   Header file for the shared-memory
 *   extension utility functions.
 */

#ifndef _mitshm_h_
#define _mitshm_h_  1
```

```
#include <X11/Intrinsic.h>
#include <X11/StringDefs.h>
#include <X11/Shell.h>

#ifdef MITSHM

#ifdef HPUX
#define _INCLUDE_XOPEN_SOURCE
#endif /* hpux fix */


#include  <sys/ipc.h>

#ifdef HPUX
#undef _INCLUDE_XOPEN_SOURCE
#endif /* hpux fix */

#include  <sys/shm.h>
#include  <X11/extensions/XShm.h>

#endif /* MITSHM */

/*
 *      Shared-memory functions.
 */
extern
int QueryShm(Display* display,
        int* major_ver,    /* major version number */
        int* minor_ver,    /* minor version number */
        Bool* pixmaps);    /* Supports shared Pixmaps? */


extern
```

```
int QueryAndPrintShm(Display* display);


#ifdef MITSHM


extern
XImage* CreateShmImageFromWidget(Widget shell_widget,
    int width, int height,
    XShmSegmentInfo** shminfo);  /* RETURN */


extern
XImage* CreateShmImage(Display* display,
    Visual* visual,
    unsigned int depth,
    int width, int height,
    XShmSegmentInfo** shminfo);   /* RETURN */


extern
void DestroyShmImage(Display* display,
    XImage* ximage,
    XShmSegmentInfo** shminfo);


#endif /* MITSHM */


#endif  /* !_mitshm_h_ */


/* end of file mitshm.h */
```

Problems with Shared-Memory Code

We had a lot of problems with the MIT-SHM extension on Hewlett-Packard systems. HP-UX 8.07 claims to support the MIT-SHM extension, but our systems didn't have the necessary include file. (The fact that <X11/extensions/XShm.h> is missing under HP-UX 8.07 is apparently an oversight on the part of Hewlett-Packard. Contact your HP representative and ask for a Release 4 version of this file if you haven't upgraded to HP-UX 9.0 yet.) Furthermore, the HP-UX 8.07 Release 4 X server seemed to refuse all requests for using the shared-memory facilities.

Under HP-UX 9.0, this situation improves. Even so, we had to include the following code in the file `mitshm.h` to get the code to compile:

```
#ifdef HPUX

#define _INCLUDE_XOPEN_SOURCE

#endif /* hpux fix */


#include  <sys/ipc.h>


#ifdef HPUX

#undef _INCLUDE_XOPEN_SOURCE

#endif /* hpux fix */
```

When compiling under HP-UX 9.0, you'll need to define the symbol HPUX, which is used in the above code, otherwise, you'll have problems with `IPC_PRIVATE` and `IPC_RMID`.

We also had a lot of problems with programs compiled with X11 Release 5 libraries and displaying on a Release 4 X server. We generally saw `BadAccess` errors when the programs tried to use the X extension's shared-memory facilities.

A Program Using Shared-Memory XImages

To show off the MIT-SHM X extension, we developed a program that captures random areas of the screen into a shared `XImage`, then displays this `XImage` in a drawing-area widget within an X toolkit application. There are three callback functions in the following Motif and Open Look Intrinsics Toolkit (OLIT) programs:

1. The `captureCB` captures a image of the root window, based on a *global_x*, *global_y* location. Each time `captureCB` gets called, it increments the *global_x*, global_y location.

2. The `drawCB` handles `Expose` events in the lazy manner. The `drawCB` awaits the last `Expose` event in the sequence (checking for the *count* field to be 0), then refreshes the entire image.

3. The `exitCB` destroys the shared-memory `XImage` with our utility function, `DestroyShmImage`, and then calls `exit` to terminate the program. With special system resources like shared memory, it is a good idea to always return the resources to the operating system when done.

The `main` function makes all the widgets and then creates our shared-memory `XImage`.

OLIT Source for the Sample Program

The OLIT source code for the sample program is stored in the file `o_chap22.c`:

```
/*
 *   o_chap22.c
 *   OLIT test program for Chapter 22,
 *   which creates a shared-memory XImage.
 */
#include "olit.h"
#include "mitshm.h"
#include <X11/Xutil.h>
#include <Xol/DrawArea.h>
#include <stdio.h>


/*
 *   Globals
 */
```

```
Display*           global_display;
Window             global_window;
GC                 global_gc;
int                global_x, global_y;
int                global_width, global_height;
XImage*            global_ximage;
XShmSegmentInfo*   global_shminfo;


/*
 * Callback to capture
 * a new image.
 */
void captureCB(Widget widget,
    XtPointer client_data,
    XtPointer call_data)


{   /* captureCB */

    if (global_ximage != (XImage*) NULL) {

#ifdef MITSHM

        /*
         * We increment the position
         * each time the callback gets
         * called.
         */
        global_x += 100;
        global_y += 100;

        /*
```

```
     * Make sure ranges are
     * within screen.
     */
    if ((global_x + global_width) >=
        DisplayWidth(global_display,
            DefaultScreen(global_display) ) ) {

        global_x = 0;
    }


    if ((global_y + global_height) >=
        DisplayHeight(global_display,
            DefaultScreen(global_display) ) ) {

        global_y = 0;
    }


    /*
     * Capture an image from
     * somewhere on the screen.
     */
    XShmGetImage(global_display,
        DefaultRootWindow(global_display),
        global_ximage,
        global_x,
        global_y,
        AllPlanes); /* plane mask */


    /*
     * Place the image in
     * the window.
```

```
            */
        XShmPutImage(global_display,
            global_window,
            global_gc,
            global_ximage,
            0, 0,  /* src */
            0, 0,  /* dest */
            global_width,
            global_height,
            True);

    }

#endif /* MITSHM */

}   /* captureCB */

/*
 * Destroy the shared image,
 * then exit.
 */
void exitCB(Widget widget,
    XtPointer client_data,
    XtPointer call_data)

{   /* exitCB */

    if (global_ximage != (XImage*) NULL) {

#ifdef MITSHM

        DestroyShmImage(global_display,
```

```
                 global_ximage,
                 &global_shminfo);

#endif /* MITSHM */

    }

    /* Quit program. */
    exit(0);

}   /* exitCB */

/*
 * Callback to refresh drawing area.
 */
void drawCB(Widget widget,
    XtPointer client_data,
    XtPointer call_data)

{   /* drawCB */
    OlDrawAreaCallbackStruct* ptr;

    ptr = (OlDrawAreaCallbackStruct*) call_data;

    if (ptr->reason == OL_REASON_EXPOSE) {
            if ((ptr->event->xexpose.count == 0) &&
                (global_ximage != (XImage*) NULL)) {

#ifdef MITSHM

                XShmPutImage(global_display,
```

```
                    global_window,

                    global_gc,

                    global_ximage,

                    0, 0,   /* src */

                    0, 0,   /* dest */

                    global_width,

                    global_height,

                    True);


#endif /* MITSHM */



        }

    }


}   /* drawCB */


int main(int argc, char** argv)


{   /* main */
    XtAppContext    app_context;
    Display*        display;
    Widget          parent, drawingarea;
    Widget          mainwindow;
    Widget          menubar;
    Widget          filemenu;
    Widget          capture;
    Widget          exitchoice;
    Arg             args[20];
    int             n;


    /* Set size of our image. */
```

```
global_width  = 250;
global_height = 250;


/* Initialize X toolkit */
OlToolkitInitialize( (XtPointer) NULL);


n = 0;


XtSetArg(args[n], XtNmappedWhenManaged, False); n++;
XtSetArg(args[n], XtNwidth,  global_width); n++;
XtSetArg(args[n], XtNheight, global_height + 40); n++;



parent = XtAppInitialize(&app_context,
        "ProX",                     /* app class */
        (XrmOptionDescList) NULL,   /* options */
        0,                          /* num options */
        ARGC_PTR &argc, argv,       /* cmd line */
        (String*) NULL,             /* fallback res. */
        args, n);



/* Create Main Window. */
mainwindow = CreateMainWindow(parent, "main");


/* Create menu bar. */
menubar = CreateMenuBar(mainwindow, "menubar");


/* Create the file menu. */
filemenu = CreateMenu(menubar, "filemenu");
```

```
/*
 * Create a menu choice to
 * capture new images.
 */
capture = CreateMenuChoice(filemenu,
             "capture",
             (XtCallbackProc) captureCB,
             (XtPointer) NULL);


/* Create a menu choice to exit the program. */
exitchoice = CreateMenuChoice(filemenu,
             "exitchoice",
             (XtCallbackProc) exitCB,
             (XtPointer) NULL);




/* Create a drawing area widget. */
drawingarea = CreateDrawingArea(mainwindow,
             "drawingarea",
             global_width, global_height,
             (XtCallbackProc) drawCB,
             (XtPointer) NULL);


SetMainAreas(mainwindow,
         menubar,
         drawingarea);


XtRealizeWidget(parent);

/*
 * Now that we have the windows, we
```

```
 * can get the window IDs.
 */


global_display = XtDisplay(drawingarea);
global_window  = XtWindow(drawingarea);


/*
 * Create a graphics context.
 */
global_gc = XCreateGC(global_display,
                global_window,
                0L, (XGCValues*) NULL);


/*
 * Create an XImage.
 */
if (QueryAndPrintShm(global_display) == True) {

#ifdef MITSHM

        global_ximage = CreateShmImageFromWidget(parent,
                        global_width,
                        global_height,
                        &global_shminfo);

        if (global_ximage == (XImage*) NULL) {
            printf(
                "Error: failure to create shared image.\n");
            exit(-1);
        }
```

```
        /*
         * Capture an image from
         * somewhere on the screen.
         */
        global_x = 0;
        global_y = 0;

        XShmGetImage(global_display,
            DefaultRootWindow(global_display),
            global_ximage,
            global_x,
            global_y,
            AllPlanes); /* plane mask */

#endif /* MITSHM */

    } else {
        exit(-1);
    }

    /*
     * Set global position to 0, 0.
     */
    global_x = 0;
    global_y = 0;

    /* Map parent */
    XtMapWidget(parent);
    XtAppMainLoop(app_context);

    return 0;
```

```
}   /* main */


/* end of file o_chap22.c */
```

The sample program captures a chunk of the root window and displays that in the drawing area widget. Each time the `captureCB` function is called when the user chooses the *Capture New Image* menu choice, the program increments the `global_x` and `global_y`, which are, in turn, passed to `XShmGetImage`. `XShmGetImage` captures part of the root window's image, and the program then calls `XShmPutImage` to display the image in our drawing area widget.

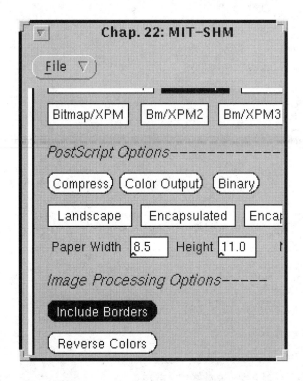

Figure 22.1   *The shared-memory image-capture program.*

Motif Source

The Motif program acts just like the OLIT program and is stored in the file `m_chap22.c`:

```
/*
 *  m_chap22.c
 *  Motif test program for Chapter 22,
 *  which creates a shared-memory XImage.
 */
#include "motif.h"
#include "mitshm.h"
#include <X11/Xutil.h>
#include <stdio.h>


/*
 *  Globals
 */
Display*            global_display;
Window              global_window;
GC                  global_gc;
int                 global_x, global_y;
int                 global_width, global_height;
XImage*             global_ximage;


#ifdef MITSHM
XShmSegmentInfo*    global_shminfo;


#endif /* MITSHM */


/*
 * Callback to capture
```

```
 * a new image.
 */
void captureCB(Widget widget,
    XtPointer client_data,
    XtPointer call_data)


{    /* captureCB */

    if (global_ximage != (XImage*) NULL) {

#ifdef MITSHM

        /*
         * We increment the position
         * each time the callback gets
         * called.
         */
        global_x += 100;
        global_y += 100;

        /*
         * Make sure ranges are
         * within screen.
         */
        if ((global_x + global_width) >=
            DisplayWidth(global_display,
                DefaultScreen(global_display) ) ) {

            global_x = 0;
        }
```

```
if ((global_y + global_height) >=
    DisplayHeight(global_display,
        DefaultScreen(global_display) ) ) {

    global_y = 0;
}


/*
 * Capture an image from
 * somewhere on the screen.
 */
XShmGetImage(global_display,
    DefaultRootWindow(global_display),
    global_ximage,
    global_x,
    global_y,
    AllPlanes); /* plane mask */


/*
 * Place the image in
 * the window.
 */
XShmPutImage(global_display,
    global_window,
    global_gc,
    global_ximage,
    0, 0,  /* src */
    0, 0,  /* dest */
    global_width,
    global_height,
    True);
```

```
        }

#endif /* MITSHM */

}    /* captureCB */

/*
 * Destroy the shared image,
 * then exit.
 */
void exitCB(Widget widget,
    XtPointer client_data,
    XtPointer call_data)

{    /* exitCB */

    if (global_ximage != (XImage*) NULL) {

#ifdef MITSHM

        DestroyShmImage(global_display,
            global_ximage,
            &global_shminfo);

#endif /* MITSHM */

    }

    /* Quit program. */
    exit(0);
```

```
}    /* exitCB */


/*
 * Callback to refresh drawing area.
 */
void drawCB(Widget widget,
    XtPointer client_data,
    XtPointer call_data)


{    /* drawCB */
    XmDrawingAreaCallbackStruct* ptr;


    ptr = (XmDrawingAreaCallbackStruct*) call_data;


    if (ptr->reason == XmCR_EXPOSE) {
            if ((ptr->event->xexpose.count == 0) &&
                (global_ximage != (XImage*) NULL)) {

#ifdef MITSHM


                XShmPutImage(global_display,
                    global_window,
                    global_gc,
                    global_ximage,
                    0, 0,  /* src */
                    0, 0,  /* dest */
                    global_width,
                    global_height,
                    True);
```

```
#endif /* MITSHM */


        }

    }


}    /* drawCB */


int main(int argc, char** argv)

{    /* main */
    XtAppContext    app_context;
    Display*        display;
    Widget          parent, drawingarea;
    Widget          mainwindow;
    Widget          menubar;
    Widget          filemenu;
    Widget          capture;
    Widget          exitchoice;
    Arg             args[20];
    int             n;


    /* Set size of our image. */
    global_width  = 250;
    global_height = 250;


    /* Initialize X toolkit */
    n = 0;


    XtSetArg(args[n], XmNmappedWhenManaged, False); n++;
    XtSetArg(args[n], XmNallowResize, True); n++;
    XtSetArg(args[n], XmNwidth, global_width); n++;
```

```
XtSetArg(args[n], XmNheight, global_height + 40); n++;



parent = XtAppInitialize(&app_context,
        "ProX",                        /* app class */
        (XrmOptionDescList) NULL,      /* options */
        0,                             /* num options */
        ARGC_PTR &argc, argv,          /* cmd line */
        (String*) NULL,                /* fallback res. */
        args, n);



/* Create Main Window. */
mainwindow = CreateMainWindow(parent, "main");


/* Create menu bar. */
menubar = CreateMenuBar(mainwindow, "menubar");


/* Create the file menu. */
filemenu = CreateMenu(menubar, "filemenu");


/*
 * Create a menu choice to
 * capture new images.
 */
capture = CreateMenuChoice(filemenu,
                "capture",
                (XtCallbackProc) captureCB,
                (XtPointer) NULL);


/* Create a menu choice to exit the program. */
```

```
exitchoice = CreateMenuChoice(filemenu,
                "exitchoice",
                (XtCallbackProc) exitCB,
                (XtPointer) NULL);

/* Create a drawing area widget. */
drawingarea = CreateDrawingArea(mainwindow,
                "drawingarea",
                global_width, global_height,
                (XtCallbackProc) drawCB,
                (XtPointer) NULL);

SetMainAreas(mainwindow,
            menubar,
            drawingarea);

XtRealizeWidget(parent);

/*
 * Now that we have the windows, we
 * can get the window IDs.
 */

global_display = XtDisplay(drawingarea);
global_window  = XtWindow(drawingarea);

/*
 * Create a graphics context.
 */
global_gc = XCreateGC(global_display,
                global_window,
```

```
                    0L, (XGCValues*) NULL);


    /*
     * Create an XImage.
     */
    if (QueryAndPrintShm(global_display) == True) {

#ifdef MITSHM

        global_ximage = CreateShmImageFromWidget(parent,
                           global_width,
                           global_height,
                           &global_shminfo);


        if (global_ximage == (XImage*) NULL) {
            printf(
                "Error: failure to create shared XImage.\n");
            exit(-1);
        }


        /*
         * Capture an image from
         * somewhere on the screen.
         */
        global_x = 0;
        global_y = 0;


        XShmGetImage(global_display,
            DefaultRootWindow(global_display),
            global_ximage,
            global_x,
```

```
                    global_y,
                    AllPlanes);  /* plane mask */

#endif /* MITSHM */

        } else {
            exit(-1);
        }

        /*
         * Set global position to 0, 0.
         */
        global_x = 0;
        global_y = 0;

        /* Map parent */
        XtMapWidget(parent);
        XtAppMainLoop(app_context);

        return 0;

    }    /* main */


/* end of file m_chap22.c */
```

Resource File for the Sample Program

Name this file ProX and place it in your home directory:

```
! ProX
! Resource file for Chapter 22 of
```

```
! Professional Graphics

! Programming in the X Window System.

!

! Place this file in your

! home directory.

!

! Generic resources.
*background:      #cccccc
*title:           Chap. 22: MIT-SHM


! Motif resources.
*fontList: lucidasans-12


*filemenu.labelString:    File
*filemenu.mnemonic:       F


*capture.labelString:     Capture New Image
*capture.mnemonic:        C


*exitchoice.labelString:  Exit
*exitchoice.mnemonic:     x


! OLIT
*filemenu.label:       File
*capture.label:        Capture New Image
*exitchoice.label:     Exit


! end of file ProX
```

Shared-Memory X Pixmaps

Shared-memory X pixmaps are much more problematic than shared-memory XImages. For one thing, not all servers support shared-memory pixmaps—a subset of those servers that offer the MIT-SHM extension support shared pixmaps. Moreover, most X servers will support only one format (XYBitmap, XYPixmap, or ZPixmap) for a shared pixmap—and the X server chooses the format. Which format is supported? You can call XShmPixmapFormat to find out:

```
int XShmPixmapFormat(Display* display)
```

XShmPixmapFormat returns the supported format; for instance, ZPixmap. Note that none of the shared pixmap routines will work unless XShmQueryVersion, (discussed above, under Detecting the MIT-SHM Extension) returned a True flag that indicated shared pixmaps are supported.

Once you determine which pixmap format is supported, and if your application can deal with whatever is the necessary way to allocate the data, you can create a shared-memory pixmap with XShmCreatePixmap:

```
Pixmap XShmCreatePixmap(Display* display,
        Drawable drawable,
        char* data,
        XShmSegmentInfo* shminfo,
        unsigned int width,
        unsigned int height,
        unsigned int depth)
```

Before calling XShmCreatePixmap, you need to set up the shared-memory segment just like we showed above in the code that creates shared XImages (under A Utility Function for Creating Share-Memory XImages). The *data* parameter points at the shared-memory segment, and should be the same value as the *shmaddr* field of the XShmSegmentInfo structure.

With a shared-memory pixmap, you can modify the *data* directly, should your application know how the data is formatted in memory. You destroy a shared-memory pixmap with XFreePixmap, just like you destroy normal pixmaps. You'll also need to detach and remove the shared-memory segment, like we described above.

The X Image Extension (XIE)

While the shared-memory extension can help reduce the amount of image data sent to the X server, with the *X Image Extension*, or *XIE*, you can ask the X server to perform a lot of image-manipulation routines for you. You can send an image to the X server and then ask the X server to rotate, crop, and filter the image, for example. All this processing takes place in the X server (with prodding by the X client program). This is especially popular for document imaging systems, where the goal is to place cheap X terminals at the desk of every user and to eliminate many of the paper forms currently in use. Such a system doesn't want to place too much of a load on the central processing unit (CPU) hosts. Instead, all the image processing that can be done in the X terminal off-loads the host, lowers the cost, and improves the overall performance.

The main problem with XIE is that it's not yet available in standard form. XIE is proposed for X11 Release 6. As of this writing, though, we're using the public review draft version 4.12 of the XIE protocol. Because the XIE protocol is subject to change, we're unable to provide any example programs. Instead, we can only provide an overview of this *huge* extension. While the MIT-SHM extension comes with five short pages of documentation (and could use more), the XIE protocol document alone is 185 pages long. XIE, of course, has a much larger task before it than the MIT-SHM extension.

XIE was mainly developed by Digital Equipment Corp. (DEC). If you have access to a version of XIE that predates Release 6, then chances are you're using the DEC version. This version will change in the final standard. One of the changes came out of a major controversy over the extension.

The controversy concerned how demanding XIE should be. The latest draft protocol merges in DEC's XIE with concepts from a simpler imaging extension developed by X terminal manufacturer NCD. This *Simple Imaging Extension*, or *SIE*, is more in tune with office document imaging systems running on low-cost hardware (X terminals or PCs running X emulators). The problem with SIE is lack of availability. Because of the above controversy, XIE allows for subsets, which means that not all services will be available on a given workstation. The main subset, the *document imaging subset*, is based in a large part on the SIE extension.

XIE was adopted as a core technology as part of the *Common Open Systems Environment*, or *COSE*.

XIE Features

Like the MIT-SHM extension, you can query whether the X server supports XIE. You can also check whether your X server provides full support or just the document imaging subset. XIE offers a number of imaging features, including:

✦ Compressed image transport, such as JPEG (Joint Photographic Experts Group), G3, and G4 fax formats;

✦ Image enhancement, including filtering and contrast adjustment;

✦ Image transformation, allowing you to scale, rotate, translate, mirror, and crop images; and

✦ Color modification, e.g., dithering, color resampling, and color mapping.

For color spaces, XIE supports:

✦ CIE XYZ;

✦ CIE Lab;

✦ YCbCr; and

✦ YCC.

XIE provides support for a number of image formats, including:

✦ CCIT G3 and G4;

✦ JPEG and lossless JPEG; and

✦ TIFF (Tagged Image File Format) and packed-bits TIFF.

Photoflos and Photomaps

One of the new concepts introduced by XIE is the photoflo. A *photoflo* is a sequence of image-processing operations. A *photomap*, an XID, is used to store image data in the X server. XIE provides functions to query, create, destroy, and modify both photoflos and photomaps, along with *color lookup tables* (LUTs), *rectangles of interest* (a new definition of the common acronym ROI), and imaging techniques. All these terms have new meanings under XIE.

We eagerly await the widespread availability of XIE, which should help push the X Window System into new applications.

Summary

To avoid having to change the core X11 protocol, the X Window System defines a way for adding extensions to the base protocol. These extensions, especially the SHAPE extension for nonrectangular windows, such as round analog clocks, have proven very popular. Two X extensions, in particular, support extra image-processing options. The MIT-SHM (shared-memory) extension allows you to store images into segments of memory shared between the client application and X server. This eliminates a number of expensive transmissions of data between your application and the X server. The proposed X Image Extension, or XIE, provides for a number of image-processing routines to reside in the X server, freeing your application from these tasks.

The MIT-SHM extension provides a means to place an XImage or pixmaps into memory shared between your application and the X server, avoiding the potentially large overhead of sending huge `XImages` over the wire to the X server. Additionally, if the X server supports shared-memory pixmaps, you can write directly into the pixmap data without the overhead of the X library function calls that send drawing request packets over the wire to the X server.

To do so, the MIT-SHM extension uses the System V UNIX notion of shared memory, using routines such as `shmget` and `shmat`. This does not include the alternative UNIX style of shared memory, based on `mmap`. The System V UNIX style of shared memory, based on `shmget`, is also supported by the X/Open Portability Guide, or XPG.

Your system must have the MIT-SHM extension to the X server *and* it must support System V shared memory. These requirements eliminate a number of other operating systems, such as DOS, right away. You also must run your X application program on the same machine as the X server, or the shared memory won't work. While there is some support in X11 Release 4, you pretty much need Release 5 to use the MIT-SHM extension.

To detect whether the shared-memory extension is available, you can run the xdpyinfo program or the xext program, the latter of which is shown in this chapter. Examine the output of xdpyinfo for the section that covers supported extensions.

By sharing XImage data between the client application and the X server, you can save a lot of data transfers. Therefore, the shared-memory extension provides a special means to create a sharable XImage. To do so, follow these six steps:

1. Allocate an XShmSegmentInfo structure for use with the XImage.
2. Create the shared XImage with XShmCreateImage.
3. Create a shared-memory segment for the XImage data using shmget.
4. Attach this shared-memory segment with shmat.
5. Decide whether the X server can write to the XImage data.
6. Tell the X server to attach your shared-memory segment with XShmAttach.

X Library Functions and Macros Introduced in This Chapter

XFreeExtensionList

XListExtensions

MIT-SHM Functions and Macros Introduced in This Chapter

XShmAttach

XShmCreatePixmap

XShmDetach

XShmGetEventBase

XShmPixmapFormat

XShmQueryExtension

Animation

This final section brings together much of the preceding book in a discussion of basic animation techniques and how they apply to the X Window System. Some of the topics covered include.

- How animation can enhance your applications.
- The problems with animation under X.
- In-betweening to cheat on animations.
- Types of animation.
- Using animation in the user interface.
- Basic X animation techniques.
- Using color cycling.
- Double and multibuffering.
- Rules for effective animation.
- How to animate X bitmaps and pixmaps.
- Xt timers and work procedures.
- Writing a periodic Xt-timer package.

935

✦ Using timer callback functions.

✦ Creating reusable timers.

✦ Animating the Spaceship Earth.

✦ Cheating with the `select` function.

✦ Using color planes for double buffering.

✦ Setting up pixel fields for double buffering.

✦ Filling in red, green, and blue (RGB) values for double buffering.

✦ How to create a program utilizing double buffering.

✦ Using the Multi-Buffering X extension for buffering.

✦ The QuickTime format.

✦ The JFIF format.

✦ The TIFF JPEG format.

✦ The MPEG format.

Chapter 23

Basic Animation Techniques

This chapter covers:

- ✦ How animation can enhance your applications
- ✦ The problems with animation under X
- ✦ In-betweening to cheat on animations
- ✦ Types of animation
- ✦ Using animation in the user interface
- ✦ Basic X animation techniques
- ✦ Using color cycling
- ✦ Double- and multibuffering
- ✦ Rules for effective animation

937

Animation

Animation opens up a whole new world for X applications. You can show the planets in motion, document the coming ice age, and create awesome special effects in your programs.

Animation is applying motion to computer graphics. As such, animation pulls together all of the techniques introduced so far in this book. Animation is used for user-interface effects, television commercials, arcade games, architectural walk-throughs, industrial simulation, visualizing weather patterns, reproducing automobile accidents in courts of law, charting the growth of the Sahara Desert, and much, much more.

Flight simulators use real-time animation to display 3D scenes for pilot training. While the state of the art is not yet a complete substitute for in-flight training, such simulated flight is normally cheaper than real flight.

As virtual reality and multimedia systems become a reality, we'll see more and more computer animation. Unfortunately, implementing animation with X is problematic. In this and the next three chapters, we discuss different animation techniques and how to implement them with X-based applications.

The Problem with Animation

The main problem with traditional animation is sheer volume. There's simply too much work to do to draw everything by hand, especially for a feature-length film. The labor-intensive process of animators hand-drawing every animation cel simply costs too much and takes too much time. These high costs in both money and time also inhibit the ability of animators to try out different sequences, or, in computer terms, to prototype parts of the animation. Because of this, animators have turned more and more to computers in recent years.

The Disney film *Beauty and the Beast*, for example, used extensive computer animation for the ballroom dancing scene. The use of 3D modeling for the ballroom allowed animators to move a "camera" about the computer-created edifice.

The main purpose for applying computer techniques to traditional animation is to have the computer, rather than the human animator, fill in a lot of work. With 24 frames-per-second, a full-length animated move has a *lot* of frames of animation. Every place the computer can automatically create frames or parts of frames means less work for the human animators. One such technique for computer-generated frames is called in-betweening.

In-Betweening

In-betweening or *tweening* is where the computer fills in the blanks in between key frames. In-betweening comes from the practice at the Disney studios whereby the more experienced animators create *key frames*, the frames that establish the key animation and major transitions. Less-experienced animators were then passed the job of creating the frames in between these key frames.

Computer-based in-betweening is where the computer acts as the less experienced animators and fills in between the key frames.

Types of Animation

There are a number of different types of animation, usually based on the implementation techniques. Each technique tries to reduce the conceptual load on the animator by automating part of the animation. Many of these types of animation try to use a high level of abstraction over the process of animation. At its base level, unfortunately, the X Window System provides only very low-level animation building blocks.

Scripted Animation

With scripted animation, the animator creates a script and the animation follows this script or program. Traditional cel-based animation is considered scripted, even though no scripting languages are used. Much of scripted animation is devoted to *staging*, the placement of animated actors on a stage.

The scripting language allows the animator to place backgrounds and actors and set the whole thing in motion. One major problem with scripted animation is that it depends on expertise in the scripting language. Animators traditionally come from the artistic community, not the computer-programming community.

Procedural Animation

Procedural animation, as you can guess, follows a procedure to determine the position of all the objects in time. Procedural animation, also called *actor animation*, is often used in simulating factory-floor assembly lines or other manufacturing processes.

What you do is come up with a set of functions or procedures that define the positions of all the animated objects. In many cases, these positions depend on other parts of the animation. You often have to define positions in terms of other objects.

In a factory-floor animation, for instance, you cannot show liquid moving through a pipe unless the valve is opened. Much of what happens in procedural animation is arbitrarily determined by your code.

Kinematic Animation

Kinematic animation uses the laws of physics to control and constrain the position of the objects. As such, kinematic animation is a lot like procedural animation, but it tends to follow the laws of physics, whereas procedural animation doesn't have this constraint. There are four main types of calculations you do with kinematic animation.

With kinematic animation, you often need to calculate the forces of nature, such as gravity, mass, forces, loads, and so forth, on an object. This process is called *forward dynamics*.

Forward kinematics is similar, but is concerned with acceleration and velocity. With forward kinematics, you work with the motion. You can use this process to calculate collisions between objects.

Inverse dynamics is the process you go through when you have the position first and need to calculate the dynamics, the forces, used to move the object to that place.

With inverse kinematics, you similarly start with a position. *Inverse kinematics* involves calculating the velocity or acceleration that was required to move an object to its current position.

Major uses for kinematic animation include fluid dynamics and other forms of scientific visualization.

Frame Animation

In frame-based animation, the animator creates a sequence of frames and then animates them. In many cases, the frames are static or predetermined, such as when you animate a series of bitmap images. This is a more low-level type of animation than the types listed above. Frame animation is important because that's how most animation is created on X.

Oftentimes, these frames are bitmaps or `XImages`.

Animation Effects in the User Interface

Another use for animation is in creating effects in the user interface. This low-level type of animation typically uses shorter sequences or *spot animation*, since the effects are mostly for presenting feedback to the user. For example, the Hewlett-Packard VUE interface animates a piece of paper coming out of the printer when you print out a file (see the next chapter).

Animation effects in the user interface usually fit into three categories:

1. **Feedback.** This includes rubber-banding lines to allow users to resize windows, drag and drop effects showing the "motion" of data from the drag source to the drop site, blinking to attract the user's attention, and animated effects like the animated bitmap of the VUE printer mentioned above.

2. **Progress indicators.** Programs that perform time-consuming tasks should present some sort of progress indicator to the user, if only to tell the user that the program hasn't locked up. At the simplest level, these progress indicators show a bar chart that gradually goes from 0 to 100 percent done. Other variations on this include animated bitmaps showing a runner running from the starting line (0 percent done) to the finish line (100 percent done), where the runner jumps up in satisfaction for a job well done. Another progress indicator is the animated busy cursor introduced in Chapter 19.

3. **Online tutorials.** Apple Computer's Guided Tour of the Macintosh is one such animated tutorial. In such tutorials, the animation shows the mouse cursor moving about and presents feedback from the parts of the interface selected by the tutorial. You'll rarely find online tutorials for X programs—unfortunately.

Using Animation to Improve the Interface

Animation can improve the user interface by helping the user to answer a number of questions, according to a very interesting paper by Baecker, Small, and Mandert ("Bringing Icons to Life," in the *SIGCHI 91 Proceedings* from the Association for Computing Machinery [ACM]).We summarize the questions and answers in Table 23.1.

Table 23.1 *Ways animation can help the user.*

Way to Help User	Question it Answers
Choice	What can I do now?
Demonstration	What can I do with this?
Explanation	How do I do this?
Feedback	What is happening?
Guidance	What should I do now?
History	What have I done?
Identification	What is this?
Interpretation	Why did that happen?
Orientation	Where am I?
Transition	Where have I come from and gone to?

Animated Tool Palettes

An interesting variant of using animated effects in the interface is to animate bitmaps in a tool palette. Tool palettes are common in drawing applications and contain bitmap "tools" such as a line-drawing tool, a rectangle-drawing tool, and an erasing tool.

In this model, when the mouse cursor enters a part of the tool palette, the tool bitmap starts to animate. The intention is that this animation provides a *demonstration* (see Table 23.1) of what the user can do with the tool.

When the mouse enters the tool, the application waits a delay time and then, if the mouse is still within the tool, the animation proceeds. The delay time is so that the user can move the mouse over the tool palette to select a tool without the animation starting up for every tool the mouse crosses. The animations should be short, say 20 frames long. You may want to cycle through the animation continuously while the mouse is in the tool, or just run through the cycle once.

From an X perspective, the tool is probably a window (tied to a widget). You can then track `EnterNotify` events, generated when the mouse cursor enters the window, and `LeaveNotify` events, generated when the cursor leaves the window. This allows you to start and stop the sequence. With Xt-based toolkits, you can call `XtAddEventHandler` to track these events. See Chapter 4.

Animation from an X Perspective

The key to animation is motion. Animation is applying motion to computer graphics. To create animation, we need a way to generate the motion. This motion typically requires a central controlling loop which draws all the parts of the animation. The loop may draw frames, parts of frames, or moving sprites.

There are three main ways to implement animation from an X Window perspective. There's *fixed-loop animation* in which your application takes over and draws the animation until it's done, with no event-processing or delays. Such applications are generally not considered well-behaved if the animation lasts more than a second.

Idle-loop animation, as the name implies, makes use of the fact that X events normally arrive few and far between. There's plenty of time to perform animation during the period in which the application is idle, awaiting events. With idle-loop animation, the application gets control from the X toolkit when there are no events waiting in the event queue.

Timer-based animation is a lot like idle-loop animation, but instead of using every free moment between events, the application sets up a timer. When the timer goes off, the application draws the next frame of the animation. We consider timer-based animation superior because it results in a more even spacing between frames. This means your animation has a more professional and less jerky feel.

Inside the controlling loop, there are a number of techniques to create animated effects.

X Animation Techniques

The basic animation techniques available to the X Window developer include the following:

✦ Color cycling;

✦ Blinking;

✦ Image transforms, flipping and other transitions;

✦ In-betweening or tweening;

✦ Bitmap frame animation;

✦ Using delta frames to just draw the differences between frames;

✦ Compression, including MPEG and QuickTime;

✦ Drawing, erasing, and drawing again;

✦ Double- and multibuffering; and

✦ Sprite animation in overlay planes.

Many times, you'll combine techniques. (Each technique is described in detail below.) For example, if you use color planes for double buffering (described in Chapter 25), a common technique is to draw into one buffer and display it. Succeeding frames require you to erase the old contents of a buffer and draw the new contents.

Color Cycling

Color cycling is one of the more primitive forms of animation. Basically, we "animate" by changing the colors of an object. The object itself doesn't change, just its colors. This form of animation just requires modification to the colormap instead of to the image in the window—the X server is responsible for changing the image in the window.

There's not a lot you can do with color cycling, because you only change colors. Even so, you can use color to present the illusion of motion. A theater marquee, for example, turns on and off stationary light bulbs. Yet, the marquee creates the illusion of motion, going around and around.

The basic means to implement color cycling is to play with the colormap. We normally use XStoreColors, which we introduced in Chapter 9, to change the definitions of the color cells you want to animate or cycle. With each pass through the animation control loop, you call

XStoreColors with the new color definitions. Typically, the colors repeat in a cycle.

With color cycling, you can also make things blink.

Blinking

One of the simplest colormap-manipulation schemes is *blinking*. In many industrial applications, for instance, you need to draw the user's attention to alarm conditions, and blinking a section of the screen is one way to accomplish this.

At the base level, the X library provides no means to implement blinking colors. One way to implement blinking colors is to change the colormap entries with XStoreColors.

The basic idea is to dynamically change the color used for an object on the screen. Let's say you want to blink a number of objects in your application's windows using four separate colors. What you can do is just change the color definitions with XStoreColor or XStoreColors. Your application doesn't have to worry about what is in the windows, as it just changes a few colors.

To blink objects in the window, you need to alternate between two colors for each object. If you want to blink four colors, then, you need two sets of four colors each: the blink-on colors and the blink-off colors. Since we're using XStoreColor or XStoreColors, it's a good idea to store the blink-on and -off colors in an array of XColor structures, as these structures are needed for the calls to XStoreColor or XStoreColors. Note that *both* sets of colors share the same color indexes or pixel values.

To make this work, you need to draw the objects with the blink colors (that is, the pixel field of the XColor structure must match one of your blink colors).

The following code snippet shows how to blink objects in the window:

```
#define BLINK_ON 1
#define BLINK_OFF    2

#define NUMBER_COLORS   4  /* arbitrary number */
```

```
XColor blink_on_colors [NUMBER_COLORS+1];
XColor blink_off_colors[NUMBER_COLORS+1];
int    blink = BLINK_OFF;


/* Allocate the color cells... */


/* Set up the colors... */


/* Switch the colors to "blink". */
if (blink == BLINK_ON) {

    XStoreColors(display, colormap,
        blink_on_colors, NUMBER_COLORS);

    blink = BLINK_OFF;
} else {
    XStoreColors(display, colormap,
        blink_off_colors, NUMBER_COLORS);

    blink = BLINK_ON;
}
```

To implement this, you need some means to generate a timing event. That is, you may want to use the "on" colors for five-tenths of a second and then switch to the "off" colors for five-tenths of a second. You need a means to tell your application when to switch.

In the next chapter, we discuss a number of ways to generate such timer events, including using Xt timers.

Image Transforms

Many presentation packages provide an array of image transformations to handle the transition from one scene to the next. For example, a new scene can come in from stage left or stage right. Another common transition is to gradually replace the bits of the original scene with the bits of the next scene. You can also use page-flipping to "flip" through the various pages.

Bitmap Frame Animation

Covered in the next chapter, *bitmap frame animation* uses XCopyArea or XCopyPlane to draw succeeding pixmaps. You could also use XImages with XPutImage or XShmPutImage. The basic idea for this technique is to draw and draw and draw. That is, with each pass through the control loop, your application draws the next frame, a bitmap, pixmap, or XImage.

Delta Frames

Since the time it takes to draw a frame limits how many frames you can display a second, one idea is to cut down on the amount of drawing. If you just kept the whole picture for a few key frames and then the *deltas*, or differences, for the frames in between, your application could draw smarter instead of drawing harder.

Using the delta-frame technique also helps cut down on the massive amount of data needed for long animations in large windows.

Compression

Another means for cutting down on the massive amounts of data required for animation is to use some form of *compression*. Much of the work in computer video and multimedia applications includes schemes to compress images for animation.

A common compression format is Apple's *QuickTime*, which runs on the Macintosh, Microsoft Windows, and Silicon Graphics workstations. QuickTime describes more than just compression, but cutting down on the data needed for animation is a major component of QuickTime. See Chapter 26 for more on QuickTime.

Another common compression format is *MPEG*, named for the *Motion Picture Experts Group*. MPEG is considered a lossy compression format, where, at least in the default case, you trade loss of image quality for compression. When you decompress an MPEG frame, you don't get back the same picture you compressed in the first place. (This is also true of QuickTime.) Even so, what you do get back looks a lot like what you originally compressed. For many applications, the loss of image quality isn't as important as the space savings.

Drawing, Erasing, and Drawing Again

Drawing, erasing, and drawing again is the simplest way to implement animation in X. You simply draw one frame, erase that frame and draw the new frame. If your system has enough speed, and if you place calls to XFlush judiciously, you can create fairly good-looking animation. The drawing, erasing, and drawing again technique is often used with procedural or kinematic animation. The main problem is with flicker, created when you erase the old frame.

Double Buffering

Double buffering is a technique used to reduce the flicker in animation, particularly if you use the simplistic draw, erase, and draw again model. With double buffering, you draw into two buffers, only one of which is visible at any time. The idea is that while buffer one is displayed, your application draws into buffer two. Then, using some magic means, you swap the visible buffer: buffer one becomes inactive and buffer two becomes visible. Your application then draws into buffer one.

This technique reduces a lot of the flicker associated with the draw, erase, and draw again model, because the user never sees the erase step, as this is done when the buffer is not visible.

In X, the magic means to swap buffers uses color planes in a colormap. Your application draws using the GC plane mask and then plays games with XStoreColors to swap the buffers. We describe these games in Chapter 25.

Multibuffering

Another means to implement double buffering is to use the X Multi-Buffering extension. As the term *multi* implies, you can use more than two buffers. You can also use more than two buffers with the color-plane implementation discussed above, but you soon run out of color planes. We also discuss this extension to the X Window System in Chapter 25.

Sprite Animation

The idea behind *sprite animation* is that you have a small object, the *sprite*, that resides in an overlay plane (or a color plane used as an overlay, see Chapters 11 and 25 on color planes). The sprite should be small so that it is easy to draw.

The basic idea behind sprite animation is much like that used for X cursors, an X-server-supported form of sprite animation. Sprite animation is very useful for video games.

Improving Animation Performance

The main way to improve the performance of your animation is to optimize the control loop. You want to draw each frame as quickly as possible and eliminate any unnecessary overhead in the control loop. Try to move all operations possible out of the control loop.

Another way to speed things up is to draw smarter instead of faster. A smarter animation routine tries to only draw things that change between frames, which is the delta -rame approach discussed above.

Rules for Effective Animation

There are a number of principles or rules you should follow to make your animations more realistic. John Lasseter collected a number of these rules ("Principles of Traditional Animation Applied to 3D Computer Animation," *Proceedings of SIGGRAPH 1987*, ACM), which we summarize below. Although the focus is on entertainment value, we still find these rules quite helpful. Many come from the basic idea of making sure your animations clearly convey what you want them to convey. If you animate poorly, that had you present may be very different than the message you wanted to convey. These rules from traditional noncomputer animation include the following:

✦ Soft objects in motion should *squash* and *stretch*. Only very rigid objects don't deform during motion. A bouncing ball, for example, should squash when it meets a hard surface and stretch as it bounces off that surface. The more an object squashes and stretches, the less rigid it is. Remember, though, that the object's volume must remain constant during squashing and stretching. Otherwise, the object will appear to grow or shrink.

✦ *Timing* is everything. The speed of motion can determine the emotions presented. You can speed the timing on the same motions to indicate nervousness, anger, and so forth. Slowing down the action for example, you may convey more friendliness, or even lethargy.

✦ *Anticipate* forthcoming action. The audience for your animations needs to anticipate upcoming action. If you don't provide this, your audience may miss important parts of your animation. Anticipation prepares your audience for the next action, which leads viewers to expect the action. For instance, when an animated character's arm stretches out toward a doorknob, this leads the viewer to the next action: opening the door.

✦ *Follow through* actions and allow *overlapping actions*. An action doesn't end at a clean stopping point. A baseball batter, for example, continues to swing the bat well after the baseball is on its way to a home run. This follow-through adds realism. In addition, the batter is already moving toward first base well before the swing is complete. This way, the end of one action overlaps with the start of another.

✦ *Stage* the action so that the ideas you present are absolutely clear. You need to ensure that your audience gets the message you want to convey. And, in order to do this, you must lead the audience's eye to the center of the action (which is probably not the center of the animated frame). It is also important to avoid losing your ideas in a wash of action. You should present only one idea at a time. Also, contrast the center of attention with the rest of the frame. A still object stands out if surrounded by motion. A moving object stands out on a still background. Too much simultaneous motion obscures everything.

✦ *Speed up and slow down* the action to produce snappier effects. With the bouncing ball, for instance, you want to have a number of frames to show the changes in the ball's shape (the squashing and stretching) at each end of the ball's arc of motion. But, use very few frames between these two extremes and the ball will appear to move faster. The basic concept is to "slow in" to one position and "slow out" on the way to the next position. In between, the motion speeds up.

✦ Have real-life objects move in *arcs*. If your objects move in straight lines, you'll get a more wooden, stiff, computer-looking animation. Natural objects, in particular, almost always move in arcs.

✦ *Exaggerate* action and expressions to convey your ideasmore clear-ly.

✦ Make your animations *appealing*. This doesn't mean making all your characters look like Barney the dinosaur (a popular character in children's TV shows). It does mean using techniques that add appeal. One way to do this is to avoid so-called "twins." A *twin* is when, for example, both arms or legs of a human character are in the exact same position. Remember that humans are not symmetri-cal (except for Marlene Dietrich, of course).

Summary

This chapter introduces the basics of animation and how they relate to the X Window System. In the following chapter, we put the basics into use.

C h a p t e r   2 4

Bitmap Animation

This chapter covers:

- ✦ How to animate X bitmaps and pixmaps
- ✦ Xt timers and work procedures
- ✦ Writing a periodic Xt-timer package
- ✦ Using timer callback functions
- ✦ Creating reusable timers
- ✦ Animating the Spaceship Earth
- ✦ Cheating with the `select` function

953

Bitmap Animation

Bitmap animation is especially useful in the user interface. Oftentimes, you have small bitmaps that you want to animate to provide improved feedback or good-looking effects. For example, Hewlett-Packard's VUE interface animates the printer when you print out a file, as shown in Figure 24.1.

Figure 24.1 *The HP VUE printer.*

The animation effects show a new piece of paper coming out of the top of the laser printer. The effects tell the user that, yes, the software *is* trying to print. Drag-and-drop interfaces often provide some animated feedback effects to tell you whether a drop operation succeeded or failed.

Bitmap Animation in X

Computer graphics and interfaces are full of bitmap imagery that you may want to animate. Whether you start with bitmaps, pixmaps, XImages, or your own image formats, the techniques are largely the same. There is a problem of scale, though, as larger images will take longer to draw, obviously. Even so, you generally follow these steps for bitmap animation:

First, you need to draw the initial frame of the animation. If you're using a bitmap or pixmap, XCopyPlane or XCopyArea may be what you need to draw your frame. If you're using XImages, XPutImage or XShmPutImage are the functions to call.

Next, you want to wait a given period and then draw the next frame. After each frame, you want to wait the same period of time, to make sure the animation appears even and not jerky.

The key is getting an even time interval, and that isn't always easy. One of the main constraints is that you normally don't want to lock up your application while animating. If you want to quit in the middle of a 20-minute animation, you should be able to. Your X application must continue to check for X events even while animating.

Xt Timers and Work Procedures

The Xt Intrinsics provide two main means for performing short tasks in the background, while the user interface remains responsive to incoming events: *timers* and *work procedures*. Both means involve the use of callback functions. When a certain condition occurs, that is, when either a timer times out or the Xt main loop is simply not busy, your callback function gets executed. In general, we find that timers are better because they allow for more evenly spaced animation effects.

First we'll deal with work procedures.

Work Procedures

A work procedure is sort of an Xt background task. When the Xt Intrinsics aren't busy doing anything else, the main event-handling loop can call work procedures. These work procedures are supposed to be small functions that perform work in the background, while the user interface remains fully responsive. The idea here is that most applications remain idle—waiting for user input—most of the time. With a work procedure, your application can take advantage of this idle time and put it to good use.

For instance, a spreadsheet application could set up a work procedure to recalculate values based on modified cells. The key here is that if the user modifies a single cell in the spreadsheet, you don't want the user to wait a potentially long time while the spreadsheet recalculates all the cells that are linked to the modified cell. So you could set up a work procedure to perform a gradual recalculation. This work procedure, for example, could update one cell every time it is called. After a short period of time, all the required cells would be updated. But the user interface still remains responsive during this entire time.

A LISP or Smalltalk programming system could reclaim unused memory, implementing garbage collection, using Xt work procedures. Since most of us aren't writing spreadsheets or LISP systems, a more common use is to create Xt widgets with work procedures. Many users complain of the long time it takes to get an X application started up. One reason for this time is that applications may be creating a number of widgets and every widget creation involves at least one call to `malloc`—a routine not known for its speed. So you're left with a dilemma: do you create all the dialog and other widgets at once, or do you create these widgets only when needed? Either way, you're just spreading around the time it takes to create these widgets. Users don't want to wait for a dialog to appear (while your application creates and then manages the dialog widgets) and users don't want to wait a long time while the application first starts up. One possible solution is to set up a work procedure at start-up. Then the work procedure gradually creates widgets—say one for each call to the work-procedure callback. This makes the application start up faster and also provides better performance during execution.

There are a whole host of reasons why you might want to use work procedures. But, to get more to the point of this chapter, your application could animate frames using work procedures, to perform idle-loop animation, as we discussed in the last chapter.

To set up a work procedure, call `XtAppAddWorkProc`:

```
XtWorkProcId XtAppAddWorkProc(XtAppContext app_context,

    XtWorkProc callback,

    XtPointer client_data)
```

`XtAppAddWorkProc` sets up a work procedure and returns the work procedure ID. Any time you want to terminate the work procedure, you can pass this ID to `XtRemoveWorkProc`:

```
void  XtRemoveWorkProc(XtWorkProcId work_id)
```

You pass a *callback* function to `XtAppAddWorkProc`. This is the function that gets executed when the main Xt event loop is idle. The formal type of this *callback* function is `XtWorkProc`, which has the following format:

```
typedef Boolean (*XtWorkProc) (XtPointer client_data);
```

Your work procedure, a C callback function, should then take the following format:

```
Boolean callback(XtPointer client_data)

{    /* callback */

    /*
     * Perform a SMALL amount of work.
     */


    /*
     * Make sure we get called again.
     */
    return False;


}    /* callback */
```

In your callback function, you return `False` if you want the callback to get executed again. If your work procedure is all done with its work, then return `True`. If the return value is `True`, the work procedure is automatically unregistered.

WARNING There's a bug in pre-R5 systems. If your code is running with X11 Release 4 or earlier libraries, and your work procedure returns `True`, chances are you'll face a memory leak. This bug was fixed in Release 5.

The work procedure should perform only a small amount of work and should return in a very short period of time, or your application will not be very responsive to the user. The whole idea of a work procedure is that of a cooperative background function. So, if your function doesn't cooperate, you can mess up the application's responsiveness. Sometimes this is necessary, but most times it isn't.

Timers

As we stated above, we prefer to use timers for animation work, rather than work procedures. Timers allow us to perform more evenly paced animation effects. To set up an Xt timer callback, use `XtAppAddTimeOut`:

```
XtIntervalId XtAppAddTimeOut(XtAppContext app_context,
    unsigned long interval,  /* milliseconds */
    XtTimerCallbackProc callback,
    XtPointer client_data)
```

`XtAppAddTimeOut` sets up a *one-time timer callback*. That is, sometime after `interval` milliseconds have elapsed, the Xt Intrinsics will call your `callback` function. The Intrinsics make no guarantee that the timer will be exact, but normally the times are close to the desired `interval`. It all depends on what happens between the time you set up the timer and the time Xt notices your timer has expired. If a flurry of `Expose` events arrive during this interval, your time-out will most likely be late. Even with this imprecision, this is about the best you can get in a portable fashion. And, normally, it's good enough, unless you require exacting timers. Our advice is to try out `XtAppAddTimeOut` and see if it works well enough. If not, there are a few other techniques you can try (see the section entitled Faster Timers later in this chapter).

    `XtAppAddTimeOut` returns a timer ID. If for some reason you don't want the timer to go off, you can remove the timer with `XtRemoveTimeOut`:

```
void XtRemoveTimeOut(XtIntervalId timer_id)
```

Prior to X11 Release 4, the old method for creating an Xt timer was to call `XtAddTimeOut`. With Release 4 and higher, you should call the newer *XtApp* routines, such as `XtAppAddTimeOut`.

WARNING

Timer Callback Functions

The callback function type, `XtTimerCallbackProc`, is defined as:

```
typedef void (*XtTimerCallbackProc)
   (XtPointer client_data,
    XtIntervalId* timer_id);
```

Your callback should look like the following code template:

```
void callback(XtPointer client_data,
      XtIntervalId* timer_id)


{    /* callback */
}    /* callback */
```

Since your callback is called from within the main Xt event loop, `XtAppMainLoop`, it should execute quickly. Your callback function should also refrain from calling its own event loop, as event loops within event callbacks (and a timer is, in a sense, an event) can confuse the Xt Intrinsics.

Setting Up Periodic Timers

Because `XtAppAddTimeOut` only sets up a one-time timer, you need to do more work if you want a periodic timer callback. In animation, you typically want to draw more than one frame, so we need to set up a periodic timer the hard way. This manual method is to simply call `XtAppAddTimeOut` from within our timer callback:

```
void callback(XtPointer client_data,
      XtIntervalId* timer_id)


{    /* callback */
    TimerStruct*    timer_struct;

    /*
     * Perform your work here...
     */
```

```
/*
 * Set up timer again. Note that
 * we pass the key information
 * with the client_data.
 */
timer_struct = (TimerStruct*) client_data;


timer_struct->times_called += 1;


if (timer_struct->times_called <
    timer_struct->max_times) {
    timer_struct->timer_id =
        XtAppAddTimeOut(timer_struct->app_context,
            timer_struct->interval,
            (XtTimerCallbackProc) callback,
            client_data);
}


}    /* callback */
```

In the code above, we set up the same function to be called again using a new timer set up via XtAppAddTimeOut. In doing this, we have a problem. XtAppAddTimeOut requires both an interval and an application context. To get around this problem, we pass this information as the *client_data*. We invent our own convenience structure to hold the necessary data, the TimerStruct:

```
typedef struct {
    XtAppContext    app_context;
    unsigned long   interval;
    XtIntervalId    timer_id;
```

```
    int             times_called;
    int             max_times;
} TimerStruct;
```

The *times_called* field allows us to keep track of how many times the timer was called. The *max_times* field allows us to turn off the timer when done. We then pass a pointer to this TimerStruct as the *client_data* when we call XtAppAddTimeOut.

Reusable Periodic Timers

To make our periodic timers more generic and reusable, we can place a user callback function within our TimerStruct. If we do this, it's probably a good idea to add in a pointer to any user data, much like Xt's notion of the *client_data* passed to every callback function. Our extended TimerStruct looks like the following:

```
typedef struct {
    XtAppContext    app_context;
    unsigned long   interval;
    XtIntervalId    timer_id;
    int             times_called;
    int             max_times;

    /* User data */
    TimerFunc       user_callback;
    XtPointer       user_data;
} TimerStruct;
```

The TimerFunc is the callback template defined by us:

```
typedef void (*TimerFunc)(XtPointer user_data,
    int times_called);
```

For animation purposes, we can use the *times_called* parameter to tell us which frame to draw. Your periodic-timer callback then should follow the code template below:

```
void user_callback(XtPointer user_data,
       int times_called)


{   /* user_callback */
}   /* user_callback */
```

Note that in using this technique we do incur the extra overhead of another function call during each timer callback. You'll have to decide whether this performance hit is worth it.

Using this technique, we need functions to set up a periodic timer and remove a periodic timer, and we need the Xt timer callback that both calls the user-callback function and sets up another timer to maintain the periodic system.

Setting Up Periodic Timers

To set up a periodic timer, we obviously need to call XtAppAddTimeOut. The function, AddPeriodic, below, adds a periodic timer based on your TimerStruct:

```
void AddPeriodic(TimerStruct* timer_struct,
    XtAppContext app_context,
    unsigned long interval,
    int max_times,
    TimerFunc user_callback,
    XtPointer user_data)


{   /* AddPeriodic */


    /*
```

```
 * Fill in timer structure.
 */
timer_struct->app_context   = app_context;
timer_struct->interval      = interval;
timer_struct->times_called  = 0;
timer_struct->max_times     = max_times;
timer_struct->user_callback = user_callback;
timer_struct->user_data     = user_data;


/*
 * Set up Xt timer.
 */
timer_struct->timer_id =
    XtAppAddTimeOut(app_context,
        interval,
        (XtTimerCallbackProc) PeriodicCallback,
        (XtPointer) timer_struct);


}   /* AddPeriodic */
```

AddPeriodic basically fills in the TimerStruct with the user-passed parameters and then calls XtAppAddTimeOut. We use our own callback function, PeriodicCallback, to maintain the callback. We pass a pointer to the TimerStruct as the client data. The pointer is then used in the callback function, PeriodicCallback.

Maintaining a Periodic Timer

In our Xt-timer callback function, we need to execute the user-callback function and then set up the Xt timer again, using XtAppAddTimeOut, because Xt timers only work one time. By setting up the timer again in each callback, we then create a periodic timer.

The function PeriodicCallback handles this:

```
static void
PeriodicCallback(XtPointer client_data,
        XtIntervalId* timer_id)

{    /* PeriodicCallback */
    TimerStruct*    timer_struct;

    /*
     * Extract our timer structure.
     */
    if (client_data == NULL) {
        return;
    }

    timer_struct = (TimerStruct*) client_data;

    /* Increment the count. */
    timer_struct->times_called += 1;

    /*
     * Call user callback here.
     */
    if (timer_struct->user_callback != NULL) {

        (*timer_struct->user_callback)
                (timer_struct->user_data,
                 timer_struct->times_called);

    }

    /*
```

```
        * Set up timer again. Note that
        * we pass the key information
        * with the client_data.
        */
    if (timer_struct->times_called <
        timer_struct->max_times) {

        timer_struct->timer_id =
            XtAppAddTimeOut(timer_struct->app_context,
                timer_struct->interval,
                (XtTimerCallbackProc) PeriodicCallback,
                client_data);

    }


    }    /* PeriodicCallback */
```

First, PeriodicCallback casts the *client_data* to a pointer to a TimerStruct. This data was originally passed to XtAppAddTimeOut in the function AddPeriodicWithStruct, above. Second, the function increments the count of the number of times the callback has been executed, stored in the *times_called* field of the TimerStruct.

Third, PeriodicCallback calls the user-callback function, stored in the *user_callback* field of the TimerStruct. Finally, if the number of times this periodic timer has been called is less than the maximum allowed, stored in the *max_times* field of the TimerStruct, we set up the timer to go again, using XtAppAddTimeOut. This keeps the timer in its periodic look.

WARNING

Your *user_callback* code, in addition to the timer-callback code in PeriodicCallback, above, needs to complete within the time passed as the *interval*. (The interval is in milliseconds.) If your callback takes too long, nothing worrisome will happen, but your animation will slow down and look jerky.

Removing a Periodic Timer

You may want to remove a periodic timer before it has expired, that is, before the *user_callback* has been called the maximum number of times. To remove a periodic timer before its time, call the function RemovePeriodic:

```
void RemovePeriodic(TimerStruct* timer_struct)


{    /* RemovePeriodic */


    if (timer_struct != (TimerStruct*) NULL) {
        /*
         * Remove Xt timer.
         */
    if (timer_struct->timer_id != 0) {
            XtRemoveTimeOut(timer_struct->timer_id);
    }


    timer_struct->timer_id = 0;
     }


}   /* RemovePeriodic */
```

RemovePeriodic simply calls XtRemoveTimeOut to cancel the pending timer and the sets the *timer_id* value to 0.

Source Code for the Periodic Timer Routines

The code for the timer routines is stored in the file timeout.c:

```
/*
 *   timeout.c
 *   Code for periodic generic Xt timers.
```

```
 */
#include "xlib.h"
#include "timeout.h"

/*
 * This Xt timer callback
 * maintains our generic
 * periodic timers.
 */
static void
PeriodicCallback(XtPointer client_data,
        XtIntervalId* timer_id)

{    /* PeriodicCallback */
    TimerStruct*    timer_struct;

    /*
     * Extract our timer structure.
     */
    if (client_data == NULL) {
        return;
    }

    timer_struct = (TimerStruct*) client_data;

    /* Increment the count. */
    timer_struct->times_called += 1;

    /*
     * Call user callback here.
     */
```

```
            if (timer_struct->user_callback != NULL) {

                (*timer_struct->user_callback)
                        (timer_struct->user_data,
                          timer_struct->times_called);


            }


            /*
             * Set up timer again. Note that
             * we pass the key information
             * with the client_data.
             */
            if (timer_struct->times_called <
                timer_struct->max_times) {
                timer_struct->timer_id =
                    XtAppAddTimeOut(timer_struct->app_context,
                        timer_struct->interval,
                        (XtTimerCallbackProc) PeriodicCallback,
                        client_data);
            }


    }    /* PeriodicCallback */


/*
 * Set up a periodic timer from
 * a preallocated timer structure.
 */
void AddPeriodic(TimerStruct* timer_struct,
    XtAppContext app_context,
    unsigned long interval,
    int max_times,
```

```
         TimerFunc user_callback,
         XtPointer user_data)


{    /* AddPeriodic */



     /*
      * Fill in timer structure.
      */
     timer_struct->app_context  = app_context;
     timer_struct->interval     = interval;
     timer_struct->times_called = 0;
     timer_struct->max_times    = max_times;
     timer_struct->user_callback = user_callback;
     timer_struct->user_data    = user_data;


     /*
      * Set up Xt timer.
      */
     timer_struct->timer_id =
        XtAppAddTimeOut(app_context,
            interval,
            (XtTimerCallbackProc) PeriodicCallback,
            (XtPointer) timer_struct);


}    /* AddPeriodic */


void RemovePeriodic(TimerStruct* timer_struct)


{    /* RemovePeriodic */


     if (timer_struct != (TimerStruct*) NULL) {
```

```
        /*
         * Remove Xt timer.
         */
        if (timer_struct->timer_id != 0) {
            XtRemoveTimeOut(timer_struct->timer_id);
        }

        timer_struct->timer_id = 0;
    }


}   /* RemovePeriodic */


/* end of file timeout.c */
```

The code in `timeout.c` requires the header file `timeout.h`:

```
/*
 *   timeout.h
 *   Header file for periodic
 *   generic Xt timers.
 */
#ifndef timeout_h_
#define timeout_h_   1

#include <X11/Intrinsic.h>

typedef void (*TimerFunc)(XtPointer user_data,
    int times_called);

typedef struct {
    XtAppContext    app_context;
```

```
    unsigned long    interval;
    XtIntervalId     timer_id;
    int              times_called;
    int              max_times;

    /* User data */
    TimerFunc        user_callback;
    XtPointer        user_data;
} TimerStruct;

/*
 * Timer functions
 */
extern void
AddPeriodic(TimerStruct* timer_struct,
    XtAppContext app_context,
    unsigned long interval,
    int max_times,
    TimerFunc user_callback,
    XtPointer user_data);

extern void
RemovePeriodic(TimerStruct* timer_struct);

#endif /* !timeout_h_ */
/* end of file timeout.h */
```

A Program to Test Bitmap Animation

We put together a simple program that animates a number of colored pixmaps, in our case, pixmaps of Spaceship Earth. The program used frame-based animation to display each frame—a pixmap—one at a time. Xt timers then provide evenly spaced frames (as even as possible under Xt's constraints). We choose multiplane pixmaps rather than simple bitmaps because pixmaps allow for color (on color systems) and require greater overhead to animate, thus creating a better test. For our pixmaps, we used the Xpm file format described in Chapter 18 to create 13 80 x 80 pixel frames of the planet earth, in living color.

Figure 24.2 *Spaceship Earth—love it or leave it.*

N O T E

We include the 13 Xpm files on the source-code diskette (see Appendix F). Rather than filling up 20 to 30 pages of this book with raw Xpm data, we encourage you to edit your own. We used Sun's `iconedit` program to create these Xpm files. See Chapter 18 for a description of other programs, such as `pixmap`, that edit Xpm files. However, the Xpm library may not be available on your system. In that case, we suggest you use bitmaps or create your own pixmaps the hard way, by rendering into them on the fly. If you use bitmaps, you'll need to call `XCopyPlane` instead of `XCopyArea`, in `CopyFrame`, below.

As usual, we created two programs, using Motif and OLIT. Both programs share a lot of code that performs the actual animation.

To draw a frame, the `CopyFrame` function, below, calls `XCopyArea` to copy one frame—one pixmap—to the output drawable, in this case a drawing-area widget. The `StepAnimation` function steps ahead one position in the *global_pixmaps* array and then calls `CopyFrame` to draw the frame. The `startAnimateCB` callback function sets up a periodic timer as we described above (`animateCB` is the function called back by the periodic timer). LoadFrames loads up a set of 13 Xpm files using the Xpm convenience function LoadXpmPixmap, which we created in Chapter 18.

The StopAnimation function stops the animation by removing the periodic timer. And, stopAnimateCB and stepAnimateCB act as wrappers for Xt callback functions. stepAnimateCB steps to the next frame. stopAnimateCB stops the animation. Both stopAnimateCB and stepAnimateCB are callbacks from menu choices.

This generic animation code is stored in the file animate.c:

```
/*
 *   animate.c
 *   Generic animation code for Chapter 24.
 */
#include "xlib.h"
#include "xpm.h"
#include "timeout.h"
#include <X11/Xutil.h>
#include <stdio.h>


/*
 *   Globals and externals.
 */
extern XtAppContext    global_context;
extern Display*        global_display;
extern Window          global_window;
extern GC              global_gc;


TimerStruct      global_timer;
int              global_frame  = 0;
int              global_width  = 80;
int              global_height = 80;
```

```
/*
 * Pixmaps for animating.
 */
#define MAX_PIXMAPS   13

Pixmap      global_pix[MAX_PIXMAPS+1];

void CopyFrame(Display* display,
    Window window,
    GC gc)

{   /* CopyFrame */

    XCopyArea(global_display,
        global_pix[global_frame],
        global_window,
        global gc,
        0, 0,
        global_width,
        global_height,
        60, 60);   /* destination */

}   /* CopyFrame */

void StepAnimation()

{   /* StepAnimation */

    /*
     * Increment count to next frame.
```

```
    */
    global_frame++;

    if (global_frame >= MAX_PIXMAPS) {
        global_frame = 0;
    }

    XFlush(global_display);

    /*
     * Copy current frame to window.
     */
    CopyFrame(global_display,
        global_window,
        global_gc);

}   /* StepAnimation */

/*
 * Callback to draw the next frame.
 */
void animateCB(XtPointer user_data,
    int times_called)

{   /* animateCB */

    StepAnimation();

}   /* animateCB */

/*
```

```
 * Callback to start a timer.
 */
void startAnimateCB(Widget widget,
    XtPointer client_data,
    XtPointer call_data)

{   /* startAnimateCB */
    int interval;

    /*
     * We pass the interval
     * time via the client_data.
     */
    interval = (int) client_data;

    /*
     * Destroy any existing timer.
     */
    RemovePeriodic(&global_timer);

    /*
     * Start at the frame we left off,
     * so don't change global_frame.
     */

    /*
     * Set up new timer.
     */
    AddPeriodic(&global_timer,
        global_context,
        interval,
```

```
               64000,
               (TimerFunc) animateCB,
               (XtPointer) NULL);


}   /* startAnimateCB */


/*
 * Load up the pixmaps for the
 * animation frames.
 */
void LoadFrames(Widget widget)


{   /* LoadFrames */
    char    filename[100];
    int     i;


    for (i = 0; i < MAX_PIXMAPS; i++) {


        /* Determine filename. */
        sprintf(filename, "earth%d.xpm", (i+1) );


        printf("Loading %s.\n", filename);


        /* Load Xpm file. */
        global_pix[i] = LoadXpmPixmap(widget,
                           filename);


        if (global_pix[i] == (Pixmap) None) {
            printf("Error reading in %s.\n",
                filename);
            exit(1);
```

```
        }

    }

} /* LoadFrames */

void StopAnimation()

{   /* StopAnimation */

    /*
     * Destroy any existing timer.
     */
    RemovePeriodic(&global_timer);

}   /* StopAnimation */

void stepAnimateCB(Widget widget,
    XtPointer client_data,
    XtPointer call_data)

{   /* stepAnimateCB */
    int frame;

    frame = global_frame + 1;

    if (frame >= MAX_PIXMAPS) {
        frame = 0;
    }

    printf("Stepping to frame %d.\n", frame);
```

```
        StepAnimation();

}   /* stepAnimateCB */


void stopAnimateCB(Widget widget,
        XtPointer client_data,
        XtPointer call_data)


{   /* stopAnimateCB */


        StopAnimation();


}   /* stopAnimateCB */


/* end of file animate.c */
```

When we animate, the timer intervals all passed by the program. This is because we provide an *Animate* menu with a number of different intervals, from 10 to 750 milliseconds, for your testing. One hundred milliseconds is a good value for animating the Spaceship Earth pixmaps, but your animations may require faster or slower speeds. The faster you go, the more central processing unit (CPU) resources you use up.

Motif Code for the Sample Program

The Motif program sets up a *File* menu with an *Exit* choice and an *Animate* menu with menu choices for 10-, 20-, 50-, 100-, 200-, 300-, 500-, and 750-millisecond animation, as well as choices to stop the animation and step through a single frame. The `CreateAniMenu` function sets up the *Animate* menu. The rest of the program is fairly straightforward, as most of the tough work is done in the shared callback functions in *animate.c*, above.

The Motif code for the sample program is stored in the file `m_chap24.c`:

```
/*
 *  m_chap24.c
 *  Motif animation program for Chapter 24.
 */
#include "motif.h"
#include "timeout.h"
#include <X11/Xutil.h>
#include <stdio.h>

/*
 *  Globals
 */
Display*      global_display;
Window        global_window;
GC            global_gc;
XtAppContext  global_context;

/*
 *  External functions.
 */
extern void CopyFrame(Display* display,
        Window window,
        GC gc);


extern void startAnimateCB(Widget widget,
    XtPointer client_data,
    XtPointer call_data);


extern void stepAnimateCB(Widget widget,
    XtPointer client_data,
    XtPointer call_data);
```

```
extern void stopAnimateCB(Widget widget,
    XtPointer client_data,
    XtPointer call_data);


extern void LoadFrames(Widget widget);


/*
 * Callback to refresh drawing area.
 */
void drawCB(Widget widget,
    XtPointer client_data,
    XtPointer call_data)


{   /* drawCB */
    XmDrawingAreaCallbackStruct* ptr;


    ptr = (XmDrawingAreaCallbackStruct*) call_data;


    if (ptr->reason == XmCR_EXPOSE) {
        if (ptr->event->xexpose.count == 0) {
            /*
             * Copy current frame to window.
             */
            CopyFrame(global_display,
                global_window,
                global_gc);


        }
    }
```

```
}    /* drawCB */

Widget CreateAniMenu(Widget menubar)

{    /* CreateAniMenu */
     Widget  menu;

     menu = CreateMenu(menubar, "animenu");

     /*
      * Create menu choices.
      */
     (void) CreateMenuChoice(menu,
                    "anim_10",
                    (XtCallbackProc) startAnimateCB,
                    (XtPointer) 10);

     (void) CreateMenuChoice(menu,
                    "anim_20",
                    (XtCallbackProc) startAnimateCB,
                    (XtPointer) 20);

     (void) CreateMenuChoice(menu,
                    "anim_50",
                    (XtCallbackProc) startAnimateCB,
                    (XtPointer) 50);

     (void) CreateMenuChoice(menu,
                    "anim_100",
                    (XtCallbackProc) startAnimateCB,
                    (XtPointer) 100);
```

```
(void) CreateMenuChoice(menu,
              "anim_200",
              (XtCallbackProc) startAnimateCB,
              (XtPointer) 200);

(void) CreateMenuChoice(menu,
              "anim_300",
              (XtCallbackProc) startAnimateCB,
              (XtPointer) 300);

(void) CreateMenuChoice(menu,
              "anim_500",
              (XtCallbackProc) startAnimateCB,
              (XtPointer) 500);

(void) CreateMenuChoice(menu,
              "anim_750",
              (XtCallbackProc) startAnimateCB,
              (XtPointer) 750);

(void) CreateMenuChoice(menu,
              "stop",
              (XtCallbackProc) stopAnimateCB,
              (XtPointer) NULL);

(void) CreateMenuChoice(menu,
              "step",
              (XtCallbackProc) stepAnimateCB,
              (XtPointer) NULL);
```

```
        return menu;


}    /* CreateAniMenu */


int main(int argc, char** argv)


{    /* main */
      Display*     display;
      Widget       parent, drawingarea;
      Widget       mainwindow;
      Widget       menubar;
      Widget       filemenu;
      Widget       animenu;
      Widget       exitchoice;
      Arg          args[20];
      int          n;


      /* Initialize X toolkit */
      n = 0;


      XtSetArg(args[n], XmNmappedWhenManaged, False); n++;
      XtSetArg(args[n], XmNallowResize, True); n++;
      XtSetArg(args[n], XmNwidth,  200); n++;
      XtSetArg(args[n], XmNheight, 240); n++;



      parent = XtAppInitialize(&global_context,
            "ProX",                        /* app class */
            (XrmOptionDescList) NULL,  /* options */
            0,                         /* num options */
            ARGC_PTR &argc, argv,      /* cmd line */
```

```
                    (String*) NULL,              /* fallback res. */
                    args, n);



/* Create Main Window. */
mainwindow = CreateMainWindow(parent, "main");


/* Create menu bar. */
menubar = CreateMenuBar(mainwindow, "menubar");


/* Create the file menu. */
filemenu = CreateMenu(menubar, "filemenu");


/* Create a menu choice to exit the program. */
exitchoice = CreateExitChoice(filemenu,
                "exitchoice");


/*
 * Create Animation menu.
 */
animenu = CreateAniMenu(menubar);


/* Create a drawing area widget. */
drawingarea = CreateDrawingArea(mainwindow,
                "drawingarea",
                200, 200,
                (XtCallbackProc) drawCB,
                (XtPointer) NULL);


SetMainAreas(mainwindow,
            menubar,
```

```
                    drawingarea);

    XtRealizeWidget(parent);

    /*
     * Now that we have the windows, we
     * can get the window IDs.
     */

    global_display = XtDisplay(drawingarea);
    global_window  = XtWindow(drawingarea);

    /*
     * Create a graphics context.
     */
    global_gc = XCreateGC(global_display,
                    global_window,
                    0L, (XGCValues*) NULL);

    /*
     * Load up all the Xpm
     * pixmaps for our
     * animation sequence.
     */
    printf("Loading animation sequence.\n");

    LoadFrames(parent);

    /* Map parent */
    XtMapWidget(parent);
    XtAppMainLoop(global_context);
```

```
      return 0;

  }   /* main */


/* end of file m_chap24.c */
```

OLIT Code for the Sample Program

The Open Look Intrinsics Toolkit (OLIT) program, as you expect, mimics
the Motif program. The OLIT source code for the example program is
stored in the file o_chap24.c:

```
/*
 *  o_chap24.c
 *  OLIT animation program for Chapter 24.
 */
#include "olit.h"
#include "timeout.h"
#include <X11/Xutil.h>
#include <stdio.h>
#include <Xol/DrawArea.h>


/*
 *  Globals
 */
Display*        global_display;
Window          global_window;
GC              global_gc;
XtAppContext    global_context;

/*
```

```
 * External functions.
 */
extern void CopyFrame(Display* display,
        Window window,
        GC gc);

extern void startAnimateCB(Widget widget,
    XtPointer client_data,
    XtPointer call_data);

extern void stepAnimateCB(Widget widget,
    XtPointer client_data,
    XtPointer call_data);

extern void stopAnimateCB(Widget widget,
    XtPointer client_data,
    XtPointer call_data);

extern void LoadFrames(Widget widget);

/*
 * Callback to refresh drawing area.
 */
void drawCB(Widget widget,
    XtPointer client_data,
    XtPointer call_data)

{   /* drawCB */
    OlDrawAreaCallbackStruct* ptr;

    ptr = (OlDrawAreaCallbackStruct*) call_data;
```

```
        if (ptr->reason == OL_REASON_EXPOSE) {

            if (ptr->event->xexpose.count == 0) {

                /*
                 * Copy current frame to window.
                 */

                CopyFrame(global_display,
                    global_window,
                    global_gc);


            }

        }


}    /* drawCB */


Widget CreateAniMenu(Widget menubar)

{    /* CreateAniMenu */
    Widget  menu;


    menu = CreateMenu(menubar, "animenu");


    /*
     * Create menu choices.
     */
    (void) CreateMenuChoice(menu,
                    "anim_10",
                    (XtCallbackProc) startAnimateCB,
                    (XtPointer) 10);


    (void) CreateMenuChoice(menu,
```

```
                              "anim_20",
                              (XtCallbackProc) startAnimateCB,
                              (XtPointer) 20);

        (void) CreateMenuChoice(menu,
                              "anim_50",
                              (XtCallbackProc) startAnimateCB,
                              (XtPointer) 50);

        (void) CreateMenuChoice(menu,
                              "anim_100",
                              (XtCallbackProc) startAnimateCB,
                              (XtPointer) 100);

        (void) CreateMenuChoice(menu,
                              "anim_200",
                              (XtCallbackProc) startAnimateCB,
                              (XtPointer) 200);

        (void) CreateMenuChoice(menu,
                              "anim_300",
                              (XtCallbackProc) startAnimateCB,
                              (XtPointer) 300);

        (void) CreateMenuChoice(menu,
                              "anim_500",
                              (XtCallbackProc) startAnimateCB,
                              (XtPointer) 500);

        (void) CreateMenuChoice(menu,
                              "anim_750",
```

```
                          (XtCallbackProc) startAnimateCB,
                          (XtPointer) 750);


        (void) CreateMenuChoice(menu,
                          "stop",
                          (XtCallbackProc) stopAnimateCB,
                          (XtPointer) NULL);


        (void) CreateMenuChoice(menu,
                          "step",
                          (XtCallbackProc) stepAnimateCB,
                          (XtPointer) NULL);


        return menu;


}    /* CreateAniMenu */


int main(int argc, char** argv)


{    /* main */
     Display*      display;
     Widget        parent, drawingarea;
     Widget        mainwindow;
     Widget        menubar;
     Widget        filemenu;
     Widget        animenu;
     Widget        exitchoice;
     Arg           args[20];
     int           n;


     /* Initialize X toolkit */
```

```
OlToolkitInitialize( (XtPointer) NULL);

n = 0;

XtSetArg(args[n], XtNmappedWhenManaged, False); n++;
XtSetArg(args[n], XtNwidth,   200); n++;
XtSetArg(args[n], XtNheight, 240); n++;


parent = XtAppInitialize(&global_context,
        "ProX",                     /* app class */
        (XrmOptionDescList) NULL,   /* options */
        0,                          /* num options */
        ARGC_PTR &argc, argv,       /* cmd line */
        (String*) NULL,             /* fallback res. */
        args, n);


/* Create Main Window. */
mainwindow = CreateMainWindow(parent, "main");

/* Create menu bar. */
menubar = CreateMenuBar(mainwindow, "menubar");

/* Create the file menu. */
filemenu = CreateMenu(menubar, "filemenu");

/* Create a menu choice to exit the program. */
exitchoice = CreateExitChoice(filemenu,
                "exitchoice");
```

```
/*
 * Create Animation menu.
 */
animenu = CreateAniMenu(menubar);

/* Create a drawing area widget. */
drawingarea = CreateDrawingArea(mainwindow,
                "drawingarea",
                200, 200,
                (XtCallbackProc) drawCB,
                (XtPointer) NULL);

SetMainAreas(mainwindow,
            menubar,
            drawingarea);

XtRealizeWidget(parent);

/*
 * Now that we have the windows, we
 * can get the window IDs.
 */

global_display = XtDisplay(drawingarea);
global_window  = XtWindow(drawingarea);

/*
 * Create a graphics context.
 */
global_gc = XCreateGC(global_display,
                global_window,
```

```
                    0L, (XGCValues*) NULL);


    /*
     * Load up all the Xpm
     * pixmaps for our
     * animation sequence.
     */
    printf("Loading animation sequence.\n");


    LoadFrames(parent);


    /* Map parent */
    XtMapWidget(parent);
    XtAppMainLoop(global_context);


    return 0;


}    /* main */


/* end of file o_chap24.c */
```

Resource File for the Sample Program

Name this file ProX and place it in your home directory:

```
! ProX
! Resource file for chapter 24 of
! Professional Graphics
! Programming in the X Window System.
!
! Place this file in your
! home directory.
```

```
!
! Generic resources.
!
*background:      #cccccc
*title:           Animate


*drawingarea.background: white


! Motif resources.
*fontList: lucidasans-12


*filemenu.labelString:    File
*filemenu.mnemonic:       F


*animenu.labelString:     Animate
*animenu.mnemonic:        A


*anim_10.labelString:     Every 10 ms.
*anim_20.labelString:     Every 20 ms.
*anim_50.labelString:     Every 50 ms.
*anim_100.labelString:    Every 100 ms.
*anim_200.labelString:    Every 200 ms.
*anim_300.labelString:    Every 300 ms.
*anim_500.labelString:    Every 500 ms.
*anim_750.labelString:    Every 750 ms.
*stop.labelString:        Stop Animation
*step.labelString:        Step to next frame


*exitchoice.labelString:  Exit
*exitchoice.mnemonic:     x
```

```
! OLIT
*filemenu.label:      File
*exitchoice.label:    Exit


*animenu.label:       Animate


*anim_10.label:       Every 10 ms.
*anim_20.label:       Every 20 ms.
*anim_50.label:       Every 50 ms.
*anim_100.label:      Every 100 ms.
*anim_200.label:      Every 200 ms.
*anim_300.label:      Every 300 ms.
*anim_500.label:      Every 500 ms.
*anim_750.label:      Every 750 ms.
*stop.label:          Stop Animation
*step.label:          Step to next frame
! end of file ProX
```

The long resource file above fills in all the menu choices for the *Animate* menu.

Faster Timers

XtAppAddTimeOut, described earlier in this chapter, is really a front end to CPU-intensive UNIX calls to implement timers. Because of this, you might find that your Xt-based timers consume too many CPU resources. If that's the case, you may need to implement your own timers.

One way to work on your own pseudotimer is to use the UNIX System V Release 4 (SVR4) and Berkeley function select. You can use the select function to multiplex between a number of descriptors of open files. X, remember, typically uses a file descriptor for the connection to the X server, at least on UNIX-based systems. With select, you tell the function the file descriptors you're interested in; what conditions you're interested in, such if new data is ready to be read on a given file descriptor; and how long you want to wait for activity on any of the file descriptors. This last part, the delay factor, can be used to multiplex a timer and X event handling.

The `select` call takes the following format:

```
#include <time.h>
#include <sys/time.h>   /* timeval */
#include <sys/types.h> /* fd_set */
#include <unistd.h>      /* may have func proto */


int select(size_t number_fd_bits,
      fd_set* read_fd_bitmasks,
      fd_set* write_fd_bitmasks,
      fd_set* except_fd_bitmasks,
      const struct timeval* timeout)
```

Older definitions of `select` used the following:

```
int select(size_t number_fd_bits,
      int* read_fd_bitmasks,
      int* write_fd_bitmasks,
      int* except_fd_bitmasks,
      const struct timeval* timeout)
```

If no activity occurs on any of the file descriptors within the time-out period, `select` blocks for the amount of time stored in the *timeout* parameter. If activity takes place on any of the file descriptors, then `select` marks the bitmasks to show which file descriptors had activity and quits right away. Thus, `select` provides a form of event control with timed waits. It returns the number of file descriptors that had activity.

WARNING

Select is specific to the UNIX operating system, particularly BSD, SVR4 UNIX, and their derivatives. Even so, some systems don't provide `select`, so that if you use `select`, your code is not be portable.

The Timeval Structure

The `timeval` structure has the following fields:

```
struct timeval {
    long  tv_sec;   /* seconds */
    long  tv_usec;  /* and microseconds */
};
```

There are three ways to interpret the `timeval` structure values. First, if you pass a NULL to `select` for the `struct timeval` pointer, this means your application wants to block forever. We generally don't want this. If both the *tv_sec* and *tv_usec* fields are set to zero, then `select` won't wait at all—it will just check whether any of the file descriptors are ready for the given conditions. The third way is to pass a number of seconds in the tv_sec field, most likely zero seconds for our uses, and a number of microseconds in the tv_usec field, which is useful for setting up a short timeout.

Calling the Select Function

Calling the `select` function directly is fraught with problems. First, many systems don't support `select`, although a similar function, `poll`, may help. Second, in the beginning, `select` was based on the model that only supported 32 file descriptors were allowed per process and that integers are 32 bits long. Hence, `select` uses bitmasks to indicate all the files. These assumptions are no longer valid on many systems, so you have to go through some contortions to use `select`.

There are four steps to calling `select` to check for X events and provide a time-out, which we go through in depth below:

1. Fill in the time-out values in the `struct timeval`.
2. Get the file descriptor for the X connection.
3. Fill in the bitmasks with the desired file descriptors.
4. Call the `select` function itself.

The first step, filling in the time-out values in the `struct timeval`, is easy:

```
struct timeval timeout;


timeout.tv_sec = 0;  /* 0 full seconds */
timeout.tv_usec = 5000000;
```

The second step, getting the X file descriptor, uses a special macro. Your application's connection to the X server typically uses a file descriptor, normally a TCP socket, which you can get from the `ConnectionNumber` macro:

```
int ConnectionNumber(Display* display)
```

The third step, filling in the bitmasks, is the least portable. Assuming connection holds the file descriptor of the X connection, retrieved with the `ConnectionNumber` macro, you fill in a special data type, the `fd_set`, as follows:

```
int        connection;
fd_set     read_set;


FD_ZERO(&read_set);


FD_SET(connection, &read_set);
```

The FD_ZERO macro zeros out the `fd_set` data type. FD_SET sets a file descriptor into an `fd_set` data type. (The `fd_set` data type exists only for this purpose.) We only want to set up the read mask because we want to either wait for a given time-out, or stop if there's an incoming X event waiting.

WARNING

The `fd_set` data type and the FD_ZERO and FD_SET macros won't be supported on some systems that do support `select`.

With this set up, we can call `select`:

```
status = select(1,   /* one useful bit */
          &read_set,
          0, 0,
          &timeout);
```

To put it all together, you can call `select` to check for X events as follows:

```
#include <sys/types.h>
#include <sys/time.h>   /* timeval */
#include <unistd.h>     /* may have func proto */
#include <time.h>
#include <sys/types.h>
#include <X11/Xlib.h>


int           status;
struct timeval timeout;
Display*      display;
XEvent        event;
int           connection;
fd_set        read_set;


/* Set up timeout. */
timeout.tv_sec = 0;   /* 0 full seconds */
timeout.tv_usec = 5000000;


/* Get X connection fd */
connection = ConnectionNumber(display);



/* Set up read mask. */
FD_ZERO(&read_set);
```

```
    FD_SET(connection, &read_set);

/* Call select */
status = select(1,  /* one useful bit */
            &read_set,
            0, 0,
            &timeout);

if (status == 0) {

    /* We timed out with no activity. */

    /* Perform animation... */

} else {

    /* We had activity on the X socket */

    if (XEventsQueued(display, QueuedAfterReading ) > 0) {

        /* Get X event. */
        XNextEvent(display, &event);

        /* Process the X event... */
    }
}
```

The above code checks only for activity on the X-connection file descriptor. This file descriptor will have read activity when new X events arrive. Our assumption is that if an X event comes in, we want to process it right away. Otherwise, we wait for the given time-out period. Your applications, on the other hand, may have a number of file descriptors open and may therefore want to check for activity on all these file descriptors.

The XNextEvent function blocks awaiting the next event from the X server:

```
XNextEvent(Display* display,
    XEvent* event) /* RETURN */
```

We can avoid blocking if we only call XNextEvent if we're sure that an event has arrived. We're sure an event has arrived because of the call to XEventsQueued:

```
int XEventsQueued(Display* display, int queue_mode)
```

XEventsQueued returns the number of X events waiting in the event queue. The *queue_mode* can be one of QueuedAfterFlush, QueuedAfterReading, or QueuedAlready. With QueuedAfterFlush, XEventsQueued first checks the internal queue. If there are no events waiting in the queue, then XEventsQueued calls XFlush and checks again. With QueuedAfterReading, if there are no events waiting in the queue, XEventsQueued attempts to read events from the connection to the X server, but does not flush out X requests waiting on an XFlush. With QueuedAlready, XEventsQueued checks only the internal queue for events.

Using Select with the Xt Intrinsics

With the Xt Intrinsics, you'll want to call XtAppNextEvent instead of XNextEvent:

```
void XtAppNextEvent(XtAppContext app_context,
        XEvent* event) /* RETURN */
```

Both functions block awaiting the next event from the X server.

With all this, you can make an end-run around XtAppMainLoop, which we discussed in Chapter 5, but to be honest, this isn't always worth it. We suggest trying XtAppMainLoop first, then using code such as that above if you find performance or other problems.

Summary

Bitmap animation is especially useful in the user interface. Oftentimes, you have small bitmaps that you want to animate to provide improved feedback or good-looking effects.

Computer graphics and interfaces are full of bitmap imagery that you may want to animate. Whether you start with bitmaps, pixmaps, `XImages`, or your own image formats, the techniques are largely the same. There is a problem of scale, though, as larger images will take longer to draw, obviously. Even so, you generally follow these steps for bitmap animation:

First, you need to draw the initial frame of the animation. If you're using a bitmap or pixmap, `XCopyPlane` or `XCopyArea` may be what you need to draw your frame. If you're using `XImages`, `XPutImage` or `XShmPutImage` are the functions to call.

Next, you want to wait a given period and then draw the next frame. After each frame, you want to wait the same period of time, to make sure the animation appears even and not jerky.

The key is getting an even time interval, and that isn't always easy. One of the main constraints is that you normally don't want to lock up your application while animating. If you want to quit in the middle of a 20-minute animation, you should be able to. Your X application must continue to check for X events even while animating.

The Xt Intrinsics provide two main means for performing short tasks in the background, while the user interface remains responsive to incoming events: *timers* and *work procedures*. Both means involve the use of callback functions. When a certain condition occurs, that is, when either a timer times out or the Xt main loop is simply not busy, your callback function gets executed. In general, we find that timers are better because they allow for more evenly spaced animation effects.

To make our periodic timers more generic and reusable, we can place a user callback function within our `TimerStruct`. If we do this, it's probably a good idea to add in a pointer to any user data, much like Xt's notion of the `client_data` passed to every callback function.

We put together a simple program that animates a number of colored pixmaps, in our case, pixmaps of Spaceship Earth. The program used frame-based animation to display each frame—a pixmap—one at a time. Xt timers then provide evenly spaced frames (as even as possible under Xt's constraints). We choose multiplane pixmaps rather than simple bitmaps because pixmaps allow for color (on color systems) and require greater overhead to animate, thus creating a better test. For our pixmaps, we used the Xpm file format described in Chapter 18 to create 13 80 x 80 pixel frames of the planet earth, in living color.

Xt Functions and Macros Introduced in This Chapter

XtAppAddTimeOut

XtAppAddWorkProc

XtAppNextEvent

XtRemoveTimeOut

XtRemoveWorkProc

XLibrary Functions and Macros Introduced in This Chapter

XEventsQueued

XNextEvent

Chapter 25

Double Buffering for Smooth Animation

This chapter covers:

- ✦ Using color planes for double buffering
- ✦ Setting up pixel fields for double buffering
- ✦ Filling in red, green, and blue (RGB) values for double buffering
- ✦ How to create a program utilizing double buffering
- ✦ Using the Multi-Buffering X extension for buffering

Software Double Buffering

Double buffering is the process of drawing into two buffers to make smoother animations. The technique is used to reduce the flicker in animation, particularly if you employ the simplistic draw, erase, and draw again model. With double buffering, you draw into two buffers, only one of which is visible at any time. The idea is that while buffer 1 is displayed, your application draws into buffer 2. Then, using some magic means, you swap the visible buffer: buffer 1 becomes inactive and buffer 2 becomes visible. Your application then draws into buffer 1.

This technique reduces a lot of the flicker associated with the draw, erase, and draw again model, because the user doesn't see all the redrawing and erasing that goes on in the hidden buffer. You end up with a smoother transition between frames of your animation.

In X, the magic means to swap buffers uses color planes in a colormap. Your application draws using the GC (graphics context) plane mask and then plays games with XStoreColors to swap the buffers.

In this chapter, we discuss two means for implementing double buffering. One uses color planes and should work on any X system with a writable visual, such as DirectColor, GrayScale, or PseudoColor. The other uses the Multi-Buffering X extension and is therefore not available on all systems.

Double Buffering Using Color Planes

In Chapter 11, we used color planes as overlays. Now we're going to use color planes to support double buffering. The concepts are very close, but we need a few more tricks for working with double buffering.

The basic strategy for drawing with color-plane double buffering follows. On every time-out callback, you want to draw the next animation frame:

1. Set up the plane mask.
2. Clear the old frame data in the current buffer with XFillRectangle.
3. Draw your animation frame.

4. Make the frame visible by calling `XStoreColors`.

5. Switch the buffer number, from 0 to 1 or 1 to 0.

First, you set up the color planes. When you draw, you draw into buffer 0, display buffer 0, and then start drawing into buffer 1. On every time-out, you swap buffers. You *always* draw into the hidden buffer, to ensure that the user doesn't see any odd effects created while drawing.

Sound easy? To set up color-plane double buffering, first you need to allocate a number of color planes for the buffering. You must determine how many planes are necessary based on the number of colors you use and then double it (for the double buffer). Once you allocate the planes, you need to split the planes into the two buffers and fill in the all color cells your application now owns. You then need to set up the plane masks for the graphics contexts you use for the proper planes.

To swap the buffers, you need to change the plane mask on your GC and then call `XStoreColors` to store in the next buffer's color definitions. We cover all of this in depth below, starting with the process you follow to determine how many color planes you really need. The idea is to use as few as possible, since they are usually a precious resource on most systems.

Determining How Many Color Planes Are Needed

To determine the number of color planes needed, determine how many colors to draw, including any background colors. Let's say, for example, that we want to draw with three colors, including the background. In our case, we'll draw with *slateblue* and *cadetblue*, using *black* as the background color.

To determine the number of color planes, we need to find the closest power of 2 that holds at least three colors. It doesn't take a rocket scientist to pick 4, or 2^2. Thus, we need to allocate 2 color planes for our colors. Since we also want to double-buffer our graphics output, we need to double the number of color planes allocated, to 4.

We always allocate one pixel as well as the planes, so that we have a pixel value to use as a base pixel to build up the color cells we own.

So, the total number of colors we're allocating is 1 (pixel) * 2^4, or 16 colors total, which we allocate with `XAllocColorCells`, requesting one pixel and four planes:

```
#define NUMBER_PLANES    4
#define NUMBER_PIXELS    1

Display*        display;
Colormap        colormap
unsigned long   planes[NUMBER_PLANES+1];
unsigned long   pixels[NUMBER_PIXELS+1];
int             status;

status = XAllocColorCells(display,
        colormap,
        False,   /* no need to be contiguous */
        planes,
        NUMBER_PLANES,
        pixels,
        NUMBER_PIXELS);

if (status == 0) {
    /* error ... */
}
```

To visualize the result of the call to `XAllocColorCells` (if this call is successful), let's assume the one pixel we allocate has a value of 0x80, or 1000000 in binary, and the four planes are 0x08, 0x04, 0x02, and 0x01. The final pixels we own are all combinations of the base pixel (0x80 for our example) and the four planes. To put this all together, we own the pixel values listed in Table 25.1.

Table 25.1   *Color cells from allocating 4 planes.*

Cell	Planes	Final Pixel
0	0000	10000000

1	0001	10000001
2	0010	10000010
3	0011	10000011
4	0100	10000100
5	0101	10000101
6	0110	10000110
7	0111	10000111
8	1000	10001000
9	1001	10001001
10	1010	10001010
11	1011	10001011
12	1100	10001100
13	1101	10001101
14	1110	10001110
15	1111	10001111

Your call to XAllocColorCells often won't result in such nice, neat values. By using the example, we hope to clearly show which color planes you need to fill in with which colors.

Filling in the Color Planes

To fill in these planes, we need to place one of our three colors in each of the 16 color cells our application now owns. For double buffering, we'll use planes 0 and 1 for buffer 0 and planes 2 and 3 for buffer 1. To do this, we split the color planes right down the middle, as listed in Table 25.2.

Table 25.2 *Color planes to buffers.*

Cell	Buffer 0	Buffer I
0	00	00
1	00	01
2	00	10

3	00	11
4	01	00
5	01	01
6	01	10
7	01	11
8	10	00
9	10	01
10	10	10
11	10	11
12	11	00
13	11	01
14	11	10
15	11	11

We need to create two 16-element XColor arrays to fill in the color planes. The first array will hold the colors for buffer 0, the second those for buffer 1. Note that the pixel value is the same for both buffers, but we want to place different red, green, and blue (RGB) values into the two buffers. Why? Because we want XStoreColors, in combination with a GC plane mask, to change the image from buffer 0 to buffer 1. To do this, we need to play some tricks with the color cells.

The main trick is simple: wherever we have both bits on, we use the background color. Wherever we have only one bit on, we use the proper color. Where no bits are on, we use the background (black). To color buffer 0, we use the scheme listed in Table 25.3.

Table 25.3 *Coloring buffer 0.*

Cell	Buffer 0	Color
0	00	black
1	00	black
2	00	black
3	00	black

4	01	slateblue
5	01	slateblue
6	01	slateblue
7	01	slateblue
8	10	cadetblue
9	10	cadetblue
10	10	cadetblue
11	10	cadetblue
12	11	black
13	11	black
14	11	black
15	11	black

There are four combinations with our background color, `black`; four combinations with our first color, `slateblue`; and four combinations with our second color, `cadetblue`. We also have four combinations left over, because we allocated for four color cells, not three, as 4 is a power of 2. We set these combinations, where both plane-mask bits are on, to the background color, `black`.

We color buffer 1 similarly, as listed in Table 25.4.

Table 25.4 *Coloring buffer 1.*

Cell	Buffer 1	Color
0	00	black
1	01	slateblue
2	10	cadetblue
3	11	black
4	00	black
5	01	slateblue
6	10	cadetblue
7	11	black

8	00	black
9	01	slateblue
10	10	cadetblue
11	11	black
12	00	black
13	01	slateblue
14	10	cadetblue
15	11	black

The two buffers are different in how you lay out the colors to the combinations. This is the key to making the color planes act as a double buffer. To put the two buffers together, we use the setting listed in Table 25.5.

Table 25.5 *16 colors by planes.*

Cell	Planes	Buffer 0	Buffer 1
0	0000	black	black
1	0001	black	slateblue
2	0010	black	cadetblue
3	0011	black	black
4	0100	slateblue	black
5	0101	slateblue	slateblue
6	0110	slateblue	cadetblue
7	0111	slateblue	black
8	1000	cadetblue	black
9	1001	cadetblue	slateblue
10	1010	cadetblue	cadetblue
11	1011	cadetblue	black
12	1100	black	black
13	1101	black	slateblue
14	1110	black	cadetblue
15	1111	black	black

Each color cell is created by ORing the proper plane masks and the single pixel value we allocated with XAllocColorCells. For now, though, the actual values of the pixel and plane masks don't matter.

After we allocate the planes and pixel, the next step is to initialize the two buffers.

Initializing the Double Buffers

We need to initialize the plane masks that we'll later on use for drawing, and then need to start initializing all the color cells we own. To initialize the plane masks, we want the mask for buffer 0 to hold *all* color planes *except* the planes in buffer 1. We then want the plane mask for buffer 1 to hold all the color planes except for the planes in buffer 0. The code to do this follows, and uses the PictureMask function from Chapter 11:

```
#define NUMBER_PLANES    4

unsigned long   planes[NUMBER_PLANES+1];
unsigned long   plane_mask[2];
int             i;

plane_mask[0] =
    PictureMask(planes, NUMBER_PLANES);
plane_mask[1] =
    PictureMask(planes, NUMBER_PLANES);

/*
 * Now, set plane_mask[0] to
 * the lower half of our planes.
 */
for (i = 0; i < NUMBER_PLANES/2; i++) {
    plane_mask[0] |= planes[i];
}

/*
```

```
 * Now, set plane_mask[1] to
 * the upper half of our planes.
 */
for (i = NUMBER_PLANES/2; i < NUMBER_PLANES; i++) {
    plane_mask[1] |= planes[i];
}
```

Once the plane masks are set up, we initialize all 16 colors we own:

```
/*
 * Initialize color cells to all black.
 */
int           i;
unsigned long xcolor_array[2][16];

for (i = 0; i < 16; i++) {
    xcolor_array[0][i].flags =
            DoRed | DoGreen | DoBlue;
    xcolor_array[0][i].red   = 0;
    xcolor_array[0][i].green = 0;
    xcolor_array[0][i].blue  = 0;

    xcolor_array[1][i].flags =
            DoRed | DoGreen | DoBlue;
    xcolor_array[1][i].red   = 0;
    xcolor_array[1][i].green = 0;
    xcolor_array[1][i].blue  = 0;
}
```

We set all the color cells so that the XColor structure *red, green,* and *blue* fields all hold 0. We initialize all the colors to *black*. Why? Because black is our background color and most of the color tables are to be filled

with *black* anyway. We also set all the *flags* fields to DoRed |
DoGreen | DoBlue so that XStoreColors, called later on, will use all
the RGB components.

Setting Up the Pixel Fields

The next step is to set up the *pixel* fields for the 16 color cells we own.
Each color cell, or pixel value, is formed by the proper plane mask and the
base pixel value that we got back from *XAllocColorCells*, above. We
OR together the plane masks and the pixel value. To do so, we use a simple
trick. Since our buffering scheme uses bits to represent the planes, we can
treat an integer loop variable, *i*, as a binary number. We can set up a result
like that of Table 25.1, except that instead of using the binary values as the
pixel value, we instead use the values returned from XAlloc-
ColorCells:

```
unsigned long     new_pixel;


for (i = 0; i < 16; i++) {


    /* Initialize each time. */
    new_pixel = pixels[0];


    /*

     * We basically count up, using

     * i as a binary number.

     */


    /* Plane 0. */
    if (i & 0x08) {
        new_pixel |= planes[0];
    }


    /* Plane 1 */
```

```
if (i & 0x04) {
    new_pixel |= planes[1];
}


/* Plane 2 */
if (i & 0x02) {
    new_pixel |= planes[2];
}


/* Plane 3 */
if (i & 0x01) {
    new_pixel |= planes[3];
}


xcolor_array[0][i].pixel = new_pixel;
xcolor_array[1][i].pixel = new_pixel;
}
```

Note that both arrays of XColors use the same *pixel* values. The RGB values will be different (see Table 25.5, above), but the *pixel* fields are all the same. Once we have all the pixels filled in, the next step is to fill in the RGB values for the same colors.

Filling in the RGB Values

To fill in the RGB values for the colors, we cheat. First off, we know that most of the cells will use black, which has a 0,0,0 RGB value. Because of this, we showed above how we set all the color cells so that the XColor structure *red*, *green*, and *blue* fields all hold 0. We also set all the *flags* fields to DoRed | DoGreen | DoBlue so that XStoreColors will use all the RGB components. Once this is done, we only have to set the RGB values for the *slateblue* and *cadetblue* cells.

To further cheat, we can look up *slateblue* and *cadetblue* in our rgb.txt file (see Appendix A) and we find the RGB values are 106, 90, 205 for *slateblue* and 95, 158, 160 for *cadetblue*. Remember that we have to scale the 0 to 255 RGB value from the rgb.txt file into a 0 to 65,535 value suitable for use with X. To do this, we use the ConvertTo64K macro from Chapter 9:

```
#define ConvertTo64K(c)    ((65535 * (long) c)/256)
```

All the tedious code for setting the RGB values is in the function InitDblBuffer, shown later under Double-Buffering Code. Even with only 16 color cells, you can see how tedious the process of setting up all the RGB values is. We leave it to you to find the most efficient way to set up these RGB values.

Choosing the Drawing Colors

From the set of 16 color cells, we choose a set of three drawing colors so that the rest of the code never has to worry about which buffer we are drawing in. Because of this, we need to choose the cells where our color value is the same in each buffer, as we can see in Table 25.6.

Table 25.6   *Matched colors in both buffers.*

Cell	Planes	Buffer 0	Buffer 1
0	0000	black	black
5	0101	slateblue	slateblue
10	1010	cadetblue	cadetblue

What we want is for the rest of the code to draw using a given pixel value and have it paint the desired color into either buffer. We use color cells 0, 5, and 10, as shown above.

If we do this, we also must set up the proper plane mask for the graphics context (GC) we use when drawing. Why? Because if we don't, we defeat the double buffering, as our colors will show through onto the other buffer. Since we choose to use the pixels that have color bits in both buffers turned on, it means we can share the GC used to draw, but we *must* set up the proper plane mask to mask out the other buffer. Each plane mask must include all planes *except* for the planes in the other buffer. The plane mask for buffer 0 holds all the planes outside of each buffer, and then the bits for the planes in buffer 0.

Additionally, we can draw with the three colors into another, non-buffered window, using the same color cells and have no ill effects.

Swapping the Buffers

To improve efficiency, and to hide some of the code for double buffering, we use one step to swap the color buffer and set up the plane masks for drawing. Because we set up the plane masks, we need to call this code *first*, before drawing. This leads to the old which-came-first, chicken or the egg, problem: how can we swap buffers if we've drawn nothing in the buffer? Well, we let the toolkit clear the window originally and then we really don't care.

The very first time our time-out callback is executed, it will draw into a buffer that isn't visible yet. The second call to the callback will display *that* buffer, while the code draws into the other buffer. The animation will always be one step ahead of what the user sees. Other than that, we have no problems with placing all the swapping code together. Why do we want to do this? Because we may want to change the whole method we use for double buffering. In fact, in the last sections of this chapter, we'll show you how to use the Multi-Buffering extension in place of color planes for buffering, and we'll use the same program.

To swap buffers, we need to do three things:

1. Call `XStoreColors` to show the previous buffer.
2. Swap our buffer number.
3. Call `XSetPlaneMask` to set up the drawing plane mask.

Note that we do these three things *before* drawing into a buffer:

```
int   which_buffer;
GC    gc;


/*
 * Show the current buffer.
```

```
 */
XStoreColors(display,
    colormap,
    xcolor_array[which_buffer],
    16);

/*
 * Set GC to write into
 * hidden buffer.
 */
if (which_buffer == 1) {

    which_buffer = 0;
} else {
    which_buffer = 1;
}

XSetPlaneMask(display,
    gc,
    plane_mask[which_buffer]);
```

This is confusing as all heck, isn't it? Apparently, you're either just supposed to know this stuff or figure it out from the brief, obscure reference manuals. The code above becomes more clear when seen inside a working program. But you'll probably have to spend a long time tweaking and just thinking about the problem. This material is tough.

A Program to Show Double Buffering

This section is devoted to explaining a program that shows color-plane double buffering in action. What we do is create two drawing area widgets. In the top widget, we'll use old-fashioned single buffering, so you'll see a lot of flickering. In the bottom widget, we'll use color-plane double buffering. In the last part of this chapter, we'll use the Multi-Buffering extension for double buffering in the bottom widget.

To place some structure over the buffering, and to avoid passing around lots of parameters, we collect all the information necessary for our double buffering into a C structure:

```
#define  MAX_COLORS 3


typedef struct {
       Display*         display;
       Colormap         colormap;
       Window           window_top, window_bot;
       GC               gc_top, gc_bot;
       int              width, height;
       int              which_buffer;
       unsigned long    plane_mask[2];
       unsigned long    colors[MAX_COLORS+1];
       XColor           xcolor_array[2][16];
} DblBuffStruct;
```

The *window_top* and *window_bot* hold the window IDs of the top and bottom drawing area widgets, respectively. Similarly, the graphics contexts are *gc_top* and *gc_bot*. The *which_buffer* flag is used in the double-buffering routines to hold the buffer we're currently drawing into, 0 or 1. The drawing software just passes around an DblBuffStruct structure. It doesn't worry about this internal detail. The *plane_mask* array holds the plane masks we set into the *gc_bot* GC. Note that we never mess with the *gc_top* GC, because that window is single buffered.

The *colors* array holds the three drawing colors, which we showed how to set up above. Finally, the *xcolor_array* is used to swap the buffers in the call to XStoreColors.

An expanded version of this structure is defined in chap25.h, shown later under Drawing Code.

Double-Buffering Code

To work with the `DblBuffStruct` structure, we define two functions. These functions, `InitDblBuffer` and `SwapBuffer`, encapsulate all the double-buffering code and allow us to later switch double-buffering methods. `InitDblBuffer` initializes the two buffers, using code we described above. `SwapBuffer`, as you guessed, swaps the buffers. The functions take the following parameters:

```
void InitDblBuffer(DblBuffStruct* dblbuff,
    Widget draw1, Widget draw2,
    int width, int height)


void SwapBuffer(DblBuffStruct* dblbuff)
```

The code for these functions is stored in the file `dblbuff.c`:

```
/*
 *  dblbuff.c
 *  double buffering routines for Chapter 25.
 */
#include "xlib.h"
#include <X11/Intrinsic.h>
#include <stdio.h>
#include "chap25.h"

extern unsigned long
PictureMask(unsigned long* planes,
        unsigned int number_planes);

/*
 * Convert an RGB value from a 0-255
 * scale to X's 0-65535 scale.
 */
```

```
#define ConvertTo64K(c)    ((65535 * (long) c)/256)


#define NUMBER_PLANES    4    /* 2 planes for each buffer. */
#define NUMBER_PIXELS    1

void InitDblBuffer(DblBuffStruct* dblbuff,
    Widget draw1, Widget draw2,
    int width, int height)


{    /* InitDblBuffer */
    int             i, status;
    unsigned long   planes[NUMBER_PLANES+1];
    unsigned long   pixels[NUMBER_PIXELS+1];
    unsigned long   new_pixel;


    InitDblWindows(dblbuff,
        draw1, draw2,
        width, height);


    /*
     * Allocate color planes.
     */
    status = XAllocColorCells(dblbuff->display,
            dblbuff->colormap,
            False,  /* no need to be contiguous */
            planes,
            NUMBER_PLANES,
            pixels,
            NUMBER_PIXELS);


    if (status == 0) {
```

```
        fprintf(stderr, "ERROR allocating color cells.\n");
        exit(1);
    }


    /*
     * Set up plane masks. Initialize
     * both to everything EXCEPT for
     * the planes we allocated.
     */
    dblbuff->plane_mask[0] =
        PictureMask(planes, NUMBER_PLANES);
    dblbuff->plane_mask[1] =
        PictureMask(planes, NUMBER_PLANES);


    /*
     * Now, set plane_mask[0] to
     * the lower half of our planes.
     */
    for (i = 0; i < NUMBER_PLANES/2; i++) {
        dblbuff->plane_mask[0] |= planes[i];
    }


    /*
     * Now, set plane_mask[1] to
     * the upper half of our planes.
     */
    for (i = NUMBER_PLANES/2; i < NUMBER_PLANES; i++) {
        dblbuff->plane_mask[1] |= planes[i];
    }


    /*
```

```
 * Initialize color cells to all black.
 */
for (i = 0; i < 16; i++) {
    dblbuff->xcolor_array[0][i].flags =
        DoRed | DoGreen | DoBlue;
    dblbuff->xcolor_array[0][i].red   = 0;
    dblbuff->xcolor_array[0][i].green = 0;
    dblbuff->xcolor_array[0][i].blue  = 0;

    dblbuff->xcolor_array[1][i].flags =
        DoRed | DoGreen | DoBlue;
    dblbuff->xcolor_array[1][i].red   = 0;
    dblbuff->xcolor_array[1][i].green = 0;
    dblbuff->xcolor_array[1][i].blue  = 0;
}


/*
 * Set up all the pixel values
 */
for (i = 0; i < 16; i++) {

    /* Initialize each time. */
    new_pixel = pixels[0];

    /*
     * We basically count up, using
     * i as a binary number.
     */

    /* Plane 0. */
    if (i & 0x08) {
```

```
        new_pixel |= planes[0];
    }

    /* Plane 1 */
    if (i & 0x04) {
        new_pixel |= planes[1];
    }

    /* Plane 2 */
    if (i & 0x02) {
        new_pixel |= planes[2];
    }

    /* Plane 3 */
    if (i & 0x01) {
        new_pixel |= planes[3];
    }

    dblbuff->xcolor_array[0][i].pixel = new_pixel;
    dblbuff->xcolor_array[1][i].pixel = new_pixel;
}


/*
 * Fill in buffer 0.
 */

/* slateblue */
for (i = 4; i < 8; i++) {
    dblbuff->xcolor_array[0][i].red   =
        ConvertTo64K(106);
    dblbuff->xcolor_array[0][i].green =
```

```
            ConvertTo64K(90);
        dblbuff->xcolor_array[0][i].blue  =
            ConvertTo64K(205);
    }


    /* cadetblue */
    for (i = 8; i < 12; i++) {
        dblbuff->xcolor_array[0][i].red   =
            ConvertTo64K(95);
        dblbuff->xcolor_array[0][i].green =
            ConvertTo64K(158);
        dblbuff->xcolor_array[0][i].blue  =
            ConvertTo64K(160);
    }


    /*
     * Fill in buffer 1.
     */


    /* slateblue */
    i = 1;
    while (i < 16) {
        dblbuff->xcolor_array[1][i].red   =
            ConvertTo64K(106);
        dblbuff->xcolor_array[1][i].green =
            ConvertTo64K(90);
        dblbuff->xcolor_array[1][i].blue  =
            ConvertTo64K(205);
        i += 4;
    }
```

```
/* cadetblue */
i = 2;
while (i < 16) {
    dblbuff->xcolor_array[1][i].red   =
        ConvertTo64K(95);
    dblbuff->xcolor_array[1][i].green =
        ConvertTo64K(158);
    dblbuff->xcolor_array[1][i].blue  =
        ConvertTo64K(160);
    i += 4;
}


/*
 * We start with buffer 0.
 */
dblbuff->which_buffer = 0;


/*
 * Set up drawing colors.
 */
dblbuff->colors[0] = dblbuff->xcolor_array[0][15].pixel;

/* This is where the slateblue match occurs. */
dblbuff->colors[1] = dblbuff->xcolor_array[0][5].pixel;

/* This is where the cadetblue match occurs. */
dblbuff->colors[2] = dblbuff->xcolor_array[0][10].pixel;

}   /* InitDblBuffer */


/*
```

```
 * Swaps from one to the next buffer.
 * We see the current buffer and
 * write into the hidden buffer.
 */
void SwapBuffer(DblBuffStruct* dblbuff)


{   /* SwapBuffer */

    /*
     * Show the current buffer.
     */
    XStoreColors(dblbuff->display,
        dblbuff->colormap,
        dblbuff->xcolor_array[dblbuff->which_buffer],
        16);


    /*
     * Set GC to write into
     * hidden buffer.
     */
    if (dblbuff->which_buffer == 1) {

        dblbuff->which_buffer = 0;
    } else {
        dblbuff->which_buffer = 1;
    }


    XSetPlaneMask(dblbuff->display,
        dblbuff->gc_bot,
        dblbuff->plane_mask[dblbuff->which_buffer]);
```

```
}   /* SwapBuffer */


/* end of file dblbuff.c */
```

Drawing Code

Once we have the buffers set up, we need to draw an animated picture. The generic code that runs with both programs and either color-plane double buffering or X extension multibuffering is placed in the file `chap25.c`:

```
/*
 *  chap25.c
 *  double buffering routines for Chapter 25.
 */
#include "xlib.h"
#include <X11/Intrinsic.h>
#include "chap25.h"
#include "timeout.h"


TimerStruct global_timer;
int         global_x1, global_y1;
int         global_x2, global_y2;
int         global_dir_x1, global_dir_y1;
int         global_dir_x2, global_dir_y2;


extern void
PolygonTest(Display* display, Window window,
    GC gc, int x, int y, int fill_rule);


/*
 * Initialize the window and
 * colormap in the DblBuffStruct.
```

```
    */

void InitDblWindows(DblBuffStruct* dblbuff,
    Widget draw1, Widget draw2,
    int width, int height)

{   /* InitDblWindows */

    dblbuff->display  = XtDisplay(draw1);

    dblbuff->colormap =
        DefaultColormap(XtDisplay(draw1),
            DefaultScreen(XtDisplay(draw1) ) );

    dblbuff->window_top  = XtWindow(draw1);
    dblbuff->gc_top = XCreateGC(XtDisplay(draw1),
                    XtWindow(draw1),
                    0L, (XCCValues*) NULL);

    dblbuff->window_bot  = XtWindow(draw2);
    dblbuff->gc_bot = XCreateGC(XtDisplay(draw1),
                    XtWindow(draw2),
                    0L, (XGCValues*) NULL);

    dblbuff->width   = width;
    dblbuff->height  = height;

}   /* InitDblWindows */

/*
 * Simple function to adjust the x, y position
```

```
 * of an animated object, based on its
 * direction.
 */


void AdjustPosition(int width, int height,
    int xoffset, int yoffset,
    int* x,           /* input/output */
    int* y,           /* input/output */
    int* xdirection,  /* input/output */
    int* ydirection)  /* input/output */


{   /* AdjustPosition */

    /* Adjust X. */
    if (*xdirection > 0) {
        *x = *x + 7;
    } else {
        *x = *x - 7;
    }


    if (*x < 0) {
        *xdirection = 1;
        *x = 0;
    }


    if ((*x + xoffset) > width) {
        *xdirection = -1;
        *x = width - xoffset;
    }


    /* Adjust Y. */
```

```
    if (*ydirection > 0) {
        *y = *y + 5;
    } else {
        *y = *y - 5;
    }


    if (*y < 0) {
        *ydirection = 1;
        *y = 0;
    }


    if ((*y + yoffset) > height) {
        *ydirection = -1;
        *y = height - yoffset;
    }


}   /* AdjustPosition */


void drawItemsCB(XtPointer user_data,
    int times_called)


{   /* drawItemsCB */
    DblBuffStruct*  dblbuff;


    dblbuff = (DblBuffStruct*) user_data;


    /* Adjust position. */
    AdjustPosition(dblbuff->width,
        dblbuff->height,
        110, 80,
        &global_x1, &global_y1,
```

```
              &global_dir_x1, &global_dir_y1);


AdjustPosition(dblbuff->width,
      dblbuff->height,
      80, 80,
      &global_x2, &global_y2,
      &global_dir_x2, &global_dir_y2);


/*
 * Swap buffers.
 *  1. Display current buffer.
 *  2. Switch to new buffer.
 *  3. Set GC plane masks.
 */
SwapBuffer(dblbuff);


/* Clear old pictures. */
XSetForeground(dblbuff->display,
     dblbuff->gc_top,
     dblbuff->colors[0]);


XFillRectangle(dblbuff->display,
     dblbuff->window_top, dblbuff->gc_top,
     0, 0,
     dblbuff->width, dblbuff->height);


XSetForeground(dblbuff->display,
     dblbuff->gc_bot,
     dblbuff->colors[0]);


XFillRectangle(dblbuff->display,
```

```
        dblbuff->window_bot, dblbuff->gc_bot,
        0, 0,
        dblbuff->width, dblbuff->height);

    /* Draw new pictures. */
    XSetForeground(dblbuff->display,
        dblbuff->gc_top,
        dblbuff->colors[1]);

    PolygonTest(dblbuff->display,
        dblbuff->window_top, dblbuff->gc_top,
        global_x1, global_y1,
        EvenOddRule);

    XSetForeground(dblbuff->display,
        dblbuff->gc_bot,
        dblbuff->colors[1]);

    PolygonTest(dblbuff->display,
        dblbuff->window_bot, dblbuff->gc_bot,
        global_x1, global_y1,
        EvenOddRule);

    XSetForeground(dblbuff->display,
        dblbuff->gc_top,
        dblbuff->colors[2]);

    XFillRectangle(dblbuff->display,
        dblbuff->window_top, dblbuff->gc_top,
        global_x2, global_y2,
        80, 80);
```

```
    XSetForeground(dblbuff->display,
        dblbuff->gc_bot,
        dblbuff->colors[2]);

    XFillRectangle(dblbuff->display,
        dblbuff->window_bot, dblbuff->gc_bot,
        global_x2, global_y2,
        80, 80);

    /* Flush out requests. */
    XFlush(dblbuff->display);

}    /* drawItemsCB */

/*
 * Sets up timer to draw double-buffered items.
 */
void StartBufferTimer(XtAppContext app_context,
    unsigned long interval,
    DblBuffStruct* dblbuff)

{    /* StartBufferTimer */

    /* Initialize objects. */
    global_x1 = 0;
    global_y1 = 20;
    global_dir_x1 = 1;
    global_dir_y1 = 1;

    global_x2 = 140;
```

```
        global_y2 = 127;
        global_dir_x2 = 1;
        global_dir_y2 = 1;

        /* Set up timer. */
        AddPeriodic(&global_timer,
            app_context,
            interval,
            64000,  /* max times */
            (TimerFunc) drawItemsCB,
            (XtPointer) dblbuff);

    }   /* StartBufferTimer */


    /* end of file chap25.c */
```

The code above is fairly straightforward. The `StartBufferTimer` function sets up a periodic timer, discussed in the last chapter, for our animation. The timer-callback function is `drawItemsCB`. This function swaps the buffers and draws two objects, a polygon that we first introduced in Chapter 5 with the `PolygonTest` function, and a simple rectangle. We draw everything twice, once in the top (single-buffered) window and once in the bottom (double-buffered) window.

Motif Code for the Sample Program

The Motif toolkit code is also straightforward for our example program. We use an `XmPanedWindow` widget to hold the two drawing areas. The Motif code for the sample program is stored in the file `m_chap25.c`:

```
/*
 *  m_chap25.c
 *  Motif double buffering program for Chapter 25.
 */
```

```
#include "motif.h"
#include "chap25.h"
#include <X11/Xutil.h>
#include <stdio.h>
#include <Xm/PanedW.h>


/*  Globals */
DblBuffStruct    global_dblbuff;


/*
 * Callback to refresh drawing area.
 */
void drawCB(Widget widget,
    XtPointer client_data,
    XtPointer call_data)


{   /* drawCB */
    XmDrawingAreaCallbackStruct* ptr;
    static int      one_shot = 0;
    XtAppContext    app_context;
    Dimension       width, height;


    app_context = (XtAppContext) client_data;


    ptr = (XmDrawingAreaCallbackStruct*) call_data;


    if (ptr->reason == XmCR_EXPOSE) {

        if (ptr->event->xexpose.count == 0) {
            /*
             * If first time, set up timer.
```

```
        */
       if (one_shot == 0) {
           StartBufferTimer(app_context,
               100, /* interval */
               &global_dblbuff);


           one_shot = 1;
       }


       /*
        * We don't worry about redrawing because
        * the animation redraws every frame on
        * each timer tick anyway.
        */
      }
   }


   if (ptr->reason == XmCR_RESIZE) {

      XtVaGetValues(widget,
              XmNwidth,  &width,
              XmNheight, &height,
              NULL);


      if (XtWindow(widget) == global_dblbuff.window_bot) {
         global_dblbuff.width  = (int) width;
         global_dblbuff.height = (int) height;
      }
   }


} /* drawCB */
```

```
int main(int argc, char** argv)

{   /* main */
    XtAppContext    app_context;
    Display*        display;
    Widget          parent;
    Widget          contain;
    Widget          draw1, draw2;
    Widget          mainwindow;
    Widget          menubar;
    Widget          filemenu;
    Widget          exitchoice;
    Arg             args[20];
    int             n;


    /* Initialize X toolkit */
    n = 0;
    XtSetArg(args[n], XmNmappedWhenManaged, False); n++;
    XtSetArg(args[n], XmNwidth,  420); n++;
    XtSetArg(args[n], XmNheight, 480); n++;



    parent = XtAppInitialize(&app_context,
            "ProX",                         /* app class */
            (XrmOptionDescList) NULL,    /* options */
            0,                              /* num options */
            ARGC_PTR &argc, argv,        /* cmd line */
            (String*) NULL,              /* fallback res. */
            args, n);
```

```
/* Create Main Window. */
mainwindow = CreateMainWindow(parent, "main");

/* Create menu bar. */
menubar = CreateMenuBar(mainwindow, "menubar");

/* Create the file menu. */
filemenu = CreateMenu(menubar, "filemenu");

/* Create a menu choice to exit the program. */
exitchoice = CreateExitChoice(filemenu,
                "exitchoice");


/*
 * Create container for 2 draw areas.
 */
n = 0;
XtSetArg(args[n], XmNwidth,  410); n++;
XtSetArg(args[n], XmNheight, 410); n++;
contain = XmCreatePanedWindow(mainwindow, "contain",
            args, n);

XtManageChild(contain);

/* Create drawing area widgets. */
draw1 = CreateDrawingArea(contain,
            "draw1",
            400, 200,
            (XtCallbackProc) drawCB,
```

```
                    (XtPointer) app_context);

    draw2 = CreateDrawingArea(contain,
                "draw2",
                400, 200,
                (XtCallbackProc) drawCB,
                (XtPointer) app_context);

    SetMainAreas(mainwindow,
        menubar,
        contain);

    XtRealizeWidget(parent);

    /*
     * Set up double buffering information.
     */
    InitDblBuffer(&global_dblbuff,
        draw1, draw2,
        400, 200);

    /* Map parent */
    XtMapWidget(parent);
    XtAppMainLoop(app_context);

    return 0;

}   /* main */


/* end of file m_chap25.c */
```

The call to `InitDblBuffer` near the end of the program sets up the double buffers using color planes. The drawing-area callback function, `drawCB`, uses a static *one_shot* to start the animation timer. When a resize event occurs, we only track resizes to the bottom window, the double-buffered window.

OLIT Code for the Sample Program

The OLIT code for the same program is nearly identical to the Motif code. This code is stored in the file `o_chap25.c`:

```
/*
 *   o_chap25.c
 *   OLIT double buffering program for Chapter 25.
 */
#include "olit.h"
#include "chap25.h"
#include <X11/Xutil.h>
#include <stdio.h>
#include <Xol/ControlAre.h>
#include <Xol/DrawArea.h>


/*  Globals */
DblBuffStruct    global_dblbuff;


/*
 * Callback to refresh drawing area.
 */
void drawCB(Widget widget,
    XtPointer client_data,
    XtPointer call_data)

{    /* drawCB */
```

```
OlDrawAreaCallbackStruct* ptr;
static int      one_shot = 0;
XtAppContext    app_context;
Dimension       width, height;


app_context = (XtAppContext) client_data;


ptr = (OlDrawAreaCallbackStruct*) call_data;


if (ptr->reason == OL_REASON_EXPOSE) {

    if (ptr->event->xexpose.count == 0) {
        /*
         * If first time, set up timer.
         */
        if (one_shot == 0) {
            StartBufferTimer(app_context,
                100, /* interval */
                &global_dblbuff);

            one_shot = 1;
        }


        /*
         * We don't worry about redrawing because
         * the animation redraws every frame on
         * each timer tick anyway.
         */
    }
}
```

```
        if (ptr->reason == OL_REASON_RESIZE) {

            XtVaGetValues(widget,
                    XtNwidth,  &width,
                    XtNheight, &height,
                    NULL);

            if (XtWindow(widget) == global_dblbuff.window_bot) {
                global_dblbuff.width  = (int) width;
                global_dblbuff.height = (int) height;
            }
        }


}   /* drawCB */


int main(int argc, char** argv)

{   /* main */
    XtAppContext    app_context;
    Display*        display;
    Widget          parent;
    Widget          contain;
    Widget          draw1, draw2;
    Widget          mainwindow;
    Widget          menubar;
    Widget          filemenu;
    Widget          exitchoice;
    Arg             args[20];
    int             n;


    /* Initialize X toolkit */
```

```
OlToolkitInitialize( (XtPointer) NULL);

n = 0;
XtSetArg(args[n], XtNmappedWhenManaged, False); n++;
XtSetArg(args[n], XtNwidth,  420); n++;
XtSetArg(args[n], XtNheight, 480); n++;


parent = XtAppInitialize(&app_context,
        "ProX",                     /* app class */
        (XrmOptionDescList) NULL,   /* options */
        0,                          /* num options */
        ARGC_PTR &argc, argv,       /* cmd line */
        (String*) NULL,             /* fallback res. */
        args, n);


/* Create Main Window. */
mainwindow = CreateMainWindow(parent, "main");

/* Create menu bar. */
menubar = CreateMenuBar(mainwindow, "menubar");

/* Create the file menu. */
filemenu = CreateMenu(menubar, "filemenu");

/* Create a menu choice to exit the program. */
exitchoice = CreateExitChoice(filemenu,
                "exitchoice");

/*
```

```
 * Create container for 2 draw areas.
 */
contain = XtVaCreateManagedWidget("contain",
          controlAreaWidgetClass,
          mainwindow,
          XtNmappedWhenManaged, True,
          XtNlayoutType, OL_FIXEDCOLS,
          XtNalignCaptions, TRUE,
          NULL);

/* Create drawing area widgets. */
draw1 = CreateDrawingArea(contain,
          "draw1",
          400, 200,
          (XtCallbackProc) drawCB,
          (XtPointer) app_context);

draw2 = CreateDrawingArea(contain,
          "draw2",
          400, 200,
          (XtCallbackProc) drawCB,
          (XtPointer) app_context);

SetMainAreas(mainwindow,
     menubar,
     contain);

XtRealizeWidget(parent);

/*
 * Set up double buffering information.
```

```
    */
    InitDblBuffer(&global_dblbuff,
        draw1, draw2,
        400, 200);

    /* Map parent */
    XtMapWidget(parent);
    XtAppMainLoop(app_context);

    return 0;

}   /* main */


/* end of file o_chap25.c */
```

Resource File for the Sample Program

Name this file ProX and place it in your home directory:

```
! ProX
! Resource file for Chapter 25 of
! Professional Graphics
! Programming in the X Window System.
! Place this file in your
! home directory.
!
! Generic resources.
!
*background:    #cccccc
*title:         Chapter 25: Buffering Test
```

```
*draw1.background: black
*draw2.background: black

! Motif resources.
*fontList: lucidasans-12

*filemenu.labelString:    File
*filemenu.mnemonic:       F

*exitchoice.labelString:  Exit
*exitchoice.mnemonic:     x

! OLIT
*filemenu.label:    File
*exitchoice.label:  Exit

! end of file ProX
```

Header File for the Sample Program

The sample program requires a header file to define the DblBuffStruct structure. You'll note from the definition below that we need some prior knowledge of the Multi-Buffering X extension, which we cover in the next section.

Finally, we present the header file for the sample program, chap25.h:

```
/*
 *   chap25.h
 *   double buffering header for Chapter 25.
 */
#ifndef chap25_h_
#define chap25_h_   1
```

```
#ifdef MULTIBUFFER
#include <X11/extensions/multibuf.h>
#endif /* MULTIBUFFER */


/*
 * Structure to hold dbl-buffer info.
 */
#define  MAX_COLORS 3


typedef struct {
    Display*        display;
    Colormap        colormap;
    Window          window_top, window_bot;
    GC              gc_top, gc_bot;
    int             width, height;
    int             which_buffer;
    unsigned long   plane_mask[2];
    unsigned long   colors[MAX_COLORS+1];
    XColor          xcolor_array[2][16];


#ifdef MULTIBUFFER
    Multibuffer     multibuffers[2];
#endif /* MULTIBUFFER */


} DblBuffStruct;


extern void
StartBufferTimer(XtAppContext app_context,
    unsigned long interval,
    DblBuffStruct* dblbuff);
```

```
extern void
InitDblWindows(DblBuffStruct* dblbuff,
    Widget draw1, Widget draw2,
    int width, int height);


extern void
InitDblBuffer(DblBuffStruct* dblbuff,
        Widget draw1, Widget draw2,
        int width, int height);


extern void
SwapBuffer(DblBuffStruct* dblbuff);


#endif  /* ! chap25_h_ */
/* end of file chap25.h */
```

When you run the sample program, you should see the top buffer animate with a lot of flashing and flickering. The bottom buffer should appear a lot smoother. You can use this color-plane double buffering technique in your animations, or in dynamic rotations of complex 3D models—or whatever you want.

Besides the color-plane method for double buffering, you can also use the X Multi-Buffering extension.

The X Multi-Buffering Extension

Another means to implement double buffering is to use the X Multi-Buffering extension. As the term *multi* implies, you can use more than two buffers. You can also use more than two buffers with the color-plane implementation discussed above, but you soon run out of color planes. (With the Multi-Buffering extension, you can run out of buffers and RAM.)

Programming with the Multi-Buffering Extension

Programming with the Multi-Buffering extension is lot like programming with any X extension. The extension has its own set of functions, stored in the `libXext.a` library (like the code for the MIT-SHM extension). The extension also has its own required header file. All of the Multi-Buffering functions require the `<X11/extensions/multibuf.h>` include file:

```
#include <X11/extensions/multibuf.h>
```

If you don't have this file, as the Hewlett-Packard systems we tested surprisingly didn't, then you won't have much luck using this technique. If you are not able to use this code, you can use conditional compilation:

```
#ifdef MULTIBUFFER


#endif /* MULTIBUFFER */
```

If you want to compile the example file, you'll need to `#define MULTI-BUFFER`.

Determining If the Multi-Buffering Extension Is Available

To determine whether the Multi-Buffering extension is available, call `XmbufQueryExtension`:

```
Bool XmbufQueryExtension(Display* display,
        int* event_base,  /* RETURN */
        int* error_base)  /* RETURN */
```

`XmbufQueryExtension` returns `True` if the Multi-Buffering extension is available; `False` otherwise. The *event_base* is the base event number that you add on to the event constants `MultibufferClobberNotify` and `MultibufferUpdateNotify` to get the actual event numbers. The *error_base* acts similarly for the base error number. Add this value to the constant `MultibufferBadBuffer` for thc crror code.

Once you've determined that the Multi-Buffering extension is available, you can call `XmbufGetVersion` to get the major and minor version numbers:

```
Status XmbufGetVersion(Display* display,
        int *major_version, /* RETURN */
        int *minor_version) /* RETURN */
```

The only reason to get the version numbers is if you think there's a version incompatibility.

Creating Multibuffers

The whole purpose of the Multi-Buffering extension is to create multiple drawing buffers. To support these drawing buffers, the extension adds a new data type, `Multibuffer`. A `Multibuffer` is like a `Drawable`, in that you can draw into it using Xlib functions such as `XDrawLine`. In fact, a `Multibuffer` is an `XID`, same as a `Window` or `Pixmap`:

```
typedef XID Multibuffer;
```

To create a number of buffers associated with a given window, call `XmbufCreateBuffers`:

```
int XmbufCreateBuffers(Display* display,
        Window window,
        int number_requested,
        int update_action,
        int update_hint,
        Multibuffer* buffers)  /* RETURN */
```

`XmbufCreateBuffers` returns the number of buffers actually created. If this number doesn't match the *number_requested*, you have a problem. If `XmbufCreateBuffers` created the right number of buffers, then the buffer IDs are stored in the *buffers* array. Be sure to allocate the proper number of `Multibuffers` in the *buffers* array. If an error occurs, then `XmbufCreateBuffers` returns 0.

The *update_action* and *update_hint* parameters need more explanation. The *update_action* defines what happens to an *old* buffer when you display a new one, that is, what happens to the buffer that was last displayed. The *update_action* can be one of `Multibuffer-UpdateActionBackground`, `MultibufferUpdateActionCopied`, `MultibufferUpdateActionUndefined`, or `MultibufferUpdate-ActionUntouched`.

`MultibufferUpdateActionBackground` means that the last-displayed buffer is painted with the window's background color. We use this *update_action* because it's efficient and fast.

`MultibufferUpdateActionCopied` means that the contents of the current buffer will be copied into the buffer that was last displayed. You can use this for delta-style animation where you only draw what changed between frames. Note that this *update_action* uses a lot of memory.

`MultibufferUpdateActionUndefined` means that the buffer that was last displayed can be trashed, or undefined. Using this *update_action* allows the X server to reclaim the memory if necessary and so is very efficient.

`MultibufferUpdateActionUntouched` means that the contents of the last-displayed buffer will be untouched after you call `XmbufDisplayBuffers` to display another buffer. This is used for animations that cycle through a set of buffers and then repeat.

The *update_hint* parameter sends a hint to the X server about how often you intend to display different buffers. This lets smart X servers plan accordingly. You can set the *update_hint* parameter to one of `MultibufferUpdateHintFrequent`, `MultibufferUpdate-HintIntermittent`, or `MultibufferUpdateHintStatic`.

`MultibufferUpdateHintFrequent`, as you guessed, means that you intend to display buffers with `XmbufDisplayBuffers` frequently. We use `MultibufferUpdateHintFrequent` because, with our animation, we do intend to change `Multibuffers` frequently.

`MultibufferUpdateHintIntermittent` means that you intend to change the buffer at a rate slower than one second (the official documentation states "every so often").

`MultibufferUpdateHintStatic` means that you won't change the displayed buffer any time soon, such as during a pause in the animation.

The `Multibuffers` are created to the size of your window.

Using XmbufCreateBuffers in Your Code

We call `XmbufCreateBuffers` in our code as follows:

```
#include <X11/extensions/multibuf.h>


int         status;
Display*    display;
Window      window_bot;
Multibuffer multibuffers[2];


status = XmbufCreateBuffers(display,
             window_bot,
             2,  /* number buffers */
             MultibufferUpdateActionBackground,
             MultibufferUpdateHintFrequent,
             multibuffers);


if (status < 2) {
    /* error... */
}
```

We only need two buffers, because all the code so far is only set up for two buffers, although we could ask for more. We use the `MultibufferUpdateActionBackground` update action, because this reduces some of the garbage effects we saw at the edges of our window. We also use the `MultibufferUpdateHintFrequent` update hint, because we request a timer interval of 100 milliseconds and this is considered frequent.

Once you've created a `Multibuffer`, you can draw into it just like you draw into windows or pixmaps. When you're done with the buffers, free them.

Freeing Multibuffers

To free up all the buffers associated with a window, call `XmbufDestroyBuffers`:

```
void XmbufDestroyBuffers(Display* display,
        Window window)
```

Displaying Buffers

Once you've created all the buffers and drawn into them, you can display the buffers with `XmbufDisplayBuffers`. It displays a set of buffers within *max_delay* milliseconds after *min_delay* milliseconds have passed:

```
void XmbufDisplayBuffers(Display* display,
        int number_buffers,
        Multibuffer* buffers,
        int min_delay,
        int max_delay)
```

The *buffers* are displayed in their associated windows. `XmbufDisplayBuffers` is confusing, but at least it's the last Multi-Buffering function you really need. `XmbufDisplayBuffers` seems to imply that you pass it all the `Multibuffers` you created with `XmbufCreateBuffers` and it will take care of the animation. Wrong.

WARNING

No two of the `Multibuffers` in the *buffers* array may be associated with the same window.

What do you use `XmbufDisplayBuffers` for? You use it to display *one* of your buffers. We draw into one of our two `Multibuffers` and then call `XmbufDisplayBuffers` to display it:

```
#ifdef MULTIBUFFER
Multibuffer tempbuffers[1];
Multibuffer multibuffers[2];
Display*    display;

tempbuffers[0] =
   multibuffers[which_buffer];

XmbufDisplayBuffers(display,
    1, /* 1 buffer */
    tempbuffers,
    0, 0);


#endif /* MULTIBUFFER */
```

Note how we use no time delay. This is the easiest way to call XmbufDisplayBuffers. If your application had a number of windows with Multibuffers, you could display a number of these buffers, up to one per window, with XmbufDisplayBuffers.

That's all you really need to know about the Multi-Buffering extension. You can also create stereo windows, and query and modify buffer/window parameters. Look in the <X11/extensions/multibuf.h> include file, the online manual pages, and in the sparse document, Extending X For Double Buffering, Multi-Buffering and Stereo, part of the documentation that comes with the X Window System from the MIT X Consortium, for more information.

Strategies for Using Multiple Buffers

We can use the Multi-Buffering extension in our code in place of the color-plane double buffering used above. To do this, we merely need to extend our definition of the DblBuffStruct structure, which we previewed in chap25.h, above (under Drawing Code), and then replace two functions from dblbuff.c: InitDblBuffer and SwapBuffer. This code is stored in the file mulbuff.c:

```
/*
 *  mulbuff.c
 *  Multi-buffering routines for Chapter 25.
 */
#include "xlib.h"
#include <X11/Intrinsic.h>
#include <stdio.h>
#include "chap25.h"

#define NUMBER_PLANES   4   /* 2 planes for each buffer. */
#define NUMBER_PIXELS   1

void InitDblBuffer(DblBuffStruct* mulbuff,
    Widget draw1, Widget draw2,
    int width, int height)

{   /* InitDblBuffer */
    int             i, status, event_base, error_base;
    unsigned long   planes[NUMBER_PLANES+1];
    unsigned long   pixels[NUMBER_PIXELS+1];
    unsigned long   new_pixel;

    InitDblWindows(mulbuff,
        draw1, draw2,
        width, height);

#ifdef MULTIBUFFER

    /*
     * Is the Multi-Buffering extension supported?
     */
```

```
        status = XmbufQueryExtension(mulbuff->display,
                &event_base,
                &error_base);


        if (status != True) {
            fprintf(stderr,
                "MULTIBUFFER extension not available.\n");
            exit(1);
        }


        /*
         * Allocate two buffers.
         */
        status = XmbufCreateBuffers(mulbuff->display,
                    mulbuff->window_bot,
                    2,  /* number buffers */
                    MultibufferUpdateActionBackground,
                    MultibufferUpdateHintFrequent,
                    mulbuff->multibuffers);


        if (status < 2) {
            fprintf(stderr,
                "Could not allocate 2 multibuffers.\n");
            exit(1);
        }


#else  /* no MULTIBUFFER */


    fprintf(stderr,
        "MULTIBUFFER extension not available.\n");
    exit(1);
```

```
#endif /* MULTIBUFFER */

    /*
     * Allocate color cells.
     */
    mulbuff->colors[0] =
        AllocNamedColor(mulbuff->display,
            mulbuff->colormap,
            "black",
            BlackPixel(mulbuff->display,
                DefaultScreen(mulbuff->display) ) );


    mulbuff->colors[1] =
        AllocNamedColor(mulbuff->display,
            mulbuff->colormap,
            "slateblue",
            WhitePixel(mulbuff->display,
                DefaultScreen(mulbuff->display) ) );
    mulbuff->colors[2] =
        AllocNamedColor(mulbuff->display,
            mulbuff->colormap,
            "cadetblue",
            WhitePixel(mulbuff->display,
                DefaultScreen(mulbuff->display) ) );


}   /* InitDblBuffer */

/*
 * Swaps from one to the next buffer.
 * We see the current buffer and
```

```
 * write into the hidden buffer.
 */
void SwapBuffer(DblBuffStruct* mulbuff)


{   /* SwapBuffer */


    /*
     * Show the current buffer.
     */
#ifdef MULTIBUFFER
    Multibuffer multibuffers[1];


    multibuffers[0] =
        mulbuff->multibuffers[mulbuff->which_buffer];


    XmbufDisplayBuffers(mulbuff->display,
        1, /* 1 buffer */
        multibuffers,
        0, 0);


#endif /* MULTIBUFFER */


    /*
     * Set to next buffer.
     */
    if (mulbuff->which_buffer == 1) {


        mulbuff->which_buffer = 0;
    } else {
        mulbuff->which_buffer = 1;
    }
```

```
        /*
         * Set up window ID to buffer.
         */
#ifdef MULTIBUFFER

        mulbuff->window_bot =
            mulbuff->multibuffers[mulbuff->which_buffer];

#endif /* MULTIBUFFER */

    }   /* SwapBuffer */


/* end of file mulbuff.c */
```

You can link in `mulbuff.c` instead of `dblbuff.c` to use the Multi-Buffering extension.

The `InitDblBuffer` function doesn't need to grab any color planes. Instead, it creates two `Multibuffers` and uses the `AllocNamedColor` utility function from Chapter 7 to allocate just three colors, rather than 16.

The `SwapBuffer` function displays the current `Multibuffer` and then actually swaps the "window" ID used to draw into the bottom drawing area widget. This way, the rest of the drawing code doesn't know that it is drawing into a `Multibuffer` instead of a window.

Summary

Double buffering is the process of drawing into two buffers to make smoother animations. The technique is used to reduce the flicker in animation, particularly if you employ the simplistic draw, erase, and draw again model. With double buffering, you draw into two buffers, only one of which is visible at any time. The idea is that while buffer 1 is displayed, your application draws into buffer 2. Then, using some magic means, you swap the visible buffer: buffer 1 becomes inactive and buffer 2 becomes visible. Your application then draws into buffer 1.

This technique reduces a lot of the flicker associated with the draw, erase, and draw again model, because the user doesn't see all the redrawing and erasing that goes on in the hidden buffer. You end up with a smoother transition between frames of your animation.

In X, the magic means to swap buffers uses color planes in a colormap. Your application draws using the GC (graphics context) plane mask and then plays games with XStoreColors to swap the buffers.

In this chapter, we discuss two means for implementing double buffering. One uses color planes and should work on any X system with a writable visual, such as DirectColor, GrayScale, or PseudoColor. The other uses the Multi-Buffering X extension and is therefore not available on all systems.

Multi-Buffer Extension Functions and Macros Introduced in This Chapter

```
XmbufCreateBuffers

XmbufDestroyBuffers

XmbufDisplayBuffers

XmbufGetVersion

XmbufQueryExtension
```

Animation Standards

This chapter covers:

- ◆ The QuickTime format
- ◆ The JFIF format
- ◆ The TIFF JPEG format
- ◆ The MPEG format
- ◆ The FLI format
- ◆ The Video for Windows format
- ◆ The ANIM format

Nonstandard Animations

The animation field is wide open when it comes to standards, so it's best you are at least aware of the major animation players and their formats. Basically, no file or compression format has caught on enough to dominate the market. This information was cobbled from various sources, including some postings on the Internet.

Most of the formats covered below support some form of data compression, as the huge data requirements for most animations strain even the most powerful workstations and soon fill even the largest disk.

The QuickTime Format

The building block of Apple's multimedia strategy, the QuickTime format (incorporating compression and playback schemes) has transcended Apple's original goal of MacMovies into something representing a bona-fide industry standard—a standard helped by Apple's willingness to implement a Windows version of QuickTime, as well as the firm's eagerness to enter the UNIX market by offering QuickTime to Silicon Graphics. With major players like Apple and Silicon Graphics in association, QuickTime is a format that should be heeded.

However, there's a price to pay when dealing with QuickTime: the compression scheme was designed as a down-and-dirty implementation of video compression for personal computers, and so bears the mark of compromise, at all times sacrificing image quality for compression. Such a compression scheme is called *lossy*, because you lose quality on decompression. You'll see when in the following explanation of the actual QuickTime scheme.

Generally, video runs at 30 frames per second. QuickTime begins with a compromise in slicing this down to 15 frames per second or *fps* (that alone accounts for much of the jerkiness of the final output); playback can be trimmed down to as low as 12 fps in a small window on a Macintosh.

QuickTime also drops the resolution when digitizing the QuickTime file on the Mac, making the file of lower resolution than even the relatively low-resolution Macintosh screen. A QuickTime 1.5 movie runs at a resolution of 320 x 240 pixels; the Mac screen is 640 x 480 pixels. Of course, this resolution leads to a tremendous savings when it comes to file size—but makes the image much blurrier.

Finally, QuickTime also eliminates some colors from the final product, starting with 24 bits of color and ending up with 16 bits of color. Most images do not suffer under this restriction, however.

In the end, there are a lot of compromises when it comes to QuickTime. Quite honestly, the resolution for video is pretty awful. QuickTime is more appropriate for smaller animations created expressly for QuickTime playback.

If you're interested in QuickTime, contact your local Apple regional office.

The JPEG Format

The *Joint Photographic Experts Group (JPEG)* compression, while sacrificing some resolution and clarity while expediting efficient compression, remains a high-performance compression scheme.

JPEG started life as a hardware/software combo (requiring a specialized compression board), but now exists in software-only form.

JPEG-compressed files come in two forms: the *JFIF (JPEG File Interchange Format)* JPEG and the *TIFF (Tagged Image File Format)* JPEG formats. The TIFF format is considered the more robust; JFIF, designed solely to allow the exchange of JPEG-compressed images, is recommended for low-end image transfer, while the TIFF format contains more information about the image. However, there's a price to pay for using the TIFF format: images are less portable because there's not one single TIFF format out there; different application developers have implemented different subsets of TIFF. Both work similarly (though not identically) when it comes to the actual compression.

JPEG compression separates an image into its three RGB (red, green, blue) components, and from there breaks down each color by foreground and background. Finally, each of these components is divided into 8-pixel x 8-pixel blocks, eliminating superfluous color data and compressing the rest. How much color data is eliminated depends on your compression ratio.

If you want to implement JPEG, you're going to have to go through some work, since the specifications are not available online, nor are they widely distributed to the software-development industry. And there's less to the specifications than meets the eye: JPEG does not impose a file format, but rather merely a set of compression algorithms. While not getting into the debate surrounding the distribution of American National Standards Institute, or ANSI, documents, it seems like a rather stupid move to charge (and charge quite a bit, as it ends up—$142 for the entire documentation) for a set of compression standards. Call ANSI Sales at 212/642-4900 for information.

Once you have the compression information, you can move ahead and learn more about the file formats. `jfif.ps.Z` (the JFIF specification in PostScript format) and `TIFF6.ps.Z` (the TIFF 6.0 specification in PostScript format) are both available by anonymous ftp from sgi.com (192.48.153.1), in the `graphics/tiff` directory.

The MPEG Format

Like the Joint Photographic Experts Group responsible for the JPEG format, the *Motion Picture Experts Group* defines a digital video and audio compression format, called *MPEG*. Like JPEG compression, MPEG is a lossy format; you lose quality on decompression.

There are two main types of MPEG compression: MPEG-I and MPEG-II. MPEG-I is the most developed and concentrates on a data bandwidth of 1.5 megabits/second, which just happens to be the data rate of audio compact discs (CD) and digital audio tape (DAT). The MPEG-I frame size is 352 x 240 pixels with 30 frames per second.

The output format is small, but the input starts with CD-quality audio and the video from CCIR-601 digital television video.

MPEG compression uses the delta format described in Chapter 23. That is, MPEG tries to keep only the changes from the last frame, eliminating all redundant data and speeding the frame drawing rate. The compression is done using discrete cosine transforms or DCTs, with a basic block size of 16 x 16 pixels. MPEG compressors then try to find a close match to a given 16 x 16-pixel block in the next frame. (You can also go backward in MPEG.)

MPEG-I provides about a 6:1 compression ratio for audio and claims a total video compression rate of about 26:1, which is somewhat hard to believe. This compression is achieved, though, at considerable cost in image quality. This is simply not acceptable for many uses of digital video, which leads to MPEG-II.

MPEG-II is still in the definition stages, but hopes to increase the MPEG-I data rate to 4 megabits/second (or at least, somewhere in the 3 to

10 megabits/second range), which dramatically increases the image quality. Problems with interlacing make simply extending MPEG-II tough, which is why there's work on a new format (MPEG-II).

Like JPEG, MPEG works best with a hardware assist. Both JPEG and MPEG are organized under the *International Standards Organization*, or *ISO*, so both are sure to be future standards. There's also related work called JBIG, used for faxes and other binary imagery and MHEG, a multimedia standards effort.

As with JPEG, you can order MPEG documents from ANSI. Call ANSI Sales at 212/642-4900 for information.

The FLI Format

AutoDesk uses the FLI format in its various Animator packages. As such, it carries a certain weight in terms of potential market share. Consequently, you should be familiar with an FLI file format. This file format is fairly complex: a 128-byte header followed by frames that make up the actual animation. The frames achieve their efficiency by not passing on redundant information from frame to frame: why pass on information that's really not needed anyway? As a result, FLI-formatted resolution plays back very well, though the resulting files are not as small as those found in the QuickTime or JPEG formats.

AutoDesk is very open about what exactly makes up an FLI file; with this information (which occasionally pops up on the Internet), you could easily support FLI playbacks in your application. You can also call AutoDesk at 415/332-2344.

The Video for Windows Format

Like the Macintosh, the Windows platform carries a lot of power when it comes to establishing standards. Unfortunately, Microsoft's plans for Video for Windows, its competing technology to QuickTime, are slightly on the fuzzy side.

Microsoft has a tendency to talk out of both sides of its mouth, declaring in a position statement that "Audio Video Interleaved (AVI) is the file format for digital video under Windows. The file format itself is designed to be cross-platform compatible, allowing content on Windows-based systems to play on other operating systems as well." But Microsoft hasn't been so open in releasing Video for Windows standards to other players, preferring to center its attention on the Windows and Windows NT worlds.

That's too bad, because the Video for Windows setup has some distinct advantages. For instance, support for video is built directly into the operating system via Windows, instead of relying on the kindness of applications.

In addition, Video for Windows is completely scalable: like Windows, image quality depends on the hardware setup and memory requirements, not on the resolution of the image itself. This scalability is accomplished through a partnership with Intel.

But by withholding information about Video for Windows to the development community, Microsoft is not providing enough information to really catch their attention—and in doing so leaves the field wide open for the other animation standards listed above.

If you want to bug Microsoft for more information about Video for Windows, call 800/426-9400.

The ANIM Format

Those outside of the Amiga and video-editing worlds might not know much about the ANIM format. However, this format is gaining in popularity as a device-independent video format and an extension of the *IFF* (*Interchange File Format*) format, which is flexibly defined in the Amiga world as comprising almost anything (video, text, sound). The ANIM file standard as well as its compression specifications is available via the *Byte Information eXchange* (*BIX*) or from the plan's originator, Sparta Inc. (714/768-8161).

Summary

This short chapter briefly covers the major animation standards, as well as how to get further information about them.

The X RGB Color Database

The X Window System provides a database of English color names and their RGB values. You can use these names with functions such as XAllocNamedColor, XLookupColor, XParseColor, and XStore-NamedColor. You can also use these color names in your resource files for Motif and Open Look Intrinsics Toolkit (OLIT) programs.

The RGB color database is normally stored in a file named rgb.txt in the /usr/lib/X11 directory. Your system may use a different directory, such as /usr/openwin/lib/X11 on systems using OpenWindows. Consult your system documentation if you cannot find the proper directory.

The rgb.txt file contains the database in text format, so that you can read it. The X server normally uses the compiled format, stored in the rgb.pag and rgb.dir files. We reproduce the rgb.txt file from X11 Release 5 below. These colors should be available on all systems supporting R5 and higher X releases.

A number of vendors extend the generic R5 list. Silicon Graphics, for example, adds a number of shades of grays and blues, including the bluish-purple color used for its Indigo workstation. Other vendors also add in colors.

In the list below, the color values are given in the common scale of 0 to 255. To use these colors with X, you'll need to convert the scale to 0 to 65,535, as we showed in Chapter 9. In addition, the names are not sensitive to case. That is, you can use the names all uppercase, lowercase, or mixed case.

Red Grn Blue	Color Name
255 250 250	snow
248 248 255	ghost white
248 248 255	GhostWhite
245 245 245	white smoke
245 245 245	WhiteSmoke
220 220 220	gainsboro
255 250 240	floral white
255 250 240	FloralWhite
253 245 230	old lace
253 245 230	OldLace
250 240 230	linen
250 235 215	antique white
250 235 215	AntiqueWhite
255 239 213	papaya whip
255 239 213	PapayaWhip
255 235 205	blanched almond
255 235 205	BlanchedAlmond
255 228 196	bisque
255 218 185	peach puff
255 218 185	PeachPuff
255 222 173	navajo white
255 222 173	NavajoWhite
255 228 181	moccasin
255 248 220	cornsilk
255 255 240	ivory

255	250	205	lemon chiffon
255	250	205	LemonChiffon
255	245	238	seashell
240	255	240	honeydew
245	255	250	mint cream
245	255	250	MintCream
240	255	255	azure
240	248	255	alice blue
240	248	255	AliceBlue
230	230	250	lavender
255	240	245	lavender blush
255	240	245	LavenderBlush
255	228	225	misty rose
255	228	225	MistyRose
255	255	255	white
0	0	0	black
47	79	79	dark slate gray
47	79	79	DarkSlateGray
47	79	79	dark slate grey
47	79	79	DarkSlateGrey
105	105	105	dim gray
105	105	105	DimGray
105	105	105	dim grey
105	105	105	DimGrey
112	128	144	slate gray
112	128	144	SlateGray
112	128	144	slate grey
112	128	144	SlateGrey
119	136	153	light slate gray
119	136	153	LightSlateGray
119	136	153	light slate grey

119	136	153	LightSlateGrey
190	190	190	gray
190	190	190	grey
211	211	211	light grey
211	211	211	LightGrey
211	211	211	light gray
211	211	211	LightGray
25	25	112	midnight blue
25	25	112	MidnightBlue
0	0	128	navy
0	0	128	navy blue
0	0	128	NavyBlue
100	149	237	cornflower blue
100	149	237	CornflowerBlue
72	61	139	dark slate blue
72	61	139	DarkSlateBlue
106	90	205	slate blue
106	90	205	SlateBlue
123	104	238	medium slate blue
123	104	238	MediumSlateBlue
132	112	255	light slate blue
132	112	255	LightSlateBlue
0	0	205	medium blue
0	0	205	MediumBlue
65	105	225	royal blue
65	105	225	RoyalBlue
0	0	255	blue
30	144	255	dodger blue
30	144	255	DodgerBlue
0	191	255	deep sky blue
0	191	255	DeepSkyBlue

135	206	235	sky blue
135	206	235	SkyBlue
135	206	250	light sky blue
135	206	250	LightSkyBlue
70	130	180	steel blue
70	130	180	SteelBlue
176	196	222	light steel blue
176	196	222	LightSteelBlue
173	216	230	light blue
173	216	230	LightBlue
176	224	230	powder blue
176	224	230	PowderBlue
175	238	238	pale turquoise
175	238	238	PaleTurquoise
0	206	209	dark turquoise
0	206	209	DarkTurquoise
72	209	204	medium turquoise
72	209	204	MediumTurquoise
64	224	208	turquoise
0	255	255	cyan
224	255	255	light cyan
224	255	255	LightCyan
95	158	160	cadet blue
95	158	160	CadetBlue
102	205	170	medium aquamarine
102	205	170	MediumAquamarine
127	255	212	aquamarine
0	100	0	dark green
0	100	0	DarkGreen
85	107	47	dark olive green
85	107	47	DarkOliveGreen

143	188	143	dark sea green
143	188	143	DarkSeaGreen
46	139	87	sea green
46	139	87	SeaGreen
60	179	113	medium sea green
60	179	113	MediumSeaGreen
32	178	170	light sea green
32	178	170	LightSeaGreen
152	251	152	pale green
152	251	152	PaleGreen
0	255	127	spring green
0	255	127	SpringGreen
124	252	0	lawn green
124	252	0	LawnGreen
0	255	0	green
127	255	0	chartreuse
0	250	154	medium spring green
0	250	154	MediumSpringGreen
173	255	47	green yellow
173	255	47	GreenYellow
50	205	50	lime green
50	205	50	LimeGreen
154	205	50	yellow green
154	205	50	YellowGreen
34	139	34	forest green
34	139	34	ForestGreen
107	142	35	olive drab
107	142	35	OliveDrab
189	183	107	dark khaki
189	183	107	DarkKhaki
240	230	140	khaki

238	232	170	pale goldenrod
238	232	170	PaleGoldenrod
250	250	210	light goldenrod yellow
250	250	210	LightGoldenrodYellow
255	255	224	light yellow
255	255	224	LightYellow
255	255	0	yellow
255	215	0	gold
238	221	130	light goldenrod
238	221	130	LightGoldenrod
218	165	32	goldenrod
184	134	11	dark goldenrod
184	134	11	DarkGoldenrod
188	143	143	rosy brown
188	143	143	RosyBrown
205	92	92	indian red
205	92	92	IndianRed
139	69	19	saddle brown
139	69	19	SaddleBrown
160	82	45	sienna
205	133	63	peru
222	184	135	burlywood
245	245	220	beige
245	222	179	wheat
244	164	96	sandy brown
244	164	96	SandyBrown
210	180	140	tan
210	105	30	chocolate
178	34	34	firebrick
165	42	42	brown
233	150	122	dark salmon

233	150	122	DarkSalmon
250	128	114	salmon
255	160	122	light salmon
255	160	122	LightSalmon
255	165	0	orange
255	140	0	dark orange
255	140	0	DarkOrange
255	127	80	coral
240	128	128	light coral
240	128	128	LightCoral
255	99	71	tomato
255	69	0	orange red
255	69	0	OrangeRed
255	0	0	red
255	105	180	hot pink
255	105	180	HotPink
255	20	147	deep pink
255	20	147	DeepPink
255	192	203	pink
255	182	193	light pink
255	182	193	LightPink
219	112	147	pale violet red
219	112	147	PaleVioletRed
176	48	96	maroon
199	21	133	medium violet red
199	21	133	MediumVioletRed
208	32	144	violet red
208	32	144	VioletRed
255	0	255	magenta
238	130	238	violet
221	160	221	plum

218	112	214	orchid
186	85	211	medium orchid
186	85	211	MediumOrchid
153	50	204	dark orchid
153	50	204	DarkOrchid
148	0	211	dark violet
148	0	211	DarkViolet
138	43	226	blue violet
138	43	226	BlueViolet
160	32	240	purple
147	112	219	medium purple
147	112	219	MediumPurple
216	191	216	thistle
255	250	250	snow1
238	233	233	snow2
205	201	201	snow3
139	137	137	snow4
255	245	238	seashell1
238	229	222	seashell2
205	197	191	seashell3
139	134	130	seashell4
255	239	219	AntiqueWhite1
238	223	204	AntiqueWhite2
205	192	176	AntiqueWhite3
139	131	120	AntiqueWhite4
255	228	196	bisque1
238	213	183	bisque2
205	183	158	bisque3
139	125	107	bisque4
255	218	185	PeachPuff1
238	203	173	PeachPuff2

205	175	149	PeachPuff3
139	119	101	PeachPuff4
255	222	173	NavajoWhite1
238	207	161	NavajoWhite2
205	179	139	NavajoWhite3
139	121	94	NavajoWhite4
255	250	205	LemonChiffon1
238	233	191	LemonChiffon2
205	201	165	LemonChiffon3
139	137	112	LemonChiffon4
255	248	220	cornsilk1
238	232	205	cornsilk2
205	200	177	cornsilk3
139	136	120	cornsilk4
255	255	240	ivory1
238	238	224	ivory2
205	205	193	ivory3
139	139	131	ivory4
240	255	240	honeydew1
224	238	224	honeydew2
193	205	193	honeydew3
131	139	131	honeydew4
255	240	245	LavenderBlush1
238	224	229	LavenderBlush2
205	193	197	LavenderBlush3
139	131	134	LavenderBlush4
255	228	225	MistyRose1
238	213	210	MistyRose2
205	183	181	MistyRose3
139	125	123	MistyRose4
240	255	255	azure1

224	238	238	azure2
193	205	205	azure3
131	139	139	azure4
131	111	255	SlateBlue1
122	103	238	SlateBlue2
105	89	205	SlateBlue3
71	60	139	SlateBlue4
72	118	255	RoyalBlue1
67	110	238	RoyalBlue2
58	95	205	RoyalBlue3
39	64	139	RoyalBlue4
0	0	255	blue1
0	0	238	blue2
0	0	205	blue3
0	0	139	blue4
30	144	255	DodgerBlue1
28	134	238	DodgerBlue2
24	116	205	DodgerBlue3
16	78	139	DodgerBlue4
99	184	255	SteelBlue1
92	172	238	SteelBlue2
79	148	205	SteelBlue3
54	100	139	SteelBlue4
0	191	255	DeepSkyBlue1
0	178	238	DeepSkyBlue2
0	154	205	DeepSkyBlue3
0	104	139	DeepSkyBlue4
135	206	255	SkyBlue1
126	192	238	SkyBlue2
108	166	205	SkyBlue3
74	112	139	SkyBlue4

176	226	255	LightSkyBlue1
164	211	238	LightSkyBlue2
141	182	205	LightSkyBlue3
96	123	139	LightSkyBlue4
198	226	255	SlateGray1
185	211	238	SlateGray2
159	182	205	SlateGray3
108	123	139	SlateGray4
202	225	255	LightSteelBlue1
188	210	238	LightSteelBlue2
162	181	205	LightSteelBlue3
110	123	139	LightSteelBlue4
191	239	255	LightBlue1
178	223	238	LightBlue2
154	192	205	LightBlue3
104	131	139	LightBlue4
224	255	255	LightCyan1
209	238	238	LightCyan2
180	205	205	LightCyan3
122	139	139	LightCyan4
187	255	255	PaleTurquoise1
174	238	238	PaleTurquoise2
150	205	205	PaleTurquoise3
102	139	139	PaleTurquoise4
152	245	255	CadetBlue1
142	229	238	CadetBlue2
122	197	205	CadetBlue3
83	134	139	CadetBlue4
0	245	255	turquoise1
0	229	238	turquoise2
0	197	205	turquoise3

0	134	139	turquoise4
0	255	255	cyan1
0	238	238	cyan2
0	205	205	cyan3
0	139	139	cyan4
151	255	255	DarkSlateGray1
141	238	238	DarkSlateGray2
121	205	205	DarkSlateGray3
82	139	139	DarkSlateGray4
127	255	212	aquamarine1
118	238	198	aquamarine2
102	205	170	aquamarine3
69	139	116	aquamarine4
193	255	193	DarkSeaGreen1
180	238	180	DarkSeaGreen2
155	205	155	DarkSeaGreen3
105	139	105	DarkSeaGreen4
84	255	159	SeaGreen1
78	238	148	SeaGreen2
67	205	128	SeaGreen3
46	139	87	SeaGreen4
154	255	154	PaleGreen1
144	238	144	PaleGreen2
124	205	124	PaleGreen3
84	139	84	PaleGreen4
0	255	127	SpringGreen1
0	238	118	SpringGreen2
0	205	102	SpringGreen3
0	139	69	SpringGreen4
0	255	0	green1
0	238	0	green2

0	205	0	green3
0	139	0	green4
127	255	0	chartreuse1
118	238	0	chartreuse2
102	205	0	chartreuse3
69	139	0	chartreuse4
192	255	62	OliveDrab1
179	238	58	OliveDrab2
154	205	50	OliveDrab3
105	139	34	OliveDrab4
202	255	112	DarkOliveGreen1
188	238	104	DarkOliveGreen2
162	205	90	DarkOliveGreen3
110	139	61	DarkOliveGreen4
255	246	143	khaki1
238	230	133	khaki2
205	198	115	khaki3
139	134	78	khaki4
255	236	139	LightGoldenrod1
238	220	130	LightGoldenrod2
205	190	112	LightGoldenrod3
139	129	76	LightGoldenrod4
255	255	224	LightYellow1
238	238	209	LightYellow2
205	205	180	LightYellow3
139	139	122	LightYellow4
255	255	0	yellow1
238	238	0	yellow2
205	205	0	yellow3
139	139	0	yellow4
255	215	0	gold1

238	201	0	gold2
205	173	0	gold3
139	117	0	gold4
255	193	37	goldenrod1
238	180	34	goldenrod2
205	155	29	goldenrod3
139	105	20	goldenrod4
255	185	15	DarkGoldenrod1
238	173	14	DarkGoldenrod2
205	149	12	DarkGoldenrod3
139	101	8	DarkGoldenrod4
255	193	193	RosyBrown1
238	180	180	RosyBrown2
205	155	155	RosyBrown3
139	105	105	RosyBrown4
255	106	106	IndianRed1
238	99	99	IndianRed2
205	85	85	IndianRed3
139	58	58	IndianRed4
255	130	71	sienna1
238	121	66	sienna2
205	104	57	sienna3
139	71	38	sienna4
255	211	155	burlywood1
238	197	145	burlywood2
205	170	125	burlywood3
139	115	85	burlywood4
255	231	186	wheat1
238	216	174	wheat2
205	186	150	wheat3
139	126	102	wheat4

255	165	79	tan1
238	154	73	tan2
205	133	63	tan3
139	90	43	tan4
255	127	36	chocolate1
238	118	33	chocolate2
205	102	29	chocolate3
139	69	19	chocolate4
255	48	48	firebrick1
238	44	44	firebrick2
205	38	38	firebrick3
139	26	26	firebrick4
255	64	64	brown1
238	59	59	brown2
205	51	51	brown3
139	35	35	brown4
255	140	105	salmon1
238	130	98	salmon2
205	112	84	salmon3
139	76	57	salmon4
255	160	122	LightSalmon1
238	149	114	LightSalmon2
205	129	98	LightSalmon3
139	87	66	LightSalmon4
255	165	0	orange1
238	154	0	orange2
205	133	0	orange3
139	90	0	orange4
255	127	0	DarkOrange1
238	118	0	DarkOrange2
205	102	0	DarkOrange3

139	69	0	DarkOrange4
255	114	86	coral1
238	106	80	coral2
205	91	69	coral3
139	62	47	coral4
255	99	71	tomato1
238	92	66	tomato2
205	79	57	tomato3
139	54	38	tomato4
255	69	0	OrangeRed1
238	64	0	OrangeRed2
205	55	0	OrangeRed3
139	37	0	OrangeRed4
255	0	0	red1
238	0	0	red2
205	0	0	red3
139	0	0	red4
255	20	147	DeepPink1
238	18	137	DeepPink2
205	16	118	DeepPink3
139	10	80	DeepPink4
255	110	180	HotPink1
238	106	167	HotPink2
205	96	144	HotPink3
139	58	98	HotPink4
255	181	197	pink1
238	169	184	pink2
205	145	158	pink3
139	99	108	pink4
255	174	185	LightPink1
238	162	173	LightPink2

205	140	149	LightPink3
139	95	101	LightPink4
255	130	171	PaleVioletRed1
238	121	159	PaleVioletRed2
205	104	137	PaleVioletRed3
139	71	93	PaleVioletRed4
255	52	179	maroon1
238	48	167	maroon2
205	41	144	maroon3
139	28	98	maroon4
255	62	150	VioletRed1
238	58	140	VioletRed2
205	50	120	VioletRed3
139	34	82	VioletRed4
255	0	255	magenta1
238	0	238	magenta2
205	0	205	magenta3
139	0	139	magenta4
255	131	250	orchid1
238	122	233	orchid2
205	105	201	orchid3
139	71	137	orchid4
255	187	255	plum1
238	174	238	plum2
205	150	205	plum3
139	102	139	plum4
224	102	255	MediumOrchid1
209	95	238	MediumOrchid2
180	82	205	MediumOrchid3
122	55	139	MediumOrchid4
191	62	255	DarkOrchid1

178	58	238	DarkOrchid2
154	50	205	DarkOrchid3
104	34	139	DarkOrchid4
155	48	255	purple1
145	44	238	purple2
125	38	205	purple3
85	26	139	purple4
171	130	255	MediumPurple1
159	121	238	MediumPurple2
137	104	205	MediumPurple3
93	71	139	MediumPurple4
255	225	255	thistle1
238	210	238	thistle2
205	181	205	thistle3
139	123	139	thistle4
0	0	0	gray0
0	0	0	grey0
3	3	3	gray1
3	3	3	grey1
5	5	5	gray2
5	5	5	grey2
8	8	8	gray3
8	8	8	grey3
10	10	10	gray4
10	10	10	grey4
13	13	13	gray5
13	13	13	grey5
15	15	15	gray6
15	15	15	grey6
18	18	18	gray7
18	18	18	grey7

20	20	20	gray8
20	20	20	grey8
23	23	23	gray9
23	23	23	grey9
26	26	26	gray10
26	26	26	grey10
28	28	28	gray11
28	28	28	grey11
31	31	31	gray12
31	31	31	grey12
33	33	33	gray13
33	33	33	grey13
36	36	36	gray14
36	36	36	grey14
38	38	38	gray15
38	38	38	grey15
41	41	41	gray16
41	41	41	grey16
43	43	43	gray17
43	43	43	grey17
46	46	46	gray18
46	46	46	grey18
48	48	48	gray19
48	48	48	grey19
51	51	51	gray20
51	51	51	grey20
54	54	54	gray21
54	54	54	grey21
56	56	56	gray22
56	56	56	grey22
59	59	59	gray23

59	59	59	grey23
61	61	61	gray24
61	61	61	grey24
64	64	64	gray25
64	64	64	grey25
66	66	66	gray26
66	66	66	grey26
69	69	69	gray27
69	69	69	grey27
71	71	71	gray28
71	71	71	grey28
74	74	74	gray29
74	74	74	grey29
77	77	77	gray30
77	77	77	grey30
79	79	79	gray31
79	79	79	grey31
82	82	82	gray32
82	82	82	grey32
84	84	84	gray33
84	84	84	grey33
87	87	87	gray34
87	87	87	grey34
89	89	89	gray35
89	89	89	grey35
92	92	92	gray36
92	92	92	grey36
94	94	94	gray37
94	94	94	grey37
97	97	97	gray38
97	97	97	grey38

99	99	99	gray39
99	99	99	grey39
102	102	102	gray40
102	102	102	grey40
105	105	105	gray41
105	105	105	grey41
107	107	107	gray42
107	107	107	grey42
110	110	110	gray43
110	110	110	grey43
112	112	112	gray44
112	112	112	grey44
115	115	115	gray45
115	115	115	grey45
117	117	117	gray46
117	117	117	grey46
120	120	120	gray47
120	120	120	grey47
122	122	122	gray48
122	122	122	grey48
125	125	125	gray49
125	125	125	grey49
127	127	127	gray50
127	127	127	grey50
130	130	130	gray51
130	130	130	grey51
133	133	133	gray52
133	133	133	grey52
135	135	135	gray53
135	135	135	grey53
138	138	138	gray54

138	138	138	grey54
140	140	140	gray55
140	140	140	grey55
143	143	143	gray56
143	143	143	grey56
145	145	145	gray57
145	145	145	grey57
148	148	148	gray58
148	148	148	grey58
150	150	150	gray59
150	150	150	grey59
153	153	153	gray60
153	153	153	grey60
156	156	156	gray61
156	156	156	grey61
158	158	158	gray62
158	158	158	grey62
161	161	161	gray63
161	161	161	grey63
163	163	163	gray64
163	163	163	grey64
166	166	166	gray65
166	166	166	grey65
168	168	168	gray66
168	168	168	grey66
171	171	171	gray67
171	171	171	grey67
173	173	173	gray68
173	173	173	grey68
176	176	176	gray69
176	176	176	grey69

179	179	179	gray70
179	179	179	grey70
181	181	181	gray71
181	181	181	grey71
184	184	184	gray72
184	184	184	grey72
186	186	186	gray73
186	186	186	grey73
189	189	189	gray74
189	189	189	grey74
191	191	191	gray75
191	191	191	grey75
194	194	194	gray76
194	194	194	grey76
196	196	196	gray77
196	196	196	grey77
199	199	199	gray78
199	199	199	grey78
201	201	201	gray79
201	201	201	grey79
204	204	204	gray80
204	204	204	grey80
207	207	207	gray81
207	207	207	grey81
209	209	209	gray82
209	209	209	grey82
212	212	212	gray83
212	212	212	grey83
214	214	214	gray84
214	214	214	grey84
217	217	217	gray85

217	217	217	grey85
219	219	219	gray86
219	219	219	grey86
222	222	222	gray87
222	222	222	grey87
224	224	224	gray88
224	224	224	grey88
227	227	227	gray89
227	227	227	grey89
229	229	229	gray90
229	229	229	grey90
232	232	232	gray91
232	232	232	grey91
235	235	235	gray92
235	235	235	grey92
237	237	237	gray93
237	237	237	grey93
240	240	240	gray94
240	240	240	grey94
242	242	242	gray95
242	242	242	grey95
245	245	245	gray96
245	245	245	grey96
247	247	247	gray97
247	247	247	grey97
250	250	250	gray98
250	250	250	grey98
252	252	252	gray99
252	252	252	grey99
255	255	255	gray100
255	255	255	grey100

Appendix B

Rounded-Corner Rectangles

Many X toolkits, particularly Open Look Intrinsics Toolkit (OLIT), XView, and the Athena widget set, use rounded-corner rectangles for interface elements. Motif, however, uses 3D beveled rectangles instead of rounded-corner rectangles.

There are no Xlib functions to draw and fill a rounded-corner rectangle, although there are such functions in the X miscellaneous utilities library, or Xmu, called `XmuDrawRoundedRectangle` and `XmuFillRoundedRectangle`.

There are a number of ways you can build a rounded-corner rectangle from the primitive Xlib drawing functions.

A rounded-corner rectangle is really four straight lines and four arcs connecting the corners. If we draw it this way, however, we must be careful, because if we draw any pixel more than once, such as where the arcs meet the lines, we may inadvertently mess up drawing modes like exclusive-OR (or XOR, used in drawing rubber-band shapes).

1095

To draw a rounded-corner rectangle, `XmuDrawRoundedRectangle` uses eight arcs in a call to `XDrawArcs`. Four of the arcs are very flat and are used instead of straight lines. Drawing arcs, though, requires a number of calculations, which slows things down. Hence, our routines to draw and fill arcs use lines and rectangles along with just four arcs for the corners.

Filled Rounded-Corner Rectangles

We can draw a filled rounded-corner rectangle with four filled arcs for the corners and three rectangles for the rest.

Source Code for Rounded-Corner Rectangles

The following routines draw and fill rounded-corner rectangles and provide good examples of the multiline, multirectangle, and multiarc routines. This code does draw some pixels more than once, which may create problems with certain graphics modes, like XOR.

The file `drawrnd.c` contains these functions:

```
/*
 *  drawrnd.c
 *  Routines for drawing and filling rounded-
 *  corner rectangles.
 */
#include "draw.h"

#define NINETY_DEGREES  (90*64)

void DrawRoundRect(Display* display,
       Drawable drawable,
       GC gc,
       int x, int y,
       int width, int height,
       int arc_width,
       int arc_height)
```

```
{   /* DrawRoundRect */
    XArc        arc_array[20];
    XSegment    segment_array[10];

    if (width < 1) {
        width = 1;
    }

    if (height < 1) {
        height = 1;
    }

    /*
     * Check if too small. If so,
     * just draw a rectangle.
     */
    if ((width < 12) && (height < 12)) {
        XDrawRectangle(display, drawable, gc,
                x, y, width, height);
        return;
    }

    /*
     * Do the four corners first.
     */
    arc_array[0].x = x;
    arc_array[0].y = y;
    arc_array[0].width = arc_width;
    arc_array[0].height = arc_height;
    arc_array[0].angle1 = NINETY_DEGREES;
```

```
arc_array[0].angle2 = NINETY_DEGREES;


arc_array[1].x = x + width - arc_width;
arc_array[1].y = y;
arc_array[1].width = arc_width;
arc_array[1].height = arc_height;
arc_array[1].angle1 = 0;
arc_array[1].angle2 = NINETY_DEGREES;


arc_array[2].x = x + width - arc_width;
arc_array[2].y = y + height - arc_height;
arc_array[2].width = arc_width;
arc_array[2].height = arc_height;
arc_array[2].angle1 = 0;
arc_array[2].angle2 = (-1) * NINETY_DEGREES;


arc_array[3].x = x;
arc_array[3].y = y + height - arc_height;
arc_array[3].width = arc_width;
arc_array[3].height = arc_height;
arc_array[3].angle1 = 2 * NINETY_DEGREES;
arc_array[3].angle2 = NINETY_DEGREES;


/*
 * Now, set up the four straight lines.
 */
segment_array[0].x1 = x + (arc_width/2);
segment_array[0].y1 = y;
segment_array[0].x2 = x + width - (arc_width/2);
segment_array[0].y2 = y;
```

```
    segment_array[1].x1 = x + width;

    segment_array[1].y1 = y + (arc_height/2);

    segment_array[1].x2 = x + width;

    segment_array[1].y2 = y + height - (arc_height/2);


    segment_array[2].x1 = x + width - (arc_width/2);

    segment_array[2].y1 = y + height;

    segment_array[2].x2 = x + (arc_width/2);

    segment_array[2].y2 = y + height;


    segment_array[3].x1 = x;

    segment_array[3].y1 = y + (arc_height/2);

    segment_array[3].x2 = x;

    segment_array[3].y2 = y + height - (arc_height/2);


    /*
     * Draw the arcs and lines.
     */
    XDrawArcs(display, drawable, gc,
        arc_array, 4);
    XDrawSegments(display, drawable, gc,
        segment_array, 4);


}   /* DrawRoundRect */


void FillRoundRect(Display* display,
        Drawable drawable,
        GC gc,
        int x, int y,
        int width, int height,
        int arc_width,
```

```
              int arc_height)

{    /* FillRoundRect */
     XArc          arc_array[20];
     XRectangle    rectangle_array[4];
     XGCValues     xgcvalues;

     if (width < 1) {
         width = 1;
     }

     if (height < 1) {
         height = 1;
     }

     /*
      * Determine current arc-filling mode.
      * Note: this requires X11R4 or higher.
      */
     XGetGCValues(display, gc, GCArcMode, &xgcvalues);

     if (xgcvalues.arc_mode != ArcPieSlice) {
         XSetArcMode(display, gc, ArcPieSlice);
     }

     /*
      * Check if too small. If so,
      * just fill a rectangle.
      */
     if ((width < 12) && (height < 12)) {
         XFillRectangle(display, drawable, gc,
```

```
            x, y, width, height);
        return;
    }


    /*
     * Do the four corners first.
     */
    arc_array[0].x = x;
    arc_array[0].y = y;
    arc_array[0].width = arc_width;
    arc_array[0].height = arc_height;
    arc_array[0].angle1 = NINETY_DEGREES;
    arc_array[0].angle2 = NINETY_DEGREES;


    arc_array[1].x = x + width - arc_width;
    arc_array[1].y = y;
    arc_array[1].width = arc_width;
    arc_array[1].height = arc_height;
    arc_array[1].angle1 = 0;
    arc_array[1].angle2 = NINETY_DEGREES;


    arc_array[2].x = x + width - arc_width;
    arc_array[2].y = y + height - arc_height;
    arc_array[2].width = arc_width;
    arc_array[2].height = arc_height;
    arc_array[2].angle1 = 0;
    arc_array[2].angle2 = (-1) * NINETY_DEGREES;


    arc_array[3].x = x;
    arc_array[3].y = y + height - arc_height;
    arc_array[3].width = arc_width;
```

```
arc_array[3].height = arc_height;
arc_array[3].angle1 = 2 * NINETY_DEGREES;
arc_array[3].angle2 = NINETY_DEGREES;

/*
 * Now, set up three rectangles.
 */
rectangle_array[0].x = x + (arc_width/2);
rectangle_array[0].y = y;
rectangle_array[0].width = width - arc_width;
rectangle_array[0].height = height;

rectangle_array[1].x = x;
rectangle_array[1].y = y + (arc_height/2);
rectangle_array[1].width = (arc_width/2);
rectangle_array[1].height = height - arc_height;

rectangle_array[2].x = x + width - (arc_width/2);
rectangle_array[2].y = y + (arc_height/2);
rectangle_array[2].width = (arc_width/2);
rectangle_array[2].height = height - arc_height;

/*
 * Fill the arcs and rectangles.
 */
XFillArcs(display, drawable, gc,
    arc_array, 4);
XFillRectangles(display, drawable, gc,
    rectangle_array, 3);

/*
```

```
      * Restore original arc mode.
      */
     if (xgcvalues.arc_mode != ArcPieSlice) {
         XSetArcMode(display, gc, xgcvalues.arc_mode);
     }


 }          /* FillRoundRect */


/* end of file drawrnd.c */
```

The calls to XGetGCValues and XSetArcMode make sure that we use the proper arc-filling mode, ArcPieSlice, and then restore the previous arc-filling mode, if necessary.

The header file draw.h provides standard C function prototypes for both drawoval.c and drawrnd.c, and includes the necessary Xlib header file, <X11/Xlib.h>:

```
/*
 *   draw.h
 *   Header file for oval and rounded-corner
 *   rectangle drawing routines.
 */
#ifndef draw_h_
#define draw_h_ 1


        /* Bug fix for HP-UX 8.0. */
#ifdef HPUX_FIX
typedef char*    caddr_t;
#endif  /* HPUX_FIX  */


#include <X11/Xlib.h>


/* Ovals */
```

```
void DrawOval(Display* display,
      Drawable drawable,
      GC gc,
      int x, int y,
      int width, int height);


void FillOval(Display* display,
      Drawable drawable,
      GC gc,
      int x, int y,
      int width, int height);


/* Rounded-Corner Rectangles */
void DrawRoundRect(Display* display,
      Drawable drawable,
      GC gc,
      int x, int y,
      int width, int height,
      int arc_width,
      int arc_height);


void FillRoundRect(Display* display,
      Drawable drawable,
      GC gc,
      int x, int y,
      int width, int height,
      int arc_width,
      int arc_height);

#endif  /* !draw_h_ */
/* end of file draw.h */
```

The definition of `caddr_t`, above, fixes a problem we faced under Hewlett-Packard's HP-UX 8.0.7 operating system when compiling C files with ANSI C function prototypes. This problem is fixed in HP-UX 9.0, so we put in a define, *HPUX_FIX*, to deal with this. If you're running under HP-UX and have problems compiling any of the X header files, such as `<X11/Xlib.h>`, then define *HPUX_FIX*, either with an option to the C compiler, `-DHPUX_FIX`, or with a `#define` statement.

Appendix C

Handling X Errors

An Introduction to Handling X Errors

Working with sophisticated color and complex image-handling in X programs is fraught with danger. One of the main problems that may strike your applications is the dreaded X error. Most Xlib functions don't return a status that indicates success or failure. Instead, these functions, such as `XDrawImageString`, generate an X error on failure, like the one below:

```
X Error of failed request: BadDrawable (invalid Pixmap or
Window parameter)
    Major opcode of failed request:  76 (X_ImageText8)
    Minor opcode of failed request:  0
    Resource id in failed request:  0x1
    Serial number of failed request:  12
    Current serial number in output stream:  13
```

By default, X programs terminate on any X-related error, since the default error-handling function calls *exit.*

Remember that X is an asynchronous client-server system. Your application, the client, sends request packets over a network link to the X server. To speed up the process, most client requests, such as that generated by XDrawLine, are sent blind. That is, your application sends off the request and proceeds merrily on its way, without waiting for any status return. To make matters more complex, your application buffers up X requests so that it can send a number of request packets together. This is, again, to improve performance by reducing the network overhead.

There are a number of conditions that cause your application to flush its buffer of cached X requests and send all the packets to the X server. The XFlush function, for example, explicitly flushes the buffer, as does XSync. If the buffer fills up, then the X library automatically flushes the buffer—if your Xlib works properly. The buffer rarely fills up in real-life practice, though.

Some functions, like XNextEvent, implicitly flush the buffer, as do functions that require a round-trip to the X server, like XGetGeometry.

The packets from your application then arrive at the X server sometime later, although the delay is usually short. The X server handles your application's requests and then also buffers up its responses to send back to your application, creating another delay. Again, this delay is usually short.

If the X server detects an error, it sends back an error packet, or *error event*, to your application. Your application, in turn, reads events from the X server, with a call to, say, XNextEvent, and detects the error event.

When an error event arrives at your application, the X library automatically calls the current *error-handling function.* The default error-handling function prints out an error message and then calls exit to terminate your program.

While the error message and program termination may actually help you while you're debugging your application, this behavior is generally frowned upon in commercial-grade applications. Accordingly, your applications must be on the lookout for X error events. To do this, you must register an error-handling function. An error handler will intercept the X error and allow your routine to process the error, rather than force a nasty program termination. To make any sort of commercial-quality software, you must set up functions to handle X errors.

N O T E   Your X toolkit may provide higher-level functions for dealing with X errors. For now, however, we intend to concentrate on the low-level process for handling errors. Even if you use the higher-level routines provided by your X toolkit, you still need to understand how X deals with errors.

If you stick with the low-level X library, though, you'll find that errors are divided into two types: *I/O* (short for Input/Output) errors and *normal* errors. The I/O errors are generated when your connection to the X server breaks somehow, generally in a network failure of some kind. These are considered fatal errors and there's not a lot you can do if your network goes down. Most programs try to save data files in such a case. But, be careful, as you cannot call any Xlib functions from within a fatal I/O error-handler function.

You register your fatal X error-handler function by calling `XSetIOErrorHandler`:

```
XIOErrorHandler

XSetIOErrorHandler(XIOErrorHandler handlerfunc)
```

The `XIOErrorHandler` function pointer is then defined as:

```
typedef int (*XIOErrorHandler)(Display* display);
```

`XSetIOErrorHandler` returns a pointer to the previous fatal error-handling function. Your fatal error-handling function will then use the following template:

```
FatalErrorHandler(Display* display)


{    /* FatalErrorHandler */
}    /* FatalErrorHandler */
```

Nonfatal X Errors

The other type of errors are simpler and generally easier to handle. If you pass a bad window ID to `XDrawLine`, for instance, you'll generate a `BadDrawable` error. If the X server runs out of memory, you'll get the dreaded `BadAlloc` error. You register your nonfatal X error-handler function by calling `XSetErrorHandler`:

```
XErrorHandler
XSetErrorHandler(XErrorHandler handlerfunc)
```

The `XErrorHandler` function pointer is then defined as:

```
typedef int (*XErrorHandler)(Display* display,
    XErrorEvent* error_event);
```

`XSetErrorHandler` returns a pointer to the old error-handling function. Your *handlerfunc* function will be passed the `Display` pointer and a pointer to the error event:

```
int ErrorHandler(Display* display,
    XErrorEvent* event)


{   /* ErrorHandler */
}   /* ErrorHandler */
```

The error-handling function can return if you judge the errors recoverable. Most of them are.

The XErrorEvent Structure

Your error-handling function is passed a pointer to an `XErrorEvent`:

```
typedef struct {
    int            type;
    Display*       display;
    unsigned long  serial;
    unsigned char  error_code;
    unsigned char  request_code;
    unsigned char  minor_code;
```

```
    XID              resourceid;

} XErrorEvent;
```

The X library delivers `XErrorEvent` structures to the error-handling function set up with `XSetErrorHandler`. These error events arrive asynchronously, which makes it hard to associate the error with the offending routine. You can pull some useful information from the `XErrorEven` structure, though.

The *resourceid*, an `XID`, is the ID of the offending resource, such as a window or pixmap. It is usually defined as an unsigned long (check the include file `<X11/X.h>` to see your system's definition). The *serial* field is the serial number of the request, which usually isn't very helpful unless you are debugging an X server.

The *request_code* is the X protocol request number for the routine that actually caused the error. This can help when associating the error to the offending part of your code. The *minor_code* is, appropriately enough, the minor op-code of the failed X request.

Decoding Errors

The *error_code* field of the `XErrorEvent` structure tells what type of error happened. The `XGetErrorText` Xlib function returns the text message for a given error code:

```
XGetErrorText(Display* display,

    int error_code,

    char* buffer,  /* RETURN */

    int   buffer_length)
```

`XGetErrorText` retrieves an error message associated with an error number and places that message in a character *buffer*, which your application must allocate. You also need to pass the maximum length for a buffer that your code can accept. In your code, you can call `XGetErrorText`, as shown below:

```
#define BUFFER_LENGTH   200
```

```
void PrintErrorText(Display* display,
    XErrorEvent* event)


{   /* PrintErrorText */
    char    buffer[BUFFER_LENGTH+1];


    /*
     * Get the text associated
     * with the X error.
     */
    XGetErrorText(display,
        event->error_code,
        buffer,
        BUFFER_LENGTH);


    /* Print the text. */
    (void) fprintf(stderr, "\n\nX Error:\n\t%s\n", buffer);


}   /* PrintErrorText */
```

Armed with XGetErrorText, we can try to decode the often cryptic error messages. A common error message, printed by the default error-handling function, follows:

```
X Error of failed request: BadDrawable (invalid Pixmap or
        Window parameter)
    Major opcode of failed request:  76 (X_ImageText8)
    Minor opcode of failed request:  0
    Resource id in failed request:  0x1
    Serial number of failed request:  12
    Current serial number in output stream:  13
```

The `BadDrawable` error tells us that the error involved a bad drawable ID: a bad window or pixmap. In addition, we can guess from the op-code of 76 (`X_ImageText8`) that the error had to do with a call to `XDraw-ImageString` or some similar function that outputs text. Finally, the resource ID of the failed request is `0x1`, which is normally a bad value. Later, when drawing to this nonexistent, bad window (or pixmap), the application faulted. The serial numbers and minor op-codes don't do you a lot of good.

Common Problems

Common errors, besides the `BadDrawable` error, mentioned above, include:

✦ `BadFont`, an invalid font;
✦ `BadMatch`, usually involving attempts to copy data between drawables with different depths; and
✦ `BadAlloc`, the out-of-memory error.

X Error Numbers

The `XErrorEvent` reports the error number in the *error_code* field (see Table C.1).

Table C.1 *X error numbers.*

Error Code	Value	Meaning
Success	0	No error
BadRequest	1	Bad request code
BadValue	2	Integer parameter out of range
BadWindow	3	Parameter not a valid window
BadPixmap	4	Parameter not a valid pixmap
BadAtom	5	Parameter not a valid atom
BadCursor	6	Parameter not a valid cursor
BadFont	7	Parameter not a valid font

BadMatch	8	Parameter mismatch
BadDrawable	9	Parameter not a valid pixmap or window
BadAccess	10	Attempt to perform an illegal operation
BadAlloc	11	Insufficient resources or memory
BadColor	12	No such colormap
BadGC	13	Parameter not a valid graphics context
BadIDChoice	14	Choice not in range or already used
BadName	15	Font or color name doesn't exist
BadLength	16	Request length incorrect
BadImplementation	17	Server is defective

X Protocol Numbers

The XErrorEvent also reports the protocol number, in the *request_code* field. This helps you identify the X library function that caused the error. The X server doesn't deal with Xlib functions; it only deals with the low-level X protocol. (Your application, for example, could be written in the Ada or Modula-3 programming languages, instead of C. In this case, the Xlib C function wouldn't be much use.) Because of this, you need to map the X protocol number to an Xlib function. This process usually isn't all that hard, because of the close correspondence.

The standard X protocol request numbers are listed in Table C.2. X extensions may extend this set. These numbers reside in the file <X11/Xproto.h>.

Table C.2 *X protocol numbers.*

Request Name	Number
CreateWindow	1
ChangeWindowAttributes	2

GetWindowAttributes	3
DestroyWindow	4
DestroySubwindows	5
ChangeSaveSet	6
ReparentWindow	7
MapWindow	8
MapSubwindows	9
UnmapWindow	10
UnmapSubwindows	11
ConfigureWindow	12
CirculateWindow	13
GetGeometry	14
QueryTree	15
InternAtom	16
GetAtomName	17
ChangeProperty	18
DeleteProperty	19
GetProperty	20
ListProperties	21
SetSelectionOwner	22
GetSelectionOwner	23
ConvertSelection	24
SendEvent	25
GrabPointer	26
UngrabPointer	27
GrabButton	28
UngrabButton	29
ChangeActivePointerGrab	30
GrabKeyboard	31
UngrabKeyboard	32
GrabKey	33

Trapping Errors in Your Code

To trap an X error, you need to set up an error-handling function with XSetErrorHandler, as described above. You then need to flesh out this error-handling function. We can build a simple error-handling function, using the PrintErrorText function presented above:

```
int ErrorHandler(Display* display,
    XErrorEvent* event)

{   /* ErrorHandler */

    /*
     * Get the text associated
     * with the X error and print it.
     */
    PrintErrorText(display, event);

    /* Print error event. */
    (void) fprintf(stderr,
        "\tSerial number of request: %ld\n",
        event->serial);

    (void) fprintf(stderr,
        "\tOp Code: %d.%d \n",
        event->request_code,
        event->minor_code);

    (void) fprintf(stderr,
        "\tError Code: %d\n",
        event->error_code);

    (void) fprintf(stderr,
        "\tResource ID of failed request: %ld\n",
        event->resourceid);

    (void) fprintf(stderr,
        "\ton display %s.\n",
```

```
      DisplayString(display) );


   /*
    * Your code to deal with
    * the error should go here.
    */


} /* ErrorHandler */
```

This function does nothing more than print out an error message. When an error occurs, you'll see an error message like the following:

```
X Error:
       BadGC (invalid GC parameter)
       Serial number of request: 102
       Op Code: 72.0
       Error Code: 13
       Resource ID of failed request: 29360155
       on display nicollet:0.0.
```

In your code, though, you should also come up with a way to deal with the X error. If you don't, you'll find that your code may generate a flurry of error messages as a bad X ID, such as a window or pixmap, is used over and over again, generating an X error each time.

`XSetErrorHandler` sets up a function called for any regular X error, like when a bad window ID is passed to a drawing function. Other X errors, though, are fatal to an X program, especially errors involving loss of the server connection. This type of error could happen if the X-server program itself tipped over, or if the network communication went down. You can, however, set up a fatal-error-handler function, much like the regular error-handler function. A fatal error-handling function would then look like:

```
FatalErrorHandler(Display* display)


{   /* FatalErrorHandler */
```

```
(void) fprintf(stderr,

    "X Error: Fatal IO error on display %s.\n",

    DisplayString(display) );


/*

 * Save files, perform any

 * necessary cleanup here.

 */


/*

 * Exit the program.

 */

exit(-1);


}    /* FatalErrorHandler */
```

Again, we leave a blank spot for you to fill in. When a fatal error occurs, you need to save any data files and generally clean up your application. This fatal error-handling function, though, will be the last routine that your program executes. Why? Because the X library claims to call `exit` when a fatal error-handling function returns (not all versions of Xlib do this, however). The loss of connection to the X server is considered a fatal error. It seems rather arrogant for X to decide that it will terminate your program on a fatal I/O error, since it might be better if you could try to reopen a display connection at a later time, but that's what you have to live with.

From a fatal-error handler, you cannot use any Xlib routines that would generate a request of the X server (an I/O error means that the link to the X server is severed).

Setting Up Error-Handling Functions

We've put together a convenience function to set up the error-handling functions presented above. `RegisterErrorFuncs`, below, registers `ErrorHandler` and `FatalErrorHandler` as event-handling functions:

```
void RegisterErrorFuncs()

{   /* RegisterErrorFuncs */

    (void) XSetErrorHandler(ErrorHandler);

    (void) XSetIOErrorHandler(FatalErrorHandler);

}   /* RegisterErrorFuncs */
```

Source Code for the Error-Handling Routines

Our error-handling routines are stored in the file `error.c`:

```
/*
 *   error.c
 *   Routines to handle X errors.
#include "xlib.h"
#include <stdio.h>

/*
 * Get the text associated
 * with an X error and
 * print it to stderr.
 */

#define BUFFER_LENGTH    200

void PrintErrorText(Display* display,
     XErrorEvent* event)
```

```
{   /* PrintErrorText */
    char    buffer[BUFFER_LENGTH+1];

    /*
     * Get the text associated
     * with the X error.
     */
    XGetErrorText(display,
        event->error_code,
        buffer,
        BUFFER_LENGTH);

    /* Print the text. */
    (void) fprintf(stderr,
        "\n\nX Error:\n\t%s\n", buffer);

}   /* PrintErrorText */

/*
 * Handle Xlib errors. This routine just prints
 * out an error message and doesn't deal with
 * the error. Your code should deal with the
 * error.
 */
int ErrorHandler(Display* display,
    XErrorEvent* event)

{   /* ErrorHandler */

    /*
     * Get the text associated
```

```
 * with the X error and print it.
 */
PrintErrorText(display, event);

/* Print error event. */
(void) fprintf(stderr,
    "\tSerial number of request: %ld\n",
    event->serial);

(void) fprintf(stderr,
    "\tOp Code: %d.%d \n",
    event->request_code,
    event->minor_code);

(void) fprintf(stderr,
    "\tError Code: %d\n",
    event->error_code);

(void) fprintf(stderr,
    "\tResource ID of failed request: %ld\n",
    event->resourceid);

(void) fprintf(stderr,
    "\ton display %s.\n",
    DisplayString(display) );

/*
 * Your code to deal with
 * the error should go here.
 */
```

```
}   /* ErrorHandler */


/*
 * This routine handles fatal I/O
 * errors, like the loss of the
 * network connection to the X
 * server. Xlib claims to call
 * exit when this routine returns,
 * so you must save any necessary
 * files, etc, before returning
 * from this routine. In addition,
 * you must NOT call X functions
 * from within this routine.
 */


FatalErrorHandler(Display* display)


{   /* FatalErrorHandler */

    (void) fprintf(stderr,
        "X Error: Fatal IO error on display %s.\n",
        DisplayString(display) );

    /*
     * Save files, perform any
     * necessary cleanup here.
     */

    /*
     * Exit the program.
     */
```

```
        exit(-1);

}    /* FatalErrorHandler */

/*
 * Convenience function to set up
 * Xlib error-handling functions.
 */

void RegisterErrorFuncs()

{    /* RegisterErrorFuncs */

    (void) XSetErrorHandler(ErrorHandler);

    (void) XSetIOErrorHandler(FatalErrorHandler);

}    /* RegisterErrorFuncs */

/* end of file error.c */
```

X Library Functions and Macros Introduced in This Appendix

```
XSetErrorHandler
XSetIOErrorHandler
```

A Makefile for the Sample Programs

Since we work on a number of disparate platforms, we use a combination of a generic `Makefile` and a system-specific shell script to compile and link all the example programs. To set this up, you should be able to use the `Makefile` as is, but you'll need to create the system-specific shell script for your system's configuration.

First, we present the generic `Makefile`, then we present and explain the system-specific shell scripts. The huge `Makefile` follows:

```
#
#    Makefile for the sample sources for
#    Professional Graphics
#    Programming in the X Window System.
#
# To use this Makefile, you'll need to set a
# number of make variables:
```

```
#
#     Variable     Usage
#     CC           C compiler, e.g., cc or gcc
#     CFLAGS       Flags to CC, e.g., -g
#     X_LIBS       Low-level X lib, -lX11
#     XT_LIBS      Xt library, -lXt
#     MOTIF_LIBS   Motif library, -lXm
#     OLIT_LIBS    OLIT library, -lXol
#     RANLIB_CMD   ranlib or echo
#     MULTI        -DMULTIBUFFER if you have the Multi-Buffer
#                  header and libraries.
#     SHM          -DMITSHM if you have MIT-SHM extension
#     TOOL_INC     Motif or OLIT include directories,
#                  e.g. /usr/openwin/include
#     X_INC        X include directories, if nonstandard
#
#
CC_CMD= $(CC) $(CFLAGS) $(TOOL_INC) $(X_INC)


AR_CMD=    ar qv


#
#   Motif support library files.
#
MOTIF_OBJS= m_draw.o   \
        m_exit.o    \
        m_mainw.o   \
        m_menu.o    \
        m_pixmap.o  \
        m_prompt.o  \
        m_push.o    \
```

```
        m_shell.o   \
        m_slider.o  \
        m_string.o

#
#   OLIT support library files.
#
OLIT_OBJS=  o_draw.o    \
        o_exit.o    \
        o_mainw.o   \
        o_menu.o    \
        o_prompt.o  \
        o_push.o    \
        o_shell.o   \
        o_slider.o

#
#   Xlib support library files.
#
X_OBJS=     busy.o      \
        chgcolor.o  \
        color.o     \
        colorcms.o  \
        colormap.o  \
        convert.o   \
        drawoval.o  \
        drawrnd.o   \
        error.o     \
        fractal.o   \
        getvis.o    \
        iconchk.o   \
```

```
            iconwid.o    \
            mitshm.o     \
            overlay.o    \
            pixmap.o     \
            pixwidgt.o   \
            region.o     \
            stdcmap.o    \
            timeout.o    \
            visual.o     \
            ximage.o

#
#    Motif
#
MOTIF_PROGS=    chap5 chap9 m_chap20 m_chap8 mcolor \
        m_chap10 m_chap11 m_chap15 m_chap17 \
        m_chap19 m_chap21 m_chap22 m_chap24 m_chap25


MOTIF_LIBRARY=  libProXm.a


motif:      $(MOTIF_LIBRARY) $(MOTIF_PROGS)


$(MOTIF_LIBRARY):   $(MOTIF_OBJS) $(X_OBJS)
        /bin/rm -f $(MOTIF_LIBRARY)
        $(AR_CMD) $(MOTIF_LIBRARY) $(MOTIF_OBJS) $(X_OBJS)
        $(RANLIB_CMD) $(MOTIF_LIBRARY)


#
#    OLIT
#
OLIT_PROGS= chap6 o_chap8 o_chap10 o_chap11 \
```

```
            o_chap15 o_chap17 o_chap19 o_chap20 \
            o_chap21 o_chap22 o_chap25


OLIT_LIBRARY=    libProXo.a


olit:        $(OLIT_LIBRARY) $(OLIT_PROGS)


$(OLIT_LIBRARY):    $(OLIT_OBJS) $(X_OBJS)
        /bin/rm -f $(OLIT_LIBRARY)
        $(AR_CMD) $(OLIT_LIBRARY) $(OLIT_OBJS) $(X_OBJS)
        $(RANLIB_CMD) $(OLIT_LIBRARY)


clean:
    /bin/rm -f core xext xvisinfo chap5 \
    m_chap8 chap9 *.o libProXm.a libProXo.a \
    o_chap8 chap6 mcolor liststdc m_chap10 \
    o_chap10 m_chap11 o_chap11 m_chap15 \
    o_chap15 m_chap17 o_chap17 m_chap19 \
    o_chap19 m_chap20 o_chap20 m_chap21 \
    o_chap21 m_chap22 o_chap22 m_chap24 \
    o_chap25 m_chap25


#
#    Motif C files.
#
m_draw.o:    m_draw.c motif.h
    $(CC_CMD) -c m_draw.c


m_exit.o:    m_exit.c motif.h
    $(CC_CMD) -c m_exit.c
```

```
m_mainw.o:   m_mainw.c motif.h
    $(CC_CMD) -c m_mainw.c


m_menu.o:    m_menu.c motif.h
    $(CC_CMD) -c m_menu.c


m_pixmap.o: m_pixmap.c motif.h
    $(CC_CMD) -c m_pixmap.c


m_prompt.o: m_prompt.c motif.h
    $(CC_CMD) -c m_prompt.c


m_push.o:    m_push.c motif.h
    $(CC_CMD) -c m_push.c


m_shell.o:   m_shell.c motif.h
    $(CC_CMD) -c m_shell.c


m_slider.o: m_slider.c motif.h
    $(CC_CMD) -c m_slider.c


m_string.o: m_string.c motif.h
    $(CC_CMD) -c m_string.c


motif.h:


#
#   OLIT C files.
#
o_draw.o:    o_draw.c olit.h
    $(CC_CMD) -c o_draw.c
```

```
o_exit.o:    o_exit.c olit.h
    $(CC_CMD) -c o_exit.c


o_mainw.o:  o_mainw.c olit.h
    $(CC_CMD) -c o_mainw.c


o_menu.o:    o_menu.c olit.h
    $(CC_CMD) -c o_menu.c


o_prompt.o: o_prompt.c olit.h
    $(CC_CMD) -c o_prompt.c


o_push.o:    o_push.c olit.h
    $(CC_CMD) -c o_push.c


o_shell.o:   o_shell.c olit.h
    $(CC_CMD) -c o_shell.c


o_slider.o: o_slider.c olit.h
    $(CC_CMD) -c o_slider.c


olit.h:

#
#   Xlib C files.
#
busy.o:        busy.c xlib.h
    $(CC_CMD) -c busy.c


chgcolor.o:        chgcolor.c xlib.h
```

```
    $(CC_CMD) -c chgcolor.c


color.o:         color.c xlib.h
    $(CC_CMD) -c color.c


colorcms.o:        colorcms.c xlib.h
    $(CC_CMD) -c colorcms.c


colormap.o:        colormap.c xlib.h
    $(CC_CMD) -c colormap.c


convert.o:        convert.c convert.h
    $(CC_CMD) -c convert.c


drawoval.o:     drawoval.c draw.h
    $(CC_CMD) -c drawoval.c


drawrnd.o:      drawrnd.c draw.h
    $(CC_CMD) -c drawrnd.c


error.o:    error.c xlib.h
    $(CC_CMD) -c error.c


fractal.o:    fractal.c xlib.h
    $(CC_CMD) -c fractal.c


getvis.o:        getvis.c xlib.h
    $(CC_CMD) -c getvis.c


iconchk.o:    iconchk.c xlib.h
    $(CC_CMD) -c iconchk.c
```

```
iconwid.o:      iconwid.c xlib.h
    $(CC_CMD) -c iconwid.c


mitshm.o:       mitshm.c mitshm.h
    $(CC_CMD) $(SHM) -c mitshm.c


overlay.o:      overlay.c xlib.h
    $(CC_CMD) -c overlay.c


pixmap.o:       pixmap.c xlib.h
    $(CC_CMD) -c pixmap.c


pixwidgt.o:        pixwidgt.c
    $(CC_CMD) -c pixwidgt.c


region.o:       region.c xlib.h
    $(CC_CMD) -c region.c


stdcmap.o:      stdcmap.c xlib.h
    $(CC_CMD) -c stdcmap.c


timeout.o:        timeout.c timeout.h xlib.h
    $(CC_CMD) -c timeout.c


visual.o:       visual.c xlib.h
    $(CC_CMD) -c visual.c


ximage.o:     ximage.c xlib.h
    $(CC_CMD) -c ximage.c
```

```
xlib.h:

draw.h:

mitshm.h:

convert.h:

timeout.h:

########################################
# Example Programs, by chapter.
########################################
#
#    Chapter 5, Motif test program.
#
M_LIBS= -L. -lProXm $(MOTIF_LIBS)

chap5:  chap5.o drawtest.o $(MOTIF_LIBRARY)
    $(CC_CMD) -o chap5 chap5.o drawtest.o $(M_LIBS)

chap5.o:    chap5.c
    $(CC_CMD) -c chap5.c

drawtest.o: drawtest.c
    $(CC_CMD) -c drawtest.c

#
#    Chapter 6, OLIT test program.
#
O_LIBS= -L. -lProXo $(OLIT_LIBS)
```

```
chap6:   chap6.o drawtest.o $(OLIT_LIBRARY)
    $(CC_CMD) -o chap6 chap6.o drawtest.o $(O_LIBS)


chap6.o:    chap6.c
    $(CC_CMD) -c chap6.c


#
#   Chapter 8, Turtle Graphics, generic sources.
#
TURTLE_OBJS=    chap8.o turtle.o lsystem.o


chap8.o:    chap8.c
    $(CC_CMD) -c chap8.c


turtle.o:   turtle.c
    $(CC_CMD) -c turtle.c


lsystem.o:  lsystem.c
    $(CC_CMD) -c lsystem.c


#
#   Chapter 8, Turtle Graphics, Motif program.
#
m_chap8:    m_chap8.o $(TURTLE_OBJS) $(MOTIF_LIBRARY)
    $(CC_CMD) -o m_chap8 m_chap8.o \
        $(TURTLE_OBJS) $(M_LIBS) -lm


m_chap8.o:  m_chap8.c
    $(CC_CMD) -c m_chap8.c
```

```
#
#    Chapter 8, Turtle Graphics, OLIT program.
#
o_chap8:    o_chap8.o $(TURTLE_OBJS) $(OLIT_LIBRARY)
        $(CC_CMD) -o o_chap8 o_chap8.o \
            $(TURTLE_OBJS) $(O_LIBS) -lm


o_chap8.o:  o_chap8.c
        $(CC_CMD) -c o_chap8.c


#
#    Chapter 9, Motif color calc.
#
mcolor: mcolor.o
        $(CC_CMD) -o mcolor mcolor.o $(M_LIBS)


mcolor.o:   mcolor.c
        $(CC_CMD) -c mcolor.c


#
#    Chapter 9, 3D Bevel colors.
#
chap9:  chap9.o bevel.o $(MOTIF_LIBRARY)
        $(CC_CMD) -o chap9 chap9.o bevel.o $(M_LIBS)


chap9.o:    chap9.c
        $(CC_CMD) -c chap9.c


bevel.o:    bevel.c
        $(CC_CMD) -c bevel.c
```

```
#
#   Chapter 10, Visuals and colormaps.
#
m_chap10:   m_chap10.o $(MOTIF_LIBRARY)
    $(CC_CMD) -o m_chap10 m_chap10.o $(M_LIBS) -lm


m_chap10.o: m_chap10.c
    $(CC_CMD) -c m_chap10.c


o_chap10:   o_chap10.o $(OLIT_LIBRARY)
    $(CC_CMD) -o o_chap10 o_chap10.o $(O_LIBS) -lm


o_chap10.o: o_chap10.c
    $(CC_CMD) -c o_chap10.c


xvisinfo:   xvisinfo.c
    $(CC_CMD) -o xvisinfo xvisinfo.c $(X_LIBS)


#
#   Chapter 11, Color Overlay Planes.
#
m_chap11:   m_chap11.o chap11.o $(MOTIF_LIBRARY)
    $(CC_CMD) -o m_chap11 m_chap11.o chap11.o \
        $(M_LIBS) -lm


m_chap11.o: m_chap11.c
    $(CC_CMD) -c m_chap11.c


o_chap11:   o_chap11.o chap11.o $(OLIT_LIBRARY)
    $(CC_CMD) -o o_chap11 o_chap11.o chap11.o \
        $(O_LIBS) -lm
```

```
o_chap11.o: o_chap11.c
    $(CC_CMD) -c o_chap11.c


chap11.o:   chap11.c
    $(CC_CMD) -c chap11.c


#
#   Chapter 12, Standard Colormaps.
#
liststdc:   liststdc.c
    $(CC_CMD) -o liststdc liststdc.c $(X_LIBS)


#
#   Chapter 15, Fonts and X Toolkits, Motif.
#
m_chap15:   m_chap15.o $(MOTIF_LIBRARY)
    $(CC_CMD) -o m_chap15 m_chap15.o $(M_LIBS)


m_chap15.o: m_chap15.c motif.h
    $(CC_CMD) -c m_chap15.c


#
#   Chapter 15, Fonts and X Toolkits, OLIT.
#
o_chap15:   o_chap15.o $(OLIT_LIBRARY)
    $(CC_CMD) -o o_chap15 o_chap15.o $(O_LIBS)


o_chap15.o: o_chap15.c olit.h
    $(CC_CMD) -c o_chap15.c
```

```
#
#    Chapter 17, Pixmaps and Bitmaps.
#
m_chap17:    m_chap17.o $(MOTIF_LIBRARY)
    $(CC_CMD) -o m_chap17 m_chap17.o $(M_LIBS)


m_chap17.o: m_chap17.c
    $(CC_CMD) -c m_chap17.c


o_chap17:    o_chap17.o $(OLIT_LIBRARY)
    $(CC_CMD) -o o_chap17 o_chap17.o $(O_LIBS)


o_chap17.o: o_chap17.c
    $(CC_CMD) -c o_chap17.c


#
#    Chapter 18, Xpm
#    Note: You must have the Xpm library,
#    libXpm.a, to do any good with this.
xpm.o:   xpm.c
    $(CC_CMD) -c xpm.c


#
#    Chapter 19, Bitmap Cursors.
#
m_chap19:    m_chap19.o $(MOTIF_LIBRARY)
    $(CC_CMD) -o m_chap19 m_chap19.o $(M_LIBS)


m_chap19.o: m_chap19.c
    $(CC_CMD) -c m_chap19.c
```

```
o_chap19:    o_chap19.o $(OLIT_LIBRARY)
    $(CC_CMD) -o o_chap19 o_chap19.o $(O_LIBS)


o_chap19.o: o_chap19.c
    $(CC_CMD) -c o_chap19.c


#
#    Chapter 20, Icon Windows.
#
m_chap20:    m_chap20.o $(MOTIF_LIBRARY)
    $(CC_CMD) -o m_chap20 m_chap20.o $(M_LIBS)


m_chap20.o: m_chap20.c
    $(CC_CMD) -c m_chap20.c


o_chap20:    o_chap20.o $(OLIT_LIBRARY)
    $(CC_CMD) -o o_chap20 o_chap20.o $(O_LIBS)


o_chap20.o: o_chap20.c
    $(CC_CMD) -c o_chap20.c


#
#    Chapter 21, XImages and fractals.
#
m_chap21:    m_chap21.o chap21.o $(MOTIF_LIBRARY)
    $(CC_CMD) -o m_chap21 m_chap21.o chap21.o \
        $(M_LIBS)


m_chap21.o: m_chap21.c
    $(CC_CMD) -c m_chap21.c
```

```
o_chap21:    o_chap21.o chap21.o $(OLIT_LIBRARY)
    $(CC_CMD) -o o_chap21 o_chap21.o chap21.o \
        $(O_LIBS)


o_chap21.o: o_chap21.c
    $(CC_CMD) -c o_chap21.c


chap21.o:    chap21.c
    $(CC_CMD) -c chap21.c


#
#    Chapter 22, X Extensions.
#    and shared images.
#
xext:    xext.c
    $(CC_CMD) -o xext xext.c $(X_LIBS)


m_chap22:    m_chap22.o $(MOTIF_LIBRARY)
    $(CC_CMD) -o m_chap22 m_chap22.o $(M_LIBS)


m_chap22.o: m_chap22.c mitshm.h
    $(CC_CMD) $(SHM) -c m_chap22.c


o_chap22:    o_chap22.o $(OLIT_LIBRARY)
    $(CC_CMD) -o o_chap22 o_chap22.o $(O_LIBS)


o_chap22.o: o_chap22.c mitshm.h
    $(CC_CMD) $(SHM) -c o_chap22.c


#
#    Chapter 24, Bitmap Animation.
```

```
#    You need Xpm for this.
#
ANIM=    animate.o xpm.o
m_chap24:    m_chap24.o $(ANIM) $(MOTIF_LIBRARY)
    $(CC_CMD) -o m_chap24 m_chap24.o \
        $(ANIM) -L. -lXpm $(M_LIBS)


m_chap24.o: m_chap24.c motif.h
    $(CC_CMD) -c m_chap24.c


animate.o:  animate.c
    $(CC_CMD) -c animate.c


o_chap24:    o_chap24.o $(ANIM) $(OLIT_LIBRARY)
    $(CC_CMD) -o o_chap24 o_chap24.o \
        $(ANIM) -L. -lXpm $(O_LIBS)


o_chap24.o: o_chap24.c olit.h
    $(CC_CMD) -c o_chap24.c


#
#    Chapter 25, Double-
#    and multibuffering.
#
CHAP25=     chap25.o drawtest.o dblbuff.o


o_chap25:    o_chap25.o $(CHAP25) $(OLIT_LIBRARY)
    $(CC_CMD) -o o_chap25 o_chap25.o $(CHAP25) $(O_LIBS)


o_chap25.o: o_chap25.c olit.h chap25.h
    $(CC_CMD) $(MULTI) -c o_chap25.c
```

```
m_chap25:    m_chap25.o $(CHAP25) $(MOTIF_LIBRARY)
    $(CC_CMD) -o m_chap25 m_chap25.o $(CHAP25) $(M_LIBS)

m_chap25.o: m_chap25.c motif.h chap25.h
    $(CC_CMD) $(MULTI) -c m_chap25.c

chap25.o:    chap25.c chap25.h
    $(CC_CMD) $(MULTI) -c chap25.c

dblbuff.o:   dblbuff.c chap25.h
    $(CC_CMD) $(MULTI) -c dblbuff.c

chap25.h:

#
#    Multibuffers.
#
CHAP25_MUL=      chap25.o drawtest.o mulbuff.o

mulbuff.o:   mulbuff.c chap25.h
    $(CC_CMD) $(MULTI) -c mulbuff.c

m_chap25mul:    m_chap25.o $(CHAP25_MUL)
    $(CC_CMD) -o m_chap25mul m_chap25.o \
        $(CHAP25_MUL) $(M_LIBS)

o_chap25mul:    o_chap25.o $(CHAP25_MUL)
    $(CC_CMD) -o o_chap25mul o_chap25.o \
        $(CHAP25_MUL) $(O_LIBS)

#    end of Makefile
```

System-Specific Shell Scripts

The shell scripts allow us to compile our sources on a number of different platforms, many of which don't have the X utility called `imake` (a `Makefile`-builder). Because of the lack of `imake`, we instead use simple shell scripts that merely set the proper make variables. Here's a sample script for a Silicon Graphics IRIX 4.0.5 platform:

```
make CC=cc "X_LIBS=-1Xext -1X11" \
    "XT_LIBS= -1Xt" \
    "CFLAGS= -g" \
    "SHM=-DMITSHM" \
    "MULTI= -DMULTIBUFFER" \
    "MOTIF_LIBS=-1Xm $(XT_LIBS) $(X_LIBS)" \
    "RANLIB_CMD= echo" \
    $*
```

We named this script `makesgi`. To use such a shell script, you call it just like `make`. To compile the program named `chap5`, you'd use the following command:

```
makesgi chap5
```

The system-specific shell script sets up a number of `make` variables, including those listed in Table D.1.

Table D.1   *Make variables to set.*

Variable	Usage
CC	C compiler
CFLAGS	Extra flags for ANSI C
X_INC	Flag for X include files
TOOL_INC	Flag for toolkit include files
MOTIF_LIBS	Flags for Motif libraries

`OLIT_LIBS`	Flags for OLIT libraries
`X_LIBS`	Flags for low-level X and Xext libraries
`XT_LIBS`	Flags for Xt library
`MULTI`	Flags to compile in Multi-buffer code
`SHM`	Flags to compile in MIT-SHM (shared-memory) code
`RANLIB_CMD`	ranlib if you need this command, or echo otherwise

The way to set these flags is to examine your system. The default C compiler is cc, but some systems use `gcc` (the GNU C compiler) or `acc` (the Sun ANSI C compiler). For a more extended example, Hewlett-Packard HP-UX 9.01 uses the settings listed in Table D.2.

Table D.2   Make variables for HP-UX 9.01.

Variable	**HP-UX 9**
`CC`	`cc`
`CFLAGS`	`-Aa -g -Dhpux -Dunix`
`X_INC`	`-I/usr/include/X11R5`
`TOOL_INC`	`-I/usr/include/Motif1.2`
`MOTIF_LIBS`	`-L/usr/lib/Motif1.2 -1Xm $(XT_LIBS) $(X_LIBS)`
`OLIT_LIBS`	(not applicable)
`X_LIBS`	`-L/usr/lib/X11R5 -1Xext -1X11`
`XT_LIBS`	`-L/usr/lib/X11R5 -1Xt`
`MULTI`	(not applicable)
`SHM`	`-DMITSHM -DHPUX`
`RANLIB_CMD`	`echo`

HP-UX places the X and Motif include files in odd places—/usr/include/X11R5 and /usr/include/Motif1.2, respectively. HP-UX also requires a complicated set of linking flags, and the C compiler needs the -Aa flag to use ANSI C function prototypes. For some odd reason, both HP-UX 8.0 and 9.0 don't have the include file `<X11/extensions/multibif.h>`, so you cannot try out the multibuffering example from Chapter 25 unless you somehow get this file.

The `makehp.r5` script then follows:

```
#!/bin/sh
################################################
# Hewlett-Packard HP-UX 9.0 (X11R5 Motif 1.2)
################################################

make CC=cc X_INC=-I/usr/include/X11R5 \
"TOOL_INC=-I/usr/include/Motif1.2" \
"X_LIBS=-L/usr/lib/X11R5 -1Xext -1X11" \
"XT_LIBS=-L/usr/lib/X11R5 -1Xt" \
"SHM=-DMITSHM -DHPUX " \
"CFLAGS= -Aa -g -Dhpux -Dunix " \
"MOTIF_LIBS=-L/usr/lib/Motif1.2 -1Xm $(XT_LIBS) $(X_LIBS)" \
"RANLIB_CMD= echo" \
$*

# end of script
```

More System-Specific Shell Scripts

We include a number of system-specific shell scripts below to help you to create one that's customized for your system. Unfortunately, the documentation that describes many of these settings is often hard to find or even nonexistent. Even so, with a little experimentation, you should be able to discover what you need. On the HP systems, for instance, we ran the `xext` program from Chapter 22 and discovered that HP-UX supports the multibuffering X extension. We then tried to compile our example file and soon discovered that HP doesn't ship the necessary include file. Using trial and error can be frustrating, but there's no standard for system installations, either from vendors or users. Use these scripts as examples.

For HP-UX 8.07, use the `makehp` script:

```
#!/bin/sh
###################################################
# Hewlett-Packard HP-UX 8.0 (X11R4 Motif 1.1)
###################################################

make CC=cc X_INC=-I/usr/include/X11R4 \
"TOOL_INC=-I/usr/include/Motif1.1" \
"X_LIBS=-L/usr/lib/X11R4 -lXext -lX11" \
"XT_LIBS=-L/usr/lib/X11R4 -lXt" \
"CFLAGS= -Aa -g -Dhpux -Dunix -DHPUX_FIX " \
"SHM=-DMITSHM -DHPUX" \
"MOTIF_LIBS=-L/usr/lib/Motif1.1 -lXm $(XT_LIBS) $(X_LIBS)" \
"RANLIB_CMD= echo" \
$*


#    end of script
```

For Solaris 2.1 systems, use the `makesol` script:

```
#!/bin/sh
#######################################################
# Solaris 2.1, running OpenWindows 3.1, with ANSI C
#######################################################
#
/usr/ccs/bin/make CC=cc X_INC=-I/usr/openwin/include \
"X_LIBS=-L/usr/openwin/lib -lXext -lX11" \
"XT_LIBS=-L/usr/openwin/lib -lXt" \
"CFLAGS= -g" \
```

```
"SHM= -DMITSHM" \
"MULTI= -DMULTIBUFFER" \
"OLIT_LIBS=-L/usr/openwin/lib -lXol $(XT_LIBS) $(X_LIBS)" \
"RANLIB_CMD=echo"\
$*


#   end of script
```

For Silicon Graphics systems, use the `makesgi` script:

```
#!/bin/sh
######################################
# Silicon Graphics (SGI) IRIX 4.0.5
######################################

make CC=cc "X_LIBS=-lXext -lX11" \
    "XT_LIBS= -lXt" \
    "CFLAGS= -g" \
    "SHM=-DMITSHM" \
    "MULTI= -DMULTIBUFFER" \
    "MOTIF_LIBS=-lXm $(XT_LIBS) $(X_LIBS)" \
    "RANLIB_CMD= echo" \
    $*


#   end of script
```

For Interactive/SunSoft UNIX SVR3.2, version 3.0 on the 486, we support both the X Consortium Release 5 and the built-in X11 Release 4. We use the `gcc` C compiler on both. For Release 5, use the `makeisc.r5` script:

```
#!/bin/sh
##############################################################
# Interactive/SunSoft SVR3.2, ver. 3.0, XFree86 X11R5
##############################################################
```

```
make CC=gcc X_INC=-I/usr/local/X11R5/include \
    "CFLAGS=-g " \
    "SHM=-DMITSHM" \
    "MULTI=-DMULTIBUFFER" \
    "X_LIBS=-L/usr/local/X11R5/lib -1Xext -1X11 -1inet" \
    "XT_LIBS=-L/usr/local/X11R5/lib -1Xt" \
    "MOTIF_LIBS=-1Xm $(XT_LIBS) $(X_LIBS)" \
    RANLIB_CMD=echo \
    $*
```

For Release 4, use the `makeisc` script:

```
#!/bin/sh
#######################################################
# Interactive/SunSoft SVR3.2, ver. 3.0, built-in X11R4
#######################################################

make CC=gcc "CFLAGS=-g " \
    "X_LIBS= -1Xext -1X11 -1nsl_s" \
    "XT_LIBS= -1Xt" \
    "SHM=-DMITSHM" \
    "MULTI=-DMULTIBUFFER" \
    "MOTIF_LIBS=-1Xm $(XT_LIBS) $(X_LIBS)" \
    RANLIB_CMD=echo \
    $*


#    end of script
```

NOTE

Even if you use similar systems to ours, you may need to customize these shell scripts. We provided a number of the scripts so that you can use these as examples.

Appendix E

For More Information

There's no way one book can cover everything you want to learn. We've concentrated on showing you how to get going with drawing professional graphics using X, Motif, and Open Look Intrinsics Toolkit (OLIT). Here's a sampling of other sources for information.

Books and Documents

We found the following books, articles, and documents helpful.

Graphics

Foley, James, Andries van Dam, Steven Feiner, and John Hughes, *Computer Graphics: Principles and Practice*, second edition, Addison-Wesley, 1990. The bible of computer graphics, which includes a long section on color and the CIE model.

1153

Fractals and L-Systems

Oliver, Dick, *FractalVision: Put Fractals to Work for You*, SAMS, 1992. A good book to introduce the concepts of fractals. Particularly useful if you have a DOS-based PC so you can run the associated software.

Peitgen, Heinz-Otto, Hartmut Juergens, and Dietmar Saupe, *Chaos and Fractals: New Frontiers of Science*, Springer-Verlag, 1992. More discussions of L-systems, Mandelbrot sets, and other fractal-based systems, with pseudocode and BASIC programs.

Prusinkiewicz, Przemyslaw, and Aristid Lindenmayer, *The Algorithmic Beauty of Plants*, Springer-Verlag, 1990. An introduction to L-systems and modeling plant growth with software, by the creators of L-systems—the *L* stands for Lindenmayer.

Animation

There's not a lot of material available if you want to learn computer animation. Most books assume you know a *lot* about 3D graphics. Here's a few good references:

Adams, Lee, *C For Windows Animation Programming*, Windcrest, 1993. While devoted to Microsoft Windows programming, this is one of the few books to take on animation from a raster graphics perspective.

Baecker, Ronald, Ian Small, and Richard Mander, "Bringing Icons to Life," in the *SIGCHI 91 Proceedings*, Association for Computing Machinery.

Lasseter, John, "Principles of Traditional Animation Applied to 3D Computer Animation," *Proceedings of SIGGRAPH 1987*, ACM. We summarized this excellent paper in Chapter 23.

Thomas, F. and O. Johnston, *Disney Animation: The Illusion of Life*, Abbeyville, 1981. This book covers traditional, noncomputer animation from the Disney perspective.

Vince, John, *3-D Computer Animation*, Addison-Wesley, 1992.

Watt, Alan, and Mark Watt, *Advanced Animation and Rendering Techniques: Theory and Practice*, Addison-Wesley, 1992.

There is scant material on the Multi-Buffering X extension, described in

Chapter 25. There's one official document and an online manual entry. That's it.

Friedberg, Jeffrey, Larry Seiler, and Jeff Vroom, "Extending X For Double-Buffering, Multi-Buffering and Stereo." Part of the documentation that comes with the X Window System from the MIT X Consortium.

Images

Heckbert, Paul, "Color Image Quantization for Frame Buffer Display," *Proceedings of SIGGRAPH 1982*, ACM. This excellent, if old, paper describes what to do when you have to reduce the number of colors used by an image, to, for example, display a 24-bit image on an 8-bit display.

Kay, David, and John Levine, *Graphics File Formats*, Windcrest, 1992. This book covers a plethora of image file formats, including PCX, JPEG, TIFF, and GIF.

Fonts

Adobe Systems, *Bitmap Distribution Format*. Part of the documentation that comes with the X Window System from the MIT X Consortium.

Flowers, Jim, *X Logical Font Description Conventions*. Part of the documentation that comes with the X Window System from the MIT X Consortium.

Fulton, Jim, *The X Font Service Protocol*. Part of the documentation that comes with the X Window System from the MIT X Consortium.

Interface Design

Kobara, Shiz, *Visual Design With OSF/Motif*, Addison-Wesley, 1991. An excellent book showing how to create good-looking Motif displays. This is not a programming book, but is very useful for interface designers.

X, Motif, and Open Look

Asente, Paul J. and Ralph R. Swick, *X Window System Toolkit*, Digital Press, 1990. The bible of the Xt Intrinsics.

Corbet, Jonathan, and Keith Packard, "MIT-SHM—The MIT Shared Memory Extension: How the shared memory extension works." Part of the documentation with the X releases from the MIT X Consortium, this describes, in excruciatingly brief detail, how the MIT-SHM extension works.

Johnson, Eric F., and Kevin Reichard, *Advanced X Window Applications Programming*, MIS:Press, 1990. Hey, we're biased, right?

Johnson, Eric F., and Kevin Reichard, *Power Programming Motif*, MIS:Press, 1991. This book introduces Motif and includes a host of example source code to jump-start the Motif learning curve.

Johnson, Eric F., and Kevin Reichard, *Using X*, MIS:Press, 1992. Covers X resources and how to work with, troubleshoot, and conquer the X Window System.

Johnson, Eric F., and Kevin Reichard, *X Window Applications Programming*, second edition, MIS:Press, 1992. Introduces X library programming.

Open Software Foundation, *OSF/Motif Programmer's Reference, Revision 1.2*, *OSF/Motif Style Guide, Revision 1.2*, and *OSF/Motif Programmer's Guide, Revision 1.2*, all Prentice Hall, 1993. These form the official Motif manuals.

Scheifler, Robert W., and James Gettys, with Jim Flowers, Ron Newman, and David Rosenthal, third edition., *X Window System: The Complete Reference to Xlib, X Protocol, ICCCM, XLFD*, Digital Press, 1992.

Young, Douglas, and John Pew, *The X Window System: Programming and Applications with Xt*, Open Look edition, Prentice Hall, 1992. One of the few books available on OLIT programming.

PEX and PEXlib

The best place for PEX and PEXlib information is with your X Window System documentation. X11 Release 5 includes PEX and a number of documents, with most of them stored in `mit/doc/extensions/PEX`. Much of the PEXlib material comes with fix 18 for X11 Release 5.

Since PEX supports the PHIGS API, look for most PHIGS books, especially recent ones, to cover PEX. New books on PHIGS seem to appear every day, such as:

Gaskins, Tom, *PEXlib Programming Manual*, O'Reilly, 1992.

Gaskins, Tom, *PHIGS Programming Manual*, O'Reilly, 1992.

Howard, Toby, Terry Hewitt, R. J. Hubbold, and K.M. Wyrwas, *A Practical Introduction to PHIGS and PHIGS PLUS*, Addison-Wesley, 1991.

General Programming

Stevens, W. Richard, *UNIX Network Programming*, Prentice Hall, 1990. This book covers more than you want to know about UNIX interprocess communication, including shared memory.

Obtaining the X Window Source Code

The official source for X Window source code is the MIT X Consortium. As of this writing, the X Consortium sells a slew of documentation and the source code on 1,600-dpi or QIC-24 tapes in UNIX tar format. You can write:

MIT Software Distribution Center
Technology Licensing Office
Room E32-300
77 Massachusetts Av.
Cambridge, MA 02139
617/258-8330

You can also grab X from your local Internet archive.

In addition, many vendors (e.g., O'Reilly & Associates) sell the complete X Window source on CD-ROM. Check a current issue of *UNIX Review* for vendors advertising X CD-ROMs.

Appendix F

Obtaining the Example Source Code for This Book

We've put together a companion source code diskette for *Professional Graphics Programming with the X Window System*, containing all the example programs in the book. This diskette is an MS-DOS-formatted disk containing the C sources in ASCII files.

All files on the source code diskette should be straight ASCII files. All examples are in standard ANSI/ISO C. When you transfer these files to a UNIX machine, you probably want to convert the file names to lower case (except for the Makefile). There are no special subdirectories: all files should be in the root directory on the floppy disk—place the files in any directory you like in your user account.

To use the source code diskette, you will need some way to transfer these files from the DOS-formatted diskette to your X development system. You can look at Kermit, Ethernet FTP, NFS, or read the DOS diskette

1159

directly on your UNIX box. (Many UNIX workstations, e.g., the Sun SPARC-10, come with a disk drive and software that can read DOS-formatted diskettes.)

We tested our code on a number of platforms, including those in Table F.1.

Table F.1   *Tested platforms.*

Hardware	O.S.	X ver.	Motif/OLIT ver.
HP 705	HP-UX 8.07	R4	Motif 1.1
HP 720	HP-UX 9.01	R5	Motif 1.2
SGI	IRIX 4.0.5	R4	Motif 1.1
486	ISC SVR3.2 3.0	R4	Motif 1.1
486	ISC SVR3.2 3.0	R5	Motif 1.1
SPARCclassic	Solaris 2.1	R4/OW 3.1	OLIT 3.x
SPARC-10	SunOS 4.1.3	R4/OW 3.0	OLIT 3
SPARC-10	Solaris 2.1	R4/OW 3.1	OLIT 3.x

We focus on writing portable code, so the example programs should work on most configurations. A few of the chapters require certain extensions to X (MIT-SHM in Chapter 22 and Multi-Buffering in Chapter 25) or extra libraries (Xpm is used in Chapters 18 and 24). In the text, we documented a number of problems on the various platforms. Due to configuration differences, you may experience problems on your system.

Contact MIS:Press for ordering information.

3D Graphics with PEX and PEXlib

This books focuses on using general graphics techniques with your X applications. Even so, we find that three-dimensional applications are becoming more and more common. This appendix briefly introduces some portable X features for 3D graphics, including PEX, PEXlib, and PHIGS.

Three-dimensional graphics requires a lot of computing horsepower. But, as UNIX workstations drop in price and gain more and more in power, three-dimensional graphics become possible and affordable. Three-dimensional graphics can display large data spaces in a meaningful way, present business graphics with pizzazz, or provide the latest in hot new experimental interfaces.

The problem with 3D processing is that despite numerous graphic standards, nothing seems, well, standardized. In a multivendor environment, for every standard like GKS, GKS-3D, or PHIGS, you'll find a lack of support for at least one of your platforms. Or you may find support, but with zillions of incompatible offerings. If you can stick with just one vendor forever, you won't have many problems, but this defeats the whole idea of using open systems.

If you're trying to deliver 3D applications in a multivendor environment, such as on Sun, Hewlett-Packard, IBM, or Silicon Graphics workstations, you don't have a lot of options if you want to write just one set of source code. Yet, you can pretty much do the same with 2D X applications, using an X toolkit like Motif, as we've described in this book. This, of course, raises our expectations with 3D graphics to the same level.

The X Window System's answer for this 3D dilemma is called *PEX*, which is short for the PHIGS (and PHIGS-PLUS) Extension to X.

PHIGS, in turn, stands for Programmer's Hierarchical Interactive Graphics System and is one of many graphics standards.

Standardized as ISO 9592, PHIGS includes C and FORTRAN bindings to a library of 3D routines. PEX provides added support in the X server—a lot of added support—for PHIGS graphics and includes a library for the C bindings to PHIGS. Even though PEX is an extension to X, you can call the PHIGS routines to create PHIGS programs, which makes much of X transparent. This is all well and good, but we've found that for most real applications, you need to jump down to the lower levels, just like you have to jump down beneath the Motif and Open Look Intrinsics Toolkit (OLIT) toolkits.

The PEX Protocol

PEX seems intimately tied to PHIGS, but PEX really is just a network protocol, much like the X protocol. PEX is an extension to the X Window System. PEX applications, therefore, generate PEX network requests under the hood. (And PEX network requests are just extended X network requests.) Of course, to generate these requests, most of us prefer to use a C library that takes care of these low-level details. And that's where the PHIGS library for PEX comes in.

This separation of protocol and library follows the MIT X Consortium's oft-stated goal of providing mechanism, not policy. Even so, while one could conceivably layer any sort of 3D library, such as Silicon Graphics' GL, on top of PEX, it's harder than it seems, because of differing models of how to handle the display of 3D objects. Most PEX developers will end up using a PHIGS binding to PEX. PEX, in fact, makes no provision for certain aspects of the GL architecture, belying PEX's supposed neutrality.

And, that was the point originally, to follow existing 3D standards. Now, however, PEX has broadened to allow more than merely a PHIGS binding.

The whole idea of PEX is to provide a widespread base level of support for 3D graphics. The key is widespread, as all 3D standards so far haven't been all that standard, except on a few platforms. With PEX, the hope is that any X server (provided it offered PEX) could then run the same 3D graphics software.

PEX, however, comes only as a unoptimized sample implementation with X11 Release 5. It's up to individual vendors to optimize PEX for their hardware, much the same as the X server, although the base X server from the X Consortium often beats vendors at their own game. The PEX extension, so far, isn't known for speed. We certainly hope this will improve in the future.

Tektronix and NCD, among others, sell X terminals that support PEX.

PEX Versions

PEX, the PHIGS 3D extension to X, is off and running to a rocky start. PEX 5.1, which should be out now, fixes a number of problems with the initial 5.0 specification that came out in X11 Release 5.

The next release, PEX 6.0, tackles some of the tougher, noncompatible issues that have dogged PEX. Some of the goals of PEX 6.0 include full support for PHIGS-PLUS features. PEX 6.0 should appear with X11 Release 6. Even so, it will be a few years before commercial vendors start supporting PEX 6.0. When this changeover occurs, though, you need to be prepared to upgrade your code and deal with compatibility issues and vendors all operating on different schedules.

PEX Sample Implementation

The PEX sample implementation, or PEX-SI, allows anyone with the extension and the programming libraries to start coding PHIGS applications today. Unfortunately, though, with PEX-SI, the emphasis is on *sample* implementation. PEX-SI tends toward very slow program execution and it doesn't support double buffering for animation. Moreover, PEX-SI only works on color screens.

Even with these limitations, there's been a lot of 3D momentum with X. After all, you no longer need special hardware to run portable 3D applications. Furthermore, other 3D libraries, such as SGI's GL, have opened considerably in an effort to remain competitive, as we cover below.

Programming PEX

Before you can begin programming with PEX and PHIGS, you need to make sure your system supports the PEX extension. As with other X extension, use the xdpyinfo program and look in the list of extensions for X3D-PEX:

```
number of extensions:      6
     XTestExtension1
     SHAPE
     MIT-SHM
     X3D-PEX
     Multi-Buffering
     MIT-SUNDRY-NONSTANDARD
```

You can also use the xext program from Chapter 22.

Programming PEX with PHIGS

In addition to the X server extension, you also need application support in terms of programmer libraries and include files. You'll need the standard PHIGS header files, especially <phigs/phigs.h>, which is normally stored in /usr/include/X11/phigs. The PEX PHIGS API library, libphigs.a, should be with your other X libraries. You'll need to link with this library, as well as with the X library, libX11.a, and most likely the C math library, libm.a, for example:

```
cc -o foo foo.c -lphigs -lX11 -lm
```

Or

```
cc -DPEX_SI_PHIGS -o foo foo.c \
    -lphigs -lX11 -lm
```

We find the `PEX_SI_PHIGS` definition is often helpful when compiling PEX/PHIGS programs.

The `libphigs.a` library contains PHIGS functions, such as `phigs_ws_type_create` and `pset_line_ind`, as well as PHIGS-PLUS functions like `pset_int_shad_meth`. PHIGS is far too big a topic for this book to cover its functions in depth. Refer to Appendix E for more information on PEX and PHIGS.

The X11 R5 PEX-SI only supports color screens, so if you have a monochrome systems, you're in for a lot of code hacking.

PEX Examples

There are a few PHIGS examples with the X11R5 sources, stored in `mit/demos/auto_box` and `mit/demos/beach_ball`. These examples should give you a good idea of how to get PHIGS programs working with PEX.

Before you run either the `auto_box` or especially the `beach_ball` program, though, watch out. Both these programs send a flurry—more like a hurricane—of X requests and usually lock up your X server for a *long* while. Be prepared to terminate these programs using the UNIX `kill` command or the window manager. The `auto_box` program tends to end of its own free will much sooner than `beach_ball`, which runs in a continuous loop.

PEX Support Files

The PEX configuration files are in `/usr/lib/X11/PEX`, which also contains the `phigsmon` program. *Phigsmon* stands for the *PHIGS Monitor*, a run-time program that is (optionally) executed as a child process from your PHIGS applications. Luckily, this process is generally automatic. `Phigsmon` is used for input and client-side structure storage.

If you don't need `phigsmon`, you can turn it off with the following command from the C shell, `csh`:

```
setenv PEX_SI_API_NO_PM 1
```

You might need to do this if you see errors regarding PEX IPC (interprocess communication).

PEX supports its own set of fonts, which are normally stored in `/usr/lib/X11/fonts/PEX`.

Problems with PEX

The major problems with current PEX implementations are speed and size. PEX is a very complex protocol, especially with a PHIGS binding layered on top. Also, most 3D applications generate very large amounts of data—this is the whole point of 3D applications. Somehow, all this data needs to travel over a network link to the PEX part of the X server. This is one of the rationales for direct-to-hardware libraries like GL.

PEX programs in fact, often generate flurries of X protocol requests. This leads to noticeable performance problems, especially since the X server—at least in most implementations—supports only a single thread of execution and must complete the entire PEX request before servicing other X applications. This tends to make your screen lock up while the X server handles the incoming storm of PEX requests.

To see this in action, try the PEX demo called `beach_ball`. This program comes with X11 Release 5 (from the X Consortium) and can slow down most any system to a crawl.

These flurries of large packets tend to exceed the limits on the maximum size of X requests, and provide the impetus for *multithreaded* X servers.

With multiple threads of execution, an X server could service other X applications at the same time it divides up a huge block of PEX requests into smaller chunks. This would change the appearance of your workstation from a single-tasking dead-in-the-water boat anchor back to a true multi-tasking workstation. The problem is that both the X server and X programmer libraries weren't written with multiple threads in mind. X11 Release 6, though, should improve this situation for those who have operating-system support for multiple threads. In fact, problems with PEX form one of the main driving forces behind the movement for a multithreaded X server.

New Directions in PEX

The current version of PEX is PEX 5.1, which is mostly compatible with the original PEX 5.0 that came with X11 Release 5. The PEX protocol, though, will be subject to a major revision with PEX 6.0. This later revision should include the standardized PHIGS-PLUS and a host of new features.

PEXIM, for PEX Immediate Mode, adds an API for immediate-mode graphics. PEX already supports an immediate mode, but PHIGS doesn't—yet.

Some of these problems with PEX have dampened enthusiasm for PHIGS. Because of this, there's a new library called *PEXlib*.

PEXlib

In addition to the PEX protocol itself, a low-level library called *PEXlib* provides access to the low-level PEX protocol. Based on work by DEC and available on the X11R5 contributed software tapes, PEXlib is a lot like the X library, Xlib. Xlib sits on top of the low-level X protocol, while PEXlib sits on top of the low-level PEX protocol. Even though PEXlib is considered low level, it is really a high-level library with a complex graphics pipeline. PEXlib is more down and dirty than PHIGS, but PEXlib still allows you to work with three-dimensional graphics at a high level of abstraction.

Most programmers, however, use a toolkit that sits on top of the Xlib. The PEX world promises to evolve in the same way. PEXlib is supposed to be policy free, that is, PEXlib is not tied to PHIGS.

The PHIGS C binding, the PHIGS library, could be implemented on top of PEXlib, much like X toolkits sit on top of Xlib. PEXlib and PHIGS both support the same model for defining and rendering scenes as well as the same graphics primitives.

The hope is also that other 3D libraries and toolkits could also sit on top of PEXlib, such as Hewlett-Packard's Starbase or Silicon Graphics' GL (Graphics Library). When the X Consortium says you could implement a number of other 3D libraries on top of PEXlib, however, they don't mean OpenGL, a 3D API promoted by Silicon Graphics. While we're sure there's a technical reason for this, it seems but yet another salvo in an apparently bitter war between the various 3D partisans.

Acquiring PEXlib

PEXlib started out in the contributed code for X11 Release 5. The official PEXlib was first released as part of fix 19 for X11 Release 5. X11 Release 6 should include PEXlib as part of the standard system, along with PEX 6.0.

Because of this, you may have to go through some contortions to get PEXlib set up on your system. We acquired PEXlib from the X

Consortium's e-mail server and compiled the library ourselves against a generic X11 Release 5 system.

Programming with PEXlib

PEXlib is another library that sits on top of PEX. The PHIGS library also sits on top of PEX, which tends to confuse things. Just remember that you have the choice to use the library you want.

PEXlib uses a lot of complex X features like standard colormaps and nondefault visuals. We'll go over some of the barest basics and refer you to Appendix E for a listing of PEX and PEXlib books, along with other sources of information.

PEXlib supports a number of features such as structure-mode or immediate-mode graphics, internalized text display, geometric transformations, different views of data, light sources, shading, double buffering, and picking. Some of these terms need explaining. *Structure mode* is where you store graphics primitives in a database for later rendering to the screen. *Immediate mode* is where you send the graphics primitives to PEX one by one and they are displayed immediately—or as quickly as your workstation supports. PEX does not support ray tracing, radiosity, or texture mapping.

The main PEXlib include file is `<X11/PEX5/PEXlib.h>`, normally in the `/usr/include/X11/PEX5` directory. All PEXlib code must include this file:

```
#include  <X11/PEX5/PEXlib.h>
```

We expect the PEX5 subdirectory to change to PEX6 when PEX 6.0 arrives.

Initializing the PEXlib

Like all X extensions, PEX requires you to call a function to test if the extension is available. This function, `PEXInitialize`, also initializes the PEX extension code in the X server:

```
#include  <X11/PEX5/PEXlib.h>
```

```
int PEXInitialize(Display* display,
    PEXExtensionInfo** pex_info,  /* RETURN */
    int message_length,
    char* error_message)          /* RETURN */
```

The *error_message* may contain a message if PEXInitialize fails. You must specify that maximum length of this message with the *message_length* parameter. A good *message_length* is PEXError-StringLength, which is often 80 bytes.

PEXInitialize returns 0 on success; PEXBadExtension, PEXBadFloatConversion, PEXBadLocalAlloc, or PEXBad-ProtocolVersion on errors.

PEXBadExtension means that the X server does not support PEX. There's not much you can do if this is the case.

PEXBadFloatConversion means your application and the X server cannot agree on a PEX floating-point format.

PEXBadLocalAlloc means that your application couldn't allocate space for all the PEX global variables and structures.

PEXBadProtocolVersion means that the PEX protocols don't match between your application and the X server. PEXBadProtocol-Version may become a common error as older PEX 5.1 programs run against a PEX 6.0 X server, or PEX 6.0 applications run against old vendor-supported PEX 5.1 X servers.

The *pex_info* parameter contains information returned about the PEX code in the X server, stored in a PEXExtensionInfo structure. The PEXExtensionInfo structure looks like:

```
typedef struct {
    unsigned short    major_version;
    unsigned short    minor_version;
    unsigned long     release;
    unsigned long     subset_info;
    char*             vendor_name;
    int               major_opcode;
```

```
    int             first_event;
    int             first_error;
} PEXExtensionInfo;
```

For most X servers, the *major_version* will be 5 until PEX 6.0 comes out with X11 Release 6. If the *major_version* is 5, the *minor_version* will be 0 or 1, for PEX 5.0 or 5.1. The *release* is a number that the PEX server vendor can use. For the sample implementation that comes with X11 Release 5, the release number is 0.

The *vendor_name* can also be filled in by the PEX server vendor. A common *vendor_name* is "X3D-PEX Sample Implementation."

PEX Subset Information

Because PEX is so huge, many X servers, particularly X terminals, may have a hard time implementing the whole thing. PEX, like the X Image Extension covered in Chapter 22, supports the idea of subsets. Information on the supported subsets is stored in the *subset_info* field of the PEXExtensionInfo structure, which holds a set of bit-flags, as shown in Table 6.1.

Table G.1   PEX subset bit flags.

Flag	Value
PEXCompleteImplementation	0x0
PEXImmediateMode	0x1
PEXWorkstationOnly	0x2
PEXStructureMode	0x3

These bit-flags indicate which subsets of PEX your X server supports. If you're lucky, you'll get a complete implementation (PEXComplete-Implementation). Otherwise, your X server may support immediate-mode graphics (PEXImmediateMode), the PEX structure mode (PEX-StructureMode), PHIGS workstation resources (PEXWorkstation-Only), or any combination of all three.

The *major_opcode* isn't really important. The *first_event* is the first event code for PEX events, and the *first_event* is the first error code for PEX errors.

You can print out the fields of the PEXExtensionInfo structure using the code below:

```
void PrintPEXlibInfo(PEXExtensionInfo* pex_info)

{   /* PrintPEXlibInfo */

    printf("PEX version %d.%d\n",
        pex_info->major_version,
        pex_info->minor_version);

    printf("PEX vendor: %s with release %ld\n",
        pex_info->vendor_name,
        pex_info->release);

    printf("Major opcode %d\n",
        pex_info->major_opcode);

    printf("first event %d, first error %d\n",
        pex_info->first_event,
        pex_info->first_error);

    printf("This implementation of PEX supports: \n");

    if (pex_info->subset_info ==
        PEXCompleteImplementation) {

        printf("\t A complete PEX implementation.\n");

    } else {
```

```
            if (pex_info->subset_info & PEXImmediateMode) {
                printf("\t Immediate-mode graphics.\n");
            }


            if (pex_info->subset_info & PEXWorkstationOnly) {
                printf("\t PHIGS workstation resources.\n");
            }


            if (pex_info->subset_info & PEXStructureMode) {
                printf("\t PEX structures.\n");
            }
        }


    }   /* PrintPEXlibInfo */
```

Calling PEXInitialize

Putting all this together, you can call PEXInitialize as shown in the
code below:

```
    Display*            display;
    int                 status;
    PEXExtensionInfo*   pex_info;

    char  error_message[PEXErrorStringLength+1];


    status = PEXInitialize(display,
                &pex_info,
                PEXErrorStringLength,
                error_message);
```

Sample Program to Initialize PEX

We've put together one of the shortest possible PEXlib programs. The simple sample program below shows the call to PEXInitialize. This program doesn't do much other than print out information on your X server's PEX implementation. This code is stored in the file pexinfo.c:

```
/*
 *  pexinfo.c
 *  PEXlib program prints out PEX info.
 */
#include  <X11/PEX5/PEXlib.h>
#include  <stdio.h>


/* Prints info on PEX. */


void PrintPEXlibInfo(PEXExtensionInfo* pex_info)


{   /* PrintPEXlibInfo */

    printf("PEX version %d.%d\n",
        pex_info->major_version,
        pex_info->minor_version);

    printf("PEX vendor: %s with release %ld\n",
        pex_info->vendor_name,
        pex_info->release);

    printf("Major opcode %d\n",
        pex_info->major_opcode);

    printf("first event %d, first error %d\n",
```

```
                pex_info->first_event,
                pex_info->first_error);


        printf("This implementation of PEX supports: \n");


        if (pex_info->subset_info
            == PEXCompleteImplementation) {


            printf("\t A complete PEX implementation.\n");


        } else {


            if (pex_info->subset_info & PEXImmediateMode) {
                printf("\t Immediate-mode graphics.\n");
            }


            if (pex_info->subset_info & PEXWorkstationOnly) {
                printf("\t PHIGS workstation resources.\n");
            }


            if (pex_info->subset_info & PEXStructureMode) {
                printf("\t PEX structures.\n");
            }
        }


} /* PrintPEXlibInfo */


int main(int argc, char** argv)


{   /* main */
    Display*            display;
```

```
PEXExtensionInfo*  pex_info;
int                status;

char  error_message[PEXErrorStringLength+1];

/* Open display connection. */
display = XOpenDisplay(NULL);

if (display == (Display*) NULL) {
    fprintf(stderr,
        "Error opening display.\n");
    exit(-1);
}

/*
 * Initialize PEX.
 */
status = PEXInitialize(display,
        &pex_info,
        PEXErrorStringLength,
        error_message);

if (status != 0) {
    switch(status) {
        case PEXBadExtension:
            printf("Bad Extension.\n");
            break;
        case PEXBadProtocolVersion:
            printf("Bad Protocol Version.\n");
            break;
        case PEXBadFloatConversion:
```

```
                    printf("Bad Float Conversion.\n");
                    break;
              case PEXBadLocalAlloc:
                    printf("Bad Local Memory Alloc.\n");
                    break;
          }


          XCloseDisplay(display);
          exit(-1);
      }


      /* Print PEX info. */
      PrintPEXlibInfo(pex_info);


      XCloseDisplay(display);


  }    /* main */


  /* end of file pexinfo.c */
```

Compiling and Linking PEX Programs

PEXlib programs require the PEX5 library (`libPEX5.a`) the X library (`libX11.a`), and most likely the C math library (`libm.a`). You can compile and link a PEXlib program using a command like the following:

```
cc -o pexinfo pexinfo.c -lPEX5 -lX11 -lm
```

When you run the `pexinfo` program shown above, you'll get an output like the following—if your system supports PEX:

```
PEX version 5.0
PEX vendor: X3D-PEX Sample Implementation with release 0
Major opcode 131
first event 0, first error 129
```

```
This implementation of PEX supports:
        A complete PEX implementation.
```

PEX and GL

The *Graphics Library*, or *GL*, from Silicon Graphics Inc. (SGI) remains the primary competitor of PHIGS and PEX. Unlike PHIGS, GL supports immediate-mode graphics. PEX also supports immediate-mode graphics, but PHIGS does not. This has led to a number of battles between PHIGS/PEX and GL.

The main difference between GL and PEX is that up until recently, GL was proprietary to Silicon Graphics and a few other vendors. In the last year, however, SGI opened up GL to other vendors, forming what it calls *OpenGL*. OpenGL is open mainly because of the competition from PEX and PHIGS. SGI, obviously, hopes GL will win the battle for the hearts and minds of software developers.

If PEX catches on and becomes widely available, OpenGL may also fall by the wayside. But there are a large number of vendors aligned behind the GL movement, including IBM, Microsoft, and, of course, Silicon Graphics. We think OpenGL will hang in there and the resulting competition will be good for both PEX and GL.

One touted benefit of GL is that it can write to local graphics hardware directly. To provide anything close to good performance, a 3D library needs to have direct access to the underlying hardware. GL supporters highlight this as a benefit of their approach. But, PEX servers can—and should—directly access the underlying hardware, even though you'll still have the overhead of the X protocol.

The advantage of PEX is that you can already buy PEX X terminals, from vendors such as Tektronix and NCD.

And, in the end, you may be able to run GL applications on top of the PEX protocol, giving you the portability of PEX and the features of GL. There's already one GL-like library that runs under PEX, called *PEXtk*. The free PEXtk is written by ShoGraphics and sits on top of PEXlib, which improves the performance and decreases the complexity from a full-blown PHIGS implementation.

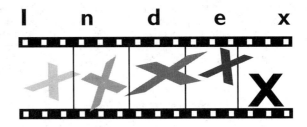

Index

1179

PROGRAM LISTINGS ON DISKETTE

MIS:PRESS

This diskette contains the complete listings for all programs and applications contained in this book—it eliminates the need to type in pages of program code.

Professional Graphics Programming in the X Window System

Eric Johnson and Kevin Reichard

ISBN: 1-55828-256-4

MIS.Press

If you did not buy this book with a diskette, use this form to order now. *Only*

$29⁹⁵

MIS:PRESS
4375 West 1980 South
Salt Lake City, Utah 84104
(810) 972-2221

_____

NAME (PLEASE PRINT OR TYPE)

_____

ADDRESS

_____

CITY   STATE   ZIP

Call toll-free
1-800-488-5233
1-800-628-9658

Professional Graphics Programming in the X Window System
ISBN: 1-55828-256-4 Only $29.95
Please add $2.00 for shipping and handling (Foreign $6.00)

Check one:
❏ VISA   ❏ Mastercard
❏ American Express
❏ Check enclosed $ _____

_____

ACCOUNT NO.

_____

EXP. DATE

_____

SIGNATURE